AN ARMY FOR EMPIRE

THE UNITED STATES ARMY
IN THE SPANISH-AMERICAN WAR

Graham A. Cosmas

 White Mane Publishing Company, Inc.

The acid-free paper used in this book meets the guidelines for permanence and durability of the Committee on Production Guidelines for Book Longevity of the Council of Library Resources.

First Printing, 1971
Second Printing, 1994 with supplemental materials

First Printing by
The Curators of the University of Missouri, University of Missouri Press,
Columbia, Missouri 65201

Second Printing by
White Mane Publishing Co., Inc., Shippensburg, PA USA

For a complete list of available publications
please write
White Mane Publishing Company, Inc.
P.O. Box 152
Shippensburg, PA 17257

ISBN 0-942597-49-4 (formerly ISBN 0-8262-0107-5 -   formerly Library of Congress Catalog Number 76-149010)

Library of Congress Cataloging-in-Publication Data

Cosmas, Graham A.
        An army for empire : the United States Army in the Spanish
-American War / Graham A. Cosmas.
              p.   cm.
        Originally published: Columbia : University of Missouri Press.
1971.
        Includes bibliographical references and index.
        ISBN 0-942597-49-4 :
        1. United States.   Army--History--Spanish-American War, 1898.
I. Title.
E725.3.C6   1994
973.8'93--dc20   93-48947
                                                                         CIP

PRINTED IN THE UNITED STATES OF AMERICA

To Jean Carter Cosmas

and George Cosmas

Acknowledgments

I should like to thank the staffs of the following libraries and archives, without whose gracious and unstinting assistance this book never could have been written:

The Ainsworth Search Room, National Archives, Washington, D.C.

The Manuscripts Division, Library of Congress, Washington, D.C.

The State Historical Society of Wisconsin, Madison, Wisconsin

The Michigan Historical Collections, Ann Arbor, Michigan

The William L. Clements Library, Ann Arbor, Michigan

Thanks are also due to my graduate advisers, Professor Edward M. Coffman and Professor Richard N. Current, for their invaluable guidance and support at every stage of the project and to Professor Bernard H. Cohen and the directors of the National Security Studies Group at The University of Wisconsin for financial assistance that made possible a year of research in Washington, D.C.

G.A.C.
Arlington, Virginia
May, 1973

Contents

List of Illustrations and Maps

Guide to Footnote Abbreviations

For the reader's convenience, a number of frequently cited sources with long, complicated titles are abbreviated as follows, throughout the footnotes.

AGO Records: Records of The Adjutant General's Office.

Correspondence: *Correspondence Relating to the War with Spain and Conditions Growing out of the Same, . . . between The Adjutant General of the Army and Military Commanders in the United States, Cuba, Porto Rico, China, and the Philippine Islands, from April 15, 1898, to July 30, 1902.*

GO [number], HQA, [date]:   General Order No. _____, Headquarters of the Army, [date].

GO [number], WD, [date]:   General Order No. _____, War Department, [date].

GO/AGO, 1898:   *General Orders and Circulars, Adjutant General's Office, 1898.*

GO/AGO, 1899:   *General Orders and Circulars, Adjutant General's Office, 1899.*

JMSI: *Journal of the Military Service Institution of the United States.*

OQMG Records: Records of the Office of the Quartermaster General.

RSW, [year]:   *Report of the Secretary of War,* or *Annual Report of the War Department* (depending on the year). House Executive Documents, various sessions, 1880-1904.

War Investigating Commission: *Report of the Commission appointed by the President to Investigate the Conduct of the War Department in the War with Spain.* Senate Document No. 221, 56th Cong., 1st sess., 1900.

Preface to the Second Edition

During the twenty years since *An Army for Empire* was published by the University of Missouri Press, the literature on the Spanish-American War era has expanded in both subject matter and sophistication. However, no new study has appeared to duplicate or replace this volume as an account of the organization and administration of the Spanish-American War Army and of the response of the War Department to the conflict of 1898 and the challenges of overseas empire.

Most of the new literature deals with topics either broader or narrower than the focus of *An Army for Empire*, though many authors elaborate upon or reinforce points made in that work. David F. Trask and Philip S. Foner have produced major studies of the Spanish-American War as a whole. In addition, George J. A. O'Toole has written a popular survey of the war.[1] Both Trask and Foner, although interpreting the war differently, have written international histories which draw upon Spanish and Cuban as well as American sources and broaden our understanding of wartime diplomacy and strategy. Neither they nor O'Toole go much beyond *An Army for Empire* in their treatment of the U.S. Army in the conflict.

Military reform in the United States armed forces during the late nineteenth and early twentieth centuries has received increasing scholarly attention. James W. Abrahamson's *America Arms for a New Century* is a major survey of the period, with emphasis on the ideas of reform intellectuals in both the Army and the Navy. For the Army in particular, recent writers have challenged the thesis advanced by Samuel P. Huntington in *The Soldier and the State* that the officer corps before the Spanish War lived in monastic isolation from civilian society. This thesis is convincingly demolished by, among others, John M. Gates in his important article "The Alleged Isolation of US Army Officers in the Late 19th Century." Edward M. Coffman also attacks the Huntington thesis. Timothy Nenninger recounts the development of the Army's embryonic staff college at Fort Leavenworth, covering both the pre- and post-Spanish War years. Allan Millett, in the introduction to his biography of Robert L. Bullard, analyzes the development of professionalism in the Spanish War-era Army. These works reinforce and expand the thesis expressed in *An Army for Empire* that the basic agenda for Army reform was set well before the outbreak of war with Spain.[2]

1. David F. Trask, *The War with Spain in 1898* (New York: Macmillan Publishing Co., Inc., 1981). Philip S. Foner, *The Spanish-Cuban-American War and the Birth of American Imperialism, 1898-1902* (2 vols. New York and London: Monthly Review Press, 1972). G. J. A. O'Toole, *The Spanish War: An American Epic, 1898* (New York: W. W. Norton & Co., 1984).

2. James L. Abrahamson, *America Arms for a New Century: The Making of a Great Military Power* (New York: The Free Press, 1981). John M. Gates, "The Alleged Isolation of US Army Officers in the Late 19th Century," *Parameters: Journal of the US Army War College*, X, no. 3 (1980), 32-45. Edward M. Coffman, "The Long Shadow of *The Soldier and the State*," *The Journal of Military History*, LV, no. 1 (January 1991), 69-82. Timothy K. Nenninger, *The Leavenworth Schools and the Old Army: Education, Professionalism, and the Officer Corps of the United States Army, 1881-1918* (Westport: Greenwood Press, 1978). Allan R. Millett, *The General: Robert L. Bullard and Officership in the United States Army, 1881-1925* (Westport: Greenwood Press, 1975).

Recent literature on the late Nineteenth Century Army reflects the influence of the so-called "New Military History," an approach to the subject that gives institutional, technological, and sociological aspects of armies and warfare equal weight with accounts of campaigns and battles. Jack D. Foner analyzes reform in the condition of the Army's enlisted force. Marvin Fletcher and Willard Gatewood tell the story of black soldiers and officers of the era. Useful information on black troops in the Spanish War also can be found in Bernard Nalty's survey of Blacks in the American military, *Strength for the Fight*, and in the documentary collection edited by Nalty and Morris MacGregor. Much of the recent work in the social history of the Army up to 1898, as well as prodigious primary source research, is synthesized in Edward M. Coffman's monumental survey, *The Old Army*. Coffman now is working on a similar volume dealing with the period from the war with Spain to the outbreak of World War II. Part social, part institutional, and part technical history is Mary C. Gillett's *The Army Medical Department, 1865-1917,* the third of a projected four volumes on the Medical Department in preparation by the Army Center of Military History.[3]

The history of the National Guard and its role in the Spanish-American War are the subjects of a number of studies published since *An Army for Empire*. John K. Mahon has produced a long-needed general history of state militia forces, with coverage of their role in the Spanish-American and other wars. Gerald F. Linderman, in an examination of American society during the conflict with Spain, provides fascinating insights into the influence of state volunteers' values and attitudes to military service on their conduct in camp and field. Useful state studies include Jerry M. Cooper's account of the Wisconsin National Guard in the war and Robert H. Ferrell's edition of the previously unpublished memoirs of Colonel Curtis V. Hard of the 8th Ohio U.S. Volunteers.[4]

3. Jack D. Foner, *The United States Soldier between Two Wars* (New York: Humanities Press, 1970). Marvin Fletcher, *The Black Soldier and Officer in the United States Army, 1891-1917* (Columbia: University of Missouri Press, 1974). Willard B. Gatewood, Jr., *Black Americans and the White Man's Burden, 1898-1903* (Champaign, Ill.: University of Illinois Press, 1975); *Smoked Yankees* (Fayetteville, Ark.: University of Arkansas Press, 1987); *Smoked Yankees and the Struggle for Empire: Letters from Negro Soldiers, 1898-1902* (Ann Arbor, Mich.: Books on Demand, n. d.). Bernard C. Nalty, *Strength for the Fight: A History of Black Americans in the Military* (New York: The Free Press, 1986). Morris J. MacGregor and Bernard C. Nalty, eds., *Blacks in the United States Armed Forces: Basic Documents* (13 vols. Wilmington, Del.: Scholarly Resources, Inc., 1977); see especially vol. III. Edward M. Coffman, *The Old Army: A Portrait of the American Army in Peacetime, 1784-1898* (New York: Oxford University Press, 1986). Mary C. Gillett, *The Army Medical Department, 1865-1917* (Washington: U.S. Army Center of Military History, forthcoming).

4. John K. Mahon, *History of the Militia and the National Guard* (New York: The Macmillan Company, 1983). Gerald F. Linderman, *The Mirror of War: American Society and the Spanish-American War* (Ann Arbor: University of Michigan Press, 1974). Jerry M. Cooper, "National Guard Reform, the Army, and the Spanish-American War: The View from Wisconsin," *Military Affairs*, XLII (1978), 20-23. Robert H. Ferrell, ed., *Banners in the Air: The Eighth Ohio and the Spanish-American War* (Kent, Oh.: Kent State University Press, 1988).

Postwar conflicts and military reform have been the subjects of important work. The war in Vietnam led to a revival of interest in America's earlier large-scale counterinsurgency campaign in the Philippines at the turn of the century, with particular attention to why and how the U.S. Army prevailed over the nationalist guerrillas of Emilio Aguinaldo. To this question, works by John Gates and Stuart C. Miller offer opposing answers, the former author emphasizing Army benevolence toward the Filipinos and the latter pointing to prevalent racism and brutality in the conduct of the war. Recently, something of a synthesis has emerged in the works of writers such as Brian Linn and Glenn A. May. These authors point out that the Army's tactics varied with the nature of the resistance in different locations and argue that the American victory must be explained in large measure in terms of the social and political divisions and weaknesses of the Filipino resistance.[5]

Postwar reform is treated in the works of Abrahamson and Nenninger cited previously. James E. Hewes's *From Root to McNamara* chronicles the creation of the Army's general staff and its effects on military administration. A new history of the Army War College, a major product of the Root reforms, now is available to supplement the earlier work by George S. Pappas.[6]

Most high-level War Department and Army figures of the Spanish-American War period still lack full-scale scholarly biographies. They include Secretary of War Russell A. Alger, Commanding General of the Army Nelson A. Miles, and Adjutant-General Henry C. Corbin. However, useful works have been produced on Major Generals Wesley Merritt and William R. Shafter. Don E. Alberts's biography of Merritt details that general's important part in the pre-1898 Army reform movement, providing insight into Merritt's relatively efficient conduct of the Philippine expedition. Paul Carlson's life of Shafter, unfortunately, is stronger on Shafter's frontier service than on his command at Santiago de Cuba. Nevertheless, this volume fills a gap in the literature and illuminates Shafter's relationships with Miles and other Regular Army leaders of the time. Jack C. Lane has produced a biography of Leonard Wood much less laudatory of that controversial doctor-turned-soldier than was the previous standard life by Herman Hagedorn. Valuable Spanish and Philippine War material also

5. John M. Gates, *Schoolbooks and Krags: The United States Army in the Philippines, 1898-1902* (Westport: Greenwood Press, 1973). Stuart C. Miller, *"Benevolent Assimilation": The American Conquest of the Philippines, 1899-1903* (New Haven: Yale University Press, 1982). Brian M. Linn, *The U.S. Army and Counterinsurgency in the Philippine War, 1899-1902* (Chapel Hill: University of North Carolina Press, 1989). Glenn A. May, *Battle for Batangas: A Philippine Province at War* (New Haven: Yale University Press, 1991).

6. James E. Hewes, *From Root to McNamara: Army Organization and Administration, 1900-1963* (Washington: U.S. Army Center of Military History, 1975). George S. Pappas, *Prudens Futuri: The U.S. Army War College, 1901-1967* (Carlisle Barracks, Pa.: Alumni Association, U.S. Army War College, ca 1968). Col. Harry P. Ball, USA (Ret.), *Of Responsible Command: A History of the U.S. Army War College* (Carlisle Barracks, Pa.: U.S. Army War College Alumni Association, 1983).

can be found in Millett's work on Robert L. Bullard and in the first volume of Donald Smythe's definitive biography of General John J. Pershing.[7]

As the centennial of the Spanish-American War approaches, *An Army for Empire* continues to stand the test of time as an account of the Army's part in that conflict. This White Mane edition is identical to the original except for the inclusion of this preface, of additional illustrations, and of revisions in three chapters. In Chapter 4, expanded treatment is given to the role of black Americans in the Spanish War Army. Chapter 7 now includes a new section analyzing the war's only major land engagements at San Juan Hill and El Caney. This section is based on the author's additional research on those engagements for a chapter in an anthology on America's first battles sponsored by the U.S. Army Combat Studies Institute at Fort Leavenworth.[8] Finally, the first part of Chapter 9 has been enlarged to provide fuller coverage of the period between the armistice in mid-August 1898 and Secretary Alger's departure a year later. During this time, the Army made the transition from the war with Spain to the new conflicts and responsibilities of America's overseas empire. The expanded treatment of these events better shows the working out of wartime developments and establishes the state of the War Department and Army as Secretary of War Elihu Root began his campaign for reform. The author and the publisher hope that, with these revisions, this new edition of *An Army for Empire* will continue to be useful to students of the Spanish-American War for many years to come.

7. Don E. Alberts, *Brandy Station to Manila Bay: A Biography of General Wesley Merritt* (Austin, Tex.: Presidial Press, 1981). Paul H. Carlson, *"Pecos Bill": A Military Biography of William R. Shafter* (College Station: Texas A&M University Press, 1989). Jack C. Lane, *Armed Progressive: General Leonard Wood* (San Rafael, Cal.: Presidio Press, 1978). Donald Smythe, *Guerrilla Warrior: The Early Life of John J. Pershing* (New York: Charles Scribner's Sons, 1973).

8. Graham A. Cosmas, "San Juan Hill and El Caney, 1-2 July 1898," in Charles E. Heller and William A. Stofft, eds., *America's First Battles, 1776-1965* (Lawrence: University Press of Kansas, 1986), 109-48.

Introduction

Tales of romantic heroism, charges of official mismanagement, and allegations of negligence and corruption dominate most accounts of the United States Army's part in the Spanish-American War. In the accepted version, elderly, hidebound staff officers, aided and abetted by a weak President and his incompetent Secretary of War, blunder into the conflict unprepared, shape an amateurish, aimless strategy, and fail abysmally in the procurement and distribution of supplies. Because of this ineptitude on the official level, American soldiers confront the enemy with obsolete weapons while their comrades in the home camps die by hundreds in preventable epidemics. Only the Spaniards' incompetence—even more monumental than our own—the efficiency of the Navy, and the gallantry of the troopers at San Juan Hill—popularly typified by Theodore Roosevelt and his immortal Rough Riders—save the day for America.

Many of the facts support this version of the story. Confusion, bordering at times on chaos, did surround the first mustering of troops. Supplies were indeed scarce early in the war, and what supplies were available did not always reach the men who needed them. Sanitation in many camps broke down disastrously, partly as the result of shortages of equipment and partly through official errors. The Santiago expedition embarked in confusion, entered battle in disorder, and stampeded home in panic before the specter of yellow fever. By concentrating only on these events, one can make a good case for dismissing the Army's administration of the war in 1898 as a black comedy of blunders.

Yet, all the accounts of the war of 1898 upon which the traditional version of the Army's conduct of it is based share one common deficiency: They view the military operations against Spain from the standpoint of every level of participant but the highest responsible civilian and uniformed officials of the War Department. They look at the Army's administration from the outside, seeing only the partial effects of decisions, not knowing why those decisions were made or that, in many instances, initially wrong decisions were reversed. Theodore Roosevelt, along with innumerable soldier-memoirists, viewed the War Department's actions from subordinate positions in the field—not the most flattering perspective on the high command in any war. The newspaper correspondents, whose indignant eloquence did much to shape the popular conception of the campaigns, wrote from essentially the same viewpoint. The naval officer and historian French Ensor Chadwick, in what remains the most thorough and judicious military account of the conflict, brought to his work little firsthand information about the inner workings of the War Department. Such recent historians as Margaret Leech and H. Wayne Morgan echo in their accounts of the McKinley Administration the bewildered impatience of a President and his civilian advisers who created difficulties for the War Department while never quite understanding the handicaps under which that agency labored.

War Department officials themselves biased the record by their silence. Of the civilian and uniformed men in charge of the department in 1898, only Secretary of War Russell A. Alger left a memoir of his tenure. While it contains much useful information and many revealing documents, his book avoids discussing many of what are, to the historian, the most interesting questions about how military policy was made and implemented. The published reminiscences of the commanding general of the Army, Nelson A. Miles, are little more than recapitulations of his official reports. The bureau chiefs, including the influential Adjutant General, Henry Clark Corbin, confined their accounts to their annual reports and to their testimony before official investigating bodies—much of which is pertinent but fragmentary. Because the men at the top remained virtually silent, many of their decisions went unexplained, unanalyzed, and undefended; therefore, the historical record of the war has remained incomplete.

This account is an effort to reconstruct the War Department's story of the war, to trace the course of the department's effort to organize and equip an army and then deploy it to secure the objectives of national policy. It analyzes each major decision concerning these matters, why it was made, and the results it produced. The story has for its protagonists the President, the Secretary of War, the Commanding General of the Army, the chiefs of the supply and administrative bureaus, and the commanders of expeditions, training camps, and army corps. Members of Congress and of the Regular Army officer corps, along with the leaders of the National Guard, play crucial supporting (and sometimes disrupting) roles in the drama. How all of these men viewed the military problems of the war, how they planned to wage the war, and how they implemented their plans constitute the substance of the plot. Clearly, this account is not a full history of the Spanish-American War. It ignores naval and diplomatic developments except as they affected the conditions under which the War Department did its work. It treats of the conduct of campaigns in the field and the conditions under which soldiers lived, fought, and sometimes died only as they, or officials' perceptions of them, shaped command and policy decisions.

To reconstruct the forming of military policies in 1898, I have supplemented the published government documents, the war memoirs, and the correspondents' dispatches with material from the hitherto largely unexploited files of The Adjutant General's and the Quartermaster General's offices, both of which collections are preserved in the National Archives. These massive accumulations of reports, telegrams, personal and official letters, and miscellaneous material including original samples of khaki uniform cloth close many gaps in the printed accounts and enable the historian to see the day-to-day progress of the war as officials saw it at the time. The personal manuscripts of President McKinley, Secretary of War Alger, Adjutant General Corbin, and other officials fill in the details of internal War Department politics and cast light on the background of many decisions. Much can be learned, also, simply from following through contemporary newspapers and periodicals the growth of War Department policies, pursuing the course of developments in chronological order from the destruction of the U.S.S. *Maine* in February, 1898, through the armistice with Spain six months later. Many decisions and actions that, in isolation, make little sense are comprehensible when viewed within the total context of the events of those hectic months.

It became necessary in the course of this study to range backward in time from 1898, because the way in which the Army was mobilized and the war conducted showed the influence of strategic and organizational doctrines developed by American professional soldiers during the twenty years before the *Maine* exploded in Havana harbor. The pages of late-nineteenth-century military periodicals and the writings of such Army reformers as Emory Upton and John M. Schofield provide a framework of ideas within which the War Department policies of 1898 must be placed for proper evaluation.

When the entire effort to mobilize, put in the field, and support an army is examined within this framework rather than against the background of a few highly publicized incidents, the generally accepted picture of the War Department's ineptitude requires at least modification. If the management of the Santiago expedition was less than brilliant, the records show that the expedition had to be formed hastily, due to circumstances beyond the War Department's control. Further, in spite of necessary haste and improvisation, the expedition did achieve the objective set for it. In the other theaters of the war, the forces sent against Puerto Rico and Manila were much better organized and equipped. Although in the action against Cuba shortages of equipment, clothing, and weapons plagued the Army at the outset, the bureaus worked manfully to overcome them and succeeded within a short time. It is true that sanitation collapsed in some camps, but competent commanders in others prevented disastrous epidemics, with the full support of the Secretary of War and of the bureau chiefs in Washington. Many of the Army's wartime misfortunes resulted less from fundamental mistakes in policy than from efforts to implement sound policies too rapidly with too few trained men and with inadequate stock piles of supplies. The medical disasters of the war resulted as much from the inadequacies of the late-nineteenth-century epidemiology as from official errors or negligence. At home, the actions of Congress and of the National Guard's pressure group disrupted prewar planning and preparation as much as the absence of a

general staff, while abrupt changes in policy objectives and rapid alterations in the naval situation repeatedly forced disruptive adjustments in the
Army's wartime mobilization and missions.

During the brief conflict with Spain, the War Department had to
discharge its responsibilities despite simultaneous transitions in the foreign
policy of the United States and in the organization and strategic doctrine
of the Army. Secretary Alger, General Miles, and the bureau chiefs prepared
for the crisis of 1898 on the basis of new ideas, formulated within the officer corps, about the Army's missions in and mobilization for overseas offensive operations. They also worked on certain assumptions about the
political and territorial objectives of the military effort by the United States
to expel Spain from Cuba. Both sets of ideas and assumptions failed to fit
the actual circumstances of the war. Pressures from the state militia and
Congress compelled unanticipated changes in the plan for raising an army,
while alterations in President McKinley's military strategy and war aims
placed a series of constantly shifting demands upon the Army. These conditions, plus long-standing organizational deficiencies in the War Department and the Army—deficiencies the men in responsible positions in 1898
had done little to cause and could not at once remedy—made all but inevitable the mistakes and disorder of the first weeks of the war effort. Nevertheless, by working hard and in the main sensibly, officials in Washington
and commanders in the field had solved their most serious problems by early
autumn of 1898. When Elihu Root took over the War Department in
mid-1899, he inherited a military administration that was discharging efficiently its day-to-day tasks. That solid base permitted him to build a modern
staff and command system.

1

The War Department and the Army, 1898

I

On August 24, 1897, at a banquet of the Grand Army of the Republic held at Buffalo, New York, Secretary of War Russell A. Alger rose to reply to a toast "to the Army of the United States." Alger, a former national commander of the G.A.R., felt confident and expansive among his Civil War comrades. He declared that the United States Army, "as far as it went," was "the best under God's footstool." He went on to recall how an English friend in London had asked him what the United States would do if attacked by a great foreign military power. "I answered that in thirty days we could put millions of fighting men in the field, and back them up with a wall of fire in the person of the veteran."[1]

Alger's remarks received enthusiastic applause from his fellow veterans, but the staid *New York Times* four days later sharply scolded the Secretary of War for what the editor called his "foolish bragging." Alger knew perfectly well, the editor wrote, "that we could offer no resistance on either coast to a first-class or second-class naval power, and that two army corps could traverse the country as far as their commanders chose to take them without meeting any effectual opposition." The *Times* writer was not alone in his dim view of the state of America's land forces. In January of the following year, during the annual debate on Army appropriations, Representative George B. McClellan, Jr., a New York Democrat and son of a Civil War general, treated his colleagues in the House to a veritable jeremiad on the condition of the Army. That service, McClellan charged, was "little better than a clumsily organized National police force," its infantry formations would have been "considered excellent in the seventeenth century," and it lacked a modern staff, mobilization plans, and even a reserve supply of ammunition.[2]

The actual condition of the United States Army offered ample justification for the lamentations of the *Times* and of Representative McClellan. A victim of repeated economy drives in Congress, the Army in 1897 had an authorized strength of only 25,000 officers and men, insufficient even to keep its 25 infantry, 10 cavalry, and 5 artillery regiments at their minimum peacetime strength. In fact, two companies of each infantry and cavalry

1. *The New York Times*, August 25, 1897.
2. *The New York Times*, August 28, 1897, and January 18, 1898.

1

regiment existed only on paper; the officers assigned to them were dispersed to teach military science at land-grant colleges and to inspect National Guard summer encampments. The Army's manned companies and battalions, scattered across the continent in over seventy small posts, functioned mainly in police actions against rebellious Indians or striking laborers. It had no permanent troop formations larger than regiments—seldom were entire regiments assembled at a single post—and neither detailed war plans nor a staff for making them existed.[3]

Petty quarrels that were bred of boredom, frustrated ambition, and slow promotion rent the officer corps. The ambitious of all ranks tried to manipulate Army legislation to advance themselves and their friends, a practice that provoked a senator familiar with military matters to declare that he "had never known a line officer to advocate an Army bill that did not have for its purpose promotion; nor the Department bureaus to favor an Army measure that did not increase the rank and power of the staff." Rival generals resorted to the newspaper columns to discredit each other. Young officers who tried to introduce reforms sometimes were destroyed by hostile seniors in trumped-up courts-martial or driven to drink and despair by the apparent impossibility of achieving any progress. Aspirants to promotion shamelessly cultivated influential businessmen and politicians, upon whom they called for assistance in their fight for choice positions. Gen. John Gibbon wrote in 1893 of appointments to the staff: "During the past twenty-five or thirty years there has been but one period of four years where political as well as personal influence has not had an undue share in these selections."[4]

Yet the Army in 1898 was far from a somnolent, decaying force. While many of its officers quarreled and intrigued for promotion, a creative minority among them, working closely with the Navy reformers of the era, sought improvement and modernization in their service. Gen. William T. Sherman, in command of the Army from 1869 to 1883, encouraged the reformers by administrative action and personal example. The officers' schools that he helped to establish served the young innovators as both training ground and forum. In 1879, with Sherman's blessing, they founded the Military Service Institution of the United States, a voluntary society for military study and discussion that was open to both Regular and National Guard officers

3. *RSW, 1890*, I, 46-48. *Report of the Commission Appointed by the President to Investigate the Conduct of the War Department in the War with Spain*, Senate Doc. No. 221, 56th Cong., 1st sess., 1900 (hereafter cited as *War Investigating Commission*), I, 113. C. Joseph Bernardo and Eugene H. Bacon, *American Military Policy: Its Development since 1775*, 236, 238-41. Samuel P. Huntington, *The Soldier and the State: The Theory and Politics of Civil-Military Relations*, 228. John McAuley Palmer, *America in Arms: The Experience of the United States with Military Organization*, 123-24.

4. Gen. John Gibbon, "Needed Reforms in the Army," *The North American Review*, CLVI, 215. Col. Thomas M. Anderson, "Military Service Reform," *JMSI*, XII, 980, 983-84. *Army and Navy Journal*, February 5, 1898. *The New York Times*, February 8, 1891. C. P. Huntington to Russell A. Alger, December 4, 1897, Russell A. Alger Papers. William R. Shafter to Col. Henry

and headed by the Commanding General of the Army. In the institution's journal thoughtful soldiers exchanged opinions and information on a broad range of military subjects. Out of their studies, articles, and debates, the progressive officers formulated numerous proposals for Army reform, and by 1898, in a slow and halting process, those proposals were finding their way into War Department plans and congressional enactments.[5]

The Army's weaponry, for an example of the effectiveness of these proposals, underwent complete modernization. During the 1880s, Congress, in response to the recommendations of a planning board headed by Secretary of War William C. Endicott, authorized the large-scale reconstruction of the fortifications protecting the nation's principal harbors. Although never adequately financed, the coast defense program resulted in the establishment of the Army Gun Factory, which was capable of turning out all calibers of rifled steel breech-loading cannon. Private industry, encouraged by the promise of government orders, also enlarged its capacity to produce gun forgings, carriages, and even finished weapons. By 1897, only 30 of the 500 heavy guns called for in the Endicott Report and 70 of the more than 1,000 mortars had been mounted in the fortifications, but the technical and industrial problems of constructing a defense system able to repel attack by modern armored battleships had been solved. Actual construction could progress rapidly if and when Congress appropriated the money.[6]

During the eighties, the Artillery exchanged the Civil War muzzleloaders for a new arsenal of breech-loading steel guns ranging in caliber from a 3.2-inch light fieldpiece to a 5-inch siege cannon and a 7-inch howitzer. In 1893, after a decade of weapon tests by the Ordnance Department, the Infantry and Cavalry received their first general-issue magazine small arm, the 30-caliber, 5-shot Krag-Jörgensen. Named for its Scandinavian designers, this bolt-action rifle fired the new smokeless powder and in range, accuracy,

---

C. Corbin, April, 1892, Box 1, Henry C. Corbin Papers. James H. Wilson to Henry M. Flagler, September 22, 1910, Box 9; Col. Marshall I. Ludington to Wilson, June 14, 1897, Box 14, James Harrison Wilson Papers. Col. A. R. Buffington to Maj. Gen. John M. Schofield, September 20, 1890, Box 22; Senator William E. Chandler to Schofield, May 27, 1890, Box 23; Enoch Pratt to Schofield, December 6, 1890, Box 31; Frederic Remington to the Editor of *The Sun*, May 28, 1893, George M. Sternberg to Schofield, December 4, 1890, and Leland Stanford to Schofield, December 6, 1890, Box 33; E. A. Carr to Schofield, September 28, 1890, Box 38; Wesley Merritt to Schofield, December 20, 1892, and Nelson A. Miles to Schofield, January 26, 1889, Box 41; Schofield to Merritt, January 4, 1893, Box 57, John M. Schofield Papers.

5. John A. T. Hull, "The Hull Army Bill," *The Forum*, XXV, 398. For an account of the rise of military professionalism in Europe and the United States, see Huntington, *Soldier and State*, 31-32, 229-36, 243. *RSW*, 1892, I, 48.

6. *Report of the Board on Fortifications and Other Defenses Appointed by the President . . . under . . . the Act of Congress Approved March 3, 1885.* House Doc. No. 49, 49th Cong., 1st sess., 1886 (hereafter cited as *Endicott Report*), Pt. 1, pp. 5-6, 8-12, 25-30. For a running account of the building of the new defenses, see *RSW*, 1885-1898. See also Capt. Rogers Birnie, "Gun Making in the United States," *JMSI*, XII, 416-17, and Charles F. Benjamin, "The Artillery and the Ordnance," *JMSI*, VIII, 366-67.

and durability equaled or surpassed the best European military rifles of its time. Along with smokeless ammunition for the "Krag," as the troops at once nicknamed it, the Ordnance Department perfected a smokeless cartridge for each of its artillery pieces, but production facilities for this propellant, which differed radically in its chemistry and manufacture from the older charcoal or "black" powders, remained dangerously limited. So, for lack of appropriations, did reserve stocks of the Krag-Jörgensen.[7]

The procedures for promotion and training of officers underwent many reforms, most of them suggested and lobbied for by Army progressives. Congress, at the War Department's urging, altered the rules of promotion and retirement to give competent junior officers hope, at least, of achieving field rank before they grew old and gray. A system of proficiency examinations for all candidates for promotion to grades up to and including that of major, along with the annual reports on the efficiency of subordinates made to the War Department by commanders, enforced a minimal standard of professional performance. To provide officers with the specialized technical training that modern warfare required and that West Point could not furnish, the War Department during the eighties and nineties established advanced schools for officers of the Army's different branches. On the eve of the Spanish-American War, this system of higher education included schools for the Artillery, the Engineers, the Infantry and Cavalry combined, the Field Artillery and Cavalry combined, the Signal Corps, and the Hospital Corps, plus an Army Medical School to train the service's surgeons in specialized military surgery. Officers attending these institutions received classroom instruction and field and laboratory drill in their specialties. Artillery lieutenants at their branch school at Fort Monroe, for instance, learned to fire weapons of all calibers from Gatling guns to coast defense rifles, besides studying telegraphy, steam engineering, explosives, metallurgy, and other sciences related to their service.[8]

By the mid-nineties, one of these branch schools, that for Infantry and Cavalry at Fort Leavenworth, Kansas, had begun to teach that most important and least understood of the new technical specialties—the science

7. RSW, 1881, I, 19; 1882, I, xvii-xviii; 1884, I, 21; 1885, I, 31; 1886, I, 36-38; 1887, I, 27, 32; 1891, I, 8-9, III, 23-24; 1892, I, 18, III, 27-28; 1893, I, 12-13; 1894, I, 14-15; 1895, I, 26; 1896, I, 35-36; 1897, I, 44-46, 829-30, III, 27-29, 31, 38; 1898, IV, 47-48. Victor L. Mason, "New Weapons of the United States Army." The Century Magazine, XLIX, 570-71, 581-83. Capt. Stanhope E. Blunt, "The United States Magazine Rifle," Harper's Weekly, XXXVII, 619. Lt. J. P. Wisser, "A Decenium of Military Progress," JMSI, XVIII, 246-47. William Addleman Ganoe, The History of the United States Army, 367-68.

8. Huntington, Soldier and State, 237-39, 244-46. Ganoe, History of the Army, 365-66. Bernardo and Bacon, Military Policy, 309-11. RSW, 1881, I, 5; 1882, I, xxiii; 1886, I, 17-19; 1887, I, 121-22, 124-25; 1888, I, 9-11; 1889, I, 5-6, 15-16, 63, 65-66; 1890, I, 3-4; 1891, I, 20-22, 309-10; 1892, I, 11; 1895, I, 13. Wisser, JMSI, XVIII, 236. Lt. E. M. Weaver, "The Military Schools of the United States," The United Service, New Series, III, 457-66. Capt. Tasker H. Bliss to Secretary of War Daniel S. Lamont, January 9, 1897, Vol. I, Tasker H. Bliss Papers.

of high command. Lieutenants detailed to the school from their regiments studied military history, army administration, strategy, and tactics, along with more specialized branch skills. Using troops from the large Leavenworth garrison, they conducted mock company and battalion actions, and they worked out brigade, division, and corps maneuvers with models on sand tables. While chronically short of funds, facilities, and staff, this and the other schools formed the foundation of an up-to-date officer training system. Started at the urging of Army reformers, they institutionalized and perpetuated reform and began to feed a new, scientific-minded generation into the lower ranks of the officer corps.[9]

As the Indian wars gradually came to an end during the eighties, the War Department improved the instruction, deployment, recruitment, and living conditions of the Army's small standing enlisted force. New training procedures, in accord with the theories of the progressive officers, reduced the time soldiers spent on close-order drill and increased that devoted to calisthenics, physical conditioning, marksmanship, and field maneuvers. To facilitate training of large units and improve administration, the War Department began to close the Army's many little one- and two-company posts, and to concentrate regiments and battalions at major rail junctions from which they could move quickly to trouble spots in emergencies. By the late nineties, this program showed impressive progress. In 1888 the Regular Army garrisoned 120 posts; in 1896 it held 77, most of them with 3 or more companies. Ten of the 25 infantry regiments had been assembled, each at a single post. Improved recruiting procedures, better pay and rations, and reduction of the initial term of service from five to three years reduced the Army's annual desertion rate from almost 12 per cent of the total enlisted strength in 1889 to about 6 per cent two years later. The construction at army forts of gymnasiums and recreation halls and the establishment of post exchanges at which the troops could purchase at cost nonissue luxuries made more tolerable the life of the private soldier. Thanks to these changes, the small Regular Army in 1898 had become, in the words of its Commanding General, "the best conditioned . . . military body in the world. . . . The men were . . . trained athletes, well disciplined and excellent marksmen."[10]

9. On the Leavenworth school, see Lt. Arthur L. Wagner, "An American War College," *JMSI*, X, 288-96; Huntington, *Soldier and State*, 240; and Weaver, *United Service*, III, 464-66. For the deficiencies of the schools, see: Weaver, *United Service*, III, 467-68; Benjamin, *JMSI*, VIII, 364-65; Wagner, *JMSI*, X, 296-300, 303; and *RSW*, 1892, I, 12.

10. Nelson A. Miles, *Serving the Republic*, 270. *RSW*, 1880, I, vi, 5; 1882, I, i, iv; 1883, I, 9; 1884, I, 6; 1885, I, 7, 13, 64-65; 1887, I, 9; 1888, I, 16; 1889, I, 9, 11, 23, 66; 1890, I, 10-11, 15-16, 93; 1891, I, 9-10, 16, 59-60; 1892, I, 5-7; 1894, I, 9-10; 1895, I, 5, 14, 123-25; 1896, I, 5, 13-14, 75; 1897, I, 99, 151-53. Ganoe, *History of the Army*, 366-67, 369-70. George W. Latshaw, "Military Medical Service during and Immediately after the Spanish-American War, 1898-1901" (M.S. thesis, University of Wisconsin, 1958), 17-18. Bernardo and Bacon, *Military Policy*, 241-44. Maj. Gen. John M. Schofield to General Brooke, March 29, 1890, and to Secretary of War Redfield Proctor, July 18 and 21, 1890, Box 55, Schofield Papers.

II

During the eighties and nineties, a movement for reform, revival, and expansion swept the volunteer state militia that had emerged in the early nineteenth century from the wreckage of the compulsory system established by the Founding Fathers. These forces had survived the vicissitudes of war and fluctuating public interest to become the nation's traditional second line of land defense. Significant governmental and popular support for their rebuilding dated from the great railroad strikes of 1877. The states, alarmed at the failure of their militia to control the riots and disorders accompanying the strikes and made newly aware of their police value, began increasing their military budgets. They brought up to date the by-then archaic militia laws, organized new units, built new armories, and tried to improve training and leadership.[11]

By the mid-nineties, all the states and most of the territories had volunteer militia that the governors, as commanders-in-chief, could summon to duty for the maintenance of law and order or for defense against invasion. Thirty-eight of the states by this time called their troops the "National Guard." Others used such titles as "Georgia Volunteers," "Texas Volunteer Guard," or similar variants. Authorized and established by state law, militia company and regimental formations were patterned after those of the Regular Army. Men enlisted in the militia for terms ranging from three to five years, depending on the state's requirement. Continuing their civilian pursuits except when called to duty, they devoted a certain number of days per month and usually about a week in the summer to training. In most states, the troops elected their own officers, who then received commissions from the governor. Most of the money for militia uniforms, armories, pay, and equipment came from the states, which, even with the revival of interest in their forces after 1877, still varied greatly in their willingness to finance their local armies. In 1897, for instance, only two states, New York and Pennsylvania, accounted between them for a third of the $3 million appropriated that year to support the militia. The federal government annually subsidized the state troops to the amount of $400,000, apportioned among the states according to the number of their representatives in Congress. This money reached the militia in the form of allotments of weapons and equipment from federal arsenals.

The force supported by these resources aggregated in 1897, according to the War Department, about 114,000 officers and men, including 4,800 cavalry, 5,900 field and fortress artillery, 100,000 infantry, and a few thousand supply and service troops. Each state treated its militia as its own par-

11. Frederick P. Todd, "Our National Guard: An Introduction to Its History," *Military Affairs*, V, 72-73, 80-83, 156-58. William H. Riker, *Soldiers of the States: The Role of the National Guard in American Democracy*, 41-48, 50-51. Francis V. Greene, "The New National Guard," *The Century Magazine*, XXII (New Series), 483-98. Walter Millis, *Arms and Men: A Study of American Military History*, 45, 120-21, 127-30.

ticular army, and beyond the regimental level the degree of organization varied greatly. Five of the states had divisions, twenty-five kept up brigades, and the remainder had no organization beyond the regiment. Some states, most of them in the East, maintained efficient signal companies and medical units. Others had no troops of this degree of specialization. The National Guard as a whole, in proportion to its numbers, was seriously lacking in support units.[12]

Compared to the somnolent, disorganized militia of the late sixties and early seventies, the National Guard of the 1890s was much improved, but it was far from a ready reserve for war duty. To begin with, the Guard's obligations to the federal government and in fact its whole position under the law remained ambiguous. Most guardsmen assumed that the President could mobilize them for any of the three purposes for which the Constitution allowed him to use the militia—suppressing insurrections, enforcing federal law, and repelling invasions. But no established procedure existed for calling them up in war, and no one knew exactly what authority the President had over the militia, once they had entered federal service. Guardsmen disagreed, for example, on whether the President could order them to duty outside the United States. Many insisted that they were under no obligation to participate in offensive campaigns beyond the nation's borders.[13]

Doubt persisted, also, about the Guard's constitutional right to exist. Outside of the compulsory militia established in 1792 by a law that was still on the books although unenforced, the states were not allowed to maintain armies or navies, but in supporting the volunteer National Guard they could be construed as doing just that. Guardsmen, of course, claimed that their units were the militia created in 1792, but in fact their force had been enlisted on a different basis and was supported largely by state law and private initiative. While Congress for many years had spent its annual militia subsidy on the Guard and the courts from time to time had treated it as though it were the national militia, federal law as yet contained no explicit provision to that effect. Presumably, Congress still could disown the National Guard altogether, create an entirely new force of part-time soldiers, and designate this new force as beneficiary of the federal subsidy. Until Congress either formally adopted or formally disowned the state troops, their

12. *The Organized Militia of the United States, 1897* (hereafter cited as *Militia in 1897*), 380-82, 436. Latshaw, "Military Medical Service, " 20-21. Greene, *Century*, XXII, 483-98. Maj. Howard A. Giddings, "How to Improve the Condition and Efficiency of the National Guard," *JMSI*, XXI, 61-75. Harry P. Mawson, "The National Guard," *Harper's Weekly*, XXXVI, 858. Massachusetts Adjutant General's Office, *Annual Report of the Adjutant General of . . . Massachusetts for the Year Ending December 30, 1895* (hereafter cited as Adj. Gen. of Mass., *Report, 1895*), 17, 22.

13. Lt. John H. Parker, "National Guard Problem," *The Forum*, XXVIII, 190-96. Lt. Col. Walter S. Frazier, Jr., "The National Guard National in Name Only," *JMSI*, XX, 519. Capt. Arthur Williams, "Readiness for War," *JMSI*, XXI, 244-45. "Comment and Criticism: Organization of Militia Defense," *JMSI*, XIII, 1175-76. Gen. William T. Sherman, "The Militia," *JMSI*, VI, 1-26.

position in federal war plans and the arrangements for their peacetime administration and training would remain unclear.[14]

Inadequate financing, both from Congress and the states, had left the National Guard appallingly deficient in modern weapons and equipment. At the outbreak of the Spanish War, most of the state troops carried the Springfield rifle, a single-shot breech-loader that fired charcoal powder and that the Regulars had discarded in favor of the Krag-Jörgensen. Many of these Springfields were Army cast-offs, worn out and likely to explode in their users' faces when fired. Some state artillery units had received the new steel breech-loading fieldpiece, but most made do with older muzzle-loading models. National Guard units almost invariably lacked reserves of clothing and accoutrements. Many of the uniforms, cartridge belts, knapsacks, and other items in their possession were near disintegration from age. Hardly a single state had a full supply of tentage, camp equipage, or wagon transportation. Yet, in spite of these lacks, state officials often boasted of the battle-readiness of their troops and how quickly they could take the field if called out for war duty.[15]

Their boasting may be attributable to a lack of military training, a common deficiency of both the officers of the National Guard and their men. Less than half of the states conducted regular instruction courses for their officers, and even fewer required examinations for appointment or promotion. Training for enlisted men consisted of weekly company drills in their armories, supplemented by regimental or brigade drills during the week or ten days of summer camp. In both armories and camps, instruction consisted almost entirely of close-order drill, with little time given to target practice (for which most states lacked ammunition) or to exercise in the open-order tactics required for survival in combat with modern rifles and artillery. Some state troops conducted sham battles at their summer camps, but these, in the opinion of Regular officers, often were unrealistic and based on obsolete tactical systems. Few states trained either officers or men in such necessary campaigning skills as cooking and setting up camp in the field. In feeding their guardsmen, for instance, hardly any of the states kept strictly to the Army ration, on which the soldiers would have to live if ever called into federal service. Instead, units in camp supplemented the regular ration with extra delicacies, and some even hired civilian chefs to prepare their meals. With their elected officers and lax discipline, National Guard formations often

14. For arguments on this point, see Sherman, *JMSI*, VI, 23-24, and Lt. Joseph B. Bachelor, Jr., "A United States Army," *JMSI*, XIII, 57-58.

15. *Militia in 1897*, 382-83. Giddings, *JMSI*, XXI, 62-63. W. B. Wetmore, "The National Guard Bill in Congress," *The United Service*, VI, 339. Franklin F. Holbrook, *Minnesota in the Spanish-American War and the Philippine Insurrection*, 16. Maine Adjutant-General, *Annual Report of the Adjutant General of the State of Maine for the Year Ending December 31, 1894* (hereafter cited as Adj. Gen. of Maine, *Report, 1894*), 709. Adj. Gen. of Mass., *Report, 1895*, 24-25, 28-29, 34. New Hampshire Adjutant General, *Biennial Report of the Adjutant General of . . . New Hampshire, November 1, 1894, to October 1, 1896* (hereafter cited as Adj. Gen. of N.H., *Report, 1894-1896*), 3-5, 7. Ohio Adjutant General, *Annual Report of the Adjutant General . . . for the Fiscal Year Ending November 15, 1897* (hereafter cited as Adj. Gen. of Ohio, *Report, 1897*), 415-16, 459.

resembled social clubs as much as they did military units. Guardsmen in the northeastern states spent much time and money on parties, picnics, drill competitions, and elaborate dress uniforms ornamented with plumes and gold braid. A Mississippi guardsman of the nineties recalled his company's summer camp as a pleasant vacation replete with dances and entertainments at towns near the campsite. His unit was, he said, "in a few words, . . . a company of good fellows, friends who enjoyed each other's society."[16]

III

The nation in 1898 did not have an army in any operational sense of that word. It possessed instead a large collection of companies, battalions, regiments, and batteries—those of the Regular establishment well equipped, trained, and commanded, those of the state militia indifferently or poorly outfitted and led. The task of transforming this aggregation of men and weapons into a unified force for offense or defense would become in any emergency principally the work of the War Department.

That department—that is to say its highest officials stationed in Washington—conducted daily business in surroundings of subdued elegance. Since 1888 the Secretary of War, the Commanding General of the Army, and the chiefs of the staff bureaus had occupied offices in the new State, War, and Navy Building. This impressive granite pile, its facade a mass of columns, stood next to the White House on Pennsylvania Avenue and sheltered diplomats and admirals as well as generals. Within this massive edifice, the atmosphere and fittings resembled those of a prosperous law firm or solid business establishment. Only the occasional groups of battle flags in the corridors and a few glass cases displaying weapons, uniforms, and ship models reminded the casual observer that the business there carried on concerned the national security of the Republic.[17]

But much of the War Department's routine business did not in fact concern the national security. On a budget that totaled in 1897 slightly over $49 million, the department, besides maintaining the standing army, discharged a wide variety of civil responsibilities. Secretary of War Alger, in his annual report for 1897, a typical peacetime year, dealt at some length with such martial topics as reorganization of the Infantry and progress on the new coast defenses, but he devoted even more space to the exploration

16. *Militia in 1897*, 380-82, 384-85. Adj. Gen. of Maine, *Report, 1894*, 3-4, 60-61. Adj. Gen. of Mass., *Report, 1895*, 12, 14-17, 32-33, 167-80. Adj. Gen. of N.H., *Report, 1894-1896*, 5-7, 40, 44-59. Adj. Gen. of Ohio, *Report, 1897*, 419, 460-61, 485. Mawson, *Harper's Weekly*, XXXVI, 858. Riker, *Soldiers of the States*, 57-58. Todd, *Military Affairs*, V, 158-59. William Allen White, "When Johnny Went Marching Out," *McClure's Magazine*, XI, 200. James Malcolm Robertshaw, "History of Company 'C,' Second Mississippi Regiment, Spanish-American War," *Publications of the Mississippi Historical Society, Centenary Series*, I, 429. Gov. Thomas G. Jones to the Secretary of War, May 14, 1891, Box 29, Schofield Papers.

17. *RSW*, 1883, I, 21; 1888, I, 37. Rufus F. Zogbaum, "Official and Social Life of the Army and Navy in Washington," *Harper's Weekly*, XXXVII, 767.

of Alaska, the affairs of the National Soldiers' Home, flood relief in the Mississippi and Rio Grande valleys, the government's need for a hall of records, river and harbor improvements, and the condition of the water supply, public buildings, bridges, and monuments in the District of Columbia. Matters such as these occupied much of the time and energy of the Secretary and his bureau chiefs. In the department's budget, civil needs often outweighed the military. Thus, the War Department in 1897 spent twice as much on river and harbor improvements as it spent on coast defenses. A critic might observe that the department had done more to facilitate than to prevent the entry of enemy battleships into American ports.[18]

Two officials controlled the War Department and through it the military establishment. The civilian Secretary of War, usually a distinguished businessman or politician, received his appointment from the President and was in theory the agent through whom the President exercised his constitutional powers as Commander-in-chief. The Secretary directly commanded the ten adminstrative and supply bureaus that collectively were known as the "staff" of the Army. The uniformed Commanding General of the United States Army also received his assignment from the President. Legally, the President could confer this post upon any general on active duty, but in practice he invariably selected the senior major general, the service's highest-ranking officer, for whom the position constituted an honorary distinction at the end of a long career. The Commanding General controlled all troops of the "line"; that is, the regiments of infantry, cavalry, and artillery, and all orders to them from the President and the Secretary were supposed to pass through him.[19]

The War Department administered the Army's scattered garrisons through eight geographical military departments, the number and boundaries of which were established and altered by presidential order. Department commanders, who were appointed by the President, reported directly to the Commanding General in Washington. Their authority extended over all military installations and personnel in their areas except the officers' schools, arsenals, major supply depots, and recruiting stations, which the War Department controlled. Each commander carried out all military orders affecting his department and was responsible for the training, supply, health, and discipline of the troops therein. The departments normally contained only static garrisons. Their commanders could assemble temporary field forces when necessary to fight Indians, perform police duty, or conduct maneuvers, but federal law forbade the maintenance in peacetime of any

18. *RSW, 1897*, I, 3-61.

19. Lt. Col. J. G. C. Lee, "Suggestions for Consideration, Relative to the Quartermaster's Department, U.S. Army," *JMSI*, XV, 262. Lt. Henry T. Allen, "The Central Military Administrations of Five Great Powers," *JMSI*, XIX, 79-80. *War Investigating Commission*, I, 115. Maj. Gen. John M. Schofield, undated note in "Command of the Army" folder, Box 72; and "The Military System of the United States," memorandum dated 1890, Box 94, Schofield Papers.

permanent troop formation larger than the regiment. When organized in war-time, armies, corps, and divisions could act either under a department commander or independently under direct orders from Washington.

On the eve of the Spanish-American War, only one of the department commanders was a West Point graduate. The rest had entered the Union army as volunteers during the Civil War, had transferred to the Regulars after Appomattox, and then had risen in rank by seniority. While brave and experienced in small-unit combat, many of these generals—future corps, division, and brigade commanders—lacked experience in managing large troop formations. Company or regimental officers in the Civil War, they had spent the years since 1865 leading columns against the Indians or commanding garrisons of three or four companies at the largest. Elevation to the rank of general and to the command of a department had meant for these men not the weighty responsibility of control over great masses of soldiers but merely administration from an office desk of a number of small posts.[20]

Each of the ten staff bureaus concerned with administration and supply had a brigadier general as its chief. Lower-ranking officers of each bureau served in Washington and at arsenals and depots directly controlled by their chief or were attached for field service to geographical departments and line commands.

Of the three bureaus concerned with the Army's administration, The Adjutant General's Office was the most important and influential. This bureau received and transmitted correspondence between all branches and stations of the Army and it issued all the orders prepared by the Secretary of War and the Commanding General. It also kept the Army's personnel records, supervised the Military Academy and the recruiting service, directed the work of Army officers on duty with the National Guard, and contained the Army's rudimentary intelligence service. In war, it had charge of enrolling and mobilizing Regulars, volunteers, and militia. Officers of the Inspector General's Department, the second administrative bureau, periodically inspected all Army posts and installations to make sure that War Department directives were being followed and to report failures and abuses to higher authority. The third administrative bureau, the Judge-Advocate-General's Office, kept the Army's court-martial and legal records and advised the Secretary of War on questions of law.[21]

Supplies and logistical support for the Army came from the other seven bureaus, each of which purchased and issued to the troops certain items of food, clothing, and equipment and conducted research and development in

20. Gibbon, The North American Review, CLVI, 213. RSW, 1897, I, 102-10. U.S. War Department, Regulations for the Army of the United States, 1895 (hereafter cited as Army Regulations, 1895), Paragraphs 189-97. Army and Navy Journal, February 12, 1898. Palmer, America in Arms, 119-20.

21. RSW, 1894, I, 11. War Investigating Commission, I, 116-18, 121-22, 124-25; V, 1771-72. Army Regulations, 1895, Paragraphs 748, 857 and 890.

its area of responsibility. The Quartermaster's Department, largest and most diverse in its functions, furnished all of the Army's clothing, tentage, camp equipage, wagons, ambulances, horses, and mules; it rented ground for and constructed camps and posts; it made all arrangements for the movement of troops and stores by rail; and when necessary it chartered, purchased, or built transports and landing craft. The Subsistence Department fed the Army and also furnished such accessories as candles and salt. The Ordnance Department designed, tested, manufactured or purchased, and issued all weapons, ammunition, cartridge belts, cavalry and artillery horse equipment, knapsacks, haversacks, and mess kits. Besides its work in civil-engineering projects, such as the improvement of rivers and harbors, the Corps of Engineers furnished engineering tools and built forts and gun emplacements; in the field, its officers took charge of reconnaissance, laid out entrenchments and fortifications, and constructed military roads and bridges. The Medical Department purchased and issued all hospital stores, with the exception of tents, wagons, ambulances, and draught animals, which came from the Quartermaster's Department. Its surgeons, assisted by hospital corpsmen, treated the sick and wounded and acted as sanitation advisers to troop commanders. The Signal Bureau, in charge of Army communications, furnished signal flags, telephones, and telegraph equipment as well as qualified officers and men to operate them. Last but by no means least in the eyes of the soldiers, the Pay Department paid the troops.[22]

Most of these bureaus consisted only of officers and relied for their work forces on soldiers detailed from the line or on hired civilians. However, the growing technical complexity of supply and administration had created a demand for specially trained service troops, and in 1898 three bureaus had enlisted corps attached to them. The Corps of Engineers included a 500-man battalion that was expert in construction work and various mechanical trades. The Medical Department contained the Hospital Corps, founded in 1887, which numbered in 1898 about 700 soldiers specially recruited and trained in first aid, stretcher-bearing, ambulance service, and ward nursing. Hospital corpsmen served in detachments at posts and with columns in the field. Under the supervision of the Signal Bureau, the Signal Corps of 10 officers and 50 men built, maintained, and operated military telephone and telegraph systems. Impressed by the usefulness of these units, Secretaries of War and bureau chiefs during the nineties urged the enlistment of about 2,000 such service troops for the Quartermaster and Subsistence departments. The service troops, officials argued, would perform necessary tasks more efficiently than civilian employees, and creation of

22. Lee, *JMSI*, XV, 258-59. *RSW, 1897*, I, 33-34; *1898*, I, 548. *War Investigating Commission*, I, 125-26, 148-49, 169, 189-90, 195, 200. *Army Regulations, 1895*, Paragraphs 972, 1226, 1230, 1295, 1392, 1472, 1473, 1488, 1492, 1537.

a service corps would return to the line over 1,500 combat troops then tied up in staff duty. As did so many military reforms before 1898, this one foundered in Congress.[23]

Once appointed to a staff corps or bureau, an officer remained with it for the rest of his Army career. Three bureaus—the Medical Department, the Ordnance Department, and the Signal Corps—required all candidates for appointment to pass examinations covering both general education and professional skills, and the latter two accepted only officers with at least two years' previous service in the line. The other staff departments were open to both Army officers and civilians until 1894, when Congress closed them to all applicants but line officers. For both military and civilian candidates, advantageous political and social connections helped to assure the candidate's selection, and for some soldiers staff posts were rewards for gallantry in combat. Once commissioned in a bureau, an officer advanced through its ranks by seniority. In the Engineer, Ordnance, and Medical departments, the officer had to pass an examination before each promotion up to the grade of major. The President appointed the chief of each bureau from among its officers, and once appointed, the bureau chief held his post until death or retirement. As a rule, the President made his selections on the basis of length of service in the bureau, but some Chief Executives, notably Benjamin Harrison and Grover Cleveland, disregarded seniority to advance able younger men. Despite the political and social elbowing for the appointments, the bureau chiefs and their subordinates were on the whole, capable technicians, masters of their specialties. Many had served for extended periods in the line, and this experience enabled them to understand and sometimes anticipate the needs of troops on campaign.[24]

Except for The Adjutant General and for the Inspector General, who were both responsible to the Commanding General, the bureau chiefs and all staff personnel not attached to military departments or line units took orders only from the Secretary of War. Thus, if the Commanding General wanted some action by a bureau chief, he requested the Secretary to issue the order. This situation had its basis in federal law, which gave the Secretary sole power over the expenditure of Army appropriations and which

23. *RSW, 1885*, I, 24; *1886*, I, 30; *1887*, I, 22; *1892*, I, 8, 199-200; *1897*, I, 34; *1898*, I, 904; *War Investigating Commission*, I, 190, 669, 671; II, 784. Latshaw, "Medical Service," 15-16. Lt. E. F. Ladd, "A Special Service Corps for the Quartermaster's Department," *JMSI*, XIV, 1008-18. Capt. E. L. Zalinski, "The Army Organization Best Adapted to a Republican Form of Government, which Will Ensure an Effective Force," *JMSI*, XIV, 963-64. Lee, *JMSI*, XV, 279.

24. *Army Regulations, 1895*, Paragraphs 21, 22, 1394, 1489, 1490, 1538. *RSW, 1886*, I, 18; *1895*, I, 12. *War Investigating Commission*, VII, 3150, 3761. Huntington, *Soldier and State*, 247. Lee, *JMSI*, XV, 261. *The New York Times*, January 28, 1891, and May 31, 1893. Maj. Gen. John M. Schofield to the President of the United States, July 21, 1893, Box 54; Schofield, undated manuscript in "Reorganization of the Army" folder, Box 86, Schofield Papers. Hermann Hagedorn, *Leonard Wood: A Biography*, I, 46-47, describes the entry examination for the Medical Department in 1885.

commonly was interpreted as leaving the bureaus subject to him alone. Staff officers attached to department headquarters or to field forces received orders only from the general in immediate command, and they were considered as under his exclusive control. The same rule applied to engineer troops, signal parties, and hospital corpsmen attached to line formations. While it seemed to give any general full power over his staff, this arrangement contained one important ambiguity: Under the regulations, a bureau chief could correspond directly with a subordinate on detached service and give him orders on matters related to the internal management of the bureau. This provision opened the way for bureau chiefs to undermine the authority and independence of generals in the field.[25]

IV

Like the Army and militia it administered, the War Department in 1898 was a collection of disconnected agencies—each fairly efficient—rather than a unified institution animated by common plans and purposes. The lines of authority and responsibility within the department were poorly defined, so that the making of military decisions required much negotiation among independent centers of power. No organization existed to plan and coordinate the operations of the whole Army. Each bureau planned in its own field, but many military problems required for their solution a joint effort by several agencies. When confronted with such questions, the War Department all too often floundered in confusion. The lack of articulation in the department began at the top and penetrated down through all levels of the Army.

At the heart of the trouble lay a continuing conflict over authority between the Secretary of War and the Commanding General. Congress as early as 1789 had created the post of Secretary of War and had given that official theoretically absolute power over the Army as the President's deputy, but neither in 1789 nor later did Congress by law establish a uniformed head for the Army or define his powers and his relationship to the Secretary of War. For many years the Army had no uniformed chief. The Secretary commanded the troops himself through the geographical departments. Then, in 1821 Secretary of War John C. Calhoun on his own initiative created the post of Commanding General by assigning the senior major general of the Army to duty in Washington. Subsequent to Calhoun's action, the Commanding General received recognition from Congress in various laws but never a formal grant of power. The position evolved largely through administrative action and changes in the *Army Regulations* and often through

25. *Army Regulations, 1895*, Paragraphs 17, 18, 736, 737-41, 767, 1477-81, 1541. Secretary of War Robert T. Lincoln to Lt. Gen. Philip H. Sheridan, December 9, 1884, and January 17, 1885, Box 33, Schofield Papers.

accidents of personality or politics. In the person of Ulysses S. Grant, the position of Commanding General reached the pinnacle of power and prestige in 1864-1865, when President Lincoln treated Grant as chief strategic planner and director of the armies, equal in authority to the Secretary of War.[26]

In 1895, the *Army Regulations* defined the relationship between the two heads of the War Department in these words:

> The military establishment is under the orders of the Commanding General of the Army in that which pertains to its discipline and military control. The fiscal affairs of the Army are conducted by the Secretary of War, through the several staff departments.
>
> All orders and instructions from the President or Secretary of War, relating to military operations or affecting the military control and discipline of the Army, will be promulgated through the Commanding General.

Congress in law and Secretaries and bureau chiefs in practice interpreted this definition to mean that the Commanding General had no direct authority over the staff departments. His control was restricted to the actual fighting units and to individual staff officers serving with them.[27]

Neither the law nor the regulations made clear the degree of subordination of the General to the Secretary or even whether he was subordinate at all. Calhoun in the 1820s had intended the General to act as an assistant to the Secretary, directing military operations and furnishing expert advice to his civilian superior. However, events and personalities and especially the broad, independent powers wielded by Grant and his direct relationship to President Lincoln had so changed the shape of the office that in the mid-nineties many people in Congress and the Army, including usually the Commanding General himself, assumed that the General and the Secretary were equals under the President, with the General controlling military affairs and the Secretary attending to fiscal matters. Each was presumed to act directly under the President's orders, independently of the other.

Such in fact was the case in most European command systems of the time. The king, emperor, or czar commanded the forces in person, using as deputies a uniformed chief of staff and a civilian minister of war. Each of these functionaries had a clearly defined area of responsibility, and each was independent of the other's control, owing obedience only to the head of state, who coordinated their actions and resolved disputes between them.

26. Bernardo and Bacon, *Military Policy*, 251-52. Huntington, *Soldier and State*, 184-86, 208, 247. Russell F. Weigley, *Towards an American Army: Military Thought from Washington to Marshall*, 164-65. Gen. John M. Schofield, *Forty-Six Years in the Army*, 408. Maj. Gen. William Harding Carter, *Creation of the American General Staff*, Senate Doc. No. 119, 68th Cong., 1st sess., 1924, p. 19. Allen, *JMSI*, XIX, 78-79. Maj. Gen. John M. Schofield, "The Military System of the United States," 1890, memorandum in Box 94, Schofield Papers.

27. *Army Regulations, 1895*, Paragraphs 187 and 188. Secretary of War Robert T. Lincoln to Lt. Gen. Philip H. Sheridan, January 17, 1885, Box 33; Maj. Gen. John M. Schofield, "The Military System of the United States," 1890, memorandum, Box 94, Schofield Papers. Maj. H. T. Allen, "The Organization of a Staff Best Adapted to the United States Army," *JMSI*, XXVIII, 176.

In Old World armies, especially in that of Germany, the chief of staff possessed far more real power than did the minister of war, but in the United States Army the reverse was true. Lacking a large personal staff and having no control over the supply bureaus, the Commanding General was unable in reality to direct military operations or to make war plans. The bureau chiefs asserted complete independence of the General in all aspects of their work, and the Secretary, fearing any increase in the strength of his uniformed rival, upheld their autonomy.

In fact, the Secretary, who could give orders to both line and staff, took over command of the Army and left the so-called Commanding General usually idle and always frustrated. The General retaliated, when he could, through political and administrative intrigues against the Secretary to support his claim to equal authority and his right to control the bureaus. Almost invariably the General was at a disadvantage in these clashes. Raised to his position by the automatic working of seniority, he often was not in political sympathy with the President, while the Secretary, as the Chief Executive's personal deputy, usually enjoyed the President's trust and confidence. As a result, the Secretary consistently triumphed over the General in their bureaucratic confrontations. Frequently he pushed the General entirely out of the Army chain of command by issuing orders to the troops directly through The Adjutant General. One Commanding General in the 1880s complained that he never even saw the orders issued in his name until they appeared the following day in the newspapers.[28]

Through these circumstances, a civilian, frequently with no previous military experience, controlled the Army, and within the War Department there existed no body of officers able to advise him on plans or to oversee the execution of his orders. As both American and foreign soldiers realized, successful modern military operations required concerted action by many highly trained specialists and according to prearranged plans. The specialists themselves could not do the planning; they lacked the breadth of knowledge and the authority to act and were too preoccupied with day-to-day activities to devise long-term strategy. Command now had evolved into a specialty in its own right, for which officers must be expressly trained and for the exercise of which new institutions must be created.

In Old World armies, the general staff, first developed by Prussia, provided at once an agency for planning and control and a training school for commanders. Composed of line officers carefully selected for ability, the

---

28. Stephen E. Ambrose, *Upton and the Army*, 129. Bernardo and Bacon, *Military Policy*, 255. Huntington, *Soldier and State*, 208-10. Weigley, *American Army*, 165-67. Carter, *General Staff*, 61-62. *War Investigating Commission*, I, 116. Schofield, *Forty-Six Years*, 411-13, 470, 476. Lee, *JMSI*, XV, 261-62. Allen, *JMSI*, XIX, 64-70. Avery D. Andrews, "Army Controversies," *The Independent*, LI, 456-59. Maj. Gen. John M. Schofield, undated note on "Command of the Army," Box 72; Schofield, "Command as Compared with Army Administration," undated note, Box 93; Schofield, "The Military System of the United States," 1890, memorandum, Box 94, Schofield Papers.

general staff in peacetime collected military intelligence, studied strategy and tactics, supervised weapons development, and drew up mobilization orders and plans of campaign. In war, some general staff officers coordinated operations, while others served as chiefs of staff of armies, corps, and divisions. The system increased rather than reduced the freedom of action of field commanders. With their missions carefully defined in advance and with assistance by officers indoctrinated in a common theory of war, generals could be given considerable discretion in dealing with tactical emergencies and in exploiting unforeseen opportunities. This method of command contributed much to Prussia's victories over Austria in 1866 and France in 1870-1871, and other European Powers were quick to copy it.[29]

Not so the United States. The American Army had the technical experts required for waging modern war but not the staff to mold them into a smoothly functioning military machine. Planning, if it was done at all, was the task of the Secretary of War and the Commanding General, assisted informally by whatever line and staff officers seemed to know something about the problem at hand. The staff of a general in the field consisted entirely of specialists from the technical bureaus; he had no chief of staff trained to supervise and coordinate the execution of his plans. The United States in fact had no body of officers educated in army administration or in the conduct of campaigns beyond a few aging Civil War veterans who had learned by hard experience. Except for the efforts of the school at Fort Leavenworth, the Army did little to prepare its junior officers to move and supply major forces, and the infrequency of large-scale maneuvers in peacetime gave them little chance to practice what they learned. As a result, in the words of an Army reformer, "If all the captains and lieutenants of the line should be called upon for projects for moving troops, for plans for the same campaign on the same map and for the detailed orders for commencing the same, . . . crudity would be the chief characteristic of the solutions given."[30]

The division of authority in the War Department, combined with the absence of a central military staff, enhanced the power of The Adjutant General. This officer, in theory under the authority of both the Secretary and the Commanding General and responsible for the transmission of orders and correspondence, the personnel records, the recruiting service, the mobilization of troops, and the collection of military intelligence, performed many of the functions of a European general staff. Through him and

29. Ambrose, *Upton*, 92-93. Michael Howard, *The Franco-Prussian War: The German Invasion of France, 1870-1871*, 23-25. Carter, *General Staff*, 8. Capt. T. A. Bingham, "The Prussian Great General Staff and What It Contains that is Practical from an American Standpoint," *JMSI*, XIII, 666-68, 670.

30. The quotation is from Bingham, *JMSI*, XIII, 670-71. Carter, *General Staff*, 211, Allen, *JMSI*, XIX, 80-81. In the Civil War, field commanders improvised general staffs for themselves; see Maj. Gen. John M. Schofield, undated, untitled note in "Reorganization of the Army" folder, Box 86, Schofield Papers.

his bureau, a Secretary who wished to take military functions away from the Commanding General could make operational plans and issue orders to the Army. The Adjutants General, usually strong, able administrators, made the most of the situation. Some even wrote and issued orders on their own initiative without consulting either of their nominal superiors.[31]

Within the staff, the Inspector General frequently challenged The Adjutant General's supremacy. His department, also under orders of both the Secretary and the Commanding General, performed in its inspections of troops one of the tasks of a general staff. Driving toward a major role in the command of the Army, the Inspectors General fought for legislation to enlarge and strengthen their bureau and battled The Adjutants General on points of disputed administrative jurisdiction. As one among many interoffice skirmishes, chiefs of the two bureaus clashed in 1893 over the right to appoint officers to inspect and train the National Guard. Especially during the late nineties, the Inspector General allied himself with the Commanding General, while The Adjutant General sided with the Secretary of War. Backed by the Secretary's superior political influence, The Adjutant General easily repelled the attacks of his rival.[32]

The tension between the Secretary and the Commanding General was reflected throughout the Army in a running feud between staff and line officers. The latter resented the staff as an overprivileged elite within the service. They complained that their staff colleagues, usually stationed in towns or cities, enjoyed the company of their families and the amenities of civilized life, while line officers, often marooned at remote Western posts, had few luxuries to mitigate the hardships and dangers of the field. To make the injustice still more bitter, staff positions, instead of being distributed equitably to the Army on the basis of merit and faithful service, often went to men whose only qualification for them was the enjoyment of friends in high places. Line officers complained, too, that the staff was too large. They pointed out that three out of every eight officers in the Army belonged to supply or administrative bureaus and that the staff departments spent on themselves a sixth of the Army's budget. As a colonel of infantry expressed their complaints, "This thing of spending fifteen dollars to get the other eighty-five where they ought to go, is rather expensive financiering." Above all, line

31. Secretary of War Elihu Root, memorandum printed in *Army and Navy Journal*, January 16, 1904, quoted in Bernardo and Bacon, *Military Policy*, 297-98. Allen, *JMSI*, XIX, 80-82. Carter, *General Staff*, 186. Schofield, *Forty-Six Years*, 442-43, 469-70. General Orders No. 23, Headquarters of the Army, March 18, 1892, Vol. I, Bliss Papers. Maj. Gen. John M. Schofield to the President of the United States, July 15 and 21, 1893, Box 54; Schofield, undated, untitled note in "Reorganization of the Army" folder, Box 86, Schofield Papers.

32. *Army Regulations, 1895*, Paragraphs 858 and 872. Maj. Gen. John M. Schofield to Secretary of War Daniel S. Lamont, August 8, 1893, Box 57, Schofield Papers. For examples of the political maneuvering between The Adjutant General and the Inspector General, see Files No. 73705, 74750 and 81860, AGO Records.

officers complained of staff snobbery, and they accused bureau officers of unfairly lording it over the combat soldiers, who did the service's real work.[33]

Many of the line's grievances against the staff were more the result of general army conditions than of deliberate staff malice. In a small army, largely inactive or confined to frontier police duty and short of funds, line officers could expect few opportunities for distinction or advancement, and staff duty accordingly acquired an inordinate aura of privilege. Probably the establishment of new postgraduate schools, the concentration of troops at larger and more comfortable posts, and the introduction of field maneuvers and new weapons, by offering a richer professional life to officers of the combat branches would have reduced the tensions arising from the difference in living standards. The selection of all staff officers from the line by competitive examinations would have eliminated most of the favoritism and political influence from bureau appointments. The complaint about the size of the staff had validity only under peacetime conditions. When the Army expanded in emergencies, as the Spanish War was soon to demonstrate, it would need every staff officer it had and more besides. However, the conflict between staff and line went beyond these minor irritations and jealousies. It was related directly to the larger problem of command.

The reformers among Army officers, who themselves usually belonged to the line, saw preparation for combat as the only proper mission of their service. From this assumption it followed that representatives of the Infantry, Cavalry, and Artillery—the fighting force of the Army—should have the determining voice in all questions of military plans, organization, and administration. In foreign services, they had such a voice in the general staff, but in the American system the civilian Secretary of War and the uniformed technicians of the bureaus made most of the important decisions. Emory Upton, the intellectual leader of Army progressives, summed up the problem and their complaint:

> The Ordnance . . . manufactures our guns and carriages; the Engineers build the fortifications on which the guns are mounted, and both are turned over to the Army to be tested in war without an opportunity for the general in chief, or the officers who may die in their defense, to make the slightest suggestion.[34]

33. Bernard L. Boylan, "The Forty-Fifth Congress and Army Reform," *Mid-America*, XLI, 176-78. *Army and Navy Journal*, March 4, 1899. Carter, *General Staff*, 235-36. Anderson, *JMSI*, XII, 984. William T. Sherman, *Memoirs of W. T. Sherman, Written by Himself*, II, 405. For the contrasting ways of life within the Army, compare Zogbaum, *Harper's Weekly*, XXVII, 767, 770, on staff and garrison life in Washington with the description of a Western post in Hagedorn, *Wood*, I, 114.

34. Upton is quoted in Bernardo and Bacon, *Military Policy*, 290-91; see also 253-55. Huntington, *Soldier and State*, 255-56. Peter S. Michie, "The Personnel of Sea-Coast Defense," *JMSI*, VIII, 12. Anderson, *JMSI*, XII, 981-82, 985-87. Lt. J. G. Harbord, "The Necessity of a Well Organized and Trained Infantry at the Outbreak of War, and the Best Means to be Adopted by the United States for Obtaining such a Force," *JMSI*, XXI, 8, quotes General Miles on the need for line supremacy over the staff. Schofield, *Forty-Six Years*, 469. Sherman, *Memoirs*, II, 405.

In matters both small and large, this situation had annoying and potentially disastrous results for the line. For example, the housing and transportation allowances provided for officers on garrison duty were grossly inadequate, but no line representative had authority to change them and the staff officers responsible for those provisions lacked firsthand knowledge of conditions at outlying posts. Much more serious, bureau chiefs could obstruct the operations of a field commander and force changes in his plans by ordering their subordinates on his staff not to purchase or issue needed equipment. On grounds of economy or bureau policy the chiefs and their subordinates often did so. Thus, they substituted their judgment of the military situation for that of the officer in the field, upon whose shoulders responsibility rested and upon whom the blame fell when an action failed. In 1887 a disgusted department commander summed it up:

> The orders of the general commanding an army, involving the most important military operations, may be practically annulled at any moment by orders to his staff officers respecting the transportation or supplies, or even the personnel of his command, coming to them from their staff superiors in Washington, and without the knowledge of any military commander.[35]

The frustration of field commanders by bureau chiefs resulted from a general movement toward administrative centralization in the Army. Until the 1880s department and field commanders, within broad limits, had controlled the administration of their areas of responsibility through their own staffs. They had the right to spend money and purchase supplies on their own initiative. Gradually during the eighties and nineties, the War Department, seeking to prevent fraud and to enforce cuts in military spending, reduced this independent power. By the time the Spanish-American War broke out, almost every decision involving the expenditure of funds had to be made in Washington. The quartermaster of a geographical department, for instance, had to send all of his supply contracts to the Quartermaster General's Office for approval.[36]

Centralization spread administrative paralysis throughout the Army and all but assured slow reaction by the War Department to any emergency. It burdened the bureau offices in Washington with mountains of paper work, most of it concerning minor matters that should have been dealt with in the field. In Washington, so occupied were the high officials with routine detail that they lacked the time to make broad plans or consider important

35. Lt. Col. J. G. C. Lee, "Reform in Army Administration," *JMSI*, XI, 534-36. The quotation is from a report by General Schofield in *RSW, 1887*, I, 116-17. Lt. Col. J. G. C. Lee, "Centralization and Decentralization in Army Affairs," *JMSI*, XII, 752. Maj. Gen. John M. Schofield to Secretary of War S. B. Elkins, February 27, 1892. Box 56, Schofield Papers.

36. Lee, *JMSI*, XI, 530; XII, 747-48, 751-52. Anderson, *JMSI*, XII, 985. Lee, *JMSI*, XV, 263-65, 267-79. Gen. Nelson A. Miles to Maj. Gen. John M. Schofield, March 14, 1890, Box 41, Schofield Papers.

decisions; in the field, the system reduced the energy and initiative of department commanders and their staffs and created among them a psychology of delay and avoidance of responsibility. Centralization bred, too, an endless multiplication of the number of returns, reports, and papers flowing through Army channels. Under peacetime conditions the system worked after a fashion, but Army progressives warned repeatedly that in wartime it would break down under the strain of mounting transactions and the need for rapid and momentous decisions. Then, as General Sherman wrote, "a general to be successful would have, as we did in 1861, to tear up his Army Regulations and go back to first principles."[37]

V

Forward-looking Army officers, well aware of the administrative weaknesses of their service, had developed during the eighties and nineties a number of proposals for reform. Almost every reformer, whether of line or staff, agreed that the movement toward centralization must be reversed. Each subordinate commander, the reformers insisted, must have complete military and fiscal control within his sphere of authority, subject only to general policies laid down by the War Department. Each commander then could be held entirely responsible for the results of his decisions. Most officers believed also that staff selection needed reforming, but line and staff differed on what changes were imperative. The progressives among the line officers wanted to get rid of permanent staff assignments. They argued that at least the captains and lieutenants in the staff bureaus should be line officers, serving in rotation for terms of one or two years. This arrangement, they pointed out, would break down the barriers between line and staff, assure better protection of line interests, and train all officers in administration and supply, thus preparing them for higher commands in wartime. Staff officers, on the other hand, while willing to put initial appointments on a strict merit basis and to close the bureaus to all but line officers, insisted on permanent tenure. They argued that only specialists who devoted their entire careers to the task could master the technical complexities of modern supply. For bureaus like the Quartermaster and Ordnance departments, this argument carried weight, but it had less validity for The Adjutant General's and Inspector General's departments, which were strictly administrative agencies. While divided on the issue of staff rotation, most reformers, regardless of branch, favored some kind of planning agency for the Army, preferably one controlled by the Commanding General. Down to 1898, proposals for

37. Gen. William T. Sherman to Russell A. Alger, February 13, 1889, Alger Papers. Carter, *General Staff*, 17. *RSW, 1887*, I, 117; *1897*, I, 26. Lee, *JMSI*, XI, 511-32, 537, 542; XII, 748-51; and XV, 280. Anderson, *JMSI*, XII, 980-81. Zalinski, *JMSI*, XIV, 957-58. Gibbon, *The North American Review*, CLVI, 216-18.

merging The Adjutant General's and Inspector General's offices into a central bureau for administration, planning, and intelligence absorbed most of the attention of progressives interested in these problems.[38]

The question of command baffled the officer-reformers. Most of them insisted that the Commanding General must have the right to give orders to the staff bureaus on all questions concerning the armament, equipment, and supply of troops, but should the General be considered the equal or subordinate of the Secretary? Most officers took the first position. They argued that the Secretary should be excluded altogether from the chain of command and his area of decisions confined to administration and finance, as were the position and duties of the war minister of Prussia. While possessing theoretical merit, this stance was counter to the whole American tradition of civilian control over the military, and no program based on it stood any chance of adoption by Congress.[39]

Maj. Gen. John M. Schofield took a more realistic approach to the Army's dilemma over authority. Schofield, a West Pointer, had distinguished himself as a corps commander in the Civil War. He also commanded occupation troops in the border states and later served as Secretary of War under President Andrew Johnson. During the seventies and eighties, Schofield assisted Generals Sherman and Sheridan in their struggles for power against a succession of Secretaries of War. These experiences gave Schofield an unusually sophisticated understanding of the relationship between politics and military affairs.

Schofield drew three conclusions from the events in which he had participated. First, he agreed with his colleagues that the Army needed a single uniformed head, with power over the staff as well as the line. Second, unlike most other officers, he accepted the fact that in the United States the President would always make the final military decisions and use the Secretary of War as his agent for implementing them. The military head, therefore, could act effectively only if he subordinated himself to the Secretary as well as to the President. Third, Schofield pointed out that the views of the

38. Ambrose, *Upton*, 103-4. Bvt. Maj. Gen. Emory Upton, *The Armies of Asia and Europe*, 324-25. *Reorganization of the Army*, Senate Report No. 555, 45th Cong., 3d sess., 1879 (hereafter cited as *Burnside Report*), Pt. 1, pp. 2-3. *War Investigating Commission*, I, 313. Sherman, *Memoirs*, II, 406. *RSW, 1895*, I, 12-13, 71. Lee, *JMSI*, XI, 530-33, 536-37, 542; and XII, 750, 753-54. Anderson, *JMSI*, XII, 986. Maj. William C. Sanger, "The Army Organization Best Adapted to a Republican Form of Government, which Will Ensure an Effective Force," *JMSI*, XIV, 1157-59. Lee, *JMSI*, XV, 262-63, 271-74. Williams, *JMSI*, XXI, 241. Maj. Gen. John M. Schofield to Secretary of War. S. B. Elkins, May 16, 1892, Box 56, Schofield Papers.

39. Ambrose, *Upton*, 93-94, 103-4, 129-32. Weigley, *American Army*, 120-21, 167-68. Bernardo and Bacon, *Military Policy*, 253-54. Schofield, *Forty-Six Years*, 421. *Burnside Report*, Pt. 2, pp. 7-8. Gen. Henry C. Wayne in "Reviews," *JMSI*, III, 392, 394. Anderson, *JMSI*, XII, 985-86. Zalinski, *JMSI*, XIV, 956-57. Allen, *JMSI*, XIX, 79. In 1869 the General briefly possessed power over the bureaus, but he soon lost it on grounds his power was "inconsistent with the duties of the Secretary of War." See Secretary of War Robert T. Lincoln to Lt. Gen. Philip H. Sheridan, January 17, 1885, Box 33, Schofield Papers.

Courtesy *Leslie's Weekly*

Lieutenant General John M. Schofield, U.S.A.

uniformed head of the Army would carry weight with the President and the Secretary only if those officials had confidence in the soldier's political loyalty and reliability. For this reason, Schofield argued, the practice of automatically placing the senior general at the head of the Army reduced rather than expanded professional military influence in the formation of policy. If the President did not trust an officer, no matter how eminent he might be professionally, the Chief Executive would not listen to him.

From these conclusions Schofield derived a new system of command, one that he thought would conform to the spirit of American institutions without sacrificing military or administrative efficiency. In place of the commanding general, Schofield proposed the creation of a chief of staff of the Army. This officer would have no power to command in his own right, but he would issue orders to all branches of the service, including the bureaus, in the names of the President and the Secretary of War, and he would act as military adviser to the civilian officials. Instead of automatically appointing the senior general to this post, the President should have the right to select any general he wished to serve for the duration of his term. By clearly subordinating the Chief of Staff to the President and the Secretary and by assuring his political harmony with his superiors, Schofield sought to reinforce the authority of this officer, a representative of line interests, over the rest of the Army, thus achieving the unity of control desired by the military reformers.[40]

Despite the efforts of the military reformers, staff and command reform made no legislative progress before the war with Spain. During the 1870s, military progressives, allied with a few interested congressmen, introduced measures in the national legislature to place the bureaus under the Commanding General and to establish rotation in some staff posts, but all their efforts failed. Congress in that period cared little for Army reform, and staff rotation met determined, effective opposition from the bureaus. Besides resistance by the bureaus, the reformers also encountered the traditionalism and complacency of many of their Army colleagues in both staff and line. These conservatives looked with suspicion on the idea of scientific training for command and argued that leadership is a mystical art of which some are born masters and others are not. They pointed out, too, that under the existing administrative system the nation had won all of its previous wars. Why change something that worked? If it had been good enough for General Grant, it was good enough for them.[41]

40. Weigley, *American Army*, 162-63, 168-72. Schofield, *Forty-Six Years*, 408, 422, 479, 536-39. *War Investigating Commission*, I, 115-16. Maj. Gen. John M. Schofield to Secretary of War Daniel S. Lamont, August 8, 1893, Box 57; undated note in "Command of the Army" folder, Box 72; undated, untitled essay in "Reorganization of the Army" folder, Box 86; memorandum on "The Military System of the United States," 1890, Box 94, Schofield Papers.

41. Boylan, *Mid-America*, XLI, 176-81. Carter, *General Staff*, 16. Ambrose, *Upton*, 114-15. For the view of leadership as a mystical art, see Capt. James Chester, "Impending Changes in the Character of War," *JMSI*, XIX, 83-85. He also foresaw modern total war; see 86-89.

While legislative proposals for reform foundered, however, a series of practical administrative measures that were effected during the eighties and nineties alleviated some of the War Department's internal conflicts of authority and laid at least a foundation for rational military planning. In coast defense and weapons development, for example, Congress, in recognition of the need for central planning of these complex and expensive projects, compelled the establishment of machinery for consultation between staff and line. It did so in 1888 by establishing the Board of Ordnance and Fortification, composed of the Commanding General of the Army and one officer each from the Engineers, Ordnance, and Artillery. Congress empowered the board to supervise the testing of all proposed new weapons and to determine which types should be adopted for the coast defenses. It also gave the board the right to allot the annual appropriation for coast defense among the bureaus, primarily the Engineers and the Ordnance Department. The bureaus then made the necessary contracts and actually built the forts and mounted the guns. During the nineties, the Board of Ordnance and Fortification made the final selections of the Army's new artillery pieces, carriages, ammunition, propellants, and mines. Although hampered by confusion about the extent of its authority, particularly over appropriations, the board introduced order into the coast defense effort, and it brought line and staff officers together for joint planning and the exchange of ideas. Also, in what was then an important part of the Army's strategic planning and preparation for war, it gave the Commanding General at least limited control over the work of the bureaus.[42]

Within The Adjutant General's Office, meanwhile, the rudiments of an intelligence service and planning staff had been taking shape. Credit for this innovation belongs to Adj. Gen. R. C. Drum. In 1885 Drum received a request from the President for routine military information and was embarrassed to discover that the War Department possessed neither the information nor an agency for obtaining it. Determined to remedy this condition, Drum on his own authority created an intelligence unit in his office. The Military Information Division, as it came to be called, received formal recognition as an agency in a War Department general order of April 12, 1889, and three years later Secretary of War William B. Elkins reorganized it and spelled out its duties. Reflecting the Secretary's continuous drive for complete control of the military establishment, Elkins' order of March 15, 1892, placed the division under the command of an officer of The Adjutant General's department who was to be selected by the Secretary of War. The order also assigned to the information division a variety of functions

42. A quarrel between the military committees of Congress and the then Chief of Ordnance also contributed to the establishment of the board. Birnie, *JMSI*, XII, 489. Schofield, *Forty-Six Years*, 485-87. *RSW*, *1888*, I, 30-31; *1890*, I, 53-56; *1895*, I, 25-26, 851; *1896*, I, 920-22.

performed in other armies by their general staffs. Thus planned, the Military Information Division would collect and file material on the geography, economic resources, and armed forces of the United States and foreign countries; prepare instructions for American military attachés abroad and collate their reports; publish and distribute throughout the Army maps and books on military subjects; and correspond with the states on National Guard matters and instruct the Army officers detailed to train the militia. Most important, in its implications, of all the assigned functions was that which charged the division to prepare plans for the mobilization of Regulars, militia, and volunteers in the event of war. The division, Elkins made clear, would in fact make the Army's war plans. He declared:

> In connection with the collection and arrangement of the mass of military information herein described, plans will be carefully formulated and deposited in the archives of the division, intended to anticipate as far as possible contingencies that may arise in case the nation should be involved in war.[43]

Between its founding and the war with Spain, the Military Information Division expanded in both personnel and activity. In 1889 the division consisted of 1 officer, 3 clerks, and 1 messenger. Nine years later, it boasted 12 officers, 10 clerks, and 2 messengers in its Washington office, plus 40 officers on National Guard duty and 16 military attachés overseas. As to its activities during the first nine years of its existence, the division collected and recorded on thousands of index cards extensive and miscellaneous military information on this and other nations; its chief coordinated the work of Army officers with the National Guard; and the division annually published monographs on subjects presumed to be of professional interest to the officer corps. A special section of the division concentrated on Hawaii and Latin America, areas of vital diplomatic and strategic interest to the United States in the nineties. As early as 1893 this section had prepared detailed surveys, with maps, of the geography and military resources of Hawaii, Samoa, Mexico, and Cuba, and its officers wanted to extend the series to cover the rest of South America and the Caribbean. Another section collected and published military maps. At the outbreak of hostilities in 1898, it had ready detailed maps of Cuba and Puerto Rico, the likely theaters of operations. Connected with the division and feeding information to it were the military attachés at United States legations abroad. Under a system first authorized by Congress in 1888, these officers provided firsthand accounts of military developments from major European and Latin American capitals. The Military Information Division preserved and collated their reports.

43. Elizabeth Bethel, "The Military Information Division: Origin of the Intelligence Division," *Military Affairs*, XI, 17-20. *RSW, 1892*, I, 7-8, 195. Confidential Order signed by Adj. Gen. R. C. Drum, April 12, 1889; Asst. Adj. Gen. Thomas M. Vincent to the Secretary of War, October 13, 1896; General Orders No. 23, Headquarters of the Army, March 18, 1892, Vol. I, Bliss Papers.

While efficient in amassing information, the division before 1898 suffered from chronic shortages of manpower, office space, and money—deficiencies that prevented it from doing any significant military planning. Until 1894 Congress appropriated nothing for the division, and thereafter less than $4,000 per year. Yet, in spite of its scant resources the division managed to collect much information of real value and represented for the War Department at least a halting first step toward a general staff.[44]

During the late eighties and early nineties, the disruptive effect on operations caused by the War Department's internal conflict over authority all but ceased, thanks largely to the efforts of Major General Schofield, whom the seniority system in 1888 brought to the post of Commanding General. During the next seven years, as far as he could within existing laws, Schofield put into practice his theories of Army command. A shrewd bureaucratic infighter, Schofield early staked out his claims. He renounced any right to issue orders independently of the Secretary of War or to command the bureaus. He made clear that he considered himself subordinate to the Secretary as well as to the President and that he would wield power only in their names. At the same time, he insisted that all orders to the geographical departments and to troops of the line from his civilian superiors be sent to him before going to The Adjutant General, so he could read and comment on them. Schofield's tact and self-effacement won him the confidence of a series of Presidents and Secretaries of War, and he gradually gained his point, which was to restore the position of the General in the chain of command. He also upheld the authority of department commanders against the staff bureaus by stopping almost entirely the issue of orders by bureau chiefs directly to subordinates in the field. He insisted with special emphasis that no bureau chief be permitted to disallow a supply requisition until the case had been examined and ruled upon by the Secretary and the Commanding General. By the time he retired for age in 1895, Schofield, by establishing harmonious relations with his civilian superiors, had gained the power to reduce the bureaus' pretensions to independence and to uphold the authority and interests of the line. Much to his regret, Schofield failed to obtain legislation that would perpetuate his reforms, but he had proved the practicality of his ideas and had made the existing system work as smoothly as circumstances permitted.[45]

44. Bethel, *Military Affairs*, XI, 18-24. *RSW, 1892*, I, 195; *1893*, I, 24, 161-68; *1897*, I, 16; *1898*, I, 283; Asst. Adj. Gen. Thomas M. Vincent to the Secretary of War, October 13, 1896, Vol. I, Bliss Papers. Bingham, *JMSI*, XIII, 676. *Army and Navy Journal*, April 21, 1898. Capt. W. H. Bixby to Maj. Gen. John M. Schofield, August 12, 1888, Box 22, Schofield Papers.

45. Schofield, *Forty-Six Years*, 6-7, 422-23, 468-71, 480, 482-83. Weigley, *American Army*, 171-73. Bernardo and Bacon, *Military Policy*, 256. *RSW, 1888*, I, 4; *1892*, I, 50. Maj. Gen. John M. Schofield to The Adjutant General, October 29, 1888, and to Secretary of War Redfield Proctor, March 30, 1889, Box 54; Schofield to The Adjutant General, February 11 and April 3, 1890, Box 55; Schofield to Secretary of War S. B. Elkins, January 25, 1893, and to Secretary of War Daniel S. Lamont, April 3, 1893, Box 57; Schofield to Secretary of War Russell A. Alger, probably 1897, Box 64; Schofield, "Our Military and Naval Policy," memorandum written in 1888 with addition dated 1894, Box 94, Schofield Papers.

On the eve of the Spanish-American War, the War Department had a military organization capable, if properly managed, of intelligent, coordinated response to a crisis. The Board of Ordnance and Fortification and the Military Information Division had accustomed at least a few officers and bureaucrats to making decisions by consultation on the basis of systematically gathered facts, and General Schofield had demonstrated the possibility of maintaining a smooth working relationship between the department's civilian and uniformed chiefs. But, as Schofield himself wrote soon after his retirement, "My . . . plan worked well enough so long as I helped to work it. How it may be with anybody else, . . . only the future can determine."[46] The War Department's independent power centers still operated without clear statutory definitions of their authority and responsibility. Their effective teamwork depended entirely on the degree of personal cooperation established by the men who headed them. The performance of all divisions of the War Department would depend, also, on how successfully those in authority adapted to the particular situation certain general ideas the Regular officer-reformers had formulated about the Army's proper organization for and strategic role in foreign wars.

46. Schofield, *Forty-Six Years*, 480. See also undated, untitled memorandum by Schofield in "Reorganization of the Army" folder, Box 86, Schofield Papers.

2

The Men and Their Ideas

I

During the last two decades of the nineteenth century, the years in which the new generation of military professionals launched their campaigns for service reform, the United States increased her involvement in international power politics. American businessmen sought enlarged foreign markets; churchmen and philanthropists considered it their duty to liberate and uplift allegedly benighted foreign peoples; and a vocal clique of intellectuals and politicians believed that national greatness required an assertive foreign policy. Urged by these elements, the United States began to challenge European imperialism in the Far East and Latin America. Her statesmen sought trade and political influence rather than territory. They worked toward control of the projected Central American canal and its Caribbean approaches, toward American hegemony over Hawaii, and toward the establishment of island outposts in the Pacific from which to expand the American presence in Asia. The new diplomatic activism led to a series of confrontations with Old World Powers who had ambitions of their own in regions of interest to the United States. Almost every administration between 1880 and 1898 had its diplomatic incident, some more serious than others. While none of these crises escalated into war, they clearly illustrated the dangers of an assertive foreign policy and foreshadowed a test of strength between the United States and European militarism.[1]

Citing the new diplomacy's need for armed support, progressive Army and Navy officers tried to relate the service reforms they desired to the larger interests of the nation. As they developed their arguments, they broadened their definition of "national defense." Capt. Alfred Thayer Mahan, theorist and propagandist of the modern Navy, sounded the keynote:

defence means not merely defence of our territory, but defence of our just national interests, whatever they be and wherever they are. For example, the exclusion of direct European control from the Isthmus of Panama is as really a matter of national defence as is the protection of New York Harbor.[2]

1. For a comprehensive description of the new foreign policy, see Walter LaFeber, *The New Empire: An Interpretation of American Expansion, 1860-1898*, passim. H. Wayne Morgan, *America's Road to Empire: The War with Spain and Overseas Expansion*, 3. For contemporary statements, see Capt. Alfred Thayer Mahan, *The Interest of America in Sea Power, Present and Future*, passim, and Henry Cabot Lodge, "Our Blundering Foreign Policy," *The Forum*, XIX, 8-17.

2. Capt. Alfred Thayer Mahan, *Lessons of the War with Spain and Other Articles*, 298. The passage quoted was written before the war with Spain.

Mahan, whose thought ranged far beyond questions of naval strategy, weapons, and organization, laid out during the 1890s a comprehensive plan for American world power based on maritime supremacy and overseas trade. His system depended upon a fleet of armored, steam-propelled battleships able to command the sea approaches to both coasts of the Western Hemisphere and, if necessary, to attack distant enemy shores. To provide places of refuge and coaling stations for the fleet and for the merchant marine that he considered its necessary complement, Mahan urged the acquisition of bases in strategic areas like the Caribbean and the Western Pacific—not large colonial territories but small, advantageously located islands with deep, spacious, and easily fortified harbors. Above all, he stressed that the United States must control the future Central American canal. Given such a military-geographic position, Mahan argued, the United States could enforce the Monroe Doctrine, expand her commerce, and maintain her vital interests in a shrinking, increasingly competitive world. Mahan brought together in systematic and persuasive form ideas that were already current among Navy reformers and civilian expansionists, and he outlined an international posture that was attractive to many Americans. In response to the doctrines he articulated and to the pressures he helped bring to focus, the congresses and administrations of the late eighties and the nineties began to seek foreign bases and to build armored battleships and cruisers. Almost every year Congress authorized new warships. By 1898 a respectable fleet had come into being, and the Navy Department was organizing it and planning its wartime deployment on the principles Mahan had outlined.[3]

The Army officers who attended and staffed the new branch schools, joined the Military Service Institution of the United States, and contributed to its journal and similar publications reflected in their writings the late-nineteenth-century expansionist mood. A few of them advocated expansion— commercial and territorial—as a moral, economic, and racial necessity; many others simply accepted expansion as a fact of life upon which military plans and policies must be based. Most of them viewed war as an outgrowth of politics and commerce and as the instrument of political and commercial purposes. Discussing defense of a Central American canal, one officer observed: "It is very difficult to differentiate the military view from the commercial and political aspects, so intimately are they associated with each other from first to last." In suggesting the probable causes of future

3. Mahan, *Interest in Sea Power*, 16-17, 25-26, 42-48, 52-55, 101-4, 128-29, 133-34, 139-40, 156-57, 193, 198-99, 214. Mahan, *Lessons*, 301-7. LaFeber, *New Empire*, 91-92. Robert Seager, II, "Ten Years before Mahan: The Unofficial Case for the New Navy, 1880-1890," *Mississippi Valley Historical Review (Journal of American History)*, XL, 492-93, 505-11. Harold Sprout and Margaret Sprout, *The Rise of American Naval Power, 1776-1918*, 196-201, 204-5. Maj. W. A. Glassford, USV, "Porto Rico and a Necessary Military Position in the West Indies," *JMSI*, XXVIII, 16-17. For the details of the search for bases, see LaFeber, *New Empire*, 121-27, 229-41; for the building and organization of the fleet, see Sprout and Sprout, *Naval Power*, 186-98, 207-22.

wars, Army progressives expressed awareness of the objectives of the new diplomacy by pointing to commercial rivalries, European challenges to the Monroe Doctrine, and disputes over control of the Central American canal as likely to bring the United States into collision with other powers. Many of them emphasized the fact that the United States was now fully part of an interdependent world political and economic system. As one of them put it, "In our feelings, our information, our pleasures, and our business interests we are not isolated. . . . We are being continually brought into closer contact with other nations, and will ultimately be called into the deliberations of the world." Following Mahan's lead, Army officers broadened their ideas of the scope of national defense. "Now we have interests abroad," an officer at the Infantry and Cavalry School wrote in 1892, "which are endangered by threats of aggression far from our own borders, and no question can excite Europe without agitating us."[4]

For Mahan and his colleagues in the Navy, their broadened view of America's world role carried with it a complete redefinition of their service's wartime military mission, moving from the traditional harbor defense and commerce raiding to fleet actions far from the coast. The progressive Army officers made no such radical revision of their service's purposes. Instead, they rerationalized the Army's historic tasks of coast and border defense in terms of Mahan's maritime-commercial expansionism. In the process, they acepted a limited, secondary role for the Army in future wars in foreign territory. They argued that, for the United States, separated by water as she was from her potential enemies and from the main theaters of conflict—even in the Western Hemisphere—and with no interest in the conquest of large territories, the Navy must carry most of the burden of any wartime offensive. The tasks of the Army would be protection of the continental homeland, defense of outposts like the Central American canal, and the organization of small expeditionary forces to help the Navy take and hold strategic points on foreign soil. In 1897 General Schofield, recently

4. The first quotation is from Capt. Lewis D. Green, "The Nicaragua Canal in Its Military Aspects," *JMSI*, XXVI, 1; see also 3-8 and 12-13. The second is from Lt. George B. Duncan, "Reasons for Increasing the Regular Army," *The North American Review*, CLXVI, 451-52. The third is from Bachelor, *JMSI*, XIII, 55-56; see also 54-55. Other examples of this thinking follow: Lt. Arthur L. Wagner, "The Military Necessities of the United States and the Best Provisions for Meeting Them," *JMSI*, V, 238-44. Maj. William R. King, "The Military Necessities of the United States and the Best Provisions for Meeting Them," *JMSI*, V, 356. Capt. George F. Price, "The Necessity for Closer Relations between the Army and the People, and the Best Method to Accomplish the Result," *JMSI*, VI, 320-21. Lt. H. L. Hawthorne, "A Central American Oceanic Canal and Its Strategic Importance to the United States," *JMSI*, X, 576-91. Lt. Sidney E. Stuart, "The Army Organization Best Adapted to a Republican Form of Government, which Will Ensure an Effective Force," *JMSI*, XIV, 238-39. Maj. George S. Wilson, "The Army: Its Employment during Time of Peace and the Necessity for Its Increase," *JMSI*, XVIII, 494-95. Williams, *JMSI*, XXI, 249-52. Harbord, *JMSI*, XXI, 1-2. John M. Schofield, "The Monroe Doctrine," undated memorandum in Box 94, Schofield Papers. For a modern analysis, see Huntington, *Soldier and State*, 236-37, 254-63.

retired after his successful term as Commanding General and soon to help in shaping strategy against Spain, summed up the Army's place in the new military posture:

In a country having the situation of the United States, the navy is the *aggressive* arm of the national military power. Its function is to punish an enemy until he is willing to submit to the national demands. For this purpose entire freedom of action is essential; also secure depots whence supplies may be drawn and where necessary repairs may be made, and harbors where cruisers or other vessels may seek safety if temporarily overpowered. Hence arises one of the most important functions of the land defense: to give the aggressive arm secure bases of operation at all the great seaports where navy-yards or depots are located. It may be that in special cases military forces may be needed to act in support of naval operations, or to hold for a time important points in a foreign country; but such service must be only auxiliary, not a primary object. Foreign conquest and permanent occupation are not a part of the policy of this country.[5]

Supported by Mahan and his followers in the Navy, the Army's reformers assigned special importance to their service's traditional task of building, maintaining, and garrisoning the forts that defended major American harbors. Under late-nineteenth-century conditions, these defenses could not repel—and indeed were not intended to repel—invasions aimed at overrunning and occupying extensive tracts of United States soil. Such operations would require more troops than any potential European enemy could spare from other missions. Further, our neighbors Canada and Mexico could draw on neither the manpower nor the economic resources to mount significant across-the-border attacks.

Instead, the coast defenses were intended to ward off sudden, limited assaults on our great seaports and amphibious harassment of our long shoreline. Such incursions were well within the means of potential Old World enemies, any of whom, military planners estimated, could have an armored battle fleet accompanied by 40,000 to 100,000 troops on transports ready for action against the East Coast within thirty days of a declaration of war. By capturing or bombarding one or more of our major coastal cities or by dominating a vital region like Chesapeake Bay, such an enemy force could destroy huge amounts of property, disrupt land and water transportation, upset the domestic economy, demoralize the population, and deprive the Navy of needed bases. A sudden—and quite probably successful—descent on any of our coasts would give the enemy the military initiative and place the theater of conflict on United States soil. Faced with such a situation, the nation would exhaust her military strength in fighting to liberate her own

5. Lt. Gen. Schofield's words are from *Forty-Six Years*, 527-28; see also 489-90. Bvt. Brig. Gen. Samuel B. Holabird, "Some Thoughts about the Future of Our Army," *The United Service*, VIII, 26-27. Hawthorne, *JMSI*, X, 587. Lt. Peter C. Hains, "Should the Fixed Coast Defenses of the United States be Transferred to the Navy?" *JMSI*, XV, 254-56. Green, *JMSI*, XXVI, 10-12.

territory while her opponent scooped up the colonial prizes of war in Latin America or Asia.[6]

Had the United States in this period engaged in limited war with a major European nation over, say, an imperialistic incursion into the Caribbean or South America, she probably would have faced attacks of this sort. British landing parties in the War of 1812 had ravaged the shores of Chesapeake Bay and had burned the city of Washington. During the Venezuelan boundary crisis of 1896, when still another Anglo-American war seemed at least remotely possible, a British military writer suggested that, if war came, Britain should defend the Canadian border with small forces and launch her main offensive with 50,000 to 100,000 troops on the East Coast where, he said, lay the best targets for attack. German military planning in the period also ran along these lines, emphasizing sudden descents on New York and New England with fleets and armies to cover a drive for Caribbean bases and colonies.[7]

To parry such thrusts and to preserve the Navy's freedom of offensive action, Army officers, with the concurrence of Mahan and the naval theorists, urged replacement of the old masonry Civil War-era forts, upon which the nation still relied to guard the principal harbors and the entrances to coastal waterways. The new forts would consist of modern concrete and earth emplacements mounting heavy-caliber steel breech-loading rifles and mortars able to smash armored battleships. To hold enemy fleets under the fire of such guns, the officers advocated the blocking of narrow channels with mine fields. Small, swift torpedo boats also would form part of the defense. Elaborate telephone, telegraph, and fire control systems would bind all these components into a unified, massive concentration of firepower. Once in place and properly manned, strategists of the Army and Navy argued, such fortifications were almost impassable because guns in land batteries, better protected and mounted on steadier aiming platforms, could always outshoot guns on warships. Because of their size and mechanical complexity (a single

6. Wagner, *JMSI*, V, 238-44. Lt. Eugene Griffin, "Our Sea-Coast Defense," *JMSI*, VII, 416-17, 420-21. Lt. Sidney E. Stuart, "Some Principles of Organization Adapted to the Conditions Affecting the Maintenance, Instruction and Efficiency of Our Coast Artillery," *JMSI*, XII, 1224. Bachelor, *JMSI*, XIII, 56. Stuart, *JMSI*, XIV, 239-43. Zalinski, *JMSI*, XIV, 926. Sanger, *JMSI*, XIV, 1149, 1180. Lt. Louis C. Scherer, "Limitations of the National Guard," *JMSI*, XVIII, 267. Wilson, *JMSI*, XVIII, 494, 499-501. Williams, *JMSI*, XXI, 243. Lt. S. M. Foote, "Based on Present Conditions and Past Experience, How Should Our Volunteer Armies be Raised, Organized, Trained, and Mobilized for Future Wars," *JMSI*, XXII, 18-19, 24-25. Mahan, *Interest in Sea Power*, 110, 197-99, 212. Mahan, *Lessons*, 16. *RSW, 1880*, I, xvii-xx; *1884*, I, 49; *1886*, I, 32; *1890*, I, 5, 44-45. *Endicott Report*, Pt. 1, p. 7. Miles, *Serving the Republic*, 267. Maj. Gen. John M. Schofield to Charles F. Archer, April 23, 1894, Box 57, Schofield Papers.

7. For the British comment, see "War with the United States," *JMSI*, XVIII, 669-73, an article reprinted from the English journal *Broad Arrow*. The Germans in the early 1900s planned a similar campaign against the United States; see John A. S. Grenville and George B. Young, *Politics, Strategy, and American Diplomacy: Studies in Foreign Policy, 1873-1917*, 305-7.

coast-defense cannon weighed 50 tons and required a steam-driven carriage to traverse it), these fortifications, like the battleships they were intended to support, had to be built in peacetime and kept always in readiness. The nation could not improvise them during hostilities.[8]

To Captain Mahan, coast defenses of this type were an integral part of his program of commercial expansion founded on a battleship navy. He argued that only with its own bases and the principal seaports secured by land fortifications could the battle fleet, relieved of defensive tasks, perform its proper functions of engaging hostile fleets on the high seas and of blockading the enemy's shores. Army advocates of new fortifications consistently and explicitly related them, in articles, reports, and speeches, to an aggressive naval strategy and to an expansionist diplomacy. Typical of many such advocates, a general wrote in 1889: "The great sea board cities of the country can, at a moderate cost, be placed in a condition of permanent security against any possible foreign attack, while the Navy . . . may be left entirely free to protect the interests of the United States on all the seas of the world, and to pursue and attack upon the open ocean any hostile fleet which may venture near our shores." Going beyond strictly military considerations, Army theorists saw in coast defense a deterrent to enemy attack and a support for an active diplomacy. As one of them put it,

If we offer no vulnerable point to possible enemies, any position which we may take in regard to international questions or any demands we may make, will be carefully considered; and if our claims are disregarded, we shall then be in a position to determine calmly and deliberately what course of action we should adopt.[9]

II

Because of the need to construct the coast fortifications well in advance of any international crisis and because of their complementary relationship to the new fleet that was being built, War Department reports, budgets, and legislative recommendations during the eighties and nineties stressed coast defense to the point where it seemed to be the Army's only strategic

8. Mahan, *Interest in Sea Power*, 194-97. Mahan, *Lessons*, 68-69. Griffin, *JMSI*, VII, 406-15, 420, 422-27, 435. Stuart, *JMSI*, XII, 1228-29. Hains, *JMSI*, XV, 250-51, *RSW*, *1880*, I, xix-xx; *1884*, I, 17, 20-21; *1887*, I, 118-19; *1889*, I, 18. John M. Schofield, "Sea Coast Defense," Address Delivered before Coast Defense Convention, Tampa, Florida, January, 1897, in Box 95, Schofield Papers.

9. The first quotation is from *RSW*, *1889*, I, 68; see also p. 19. The second is from Maj. William C. Sanger, "Organization and Training of a National Reserve for Military Service," *JMSI*, X, 83. Mahan expresses his views in *Interest in Sea Power*, 194, and *Lessons*, 48-53, 58, 63. For Army utterances along these lines, see the following: *RSW*, *1880*, I, xix; *1890*, I, 45; *1894*, I, 62; *1895*, I, 66-67. *Endicott Report*, Pt. 1, pp. 8-9. Schofield, *Forty-Six Years*, 527-28. Wagner, *JMSI*, V, 244-49. Griffin, *JMSI*, VII, 421-22. Michie, *JMSI*, VIII, 3. Hains, *JMSI*, XV, 236, 248-50, 256. An eloquent juxtaposition of coast defense strategy with aggressive political expansionism is Schofield, "Sea Coast Defense," Box 95, Schofield Papers.

concern. However, progressive Army officers during those years also devoted much thought and argument to the organization, recruitment, and training of the troops who in future wars would man and defend the batteries and perhaps assist the Navy in offensive operations. By 1898 they had developed well-defined and widely circulated proposals on those issues.

In fact, discussion within the Army of "military policy"—by which most officers meant the recruitment, organization, and training of soldiers—antedated the rise of diplomatic expansionism and Mahanite navalism. It began in response to the revolutionary changes that industrial technology had made in the conduct of and preparations for land warfare. American officers of this era saw the single-shot, muzzle-loading musket—the standard infantry weapon for over a century—give way within a generation, first to the single-shot breechloader and then to the magazine repeater, which used smokeless powder to propel high-velocity steel-jacketed bullets and increased by four or five times the volume, range, and accuracy of infantry fire. Artillerymen abandoned their muzzle-loading iron smoothbores for rifled steel breechloading cannon that were able to throw shrapnel and high explosives with unprecedented accuracy and destructiveness. Perplexed tacticians of all arms debated the proper battlefield role of the machine gun, a device that promised to transform the "rain of bullets" from poetic image to deadly reality. Mobilization planners now were able to include in their strategy the railroads, which made possible the rapid movement and continuous supply over long distances of huge forces of men, and the telegraph lines, over which the actions of these armies could be centrally directed. Together, these inventions allowed strategic combinations of hitherto unthinkable magnitude and promised swifter-moving, more decisive campaigns than those of the past.[10]

The firepower of the new small arms and artillery, by rendering suicidal the shoulder-to-shoulder formations in which soldiers had maneuvered on battlefields from Marathon to Gettysburg, forced radical changes in tactics and training, changes that had important implications for military policy. Under fire from the new weapons, soldiers had to move and fight in small groups, the members of which must take more individual initiative and make more tactical decisions than had their ancestors who tramped forward in ranks to the beating of drums. An American military reformer summed up the change and its implications:

> The major assumes the functions of a brigade commander; a captain requires the knowledge and skill of a colonel; a lieutenant performs the duty of a captain; a sergeant takes the place of a lieutenant, and a corporal, no longer required simply to fire his musket, takes command of a squad or section.

10. Howard, *Franco-Prussian War*, 3. Capt. Francis V. Greene, "The Important Improvements in the Art of War during the Past Twenty Years, and Their Probable Effect on Future Military Operations," *JMSI*, IV, 7-13, 35-38. Wisser, *JMSI*, XVIII, 237-38, 242-49, 252-54. Duncan, *The North American Review*, CLXVI, 457.

> To all of these grades latitude is given in the management of their commands under fire, and hence an error of judgment in any one may initiate a movement that may lose a battle.[11]

To prepare them to take such initiative, all soldiers, from the lowly private on up, required intensive and varied training. No longer would mastery of close-order drill and the loading and firing of the weapon suffice. The modern soldier needed physical conditioning, instruction in marksmanship and the direction of fire, and practice in skirmishing and making use of terrain. Addition of these skills meant that the training process must be longer and more systematic than it had been in the past, and it implied further that more soldiers must be trained in advance during peacetime rather than after hostilities began. With the old mass tactics, officers argued, superior numbers, valor, and devotion to a cause sometimes could compensate for a lack of drill and discipline, but in the modern war of machines and firepower, superior training would prevail.[12]

The new conditions of battle, combined with the ability to move large armies quickly by rail and steamship, placed a premium upon peacetime preparation and planning for war. A nation that had available at all times a huge body of trained men, that could organize the men into armies within days of a declaration of war, and that could concentrate them by rail for offensive action, would be able to launch such overwhelming attacks so swiftly that an opponent less prepared would never be able to recover from the initial blow. Aware of these facts, military men in both Europe and the United States expected future wars to be short and decisive, with the better-prepared contestant always victorious. The wars of the late nineteenth century—and especially Prussia's successful actions against Austria and France—seemed to confirm this theory. Few military men before 1914 seriously considered what would happen if two equally well prepared nations collided. For pre-World War I strategists, organization and advance planning, not size of population and economic resources, were the determinants of victory.[13]

To protect themselves under such conditions, the major continental powers, with Prussia setting the example, maintained highly skilled standing armies but, in addition, created mass citizen armies, trained thoroughly

11. The quotation is from Upton, *The Armies of Asia and Europe*, 315-16; see also 270-315. Ambrose, *Upton*, 56-58. Greene, *JMSI*, IV, 14-15, 25-33. Wisser, *JMSI*, XVIII, 238-42, 247-48.

12. Maj. Gen. John M. Schofield, "Notes on the Legitimate in War," *JMSI*, II, 6. Brig. Gen. Wesley Merritt, "Important Improvements in the Art of War in the Last Twenty Years and Their Probable Effect on Future Military Operations," *JMSI*, IV, 182, 186-87. Wisser, *JMSI*, XVIII, 240-41. Williams, *JMSI*, XXI, 230. Foote, *JMSI*, XXII, 22. Holabird, *United Service*, VIII, 21-22. Duncan, *The North American Review*, CLXVI, 457.

13. Howard, *Franco-Prussian War*, 3-4, 455. For contemporary expressions by American officers on this point, see: Schofield, *JMSI*, II, 8. Greene, *JMSI*, IV, 6-7. Harbord, *JMSI*, XXI, 4-5. Williams, *JMSI*, XXI, 231-35. General Oliver O. Howard, "A Plea for the Army," *The Forum*, XXIII, 642-44. Ambrose, *Upton*, 132-35.

in time of peace, prepared for rapid mobilization, and commanded throughout by highly educated professional officers. Under this system, the standing
army functioned as the cadre and training school of the war army. Its companies, battalions, and regiments contained at all times their full complements
of officers but only a fraction of their wartime enlisted strength. The fraction under arms consisted largely of civilian conscripts who were serving a
fixed term (in Prussia three years) with their units. At the end of his term
"with the colors," the conscript passed into the reserve, in which he served ten
or twelve years, returning to the ranks periodically during that time for training and maneuvers. In time of war, the youngest and most able-bodied reservists filled up the units of the standing army while the older men, in separate
reserve formations, garrisoned fortresses, guarded lines of communication, and
performed other rear-area duties. So organized, Prussia's mass army could expand in a few days from a peacetime footing of about 500,000 men into a wartime army of over 3 million, all of them fully trained soldiers. Every level was
under command of professional officers who had been instructed in their duties
by an elaborate system of schools. The general staff, composed of officers selected
for special competence, made comprehensive war plans and defined in detail
the mission of every part of the army. After Prussia overwhelmed Austria and
France, her rivals quickly copied her military system.[14]

While they were much impressed by Prussia's war machine, few American
Army reformers wanted to adopt it entire. Given the vast sea distances that
separated her from the other powers and given her lack of interest in widespread
territorial conquests, the United States had no need for a continental-size mass
army or for the peacetime conscription required to maintain it. Nevertheless,
Army theorists insisted, even Mahan's program of maritime-commercial expansion needed the support of mobile land forces high in quality if relatively
modest in numbers. For the provision of such an army, they argued, the nation's existing small Regular establishment and decentralized, ill-equipped, poorly
trained state militia were insufficient; and the creation in wartime of large temporary volunteer armies could not compensate for the failure in peacetime to
organize and train reserves. Indeed, under the conditions of modern war,
volunteer armies could be effective only if based on a previously recruited and
instructed cadre. Therefore, Army progressives concluded, America must modify
her traditional military institutions so as to train more men in advance of trouble,
plan systematically for possible wars, and above all unify all components of
her land forces, which should at all times be under federal control exercised
by a thoroughly professional officer corps.[15]

14. Howard, *Franco-Prussian War*, 4, 21-22. Ambrose, *Upton*, 90-92, 99-100. Greene, *JMSI*, IV,
2-3. Wisser, *JMSI*, XVIII, 235-37. Millis, *Arms and Men*, 122-23.

15. Greene, *JMSI*, IV, 3-4. Wagner, *JMSI*, V, 254. Price, *JMSI*, VI, 320-21. Harbord, *JMSI*, XXI,
6. Foote, *JMSI*, XXII, 15. Capt. W. A. Glassford, "Based on Present Conditions and Past Experiences,
How Should Our Volunteer Armies be Raised, Organized, Trained, and Mobilized for Future Wars,"
JMSI, XXII, 480. Capt. Herbert Barry, "In What Way Can the National Guard be Modified so as
to Make It an Effective Reserve to the Regular Army in Both War and Peace?" *JMSI*, XXVI, 204-6.
See also Weigley, *American Army*, ix, 106-9, 118.

A decade before Mahan began promoting the new Navy, Bvt. Maj. Gen. Emory Upton of the United States Artillery outlined a plan for an army well adapted to the requirements of modern tactics and maritime expansion. By temperament and training, Upton was well suited to his task. Born in western New York State in 1839 and reared by devout parents, he combined in his character moral and physical courage, zeal for reform, and devotion to the military profession. After graduating from West Point in 1861, he earned an excellent combat record in the Civil War, having proved himself to be a brave and resourceful commander, but the incompetent leadership and needless slaughter he observed revolted him, and after the war he dedicated himself to reform of the Army. Serving as Commandant of Cadets at West Point and later as Superintendent of Instruction at the Artillery School, he adapted the Army's tactical system to the new conditions of battle and won recognition during the late 1870s as the service's most brilliant theoretician. He enjoyed the friendship and support of Commanding General Sherman. In 1875 and 1876, under War Department orders, Upton traveled around the world to study foreign military systems. His tour further impressed upon him his own country's military deficiencies and made him an admirer of the Prussian war machine. Upon his return to the United States, he began applying German principles to plans for the reform of the American Army. The results of his efforts appeared in two books that were influential at different times: *The Armies of Asia and Europe*, published in 1878, and *The Military Policy of the United States*, a comprehensive history of the conduct of America's wars, still unfinished at the time of his death in 1881 but published early in the twentieth century. In these works, Upton told his countrymen what was wrong with their military policy and made suggestions for change.[16]

Upton contrasted previous American military policy, as he saw it, with that of the European Powers. He wrote:

> If we . . . compare our military policy during the first century of the Republic with the present military policy of European nations, we shall find that the difference lies principally in . . . that, while they prosecute their wars exclusively with trained armies, completely organized in all of their parts, and led by officers specially educated, we have begun, and have prosecuted, most of our wars with raw troops, whose officers have had to be educated in the expensive school of war.[17]

In the past, Upton argued, this practice had led to wars that were needlessly bloody and prolonged, even if ultimately successful; in the future such lack of preparedness might well lead to national disaster. To prevent

16. Ambrose, *Upton, passim*. Weigley, *American Army*, 101-6. Huntington, *Soldier and State*, 232. Richard C. Brown, "General Emory Upton—the Army's Mahan," *Military Affairs*, XVII, 125-27. Upton, *Armies*, iii-iv.

17. Upton, *Armies*, 321.

this calamity, he continued, the United States should place all her land forces under federal and professional control and train more men and officers in peacetime.

His specific reorganization proposals centered on transformation of the small Regular Army into the skeleton of a war force of over 100,000 troops. Since the Army's enlisted strength of 25,000 was barely adequate to keep at half force the regiments, battalions, and companies then authorized, Congress could accomplish this reform simply by permitting the President in emergencies to add more men to existing and fully officered formations. To provide trained recruits for this expansion and to serve as the nucleus for a larger war force than the augmented Regular units could constitute, Upton called for creation of a new federal militia, which he called the "National Volunteers." Like the existing state militia, the National Volunteers would consist of civilians who devoted a certain amount of their time to drill and training and who stood ready to assemble and march off to duty when called. Unlike the state militia, which Upton would relegate to state support and local defense and police duty, the National Volunteers would be organized, officered, paid, and equipped entirely by the federal government and closely linked to the Regular Army. In his earlier writings, Upton envisioned the Volunteers as a force of modest size, one or two battalions of which would be connected to each of the twenty-five Regular infantry regiments. Later, he expanded the plan for the Volunteers by suggesting the creation of one battalion for each congressional district—over 400 in all. Along with these changes in manpower policy, Upton advocated reforms in promotion and retirement practices, the creation of advanced schools for officers, the inauguration of a reserve officer training system in civilian colleges, the establishment of a general staff, and wartime conscription.[18]

Upton did not live to see any of his major proposals adopted. Together with many high-ranking military officers and a few interested members of Congress, he waged during the late 1870s a determined but losing fight for reorganization of the Army. In December, 1878, a special congressional committee introduced a measure, the Burnside bill, which incorporated many of Upton's proposals, but partisan politics and opposition from vested interests within the Army defeated the bill. In March, 1881, depressed by the failure of the campaign for military reform and probably suffering from a brain tumor, Upton committed suicide. His brilliant career, it seemed, had led only to frustration and tragedy.[19]

18. For Upton's own expressions of his ideas, see: Upton, *Armies*, viii-ix, 323-24, 327, 329-32, 337-54, 358, 367, 368-69; and Emory Upton, *The Military Policy of the United States*, Senate Doc. No. 494, 62d Cong., 2d sess., 1912, pp. vii and xiii-xv. For modern analyses of Upton's ideas, see: Ambrose, *Upton*, 102-4, 107-8, 110, 124, 126; Weigley, *American Army*, 109, 122-24; Brown, *Military Affairs*, XVII, 127-28; and Huntington, *Soldier and State*, 234-35.

19. Ambrose, *Upton*, 112-19, 121, 136-50. Weigley, *American Army*, 124-25. Boylan, *Mid-America*, XLI, 173-76, 178-79, 185-86. *Burnside Report*, Pt. 1, p. 3, and Pt. 2, pp. 2-3, 9, 11, 23-24.

The contrary proved true. As the changed diplomatic and naval conditions of the 1880s and 1890s furnished a new rationale for military reform, Army progressives, who learned of Upton's ideas from his writings and by word of mouth, made them the foundation for their plans for modernizing their service.[20]

Variants of Upton's plan for a Regular Army that would be rapidly expansible in emergencies filled military journals, official reports, and popular magazine articles. These proposals differed in details but were similar in principles. The authors of most of them advocated a modest enlargement of the peacetime force—usually to 30,000 or 40,000 men—to enable the Army to perform adequately its garrison and police tasks and to allow the assembly of large formations for maneuvers. They called also for subdivision of each infantry regiment into three of the four-company battalions that tactical experts considered the largest formations maneuverable in open order by one officer. They asked that the President be empowered to increase the Army's size in an emergency up to a set maximum, either by adding men to existing regiments, battalions, and companies or by forming new units. The size of the expanded army varied in the different plans. In some, it would be a war force of over 200,000 men, but most reformers settled for a maximum of between 50,000 and 100,000. To provide trained men for the expanded regiments, some officers proposed a system of short two- or three-year enlistments in the Regular Army, to be followed by several years in a reserve, during which time the reservist would be subject to recall to fill the ranks in wartime. Plans for training reserve officers for the Regulars and for recalling retired officers to the colors in emergencies also had their advocates.[21]

The increasingly expansionist-minded officer-reformers envisioned for the reorganized Regular Army a strategic role out of all proportion to its modest size. Such an army, which the President could mobilize at his discretion, would give the United States a ready striking force for dealing with crises short of major war, and in a full-scale conflict it might provide the margin between victory and swift disaster. In the event of a sudden coastal incursion by hostile forces, for example, the expansible army could protect the harbor defenses against enemy infantry that was being landed out of

20. Ambrose, *Upton*, 3-4, 121-22, 151-53. Weigley, *American Army*, 125-26. Brown, *Military Affairs*, XVII, 128.

21. Wagner, *JMSI*, V, 250-53. King, *JMSI*, V, 368-71. Lt. Arthur L. Wagner, "The Military and Naval Policy of the United States," *JMSI*, VII, 257-67, 270-75, 278. Zalinski, *JMSI*, XIV, 949-51, 958-62. Sanger, *JMSI*, XIV, 1154, 1156, 1159. Wilson, *JMSI*, XVIII, 490-91, 504-5. Harbord, *JMSI*, XXI, 8-13. Williams, *JMSI*, XXI, 241-43. Foote, *JMSI*, XXII, 17, 46-47. Glassford, *JMSI*, XXII, 472-75. Holabird, *United Service*, VIII, 31. John A. T. Hull, "The Organization of the Army," *The North American Review*, CLXVIII, 388. Howard, *Forum*, XXIII, 644-45. Duncan, *The North American Review*, CLXVI, 453. *RSW, 1877*, I, vi, 47-49; *1883*, I, 47-48. Maj. Gen. John M. Schofield to the Secretary of War, January 19, 1892, Box 56; Schofield to Rep. D. Henderson, January 3, 1893, and to Daniel S. Lamont, September 15, 1893, Box 57, Schofield Papers.

range of the heavy guns. It also might play a crucial offensive role. Army theorists pointed out that in modern war a sudden assault, even on a small scale, might gain a decisive advantage. With an expansible army, the United States would have the means to launch such attacks while additional larger forces were being mobilized, thus securing victory sooner and at less cost in lives and treasure. Beyond the military sphere, officers saw the expansible army as a support for overseas commerce and diplomacy and as a deterrent to war. One of them wrote as early as 1884: "We are liable to insult and dishonor in a hundred ways, unless we are prepared to go even to the ends of the earth, not only with ships but with powerful armies in transports, to vindicate the rights of our citizens and the honor of the flag." Sounding the theme of deterrence, another officer declared, "A known preparedness to send an efficient military force wherever the exigencies of just war might demand would be the safest guarantee against such a possibility." This emphasis on the Regulars' extracontinental expeditionary function was to have an important impact on military policy and strategy in 1898.[22]

To furnish trained recruits for the expanding Regular units and to act, if necessary, as the cadre for a mass army of citizen-soldiers, most Army reformers of the eighties and nineties urged the establishment of a reserve force under federal control. They differed on its organizational details. Some revived Upton's plan for the National Volunteers and called for a full-fledged federal militia. Others suggested more modest plans for local officer cadres, appointed under the Army's supervision, who would attend classes and drills in peacetime and in wartime recruit and train temporary volunteer regiments similar to those that had fought so well in the Civil War when competently led. Whatever their details, all the plans demanded complete federal control of the system, especially of the selection and commissioning of its officers. To enlarge the nation's total pool of trained manpower, some Army officers advocated basic military drill for all boys in the public schools. Others, following Upton's lead, urged conscription in time of war.[23]

Their plans for a new federal military reserve brought Upton's followers into collision with the leaders of the expanding and politically militant state militia. During the militia's revival in the late seventies, their officers had

22. The first quotation is from King, *JMSI*, V, 359-60; see also 363-64 and 371-72. The second is from Duncan, *The North American Review*, CLXVI, 452-53. Wagner, *JMSI*, VII, 392-93, 396. Hains, *JMSI*, XV, 243. Williams, *JMSI*, XXI, 240-41. Mahan, *Interest in Sea Power*, 192-93. Schofield, *Forty-Six Years*, 526-28.

23. Wagner, *JMSI*, V, 249-50, 253-61. Price, *JMSI*, , VI, 317. Wagner, *JMSI*, VII, 399-400. Lt. A. C. Sharpe, "Organization and Training of a National Reserve for Military Service," *JMSI*, X, 11-12. Sanger, *JMSI*, X, 38. Stuart, *JMSI*, XII, 1229-35. Stuart, *JMSI*, XIV, 237, 247-48, 254-56, 276-78. Zalinski, *JMSI*, XIV, 927-33, 937-39, 943-45. Sanger, *JMSI*, XIV, 1160, 1168-71. Harbord, *JMSI*, XXI, 3, 7. Williams, *JMSI*, XXI, 255. Foote, *JMSI*, XXII, 16-17, 29-35, 43-44. Glassford, *JMSI*, XXII, 471-72, 474-79. Lt. S. M. Foote, "Our Volunteer Armies—A Reply," *JMSI*, XXII, 641. *RSW*, *1887*, I, 125-26. Schofield, *Forty-Six Years*, 366, 516-22, 524, 535. Sherman, *Memoirs*, II, 385-86.

learned to lobby effectively in state legislatures for funds and support. In 1879 they formed the United States National Guard Association and carried their campaign to Congress. Representing solid blocs of voters in most states, the Guards' officers had political power to back up their requests. A contemporary observer wrote of them: "Whatever may be said about the legality of their organization, it is a fact that they have the recognition and support of the people and that they have inconsiderable influence in politics, although this influence has never been used for any purpose but to promote the interests of the force." Campaigning for congressional recognition and federal subsidies, a growing number of militia leaders demanded that their force be assigned a larger military role than the traditional furnishing of organized units for short-term local defense and the training of individual recruits for separate wartime volunteer regiments. As their adoption of the name "National Guard" signified, they urged that the rejuvenated state militia perfom the function of Upton's National Volunteers, that their units stand beside the Regular establishment as the nucleus of the national wartime Army.[24]

Unlike Upton, who had written during the militia's decline and dismissed them with contempt, Regular Army reformers of the 1880s and 1890s no longer regarded the state forces as "a military Nazareth out of which nothing good can come," but neither were they willing to accept them as the nucleus of a wartime citizen army. Following European examples and the doctrines of Upton, they insisted that any reserve for the wartime Army must be under continuous federal command and supervision. Only then could professional officers enforce a uniform high standard of leadership, organization, training, and equipment. The Regulars pointed out that the Constitution, by reserving to the states in peacetime the crucial rights to organize, officer, and instruct their militia, prevented such federal control over the so-called National Guard. Congress could prepare plans and set standards, but it had no way to enforce them upon the states. Unless the federal government could effect radical reforms, the Regulars insisted, the militia's lack of properly trained regimental and company officers, the ignorance in all of its ranks of open-order tactics and field survival techniques, and the social-club atmosphere prevailing in so many of its units would continue to render it worthless as a ready reserve. Further to bolster their case, Regulars stressed that, since each state, not the federal government, prescribed the number and type of units in its militia, the National Guard as a whole did not contain the proper balance of infantry, cavalry, and artillery for a field army. Called up, it would provide little but infantry, the branch that the states emphasized for its police value.

24. The quotation is from Sanger, *JMSI*, XIV, 1161. Riker, *Soldiers of the States*, 55-56, 59-62. Wetmore, *United Service*, VI, 337-38. Martha Derthick, *The National Guard in Politics*, 16, 20.

The Regular reformers thus expressed their preference for a reserve cadre separate fom the militia and under federal command. They wanted to confine the National Guard in war to its historic functions—short-term local defense and the furnishing of trained officers and men to units of the national Army, whether Regular or volunteer. Regulars pointed out that the new program of coast fortification implied an enlarged and increasingly important military role for local defense forces. When completed, the projected batteries would require almost 100,000 troops, in addition to the Regular heavy artillery, to man the guns and protect them from amphibious attack. This task, Regulars suggested, could absorb the whole existing National Guard, and to this static local service Guard units were especially suited. As a home defense force and as a pool of recruits and replacements for the field armies, the Regulars considered the National Guard valuable enough to deserve continued and increased federal subsidies. They called upon Congress to give the Guard firm recognition in law and to provide it with additional funds and equipment. They favored bringing together Army and National Guard units for maneuvers and the assignment of Regular officers to help train the militia. Some suggested that the Army's schools be opened to qualified militia officers and urged that guardsmen who passed fitness examinations be commissioned in the new federal reserve. But that reserve itself, the Regulars insisted, must remain organizationally separate from the state troops, under federal command at all times and for all purposes.[25]

A strong faction within the National Guard accepted the Army's definition of their military role. Located, in large part, in East Coast and Canadian border states where there were many seaport and fortifications, these guardsmen saw ample opportunities for duty in home defense and had no desire for long-term service far away from their localities. They accordingly called upon Congress to clarify the procedures under which the President could call out the National Guard for three to six months of duty in emergencies and urged the federal government to subsidize fortress artillery regiments of militia. These guardsmen accepted, too, their role as a feeder to a separate wartime volunteer army. As a Massachusetts officer put it,

25. The following illustrate Regular Army views on the militia: Upton, *Armies*, 367. Brig. Gen. Theodore F. Rodenbough, "Militia Reform without Legislation," *JMSI*, II, 390, 397, 417-19. Wagner, *JMSI*, V, 254-55. Lt. G. N. Whistler, "The Artillery Organization of the Future," *JMSI*, V, 329-30. Sherman, *JMSI*, VI, 16-17, 25-26. Wagner, *JMSI*, X, 301-3. Stuart, *JMSI*, XII, 1231-32. Stuart, *JMSI*, XIV, 251-52. Zalinski, *JMSI*, XIV, 940-43, 945, 948. Sanger, *JMSI*, XIV, 1160-63, 1165-67, 1171-74. Scherer, *JMSI*, XVIII, 275-84. Wilson, *JMSI*, XVIII, 485-88. Harbord, *JMSI*, XXI, 16-22. Williams, *JMSI*, XXI, 243-44. Foote, *JMSI*, XXII, 17-18, 20-22, 38-41, 45. Glassford, *JMSI*, XXII, 479. Foote, *JMSI*, XXII, 641-42. *RSW, 1887*, I, 120, 125. James C. Ayres, "The National Guard and Our Sea-Coast Defence," *The Forum*, XXIV, 419. For background on the previous war roles of the militia, see Robert S. Chamberlain, "The Northern State Militia," *Civil War History*, IV, 106-8, 111, 117-18. For Prussian and French doctrine on reserves, see Barbara A. Tuchman, *The Guns of August*, 25, 35.

"The militia must be kept alive, in war as in peace, as a mother of regiments, training men for them in advance, recruiting for them when war comes, acting always as do the home battalions of some foreign services."[26]

A powerful group of Midwestern and Southern guardsmen, however, militantly rejected the Army's concept of their organization and duties. Since their areas were devoid of coast defenses and would not be threatened by enemy attack, they saw that the Regulars' plan provided little justification for the existence of their units. Without such justification they would experience difficulty in securing state and federal support. In contrast to the Eastern Guard leaders, who often were wealthy and prominent citizens, the Midwestern and Southern militia officers considered the Guard a career rather than a hobby and regarded it as a road to social prestige and political power. Extended field campaigns alongside the Regulars would afford these men opportunities for fame and promotion; hence, they were willing to undertake such duty. Brushing aside the Regular Army's doubts about their capabilities, Guard officers of this school called for recognition of the existing state troops as the organizational skeleton of any wartime force larger than the expanded Regular establishment, subject as were Regular Army formations to perform any service required by the President anywhere in the world and ready to stay in the field for two or three years if necessary. The more extreme proponents of this point of view wanted legislation that would empower the President to draft the entire National Guard into federal service in emergencies for as long as the national interest required and to use it for any purpose (including overseas offensive operations) for which he was entitled to use the Regular Army. Others, aware that many National Guardsmen considered mandatory foreign service outside their constitutional obligation, suggested that in wartime Guard units be given the opportunity to volunteer in a body under their own officers for extended federal service. Although divided on this question, guardsmen of the reservist faction agreed on two points: They opposed any separate federal reserve, although they approved of a larger Regular Army, and they insisted that in peacetime the states must retain complete authority over the organization, officering, and training of their regiments, with the federal government merely providing additional funds and equipment. Insistence on these points made their program unacceptable to the Regulars.[27]

26. The quotation is from "Comment and Criticism," *JMSI*, XXII, 432. Todd, *Military Affairs*, 162-63. Derthick, *Guard in Politics*, 23-24. *RSW, 1902*, I, 40. Sanger, *JMSI*, XIV, 1174-76. Lt. H. C. Carbaugh, "Federal Duty and Policy as to Organizing and Maintaining an Adequate Artillery Force for the United States," *JMSI*, XXI, 257-63. "Comment and Criticism," *JMSI*, XXII, 430-32, 434-35, 437-39. Ayres, *Forum*, XXIV, 416-17, 419, 421. W. R. Hamilton to Lt. T. H. Bliss, September 22, 1889, Box 27; Maj. Gen. John M. Schofield to Maj. Gen. Josiah Porter, December 5, 1894, Box 57, Schofield Papers.

27. Derthick, *Guard in Politics*, 22-24. "Comment and Criticism," *JMSI*, XIII, 1174-78. Col. James M. Rice, "The National Guard—What It Is and Its Use," *JMSI*, XV, 915-17, 921-24, 927-29, 932-35. "Comment and Criticism," *JMSI*, XXII, 429, 436-37, 440. Col. C. W. King, "United States Guard, Why Not?" *JMSI*, XXII, 644-51. Wetmore, *United Service*, VI, 339. *Proceedings of the Convention of National Guards, St. Louis, October 1, 1879*, 12-13, in Dabney H. Maury to Maj. Gen. John M. Schofield, May 13, 1891, Box 30, Schofield Papers.

During the 1890s the outlines of a compromise between the extreme Regular and National Guard positions began to emerge in the writings of some Army progressives. These realists pointed out that the creation of a federal military reserve that would be independent of the state troops was politically impossible. The National Guard would not tolerate the existence of such a competing force, and it had the political leverage to prevent its formation. Therefore, the existing National Guard must be accepted as the basis of any new reserve. The question then remained of assuring, in spite of the constitutional limits, effective federal supervision and proper standards of performance. The answer, the proponents of compromise suggested, lay in the power of the federal dollar. The national government should assume the cost of paying, arming, and equipping the state troops if, in return, the militia's enlistment terms, organization, and training conformed to standards set by the War Department, standards that, for all practical purposes would place the militia under the Army's control and transform it into Upton's National Volunteers. Under this plan of organization, the Constitution would not be violated, because the states, through their own legislation, would themselves put the federal policy into execution. This formula, which was to find far-reaching application in fields other than the military, the Regulars and National Guardsmen eventually adopted, but they did not do so until long after their disagreement over the reserve issue had disrupted mobilization plans for the Spanish War.[28]

In the decade before the Spanish-American War, Secretaries of War and Commanding Generals of the Army began incorporating the ideas of the Army progressives into their administrative actions and legislative requests. The slow rebuilding of the coast defenses, the rearmament of the Regulars with modern small arms and artillery, the reforms in promotion and education of officers, the founding of the Military Information Division, and the other pre-1898 improvements in the Regular establishment all had their origins in the writings of Upton and his followers. Secretaries and Commanding Generals repeatedly proposed legislation aimed at establishment of the expansible Regular Army. Year after year, they called upon Congress to increase the enlisted strength from 25,000 men to 30,000, the minimum number required for the Army's police and garrison duties and for its proper organization and training. They asked, also, for division of the infantry regiments into the four-company battalions recommended by tactical experts in the United States and Europe and already adopted by most foreign armies. In the American Army, the Cavalry and Artillery had organized battalions; only the Infantry remained to be reorganized. During the nineties, regimental and department commanders improvised infantry battalions for training, but it required an act of Congress to make the formations permanent and to authorize the assignment of battalion officers and staff.[29]

28. Sharpe, *JMSI*, X, 12, 14, 16-29. Bachelor, *JMSI*, XIII, 62-70.

29. *RSW*, *1880*, I, v; *1881*, I, 4; *1882*, I, iv; *1885*, I, 130-33; *1886*, I, 16; *1887*, I, 123-24; *1889*, I, 5, 65; , *1890*, I, 11-12, 46, 48-50; *1891*, I, 12, 57; *1892*, I, 3-4, 47-48; *1893*, I, 11-12, 63; *1894*,

Both Secretaries of War and Commanding Generals saw the Army, if revamped along these lines, as the base for an expansible force. In 1894, for example, Secretary of War Daniel S. Lamont called for reorganization of the Infantry and for the increase of the Army to 30,000 men. He pointed out "the great advantage of the [proposed] formation in enabling us to put a large and effective force in the field upon short notice, by merely enlisting a sufficient number of additional private soldiers, the officers and organization being always ready for this expansion." Enlargement of the Army by 5,000 men, however, proved too radical, militaristic, and expensive a step for Congress, which greeted every War Department bill with indifference or hostility. Until the war with Spain, the Army's strength remained at 25,000 men, and the Infantry struggled along in outdated formations.[30]

To avoid the controversial question of the National Guard's role as a reserve force, War Department officials before 1898 restricted their legislative recommendations to the area of agreement between Regulars and militiamen. Secretaries and Commanding Generals called for federal recognition of the National Guard and recommended increased subsidies for it. Working with the Guard's lobby, the War Department secured some minor improvements in militia law and appropriations. In 1882 Congress authorized the loan of Army cannon and mortars to militia units that were training for coast defense. Five years later, it increased the militia's annual subsidy from $200,000 to $400,000 and allowed the states to draw their allotments in clothing and camp equipage as well as in weapons and ammunition. In 1897 the Secretary of War obtained congressional permission to exchange late-model Springfield rifles from federal stock piles for other weapons turned in by the militia, the aim being to assure a uniform, if obsolescent, arming of the state forces. The War Department every year detailed scores of Regular officers to inspect National Guard encampments and to assist the states in training their troops. On the basis of the officers' reports and of the states' returns, the Military Information Division published periodic summaries of the condition of the militia. Occasionally, Regular units camped with the guardsmen for combined maneuvers. While they avoided a direct discussion of the Guard's military function, Secretaries of War and Commanding Generals in their reports repeatedly stressed the militia's importance in coast

I, 5-7, 60, 64; *1895*, I, 7-10, 69, 191; *1896*, I, 6-7; *1897*, I, 7-8, 221. Wagner, *JMSI*, VII, 396. Harbord, *JMSI*, XXI, 9-11. Hull, *Forum*, XXV, 396-97. Hull, *The North American Review*, CLXVIII, 386. Maj. Gen. John M. Schofield to John Bigelow, October 29, 1894, and to Representative J. H. Outhwaite, March 18, 1894, Box 57, Schofield Papers, printed copy of H. R. 4106, 55th Cong., 2d sess., in File No. 74259. AGO Records.

30. The quotation is from *RSW, 1894*, I, 7. For other official expressions in favor of an expansible Army, see *RSW, 1885*, I, 7: *1887*, I, 10; *1891*, I, 56-57; *1892*, I, 48; *1894*, I, 59-60; *1895*, I, 68-70.

defense and as a "training school" for citizen-soldiers. They clearly indicated that, when forced to face the issue, the War Department would adopt the Regular Army's point of view, not the National Guard's.[31]

The men in authority in the War Department in 1898 inherited a set of well-established assumptions about the Army's mission in foreign wars and about its proper organization for carrying out that mission. If unfamiliar with these principles before assuming office, they encountered them in the recommendations and proposals of their professional subordinates. Whether the ideas so received were applied with flexibility and responsiveness to the larger political and strategic situation depended on the personalities and experience of the individuals in the seats of power.

III

Secretary of War Russell Alexander Alger, who entered office early in 1897 with the McKinley Administration, had distinguished himself both in war and in business during a long, eventful career. Probably a distant relative of Horatio Alger, the writer of boys' success stories, he lived the life of an Alger hero in his rise from orphaned poverty to wealth, power, and prestige. He was born in 1836 on the Ohio frontier, the son of a pioneer couple, both of whom died when he was eleven years old, leaving him to support himself and two younger children. Through hard work as a farm hand and, later, as a part-time school teacher, he maintained himself and the other children, put himself through a local academy, and in 1857 won admission to the Ohio bar. Two years later, he moved to Grand Rapids, Michigan, where he entered the lumber business and married the daughter of an old settler and leading citizen.[32]

In August, 1861, as the nation mobilized for civil war, Alger entered the Union Army as captain of a Michigan Volunteer cavalry company he had recruited. In 1863 he commanded his own regiment, the Fifth Michigan

31. Bernardo and Bacon, *Military Policy*, 249-50. Riker, *Soldiers of the States*, 60. *Militia in 1897*, 381. Schofield, *Forty-Six Years*, 522. Rodenbough, *JMSI*, II, 391-96. King, *JMSI*, V, 386-91. Sherman, *JMSI*, VI, 11, 26. Price, *JMSI*, VI, 324-27. Giddings, *JMSI*, XXI, 62-73. "Comment and Criticism," *JMSI*, XXII, 431-32. Wetmore, *United Service*, XII, 21, 24-30. *RSW, 1880*, I, vii-viii, 245, III, viii; *1881*, I, 18-19; *1882*, I, v-vi, xx, xxiii-xxix; *1883*, I, 22; *1884*, I, 6, 49; *1885*, I, 10-11; *1886*, I, 20; *1887*, I, 12, 27-28, 80, 123, 126; *1888*, I, 14; *1889*, I, 14, 19; *1890*, I, 16-17, 51, 271; *1891*, I, 23, V, 99; *1892*, I, 13, 18, 46, 48; *1893*, I, 27-28, 62, 64-65; *1894*, I, 23-24; *1895*, I, 16-17; *1896*, I, 17-18; *1897*, I, 48-49. *Proceedings of the Convention of National Guards, St. Louis, October 1, 1879*, 8-12, in Dabney H. Maury to Maj. Gen. John M. Schofield, May 13, 1891, Box 30; Schofield to Maj. Gen. Josiah Porter, December 5, 1894, Box 57, Schofield Papers.

32. No biography of Alger has yet been written, and his career must be followed through a variety of scattered sources. For his early life, the best are: George W. Hotchkiss, *History of the Lumber and Forest Industry of the Northwest* (hereafter cited as Hotchkiss, *Lumber Industry*), 75-77. Albert Baxter, *History of the City of Grand Rapids, Michigan*, 103, 589. S. C. Bingham, *Early History of Michigan, with Biographies of State Officers, Members of Congress, Judges and Legislators*, 35-36.

Major General Nelson A. Miles

Courtesy U.S. Army Center of Military History
Secretary of War Russell Alexander Alger

Courtesy National Archives

Adjutant General Henry C. Corbin

Cavalry, in the brigade led by the dashing, controversial "boy general," George Armstrong Custer. Gallant and skillful service in the Gettysburg, Wilderness, and Shenandoah Valley campaigns won Alger repeated recommendations for advancement to brigadier general and eventually brevet promotions to brigadier general and major general "for gallant and meritorious services." On the strength of these titles, friends in later years often called him "General Alger." Ill health forced Alger's resignation from the service in September of 1864, but a quarrel, later patched up, between him and Custer left an unjustified stain on Alger's war record.[33]

After he left the Army, Alger moved with his family to Detroit and re-entered Michigan's rapidly growing lumber industry. Hard work and good fortune soon brought their rewards. By the mid-eighties, his days of poverty well behind him, Alger had won his place among the industrial and financial tycoons of the Gilded Age. In control of Alger, Smith, and Company, Michigan's largest lumbering concern, he diversified his investments by buying timberlands in the Upper and Lower peninsulas of Michigan, in California, in the South, and in Canada, and by acquiring stock in and serving as a director of banks, railroads, and manufacturing concerns. As his wealth increased, Alger acquired the trappings that went with it in late-nineteenth-century America—a fine mansion in Detroit, a private railroad car with lavish fittings, a stable of trotters, and an art collection. He made bountiful contributions to charity. He numbered Marcus A. Hanna and Marshall Field among his friends and attended banquets with J. Pierpont Morgan and Cornelius Vanderbilt. As did his wealthy contemporaries, he toured abroad, visiting the British Isles, the Continent, and Turkey.[34]

By way of involvement in Union veterans' affairs, Alger, a lifelong Republican, entered active politics. After helping to organize the Grand Army of the Republic in Michigan, he supervised establishment of the state soldiers' home, drummed up financial aid for impoverished widows of Union generals,

33. For glimpses of Alger as a cavalry officer and of the actions in which he fought, see James H. Kidd, *Personal Recollections of a Cavalryman*, 45, 54-55, 107-45, 148, 151-55, 215-23, 281, 293, 300-306, 310-11, 343, 345-48, 351, 369-71, 383. See also Philip Henry Sheridan, *Personal Memoirs of P. H. Sheridan*, I, 140-43, 160-65. For histories of the regiments with which he served, see Michigan Adjutant General, *Record of Service of Michigan Volunteers in the Civil War, 1861-1865*, XXXII, 2; XXXV, 1-3; XXXVI, 1, 3. Custer recommends Alger for promotion, in George A. Custer to Secretary of War Edwin M. Stanton, October 19, 1863, and June 26, 1864, Alger Papers. The scandal surrounding Alger's resignation, in which Custer mistakenly reported Alger absent from his regiment without leave when Alger in fact was sick in hospital, is documented exhaustively in the Alger Papers.

34. Material on the details of Alger's business career is fragmentary and scattered. The best over-all account is Hotchkiss, *Lumber Industry*, 76-77; see also Baxter, *Grand Rapids*, 590-91; Bingham, *History of Michigan*, 36; and Silas Farmer, *History of Detroit and Wayne County and Early Michigan*, 1220. For material on Alger's acquaintanceships and manner of living, see the letters, notes, newspaper clippings, invitations, and other relics preserved in the Alger Papers.

and religiously attended veterans' gatherings all over the country. In 1889 his services received their reward; his comrades elected him National Commander of the G.A.R. His personal following among the old soldiers, along with his large and frequent campaign contributions, made him a power in the Michigan Republican party. He served one term as governor of his state in 1885-1887, during which he earned dubious distinction as the first chief executive of Michigan to use the National Guard to break a strike. He also watched closely the management of the state children's homes and made detailed, humane suggestions for their improvement. In 1888 he was Michigan's favorite-son candidate for President in a Republican convention that was highlighted by charges from supporters of John Sherman, another aspirant, that Alger men had bribed Southern delegates. The following year, President-elect Benjamin Harrison considered Alger for Secretary of War in his Cabinet, but did not appoint him.[35]

Probably through business connections in Cleveland and through his friendship with Marcus A. Hanna, Alger early associated himself with the rising Republican politician William McKinley. During the 1890s, at McKinley's invitation, Alger frequently spoke in Ohio at campaign rallies. In 1894 he loaned McKinley his private railroad car for an electioneering trip, and when McKinley made his drive for the Republican presidential nomination in 1896, Alger helped secure Michigan's delegates for the Ohioan. He also spoke for McKinley to his business associates in the East to reassure them about McKinley's soundness on the gold standard. After McKinley's nomination, Alger organized a group of Union veterans and took them campaigning in his private car to strengthen McKinley's appeal to the important ex-soldier element in the Republican coalition. In January of 1897, these efforts and vigorous backing from New England and Midwestern Republican leaders brought Alger the post he long had coveted. McKinley appointed him Secretary of War.[36]

Supporters of Alger's appointment had stressed to McKinley his tact, popularity with the veterans, party loyalty, and business experience as

35. The Dictionary of American Biography (hereafter cited as DAB), I, 179-80. F. Clever Bald, Michigan in Four Centuries, 297-98. Bingham, History of Michigan, 36. Farmer, History of Detroit, 1053. For various aspects of Alger's activity in politics and veterans' affairs, see the correspondence in the Alger Papers.

36. Alger's relationship to McKinley can be followed through his correspondence with McKinley and Hanna in the Alger Papers. For the details of his appointment, see the following: Margaret Leech, In the Days of McKinley, 102-4. H. Wayne Morgan, William McKinley and His America, 260-61. William McKinley to Russell A. Alger, January 27, 1897, Alger Papers. W. M. Osborne to McKinley, January 6, 1897; Alger to J. B. Foraker, February 1, 1897; Alger to McKinley, January 11, 1897; Redfield Proctor to McKinley, January 12, 1897; William E. Chandler to McKinley, January 12, 1897; Samuel Thomas to McKinley, January 18, 1897, William McKinley Papers. R. M. Moore to James H. Wilson, February 1, 1897, Box 17; Brig. Gen. James H. Wilson to Col. Blueford Wilson, July 19, 1899, Box 44, James H. Wilson Papers.

reasons for giving him the war portfolio. These qualities were, indeed, among Alger's qualifications, but he also brought to his office what a Cabinet colleague later called "weaknesses incompatible with the direction of great movements." Sixty-two years old at the beginning of the war with Spain, the pleasant, affable veteran sported an elegant white mustache and goatee and still stood as tall, slender, and erect as the dashing young cavalryman he had been thirty-odd years earlier. In his struggles with the complexities of his job, he displayed much common sense and humanity. Officers who served under him in the War Department respected his patriotism, his devotion to the Army, and his concern for the welfare of the common soldier. They also praised his receptiveness to professional advice. However, the strains of crisis brought out Alger's less commendable qualities. For all his combat experience in the Civil War, he had no real training in large-scale military administration, never having commanded a body of troops larger than a brigade and that only briefly. He was not well informed about the changes in weapons and tactics that were revolutionizing the conduct of war. Except for his work in veterans' organizations, his one term as governor of Michigan, and his unsuccessful campaign for the Presidency, he possessed little background in politics and government—certainly nothing to fit him for management of a major federal department in wartime. Defects of temperament annoyed and bewildered his colleagues. President McKinley found him outspoken as an adviser but, in the President's words, "a little shifty" in his views and guided more by emotional impulse than by logical thought in formulating opinions. Generous and optimistic, Alger often failed to secure all the facts before committing himself to a course of action, and hence he promised more than he could deliver, to his and the Army's embarrassment. Worst of all, he revealed a vain, selfish streak, which precipitated feuds with his colleagues and subordinates over minor and usually fancied insults to his personal honor. Adj. Gen. Henry C. Corbin, an astute officer who managed to get along with Alger, remembered him as "the most egotistic man with whom I have ever come in contact."[37]

Alger's uniformed codirector of the War Department, Commanding General Nelson Appleton Miles, had taken office in 1895 when his predecessor, Schofield, reached mandatory retirement age. Like many senior generals of the 1890s, Miles was not an Academy man. Born on a

37. The comment on Alger's egotism is from Gen. H. C. Corbin to Rep. Charles H. Grosvenor, February 4, 1907, Box 1, Corbin Papers. Alger's weaknesses are stressed in James Wilson to William McKinley, July 30, 1899; see also William E. Chandler to McKinley, January 12, 1897; and draft of letter from McKinley to Alger, July, 1899, McKinley Papers. J. F. Weston to Brig. Gen. James H. Wilson, August 3, 1899, Box 26, Wilson Papers. Baxter, *Grand Rapids*, 591. Farmer, *History of Detroit*, 1053. Leech, *Days of McKinley*, 102. Laurence S. Mayo, ed., *America of Yesterday, as Reflected in the Journal of John Davis Long*, 188, 197.

Massachusetts farm in 1839 to devout Baptist antislavery parents, Miles clerked in a store until the firing on Fort Sumter. A strong Union man and abolitionist, he volunteered immediately in 1861 and entered the Army as a lieutenant of Massachusetts Volunteer infantry. He served throughout the war with the Army of the Potomac and fought in most of the hard battles on the road to Richmond. The young volunteer proved a natural combat soldier, courageous, endowed with an instinct for the quick, accurate evaluation of terrain, and able to make correct tactical decisions rapidly. Fortunate in serving under superiors who recognized his talents, Miles rose swiftly through the ranks. By 1862 he was commanding his own regiment of New York infantry, which he led gallantly at Fredericksburg and Chancellorsville. He received his commission as brigadier general of Volunteers in May of 1864. A general at twenty-five, he commanded first a brigade, then a division, and finally an army corps in the bloody Wilderness and Petersburg campaigns. At the war's end, the Army's high command marked him for future greatness.

Deciding to build his career in the military, Miles applied for a commission in the postwar Regular establishment, and in 1866 his battlefield reputation, plus the backing of Generals Grant and Sherman, won him a colonelcy. Two years later, he married Mary Hoyt Sherman, niece of General Sherman and of the powerful Senator John Sherman, Alger's bitter rival in the convention of 1888. This connection with a family of influence in Ohio Republican politics assured Miles of strong backers in government who saw that he received in full the rewards to which his professional abilities entitled him.[38]

While in command of the Fifth United States Infantry on the western plains during the climactic Indian wars of the 1860s, 1870s, and 1880s, Miles added to his Civil War fame. He and his regiment participated in most of the major campaigns of the West. They fought the Kiowa, Comanche, and Apache Indians in the Southwest, and they conducted the ruthless winter offensive that broke the Sioux and Cheyenne who overwhelmed Custer at the Little Big Horn. In other actions, they helped run down the elusive Nez Percés. As a department commander, Miles played a large role in the capture of Geronimo in 1886. During the winter of 1890-1891, he put down the Sioux Ghost Dance Revolt, the last of the Indian uprisings. In all these episodes, Miles displayed great capacity as a leader of men, aggressiveness, and tactical skill. He built up elaborate spy networks of scouts and friendly Indians and adapted conventional strategy to the peculiar demands of

38. Virginia W. Johnson, *The Unregimented General: A Biography of Nelson A. Miles*, 3-34, describes Miles's Civil War exploits and his entry into the Regular Army. The only recent biography of Miles, it leaves much to be desired. See also *DAB*, XII, 614-15.

Indian warfare. On the march, he took effective precautions against ambush, kept his troops ready for combat at all times, and made sure each of his columns remained in supporting distance of the others. Like other successful Indian fighters, he learned that constant pursuit and attack were the most effective means of wearing down Indian bands too mobile to be trapped and crushed in pitched battle. Curiously, while pursuing and defeating the Indians, he grew increasingly sympathetic to them and developed an appreciation for their way of life and for the courage of their hopeless resistance. He treated captured hostiles humanely, tried to end tribal revolts by persuasion rather than by force, and more than once battled his superiors in Washington—even the President—on behalf of honorable treatment for Indians whom he had defeated. Miles's attitude in these matters illustrated his strong sense of honor and his willingness to defend what he believed to be right—the heritage, perhaps, of his strait-laced New England upbringing.[39]

Miles's victories on the frontier brought him national fame and much publicity. Grateful for his protection, Westerners honored him with testimonial dinners, parades, and jeweled swords; in 1888 a few politicians talked of nominating him for the Presidency. More important for his career, Miles retained the respect of his military superiors. Grant considered him one of the five best officers in the Army, and Sheridan referred to him as "the only man who amounts to anything, and on whom we can count." In 1880 Miles received his commission as brigadier general in the United States Army. Ten years later, by then the senior brigadier in the service, he won promotion to major general, in those days the Army's highest rank. During these years, besides campaigning against the Indians, he commanded various geographical departments. He proved a progressive administrator who emphasized physical conditioning and combat training for his troops and organized large-scale field maneuvers. In 1894 he directed the Army contingent that was sent to disperse the Pullman strikers in Chicago. In September of the following year, as the senior major general, he succeeded Schofield as Commanding General of the Army.[40]

When he assumed his duties in Washington, Miles looked the perfect soldier. A tall, powerfully built man who took pride in his physical fitness, he loved horseback riding and in Washington mastered the bicycle as well. He followed closely the rapid changes in tactics and weapons and urged the Army to experiment with bicycles and with a new-fangled device called the automobile. His record on the frontier more than confirmed his ability

39. Johnson, *Unregimented General*, 37-299. For Miles's attitude toward the Indians and his methods of fighting them, see his *Serving the Republic*, 122, 133-35, 163-64, 196-207, 225, 230-31.

40. Johnson, *Unregimented General*, 210, 220-28, 254-57, 261-64, 303-9. Miles, *Serving the Republic*, 260. Hagedorn, *Wood*, I, 116-17, describes a sham battle by Miles near Monterey, California.

as a field commander. Yet, for all his virtues, he failed disastrously as Commanding General, and his conduct in that position paved the way for abolition of the office early in the twentieth century.

Egotism and ambition brought about Miles's downfall. In him, the earnest morality of a New England conscience had become entangled with personal vanity. He had a commendable willingness to stand up for his principles, but he often confused principle with his own wounded pride and with his desire for self-dramatization. He was courageous but pompous and conceited, politically ambitious but gullible and naive. As sensitive as Alger to slights upon his honor, Miles often suspected conspiracies against him where none existed. He irritated civilians by his posturing on horseback at the head of every parade and by his fondness for elaborate uniforms. Said the oft-quoted Mr. Dooley: "Seize Gen'ral Miles' uniform. We must strengthen th' gold resarve." Angered by Miles's grasping for publicity, Secretary of War Lamont once exploded: "General Miles is a newspaper soldier."[41]

From the day Miles joined the Army, he quarreled with colleagues and superiors. Each of his Indian campaigns left an aftermath of recrimination between him and other generals, clashes between him and the supply bureaus, and misunderstandings between him and the War Department. The fact that he often had right on his side did nothing to endear him to his opponents. Called to Washington in 1894 to receive orders for suppressing the Pullman disturbance, he openly questioned the need for interference by the Army and suggested that the trouble would subside if the federal government ignored the disorders. His attitude enraged President Cleveland and the then Commanding General Schofield. When he became Commanding General, Miles persisted in his quarrelsome ways. He clashed, early in 1898, with the House Appropriations Committee over money for coast defense and bluntly told the people's representatives that their reductions in the budget threatened national security. The post of Commanding General required tact, self-effacement, and political sophistication—all qualities he lacked. In the words of a contemporary, "His judgment in everything except the mere fighting is likely to be very defective." Worst of all, he was committed to the theory that the Commanding General owed obedience only to the President and that in war he should have exclusive control over the planning and conduct of operations. Only the confinement of the department's activity to peacetime routine and Miles's absence from Washington during the summer of 1897 prevented an early, explosive confrontation between him and the choleric Alger.[42]

41. Johnson, *Unregimented General*, 5, 17, 32, 43, 71, 183, 225-26, 274-75, 308-11. Leech, *Days of McKinley*, 200-201. Edward Ranson, "Nelson A. Miles as Commanding General, 1895-1903," *Military Affairs*, XXIX, 180-81. Miles's views on bicycles and automobiles are in *RSW, 1895*, I, 69. Maj. Gen. John M. Schofield to Maj. Gen. Nelson A. Miles, January 24, 1889, Box 54; Anonymous "Old Staff Officer" to Schofield, June 15, 1893, Box 32, Schofield Papers. Lamont is quoted in Arthur Wallace Dunn, *From Harrison to Harding*, I, 106.

42. Johnson, *Unregimented General*, 7, 28-31, 75, 88-89, 95, 210-21, 242-44, 251-54, 257, 289-90, 295. Miles's actions during the Pullman strike are described in an undated manuscript by General

IV

Among the bureau chiefs, Adj. Gen. Henry Clark Corbin stood out. Corbin was another of the many volunteers who held high rank in the Army of the 1890s. Born in 1842 in southern Ohio, he studied law until the outbreak of the Civil War, then entered the Army in July, 1862, as a lieutenant of Ohio Volunteer infantry. A year later, after passing a qualifying examination, he accepted a major's commission in the Fourteenth United States Colored Infantry, one of the Negro regiments created as a result of the Emancipation Proclamation. With this regiment, he distinguished himself in the campaigns of Atlanta and Nashville and rose to the rank of lieutenant colonel early in 1864 and to full colonel in September, 1865. He received several brevets for gallantry and faithful service. After Appomattox, on the recommendation of his superior officers, the War Department appointed him a second lieutenant of Regular infantry. Later, as captain, he joined an infantry regiment on the southwestern frontier in July, 1866. For the next ten years, as a company commander, he fought Apaches in New Mexico and patrolled the Mexican border. In the latter duty, he displayed discretion and diplomatic skill as well as military competence. As a staff officer, he participated in the Nez Percé campaign of 1877.[43]

The circumstances of Corbin's entry into the staff illustrate the role of political influence in such appointments. Ordered east on recruiting service in 1876, he made the acquaintance of Rutherford B. Hayes, the Republican presidential nominee, who was a fellow Ohioan. The following year, President-elect Hayes appointed Corbin his personal military aide. Through Hayes, Corbin joined the circle of Ohio politicians who dominated the Republican party, and he won the friendship of James A. Garfield and William McKinley, among many other powerful men. Corbin earned the confidence of the Ohio bosses by his distinguished appearance (necessary in a presidential aide), by his affable, urbane manner, and by his administrative ability. Having developed special skill in the organization of large public parades and ceremonies, he conducted several presidential

Schofield in the "Command of the Army" folder, Box 72, Schofield Papers. Miles tells a very different story in *Serving the Republic*, 253-54. Ranson, *Military Affairs*, XXIX, 199. *Army and Navy Journal*, February 5, 1898. The comment on Miles's judgment is in Brig. Gen. James H. Wilson to Anthony Higgins, August 14, 1899, Box 44; see also Wilson to H. W. Biddle, December 17, 1898, Box 43, Wilson Papers.

43. "Henry Clark Corbin, Lieutenant-General United States Army," *Army and Navy Life and the United Service*, IX, 5-7. Francis B. Heitman, *Historical Register and Dictionary of the United States Army*, 327. Nashville (Tenn.) *Banner*, March 13, 1900, clipping; *Memorandum of the Military Service of Brig. Gen. Henry C. Corbin*, 1900, 1-2; The Adjutant General's Office, Statement of the Military Service of Henry Clark Corbin, September 28, 1909; undated, untitled biographical sketch, Boxes 7 and 8, Corbin Papers.

inaugurations and, for the dedication of Grant's Tomb in New York City, moved 70,000 veterans into town in the morning and out again in the evening without delay or disorder. Presidents Hayes, Garfield, and Arthur relied on him as a confidential agent and adviser, and he was among those who stood at Garfield's bedside when the martyred President lay dying. In June, 1880, probably with the assistance of his political backers, he entered The Adjutant General's Department with the rank of major. Thereafter he rose steadily through the ranks of his bureau, serving in Washington and with various geographical departments. In February, 1898, as the senior colonel of the bureau, he was appointed Adjutant General of the Army with the rank of brigadier general.[44]

Corbin owed his position in large part to political connections, but he was far more than a mere hanger-on of the mighty. He was physically impressive—tall, erect, and heavily built, with a square, grim face that was adorned in 1898 with a thick mustache and a small, neat goatee, all turning gray. Tireless, direct in speech, and forceful in manner, he possessed a talent for administration and the will and physical condition for long hours of hard work. General Schofield, under whom he served for a time, reported in 1890 that Corbin had "shown special ability in the management of large bodies of all sorts and conditions of men" and that he "would be a good selection for any unusual service which might be required of an Army officer." While primarily an administrator, Corbin proved his physical courage on more than one occasion. In 1891, for example, on a staff assignment in Arizona, he averted an Indian outbreak by walking unarmed into the hostile camp with only one companion and persuading the rebellious chiefs to lay down their arms. Even men who disliked Corbin acknowledged his absolute personal honesty and his devotion to the interests of the Army. Line officers welcomed his elevation to Adjutant General, pointing out that he had spent more years in command of troops than had any of his predecessors and that he could be relied on to support line interests in Washington.

Above all, Corbin knew how to deal amicably with politicians without sacrificing professional integrity. He recognized, as did Schofield, that in the United States the professional soldier must be the assistant of the civilian leaders, not their master and critic. He respected the politicians and understood their problems, even as he tried to communicate to them the needs of the Army. When asked for advice, he gave it honestly and directly and upheld his position vigorously in argument. If the decision of his civilian

44. "Corbin," *Army and Navy Life and the United Service*, IX, 7-8. R. B. Hayes to Col. H. C. Corbin, November 4, 1892, Box 1; *Memorandum of the Military Service of Brig. Gen. Henry C. Corbin, 1900*, 2, 15-16, Box 7; undated, untitled biographical sketch, *The New York Times*, October 24, 1909, clipping, Box 8; *New York Tribune Illustrated Supplement*, January 8, 1898, clipping, Box 10, Corbin Papers.

superiors went against his judgment, he nevertheless executed their orders faithfully and competently. He never intrigued against them or leaked detrimental information to the press, as Miles and other generals often did. Because they trusted him, Presidents and Secretaries of War listened to Corbin and frequently followed his suggestions. The power he thus gained he used in the interests of the Army and especially of the career officers of the line. Typical of his concern for their interests was his reply when President McKinley, impressed by his work during the war with Spain, offered him a commission as major general of Volunteers. Corbin gratefully declined. He pointed out that very few vacancies in that grade were available and that all "should be given to the gallant and more deserving officers serving with troops in the field." While not a theorist (he contributed nothing to the military journals before 1898), he understood and believed in the doctrines of the Uptonian reformers and incorporated them in his advice to the politicians. Clearly, of the officers in the War Department in 1898, Corbin was the best fitted for high command. As a bureau officer later put it, "One of the most fortunate things that occurred to the Government at the beginning of the War was finding such a fellow as Corbin in the office of The Adjutant General."[45]

With the exception of the chiefs of Ordnance and of Engineers, all of the other bureau heads had entered the Army as volunteers and then transferred to the Regulars after Appomattox. All were experienced in their specialties, and many had served in the line before joining the staff.[46]

Q. M. Gen. Marshall I. Ludington was born in Pennsylvania in 1839 and served continuously in his department from the time he entered the Army during the Civil War. From Chancellorsville to Appomattox, he was chief quartermaster of the Second Corps in the Army of the Potomac. After the war he served on various staffs and commanded major supply depots until, on February 3, 1898, he took office as Quartermaster General. Courteous, kindly, and competent, Ludington had earned an excellent professional reputation. Although some acquaintances considered him indecisive and reluctant to act on his own initiative, his actions in the war crisis later gave evidence of quite the opposite administrative qualities.[47]

45. Dunn, Harrison to Harding, I, 252-53. "Corbin," Army and Navy Life and the United Service, IX, 7-8. Army and Navy Journal, January 15, 1898. Schofield's remarks are quoted in Memorandum of the Military Service of Brig. Gen. Henry C. Corbin, 1900, 17, Box 7, Corbin Papers. See also: Adj. Gen. H. C. Corbin to Secretary of War R. A. Alger, August 13, 1898; Secretary of War Elihu Root to Charles P. Miller, March 2, 1900; Lt. Gen. John M. Schofield to Secretary of War Elihu Root, May 18, 1903; Morning Oregonian, July 4, 1903, clipping; The Cablenews (Manila), June 13, 1905, clipping; The New York Times, October 24, 1909, clipping; and William E. Horton, "Memorandum Relative to General Corbin," December 15, 1909, all in Box 8; Evening Dispatch (Columbus, O.), February 25, 1898, clipping; and the Mail and Express Illustrated Saturday Magazine, June 25, 1898, clipping, Box 10, Corbin Papers. Corbin's appearance can be seen in various photographs in his papers, especially Box 10. J. F. Weston to Brig. Gen. James H. Wilson, August 3, 1899, Box 26, Wilson Papers.

46. Army and Navy Journal, February 12, 1898. RSW, 1898, I, 263; 1899, I, Pt. 2, p. 32.

47. Heitman, Historical Register, I, 646. Army and Navy Journal, February 5, 1898. Brig. Gen. James H. Wilson to Maj. James B. Aleshire, March 5, 1900, Box 45, Wilson Papers.

The Commissary General, Charles Patrick Eagan, came from immigrant stock. Born in Ireland in 1841, he crossed to America with his parents when a small boy and grew up on the Pacific Coast. He entered the service as a volunteer in 1862 and transferred to the Regulars four years later. An infantryman by original branch, he commanded troops on the frontier for several years and won respect for his almost suicidal gallantry in action. His valor especially impressed Gen. George Crook, Miles's rival for the title of greatest of the Indian fighters. Crook helped the young Irishman transfer to the Subsistence Department in 1874 and thereafter assisted and guided him. Eagan rose by seniority through the ranks of his bureau, and in May, 1898, he received his appointment as Commissary General. Although younger than most high-ranking officers in that era of slow promotion, he proved to be an able administrator. He fought aggressively for proper food for the troops, even challenging orders from Secretary Alger if he believed them in error. Handsome and charming, Eagan made many friends, but he possessed a savage temper that, in the end, helped to destroy him.[48]

Brig. Gen. George Miller Sternberg, Surgeon General of the Army, enjoyed world-wide professional renown. A native of New York State and a graduate of Columbia Medical School, Sternberg joined the Regular Army Medical Department in 1861 and remained in the service thereafter. Besides discharging the duties of a field and post surgeon, he conducted during the 1870s, 1880s, and 1890s extensive research in epidemiology and in the new science of bacteriology. He became one of the American pioneers in public health and conducted path-breaking investigations of the causes and spread of yellow fever. He ranked in 1898 as one of the world's experts on that dread disease. His work in bacteriology, especially his contributions to the study of the disease-controlling functions of the white corpuscles, paralleled and confirmed the findings of the European giants Koch, Pasteur, Lister, and Metchnikoff, all of whom held Sternberg in high respect. An eloquent speaker and prolific writer, Sternberg contributed much to the modernization of American medicine by helping to convince physicians of the value of systematic study of the causes and treatment of disease. A kind, religious man of German Lutheran background, Sternberg took office as Surgeon General in 1893, having been promoted over the heads of several seniors in recognition of his professional eminence. He proved to be a conscientious, progressive administrator, noted for his capacity to win the loyalty of subordinates. He founded the Army Medical School to improve the training of military surgeons, established new schools for the Hospital Corps, and introduced at Army hospitals such innovations as X-ray machines, biological laboratories, and programs for rehabilitating disabled veterans. To his countrymen, he represented the best in up-to-date scientific medicine.[49]

48. Heitman, *Historical Register*, I, 393. *Army and Navy Journal*, June 4, 1898, and February 4, 1899.

49. For a detailed account of Sternberg's career and of his scientific achievements, see John Mendinghall Gibson, *Soldier in White: The Life of General George Miller Sternberg, passim*. Also:

The only two West Pointers among the staff chiefs headed the technical bureaus of Ordnance and Engineers. The Chief of Ordnance, Brig. Gen. Daniel Webster Flagler, a New Yorker by birth, graduated fifth in the Academy class of 1861 and spent his entire Army career in the Ordnance Department. After serving in the field with troops in the Civil War, he commanded at one time or another most of the major arsenals, and he helped to design the Army's new coastal and field artillery. In 1891, in recognition of his expert grasp of the complex details of his specialty, President Benjamin Harrison appointed him Chief of Ordnance in preference to two senior colonels in the bureau.[50]

Brig. Gen. James Moulder Wilson, Chief of Engineers, ranked twelfth in the West Point class of 1860 and served in the Ordnance Department and in the Artillery before transferring to the Engineers in 1864. He received several brevet promotions for gallantry in action during the Civil War, then advanced through the ranks of the peacetime Corps of Engineers. He spent most of his time superintending river and harbor improvements before taking office as Chief of Engineers in February, 1897.[51]

The careers of Insp. Gen. Joseph C. Breckinridge, Chief Signal Officer Adolphus W. Greely, Paymaster-General Thomas H. Stanton, and Judge Adv. Gen. G. Norman Lieber all followed a similar pattern. All entered the Army as volunteers in the Civil War and then transferred to the Regulars. All served in the line before joining the staff, Breckinridge in the Artillery, Stanton and Lieber in the Infantry, and Greely in both Infantry and Cavalry. During the Indian campaigns, Paymaster-General Stanton acted for a while as chief of scouts for General Crook. All four officers rose by seniority through the ranks of their bureaus. All but Breckinridge, who received his appointment in 1885, became heads of their departments during the early or middle nineties.[52]

V

The War Department approached the Spanish conflict with competent and, in many cases, distinguished professional soldiers in charge of its administrative bureaus. Outside Washington, it could rely on the department commanders and their staffs to carry on most routine administrative and supply activities. The Regular Army and the National Guard constituted

Heitman, *Historical Register*, I, 921. Latshaw, "Medical Service," 14, 16-17, 19. Leech, *Days of McKinley*, 300-301. *The New York Times*, May 31, 1893.

50. Heitman, *Historical Register*, I, 424. Obituary in General Order No. 59, Headquarters of the Army, April 1, 1899, in *GO/AGO, 1899*. *The New York Times*, January 26, 1891.

51. Heitman, *Historical Register*, I, 1047. *The New York Times*, February 2, 1897.

52. Heitman, *Historical Register*, I, 242, 632, and 916. *The New York Times*, March 27, 1895.

between them a trained and partly trained cadre adequate in numbers for a wartime army of the size likely to be needed. A well-worked-out doctrine existed as a basis for planning the mobilization and employment of the land forces.

Yet, the War Department also approached the crisis with important weaknesses. In the persons of Alger and Miles, its highest leadership left much to be desired in character and ability. Supply stock piles were woefully inadequate, and trained commanders and staffs for large field forces were not available. There was no special staff to plan and coordinate operations or to anticipate and prepare solutions for the novel problems of amphibious campaigning in the tropics. Worst of all, the Regular Army's established organizational and strategic theories were fated to collide disruptively with the political, diplomatic, and naval realities of the developing conflict.

3

The Shaping of Military Policy

I

In the Spanish-American War of 1898, the Army received its first call to support the new diplomacy and its first opportunity to put into practice the ideas of Upton and his followers. The war grew out of a nationalist revolt in Cuba, Spain's most important remaining colony in the Western Hemisphere. Throughout the nineteenth century, Cuban discontent with Spanish rule had steadily increased, provoked by the politically repressive and economically ruinous policies of the mother country. Between 1868 and 1878, the Cubans carried their campaign for self-government onto the battlefield in the Ten Years' War, a conflict that won from Spain promises of reform in the island's government. The Spanish Government did not honor its promises, however, so the Cubans took up arms a second time in 1895. Led by veterans of the earlier war against the mother country and supported by exiles in the United States who furnished guns, money, and men, Cuban guerrillas spread ambush and destruction the length of the island, vowing to continue their fight this time until they won absolute independence. Spain responded with a brutal but unsuccessful campaign of repression, and three years of savage combat ensued. The conflict touched both the conscience and the pocketbook of Cuba's northern neighbor, the United States. American citizens, enraged by Spanish cruelty to the citizens and insurgents, assisted the rebel forces with funds, supplies, and volunteers. The violence in Cuba disrupted profitable trade, threatened the destruction of American property worth $50 million in the island, and jeopardized the military and political stability of the Caribbean, an area accorded great commercial and strategic importance by adherents of the new expansionist diplomacy.

From the beginning of the war, many Americans demanded that their government intervene forcibly to end it and to rescue the Cubans from their Spanish oppressors, but the Administration's policy, under Grover Cleveland until 1897 and thereafter under William McKinley, was much less militant. Influenced by business and financial leaders who opposed war for economic reasons, both Cleveland and McKinley declared the United States neutral in the Cuban conflict. Yet, at the same time, each President in diplomatic notes and public speeches made clear to Spain that the United States, in view of its citizens' extensive interests in Cuba, wanted order restored in the island, by a Spanish victory if possible or by negotiation between mother country and rebels if military action failed to bring a decision. Making veiled threats of intervention, each President in his turn informed Spain's diplomats that American patience had its limits and that, if the conflict continued too much longer, the United States would act on her own initiative to resolve it.[1]

During President McKinley's first year in office, war with Spain over Cuba remained a remote possibility. McKinley, like his predecessor, emphasized peaceable diplomatic means, not military pressure. By the end of 1897, diplomatic negotiations appeared to be resolving the Cuban crisis. A change of government in Spain during the summer brought into power a liberal ministry friendly to the United States and favorable to reform in Cuba. In October the ministry sent a new military governor to the island and promised to avoid excessive brutality in the conduct of the war. A few weeks later the ministry proposed and the Spanish parliament accepted a plan for Cuban self-government within the Spanish Empire. This plan, Spanish and American officials hoped, would form the basis of a negotiated peace between Spain and the rebels. In December, in his annual message to Congress, McKinley expressed cautious optimism about Cuba, although he coupled it with another warning that the United States expected action from Spain as well as promises. Reflecting the hopes for peace, Secretary of the Navy John D. Long planned to begin taking warships out of service and laying them up in harbor to reduce operating expenses.[2]

Officers in the War Department, especially those of the Military Information Division, paid close attention to the Cuban war. They, like their colleagues in the Navy, regarded the stricken island as the strategic key to control of any future Central American canal. As did their civilian countrymen, however, Regular soldiers disagreed on the advisability of direct American intervention in the conflict. Lieutenant General Schofield spoke out for armed action as early as January, 1897, basing his stand on moral and economic rather than military grounds. On the other side, General Miles at the time questioned the need for war and later contended that the issues between Spain and the United States could and should have been settled by peaceful means. A junior officer recalled that he and his colleagues, who were stationed at Key West late in 1897, strongly sympathized with the Cuban insurgents but saw no real possibility of American intervention. Secretary

1. Grenville and Young, *Politics, Strategy, and American Diplomacy*, 248-49. David F. Healy, *The United States in Cuba, 1898-1902: Generals, Politicians, and the Search for Policy*, 6-8. LaFeber, *New Empire*, 284-87, 334-35. Ernest R. May, *Imperial Democracy: The Emergence of America as a Great Power*, 115-16, 118-19, 124-30. Morgan, *Road to Empire*, 9-12, 19-28. Morgan, *McKinley*, 326-27, 342-43. For examples of conservative opinion on Cuba, see: Whitelaw Reid to William McKinley, December 5, 1896; Grenville M. Dodge to McKinley, February 21, 1898, McKinley Papers; and Grenville M. Dodge to Russell A. Alger, March 15, 18, and 22, 1898, Alger Papers.

2. LaFeber, *New Empire*, 337, 339-40. May, *Imperial Democracy*, 125-26, 134-35. Morgan,*Road to Empire*, 27, 29-31, 33-34. The McKinley Administration's naval plans are described in Sprout and Sprout, *Naval Power*, 224, 228-29.

of War Alger was by far the most belligerent official connected with the Army. As early as 1895 he had urged the United States to recognize the Cuban rebel government. In McKinley's Cabinet, especially as relations with Spain deteriorated early in 1898, the volatile Secretary called for an ultimatum to Spain, under the reasoning that a failure to act boldly would mean political disaster for the Republican party. Aside from the vocal Alger, Army leaders before the war expressed few opinions on Cuban policy. They properly left political decisions to the President and the diplomats. Later, after the expulsion of Spain from the island, Army commanders, given responsibility for governing Cuba, were to prove more outspoken on policy questions, but in the debate over intervention their role was a passive one.[3]

Reflecting the general relaxation of tensions, the War Department during 1897 confined itself to routine peacetime activities and displayed little sense of urgency over Cuba or, for that matter, any other possible theater of action. Officials concerned themselves with speeding up promotion, strengthening the coast defenses, and closing down the small posts to allow the concentration of regiments. Secretary Alger, jokingly congratulated by his friend Mark Hanna for having the easiest job in the Cabinet, spent the summer traveling to escape the Washington heat. Later in the year he fell seriously ill, apparently of typhoid fever, and was confined to bed until the end of January. While Alger summered on Lake Champlain, General Miles journeyed to Europe to observe the war then in progress between Greece and Turkey. Besides visiting the Balkan battle front, he represented the United States at Queen Victoria's Diamond Jubilee and then attended the autumn maneuvers of the major continental armies. The nearest thing to a crisis that the Army dealt with in 1897 occurred in Alaska rather than Cuba. Reports from that remote frontier in November bore the dire news that thousands of gold prospectors in the Yukon lacked food to carry them through the winter and would starve if not assisted immediately. The War Department set about their rescue, organized an Army expedition to take food and supplies into the wilderness, and even purchased Norwegian reindeer to build up Alaska's herds of livestock. The department discontinued its efforts in February after later reports revealed that the food shortage had been exaggerated.[4]

3. The Navy view of Cuba's importance is expressed in Mahan, *Interest in Sea Power*, 287-89, 300-313. For a similar Army view, written before Mahan's article, see Hawthorne, *JMSI*, X, 588-91. Schofield called for intervention in his speech to Coast Defense Convention, Tampa, Florida, January, 1897, Box 95, Schofield Papers. Miles's views are in his *Serving the Republic*, 268-69, and in Johnson, *Unregimented General*, 314-15. The opinions of the Key West officers are described in Brig. Gen. Thomas Cruse, *Apache Days and After*, 259-61. Alger's views are discussed in Leech, *Days of McKinley*, 174-75, 184. See also: undated draft of letter from William McKinley to Alger, probably July, 1899, McKinley Papers; and Alger to Edward F. Cragin, September 28, 1895, to G. M. Dodge, March 19, 1898, and to William McKinley, December 28, 1899, Alger Papers. Huntington, *Soldier and State*, 261-62, comments on the reluctance of nineteenth-century Army officers to express opinions on policy matters outside their narrow professional sphere.

4. Maj. Gen. Nelson A. Miles to Secretary of War R. A. Alger, April 23, May 3 and 12, and August 4, 1897; Alger to Gen. Daniel E. Sickles, July 15, 1897; A. F. Burleigh and S. H. Piles to Alger, July 22, 1897; Acting Adj. Gen. Samuel Breck to Alger, August 3, 1897; W. S. Mason

But in the first weeks of 1898 the atmosphere of business-as-usual in the War Department and elsewhere in the government gave way suddenly to a sense of crisis. In January it became apparent that Spain's program for pacifying Cuba had no chance of success. The scheme for autonomy, or Cuban self-government under Spanish sovereignty, met only contemptuous rejection from the tough rebels, who renewed their demands for total independence. At the same time, the Spanish army in the island, which opposed any concessions to the Cubans, denounced the plan. Spanish officers even led an antiautonomy riot in Havana. Reports from American diplomats in Cuba made clear that, for all the promises, Spanish brutality and Cuban suffering continued as before. In February, New York newspapers published a personal letter written to a friend in Cuba by the Spanish minister in Washington and intercepted by rebel sympathizers in Havana. The letter expressed contempt for the United States and for President McKinley and in some of its passages hinted that Spain's promises of reform in Cuba were not made in good faith. The final blow to peace fell on the night of February 15, when the United States battleship *Maine*, sent to Havana to show the flag after the January riots, blew up at her anchorage, killing more than 200 of her crew. Public opinion at once blamed Spain for this disaster. The destruction of the *Maine*, added to the other developments, provoked a loud outcry among Americans of all parties, classes, and sections for drastic action against Spain. The events also convinced President McKinley that Spain by her own efforts could not restore order in Cuba. During the month of March he intensified his diplomatic pressure on Spain and demanded that she resolve an intolerable situation at once by declaring an armistice and granting Cuban independence under United States supervision.[5]

These events changed American armed intervention in Cuba from a remote to an immediate possibility. Accordingly, President McKinley at last began military preparations. On March 7 his spokesmen in Congress introduced a bill to appropriate from surplus funds in the Treasury $50 million "for the National defense and for each and every purpose connected therewith to be expended at the discretion of the President." In an outpouring of

to Alger, November 4, 1897; William McKinley to Alger, January 13, 1898; Steffan Lipton to Alger, February 22, 1898, Alger Papers. Alger to J. B. Foraker, February 1, 1897, and to McKinley, January 12, 1898; McKinley to Alger, January 13, 1898, McKinley Papers. C. D. Sheldon to Chase S. Osborn, January 19, 1898, Chase S. Osborn Papers. Alger expresses optimism about the political and diplomatic situation in Alger to W. H. Withington, May 24, 1897, William H. Withington Papers. Miles, *Serving the Republic*, 262-66. Johnson, *Unregimented General*, 311-14. RSW, *1898*, I, 11; II, 3-4. *The New York Times*, January 9, 1898. *New York Tribune*, March 2, 1898.

5. LaFeber, *New Empire*, 342-49. Leech, *Days of McKinley*, 162, 167-68, 170-71. May, *Imperial Democracy*, 135-51. Morgan, *Road to Empire*, xi-xii, 37-54. Charles S. Olcott, *The Life of William McKinley*, II, 6-7, 12-13. U.S. Congress, *Affairs in Cuba: Message of the President of the United States on the Relations of the United States to Spain, and Report of the Committee on Foreign Relations, United States Senate, Relative to Affairs in Cuba*, prints reports of American officials on Cuban conditions; see especially 8-9, 13-14, 23, 29, 32-33, 35-36, 41, 44-46, 52-54, 466, 540, 547.

patriotic emotion, the House of Representatives passed the bill the next day by a unanimous vote. The Senate, also unanimously, followed suit on March 9, and McKinley signed the bill the same day. The President, however, had not yet abandoned hope for a peaceful resolution of the crisis. He intended the Fifty Million Bill, as it came to be called, not as a first step in a war mobilization, but rather as a measure to improve the nation's general defense posture and as a show of strength to overawe Spain.[6]

II

For the War and Navy departments, the passage of the Fifty Million Bill signaled the start of serious military preparations. Each department used the available funds to improve its standing forces, and Army and Navy officers, working through several different agencies, began planning the strategy for intervention in Cuba. The Naval War College, that service's highest-level staff school, had begun studying strategy for a war with Spain as early as 1895. By 1898 it had produced a detailed plan for operations in the Caribbean as well as in the Pacific. During March of 1898, as war preparations intensified, Secretary Long organized the Naval War Board to refine and implement the plan. Composed of Assistant Secretary of the Navy Theodore Roosevelt and three uniformed officers, the board reviewed strategic problems and coordinated the work of preparing the fleet for battle. The War Department, in keeping with its loose organization, planned less formally. Each bureau chief made his own preparations and dealt with his own problems, but periodically, Secretary Alger or General Miles called several of them together to decide some broader question. Given the maritime nature of the prospective war, the Army's role in it would depend on the actions of the Navy. Recognizing the need thus created for joint planning, Alger and Long late in March delegated two officers, one from each service, to bring the Army and Navy into strategic harmony. Alger appointed to represent the Army Lt. Col. Arthur L. Wagner, chief of the Military Information Division, a former head of the Infantry and Cavalry School, and a respected Army progressive. The two-man board met frequently during the weeks preceding the outbreak of hostilities to consider questions of coast defense and to organize a joint assault upon Cuba. While their planning, by modern standards, lacked detail and sophistication, each service by the beginning of April clearly understood its probable mission in a conflict with Spain.[7]

6. LaFeber, New Empire, 349-50. May, Imperial Democracy, 149. Walter Millis, The Martial Spirit, 115-16. Morgan, Road to Empire, 49-50. The New York Times, March 8, 9, 10, and 16, 1898. For an interpretation of the intent of this measure,. see John D. Long's comment in his "Journal," March 8, 1898, in Mayo, America of Yesterday, 173.

7. Grenville and Young, Politics, Strategy, and American Diplomacy, 272-73. John D. Long, The New American Navy, I, 162-63. War Investigating Commission, VII, 3153. Memorandum by Col. Arthur L. Wagner, May 20, 1902, File No. 198209, AGO Records. The New York Times, March 27 and April 3, 1898. Army and Navy Journal, March 26 and April 2, 1898. Bethel, Military Affairs, XI, 21.

In all their planning and preparation, the services worked without political guidance from President McKinley. A shrewd, competent politician, McKinley fully controlled his foreign policy, but his working methods created difficulties for the Army and Navy in their efforts to support him effectively. Cautious and taciturn, McKinley never revealed—even to his Cabinet—his ultimate plans for Cuba. Never, during the weeks of preparation, did he give the armed services any specific instructions about how to use the new defense fund. They were to prepare for war, but for what kind of war and for what political objective? For the Navy, this lack of guidance did not constitute a serious problem. In any conflict with Spain, whatever the kind or its objectives, the Navy's mission would be the same: to seek out and destroy the Spanish fleet, to sweep Spain's merchant marine from the seas, and to blockade or bombard the coasts of Spain and her colonies. For the Army, however, the political objective would determine the scale of the war effort. If, for example, the President proposed only to aid the rebels in expelling the Spaniards from Cuba, relatively few American troops would be needed. If, on the other hand, he envisioned a large-scale campaign of conquest against the Spanish Empire, much more extensive preparation would be required. Lacking clear presidential instructions, Army and Navy officers based their plans on their own definitions of the national objectives and on their own evaluations of the military situation in Cuba.[8]

The War, Navy, and State departments had been collecting information on the Cuban conflict since its outbreak in 1895. Thanks to the geographical proximity of Cuba to the United States and to the fact that many Americans had lived or worked in the island, sources of intelligence were plentiful. Travelers, as they returned from Cuba, often reported their observations to the War Department. Businessmen with dealings in Cuba gave valuable details on the Spaniards' purchases of supplies, the condition of the roads, and ways of combating tropical diseases. Scores of Americans had fought in the Cuban army as volunteers; they freely described their experiences to the military authorities or to the various congressional committees that were investigating the situation. Cuban exiles and refugees constituted a voluble but biased source of information. The departments as a matter of routine exchanged intelligence data among themselves. The State Department, for example, regularly passed on to the Army the reports of its consuls in Spain and her colonies, reports that often dealt with military as well as political and commercial matters.[9]

8. Morgan, McKinley, 276, 292. Grenville and Young, Politics, Strategy, and American Diplomacy, 242-43. For expressions of confusion from Cabinet members and from the military, see The New York Times, March 24 and 25 and April 12, 1898.

9. Affairs in Cuba, passim, prints the testimony of Americans who fought in the Cuban army. Stewart L. Woodford to Secretary of War Alger, December 15, 1897; William L. Ellsworth to Alger, January 31, 1898; Kellogg to Adj. Gen. H. C. Corbin, March 27, 1898, P. Brooke to _____, April 20, 1898, Alger Papers. New York Sun, March 25, 1898, clipping in Box 10, Corbin Papers. Files No. 36321, 46731, 49667, 53724, 72524, 72726, 75856, 76730, 82865, 83714, 92221, 94802, and 505104, AGO Records, contain correspondence between the State and War departments. Correspondence, II, 744-46.

Courtesy *Leslie's Weekly*

President William McKinley

For the War Department, the Military Information Division collated and evaluated this material. From research by its staff in Washington, supplemented by the reports of the American military attaché at Madrid, the division had compiled by the end of 1897 a generally accurate account of Spain's strength and position in Cuba. The division knew, to within 2,000 men of the official Spanish figure, the number of the opposing troops and where they were stationed. Before the outbreak of hostilities, it published and distributed to the Army detailed maps of Cuba and Puerto Rico, and it prepared reports on conditions in Cuba and plans of the fortifications at Havana and other points. For the coast artillery, the division published an illustrated identification manual on the Spanish fleet. During the war, the Army's embryonic intelligence agency turned out additional maps and pamphlets on Cuba, Puerto Rico, and the Philippines besides assembling information on Spain herself to guide attacks on the enemy's homeland, should strategy dictate such assaults. Until the actual declaration of war, the Army refrained from outright espionage against Spain, since officials considered such action unethical in time of peace. For this reason, in August of 1897, The Adjutant General rejected a suggestion from the Military Information Division that an officer be sent in disguise to map harbors in Cuba. Nevertheless, from the information available, the Army, like the Navy, possessed all the essential facts about the character of the Cuban war and of the forces engaged in it.[10]

Consisting of 150,000 regulars from the Iberian Peninsula and 80,000 Cuban loyalist "Guerrillas" and "Volunteers," Spain's army in Cuba appeared formidable, but poor training and the ravages of tropical disease had rendered it all but useless for intensive campaigning. Mostly young conscripts, the rank and file of the regulars had received little but elementary drill to prepare them for the partisan war they had been sent to fight. A British observer wrote of them: "It makes one sad to see the quality of the expeditions packed off in heartless shoals to Cuba, boys, to look at, at fifteen or sixteen, who have never held a rifle till this moment, and now are almost ignorant which end it fires, good lads—too good to go to such uneven butchery—with cheerful, patriotic, willing faces, but the very antithesis of a soldier." The officers commanding these unfortunates knew little of tactics and possessed few of the technical skills needed in modern warfare. To weaken their effectiveness still further, the dreaded yellow fever and other diseases decimated the troops. Since 1895 over 13,000 of them had perished from yellow fever alone.

10. Bethel, *Military Affairs*, XI, 21-24. *War Investigating Commission*, I, 118-119. *RSW, 1898*, I, 282. Maj. A. L. Wagner to The Adjutant General, June 29, 1897, File No. 58401; Adj. Gen. Samuel Breck to the Librarian of Congress, January 14, 1898, File No. 68912; Chief of Engineers to The Adjutant General, March 1, 1898, File No. 71419; The Adjutant General's Office memorandum, March 17, 1898, File No. 72391, AGO Records. *The New York Times*, March 24, 1898. Rear Adm. French Ensor Chadwick, *The Relations of the United States to Spain: The Spanish-American War* (hereafter cited as Chadwick, *Spanish-American War*), II, 358.

An estimated 25 to 30 per cent of Spain's soldiers lay sick in hospitals, and the American consul general at Havana calculated that in the whole island no more than 55,000 of them were capable of field operations. Of 18,000 Spanish troops at Manzanillo, the American consul there reported, 6,000 jammed the fever wards.[11]

The Cuban rebels mustered between 25,000 and 40,000 troops, the number varying at different times with changes in the military situation. Led by wealthy planters and business and professional men and recruited from the plantation workers, small tradesmen, and laborers, the Cuban soldiers were well prepared for the hit-and-run warfare they waged. The ability of their commanders won the respect even of European professionals. Most of the Cubans carried modern rifles, either captured from the Spaniards or smuggled in from Europe or the United States, and they relied on their practiced use of the machete—the long-bladed, heavy cane-cutting knife—in hand-to-hand combat. The Cubans usually operated in small detachments controlled by a hierarchy of regional commanders. Their strongest field force, under Gen. Calixto García, roamed the thinly populated eastern end of the island and often fought major engagements with the aid of fourteen cannon served by volunteers from the United States. To keep order in areas they controlled and to support their troops with food and equipment, the rebels maintained a civil government that had been elected by the army and in fact was dominated by it. The Cubans drew their food from the country-side by cultivating small gardens and keeping herds of cattle in remote places where the Spanish troops did not penetrate. In the eastern provinces they established crude workshops, in which they made their own shoes, saddles, and leather goods and repaired their weapons. For all their ingenuity, the Cuban soldiers often ran short of food, clothing, ammunition, and medical supplies. Their families, hidden in the hills, subsisted under the most primitive conditions and lived in fear of attack by marauding Spanish troops and the even more savage Cuban loyalists.[12]

11. Maj. Gen. Nelson A. Miles to the Secretary of War, April 9, 1898, in *RSW, 1898*, II, 5. The official Spanish statement of their losses from yellow fever is in *RSW, 1899*, I, Pt. 2, p. 497. Chadwick, *Spanish-American War*, I, 52-54. The consuls' reports are in *Affairs in Cuba*, 37, 407, 409, 546-47. Penciled note from C. D. W. W., to Colonel Gilmore, in Consul Benjamin H. Ridgely to Assistant Secretary of State William R. Day, May 10, 1898, File No. 83714, AGO Records. The United States Evacuation Commission, sent to Cuba in the fall of 1898, found about 123,000 Spanish regulars; Maj. Gen. J. F. Wade to The Adjutant General, October 1, 1898, File No. 243501, AGO Records. The comment on the quality of the Spanish troops is from Leonard Williams, "The Army of Spain: Its Present Qualities and Modern Virtue," *JMSI*, XXI, 351-52. *The New York Times*, April 15, 1898.

12. Chadwick, *Spanish-American War*, I, 51. Frederick Funston, *Memories of Two Wars: Cuban and Philippine Experiences*, 31-32, 35, 99, 117. Funston served as a volunteer with García and later joined the United States Army. Williams, *JMSI*, XXI, 350-51. *Affairs in Cuba*, 359-63, 366-69, 372-73, 376, 383-86, 393-94, 412, 426, 430, 436-43, 541-42, 546; most of this material is congressional testimony of men who served in the rebel army.

The insurgents waged a campaign of raids and ambushes and avoided large-scale battles. One of their major aims was to destroy Cuban agriculture, especially the sugar industry, which was Spain's chief source of revenue in the island. Rebel bands burned cane fields and farm buildings, and in their raids they killed many farmers or drove them into the Spanish-held towns. They allowed some large plantations to continue work, provided the planters paid "taxes," in money or in kind, to the rebel government. Unable to feed large numbers of men at one place for any length of time, they scattered their soldiers in small groups that could live off the country. When opportunities presented themselves, the groups came together to harass Spanish garrisons, dynamite trains, ambush supply columns, and occasionally destroy an isolated enemy detachment. An excellent intelligence service enabled the Cubans to fight or avoid major Spanish forces almost at will. In eastern Cuba, where Spanish garrisons were few and far apart, the insurgents several times assembled forces of nearly 5,000 men with artillery for attacks on small towns. If victorious, they would hold a captured town for as long as necessary to loot it of all usable stores and then disperse into the hills from whence they came. Unfortunately, lack of discipline in regular operations and shortages of supplies prevented the Cubans from consolidating or following up such successes.[13]

The Spaniards, on their part, followed an ineffective strategy. Instead of pursuing and attacking the rebels, they used most of their troops to garrison scores of minor towns, each fortified with blockhouses, trenches, and barbed wire. They wasted still more manpower by establishing fortified lines called *trochas*, which ran from coast to coast across the narrow island. Barbed-wire barriers guarded at intervals by blockhouses, the *trochas* were supposed to reduce the rebels' mobility. In fact, the Cubans crossed them almost at will, and the barrier-blockhouse line merely tied down more Spanish infantry in fixed defenses. Because of their faulty strategy, the Spaniards could spare relatively few men for offensive operations. The forces they did send out usually moved slowly and failed to attack aggressively if they met the enemy. Spanish columns rarely left the main roads, on which they marched from town to town while the free-moving Cubans ambushed or evaded them as they chose.[14]

Unable to crush the rebels militarily, the Spaniards tried to win the war by destroying Cuba's economy. In 1896 the island's governor-general, Valeriano Weyler, introduced the infamous "reconcentration" policy.

13. Healy, *United States in Cuba*, 8-9. Funston, *Memories*, 32, 36-62, 66-141, 144-45. Funston commanded the artillery in several Cuban sieges of Spanish-held towns. *Affairs in Cuba*, 29-30, 36-40, 42-43, 357-58, 381-82, 387-88, 427-28, 443, 541.

14. Funston, *Memories*, 145. *Affairs in Cuba*, 35-36, 369, 371, 407-8, 438, 534. *The New York Times*, February 4, 1897. *Army and Navy Journal*, April 9, 1898. Williams, *JMSI*, XXI, 349-50.

He forced the entire rural population of the four westernmost provinces, mostly small landowners and tenant farmers, into fortified zones around the towns—in effect, prison camps guarded by troops. Anyone who remained in the countryside was subject to treatment as an enemy; the Spanish army then systematically destroyed crops, buildings, and livestock. Crowded into compounds without adequate food, shelter, or medical care, the unfortunate *reconcentrados* died by thousands of disease and starvation. While reconcentration caused untold suffering and completed the work, begun by the rebels, of paralyzing Cuban agriculture, it failed to break the insurrection. The guerrillas continued to range the devastated island at will, and the Spanish army could not catch them.[15]

By early 1898 the combatants between them had reduced much of Cuba to a desert, but neither side seemed anywhere near a decisive victory. The Spanish army held the seaports, the major interior towns, and the *trochas*, while the Cubans roamed the countryside. In the western four of Cuba's six provinces and around the island's capital, Havana, the Spaniards seemed to be winning. With many garrisons located close together and connected by good roads and railways, they made the countryside almost untenable for any but small bodies of rebels. In eastern Cuba, thinly populated, mountainous, with few roads or towns, the rebels ruled everywhere outside the seaports and were often able to move in substantial force. Neither side could break down the other's strongholds. Lacking men, ammunition, and food, the Cubans could not besiege the major towns or destroy Spanish units in massed combat; the Spaniards, on their side, seemed incapable of trapping the elusive insurgents. It appeared to most foreign observers that the war would smoulder indefinitely unless financial exhaustion or American intervention forced the Spaniards to withdraw.[16]

While able to hold their own against native guerrillas, Spain's garrisons in Cuba and in her other colonies were dangerously vulnerable to attack by a regular army and fleet. For many years Spain had neglected the defense of her own coasts, not to mention those of her overseas possessions. Few ports in the Iberian Peninsula were prepared to resist assault by land or sea. Among the colonial cities, only Havana and San Juan in Puerto Rico, had modern harbor defenses, equipped with rifled cannon and mine fields. Even these fortifications were so poorly planned that they presented only weak obstacles to a determined besieger. If attacked by a navy superior to Spain's, the colonial garrisons, isolated by water and hostile warships from the 150,000 troops stationed in the mother country, would have to fight without hope of reinforcement.

15. Healy, *United States in Cuba*, 9. Eyewitness reports on the effects of reconcentration are in *Affairs in Cuba*, 16-17, 398, 400-405, 421-23, 549.

16. Funston, *Memories*, 99-100, 141-42. Healy, *United States in Cuba*, 9. *Affairs in Cuba*, 12, 370-71, 380-81, 384, 398-400, 412-13, 421, 544, 546-47. *Army and Navy Journal*, November 14, 1896. *The New York Times*, February 4, 1898. *RSW, 1898*, II, 375. Charles F. Allison to President McKinley, November 30, 1898, McKinley Papers.

The Spanish forces in Cuba were not organized or deployed to defend the colony against attack by a foreign power. The Spaniards' faulty strategy had scattered them all over the island in small garrisons, many of which had no communication with each other except by sea. The fortifications of the towns they held, designed to repel lightly armed insurgents, could not withstand regular infantry supported by heavy artillery. Faced with the threat of military intervention by the United States, the correct military course for Spain would have been to assemble her Cuban forces at a few central points, ready to act aggressively against the invader. For both political and practical reasons, the Spaniards in 1898 could not concentrate men and arms for this purpose. The drawing in of their forces to a few large cities would have meant political defeat, the abandonment of Cuba to the rebels. Even had they wished to concentrate their forces, the Spaniards could not have done so, for they had failed to stock their strongholds with reserve supplies; each place could feed only its regular garrison. Further, impassable roads and a shortage of wagons and pack animals would have prevented the assembling troops from bringing supplies with them overland. The Spaniards actually had no choice but to remain in their isolated posts until superior mobile American forces came to overwhelm them. Only around Havana was there a network of roads and railways that the Spaniards could use to mass a large army—about 40,000 strong. Supply problems made the Spanish army's position even more hopeless. Having devastated the Cuban countryside, the Spaniards depended on shipments from overseas for food and even for fodder for their horses. A naval blockade could, within a few months, starve all their garrisons into surrender.[17]

Under these conditions, Army and Navy planners in the United States considered war with Spain primarily a naval problem. They assumed that the United States did not contemplate an invasion of Spain and that Spain could at best launch only small naval raids against the United States. They assumed further that the political objective of a war with Spain would be to assist the Cubans in driving out the Spanish army and in establishing an independent nation. This object, American strategists believed, could be secured most expeditiously and at the least cost in lives by severing Spain's sea connections with Cuba. The Army might send in a small force to aid the rebels and to bring them supplies, but no major ground action would be required. Spokesmen for the Cuban rebels, apprehensive of conquest by their huge potential ally, heartily endorsed this line of reasoning. They argued that, if the American fleet blockaded the ports and if the Army sent in weapons

17. For a Spaniard's analysis of his country's military weaknesses, see Severo Gómez Nunez, *La Guerra Hispanoamericana*, III, 115-16; V, 38-41, 50, 94. Chadick, *Spanish-American War*, I, 51, 54. American observers in Cuba often commented on the Spaniards' lack of field transportation and their dependence on imported food; see *Affairs in Cuba*, 372, 408-9, 446, 449-50, 541-42. Brig. Gen. William Ludlow to Adj. Gen. H. C. Corbin, June 5, 1898, Box 1, Corbin Papers.

and ammunition, their troops alone could destroy Spanish power. Miles and other American generals also favored this approach because they feared the consequences of plunging large forces into the Cuban jungles, especially during the summer rainy season when the roads melted into quagmires and tropical fevers made the island deadly to foreign troops.[18]

This military assessment was the basis of the services' prewar strategy, and it guided their expenditure of the Fifty Million appropriation. The Naval War College plan, completed on June 1, 1896, envisioned an exclusively maritime campaign, in which the fleet would seek out and destroy Spain's battle squadrons, blockade Cuba to starve out the Spanish army, and launch a diversionary assault on Manila. Movements against Spain's coasts and commerce could follow, if necessary. On April 4, 1898, the joint Army-Navy board submitted its war plan to the service secretaries. The interservice committee repeated the Navy's proposal for a blockade of Cuba but supplemented it with a suggestion that a small Army expedition seize a port in the eastern provinces through which weapons, supplies, and technical advisers could be sent to the insurgents. The board doubted the necessity of a large-scale invasion and warned that such an undertaking would be dangerous and costly if attempted during the rainy season, then fast approaching. However, if the government should decide on an extensive land campaign, it should attack Spain's chief Cuban stronghold, Havana, with at least 50,000 troops. The joint board also favored an assault on Puerto Rico in order to deprive the Spanish fleet of a base in the Caribbean.[19]

Army officers saw the prospective struggle as essentially the Navy's war. In private letters written in March and early April, some Regulars doubted that they would see action at all, even if war were declared. The Army's missions under existing plans would be precisely those outlined by Schofield in 1897: protecting the coast and the fleet's bases and sending expeditions to help the Navy seize and hold strategic points. As the War Department's planners prepared to spend their share of the Fifty Million appropriation, coast defense appeared to be their most immediate and pressing problem. All informed persons expected naval action to decide the issue, and, according to the military doctrine of the time, if the fleet were to be

18. Chadwick, *Spanish-American War*, II, 4. Grenville and Young, *Politics, Strategy, and American Diplomacy*, 273-74. Long, *New American Navy*, I, 165-66. Sprout and Sprout, *Naval Power*, 232. Miles's views on strategy are in *RSW, 1898*, II, 6. For a warning about Cuban fevers, see Surg. Gen. George M. Sternberg to the Secretary of War, March 25, 1898, in *RSW, 1899*, I, Pt. 2, pp. 490-94. Sternberg to Adj. Gen. Corbin, January 17, 1899, File No. 194178, AGO Records. *The New York Times*, March 16 and 23, 1898. *Army and Navy Journal*, April 23, 1898. The Spaniards expected the United States to win by such a strategy; see Admiral Pascual Cervera to the Minister of Marine, February 25, 1898, in Chadwick, *Spanish-American War*, I, 100-101.

19. The Naval War College plan is summarized in Grenville and Young, *Politics, Strategy, and American Diplomacy*, 274-76. For the joint Army-Navy plan, see Capt. A. S. Barker, USN, and Asst. Adj. Gen. Arthur L. Wagner, USA, "Memorandum for the Honorable Secretary of War," April 4, 1898, File No. 198209, AGO Records. *The New York Times*, March 27 and 29, April 1, 1898. *New York Tribune*, April 14, 1898.

free to act offensively in the Caribbean, it must leave behind it an Atlantic coast securely fortified against assault by even the second-class fleet of Spain. But coastal defenses were inadequate to repel even the Spaniards. Of the more than 2,000 heavy guns and mortars called for by the Endicott Plan, only 151 were mounted and ready for action on April 1; the Ordnance Department had available less than 20 rounds of ammunition per gun. General Miles bluntly informed Congress that the nation's capital city possessed no effective land defenses whatsoever and the capital itself would have to depend on the Navy for protection.[20]

These conditions determined the order of priorities in spending the $50 million made available to the services on March 9. The Navy's needs took precedence over the Army's, since the battle fleet was to go into action at the outset and must be fully prepared. The War Department allotted most of its money to coast defense, the strategic shield that assured the fleet's mobility; it planned to use the remaining resources in organizing a small invasion force.[21]

III

President McKinley, following these priorities, allotted $29 million of the defense appropriation to the Navy. That service had begun preparing for action in January of 1898 by concentrating the scattered ships of its Atlantic Squadron at Key West and alerting the Asiatic Squadron at Hong Kong for a possible descent upon Manila. The Navy also recruited more men and began accumulating stores of coal, ammunition, and supplies. With the funds from the Fifty Million Bill, Secretary Long in March accelerated his preparations. He added to the existing stocks of fuel, shells, and powder, and under his direction and that of his enthusiastic assistant secretary, Theodore Roosevelt, the Navy purchased or chartered over 100 merchant vessels for use as supply ships, light cruisers, and scouts. In Great Britain, the Navy Department purchased two new steel cruisers, a gunboat, and a torpedo boat to augment the fleet's fighting power, and from Brazil it obtained a vessel equipped to fire dynamite bombs. By mid-April the Navy was ready for action, its ships massed at strategic points and fully manned and supplied.[22]

20. Hugh L. Scott to Mrs. Scott, March 29 and April 2, 1898, Box 1, Hugh L. Scott Papers. Assistant Secretary of the Navy Theodore Roosevelt did not expect a large Army, either; see Roosevelt to William S. Bigelow, March 29, 1898, and to Alexander Lambert, April 1, 1898, both in *The Letters of Theodore Roosevelt*, Elting E. Morison, et al., eds. (hereafter cited as Morison, *Roosevelt Letters*), II, 801-3, 807-9. McKinley's Secretary of the Treasury predicted a small war; Lyman J. Gage to Holmes Hoge, April 11, 1898, Box 6, Lyman J. Gage Papers. Russell Alexander Alger, *The Spanish-American War*, 10-11. *The New York Times*, January 22 and March 31, 1898. Maj. Gen. Nelson A. Miles to Secretary Alger, March 18, 1898, Alger Papers. Miles to Alger, March 21, 1898, File No. 192302, AGO Records. These last letters indicate Miles's concern with coast defense.

21. *The New York Times*, March 8 and 10, 1898. *Army and Navy Journal*, March 12, 1898.

22. Chadwick, *Spanish-American War*, I, 3-5, 10-19, 22-24, 32. W. A. M. Goode, *With Sampson through the War*, 7-13. Long, *New American Navy*, I, 145-48, 150-54, 159-60, 163. Sprout and Sprout, *Naval Power*, 229-30. Journal of John D. Long, March, 1898, in Mayo, *America of Yesterday*, 172-74.

Of the $19 million the War Department received from the national defense fund, Secretary Alger allotted $15 million to the Corps of Engineers and the Ordnance Department for coast defense. Like the Navy Department, these bureaus had begun preparation even before March 9. As early as January 25, the Chief of Engineers had ordered his officers to mount as quickly as possible all the available coastal guns, even if his order required them to improvise temporary emplacements. The Engineers continued this work during February and March, then used the newly allotted funds to start construction of 90 new emplacements for heavy guns. Hiring double and triple their usual staff of workmen, the Engineers pushed forward the projects—along the northern Atlantic Coast, they defied winter cold and snow to complete the defenses. The Ordnance Department could do little to increase its output of cannon. The production process for each weapon was too complicated and required too much time for immediate results. Nevertheless, the department put on extra shifts at its gun factory and at the arsenals and began working its plants almost around the clock. For the guns already available, the Ordnance Department increased production of carriages, and it ordered from American and foreign manufacturers over 200 light rapid-fire cannon, required in coast defense to protect the batteries against enemy landing parties and raids by small, fast vessels. Worried by the shortage of artillery shells, the Chief of Ordnance pressed the contractors who supplied them to increase their plant capacity. During a single week in March, he ordered 5,000 heavy-caliber projectiles. Urged by the Army and attracted by the prospect of government orders, shell and powder manufacturers enlarged their facilities, one firm by two and one-half times. Three new firms entered the business, thus adding to the available production capacity.[23]

While the Signal Corps installed electrical communications systems in the harbor forts, the Engineers prepared to lay mine fields. With funds from the Fifty Million Bill and from subsequent appropriations, the Corps of Engineers purchased for this purpose over 400 miles of cable, 150 tons of explosives, and over 1,600 mine cases, as well as numerous searchlights and other accessories. On April 3, with time running short and with much material as yet not delivered, the Chief of Engineers gave his subordinates a free hand to purchase locally whatever they needed to improvise effective mine barriers. Able to spare only 160 of his own men to tend and if necessary detonate the mines, the Chief of Engineers on March 28 ordered the enrollment at each seaport of unpaid volunteer engineer reserves. These reservists—electricians, telegraphers, and other needed specialists—would hold themselves in readiness to man their local defenses if war should be

23. Chadwick, *Spanish-American War*, I, 49. *War Investigating Commission*, I, 191-96; VI, 2855; VII, 3159, 3763-64. *RSW, 1898*, I, 15; III, Pt. 1, p. 10; IV, 7, 17-19, 42-43, 53-54. *Army and Navy Journal*, February 26 and March 5, 1898. *The New York Times*, March 12, 1898.

declared. Assisted by the Federal Lighthouse Service, the Engineers also established harbor patrols to guide friendly vessels through the mine fields and to enforce security regulations.[24]

The supposed danger of Spanish raids induced congressmen and business leaders from coastal communities not included in the Endicott Plan to demand defenses for their home towns. The Administration felt obliged to heed these requests. For many of these places, the War Department, lacking enough modern guns, resorted to improvisation. The Engineers and the Ordnance Department set up temporary batteries by mounting obsolete muzzle-loading rifles, and they put in firing condition the guns and mortars of the Civil War forts that still remained at many harbors. Of doubtful effectiveness against modern armored cruisers, these weapons at least reassured the anxious citizenry. More useful were the 21 new 8-inch breech-loading rifles that the Ordnance Department, as an emergency measure, mounted on the converted carriages of old 15-inch smoothbores. As a final concession to the seaboard communities' clamor for protection, Secretary Alger early in April sent most of the Army's big siege guns to the coastal forts, only to remove them again in May and June for use in Cuba, Puerto Rico, and the Philippines. While the bureaus frantically improvised defenses, General Miles late in March ordered every fortress commander to prepare charts and a range-finding system for the waters under his protection.[25]

Besides mounting more guns, the War Department sought men to fire them; to obtain gunners, it pushed through Congress approval for the first increase in the Regular Army in almost thirty years. When completed, the coast defenses envisioned in the Endicott Plan would require about 85,000 officers and men to garrison them. The great mass of these gunners, Army officers believed, needed little advance training and could be recruited at the outbreak of war from civilians or National Guardsmen. The duties of only about 10 per cent of the force, about 8,500 men, demanded extensive instruction, and that cadre should come from the Regular Army Artillery. The Army's existing five artillery regiments could not furnish enough men for this purpose, therefore, every year since the mid-1880s, Artillery officers, Commanding Generals, and Secretaries of War had asked Congress to add at least two more artillery regiments to the Army. Now, pushed by the chambers of commerce of the seaport cities, the Senate early in 1898 finally passed the desired legislation. Until the beginning of March, however, the bill remained stalled in the House of Representatives, its consideration blocked by the Democrats' hostility to the Regular Army and by the

24. *War Investigating Commission*, I, 192-94, 201; VII, 3161. *RSW, 1898*, III, Pt. 1, p. 12. *The New York Times*, March 29, 1898.

25. *War Investigating Commission*, I, 191. *RSW, 1898*, III, Pt. 1, p. 8; IV, 17-18, 22. John A. Porter to Secretary of War Alger, March 16, 1898, McKinley Papers, is an example of the political demands for a coast defense. GO 10, HQA, March 22, 1898. *GO/AGO, 1898*.

Republicans' reluctance to spend money, as they thought, unnecessarily. The patriotic furor surrounding the Fifty Million Bill broke up the legislative jam. Urged on by a personal plea from Secretary Alger, Speaker Thomas B. Reed brought the bill up for consideration on March 7. The House passed it with few dissenting votes the same day, and President McKinley approved it on March 8. Three days later, the War Department started recruiting the new Sixth and Seventh regiments of artillery, each consisting of ten heavy or fortress batteries and two light or field batteries. So reinforced, the Regular Artillery was to number about 6,000 officers and men, adequate as a cadre for the defenses completed by 1898. Besides enlisting these regiments from a previously assembled roster of applicants, the War Department sent gunners to man the forts that were being hastily completed. Since many of the new posts lacked barracks, the artillerymen often camped out in tents near their weapons.[26]

Begun early in 1898, the reinforcement of the coast defenses continued throughout the war with Spain. By midsummer, the Engineers and the Ordnance Department had mounted and turned over to the Artillery for service 185 new cannons and mortars, and they were building or had completed emplacements for 550 more. Between April and June, the Ordnance Department increased threefold its ammunition reserves for all calibers of coast defense guns. On April 21, when the order came to mine the harbors, the Engineers were able to block every major port with at least one row of the submarine weapons. By the end of June they had over 1,500 ready for detonation in 28 major harbors. The Chief of Engineers felt "perfectly satisfied that we could blow up any ship that attempted to enter any of the prominent seacoast harbors of the United States." Yet, with all this effort, the coast defenses remained incomplete. The Chief of Ordnance estimated in December that, even with the progress of the recent months, completion of the Endicott program would require at least six more years' effort. The weakness of the fortifications forced a division of the fleet assembled at Key West. Late in March, the Navy Department detached a strong squadron, including three of the precious armored ships, to protect the Atlantic seaboard.[27]

None of the cannon so laboriously emplaced fired a hostile shot during the Spanish-American War. The mines floated intact in the harbors

26. *RSW, 1887,* I, 119-21; *1888,* I, 65; *1889,* I, 4, 65, 69-72; *1891,* I, 13; *1892,* I, 47; *1893,* I, 6; *1895,* I, 68; *1897,* I, 7, 9. Stuart, *JMSI,* XII, 1225-26, 1230. Carbaugh, *JMSI,* XXI, 260-62. Hull, *Forum,* XXV, 399-401. Maj. Gen. Nelson A. Miles to Secretary Alger, May 4, 1897, Alger Papers. *Army and Navy Journal,* December 18, 1897. *The New York Times,* November 5, 1897; February 26, 27, and 28, March 3, 5, 8, and 12, 1898. *The New York Tribune,* March 8, 1898. *Washington Post,* March 8, 1898. GO 6, HQA, March 11, 1898, *GO/AGO, 1898.*

27. *RSW, 1898,* I, 4; II, 198; III, Pt. 1, pp. 8-12; IV, 53-54. *War Investigating Commission,* I, 193-94; VI, 2853; VII, 3159-61. *Army and Navy Journal,* March 19 and April 30, 1898. Grenville and Young, *Politics, Strategy, and American Diplomacy,* 280-81. Long, *New American Navy,* I, 148-49.

until the beginning of August, when the engineers carefully removed them to storehouses to be kept for future emergencies. Although seemingly carried out in vain, the effort to defend the nation's coasts was based on what experts at the time considered sound strategy, it guarded the country against a possible assault, and it partially quieted the alarm of the citizenry. As the events of 1898 demonstrated and as Admiral Mahan later pointed out, inadequate coast fortifications, if only by creating a sense of public apprehension that democratic war leadership could not ignore, reduced the Navy's offensive power by forcing detachments from the fleet for static defense. For the Spaniards, an amphibious attack on the Atlantic seaboard would have been a correct counter to a blockade of Cuba. Especially if the land batteries were known to be weak, such a diversionary raid might have been attempted and could have inflicted considerable damage. A well-aimed thrust against the coast would have diverted the American blockaders from Cuba and would have allowed a relief force to slip into Havana or some other port. The Spanish authorities actually planned such an attack, but the deficiencies of their fleet prevented its implementation. The Administration, in fortifying the East Coast thus displayed reasonable prudence and followed accepted military doctrine.[28]

IV

During the month of activity following the passage of the Fifty Million Bill, the War Department devoted comparatively little attention to organizing a large army or to preparing an invasion of Cuba. None of the officials responsible for organization of the Army ever satisfactorily explained this seeming inaction. Many contemporaries whose accusations have been repeated by later historians attributed this lapse of activity to incompetence among the men in charge or to the War Department's chaotic organization. Secretary Alger defended the priorities in the department by stating that the language of the Fifty Million Bill allowed only defensive preparations, thus ruling out measures that looked forward toward a Cuban invasion. His colleague, Secretary of the Navy Long, however, took no such view. Under Long's direction, the Navy during those weeks prepared for attack. Further, the actions of Alger's own department belied his explanation.[29]

28. *War Investigating Commission*, I, 194. *RSW, 1899*, I, Pt. 1, pp. 37-38. The abortive Spanish plans are described in Chadwick, *Spanish-American War*, I, 57-60, 97-99; II, 383-386. Admiral Mahan believed that the events of the Spanish-American War proved the strategic necessity of strong coast defenses; see his *Lessons*, 45-48, 66.

29. Leech, *Days of McKinley*, 217, repeats the usual charge of incompetence against Alger. Alger, *Spanish-American War*, 8-14, claims the terms of the Fifty Million Bill prevented offensive preparations.

In spite of Alger's statements to the contrary, the War Department in March and early April made preliminary arrangements for organizing and equipping an expeditionary force. Besides accumulating material for coast defense, the Ordnance Department accelerated at its arsenals the production of rifles and accoutrements. The Chief of Ordnance in March purchased over 12 million rounds of small-arms ammunition, and he conferred with private producers of magazine rifles about possible Army contracts. He also warned Army suppliers to be ready to fill large orders for cartridge belts, knapsacks, and other items of equipment on short notice. The Quartermaster General took similar steps by speeding up work at clothing depots, purchasing material for tents and uniforms, and establishing contact with firms able to manufacture Army equipment. Secretary Alger on March 12 told Surgeon General Sternberg to prepare for large emergency purchases of medical supplies. Four days later he asked Congress to add more surgeons to the Medical Department. On April 3 Alger and Quartermaster General Ludington met at the War Department with the nation's leading wagon manufacturers. Alger warned them to expect large Army orders soon and urged them to begin assembling military wagons at once. He also sent a quartermaster officer to Saint Louis with orders to form 20 pack trains, each of 75 mules. Jokingly, he told the officer: "You had better buy good ones, . . . for you'll probably go to Cuba with them!" At about the same time Alger conferred with the wagonmakers, the Quartermaster's Department began production of 10,000 experimental tropical uniforms and completed plans to charter merchant vessels for troop transports.[30]

Besides securing supplies, the War Department made other preparations for offensive war. During March and April, The Adjutant General's Office sent maps and military information on Cuba, Puerto Rico, and the Philippines to all department and regimental commanders, so they could acquaint themselves with the probable theaters of war. Secretary Alger on March 11 reorganized the Army's geographical departments to place the entire Gulf Coast, the likely base for an attack on Cuba, under one command. A week or so later, the Army-Navy planning board began studying southern harbors and railroad lines with a view to selecting an embarkation port for an invading army. The Army late in March began moving all of its field and siege artillery to posts east of the Mississippi River for possible war use, and on April 1 General Miles ordered all but three of the infantry regiments to prepare to take the field on short notice.[31]

30. *Army and Navy Journal*, February 26 and March 12, 19, and 26, 1898. *New York Tribune*, March 12, 25, and 26, 1898. *The New York Times*, March 9, 12, 15, 16, 17, and 20, April 3, 7, and 12, 1898. *War Investigating Commission*, VII, 3783. Cruse, *Apache Days and After*, 264-65, describes the conference on wagons and the order to form the mule trains. Erna Risch, *Quartermaster Support of the Army: A History of the Corps, 1775-1939* (hereafter cited as Risch, *Quartermaster Corps*), 521-22. Maj. Gen. Nelson A. Miles to Secretary Alger, April 5, 1898, File No. 192302, AGO Records. Brig. Gen. Daniel W. Flagler to Alger, March 12, 1898, Alger Papers.

31. The Adjutant General's Office, Memorandum, March 9, 1898, File No. 71772; Maj. Gen. Nelson A. Miles to The Adjutant General, April 1, 1898, File No. 192302, AGO Records. *New York Sun*, March 25, 1898, clipping in Box 10, Corbin Papers. GO 8, HQA, March 11, 1898, *GO/AGO, 1898*. *The New York Times*, March 12, 13, 14, and 30, April 2 and 6, 1898. *New York Tribune*, March 25, 1898.

The War Department's officials failed during these weeks to accumulate supplies for a large army because they did not expect to raise one. General Miles and most other Army leaders saw no need in the prospective war for a vast number of citizen-soldiers. With the National Guard available to garrison the coast defenses, they believed a compact striking force of 75,000 to 100,000 men under professional command would suffice to follow up the Navy's expected decisive victory. Miles and the Regulars wanted to assemble this elite force as rapidly as possible and to equip it from the Army's existing reserve supplies, supplemented by modest purchases. Any larger muster of troops, they thought, could be postponed until events demonstrated a need for it, which they doubted would happen. The expeditionary corps, Army planners agreed, could be organized most efficiently by enlarging the Regular Army. The influential *Army and Navy Journal* on March 12 summed up the prevailing opinion: "With a regular Army of sufficient strength to form the fighting line, and with the organized militia for local service, we should have a force quite sufficient for our needs against Spain."[32]

Following this line of thought, the War Department in March undertook a campaign for the expansible army long demanded by Upton and his followers. The department found a congressional ally in Representative John A. T. Hull, an Iowa Republican and Chairman of the House Committee on Military Affairs. Like the Regulars, Hull considered the National Guard useless for offensive action; he strongly supported an expansible army. Since 1894, when he took over the chairmanship of his committee, Hull had worked closely with the War Department on Army legislation and had pressed for increase of the Artillery and for reorganization of the Infantry into battalions. Early in March of 1898, following up the success of the Artillery bill, Hull introduced a measure that would give the Infantry its battalion organization and that would allow the President to increase the enlisted force of the Army in wartime. Meanwhile, officers of The Adjutant General's Department had prepared a similar bill. After conferring with President McKinley, Secretary Alger, and Generals Miles and Corbin, Hull on March 17 introduced the War Department's bill in the House as a substitute for his own. A spokesman for the Administration introduced the same measure simultaneously in the Senate.[33]

32. *Army and Navy Journal*, March 12, 1898; see also the issues of November 27, 1897, and March 5, 1898. General Miles's views on the size of the Army are in Maj. Gen. N. A. Miles, "The War with Spain," *The North American Review*, CLXVIII, 515-16, and in Miles, *Serving the Republic*, 270. See also Ranson, *Military Affairs*, XXIX, 184. The 25,000 Regulars were fully armed and equipped as of March, 1898; see *The New York Times*, April 2, 1898, and *War Investigating Commission*, VII, 3281-82. The Quartermaster's Department in late February, 1898, had on hand uniforms for 50,000 men and tentage for 75,000 to 80,000, according to the *Army and Navy Journal*, February 26, 1898, but this stock had diminished before the beginning of April.

33. Hull, *Forum*, XXV, 388-89, 398, and *The North American Review*, CLXVIII, 389-91. *Army and Navy Journal*, March 12 and 19, 1898. *The New York Times*, March 14, 1898. *New York Tribune*, March 18, 1898. *RSW, 1898*, I, 254-56. Memorandum signed J. M. L., no date, and Adj. Gen. H. C. Corbin to Senator J. R. Hawley, March 18, 1898, File No. 72278. AGO Records. *New York Journal*, March 18, 1898, clipping in Box 10, Corbin Papers.

Soon named "the Hull bill" after its sponsor in the House, the proposed law conformed to long-standing Army doctrine and was intended as a permanent reform, not as a temporary crisis measure. It combined reorganization of the Infantry with an expansible enlisted force. In 1898 each regiment of United States Infantry contained ten companies, eight fully manned and the remaining two skeleton units that were staffed only with officers who spent most of their time training the National Guard or teaching military science at colleges. The Hull bill grouped the eight full companies into two battalions of the size recommended by Army experts and made the two skeleton companies the nucleus of a third battalion that the President "in time of war" could organize by manning the skeleton companies and creating two new ones. The cavalry and artillery regiments, which already had battalions, the bill left as they were. The Hull bill authorized the President, "in time of war," to expand the Regular Army into a striking force of 104,000 officers and men by increasing to a prescribed maximum the enlisted strength of each infantry company, cavalry troop, and artillery battery. Additional officers for the enlarged Army would come from the commissioned and noncommissioned ranks of the Regulars and from lists of civilians selected by the President. The bill permitted the President to designate particular states as recruiting areas for each regiment and provided that in a call for volunteers men so recruited would count as part of their states' quotas. These provisions, long advocated by Army reformers, were supposed to make Regular service more popular by associating each regiment with a locality. They would also encourage the states to recruit for the Regulars, as well as for their own units, in a major war. The Hull bill avoided the sensitive issue of peacetime enlargement of the Regular force by keeping the third battalion of each infantry regiment unmanned except during war. It added to the permanent establishment only twenty-five majors, one for each infantry regiment. The promotion of twenty-five captains to fill these vacancies, Adjutant General Corbin pointed out, would speed up promotion throughout the Infantry, allow the advancement of deserving officers, and place younger men in command of companies.[34]

Along with the bill, Secretary Alger sent to Congress a letter explaining how the War Department, under the bill's provisions, could assemble in a short time all the soldiers needed for action in Cuba. In an emergency, he wrote, the department would rearrange the standing enlisted force to bring one or two battalions of each regiment up to war strength and would

34. For text of the Hull bill, see *RSW, 1898*, I, 254-55. *Army and Navy Journal*, March 19, 1898. *The New York Times*, March 18, 1898. *New York Tribune*, March 18, 1898. *Congressional Record*, 55th Cong., 2d sess., 1898, XXXI, Pt. 4, p. 3676. For the demand for territorial recruiting, see the following: Upton, *Armies*, 352-53; Zalinski, *JMSI*, XIV, 962; Sanger, *JMSI*, XIV, 1151-57; and Harbord, *JMSI*, XXI, 15. Adj. Gen. H. C. Corbin to Senator J. R. Hawley, March 18, 1898, File No. 72278, AGO Records.

mobilize the units thus reinforced for immediate service. For some purposes they would be supplemented by National Guardsmen. The remaining Regular battalions, reduced to cadres of officers, sergeants, and corporals, would proceed to assigned stations and fill their ranks with recruits. A few weeks of training under professional instructors would render the new men fit for service, and the formations so enlarged then could join the expeditionary force. Since the bill left to the President determination of what constituted a "time of war," the Army's preparations, once the bill became law, need not wait for Congress to declare war. Alger concluded his letter in Uptonian style by stressing that "the superiority of such a force made up of professional officers and noncommissioned officers skilled in their respective duties, over a hastily organized body, officered by men new to the service, both as regards effectiveness in action and economy of administration, would be incalculable."[35]

Under the War Department's plans, the Hull bill's sponsors and many Army officers made clear, state volunteers and National Guardsmen in their own units would have no part in the attack on Cuba. Representative Hull told reporters on March 17 that his bill was designed to make the Regular Army the cadre for future volunteer forces. Adjutant General Corbin a few days later said that "an Army capable of expansion from a peace basis of 27,000 to a war footing of 104,000, would answer all ordinary demands." He also urged National Guardsmen to enlist as individuals in the expanding Regular regiments. Other generals expressed similar views; they wanted only Regulars for offensive operations, and they urged the limiting of the National Guard to coast defense. The Army commander on the Atlantic Coast asked state governors for militia detachments to garrison the forts if war broke out. At the same time, the authorities in Washington refused requests from the states for field equipment, on the plea that the Army had none to spare.[36]

With the full political weight of the McKinley Administration behind it, the Hull bill at first made encouraging progress through Congress. President McKinley, Secretary Alger, and Adjutant General Corbin (who acted as legislative manager for the bill) all personally pressed for its swift passage. Prominent Army officers endorsed the bill; leading newspapers supported it; and its House and Senate sponsors predicted early and favorable action by Congress.[37]

35. Alger's letter is in *RSW, 1898*, I, 255-56.

36. *New York Journal*, March 18, 1898, and *Philadelphia Enquirer*, March 27, 1898, both clippings in Box 10, Corbin Papers. Adjutant General Corbin also wanted to fill the Regular regiments with Army veterans; see Corbin to Representative John A. T. Hull, March 23, 1898, File No. 72278, AGO Records. Columbus, *Ohio State Journal*, April 4, 1898, quoted in *Congressional Record*, 55th Cong., 2d sess., 1898, XXXI, Pt. 4, p. 3680. *New York Tribune*, April 5 and 6, 1898. *RSW, 1898*, II, 195.

37. *Army and Navy Journal*, March 26, 1898. *The New York Times*, March 14 and April 3 and 9, 1898. *New York Tribune*, March 19 and April 9, 1898. *Washington Post*, April 3 and 4, 1898. *Philadelphia Enquirer*, March 27, 1898, clipping, Box 10, Corbin Papers. Adj. Gen. H. C. Corbin to Representative John A. T. Hull, March 18, 23, and 31, 1898, and to Representative C. E. Pearce, April 1, 1898, Representative Pearce to Corbin, March 31, 1898, File No. 72278, AGO Records.

Because it required a small appropriation, the House of Representatives was first to consider the Hull bill. On March 23 the House Military Affairs Committee reported on the bill with its main provisions intact but with an amendment that required immediate reduction of the Army to its peacetime strength of 27,000 upon the cessation of hostilities. More important, the committee, over the determined opposition of some of its members, amended the bill to require a declaration of war by Congress before the President could implement the provisions for expansion. Advocates of an expansible army, who wished to enable the President to mobilize troops before war broke out, viewed the latter amendment as a severe setback. Nevertheless, the bill's key provisions had survived, and it seemed well on the way to enactment.[38]

By the end of March, 1898, the military situation appeared entirely in hand. The Navy had assembled its squadrons for combat and the War Department was preparing to defend the seacoasts. It was rapidly accumulating weapons and supplies and reorganizing the Army into an effective striking force. The press fulsomely praised the military departments, calling the Cuban crisis a blessing in disguise in the occasion it offered to put the nation's defenses on a sounder footing. An editor well informed about military affairs wrote:

> At no time in its history since the close of the Rebellion has our little Army been so alert and efficient as it is at the present moment. . . . There soon will be at all strategic points a sufficient force to cope with every possible emergency. Our oft-repeated quotation of the adage, "In time of peace, prepare for war," and our advice to follow it up, has come into its fulfillment . . ., and if war comes we can face it with courage and equanimity.[39]

Within a few short weeks, however, the expressions of praise for the Army were to turn into cries of scorn and denunciation. The causes for this about-face were the workings of politics and the ambition of an aroused, militant National Guard.

V

Beginning in mid-February of 1898, a warlike spirit swept the nation and affected all classes and sections. Bellicose citizens by the thousands, sympathetic to the Cubans and enraged by the destruction of the *Maine*, deluged state and federal authorities with offers of military service. Civil War veterans, both Union and Confederate, proclaimed their willingness

38. *Army and Navy Journal*, March 19 and April 9, 1898. *The New York Times*, March 20, 23, and 24, 1898. *New York Tribune*, March 19, 23, and 24, 1898. *Washington Post*, March 19, 1898. U.S. Congress, *House Report No. 795*, 55th Cong., 2d sess., 1898, p. 1.

39. The quotation is from the *Army and Navy Journal*, March 26, 1898; see also the issue of April 2, 1898, quoting the *New York Sun*. *The New York Times*, March 27, 29, and 30, 1898. G. M. Dodge to Secretary Alger, March 15, 1898, Alger Papers.

to march against the Spanish oppressors. Croatian coal miners in Pennsylvania, many of whom had served in the Austrian and Russian armies, offered President McKinley a division of troops. Labor union locals, Republican clubs and student and fraternal organizations declared their readiness to volunteer en masse. Millionaires offered to raise and equip regiments at their own expense. Ohio officials later added up all of the offers of service they had received and discovered that their state alone could have raised an army of 100,000 men. All across the country, enthusiasts organized their own regiments, battalions, and companies, some connected with the National Guard but many independent of it. In President McKinley's home town of Canton, Ohio, for example, 600 of "the best young men of the city" formed a regiment and announced their intention to respond within twenty-four hours to any call for troops. Civil War veterans, meeting in New York on March 25, established the "National Volunteer Reserve," to be composed of citizens who signed a pledge to enter the armed services at once in any foreign war. Before it disbanded in mid-April, this "Grand Army of Individual Americans" claimed to have enrolled 15,000 men. All of these volunteers were eager to go to war, but they wanted to go in the local units they were busy forming, not as anonymous Regular Army recruits led by strangers from West Point; the Hull bill threatened to frustrate their military ambitions.[40]

These amateur and eager soldiers would by themselves have constituted an obstacle to the War Department's plans for a neat, orderly, modest-sized mobilization. But another factor compounded the confusion. The introduction of the Hull bill brought to a head the long controversy over the wartime role of the National Guard. Guardsmen responded to the Cuban crisis with martial enthusiasm. After the destruction of the *Maine* in February, the militiamen, without waiting for orders from Washington, began to recruit their units up to full strength, accumulate supplies, and make war plans, all in expectation of a call to invade Cuba. State officials wrote to President McKinley to offer the services of their militia and to boast of their readiness for immediate action. The adjutant general of Illinois told the newspapers that his troops, 7,500 strong, could be "en route to New York for embarkation for Cuba" within twelve hours of a call. Scenting political

---

40. *The New York Times*, February 27, March 1, 10, 16, 17, 28, and 30, April 2, 3, 4, and 5, 1898. Franklin F. Holbrook, *Minnesota in the Spanish-American War and the Philippine Insurrection* (hereafter cited as Holbrook, *Minnesota in War*), 10-11. Ohio Adjutant General, *Annual Report of the Adjutant General to the Governor of the State of Ohio, for the Fiscal Year Ending November 15, 1898* (hereafter cited as *Ohio Adjutant General, 1898*), 642. John Wanamaker to Secretary Alger, March 12, 1898; Frederick D. Grant to Alger, March 13, 1898; William Astor Chanler to Alger, March 21, 1898; Lew Wallace to Alger, April 5, 1898; Maj. Gen. Wesley Merritt to Alger, April 22, 1898, Alger Papers. M. C. Butler to President McKinley, March 9, 1898; B. B. O'Dell to McKinley, March 26, 1898, McKinley Papers. Lt. Gen. John M. Schofield to Maj. Gen. A. McD. McCook, April 15, 1898, and to W. D'H. Washington, April 22, 1898, Box 64, Schofield Papers.

opportunity in the new flurry of military preparation, guardsmen who wanted their national organization recognized as a fully constituted Army reserve renewed their agitation for a law that would allow the President to use state troops in wartime for any sort of national service.[41]

Had the invasion of Cuba promised to require more men than the enlarged Regular Army could provide, thus necessitating an immediate call for volunteers, the National Guard's martial aspirations would not have endangered the Hull bill. Under those circumstances, the Guard's leaders (most of whom in principle favored an expansible army) would have concentrated their political efforts on securing legislation concerning volunteers that they could endorse. However, the War Department's intention to use only Regulars in the assault and to restrict the National Guard to home defense directly challenged the ambitions of many of the state soldiers.

National Guard leaders from seaboard states like New York and Massachusetts, sure of a summons to man the coast defenses in the event of war, supported the Army's mobilization plan, but their colleagues from interior states, rallied by the militiamen of Ohio and Pennsylvania, quickly launched an attack on the Hull bill. These guardsmen objected to the fact that under the Hull bill the reinforced Regular Army alone could furnish the 100,000 troops needed to defeat Spain. If the bill passed, units from inland states probably would not be called to service, and their members would have to join the Regular Army as individuals if they wanted to see action. The guardsmen, who considered themselves socially superior to Regular enlisted men, found this prospect personally degrading. Militia officers would not be able to serve at all, unless they gave up their commissions—an action that was unthinkable to most of them. Even more important in the long run, the Hull bill, by eliminating any immediate need for a call for volunteers, would prevent the National Guardsmen from securing through legislation the place they sought in the military system. Hoping to force a call for volunteers and to obtain clarification of their own status, militiamen, who constituted solid voting blocs in most states, put heavy and effective pressure on Congress to defeat the Hull bill. Together with Southern Democrats who still resented military reconstruction, Populists who feared an enlarged Regular Army as an instrument of internal repression, and a few dissident Army officers with technical objections to the Hull bill, the National Guardsmen formed a powerful alliance against the War Department and the Regulars.[42]

41. *Army and Navy Journal*, March 19, 1898. *The New York Times*, March 9, 10, 21, and 28, 1898. *Washington Post*, February 23, 1898. Holbrook, *Minnesota in War*, 13. T. S. Peck to John A. Porter, February 23, 1898; Governor Daniel G. Hastings of Pennsylvania to President McKinley, March 1, 1898, McKinley Papers. Col. C. L. Kennan, Capt. George T. McConnell, and Capt. Charles X. Zimmerman, Ohio National Guard, to the Secretary of War, March 25, 1898, File No. 73160, AGO Records.

42. *Army and Navy Journal*, April 2, 9, 16, and 23, 1898. *The New York Times*, March 19 and April 17, 1898. *New York Tribune*, April 8, 1898. For an example of public preference for Volunteers

Representative Hull and his backers in the War Department quickly learned how strong that alliance was. On April 6, spurred on by increasingly urgent pleas from Adjutant General Corbin, Hull brought his bill to the House floor. In two days of repetitious debate, the guardsmen and their friends demolished it. Congressmen of all parties denounced the Hull bill, concentrating their attack on its expansion provisions. The bill, they declared, by reducing the need for state Volunteers, would permit the Regular Army to monopolize unfairly the glory of future victories by the United States forces. Speaking for his state's militia, a Pennsylvania representative made clear the National Guard's objection to the measure:

> By this bill [he said] the United States infantry will almost, if not entirely, supplant the National Guard—that now valuable auxiliary to our national strength.
> The aftereffects of such a bill can be easily foreshadowed. The probabilities of the National Guard being called into service, after this bill becomes law, will be exceedingly remote, and will cause interest in the Guard to lag. This Guard will lose its importance in the eyes of the people, and, rightly or wrongly, will fall into oblivion and disappear as an efficient and inexpensive mainstay.[43]

To applause from the galleries, speaker after speaker extolled the moral virtue and fighting spirit of the Volunteers. Regulars, they said, came from the inferior classes of society and fought only for pay, while the Volunteers, recruited from the best American stock, "are no hirelings, no mercenaries; they fight for the defense of home and country, for principle and glory, for liberty and the rights of man. In time of peace they follow their usual trades, professions, and occupations. They do not menace our liberties or the stability of our free institutions." To enlarge the Regular Army even in wartime, opponents of the Hull bill proclaimed, was to take a first step toward militarism and the destruction of our cherished freedoms. Only a few congressmen offered technical criticisms of the bill. They argued that

---

over Regulars, see *Washington Post*, April 14, 1898. C. M. Moses, Adjutant General of Colorado, to Representative J. C. Bell, March 31, 1898, in *Congressional Record*, 55th Cong., 2d sess., 1898, XXXI, Pt. 4, p. 3637; see also Pt. 5, p. 4208. Hull, *Forum*, XXV, 399, and *The North American Review*, CLXVIII, 386, 389. Charles E. Creagher, *The Fourteenth Ohio National Guard—The Fourth Ohio Volunteer Infantry*, 83, reflects the guardsmen's loyalty to their own units and to their elected officers. On this point, see also Millis, *Martial Spirit*, 155-56. *New York Journal*, March 24, 1898, and *Philadelphia Enquirer*, March 27, 1898, clippings in Box 10, Corbin Papers. For the views of a National Guard leader who supported the Hull bill, see Gen. George W. Wingate, "The Reorganization of Our State Troops: Comment and Criticism," *JMSI*, XXIII, 553.

43. The quotation is from a speech by Representative Robbins of Pennsylvania reported in *Army and Navy Journal*, April 16, 1898; see also issues of April 2 and 9, 1898. *The New York Times*, April 7, 1898. *Congressional Record*, 55th Cong., 2d sess., 1898, XXXI, Pt. 4, pp. 3624-25, 3627-28, 3634-36, 3668, 3679-80, contains other expressions of fear for the National Guard's survival if the Hull bill were passed. For Corbin's efforts on behalf of the bill, see Adj. Gen. H. C. Corbin to Representative J. A. T. Hull, March 26 and April 4, 1898, to Representative Charles H. Grosvenor, April 4, 1898, and to Speaker of the House Thomas B. Reed, April 4, 1898, File No. 72278, AGO Records.

it created unmanageably large infantry companies and that, under its provisions, reduction of the Army at the close of hostilities would leave on the nation's hands hundreds of supernumerary officers. Throughout, the attack on the bill centered on the immorality of using Regulars instead of citizen Volunteers to fight America's wars.[44]

Congressman Hull and the other defenders of the bill spent most of their time trying to appease advocates of the militia and Volunteers. They pointed out that nothing in the measure prevented the President, either before or after enlarging the Regular Army, from calling for state troops. To no avail, Hull's forces tried to reassure civil libertarians that the bill allowed no peacetime increase of the Army. While vainly attempting to avoid the expansion issue, they stressed the Infantry's crying need for the modern formation the bill prescribed. A New Jersey representative and militiaman, expressing the views of East Coast guardsmen, supported the Hull bill, on the grounds that the state troops were not fit for offensive combat. Other guardsmen in the House angrily took issue with him. Adding to Mr. Hull's tribulations, Rep. Benjamin F. Marsh, a senior member of the Committee on Military Affairs, announced that he had opposed the bill all along and had endorsed it in committee only "to get it out . . . into the House, where it could have decent consideration."[45]

At the start of the second day of debate, on April 7, Hull surrendered to the opposition. He agreed to delete from his bill all the sections that authorized increasing the enlisted force if only the House would pass those that dealt with reorganization of the Infantry. Even this retreat did not satisfy the aroused representatives. By a vote of 155 to 61, they sent the Hull bill back to the Committee on Military Affairs, in effect killing it. Assisted by Democratic and Populist foes of the Regular Army and supported by the American Volunteer tradition, the National Guardsmen had demonstrated conclusively their ability to block any of the War Department's measures they disliked.[46]

VI

From the War Department's point of view, the defeat of the Hull bill could not have come at a worse time. By April 7, when the measure died in the House, the diplomatic maneuverings over Cuba were nearing their

44. The quotation is from remarks by Representative Sulzer, a New York Democrat, in *Congressional Record*, 55th Cong., 2d sess., 1898, XXXI, Pt. 4, p. 3668; for other arguments against the Hull bill, see pp. 3629, 3633-38, 3668, 3674-75, 3679, 3689-90, 3692.

45. *Congressional Record*, 55th Cong., 2d sess., 1898, XXXI, Pt. 4, pp. 3621-26, 3630-32, 3640-44, 3691.

46. *Congressional Record*, 55th Cong., 2d sess., 1898, XXXI, Pt. 4, pp. 3667-68, 3675, 3677-78, 3692-93. *The New York Times*, April 16, 1898.

end. War was, at most, weeks away. The Administration's demands, backed by the Fifty Million appropriation, had failed to frighten the Spaniards out of Cuba. At home, the longer Spain's presence continued in Cuba, the more Americans joined in the cry for immediate forcible measures to drive her out. By the beginning of April, those Americans included an alarming number of Republican senators and representatives—so many that President McKinley stood in real danger of losing control of Congress. It was in this climate that, on April 11, McKinley further increased his pressure on Spain. Going as far as he could, short of asking Congress for a declaration of war, the President, in a special message, requested authority to use the armed forces of the United States "to secure a full and final termination of hostilities between the Government of Spain and the people of Cuba."[47]

The President and his advisers apparently still hoped at this stage that Spain, her back now to the wall, would yield to the threat of force. But Spain did not yield, and the two nations moved steadily toward war. On April 19 Congress by joint resolution authorized armed American intervention. It also declared that Cuba should be free and independent, that Spain must relinquish her sovereignty and withdraw her troops, and that the United States had no desire to annex Cuba. In the next two days, Spain and the United States broke off diplomatic relations. On April 21 McKinley ordered the squadron at Key West to blockade Havana and other ports in northwestern Cuba. The ships put to sea the next day and took station off the Cuban coast on April 23. On April 25, after Spain had ignored a final American demand that she leave Cuba, Congress formally declared war. While the two nations thus swept toward collision, Secretary Alger and his colleagues hastily revamped their plans for the Army. Time was running short, so the final criterion in making decisions ceased to be military efficiency. Instead, plans had to be based on measures Congress and the National Guard would accept.[48]

The military authorities still planned on an expeditionary force of about 100,000 men, but, realizing the political damage their earlier mistake

47. LaFeber, *New Empire*, 350, 383-85, 396-97, 400, 403. Leech, *Days of McKinley*, 177-85. May, *Imperial Democracy*, 152-54, 156-59. Morgan, *Road to Empire*, ix-x, 52-62. Olcott, *McKinley*, II, 18-26. Text of McKinley's message is in *Affairs in Cuba*, 3-14; see also 540-42. *The New York Times*, March 30 and 31, April 1, 2, 5, and 7, 1898. Benjamin F. Tracy to President McKinley, April 2, 1898; H. H. Kohlsaat to McKinley, April 2, 1898, McKinley Papers.

48. Stewart L. Woodford to Secretary Alger, April 13, 1898, Alger Papers. G. B. Howland to John Russell Young, March 25, 1898; draft of letter from President McKinley to Alger, July, 1899, McKinley Papers. Stewart L. Woodford to McKinley, April 10, 1898, in Alfred L. P. Dennis, *Adventures in American Diplomacy, 1896-1906*, 73-74. Theodore Roosevelt to Henry Cabot Lodge, April 14, 1898, in *Selections from the Correspondence of Theodore Roosevelt and Henry Cabot Lodge, 1884-1918*, Henry Cabot Lodge, ed. (hereafter cited as *Roosevelt-Lodge Correspondence*), I, 297. Mayo, *America of Yesterday*, 182. Chadwick, *Spanish-American War*, I, 127-46, 156. Goode, *With Sampson*, 28-35, 42. May, *Imperial Democracy*, 158-59. Morgan, *Road to Empire*, 56-57. Olcott, *McKinley*, II, 34-35. *The New York Times*, April 19 and 26, 1898.

had wrought, they changed its structure to include a large state Volunteer contingent. A few days after his initial defeat in the House, Representative Hull secured conditional agreement from the National Guard to a revised version of his bill. The new version retained the original's provisions for reorganization of the Infantry but limited the wartime expansion of the enlisted force to about 60,000. In the thought that Congress might reject this compromise, Adjutant General Corbin was preparing other bills that would call for even more modest expansion of the Army. Any of this legislation, if passed, would allow the Regular Army to furnish about half of the contemplated force. The other half would consist of state Volunteer regiments, preferably composed of trained National Guardsmen.[49]

Two days after the defeat of the Hull bill, General Miles, assisted by officers of The Adjutant General's Department, drew up plans for an expeditionary force consisting of all the available Regulars and 40,000 or 50,000 Volunteers. Additional Volunteers or militia were to reinforce the coast defenses. The President would call on the states for the first Volunteer contingents as soon as Congress declared war, drawing as many of them as possible from the National Guard and allowing the state authorities to organize the regiments and select their officers. Further calls for Volunteers could follow later, if necessary. On April 13 the War Department brought this mobilization plan into final form. Secretary Alger appointed a board of three officers to work out procedures for assembling the Regulars and 40,000 Volunteers for field service and 20,000 more Volunteers for coast defense. The following day, the board recommended the immediate concentration of the Regulars, either at a single southern camp or at the Gulf ports of Tampa, Mobile, and New Orleans. As soon as they were called out, the Volunteers should join the Regulars at these points, where the brigades and divisions of the field army could be formed. If the War Department preferred a single camp, the board recommended Chickamauga Battlefield Park in Georgia as the site. This federal reservation, established during the Cleveland Administration, had been planned as a maneuvering ground for the Army and the National Guard. Its eleven square miles of rolling, lightly wooded terrain could accommodate up to 50,000 soldiers, and it boasted adequate water supplies and good rail connections to the Gulf cities.[50]

49. *Army and Navy Journal*, April 9 and 16, 1898. *The New York Times*, March 23 and April 4, 6, 11, 12, 14, 15, and 17, 1898. *New York Tribune*, April 5, 1898. *Washington Post*, April 14, 1898. Theodore Roosevelt to William A. Wadsworth, April 7, 1898, and to William A. Chanler, April 21, 1898, both in Morison, *Roosevelt Letters*, II, 814-19. Secretary Alger to Gen. Lew Wallace, April 6, 1898, Alger Papers. Adj. Gen. H. C. Corbin to Representative John A. T. Hull, April 11, 1898, and to Representative Benjamin F. Marsh, April 19, 1898, Asst. Adj. Gen. Theodore Schwan to Representative Hull, April 18, 1898, File No. 74259, AGO Records.

50. Maj. Gen. Nelson A. Miles to the Secretary of War, April 9 and 15, 1898, in *RSW, 1898*, II, 5-6. *Army and Navy Journal*, April 9 and 16, 1898. *The New York Times*, April 6 and 14, 1898. *New York Tribune*, April 10, 12, 15, and 16, 1898. *Washington Post*, April 14 and 16, 1898. The Adjutant General's Office to Lt. Col. Theodore Schwan, Lt. Col. Arthur L. Wagner, and Maj. William H. Carter, April 13, 1898; The Adjutant General's Office, Memorandum prepared by Schwan, Wagner, and Carter, April 14, 1898; both in Maj. Gen. William Harding Carter, *The American Army*, 206-11. Miles, *The North American Review*, CLXVIII, 517. *War Investigating Commission*, VII, 3275, 3767.

At General Miles's urging, Secretary Alger on April 15 issued orders concentrating 22 of the Regular infantry regiments at New Orleans, Mobile, and Tampa and 6 of the cavalry regiments and most of the field artillery at Chickamauga. Before leaving their peacetime stations, the commands were to equip themselves fully for war services, and they were to take along all available wagons. With the Regulars thus collected from their scattered posts and with the Infantry massed on the Gulf Coast, the War Department, once Congress authorized a call for Volunteers, could gather them at Chickamauga and quickly complete its striking force.

The Regulars moved rapidly. Within a week of the concentration order, most of the regiments had arrived at their destinations. While the troop trains rolled toward the assembly points, the staff bureaus began chartering coastal steamers for transports and accelerated the work of collecting weapons, food, equipment, and uniforms for both Regulars and Volunteers.[51]

While the Regulars deployed for action, the War Department reached agreement with the National Guard on a plan for raising the Volunteer contingents and in the process gave the guardsmen the federal recognition they desired. National Guard leaders from a number of states had come to Washington at Representative Hull's invitation to explain their objections to his bill. Many of the guardsmen appeared before the House Committee on Military Affairs on April 16. On that and the following day, the militia leaders conferred twice at the War Department and once at the White House with President McKinley, Secretary Alger, and Generals Miles and Corbin. Together, state and federal officials outlined a law to govern the organization, training, and deployment of the Volunteers. Under it, the President would limit his first call for 60,000 troops to the National Guard. According to a formula long favored by guardsmen of the reservist school, any National Guard unit the members of which volunteered in a body would be accepted by the Army as organized and would be left under the command of its elected officers. The guardsmen, assured now of being called upon in the event of war and of having their units made the nucleus of the Volunteer Army, in turn promised to support the revised Hull bill. To clarify the agreement further, Alger and Corbin publicly pledged to respect the states' right to organize and officer their Volunteers.[52]

51. Alger, *Spanish-American War*, 15-16. Text of the concentration order is in *Correspondence*, I, 7. *Army and Navy Journal*, April 16 and 23, 1898. *The New York Times*, April 16, 17, and 22, 1898. *New York Tribune*, April 13 and 21, 1898. *Washington Post*, April 15, 1898. Secretary Alger to President McKinley, April 15, 1898, McKinley Papers. Maj. Gen. Nelson A. Miles to Alger, April 11, 1898, File No. 192302; Adj. Gen. H. C. Corbin to Generals Brooke, Wade, Coppinger, and Shafter, April 16, 1898, File No. 74735; File No. 74579 contains reports on the arrival of the troops at their assembly points; Corbin to commanding Officers at Chickamauga Park, Mobile, and Tampa, April 19, 1898, File No. 75042, AGO Records.

52. *Army and Navy Journal*, April 16 and 23, 1898. *The New York Times*, April 16, 17, and 20, 1898. *New York Tribune*, April 17 and 20, 1898. *Washington Post*, April 17 and 19, 1898. Hull, *Forum*, XXV, 399.

On April 19, the day Congress authorized armed intervention in Cuba, the Administration's spokesmen in the House and Senate introduced the bill to create a Volunteer army. Intended like the Hull bill as a permanent measure, the bill embodied the agreement reached between the McKinley Administration and the National Guard. In line with Regular Army doctrine, however, it also increased federal control over the organization and officering of the Volunteers. The measure authorized the President, in wartime and only with special permission from Congress, to raise a temporary Volunteer force to serve for three years or for the duration of hostilities, whichever was shorter, and to be disbanded immediately upon the restoration of peace. The President could call upon the states for as many men as he believed necessary and could set a quota for each state, based on its population. The Volunteers would adopt the same organization, follow the same regulations, and receive the same pay and allowances as did the Regulars. To assure members of the National Guard of their position, the bill provided that, whenever a militia company, battalion, or regiment enlisted as a unit, it would be enrolled as such and its officers given Volunteer commissions corresponding in rank to those they held in the militia. However, the bill gave the President full power to appoint all Volunteer generals and staff officers. It also gave him the right to prescribe qualifying examinations, which all Volunteer regimental and company officers, nominated as usual by their state governors, must pass before receiving their commissions. The President could assign one Regular officer to any Volunteer regiment, upon request of the governor of the state to which the regiment belonged, and the bill permitted army and corps commanders to appoint boards of review to remove incompetent Volunteer officers. These provisions, Regulars hoped, would assure a minimum level of ability among Volunteer commanders. Striking at a Civil War abuse, the bill forbade any state to send new regiments into federal service in a second call for Volunteers unless its existing regiments were already at full strength.[53]

The War Department, fearing trouble with state officials and unable to risk further delay in organizing the Army, changed the bill before it reached the floor of Congress. The altered bill reserved to the governors unconditional power to commission their states' colonels, majors, captains, and lieutenants. Otherwise, the measure went through almost intact. The House passed it on April 20. The Senate did so the next day but reduced the terms of service to one year, for the convenience of businessmen in the National Guard, and authorized the President to raise special United States Volunteer units from the country at large. On April 22, after a conference committee had compromised on a two-year term and limited to 3,000 the number of United States Volunteers, the bill became law.[54]

53. *Army and Navy Journal*, April 23, 1898. *The New York Times*, April 19 and 20, 1898. *Washington Post*, April 20, 1898. Assistant Secretary of War George D. Meiklejohn to Senator Joseph Hawley and Representative John A. T. Hull, April 19, 1898, File No. 75021, AGO Records.

54. Secretary Alger to Representative John A. T. Hull, April 20, 1898, Alger Papers. *Army and Navy Journal*, April 23, 1898. *The New York Times*, April 21, 22, and 23, 1898. *Congressional Record*, 55th Cong., 2d sess., 1898, XXXI, Pt. 5, pp. 4113, 4116, 4182.

VII

On the same day that the House passed the Volunteer bill, President McKinley and his civilian and uniformed advisers met to determine the nation's strategy for the war that now seemed inevitable. Although he had given little direction to prewar preparations, McKinley, as the opening of hostilities approached, took charge of the conduct of operations. He had fought in the Civil War as a regimental officer (friends often called him "Major McKinley") and in 1865 had considered making the Regular Army his career. The President's affable, even gentle, manner concealed an instinct for power and a highly developed sense of his responsibilities that led him to concentrate in his own hands all military and diplomatic decisions. Through frequent conferences at the White House with the Secretary of War, the Secretary of the Navy, and the uniformed heads of the services, he dictated strategy on land and sea and, further, insisted that each military move should conform to and advance his diplomatic objectives. As operations expanded, he had a special "war room" fitted out on the second floor of the Executive Mansion. On its walls, large-scale maps studded with colored flags recorded the positions of troops and ships. Through an elaborate telephone and telegraph network he kept in touch with the military bureaus and with commanders at the front.[55]

While he remained aloof from the day-to-day command and administration of the Navy, McKinley, beginning early in April, intervened constantly in the internal affairs of the Army. He did so partly out of distrust of both Alger and Miles, partly because the Army seemed to be having more trouble than the Navy in carrying out its missions, and partly because the actions of the Army were closely related to his political objectives in the Spanish islands. To supplement and cross-check the counsels of his Secretary of War and Commanding General, whom he considered unreliable, McKinley turned initially to Lieutenant General Schofield, the retired head of the Army. When Schofield stopped in Washington early in April to offer his services in the crisis, McKinley retained him as a confidential adviser and installed him in an office in the State, War, and Navy Building. For several weeks he consulted Schofield daily on matters of strategy and personnel. Most of Schofield's suggestions merely echoed those of General Miles, but on the crucial question of how large an army to assemble at the outset, the two officers were to disagree, with results that disrupted the War Department's plans.[56]

55. Alger, *Spanish-American War*, 48. Dunn, *Harrison to Harding*, I, 207. Long, *New American Navy*, II, 149. Ernest R. May, ed., *The Ultimate Decision: The President as Commander-in-Chief*, 94. Morgan, *McKinley*, 15-35, 83-84, 528. Olcott, *McKinley*, II, 48-49, 51, 54-56. *Army and Navy Journal*, May 7, 1898. *The New York Times*, May 31, 1898. Draft of letter from President McKinley to Secretary Alger, undated, probably early July, 1899, McKinley Papers.

56. Lt. Gen. John M. Schofield, "General Schofield's Experiences in McKinley's Administration," undated memoir in Box 93, Schofield Papers. *Army and Navy Journal*, April 9, 1898.

As war approached, the most perplexing military questions for McKinley and his advisers were whether, when, and where to attack the Spaniards on land. Everyone agreed that the American fleet should open the conflict by blockading the ports of Cuba. The blockade alone would, in time, starve the Spaniards into surrender, and it probably would draw the enemy fleet into battle in the Caribbean, where the American ships could destroy it. McKinley and most of his advisers, including the members of the joint Army-Navy strategy board, also agreed that if any invasion were attempted its objective should be Havana, Cuba's capital and principal city. Located in the economically well-developed and thickly populated western part of the island, Havana boasted extensive coastal and land defenses and was Spain's only really formidable fortress and naval base in the Caribbean. The bulk of the Spanish army in Cuba had concentrated in Havana and in a series of satellite towns and ports linked to the capital by rail. These garrisons denied to the rebels a belt of territory about 200 miles wide and extending from the northern to the southern coast of the narrow island, thus splitting the Cuban forces into two groups that could not combine for concentrated attacks. Havana also supplied many of the smaller posts in the interior. If the city fell, the whole Spanish position in Cuba would crumble. Besides the obvious uncertainty of when the War Department could furnish the troops needed for such an attack, changing assessments of two strategic variables—the strength and intentions of the Spanish fleet and the danger of disease to American soldiers in Cuba—caused the Administration repeatedly to reverse itself on the question of assaulting Havana.[57]

American and foreign strategists agreed that seapower would determine the outcome of the war. If the United States fleet controlled the Caribbean, it could prevent the arrival of Spanish supplies and reinforcements while disembarking armies at will in Cuba and Puerto Rico. On the other hand, the Spanish fleet, simply by remaining at large and in striking range of the sea lanes between the United States and Cuba, could render an invasion all but impossible. The United States Navy thus had to dispose of the Spanish fleet before any important action could be attempted. At the time, destruction of the enemy's seapower appeared dauntingly difficult. Although rapid changes in ship design and the fact that two steam-powered armored fleets had yet to meet in battle made estimates of strength uncertain, most naval experts in the United States and abroad considered the Spanish armored squadron a match for the American. The United States had seven armored vessels in commission to challenge Spain's five, but most of the Spanish ships were faster than their American counterparts. Spain's three

57. Long, *New American Navy*, I, 201, 229-30. Mahan, *Lessons*, 42-45, 59-61, 107. Nunez, *Guerra*, III, 113. Lt. Gen. John M. Schofield, "General Schofield's Experiences in McKinley's Administration," Box 93, Schofield Papers.

armored cruisers, with the small battleship *Cristóbal Colón*, constituted a force that, on paper, could outrun the heaviest American ships and out-fight the only vessels capable of catching them. American officers believed that indifferent crews and poor maintenance might reduce the performance of the Spanish vessels, but it would be dangerous to assume these factors in advance of proof in action. At the first strategy conferences in April of 1898, American naval planners, quite sensibly, treated the Spanish fleet as a dangerous, powerful opponent.[58]

The movements of the Spanish fleet contributed to a sense of uncertainty in American naval circles. To the surprise of the Americans, the Spaniards did not mass their armored vessels at Havana in the weeks before the declaration of war. Instead, Spain's fast armored ships—the cruisers *Infanta María Teresa*, *Almirante Oquendo*, and *Vizcaya*, and the battleship *Cristóbal Colón*—concentrated in the Portuguese Cape Verde Islands. There, three torpedo-boat-destroyers joined them. Massed in the Cape Verdes, this striking force, commanded by Admiral Pascual Cervera, could not be trapped by an early American onslaught. Its presence where it could launch itself westward at any time fixed the attention of the Americans and reduced their freedom of action.[59]

Cuba's grim reputation as the breeding ground of malaria and yellow fever led many American strategists to question whether soldiers landed there would live long enough to fight. American generals were inexperienced in tropical campaigning, but most had read histories of earlier wars in the West Indies in which whole armies had succumbed to yellow fever, smallpox, and malaria. Medical science, in spite of decades of effort, had not yet isolated the microorganism that caused yellow fever or discovered how the dread killer spread. There was thus no reliable defense against the disease; laymen regarded "yellow jack," as it was popularly called, with almost superstitious terror. Action against the Spaniards would begin just at the onset of the Cuban rainy season, a time of cloudbursts and high humidity that began in late April and continued through September. During this period, Cuba's dirt roads became almost impassable and the fevers raged at their deadliest. Surgeon General Sternberg, one of the world's leading experts on yellow

58. Chadwick, *Spanish-American War*, I, 28-29, 37-40, 44-45, 55-61, 94-96, Cruse, *Apache Days and After*, 261. Long, *New American Navy*, I, 224-26. Mahan, *Lessons*, 30-31, 53-56, 75, 88-89, 108-9. Mayo, *America of Yesterday*, 167, 180. Nunez, *Guerra*, II, 222; III, 112. Sprout and Sprout, *Naval Power*, 232-33. Miles, *The North American Review*, CLXVIII, 522. *Army and Navy Journal*, April 9, 16, and 30, 1898. *The New York Times*, May 5, 1898. *Washington Post*, April 14, 1898. Theodore Roosevelt to Elihu Root, April 5, 1898, in Morison, *Roosevelt Letters*, II, 813-14. J. Warren Keifer to President McKinley, February 25, 1898; John J. McCook to McKinley, April 21, 1898, McKinley Papers.

59. Chadwick, *Spanish-American War*, I, 25-26, 62-63. Goode, *With Sampson*, 20. Long, *New American Navy*, I, 223-24. Mahan, *Lessons*, 94-96, 98. Nunez, *Guerra*, III, 117-20. *Army and Navy Journal*, March 19, 1898.

fever, was supported by Americans who had lived in Cuba in his repeated urging of President McKinley not to invade the country during the wet months. Invasion, he predicted, would mean death and disaster for the Army. These forebodings initially impressed the President to the extent that he sought to avoid an invasion if success could be achieved by other means.[60]

Early in April, while the Hull bill was being crushed in the House, Rear Adm. William T. Sampson, who commanded the Navy's principal armored squadron, then massed at Key West, brought to a head the controversy surrounding the attack on Havana. After examining intelligence reports on Havana's coast defenses and after conferring with his captains, Sampson developed a plan for capturing the city by naval action. He believed that his battleships, without danger to themselves, could silence the city's guardian forts and compel surrender of the defending forces by threatening to shell the town. The available Regular troops could then occupy Cuba's capital. Sampson pointed to the enormous political and military effect of such an early victory and asked the Navy Department for permission to carry out his plan as soon as war was declared. On April 6 Secretary of the Navy Long refused permission. He ordered the Admiral to avoid exposing his armored vessels to damage or destruction until he had met and vanquished the Spanish fleet. Three days later, Sampson replied with a vigorously worded defense of his attack scheme and indicated the small risk it involved. His arguments apparently convinced the Administration, which in mid-April tentatively adopted his proposal. When he concentrated the Regular Army's forces on April 15, Secretary Alger sent the infantry directly to the Gulf ports, from which they could have embarked to follow up the attack Sampson advocated.[61]

However, Generals Miles and Schofield, the interservice strategy board, and many other of the President's advisers expressed vehement opposition to Sampson's plan. While Miles stressed possible delays in preparing the Army, most of the dissenters argued only on naval and medical grounds. They insisted that any attack by the armored vessels upon land forts would be foolhardy. In such an assault, Spanish gunners by luck or skill might sink or cripple enough American battleships to give the enemy fleet the numerical advantage when it reached the Caribbean. The Spaniards then

60. Gibson, *Soldier in White*, 72-74, 81, describes a yellow fever epidemic in the lower Mississippi Valley in 1875 and the panic it caused. Miles, *The North American Review*, CLXVIII, 521-22. Lt. J. Hamilton Stone, "Our Troops in the Tropics—From a Surgeon's Standpoint," *JMSI*, XXVI, 358. James M. Harding to Secretary Alger, April 4, 1898, File No. 74028; Josiah Monroe to Assistant Secretary of State William R. Day, April 15, 1898, and Memorandum by Chief Signal Officer A. W. Greeley, May 16, 1898, File No. 76730, AGO Records. *The New York Times*, May 2, 1898.

61. Chadwick, *Spanish-American War*, I, 63-64, 70-88. Goode, *With Sampson*, 18-25. Lt. Gen. John M. Schofield, "General Schofield's Experiences in McKinley's Administration," Box 93, Schofield Papers. Writing from the Spanish side, Nunez, *Guerra*, III, 123-25, insists that Sampson's attack would have failed.

might win the decisive naval battle and any American troops who had succeeded in occupying Havana would be lost, cut off from supplies and reinforcements. The fleet, Sampson's opponents argued, must avoid risk and casualties until it had beaten the Spanish squadron. The advocates of caution also repeated the dire predictions of uncontrollable epidemics among American troops sent to Cuba during the hot, wet months.[62]

General Miles on April 18 offered an alternative military plan of his own. He suggested that a major invasion be postponed until the fever season passed and until the Navy destroyed the Spanish fleet. Miles would, in the meantime, rely on the blockade, supplemented by aid to the Cubans and by small-scale American raids, to wear down the enemy. He believed that such harassment by itself might force Spain to surrender and thus secure victory at the cost of few American lives. If victory did not result from this strategy, an army, carefully organized during the summer from the Volunteers soon to be called out and the Regulars who Miles hoped soon would be reinforced, could deliver the finishing thrust against Havana in the fall. As a first step in implementing his strategy, he urged that all the available Regulars be concentrated at a single camp to train in large-unit maneuvers and to be ready to exploit any Spanish weakness.[63]

Impressed by these arguments against an early attack, President McKinley on the afternoon of April 20 called together a White House conference to thresh out a firm strategy. At the meeting, attended by Secretaries Alger and Long, Generals Miles and Schofield, and two senior Navy officers, Miles once again argued against sending battleships against forts while the Spanish fleet remained at large. He again warned of the danger from disease and stressed the Army's need for time to prepare. To the disappointment of Secretary Long, who favored a more aggressive policy, the conference decided that, throughout the summer, they would blockade Cuba, send arms and supplies to the insurgents, and annoy the Spaniards with small incursions by the Army. Adopting one of Miles's suggestions, the War Department the following day diverted six of the infantry regiments originally ordered to the Gulf Coast to Chickamauga Park, where they could train with cavalry and field artillery units. The rest of the Regular infantry was to remain encamped at Tampa, Mobile, and New Orleans as first planned.[64]

62. Miles, *The North American Review*, CLXVIII, 523. *War Investigating Commission*, VII, 3249. Capt. A. S. Barker, USN, and Asst. Adj. Gen. A. L. Wagner, "Memorandum for the Honorable Secretary of War," April 4, 1898, File No. 198209, AGO Records. Lt. Gen. John M. Schofield to President McKinley, April 20, 1898, Box 64, Schofield Papers. John J. McCook to McKinley, April 21, 1898; Andrew Carnegie to McKinley, April 27, 1898; McKinley Papers. For Navy doctrine on attacking forts, see *Affairs in Cuba*, 480.

63. Maj. Gen. Miles to Secretary Alger, April 18, 1898, *Correspondence*, I, 8-9. This letter may also be found in Miles, *The North American Review*, CLXVIII, 522-23, and Chadwick, *Spanish-American War*, II, 5. Had the Army been ready to attack before the rains began, Miles might have favored a more aggressive strategy; see Miles, *The North American Review*, CLXVIII, 524.

64. *War Investigating Commission*, I, 244, 440. Alger, *Spanish-American War*, 41-42. Mayo, *America of Yesterday*, 182-83. Maj. Gen. Miles to Secretary Alger, April 21, 1898. File No. 192302, AGO Records. File No. 74759, AGO Records, contains correspondence on the massing of the Regulars at Chickamauga. *Army and Navy Journal*, April 23, 1898. *New York Tribune*, April 24 and 25, 1898. *Washington Post*, April 10, 23, and 28, 1898.

VIII

President McKinley thus had settled on a war plan that promised the Army ample time for preparation before any major offensive action was demanded of it. Having made such a decision, he was perhaps predisposed to give way when the National Guard, after the passage of the Volunteer bill, demanded a militarily unjustified last-minute enlargement of the expeditionary force. The law of April 22 assured guardsmen of the right to enter the Volunteer service in their own organizations under their own officers, but the War Department's projected call for 60,000 men would permit only about half of the organizations that wanted to enlist to do so. A call for 60,000 men would confront state officials with a most unwelcome set of alternatives. Since the number to be called for was too small to allow them to send all their battalions and regiments into service, they could allow some to volunteer while keeping others at home, or they could recruit new regiments especially for war duty from among the officers and men of existing Guard units. Either way, politically powerful militia officers would be denied Volunteer commissions and the opportunities for promotion and glory that went with them. Officers and men alike lost no time in making known their discontent. At meetings in their armories, National Guard units passed resolutions that declared they would go to war together or not at all. Typical of many, the adjutant general of Maryland warned Corbin that, if the three regiments of his state's Guard were not taken intact at the first call, none of their members would volunteer.[65]

The War Department could not ignore these threats. If they had to have a Volunteer force, officials wanted it to be composed of trained National Guardsmen, and they could obtain the militiamen's services only if they enlisted of their own free will. Even more important in the eyes of the Regulars, the Hull bill, upon which the Army depended for reorganization and expansion, had not yet been passed. The success of the Volunteer measure had not reduced the Regulars' interest in the Hull bill—if anything, the Volunteer law had increased their sense of urgency about it. Many Regulars, who distrusted the competence of militia commanders and who themselves wanted the credit for victory, planned to enlarge their own units as rapidly as possible, if the Hull bill were passed. The expanded Army then might be able to turn Miles's proposed minor thrusts into a victorious major offensive before the Volunteers, who might require as much as six months to prepare for action, would be needed. But all of these possibilities hinged on passage of the Hull bill, and to obtain that end, the Administration was forced to satisfy the National Guard.[66]

65. Creagher, *Fourteenth Ohio*, 83. Holbrook, *Minnesota in War*, 15. *The New York Times*, April 11, 14, and 17, 1898. Adj. Gen. L. A. Wilmer of Maryland to Adj. Gen. Corbin, April 22, 1898, File No. 235852, AGO Records.

66. Asst. Adj. Gen. Theodore Schwan to Representative John A. T. Hull, April 18, 1898, Adj. Gen. Corbin to Representative Hull, April 22 and 23, 1898, and to Col. George W. Steele, April 23, 1898, Memorandum for Mr. Kohr, April 22, 1898, all in File No. 74259, AGO Records. *The New York Times*, April 28, 1898. *New York Tribune*, April 7, 1898.

On April 23, when he issued his first call for Volunteers under the new law, President McKinley did so. Instead of calling for 60,000 troops—the number military officials had been expecting—the President asked the states for 125,000. He had several reasons for this drastic change in plans. General Schofield, now playing his most disruptive part in the shaping of military policy, joined with other advisers to warn McKinley against repeating Lincoln's mistake of calling for too few troops at the outset of mobilization. They urged him to take advantage now of a martial ardor that casualty lists and reports of hard fighting might dampen later on. The strategy adopted on April 20 should allow ample time to organize and equip the larger force. During the summer, the spectacle of this mighty host arming, when combined with the contemplated land and sea pressures, might help break Spain's will to resist. But more important, apparently, than any other reason, the figure 125,000 equaled or exceeded the entire enlisted strength of the National Guard. Under a call for that number, all of the militia companies, battalions, and regiments whose officers wanted to lead them into service could be taken intact into the Volunteer Army, thus saving both the national government and the states from having to offend the politically well-organized guardsmen. The increase in the Volunteer force appalled General Miles, who saw no need for such a large army and knew that the bureaus were not prepared to equip it, but the President and Secretary Alger overrode his objections. On April 25 Alger telegraphed a request to each state governor for a portion of the 125,000 men, specifying the number of regiments, companies, or batteries the state was to organize and urging that the Volunteers be recruited as much as possible from the National Guard. On the same day, Congress declared war.[67]

Satisfied now with the Administration's military policy, the National Guardsmen finally allowed the Regulars their reorganization. Even with all the concessions they had received, the guardsmen might not have done so except for the fact that the law of April 22 required that Volunteer regiments be organized in the same way as Regular regiments. Without the Hull bill, Regular infantry regiments would have no battalions and only 10 companies, while most National Guard regiments had the modern 12-company 3-battalion organization. The guardsmen would have to reorganize upon entering federal service unless the Regulars also were given the modern formation. To keep their own units intact, the militiamen supported the revised reorganization measure that Representative Hull had introduced in the House on April 21.[68]

67. The President's decision to increase the call to 125,000 did not come until about April 21. *The New York Times*, April 18, 19, 22, 23, 24, and 26, 1898. *New York Tribune*, April 20, 23, and 24, 1898. *Washington Post*, April 16 and 19, 1898. Secretary Alger to Gen. Grenville M. Dodge, May 21, 1898; Dodge to Alger, May 25, 1898, Alger Papers. Schofield's views are in "General Schofield's Experiences in McKinley's Administration," Box 93, Schofield Papers; *Forty-Six Years*, 525; and *The New York Times*, May 26, 1898. The Quartermaster General received no advance notice of a call for 125,000 men; see *War Investigating Commission*, VII, 3783. Miles's views are in Miles, *Serving the Republic*, 270.

68. Hull, *The North American Review*, CLXVIII, 386-87. *The New York Times*, April 20, 21, and 22, 1898.

The new Hull bill differed from the original only in limiting the war-time enlisted force to 61,000 and in dropping the provision for recruiting districts. Like the amended original, the revised bill required a declaration of war before the President could implement the expansion provisions and provided for the immediate reduction of the Army to 27,000 men upon the conclusion of hostilities. To assure the acceptance intact of National Guard regiments that did not have three battalions, a new section authorized the President to muster in Volunteer units as organized under state law. As they had agreed to do earlier, the National Guardsmen now threw their weight behind the bill. It passed the House on April 23 and the Senate two days later. The President signed it into law on April 26.[69]

IX

Three elements of the situation had combined to bring the War Department stumbling unprepared into war. The course of Spanish-American diplomacy until very near the break in diplomatic relations promised peace and strongly discouraged active military measures. This state of affairs had little effect on the Navy—always maintained at high readiness—but it prevented the Army, which required much more preparation, from girding itself in time. A strategic doctrine that assigned to the fleet the primary offensive mission in a war to liberate Cuba and cast doubt on the necessity of a land invasion kept the War Department's mobilization plans modest in scale and probably encouraged the playing of politics with those plans. Then, at the very last moment, pressure from the National Guard, exerted through Congress, forced the doubling of the field army and its enlistment under a system that had politics and inefficiency built into it. War Department officials who had planned one mobilization now had to conduct an entirely different one on a larger scale. This fact, combined with the Army's shortage of supplies and trained men, with its as yet unremedied organizational weaknesses, and with further disruptive changes in McKinley's war strategy, accounts for most of the mistakes and misfortunes that ensued.

69. *Army and Navy Journal,* April 30, 1898, gives the text of the revised bill. *The New York Times,* April 22, 23, 24, 25, 26, and 27, 1898. Hull, *Forum,* XXV, 399, 401-2. The proviso on state organizations also allowed National Guard regiments to keep staff personnel not authorized for Regular units; see Hull, *The North American Review,* CLXVIII, 387.

Courtesy National Archives

Major General William R. Shafter

4

Mobilization Begins; Strategy Changes

I

Under the plan adopted on April 20, military operations began. On April 23, after Congress authorized armed intervention, the squadron at Key West established a blockade of Havana, Matanzas, Mariel, and Cardenas, all ports on Cuba's north coast. Four days later, Rear Admiral Sampson extended the blockade to the port of Cienfuegos on the south shore of the island. His patrols thereby closed all the seaports with rail connection to Havana. Following the decision of April 20, Sampson avoided attacks on Spanish batteries and confined his efforts to the capture of enemy merchantmen and to raids into the harbors with his smaller vessels. Initially, Sampson left the remainder of the Cuban coast unguarded for lack of ships to patrol it. Only after June 28 was he able to seal up completely the island's southern ports.[1]

To supplement the blockade, the War Department prepared an expedition to Cuba to show the flag and bring aid to the insurgents. On April 29 General Miles, with the approval of Secretary Alger, ordered Brig. Gen. William R. Shafter to assemble at Tampa 6,000 Regular infantry, cavalry, and field artillery. Under Navy escort, Shafter and his troops, on transports then being chartered by the Quartermaster's Department, were to sail to the south coast of Cuba and land at Cape Tunas, about 70 miles east of Cienfuegos. By marching inland, Shafter's force could contact the rebel army in central Cuba, led by General Máximo Gómez. Once he had joined Gómez, Shafter would turn over to him weapons, ammunition, and other supplies brought from the United States; he would collect information on the military situation in the island; and if the opportunity arose he would cooperate with Gómez in raids against the Spaniards. Miles ordered Shafter to avoid major battles; Shafter was to stay in Cuba for only a few days, would re-embark his men at the end of that time, and would return directly to the United States. Shafter's expedition, Miles concluded, was intended as a "reconnaissance in force, to give aid and succor to the insurgents, to render the Spanish forces as much injury as possible, [while] avoiding serious injury to your own command."[2]

1. Chadwick, *Spanish-American War*, I, 55, 141-43; II, 322-25. Long, *New American Navy*, I, 233-34. Mahan, *Lessons*, 61.

2. The April 29 order to Shafter is in Alger, *Spanish-American War*, 44-45, *Correspondence*, I, 9. *War Investigating Commission*, VII, 3191. *RSW, 1898*, II, 10-11. Miles, *The North American Review*, CLXVIII, 525. Chadwick, *Spanish-American War*, II, 5-6. John D. Miley, *In Cuba with Shafter*, 1-2.

Shafter's expedition never sailed. On the same day Miles issued the orders for it, Cervera's squadron steamed away from the Cap Verdes into the Atlantic, its destination unknown. In those days before the invention of radio, radar, and airplanes, a fleet on the high seas easily could disappear for weeks at a time. So it was with Cervera's vessels; for two weeks, the United States Navy knew nothing of their whereabouts. They might have turned back to Spain or they might be ploughing westward toward Cuba and a battle with the blockading fleet or toward the Atlantic Coast of the United States. In the probability that this supposedly fast, powerful enemy squadron was heading toward him, Rear Admiral Sampson could not detach ships to escort Shafter's transports to the south coast of Cuba. Accordingly, the War Department on April 30 postponed the expedition's departure until further notice and at the same time ordered Shafter to continue his preparations. He did so. By May 6 he had assembled about 6,000 troops and seven transports at Tampa, ready to move whenever orders came.[3]

Although it postponed Shafter's expedition, the War Department sent other aid to the Cuban rebels. During May, June, and July, mixed Cuban-American forces repeatedly invaded the island to run arms, supplies, and recruits to the insurgents. Usually 200 or 300 strong, these parties went ashore at unguarded coastal points, contacted rebel bands, and transferred stores and men to them. Several of these expeditions fought skirmishes with Spanish patrols; others missed their rendezvous with the Cubans. Most of them managed to land and deliver their cargoes. On May 26, for example, a party commanded by Capt. J. H. Dorst of the Fourth United States Cavalry sailed the steamer *Florida* into a rebel-controlled harbor in eastern Cuba. There, Dorst disembarked 400 armed Cubans to reinforce General García's army, along with 7,500 Springfield rifles, more than 1 million rounds of ammunition, 20,000 rations, large amounts of miscellaneous clothing and equipment, and about 100 horses and mules. He and his detachment then returned safely to Key West. Other officers duplicated Dorst's feat on a smaller scale. By the end of May, the Army and Navy had brought cooperation with the Cubans to a routine. Rebel officers bearing messages and information passed almost daily from the coast to the blockading fleet and then to the Army base at Tampa. Army expeditions smuggled weapons and stores to the Cubans, while General Miles arranged with staff officers of Gómez and García for Cuban assistance to an American invasion when and if one took place.[4]

3. Alger, *Spanish-American War*, 45-46. Chadwick, *Spanish-American War*, I, 69-70, 153; II, 7. Long, *New American Navy*, I, 238. Mahan, *Lessons*, 101. Miles, *The North American Review*, CLXVIII, 525. *The New York Times*, May 2, 3, 4, 5, and 7, 1898.

4. Alger, *Spanish-American War*, 42-44. Chadwick, *Spanish-American War*, I, 152-53; II, 9-12, 356-58. Miles, *The North American Review*, CLXVIII, 525. *Army and Navy Journal*, April 23, 1898. *The New York Times*, April 21 and May 6, 8, 10, and 29, 1898. *Washington Post*, April 28, 1898.

As the war of blockades and gun-running got under way, the War Department began recruiting and assembling the army that had been created by the laws of April 22 and 26. Seeking reliable units to carry out the first offensive, Secretary Alger, General Miles, and Adjutant General Corbin made special efforts to bring the Regular Army up to its authorized 61,000 men. On April 27 the War Department ordered all commanders of United States Infantry regiments to form their third battalions, and it ordered units of all branches to fill their skeleton companies and recruit to the prescribed war strength. Regiments could send recruiting parties wherever they wished; the organization that first put details into an area had exclusive right to draw on its manpower. Recruiting continued under these orders for the next three months. Men who enlisted as Regulars went first to Fort McPherson, a large post near Atlanta, to receive equipment and undergo basic training. Then they departed in small detachments to join their regiments.[5]

Hampered by the competing attractions of the swollen Volunteer service, the Regular Army could not fill its ranks quickly enough to monopolize offensive tasks. Hundreds of Regular officers accepted appointments, usually with increased rank, in the Volunteer Army and left their regiments without leaders for recruiting parties. When given a choice, most prospective soldiers preferred to enlist in Volunteer units, attracted by the easier discipline and by the chance to serve with friends and neighbors under familiar commanders. Even many discharged Regulars joined Volunteer regiments. By the end of May, the Army had enlisted only 8,500 of the 36,000 men needed to bring its formations to their war strength. Most Regular regiments left the country on expeditions before their recruits could join them and went into action against the Spaniards with less than half of their prescribed manpower. Not until late August, after an armistice had been signed, did the Regular Army attain its authorized numbers.[6]

While the Regular Army sought recruits, the Volunteers were mustering in their states. The act of April 22, under which Volunteer units were organized, contained, from the standpoint of military reformers, many progressive provisions. It perpetuated state control over the organization and officering of regiments, but beyond the regimental level, it gave the War Department, through the President, complete authority over the formation of the Army. The law's provisions for keeping state regiments at full strength during a long war, for the appointment of Regular officers to Volunteer units, and for the removal of unfit state commanders promised to alleviate some of the Volunteer system's worst defects. The effectiveness of these provisions, however, depended on how strictly the President and

5. *Army and Navy Journal*, April 30, 1898. *The New York Times*, April 28 and 29, May 26, 1898. RSW, *1898*, I, 275; II, 504-5. John Bigelow, Jr., *Reminiscences of the Santiago Campaign*, 39-41.

6. *The New York Times*, May 1, 7, 9, 18, and 26, June 5, 1898. RSW, *1898*, I, 257; II, 505. *Correspondence*, I, 13, 15, 47, 49, 309. Miles, *The North American Review*, CLXVIII, 517. Asst. Adj. Gen. Ward to Maj. Gen. J. J. Coppinger, June 20, 1898, File No. 223012, AGO Records.

the Secretary of War administered the law. In the first weeks of mobilization, professional soldiers, with good reason, feared that the Volunteer muster
would turn into a political circus in which the hard-won reforms would be
nullified.

The pressures of politics began to influence the formation of the Army
as soon as Secretary Alger apportioned among the states the 125,000 men
of the first call. On April 25 he informed each governor by telegraph how
many and what kind of units his state was to contribute and prescribed the
details of their organization. Alger urged the governors to fill their quotas
with National Guard units whenever possible, "for the reason that they are
armed, equipped, and drilled." When The Adjutant General's office drew
up these state quotas so as to obtain the proper balance of infantry, cavalry,
and artillery in an army of 125,000, it ignored in the specifications the composition of the existing militia. As a result, some states found that the ap-
portionment would not let them send all their regiments to war. Others were
ordered to furnish cavalry and artillery that they did not maintain. Governors, senators, congressmen, and National Guard officers descended upon
the White House and the War Department to demand changes in their quotas;
usually they obtained them. Pennsylvania had her 10 infantry regiments
increased to 15, the number in her National Guard. Ohio was allowed to
send 1,500 men over her quota so all of her militia could go. New York
received an extra troop of cavalry so she could muster in a full squadron
and the major commanding it. The only militia units excluded from the
prevailing favoritism were those the Army badly needed: the attached signal
and hospital companies of some state regiments, for which there were no
counterparts in the Regular organization to which Volunteer regiments were
supposed to conform. Following the letter of the law, federal officials refused
to accept them along with their parent units, and the state politicians failed
to fight for inclusion of the specialized groups in the quotas.[7]

Forced by these concessions to distribute the 125,000 Volunteers among
an increasing number of regiments, battalions, companies, and batteries,
the War Department accepted into service units far smaller than those
prescribed in the law. It mustered in under the first call a total of 5 cavalry
regiments, 16 field batteries, a heavy artillery regiment, and 119 infantry

7. Secretary Alger to the Governors, April 25, 1898, File No. 84869; Adj. Gen. Corbin to Adj.
Gen. J. B. Burbank of New York, April 27, 1898, Maj. Avery D. Andrews to Corbin, April 27,
1898, Sereno E. Payne to Corbin, April 27, 1898, Lt. Gen. J. M. Schofield to Corbin, April 28,
1898, Corbin to Andrews, April 29, 1898, and to Adj. Gen. Tillinghast of New York, May 4, 1898,
File No. 253334; Corbin to Gen. Howard Carroll, April 26, 1898, File No. 253351, AGO Records.
Edward Morrell to Gen. James H. Wilson, April 27, 1898, Box 17, Wilson Papers. Creagher, *Fourteenth Ohio*, 82, 90-92; this was one of the regiments that lost its hospital company. *War Investigating
Commission*, I, 170-71. GO 98, HQA, July 15, 1898, *GO/AGO, 1898*, further illustrates the Administration's solicitude for militia officers. *The New York Times*, April 27, 29, and 30, May 1,
1898. *New York Tribune*, April 28 and 30, 1898.

regiments, plus detached battalions, batteries, and companies. Many of these formations contained too many officers and too few enlisted men for effective operations. This result pleased state politicians, who were interested in Army patronage, but it enraged professional soldiers, who were concerned with combat efficiency.[8]

With the exception of Kansas, where the Populist governor hated the militia and insisted on creating a new force for war duty, most of the states organized their Volunteers around existing National Guard units, a process the quota changes were designed to facilitate. Maine and Rhode Island, each of which furnished only one regiment under the first call, established new regiments especially for the war and recruited individual guardsmen from other units to fill their ranks. Most of the larger states tried to send their militia organizations intact. They polled the members of each regiment to find out how many would enlist in federal service, replaced stay-at-homes with new recruits, and recommissioned the regimental and company officers as colonels, majors, captains, and lieutenants of United States Volunteers. Some states, as the law of April 22 allowed, requested the assignment of Regulars to give their regiments professional stiffening. The states usually granted a leave of absence from the militia to each guardsman who volunteered. Some retained in the militia the men who did not volunteer; others discharged them. To replace the regiments that were going into national service, New York and Ohio formed temporary wartime militia. These troops were to maintain public order at home and stand ready to answer additional calls for Volunteers.[9]

Once the composition of its contingent had been settled, each state assembled its Volunteers at a central point for enrollment in the United States Army. The citizen-soldiers left their home districts, to the cheers of crowds of well-wishers and the salutes of bands, cannon, and steam whistles. Usually they spent a week or two at their state concentration camp, drilling and undergoing physical examinations. Then a mustering officer sent by the War Department swore each company into federal service. The enrollment proceeded rapidly. Arizona, New Mexico, and Massachusetts on May 2 and 3 were the first states and territories to report their men sworn in. By mid-

8. *RSW, 1898*, I, 258; *1899*, I, Pt. 2, pp. 10-11. *The New York Times*, April 29, May 1 and 26, June 2, 1898. For the revisions in company strength, see table sent with Alger to the Governors, April 25, 1898, File No. 84869, AGO Records.

9. New York Adjutant General's Office, *New York in the Spanish-American War, 1898*, I, 24-25. Maine Adjutant General, *Report for 1898*, 12-16. Ohio Adjutant General, *Report for 1898*, 630, 658, 865. Holbrook, *Minnesota in War*, 17. *Army and Navy Journal*, June 11, 1898. *The New York Times*, May 5, 1898. Gov. Andrew E. Lee of South Dakota to President McKinley, April 26, 1898, McKinley Papers. For Kansas' military policy, see Funston, *Memories*, 150-53; many guardsmen enlisted as individuals in the governor's new regiments and elected their former officers to command them.

May, according to Adjutant General Corbin, over 60,000 had been enrolled. Two weeks later, most of the 125,000 Volunteers of the first call had entered service.[10]

The War Department lost no time in planning the organization and equipping of the gathering masses. On April 26 General Miles proposed that all the Volunteers be held in their state camps for thirty days after their muster-in to receive clothing, arms, accoutrements, and basic training while the War Department appointed generals and staff officers for them, selected concentration points, and accumulated supplies. Only after these preliminaries had been completed, Miles said, should the regiments entrain for the assembly camps for organization into brigades, divisions, and army corps. McKinley and Alger adopted this plan and on May 6, following another proposal by Miles, they issued orders for the deployment of the Volunteers. Under these orders, some 37 infantry regiments and assorted cavalry and artillery units were to assemble at Chickamauga Park, and 24 more infantry regiments, plus a small force of cavalry and artillery, were to concentrate near Washington, D.C., at a new camp in northern Virginia, later named Camp Alger. These units probably would comprise the army that would invade Cuba. Smaller contingents were to mass at San Francisco, San Antonio, New Orleans, Tampa, and Mobile. General reserve and coast defense forces, consisting of 47 infantry regiments, 17 troops of cavalry, and 18 heavy and 6 light batteries, were to remain in their states, under command of the geographical departments. The regiments ordered out of their states were to move only after they had received their weapons, uniforms, and field equipment.[11]

II

By the time the War Department issued this concentration order, framed to execute the strategy set on April 20, the character of the war and, in particular, of the Army's mission in it had undergone radical change. The change occurred at the insistence of President William McKinley.

On February 16, 1899, while defending the annexation of the Philippine Islands before the Home Market Club of Boston, McKinley enunciated a remarkable doctrine of strategic fatalism.

10. Alger, *Spanish-American War*, 21. *Army and Navy Journal*, May 7, 14, and 21, 1898. *The New York Times*, May 1, 4, 7, 10, 12, 13, 15, 18, 23, 27, and 31, 1898. *RSW, 1898*, I, 260. Secretary Alger to Gen. G. M. Dodge, May 27, 1898, Alger Papers. For glimpses of the muster in the states, see Creagher, *Fourteenth Ohio*, 84-87, 89-90, 95; Holbrook, *Minnesota in War*, 18 and 48; and White, *McClure's Magazine*, XI, 199.

11. Maj. Gen. Nelson A. Miles to Secretary Alger, April 26, May 3 and 6, 1898, File No. 192302, AGO Records. The April 26 letter, with the recommended length of the Volunteers' stay in camp doubled, evidently by postwar hindsight, is in Miles, *The North American Review*, CLXVIII, 517-18. Q. M. Gen. M. I. Ludington to Chief Quartermaster, Department of the Lakes, May 8, 1898, *War Investigating Commission*, I, 440. *Army and Navy Journal*, May 14, 1898.

Major General Wesley Merritt, U.S.A., Commander of the Expedition to Manila.

President William McKinley tours an army camp.

What nation [he asked] was ever able to write an accurate programme of the war upon which it was entering, much less decree in advance the scope of its results? Congress can declare war, but a higher power decrees its bounds and fixes its relations and responsibilities. The President can direct the movement of soldiers on the field and fleets upon the sea, but he cannot foresee the close of such movements or prescribe their limits. He can not anticipate or avoid the consequences, but he must meet them. No accurate map of nations engaged in war can be traced until the war is over, nor can the measure of responsibility be fixed till the last gun is fired and the verdict embodied in the stipulations of peace.[12]

War, then, was an uncontrollable process that, once entered upon, dictated its own course and results. The statesman could do little but ride the whirlwind and cope with the chaos it left behind. This theory might be dismissed as an attempt to rationalize a policy that was under bitter public attack except for the fact that it renders comprehensible the way McKinley made military decisions in May of 1898. During that month, in response primarily to the course of naval operations, he expanded both the political and the military aims of the conflict. As he did so, he made unanticipated new demands upon the Army and forced the War Department into a period of hectic, confused improvisation.

Dramatic revelations of the Spanish Navy's weakness and inactivity precipitated McKinley's change of strategy, and the first such revelation occurred in the Far East. On May 1, 1898, the United States Navy's Asiatic Squadron, a small force of unarmored cruisers under the command of Commodore George Dewey, attacked a similarly small Spanish flotilla in Manila Bay. The Navy Department had been planning this offensive since 1896 as a diversion to keep part of the Spanish fleet out of the Caribbean. Also, Navy men hoped, pressure on her valuable colony in the Philippines would help induce Spain to withdraw from Cuba. Dewey's attack on May 1 proved unexpectedly decisive. In a few hours' combat, his vessels, without suffering serious loss or damage, sank or set on fire every Spanish ship. Dewey now controlled Manila Bay, and the city itself lay at his mercy. He telegraphed to Washington on May 7 that he could take Manila at any time, if he had the troops to occupy it. Dewey's victory opened up a new front in the war, and at the same time it indicated that Americans had overestimated the fighting power of the Spanish Navy.[13]

12. McKinley's remarks are quoted in *The New York Times*, February 17, 1899.

13. Alger, *Spanish-American War*, 318-24. Chadwick, *Spanish-American War*, I, 89-93, 154, 156-57, 170-71, 211-13. Grenville and Young, *Politics, Strategy, and American Diplomacy*, 269-70, 272, 276-77. Long, *New American Navy*, I, 181-82, 186-87. Mayo, *America of Yesterday*, 213-14. Nunez, *Guerra*, V, 113-16, 125, 131-33. Louis J. Halle, "1898: The United States in the Pacific," *Military Affairs*, XX, 70-80. Holabird, *United Service*, VIII, 26-27, urges a similar attack on India, in the event of war with Great Britain.

In the Atlantic, also, the Spanish fleet by the first week of May appeared less formidable. In fact, it had not appeared at all. The Cape Verdes squadron had left its anchorage on April 29. By the early days of May, according to American calculations based on its supposed rate of speed, it should have reached the Caribbean. Since the squadron had not yet been sighted there, American naval authorities concluded that it probably had returned to Spain to collect reinforcements before engaging the United States fleet. On May 3 Rear Admiral Sampson, with most of his armored vessels, left his station off Havana and steamed eastward toward San Juan, Puerto Rico, intending to intercept Cervera if he were heading for that port instead of Havana. On his arrival off San Juan on May 12, Sampson found no Spanish ships. After bombarding the city's fortifications for three hours with little observable result, he withdrew westward. The failure of the Spanish squadron to appear in the Caribbean opened the way for an early American invasion of Cuba and revived pressure within the Administration for a quick move by the Army.[14]

As the first step in his new aggressive policy, the President decided to send troops to Manila to exploit Dewey's victory. Because of communications difficulties, Dewey's official report of his battle did not reach Washington until May 7, but by May 3 the authorities knew from press reports the overwhelming extent of his triumph. On May 3, at the request of Secretary Alger, General Miles submitted a plan for dispatching 5,000 men to Manila. The proposed force, intended by Miles only to secure the Philippine capital, would contain two battalions of Regular infantry, two troops of Regular cavalry, three Volunteer infantry regiments, and two Volunteer heavy batteries. All the Volunteers were drawn from California, Oregon, and Washington. Then being mustered into service in their states, they easily could assemble at West Coast ports for transport. On May 4 the President directed the concentration at San Francisco of the troops designated by Miles, "for such service as may be ordered hereafter." This disposition formed part of the May 6 Volunteer deployment order. By May 13, when Dewey, now promoted to the rank of Rear Admiral, formally requested the dispatch of a garrison for Manila, the requisite troops were already gathering at San Francisco.[15]

14. Chadwick, *Spanish-American War*, I, 214-27, 229-35. Mahan, *Lessons*, 79-80, 101-2, 116. *Army and Navy Journal*, May 14, 1898. *The New York Times*, May 5, 6, 7, 10, and 11, 1898.

15. *Correspondence*, II, 635. Alger, *Spanish-American War*, 326. Chadwick, *Spanish-American War*, I, 208-11; II, 363-64. Mayo, *America of Yesterday*, 187. Miles, *Serving the Republic*, 271. Leon Wolff, *Little Brown Brother: How the United States Purchased and Pacified the Philippine Islands at the Century's Turn*, 59-60. *The New York Times*, May 2, 4, 6, 8, and 9, 1898. Rear Adm. George Dewey to the Secretary of the Navy, May 13, 1898, McKinley Papers.

During the remaining weeks of May, the Administration radically increased the size and importance of the Manila expedition. On May 11 Secretary Alger told the staff bureaus that the army would be expanded from 5,000 men to 10,000 or 12,000. The next day, the Administration appointed Maj. Gen. Wesley Merritt, a Civil War veteran with much command experience and the second-ranking officer of the Regular establishment, to lead the growing force. Merritt's assignment to Manila surprised many officers, who had expected a soldier of his rank and ability to be sent to the Caribbean, supposedly the more important theater of operations. On May 16 the War Department designated Merritt's command as the Department of the Pacific, the jurisdiction of which would extend over the entire Philippine Archipelago, and on May 29 the department assigned still more men to Merritt, increasing his force to a full 20,000 troops. On June 21, at Merritt's suggestion, the War Department reconstituted the Philippine expedition as the Eighth Army Corps.[16]

The political purpose behind this enlargement of the Manila force was obscure. Since Dewey's victory, many businessmen and politicians, interested in expanding American influence in the Far East, had been demanding that the United States annex the Philippines as a military and commercial outpost. While he prepared to invade the Islands, McKinley gave little sign whether or not he agreed with these views. Senator Henry Cabot Lodge, an expansionist Republican, believed that the President was committed to territorial aggrandizement overseas, but he relied for evidence more on his interpretation of McKinley's remarks than on any clear statement of the President's purpose. General Merritt, after his first conference with the President about the Philippines, expressed confusion, as he indicated in a letter to McKinley: "I do not yet know whether it is your desire to subdue and hold all of the Spanish territory in the islands, or merely to seize and hold the capital."[17]

Within the Army, Generals Miles and Merritt disagreed about the objectives of the Manila force. They aired their differences in mid-May in an argument over how many Regulars the enlarged Manila expedition should contain. Merritt, who demanded twice as many Regulars as Miles wanted to assign him, insisted that he needed these seasoned fighters for the task of "conquering a territory 7,000 miles from our base, defended by a regularly trained and acclimated army of from 10,000 to 20,000 men, and inhabited by 14,000,000 people, the majority of whom will regard us with the intense

16. Adj. Gen. Corbin to the Chief of Ordnance, May 11, 1898, File No. 78939, AGO Records. *Correspondence*, II, 637, 649, 680, 700-701, 703, 705-6, 708. Capt. William Thaddeus Sexton, *Soldiers in the Sun: An Adventure in Imperialism*, 19-20. *The New York Times*, May 8, 13, and 20, 1898.

17. Merritt's remarks are in *Correspondence*, II, 645-46. Henry Cabot Lodge to Theodore Roosevelt, May 24, June 15, July 12 and 23, 1898, *Roosevelt-Lodge Correspondence*, I, 299-300, 311, 323-24, 330. LaFeber, *New Empire*, 354-61, 380-92. Morgan, *Road to Empire*, 74-75.

hatred born of race and religion." Miles, in defense of his own estimate, said that Merritt exaggerated both the size of the Spanish garrison in the Philippines and the number of the archipelago's inhabitants. Besides, "The force ordered at this time is not expected to carry on a war to conquer extensive territory." Instead, it was to establish "a strong garrison to command the harbor of Manila, and to relieve the . . . fleet under Admiral Dewey with the least possible delay." Merritt clearly envisioned his army occupying the whole island group, while Miles expected only to occupy and hold the port of Manila and looked with disapproval on any suggestion of broader conquests.[18]

McKinley's formal instructions to General Merritt, issued on May 19, implied an extensive campaign but still left unclear its long-range purpose. The Navy's success, the President wrote, had made it "necessary in the further prosecution of the measures adopted by this government for the purpose of bringing about an honorable and durable peace with Spain, to send an army of occupation to the Philippines for the twofold purpose of completing the reduction of the Spanish power in that quarter and of giving order and security to the islands while in the possession of the United States." He went on to direct the establishment of a temporary American military government in the Philippines. Probably the President had not yet settled on a policy for the Islands. Following his belief in the self-controlling nature of war, he was simply taking the next logical military step, exploitation of a successful attack with fresh forces. If that exploitation led to territorial conquests, the President would decide what to do with them after the shooting stopped. While this strategy was rational from McKinley's peculiar point of view, his failure to define political objectives created complex difficulties for the generals in command at Manila. Certainly, the military prosecution of the campaign would lead to political commitments from which the nation could not easily extricate itself.[19]

Merritt eventually received about 5,000 Regulars for his expedition, three full infantry regiments, an artillery battalion, and six troops of cavalry. Volunteer infantry, cavalry, and field artillery units, most of them from states west of the Mississippi, constituted the bulk of the Eighth Corps. By late May, over half of Merritt's 20,000 men had reached San Francisco, where they drilled and received weapons and supplies while quartermasters up and down the Pacific Coast chartered steamers to carry them to Manila. The rest of the troops arrived within the next three or four weeks.[20]

18. The exchange, which took place between May 13 and 18, is printed in *Correspondence*, II, 638, 643-45, 647-49. See also *The New York Times*, May 17, 1898.

19. McKinley's instructions to Merritt are in *Correspondence*, II, 676-78. May, ed., *Ultimate Decision*, 98-100.

20. *Correspondence*, II, 659-60, 662, 664, 666, 671, 680, 683-85, 687-89, 696-700, 705-9, 715-16, 736. Chadwick, *Spanish-American War*, II, 370. *The New York Times*, May 11, 12, 13, 18, 19, 20, 23, 24, 30, and June 2, 1898.

III

At the same time that he ordered the invasion of the Philippines, McKinley reversed his earlier plans for Cuba and called for an immediate assault on Havána. A number of military and political considerations, combined with the failure of the Cape Verdes squadron to challenge the blockade of the island, led the President to this decision. The results of the first weeks of blockade generated increasing pressure within the Navy for an early land attack. The blockade absorbed most of the Navy's maneuverable forces and left the fleet without reserves to counter unexpected moves by the enemy or to strike at the Spanish mainland. The available ships were inadequate in number to close all the minor ports on Cuba's south coast; through them, supplies from Jamaica, Mexico, Europe, and even North America trickled in to the Spaniards. The blockade thus proved less decisive than the authorities had hoped. It forced the Spanish troops in Cuba to tighten their belts and caused great suffering among the urban poor as food prices shot upward, but it did not break enemy resistance. As Theodore Roosevelt had put it before the war, "Spaniards starve well." The constant patrolling was hard on the ships; hence, breakdowns in machinery plagued Sampson's fleet. If the blockade dragged on through the summer, the fleet would face danger from Caribbean hurricanes, one of which, if it should strike in the wrong place at the wrong time, could cripple the Navy. Navy officers demanded with increasing vehemence that the Army invade Cuba and thus relieve them of their onerous and possibly dangerous task. At the very least, Navy men said, troops could seize a Cuban harbor in which ships could coal, make repairs, and if necessary take refuge from the violent storms of the area. Since the beginning of the Cuban crisis, Secretary of the Navy Long, seconded by his assistant, Roosevelt, had favored an early invasion if one could be launched without risking the battle fleet. Now, in these first days of May, Long expressed the impatience of his service in Cabinet meetings and war councils.[21]

A fresh assessment of the danger from disease reinforced the Navy's demand for a more aggressive strategy. Early in May, President McKinley's medical advisers decided that they had overestimated the hazards of a rainy season campaign. Further study of the information available, along with reports from American residents of prewar Cuba, indicated to the experts that the death rates in earlier Cuban operations and among Spanish troops in the war then being waged resulted from poor sanitation rather than from any inherent deadliness in the climate. The medical authorities now argued

21. Chadwick, *Spanish-American War*, I, 150, 215-16; II, 323. Goode, *With Sampson*, 35-36. Long, *New American Navy*, I, 198-99. Mahan, *Lessons*, 66-67, 185-86, 194. Mayo, *America of Yesterday*, 188-89. Nunez, *Guerra*, III, 137-42, considers the Havana blockade more effective than do the American writers. Theodore Roosevelt to Robley Dunglison Evans, April 20, 1898, and to Benjamin F. Tracy, April 21, 1898, in Morison, *Roosevelt Letters*, II, 818-19. *Army and Navy Journal*, May 28, 1898. *The New York Times*, May 9 and 29, 1898.

that, if American troops ate the proper foods, camped on high ground, and kept themselves clean, they could march and fight in Cuba in perfectly healthy circumstances. This assessment was based on the theory, then widely accepted, that malaria and yellow fever were filth-bred diseases. Few scientists yet suspected the mosquito as the disseminator of these scourges.[22]

Political and diplomatic considerations also dictated an early invasion. To both American and European experts, it seemed likely during the first week of May that the Spaniards had decided not to risk a fleet action in the Caribbean. Instead, they would keep their warships in home waters, counting on the unreadiness of the United States Army—of which Spanish authorities were well aware—to force a long period of inactivity. During this period, European Powers friendly to Spain might intervene on her behalf. If this were Spain's strategy, only quick, decisive ground action in Cuba could frustrate it. There was also the question of American authority in Cuba after the war. Although he permitted military cooperation with the insurgents, McKinley refused to recognize them as the legal government of Cuba. He claimed for the United States an independent, dominant role in determining the political future of the island. Victories won by American troops on Cuban soil would constitute firm backing for such a claim.[23]

On May 2 President McKinley conferred at the White House with Secretaries Alger and Long, who brought with them their chief uniformed advisers, General Miles for the Army and Adm. Montgomery Sicard for the Navy. McKinley now endorsed the Navy's demand for an immediate invasion, and Secretary Alger, voicing an optimism about the readiness of the Volunteers that was not shared by General Miles, agreed to attempt it. The five men decided to attack Havana with 40,000 to 50,000 troops, a number Alger thought could be prepared for action within three or four weeks. The campaign would begin as soon as the men and ships were ready, without regard to the approaching rainy season. It would follow a plan outlined on April 4 by the Army-Navy war board, under which a vanguard of Regulars, supported by the fleet, would seize the small port of Mariel, 26 miles west of Havana, and fortify it as a base camp. As rapidly as they could be sent down, the first ready Volunteer regiments would join the Regulars at Mariel. When enough troops had arrived, the whole force would

22. *The New York Times*, May 6, 10, and 25, 1898.

23. Grenville and Young, *Politics, Strategy, and American Diplomacy*, 285-86. Healy, *United States in Cuba*, 22-28. Morgan, *Road to Empire*, 62-63, 75. *Army and Navy Journal*, May 14, 1898. *The New York Times*, May 1, 4, 8, 9, 10, and 24, 1898. Translation of article from *The Times* of Paris, November 9, 1897; Albert Shaw to John Addison Porter, March 4, 1898; L. P. Morton to President McKinley, March 20, 1898, McKinley Papers. For a Spanish report on the weakness of the United States Army and National Guard, see "Poder Militar y Naval de los Estados Unidos en 1896," in *Selected Professional Papers Translated from European Military Publications*, 140-48. McKinley based the United States military government of Cuba on the right of armed conquest; see McKinley to Maj. Gen. John R. Brooke, December 22, 1898, in Olcott, *McKinley*, II, 196-97.

advance on Havana from the west and south. Attacking along this line, the troops could capture the city's water works and bring the Cuban capital under close siege. In contrast to Sampson's earlier scheme, this plan left the hard fighting to the Army, with the fleet's action confined to covering the landings and supporting the attack with gunfire where possible. General Miles, who still opposed mounting an invasion during the rainy season and who doubted the feasibility of such an attack at this time, dissented from the May 2 decision, but McKinley, Alger, and Long overruled him.[24]

McKinley and his advisers thus had decided on a major offensive even before most of the troops required for it had taken their oaths of allegiance to the United States. Yet, to McKinley and Alger, both of whom were veteran soldiers but neither of whom ever had commanded a formation larger than a regiment, there seemed reasonable chance that the action would succeed. The Regular vanguard, about 15,000 strong, had already assembled at Chickamauga and the Gulf ports. Although under battle strength, these regiments could go into action at once if necessary. At the April 16 conferences on the Volunteer bill, state officials had been expansive in their promises of ready troops to back up the Regulars if war came. The adjutant general of Pennsylvania, for example, told McKinley his state could put 8,000 "well-armed and well-disciplined" National Guardsmen in the field within thirty-six hours of a call. The adjutant general of Ohio pledged 6,500 battle-worthy soldiers, and a New York commander promised 14,000 within twenty-four hours. Professional soldiers in the War Department, familiar with the National Guard's shortcomings, took these promises at less than their face value; nevertheless, they expected as many as 25,000 guardsmen, most of them from the efficient New York and Pennsylvania militia, to enter service in condition to take the field within five or six weeks of enrollment. Knowing the Regulars' distrust of the militia and recalling the prodigies of valor performed by green regiments in the Civil War, McKinley and Alger may well have considered this estimate overly pessimistic. Certainly the rapidity with which the states were assembling their men for muster augured well. Allowing perhaps four weeks for the best of the Volunteer regiments to complete preparations and assuming that the Regulars would require much of that time to assemble, embark, sail to Mariel, land, and fortify a base, the necessary reinforcements should be available by the time a beachhead had been secured.[25]

24. Alger, *Spanish-American War*, 46-47. Chadwick, *Spanish-American War*, II, 8. Long, *New American Navy*, II, 9. Morgan, *McKinley*, 389-90. *RSW, 1898*, I, 82. John D. Long to Secretary Alger, May 6, 1898, Alger Papers. Capt. A. S. Barker, USN, and Asst. Adj. Gen. A. L. Wagner, "Memorandum for the Honorable Secretary of War," April 4, 1898, File No. 198209, AGO Records. *The New York Times*, May 2 and 10, 1898.

25. *The New York Times*, April 17, 24, and 25, 1898. *New York Tribune*, April 22, 1898. Adj. Gen. C. W. Tillinghast of New York to Adj. Gen. Corbin, May 9, 1898, File No. 253334, AGO Records, illustrates the states' expansive promises of ready troops. Alger's optimism went back

An optimistic report from Maj. Gen. William R. Shafter, the troop commander at Tampa, confirmed McKinley's and Alger's commitment to an early start. When the War Department on April 30 canceled Shafter's reconnaissance in force, it had enjoined him to continue preparing his men and ships for an assault and had suggested that he consult the Navy commander at Key West to determine what operations would be feasible in the near future. During the first days of May, after analyzing all the information about Cuba then at hand and after sending one of his staff officers to confer with the Navy's men at Key West, Shafter concluded that the 12,000 to 15,000 Regulars then massed at Chickamauga and the Gulf ports could capture Mariel and, possibly, Havana if they were allowed to attack immediately. According to the naval officers, the blockading fleet could escort Shafter's transports and support his landing at any time, while still remaining in position to fight Cervera if he appeared off Havana. In a report written May 7 and 8, Shafter conveyed these facts to the War Department. He declared that his troops could embark for a campaign at any time after May 12. They could carry out the order of April 29, or they could "take possession of, and hold permanently, some point on the north coast of Cuba, to be used as a base of operations." Shafter sent this report and other pertinent documents to Washington by the hand of his personal aide, Lt. John D. Miley. Upon his arrival in the capital on the morning of May 9, Miley at once delivered the papers to General Miles.[26]

In response to Shafter's report that the intended vanguard was ready to move, Alger and Miles on May 9 instructed him to embark his command, along with reinforcements to be sent him from other camps. The force was to sail to Mariel, capture it, and fortify the area against counterattack. Other troops would follow him from the United States as rapidly as they were mustered in and equipped. The assault force, to be commanded when complete by General Miles, would build up to 70,000 Regulars and Volunteers and, when fully prepared, would march on Havana. The participants later differed on how soon this second phase of the operation was to begin. General Shafter said after the war that he had expected to hold Mariel with his Regulars until fall, but officials in Washington apparently planned to reinforce him with Volunteers within a few weeks of his initial landing and to launch the main attack no later than mid-June.[27]

---

to prewar days; see Long, *New American Navy*, II, 145, 151, and unsigned Memorandum, dated May, 1898, McKinley Papers. Except for shortages of equipment, the first Volunteer regiments to reach Chickamauga Park could have taken the field almost at once, in the opinion of the veteran Maj. Gen. James H. Wilson; see *War Investigating Commission*, IV, 954-55.

26. Chadwick, *Spanish-American War*, II, 8. Miley, *In Cuba*, 4-6. *War Investigating Commission*, VII, 3788-89. Brig. Gen. William Ludlow to Adj. Gen. Corbin, May 11 and 16 and June 5, 1898, Box 1, Corbin Papers. *The New York Times*, May 8, 1898.

27. Alger, *Spanish-American War*, 47. *Correspondence*, I, 11. Chadwick, *Spanish-American War*, II, 9. Miles, *Serving the Republic*, 272. Miley, *In Cuba*, 6-7. Miles, *The North American Review*, CLXVIII, 523. *War Investigating Commission*, I, 244; VII, 3191. *Army and Navy Journal*, October 15 and December 3, 1898; the latter issue quotes General Shafter's views on the intent of the campaign.

At the insistence of Secretary Long, who needed a few days to assemble warships for a convoy, the Administration on May 10 postponed Shafter's sailing until May 16. At the same time, the War Department pushed forward its preparations for the assault. Between May 9 and 14, all the Regular infantry, cavalry, and artillery at Chickamauga, under orders from General Miles, left for Tampa, Mobile, and New Orleans. They reinforced Shafter's command to about 12,000 men. On May 10 Miles instructed Shafter to embark as many of his infantry as the transports then at Tampa could accommodate and move them at once to Key West, fully supplied for the campaign. This transfer of troops would bring part of the Army closer to its objective and relieve congestion in the camps and on the docks at Tampa. Miles then announced plans to move Army headquarters to Tampa, where he would take personal command of the invasion.[28]

Shafter's Regulars were to constitute the advance guard of the attack. To provide the main body, the War Department tried to modify the Volunteer concentration plan of May 6 so as to assemble at once the best-trained and -equipped state troops for rapid dispatch to the front. On May 7, even before the attack order went to Shafter, Secretary Alger asked the governors to outfit their regiments one at a time rather than all simultaneously, so as to prepare a few for immediate action. As troops streamed into the state camps during the first week of May, Adjutant General Corbin canvassed the nation by telegraph, seeking ready or nearly ready regiments. On May 12 he reported to Alger that 30 infantry regiments and 4 field batteries, containing in all about 30,000 officers and men, most of them from the efficient National Guards of the northeastern seaboard and the upper Mississippi Valley states, had been mustered in and partially equipped for active service. The War Department promptly ordered most of these units to Chickamauga Park, which had been designated the assembly point for the first Volunteer field force. The department directed a few other units from East Coast states to Tampa and Key West. In the course of this hurried attempt at troop concentration, some regiments stumbled about under a confusing barrage of contradictory orders. The Seventy-first New York Infantry, for instance, loaded all baggage on steamers for shipment to Tampa by water, only to wait aboard ship for a day and a half and then unload it all again to go south by rail.[29]

28. *Correspondence*, I, 11 and 12. Mayo, *America of Yesterday*, 192. Miley, *In Cuba*, 8. *War Investigating Commission*, VI, 3065. Adj. Gen. Corbin to Maj. Gen. J. F. Wade, May 10, 1898, File No. 78651; Asst. Adj. Gen. J. C. Gilmore to Corbin, May 10 and 11, 1898, File No., 192302; Corbin to Maj. Gen. J. R. Brooke, May 9 and 10, 1898, Brooke to Corbin, May 10, 1898, and Corbin to Commanding General, Department of the Gulf, May 11, 1898, File No. 223021, AGO Records. *The New York Times*, May 11, 12, 13, and 15, 1898.

29. Adj. Gen. Corbin to Maj. Gen. J. R. Brooke, May 5, 1898, File No. 77608; Alger to the Governors of the States, May 13, 1898, File No. 79638; Corbin to Alger, May 12, 1898, File No. 813553; Alger to the Governors, May 7, 1898, File No. 239604; movement orders to the New York regiments are in File No. 253334, AGO Records. *Correspondence*, I, 12. *War Investigating Commission*, III, 108. *Army and Navy Journal*, May 14, 1898. *The New York Times*, May 9, 10, and 11, 1898.

In the course of these maneuvers, it became evident that even the most conservative estimates of the Volunteers' readiness had erred on the side of optimism. The authorities, beguiled by state officials' boasts that their militiamen would step forward as one in response to a call to arms, had assumed that the vast majority of the first 125,000 Volunteers would be National Guardsmen who had undergone at least elementary drill and musketry instruction. The Volunteer Army then forming did in fact consist largely of National Guard organizations. However, most of the men who filled their ranks were not the organizations' peacetime members. The latter had failed to make good the promises of their leaders. Many could not commit themselves to two years of war service for reasons eloquently summed up by an indignant New Yorker: "Does Volunteer call expect Home Guard with delicate, sickly wife with three infants all pecuniarily disadvantaged to volunteer in this stage of war, thereby causing family financial smash . . .?" The members of the Seventh Regiment of New York, one of the best-equipped and best-trained militia units in the country, voted not to enlist, in the fear that, once in federal service, their regiment would lose its identity. Out of 550 officers and men in another New York regiment, 330 including the colonel declined to enter federal service.[30]

Most National Guard units contained in peacetime only about half of the men prescribed in the law for Volunteer formations. Of their existing members, a third to a half, on the average, either refused to enlist or failed the Army physical examination. The states still might have produced a trained first line by consolidating and reorganizing units, as the smaller New England states did, but most officials regarded such action as politically unthinkable. Instead, Guard commanders brought their regiments up to the minimum strength needed for muster by filling their ranks with new recruits, most of whom had no previous military experience and some of whom later were found medically unfit for duty. The resulting Volunteer force was in reality a mass of undrilled civilians commanded by National Guard officers and stiffened by a thin cadre of old militiamen. For example, in the New York regiments, considered at the time among those most nearly ready for the field, up to half of the men were new recruits, totally untrained.[31]

30. The quotation is from W. N. Sherwood to President McKinley, April 25, 1898, McKinley Papers. *The New York Times*, May 7, 12, and 17, 1898. An internal feud in the New York National Guard also influenced the Seventh Regiment's decision; see *New York Tribune*, April 28, 1898, and *The New York Times*, February 12, 1899.

31. *RSW, 1898*, I, 697-98; *1899*, I, Pt. 2, p. 11. *War Investigating Commission*, I, 276-77, 610. Gen. W. B. Bend, "In What Way Can the National Guard be Modified so as to Make It an Effective Reserve to the Regular Army in both War and Peace?" *JMSI*, XXVII, 372-73. Hull, *The North American Review*, CLXVIII, 391. Miles, *The North American Review*, CLXVIII, 517. Carter, *American Army*, 270-71. *The New York Times*, May 13, 15, and 17, 1898.

The War Department's hopes for an early offensive by the Volunteers rested on the supposed ability of the states to clothe and equip their troops at least partially. When Secretary Alger had informed the governors of their quotas late in April, he had asked them to turn over to their Volunteers all of their militia's arms, uniforms, tentage, and transportation. The results were disappointing. Few states could arm or clothe the men they added to their regiments to meet federal standards. Of the equipment in the hands of their troops, more was obsolete or worn out than even the gloomiest prewar reports had indicated. The Chief of Ordnance, who had expected to replace the equipment of about a third of the guardsmen who volunteered, had to replace all the equipment of many regiments. Minor but crucial items of material were in short supply or nonexistent. The New York troops, for example, lacked shelter tents and mess kits. As a further complication, several governors, who distrusted federal promises of reimbursement, withheld their equipment from the Volunteers, and their recruits entrained for camp in civilian clothes. Late in May, when a considerable number of Volunteers had assembled at Chickamauga and Camp Alger, the commanders at those places could report not a single state regiment ready to take the field.[32]

At the same time that the Volunteers' unreadiness became apparent, other insurmountable obstacles ruled out an early invasion of Cuba. The transfer of the advance guard to Key West proved impractical because the island lacked a supply of fresh water adequate for that many troops. Most important, the Army had not yet amassed enough ammunition for the invasion and could not speed its manufacture for immediate delivery. After supplying the Manila expedition and establishing a reserve for coast defense, the Ordnance Department had fewer cartridges in its arsenals than were needed for one hour's fighting by 70,000 men. Although factories, both government and private, were turning out ammunition as rapidly as possible, General Miles estimated that it would take sixty days to accumulate enough for operations on the scale contemplated.[33]

Miles, who had opposed the attack on Havana from the beginning, used all these facts in an effort to have the movement canceled or at least postponed. By-passing Alger and carrying his case directly to the White

32. *War Investigating Commission*, I, 198-99; VI, 2698, 2861, 2864; VII, 3145-46. *RSW, 1898*, I, 384; IV, 15. Files No. 253334 and 253348, AGO Records, recount a typical War Department attempt to obtain state equipment. In the same record group, see: Adj. Gen. Corbin to Gens. Brooke, Shafter, and Coppinger, and to Commanding General, Department of the East, May 24, 1898, Coppinger to Corbin, May 24, 1898, Brig. Gen. Royal T. Frank to Corbin, May 25, 1898, Brooke to Corbin, May 24-25, 1898, File No. 83749. *The New York Times*, May 10, 12, 13, 22, 25, and 30, and June 3, 1898. *Army and Navy Journal*, May 28, 1898. Bend, *JMSI*, XXVII, 372-73.

33. *Correspondence*, I, 9-10. *War Investigating Commission*, I, 475. Chadwick, *Spanish-American War*, II, 9. Miles, *Serving the Republic*, 272-73, and *The North American Review*, CLXVIII, 524, describes the ammunition shortage. Maj. Gen. J. F. Wade to Adj. Gen. Corbin, May 11, 1898, Corbin to Wade, May 12, 1898, File No. 78935, AGO Records. Brig. Gen. William Ludlow to Corbin, May 11, 1898, Box 1, Corbin Papers.

House, Miles detailed for President McKinley the Army's lack of trained men, equipment, and munitions. He repeated his earlier warnings against invading Cuba during the rainy months and against committing troops overseas before the defeat of the Spanish fleet. Miles also argued that any attack on Havana was wrong in military principle. The experiences of the Civil War, he said, had proved a frontal assault on the enemy's strongest position to be strategic folly that entailed waste of lives with little likelihood of a decisive result. Miles favored instead an offensive against Spain's weaker positions in eastern Cuba and Puerto Rico, an offensive that he claimed would destroy Spanish power in the Caribbean at small cost in American casualties.[34]

General Miles's arguments gained support from an unexpected source— the Spanish Admiral Cervera. Despite the belief of the United States Navy that he was not coming to the defense of Cuba, Cervera's four cruisers and three torpedo-boat-destroyers had been steaming westward ever since they left the Cape Verdes on April 29, but mechanical deficiencies and ill-trained engine-room crews had slowed their progress far more than American experts had predicted. On May 13 the Navy finally discovered Cervera's vessels in the Caribbean, west of Martinique. With the Spanish squadron at last within striking distance, the American fleet needed all its ships for pursuit and battle; it could spare no escorts for Army transports. At the Navy's request, the War Department on May 13 indefinitely suspended all movements against Havana, at the same time ordering all commanders to continue training their troops and assembling ships and supplies. War Department officials greeted the arrival of the Spanish squadron with relief. It provided them with a publicly acceptable excuse for postponing a campaign that the Army was not yet ready to launch.[35]

Nevertheless, until the last days of May, the Administration remained committed to the assault on Havana. In spite of General Miles's objections to the strategy, the President and his advisers still planned to disregard the rainy season and to strike at the center of Spanish power. The offensive would begin as soon as the Navy disposed of Cervera and as soon as enough troops had been trained, equipped, and furnished with transportation. Some military men urged that the Regulars invade Cuba as soon as the Spanish squadron met defeat, without regard to the readiness of the Volunteers. They argued that the 12,000 troops available could seize and hold an American base

34. Miles, *Serving the Republic*, 272-74, and *The North American Review*, CLXVIII, 523-24. Johnson, *Unregimented General*, 23. *Army and Navy Journal*, May 28, 1898.

35. Alger, *Spanish-American War*, 37-39, 47-48. Chadwick, *Spanish-American War*, I, 111-26, 238-40. Mahan, *Lessons*, 115-17. Mayo, *America of Yesterday*, 193. Miley, *In Cuba*, 8-9. *War Investigating Commission*, I, 244-45. Secretary of the Navy John D. Long to Secretary Alger, May 13, 1898, Adj. Gen. Corbin to Commanding Generals at Tampa, Mobile, and New Orleans, May 13, 1898, and Asst. Adj. Gen. J. C. Gilmore to Maj. Gen. J. F. Wade, May 13, 1898, File No. 79819, AGO Records. *Army and Navy Journal*, October 15, 1898. *The New York Times*, May 14, 1898.

on the island, from which the Army could aid the rebels and *reconcentrados* and from which the main force could deploy for the attack on Havana. They also pointed out that the longer the United States delayed in establishing a beachhead in Cuba, the more time the Spaniards would have to improve their defenses and the more difficult the final assault would be. Washington observers believed that McKinley and Alger inclined toward this point of view.[36]

While the fleet hunted Cervera's squadron, preparations for the siege of Havana absorbed the attention of troop commanders and bureau chiefs. The invasion vanguard at Tampa rapidly expanded. By mid-May, three to five regiments were arriving at the Florida port every day. General Shafter reported on May 25 that he had 17,000 men in his camps—Regular infantry, cavalry, and artillery reinforced by eight Volunteer regiments. Tampa became overcrowded as regiments streamed in, and Shafter opened additional camps at Lakeland and Jacksonville. At Tampa and in the other Florida camps, soldiers drilled, cursed the heat, and loaded stores on transports. Regular Army officers, fresh from posts scattered all over the country, enjoyed reunions with friends they had not seen since graduation day at West Point or since Appomattox—brief, welcome relief from the heat and work of preparation. General Miles now asked Congress for a special fund of $350,000 to purchase entrenching tools, electric appliances, road-building machines, and railway equipment for the army of invasion. He urged that all the Army's siege guns be assembled at Tampa for eventual use in battering down Havana's guardian forts. Quartermaster General Ludington enlarged his department's orders for lightweight uniforms, hammocks, rubber blankets, and other tropical gear. His subordinates searched the Atlantic seaboard for transport steamers to carry 25,000 men, the expected first wave of the attack.[37]

IV

During the last weeks of May, Secretary Alger, General Miles, and Adjutant General Corbin revised their plans for assembling and equipping the Volunteers, so as to take into account both the Army's enlarged, revised mission and the extreme unreadiness of the state troops. On May 14 they abandoned as impractical both the plan to hold the regiments in their states until equipped and the effort to concentrate an elite Volunteer force for immediate action. Instead they decided to collect most of the regiments at

36. *Army and Navy Journal*, May 28, 1898. *The New York Times*, May 19, 20, 23, and 24, 1898. Olcott, *McKinley*, II, 55. Secretary Alger to Gen. G. M. Dodge, May 27, 1898, Alger Papers.

37. *Correspondence*, I, 13-14. Bigelow, *Santiago Campaign*, 68-69. Chadwick, *Spanish-American War*, II, 11. Miley, *In Cuba*, 11. Brig. Gen. William Ludlow to Maj. Gen. Miles, May 22, 1898, and Miles to Secretary Alger, May 23, 1898, File No. 99075; Miles to Alger, May 14, 1898, File No. 192302, AGO Records. *The New York Times*, May 8, 10, 11, 12, 15, 16, 19, and 29, 1898.

Secretary of War Russell A. Alger with Brigadier General Henry C. Corbin, the adjutant general of the Army.

Major Generals Nelson A. Miles and William R. Shafter.

123

a few large federal camps as soon as they were mustered in. At these camps, which would require fewer of the scarce staff officers for their administration, the Volunteers could train, receive arms and uniforms, and be grouped into brigades, divisions, and corps. For the overseas expeditions the War Department would select from each camp the first regiments to complete their preparations.[38]

On May 15 the War Department issued its final Volunteer concentration order. Under it, 53 infantry regiments, 11 field batteries, and some 42 troops of cavalry were to proceed to Chickamauga. Another 20 infantry regiments were to assemble at Camp Alger, the site south of Washington. The order sent a Massachusetts regiment to Key West and small contingents of southern Volunteers to camps at Mobile and New Orleans. Reflecting the new offensive commitments, the order sent 13 infantry regiments to Tampa and 10 more, plus artillery units to San Francisco. Still more regiments were subsequently diverted to the latter point. By contrast, the force left in the states for coast defense dwindled to the equivalent of 21 infantry regiments, 1½ regiments of heavy artillery, 3 field batteries, and 3 troops of cavalry.[39]

The concentration thus ordered went forward rapidly. By May 21 about 35,000 Volunteers had reached Chickamauga and another 7,000 were pitching tents at Camp Alger. At the same time, the supply bureaus rushed in carloads of food, equipment, and clothing, all of which was needed urgently. Regiments poured into the federal camps without rifles, uniforms, tentage, wagons, and medical supplies. In one division at Chickamauga, two entire regiments lacked rifles, and 30 to 40 per cent of the men in other units were unarmed. According to a staff officer, a Kentucky regiment arrived at Chickamauga "with lots of whiskey and fine horses but no arms or clothing." Similar reports from other camps soon deluged the War Department, along with pleas for vast amounts of military equipment of all sorts, much of it not yet manufactured by the overburdened contractors and government arsenals.[40]

As the Army concentrated, the War Department completed its command structure. It put the regiments allotted to the reserve and to coast

38. *The New York Times*, May 14, 15, 16, and 23, 1898. Adj. Gen. H. C. Corbin to Maj. Gen. J. R. Brooke, May 16, 1898, File No. 81314. AGO Records.

39. *The New York Times*, May 16, 1898. Memorandum for Bureau Chiefs of Assignment of Regiments to Camps, May 15, 1898, Adj. Gen. Corbin to Commanding General, Department of the East, May 15, 1898, File No. 80916, AGO Records.

40. The quotation is from Hugh L. Scott to Mrs. Scott, May 30, 1898, Box 1, Scott Papers. *Army and Navy Journal*, May 21, 1898. *The New York Times*, May 16, 17, 21, 22, and 29, 1898. *War Investigating Commission*, I, 276-77; VI, 3065-66; *Correspondence*, I, 24-25; II, 659-60. Chief Quartermaster Guy Howard to the Quartermaster General, September 20, 1898, File No. 115533, OQMG Records. Maj. Gen. J. R. Brooke to Adj. Gen. Corbin, May 16, 1898, File No. 81164; Maj. Gen. William M. Graham to Corbin, May 29, 1898, File No. 85740; Brooke to Corbin, June 7, 1898, File No. 159902; Graham to Corbin, June 8, 1898, File No. 160104, AGO Records.

Courtesy USAMHI

Volunteer soldiers at Camp George H. Thomas at Chickamauga Park, Georgia.

Courtesy USAMHI

Tenth Cavalry Officers. Although this was a black regiment, all the officers shown here at Chickamauga were white.

defense under the control of the geographical departments in which they were stationed. To command the troops massing at federal camps, it organized army corps, each of which at full strength would contain 30,000 men in three divisions. Each division consisted of three brigades and each brigade of three regiments. The corps contained only infantry; cavalry and artillery were administered independently in their own formations, although they could be attached to corps during campaigns.

General orders of May 7 and 16 created seven of these corps and appointed a major general to command each. The First, Third, and Sixth corps consisted of the troops concentrating at Chickamauga while the force at Camp Alger constituted the Second Corps. The Fourth Corps, with headquarters at Mobile, controlled the troops massed there and at other Gulf Coast points. The Fifth and Seventh corps, both with headquarters at Tampa, were responsible for organizing the troops that were assembling in Florida for the invasion of Cuba. Another War Department order on June 21 established an Eighth Corps at San Francisco, to command the 20,000 men of the Philippine expedition. All of the corps but the Sixth had regiments assigned to them during the war. The Sixth, for reasons the War Department never explained, was not manned, much to the frustration of its commander, Maj. Gen. James H. Wilson. Wilson, a distinguished Civil War veteran brought back from civilian life by the new crisis, believed himself the victim of a plot in the War Department, but he never could confirm his suspicions. Of the organized corps, the Fifth, intended to lead the invasion of Cuba, was composed largely of Regulars. The Eighth Corps contained a mixture of Regulars and Volunteers, and the Fourth Corps also included a few Regular regiments. The other four corps consisted entirely of Volunteers.[41]

Besides units of the Regular Army and regiments of the first 125,000 Volunteers, the army corps thus organized included additional formations recruited to meet the requirements of the Army's radically expanded wartime role. For large-scale operations in Cuba and the Philippines, the Army needed more specialist troops—cavalry, engineers, signalmen, and others—than either the Regulars or the state militia could furnish. The Volunteer law

41. Corps commanders were: I Corps, Maj. Gen. John R. Brooke; II Corps, Maj. Gen. William M. Graham; III Corps, Maj. Gen. James F. Wade; IV Corps, Maj. Gen. John J. Coppinger; V Corps, Maj. Gen. William R. Shafter; VI Corps, Maj. Gen. James H. Wilson; VII Corps, Maj. Gen. Fitzhugh Lee; VIII Corps, Maj. Gen. Wesley Merritt. For material on their formation, see: *RSW, 1898,* II, 183-85, 196, 207, 218-20. GO 36, HQA, May 7, 1898; GO 46, HQA, May 16, 1898, GO 73, HQA, June 21, 1898, *GO/AGO, 1898. Correspondence,* I, 13-15, 509-79. Alger, *Spanish-American War,* 25. Miley, *In Cuba,* 13-14. James Harrison Wilson, *Under the Old Flag: Recollections of Military Operations in the War for the Union, the Spanish War, the Boxer Rebellion, etc.,* II, 417-19, 422-23, recounts the frustrations of the VI Corps's commander. *The New York Times,* May 7, 22, 28, and 31, June 1, 1898. Maj. Gen. J. R. Brooke to Adj. Gen. Corbin, May 20, 1898, File No. 82770; Asst. Adj. Gen. J. C. Gilmore to Corbin, May 20, 1898, Brooke to Corbin, May 20, 1898, and Asst. Adj. Gen. Schwan to Brooke, May 21, 1898, File No. 82799; Maj. Gen. William M. Graham to Corbin, May 25, 1898, File No. 85890; Maj. Gen. Fitzhugh Lee to Corbin, June 5, 1898, File No. 160137; Graham to Corbin, June 5, 1898, File No. 160139, AGO Records.

of April 22 had provided for 3,000 United States Volunteers to be recruited, organized, and officered entirely by the federal government. Under this provision, the War Department, while the first 125,000 Volunteers mustered in the states, raised three cavalry regiments in the western territories. After the decisions to attack Havana and Manila, Congress on May 10, at the request of the War Department, authorized the enlistment of 3,500 men as United States Volunteer Engineers and 10,000 as United States Volunteer Infantry. A week later, it created the Volunteer Signal Corps, to consist of 8 officers and 55 enlisted men for each division of troops. The Volunteer engineers and signalmen were intended to provide needed specialists in construction and communications. The Volunteer infantry, enlisted from men supposedly immune to tropical diseases and hence nicknamed the "Immunes," were to be commanded by Regular officers. These regiments would join the vanguard of the Cuban invasion and remain as an occupation force after the fighting ended. Under the laws, the War Department set rules for recruiting these troops and the President commissioned all their officers.[42]

Recruiting of the three United States Volunteer cavalry regiments had begun late in April. The raising of the Engineers, Immune Infantry, and Signal Corps was under way by the first of June. The President appointed a commanding officer for each of these units and assigned him a recruiting district. The commander, under Regular Army supervision, then selected his field and company officers, who in turn enrolled the enlisted men. All recruits had to meet Regular Army physical standards. The formation of the cavalry, engineer, and signal units went smoothly, but the Immune regiments ran into trouble in Congress. Their assigned recruiting areas lay in the South, and senators from that section held up confirmation of their commanders' commissions until President McKinley gave them a veto over appointments in these regiments. The most famous of the organizations thus formed, the First United States Volunteer Cavalry, popularly known as the "Rough Riders," reached battle readiness before most state Volunteer regiments. Commanded by Leonard Wood and Theodore Roosevelt, this legendary aggregation of cowboys, Indian fighters, outlaws, Eastern aristocrats, and Ivy League athletes took part in the attack on Santiago de Cuba and wrote a gallant and bloody record during its brief existence.[43]

On May 26 President McKinley increased the Army's numbers for the last time in the war with Spain by calling on the states for 75,000 more

42. *War Investigating Commission*, I, 201. GO 44, HQA, May 13, 1898, and GO 52, HQA, May 24, 1898, in *GO/AGO, 1898*. Miles, *The North American Review*, CLXVIII, 516. *The New York Times*, May 6, 9, 10, 11, and 23, 1898.

43. Secretary Alger to Leonard Wood, April 28 and May 26, 1898, Box 26, Leonard Wood Papers. GO 55, HQA, May 26, 1898; GO 60, HQA, June 1, 1898; GO 68, HQA, June 13, 1898; GO 85, HQA, July 1, 1898; *GO/AGO, 1898*. RSW, *1898*, I, 878-79. *The New York Times*, May 21, 23, 25, 26, and 27, and June 1, 6, 8, 10, 12, 15, 22, 23, 25, 26, and 28, 1898. For the history of the Rough Riders, see Theodore Roosevelt, *The Rough Riders*, especially pp. 1-37, which describe the raising of the regiment. See also Hagedorn, *Wood*, I, 143-59, and Theodore Roosevelt to Alger, May 22, 1898, Alger Papers. *Correspondence*, I, 625, lists the regiment's battles and casualties.

Volunteers. The call came as a surprise to War Department officials, who had not expected it so soon and saw no urgent need for more men, but the President wanted to have ample reserves for the ambitious campaigns now planned.[44]

The new call set off a tug of war between the state politicians and the professional soldiers, for whom Adjutant General Corbin served as spokesman. Contrary to the results of the quarrel over the organizing of the first state contingent, sound military procedure prevailed over patronage-mongering. The politicians wanted the entire 75,000 parceled out into new regiments, a plan that would allow the governors to commission more officers and pay off more political debts. Some governors had already formed regiments, officered by their cronies, in anticipation of a second call. In opposition to the politicos, Corbin and the Regulars urged enforcement of the clause in the Act of April 22 that forbade the acceptance of new regiments from states whose existing units were under strength. They wanted to use the second Volunteer contingent to reinforce the regiments of the first call, so many of which had entered service with too few men for field efficiency. The Regulars received support in their fight from the colonels of Volunteer regiments already in service. Having learned from experience the need for the regulation number of men, these officers telegraphed state and federal authorities on behalf of the Regulars' position. At Chickamauga alone, forty Volunteer colonels publicly backed the Regulars. After several days of indecision, McKinley and Alger upheld the professional soldiers. The Administration, on May 31, informed the governors that they would have to fill up their states' existing regiments before any new ones could be mustered in.[45]

The War Department used about 40,000 men of the second Volunteer contingent to fill existing regiments. Under orders from Adjutant General Corbin, each Volunteer infantry regiment in camp sent recruiting parties back to its home district to enlist enough men to bring its companies to their prescribed war strength of 106 soldiers. Artillery and cavalry units followed the same procedure. At the same time, the War Department instructed the governors to organize and officer enough additional companies to give all their regiments three full battalions. When this organization was well under way, the War Department apportioned requests for new units among the states to supply the remaining 35,000 men, in all, 22 regiments of infantry, 16 batteries of field artillery, and 3 batteries of heavy artillery. As colonel of one of these regiments, the Third Nebraska Infantry, William Jennings Bryan, McKinley's opponent for the Presidency in 1896, entered the Army. The raising of the new Volunteers, both individuals and units, went forward

44. *Army and Navy Journal*, April 30, May 21 and 28, 1898. *The New York Times*, May 18, 19, and 26, 1898.

45. *Army and Navy Journal*, June 4, 1898. *The New York Times*, May 18, 26, 27, 28, 29, and 31, June 1, 1898. G. M. Dodge to Secretary Alger, June 10, 1898, Alger Papers. *RSW, 1898*, I, 259.

with little delay or confusion. By mid-June recruit detachments were pouring into the camps. State and federal authorities, profiting from earlier mistakes, cooperated efficiently in assembling and mustering in the new regiments and batteries.[46]

The Army grew rapidly in numbers. At the end of May more than 8,400 officers and 160,000 men were in service; by the end of July the totals had reached 11,000 officers and almost 260,000 men. In August, when the war ended, some 275,000 troops filled the federal and state camps. By that time, all of the Volunteer organizations created by the calls on the states and by federal law had been mustered and the Regular Army was approaching its authorized war strength.[47]

The deployment of this human mass followed closely the plan adopted on May 15. About 25,000 men, most of them Regulars, eventually collected at Tampa to spearhead the invasion of Cuba. The 30,000 men of the Seventh Corps, originally supposed to encamp at Tampa, assembled instead at Camp Cuba Libre near Jacksonville because the Tampa area had grown too crowded and Maj. Gen. Fitzhugh Lee, the corps commander, considered Jacksonville a desirable concentration point. The largest single concentration, Camp George H. Thomas at Chickamauga, by early June swarmed with the 60,000 men of the First and Third corps, while Camp Alger, home of the Second Corps, contained 23,500 by mid-August. The Fourth Corps, which became a catchall for units left behind by the first Cuban expedition, was divided between Mobile, Tampa, and Miami. At San Francisco the 20,000 soldiers of the Eighth Corps awaited ships to take them to Manila. On the eastern seaboard, 12,000 Volunteers remained at their state camps to support the coast defenses, while many regiments of the second call, mustered in late in the war, never left their home camps.[48]

V

In mustering troops under the second call for Volunteers, the McKinley administration paid special attention to black manpower. Some 186,000

46. *RSW, 1898*, I, 277; *1899*, I, Pt. 2, p. 11. GO 61, HQA, June 1, 1898, *GO/AGO, 1898*. *Correspondence*, I, 135; II, 686-87. *Army and Navy Journal*, May 28, 1898. *The New York Times*, May 18 and June 2, 5, 8, 10, 12, 17, 18, 19, and 26, 1898. For Bryan's relationship to the Army, see statement by Secretary Alger, July 31, 1900, Alger Papers. Secretary Alger to the Governor of Mississippi, June 19, 1898, File No. 209870, AGO Records. The arrival of regimental recruits at Chickamauga is reported in File No. 159902, AGO Records.

47. Alger, *Spanish-American War*, 27-28. *War Investigating Commission*, I, 113, 254. *RSW, 1898*, I, 260.

48. *War Investigating Commission*, I, 202, 204, 209-11; II, 213, 234-36; IV, 853; VI, 3065; VIII, 176. *RSW, 1898*, I, 263; II, 196-97; *1899*, Pt. 4, p. 2. *Army and Navy Journal*, April 9, 1898. *The New York Times*, May 14 and 22, 1898. Alger, *Spanish-American War*, 25-26. The Chickamauga camp was named after Gen. George H. Thomas. Union hero of the Civil War battle of Chickamauga; see Adj. Gen. Corbin to Maj. Gen. J. R. Brooke, April 20, 1898, File No. 75192, AGO Records. Secretary Alger seemed embarrassed at the naming of the camp near Washington after himself: Alger to W. Livingstone, June 4, 1898, Alger Papers.

African-Americans had served in the Union Army during the Civil War, and the Regular establishment in 1898 contained four segregated black regiments— two of cavalry and two of infantry. Four of the Immune U.S. Volunteer infantry regiments were composed of Blacks. However, the first 125,000 state Volunteers included few Blacks, except for small units from Ohio, Indiana, and Massachusetts (the latter a company in a white regiment), because most National Guard regiments did not accept African-American members or because states that did have black militia units gave preference to white organizations in filling their quotas.

American Blacks were quick to object to their underrepresentation in the Volunteer Army. Some black leaders, in this decade of intensifying racism throughout the nation and of proliferating segregation laws in the South, questioned whether their race, oppressed at home, should enlist to fight oppression abroad. Nevertheless, most African-Americans shared their fellow countrymen's indignation at Spain's Cuban atrocities and at the destruction of the *Maine*. Many believed that in this new war, as in that of the 1860s, honorable military service would win Blacks greater respect in the larger society, thereby assisting them in their struggle for equality. Accordingly, in mass meetings and through delegations to the White House and Congress, Blacks protested against their exclusion from the Volunteer Army on the basis that it was a denial of equal citizenship. In response to this agitation, in the second call President McKinley accepted into service black regiments from Alabama, Illinois, Kansas, North Carolina, and Virginia, most of them organized around existing state militia units. In all, the Spanish-American War Army eventually included over 13,000 Blacks, about 3,300 of them in the four Regular regiments and the rest in the federal and state Volunteer organizations.[49]

In its only action of the war that could remotely be considered an innovation in racial policy, the War Department mustered in a number of black units under officers of their own race. For the most part, the Department did this simply by accepting the decisions of state governments in officering their black Volunteers. By this means, black-officered units from Ohio, Kansas, and North Carolina entered the service. Most of these black officers were state militiamen. Like their white counterparts, they owed their positions largely to influence or popularity in their units and local communities. However, some regiments had a leavening of former Regular Army enlisted men commissioned as Volunteer officers. The only black West Point graduate then serving in the Regular Army, 1st Lieutenant Charles Young, accepted a

---

49. Bernard C. Nalty, *Strength for the Fight: A History of Black Americans in the Military*, 63-66 (hereafter Nalty, *Strength for the Fight*). First Endorsement, War Department Adjutant General's Office to Mr. James Howard, August 3, 1916, in Morris J. MacGregor and Bernard C. Nalty, eds., *Blacks in the United States Armed Forces: Basic Documents*, III, 159 (hereafter MacGregor and Nalty, *Blacks in U.S. Armed Forces*). *The New York Times*, June 22, 23, 25, 26, and 28, 1898. For a detailed account of black Volunteers in the war with Spain, see Marvin Fletcher, "The Black Volunteers in the Spanish-American War," *Military Affairs*, XXXVIII, no. 2 (April 1974), 48-53. Hereafter Fletcher, "Black Volunteers."

commission from Ohio as major and commanding officer of that state's black 9th Battalion. For units raised under federal auspices, the War Department followed a more cautious course. It retained its all-white policy in officering the black Regular regiments. However, in organizing the Immune U.S. Volunteers, it temporarily commissioned black Regular NCOs as company officers while reserving the battalion and regimental level positions for Whites.[50]

The war experience of the black units reflected the circumstances of the conflict and the times. All four black Regular regiments took part in the Santiago campaign and fought well in the engagements at Las Guasimas, San Juan Hill, and El Caney. Of the Volunteer units, only the black company of the 6th Massachusetts Regiment saw any combat, engaging in light skirmishing during the Puerto Rico campaign. A few other regiments, both state Volunteers and "Immunes," did occupation duty in Cuba. The rest of the Volunteers, like their white counterparts, spent the war in federal assembly camps, mostly in the South. There they, and the black Regulars, had their share of bitter encounters with the region's racial customs. The troops did not always accept passively the hostility they faced. A number of violent incidents occurred between soldiers and civilians and between white and black units. Corps and division commanders all too often did little to support their black troops in such difficulties. Often they segregated their black regiments in separate camps or organizations or tried to eliminate them altogether. Brigadier General William C. Oates, a Confederate veteran, objected strongly to having the 9th Ohio Battalion assigned to his brigade in the Second Corps. He acknowledged that the unit was a well-trained and behaved one, but claimed that having black troops under him would damage his political prospects when he returned to Alabama, his home state. The War Department accommodated Oates by reassigning him to an all-white brigade and giving the brigade which included the 9th Ohio to a Union Civil War veteran.[51]

While black soldiers served honorably in the war with Spain, and in the subsequent conflict in the Philippines, African-Americans' hopes that the war would lead to advancement for their race were destined for disappointment. Jim Crow, as the segregation laws were nicknamed, continued his forward march in the decade following the war. After the wartime Volunteers were mustered out, the War Department reverted to its policy of maintaining a few segregated black regiments, although a trickle of black officers found their way into the service. As the Regular Army expanded after the war, the proportion of Blacks in its ranks declined and the treatment they received became more discriminatory, as exemplified by President Theodore Roosevelt's

50. Nalty, *Strength for the Fight*, 66-67. MacGregor and Nalty, *Blacks in the U.S. Armed Forces*, III, 165, 187-88. The black officers of the Immunes reverted to enlisted rank after their regiments were mustered out: see Fletcher, "Black Volunteers," 49.

51. After action reports of the Regulars at Santiago are in MacGregor and Nalty, *Blacks in the U.S. Armed Forces*, III, 189-97; that of the 6th Mass. is in *ibid.*, 170-83. Nalty, *Strength for the Fight*, 67-72. Fletcher, "Black Volunteers," 50-51, describes racial incidents in the South. For the 9th Ohio incident, see Brig. Gen. W. C. Oates to Maj. Gen. S. B. M. Young, October 8, 1898; Adj. Gen. Corbin to Young, October 12, 1898; and Report of II Corps Movement from Camp Meade to South Carolina and Georgia, December 10, 1898; all in Samuel B. M. Young Papers, U.S. Army Military History Institute, Carlisle Barracks, Pa.

mass discharge of a battalion of the 25th Infantry after the 1906 Brownsville incident. When America entered World War I in 1917, the Regular Army contained only the four black regiments it had in 1898 and there were only three black officers on active duty, including Charles Young, then a lieutenant colonel. Another 10,000 Blacks served in the National Guards of seven states and the District of Columbia. In the Army, as in the nation as a whole, the struggle to free Cuba in 1898 did not bring greater racial freedom at home.[52]

VI

During the crisis months of March, April, and May, all the elements of the situation upon the stability of which systematic War Department planning and preparation depended had altered repeatedly. The size of the initial force to be raised, the manner in which it was to be organized and officered, and the missions on which it was to be employed all had changed in response to pressures external to the War Department and largely uncontrolled by it. In every instance, the direction of these changes had been toward a larger force than at first anticipated, which was to carry out more complex and widespread operations.

In organizing an army under the conditions prevailing in early 1898, the McKinley Administration from March onward had vacillated between two conflicting courses of action. It could have created a relatively small force at the outset, composed of the nation's trained Regulars and militiamen and equipped from the available reserve stocks of the state and federal governments supplemented by additional purchases of specialized materials. With this force and the Navy, it could have struck swiftly at Cuba. Instead, in late April, the Administration abandoned all but the most modest plans for an early offensive and at the same time decided to raise a larger army, which required more time, given the War Department's limited resources, to make ready for the field.

Then, in early May, President McKinley decided to combine both approaches. He instructed the War Department to continue preparing the enlarged army; in fact, he further expanded the number of troops. At the same time, he demanded that Secretary Alger and his subordinates draw from the swollen, untrained, partially unarmed mass an elite force for immediate assaults on Havana and Manila. He thus left the Army's administrators in a dilemma, for to discharge effectively the latter task—invasion—they would have to neglect the former—arming, clothing, and equipping the large mass of reserves. Amid these fluctuations of strategy and confronted by contradictory demands, Alger, Miles, Corbin, and the bureau chiefs struggled to overcome decades-old shortages of supplies and trained men and to surmount or evade the obstacles to action that had been created by the War Department's cumbersome, bifurcated organization.

52. Blacks' service in the Philippines is recounted in Nalty, *Strength for the Fight*, 73-77. Marvin Fletcher, *The Black Soldier and Officer in the United States Army, 1891-1917*, recounts the declining status of Blacks in the post-1898 Army. World War I figures are from Edward M. Coffman, *The War to End All Wars: The American Military Experience in World War I*, 69.

5

Command, Administration, and Supply

I

Although their initial war plans had been totally disrupted and the size and missions of the Army changed from week to week, Secretary Alger and his colleagues continued their efforts to find officers, weapons, uniforms, food, and equipment for the assembling troops. They waged war by improvisation, solving problems by trial and error as they arose. Rarely were they able to anticipate or prepare for future needs. One of their first tasks— one that they never satisfactorily completed—was to develop within the War Department a well-defined chain of command.

As a result of the war situation and of the interaction of the department's leading personalities, the diffusion of authority from which the War Department had suffered for decades was at its worst in the spring of 1898. No single man supervised all the War Department's functions or represented it and the Army in Cabinet meetings and presidential councils. At the outset, General Miles spoke for the Army on questions of strategy, but after McKinley, early in May, decided on a large-scale offensive in Cuba, he increasingly ignored Miles's advice. As was then customary for the civilian chief in both the War and Navy departments, Secretary Alger took little initiative on strategic and technical matters. In the Administration's councils he parroted the views of generals and bureau heads. He spent much of his time trying to coordinate the work of the supply departments, attempting, as he put it, to make their plans "fit as far as possible." Adjutant General Corbin oversaw the mustering and recruitment of troops, and both he and Miles recommended officers for assignments and promotions. Each of the other bureau chiefs planned and directed his department's functions under Alger's general supervision.[1]

During the early weeks of the war, General Schofield, the President's personal military adviser, dabbled in many questions of command and organization, often with disruptive results. He lent his influence, for

---

1. *Correspondence*, I, 132, 268-69. *War Investigating Commission*, VI, 2619-20, 2808-9, 2843; VII, 3764, 3769-70. *RSW, 1898*, II, 12-13. Carter, *General Staff*, 18-19, 59. Theodore Roosevelt to Henry Cabot Lodge, June 12, 1898, *Roosevelt-Lodge Correspondence*, I, 306-7. Maj. Gen. Nelson A. Miles to Secretary Alger, May 16, 1898, File No. 192302, AGO Records. Grenville M. Dodge to Alger, May 25, 1898, Alger Papers. Alger to W. H. Withington, May 24, 1897, Withington Papers. *The New York Times*, March 21, 1897, and June 7, 1898. The Navy Department was run in the same way as the War Department; see: Grenville and Young, *Politics, Strategy, and American Diplomacy*, 278-80; Mayo, *America of Yesterday*, 157, 198; Long, *New American Navy*, II, 149-50.

example, to the demand for an unnecessarily large Volunteer force. Schofield's very presence in Washington constituted an insult to General Miles, who apparently never conferred with him. Alger soon began deliberately to snub him; gradually, too, McKinley lost interest in what Schofield had to say. Finding his position increasingly uncomfortable, Schofield left Washington in June. After his departure, McKinley fell back upon the counsels of Alger and Miles, but he sought information from other War Department officers on the basis of which to evaluate for himself the advice of the nominal heads of the Army. Time and again, he turned to Adjutant General Corbin as the most reliable source of such information.[2]

The staff bureaus were the special victims of diffused responsibility and control as well as of the repeated changes in military plans. Line officers and civilian policy makers alike treated the supply services as necessary nuisances and rarely consulted their chiefs before settling upon plans of mobilization or campaign. Neither the Quartermaster General nor the Chief of Ordnance received any advance notice of the call for 125,000 Volunteers or indeed of any details of the Army's mobilization. They had to contract for supplies on the basis of whatever rumors they could ferret out and on their own estimates of probable requirements. Troop movements and changes in campaign objectives during the war repeatedly caught the bureaus by surprise, in spite of pleas from their chiefs that they be warned in advance so they could have materials ready when and where needed. Time after time, the bureaus had to improvise transportation and equipment at the last moment, often without clear guidelines for action.[3]

Under established Army practice, troop commanders in camp and field were supposed to guide the bureaus' efforts by requisitioning the material they needed to carry out their assigned missions. Thus, in late June, when the Administration decided to send an army against Puerto Rico, Secretary Alger asked General Miles, who would lead the expedition, to estimate its supply and transportation requirements. If the commanders understood clearly their responsibilities and learned of them far enough in advance of the time for action, this system could work with rough efficiency, but too often

2. Charles G. Dawes, *A Journal of the McKinley Years*, Bascom N. Timmons, ed., 158, 188. Olcott, *McKinley*, II, 49. Charles Emory Smith to Secretary of War Elihu Root, August 12, 1899, Box 8, Corbin Papers. John A. Porter to Secretary Alger, April 27 and May 14, 1898, McKinley Papers. Lt. Gen. John M. Schofield, "General Schofield's Experiences in McKinley's Administration," undated memoir in Box 93, Schofield Papers. James H. Wilson to Col. LeGrand B. Cannon, Jr., April 10, 1898, Letterbook No. 37, Wilson Papers.

3. *War Investigating Commission*, I, 510-11; III, 126-27; IV, 1240-41; VI, 2618, 2962; VII, 3139, 3149. *RSW, 1898*, IV, 14-15. Brig. Gen. D. W. Flagler to Secretary Alger, March 12, 1898, Alger Papers. J. F. Weston to Maj. Gen. James H. Wilson, April 29, May 6, and October 22, 1898, Box 26, Wilson Papers. Flagler to Adj. Gen. Corbin, July 20, 1898, File No. 103944; Memorandum from Office of the Chief of Ordnance, July 17, 1898, File No. 105774; AGO Records. *Army and Navy Journal*, June 11, 1898.

in this particular war the field commanders lacked both information and time. The size and objectives of the Cuban expedition repeatedly changed, and so did its demands for shipping and equipment. In the home camps, disagreement over the functions of the various Army corps hindered supply efforts. General Miles regarded the corps as administrative formations for the instruction and equipment of regiments that were to be transferred to other commands when ready for combat, while corps commanders like Maj. Gen. John R. Brooke of the First at Chickamauga thought they were organizing field armies. The War Department never resolved this dispute. Corps commanders, as a result, maneuvered for front-line assignments, intrigued constantly for supplies and staff, and failed to equip their camps properly for long occupation.[4]

The confusion among the corps commanders reflected a fundamental administrative deficiency of the Army in 1898: the failure of the War Department to relate command assignments to the military tasks that had to be performed. Corps organizations, for instance, proved necessary and effective in controlling field forces in Cuba and the Philippines, but in the home camps they did little but tie up scarce generals and staff officers in superfluous headquarters organizations. For training and equipping troops under conditions that prevented all regiments being brought to battle readiness simultaneously, a series of divisional camps under the geographical departments would have required fewer administrative personnel and would have suffered less disruption when the War Department drew troops from them for field service. As it was, to reinforce the Santiago expedition in July and to invade Puerto Rico, General Miles found it necessary to organize a temporary army by taking from the First, Second, and Fourth corps their best-prepared units and many of their generals and staff officers. These inroads on personnel that could train and command raw recruits left the huge troop concentration at Chickamauga in an administrative state bordering on anarchy.[5]

Important jobs went unassigned. The War Department never placed a single general with adequate staff in charge of establishing an embarkation port for the Cuban expedition or of equipping a transport fleet. Nor did it place one officer in over-all supervision of the training camps.

4. Secretary Alger to Maj. Gen. Miles, June 26, 1898, *Correspondence*, I, 268-69, asks for supply estimates for the Puerto Rican invasion. For material on the purposes of the corps, see: Miles to Alger, April 30, 1898, File No. 192302; Maj. Gen. J. R. Brooke to Adj. Gen. Corbin, June 8, 1898, File No. 215311; Brooke to Corbin, June 17, 1898, File No. 96332; Brig. Gen. Henry V. Boynton to C. A. Boynton, June 14, 1898, File No. 160115, AGO Records. Hugh L. Scott to Mrs. Scott, June 2, 1898, Box 1, Scott Papers. J. F. Weston to Maj. Gen. James H. Wilson, June 7, 1898, Box 26, Wilson Papers. *RSW, 1898*, I, 690-92.

5. Secretary Alger to President McKinley, June 18, 1898, Alger Papers, and *Correspondence*, I, 519, illustrate the disruption of corps to obtain regiments for Puerto Rico.

Instead, it left to each corps commander the problems of clothing, equipping, and training his own soldiers while Alger, Miles, Corbin, the bureau chiefs, and the department commanders all dabbled sporadically in every other phase of mobilization. Such maldistribution of authority and responsibility did as much as the absence of a general staff in Washington to prevent coherent planning and continuous supervision of the Army's war effort. Because of the resulting confusion, a postwar investigation concluded, "There was lacking in the general administration of the War Department . . . that complete grasp of the situation which was essential to the highest efficiency and discipline of the Army."[6]

Along with confusion in command, cumbersome procedures hindered the War Department's efforts. The supply bureaus labored under a system for making contracts and regulating funds that was designed to prevent fraud in peacetime rather than to assure swift action in wartime. Secretary Alger, used to simpler business methods, "got very weary of the many legal obstructions." He declared on one occasion that he would pay for needed supplies himself if regulations prevented the quick use of government funds. The War Department's complicated filing system broke down under the flood of wartime reports and messages. Documents piled up in bureau offices where the clerks lacked the time to place them in the proper pigeonholes. Much of this excess paper resulted from the old Army evil of centralization. The bureau chiefs during the war rarely vetoed actions of their subordinates in the field, but they continued to channel most major decisions across their own desks. All contracts made by depot quartermasters, for example, had to come to Quartermaster General Ludington for final approval, even though he usually rubber-stamped the decisions made at the lower levels. Their failure to delegate authority left the bureau chiefs floundering in a mass of petty details, without leisure to consider matters of general policy or to anticipate future needs. Surgeon General Sternberg admitted after the war that he had "not had time to consider important questions which I should at times have given several hours to." Each of his colleagues could truthfully have made the same confession.[7]

Alger, Corbin, and the bureau chiefs worked hard to surmount the War Department's lack of an institutional brain and nervous system. Although he preferred to leave the bureau chiefs to their own devices, Alger met with them daily during the crisis of the war to coordinate their support of field operations. When he intervened directly in their work, it was usually to press for free spending, the suspension of hampering rules, and aggressive action.[8]

6. *War Investigating Commission*, I, 116.

7. Alger describes his frustration at slow procedure, in Alger to Col. Curtis Guild, November 12, 1901, Alger Papers. *War Investigating Commission*, I, 113, 126; III, 332, 723; IV, 1133-34; V, 2185, 2317; VI, 2634, 2643, 2846, 2956. *RSW, 1898*, I, 585-86. Alger, *Spanish-American War*, 7-8. Carter, *General Staff*, 17, 33. Risch, *Quartermaster Corps*, 495-98. Lee, *JMSI*, XI, 537-38. *Army and Navy Journal*, October 1, 1898, denounces centralization in the War Department and blames it for wartime failures.

8. *War Investigating Commission*, I, 120; VI, 2961; VII, 3293, 3761-63.

Alger also tried to anticipate future needs and to plan for meeting them, especially in the matter of selecting campsites and embarkation ports. The Army's first concentration points had been chosen by different people as mobilization progressed—Chickamauga and Tampa by the Army-Navy strategy board, Camp Alger by officers from General Miles's staff and the Quartermaster's Department, Jacksonville by troop commanders in Florida. San Francisco became a point of concentration and embarkation because the Army already had a large post there and because, as California's principal city, it was the assembly point for many of that state's Volunteers. Early in June, when it became apparent that the Caribbean expeditions and the Volunteer reserves would need more camping grounds and port facilities, Alger acted to bring order into the process of site selection. He sent four officers representing The Adjutant General's Office, the Quartermaster and Medical departments, and the Corps of Engineers on a tour of the South to examine and recommend concentration points. The officers' reports, presented to Alger on June 14, analyzed the terrain, water supplies, climate, health conditions, railroad terminals, and—where they existed—the port facilities of Fernandina, Jacksonville, and Miami in Florida, Augusta, Brunswick, and Savannah in Georgia, and Charleston, Columbia, and Summerville in South Carolina. Its conclusions guided later troop movements.[9]

Partly because of his disagreement with the President's military decisions and partly because of clashes with Alger and the bureau chiefs, General Miles's authority within the War Department and the McKinley Administration steadily declined. His feuds within the War Department began early in April, when he collided with the Chief of Ordnance over procurement and selection of weapons. Miles recommended extensive purchases of guns and ammunition abroad and demanded that the Krag-Jörgensen rifle be replaced with another weapon that had earlier been tested and rejected by an Army board. On the vehement urging of the Chief of Ordnance, Alger turned down Miles's proposals. At Miles's insistence, however, the Secretary spent over $200,000 for a trial order of 10,000 Winchester rifles that, when tested, failed to meet the Army's standards of performance. Miles continued his experiments in ordnance, and, as one result, he later burdened the Santiago expedition with 100 portable shields—massive steel plates on wheeled carriages that troops were supposed to push ahead of them in battle.

9. For material on the selection of the first campsites, see: Alger, *Spanish-American War*, 411, 415. Asst. Adj. Gen. J. C. Gilmore, Endorsement on AGO File 73129, April 7, 1898, File No. 192302; Capt. A. S. Barker, USN, and Asst. Adj. Gen. A. L. Wagner, "Memorandum for the Honorable Secretary of War," April 4, 1898, File No. 198209, AGO Records. *Correspondence*, I, 7-8. *War Investigating Commission*, I, 209, 245, 248, 266; IV, 1258; V, 1965-66, 1978, 1980; VI, 2755-56; VII, 3261-62, 3273. Lt. Col. M. C. Martin to the Quartermaster General, August 31, 1898, File No. 115533, OQMG Records. *The New York Times*, May 16, 1898. For the appointment, work, and report of Alger's campsite board, see the following: *War Investigating Commission*, VII, 3361-71. File No. 121918, AGO Records. *The New York Times*, June 9 and 15, 1898.

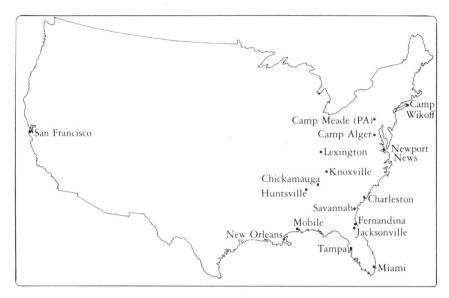

Map 1.   Camps and Embarkation Ports, 1898

The monsters, which weighed 1,000 pounds each, could not be used in the Cuban mud, and during the next several months were hauled from ship to warehouse and back again. Miles's advice on the selection of campsites proved to be both full of errors and eccentric. Repeatedly, he urged that troops be stationed at Miami, in spite of the fact that inspecting officers reported the terrain unsuitable and the water likely polluted. Eventually, at his insistence, a division spent a few weeks there, only to leave in haste after an outbreak of typhoid, probably caused by the bad water. Besides giving wrong-headed advice, Miles reopened the old conflict for supremacy between the Commanding General and the Secretary of War. He did so late in May, when Alger ordered him to make an inspection tour of the assembly camps. Storming into Alger's office, Miles angrily rejected the order and denied Alger's right to issue it. From then on, his relations with the Secretary deteriorated, along with his authority as a strategic adviser to the President.[10]

10. Chief of Ordnance D. W. Flagler to Secretary Alger, April 8 and 12, May 2, 1898; Maj. Gen. Miles to Alger, April 18, 1898; Acting Chief of Ordnance to Adj. Gen. Corbin, March 30, 1899; Chief of Ordnance A. R. Buffington to Alger, April 10, 1899; Alger to W. M. Laffan, June 29, 1900, to Corbin, November 19, 1900, and to Senator George F. Hoar, February 8, 1900, Alger Papers. H. V. Boynton to Brig. Gen. James H. Wilson, May 24, 1899, Box 4; J. F. Weston to Wilson, November 11, 1898, Box 26, Wilson Papers. Miles to Alger, May 25, 1898, File No. 85540; Miles to Alger, June 18, 1898, File No. 94797; Asst. Adj. Gen. J. C. Gilmore to Corbin, May 14, 1898, Maj. Gen. J. F. Wade to Corbin, May 17, 1898, Corbin to Maj. Gen. W. R. Shafter, May 25, 1898, File No. 121918; Miles to Secretary Alger, May 16, 1898, File No. 192302, AGO Records. *Correspondence,* I, 70-71; II, 681-82. *War Investigating Commission,* VII, 3767-68. Alger, *Spanish-American War,* 57-59. Johnson, *Unregimented General,* 317.

While Miles gradually lost his authority within the War Department, Adjutant General Corbin quietly enlarged his. Amid changing plans, conflicting orders, and clashing personalities, Corbin's calm, tact, physical endurance, and administrative efficiency held the creaking military machine on course. After the end of May, General Miles spent much of his time away from Washington, therefore, except for the actual direction of field operations, all the myriad details of army command fell upon Corbin. He supervised the recruitment and mobilization of Regulars and Volunteers and battled for full implementation of the progressive clauses of the Army legislation. He gave unified direction to the supply departments. Whenever a troop movement was ordered, he directed that copies of the order be sent at once to the bureaus. He received from the training camps daily reports on the stores available, on the number of articles issued, and on immediate additional requirements, and he referred these reports also to the bureaus for their guidance. After troops landed in Cuba, Puerto Rico, and the Philippines, he kept his office open twenty-four hours a day in order to maintain constant telegraphic communication with the expedition commanders and to pass on their reports, requisitions, and recommendations to the President and the Secretary of War. He largely controlled the assignment and transfer of officers, and field commanders praised him for putting able men in the right places. Insofar as anyone kept the press informed, he acted as public relations officer for the Army and won the respect of the Washington correspondents. He also earned the confidence of Congress. When its committees needed military information, they sent their inquiries to Corbin and received prompt, precise answers.[11]

Having lost confidence in both Alger and Miles, President McKinley began turning to Corbin for military advice and for assistance in implementing his policies. By late June he had made Corbin his *de facto* chief of staff. Everyone connected with the Administration testified to the importance of Corbin's role in the making and carrying out of policy. McKinley's postmaster-general later wrote:

General Corbin was the distinctive soldier at Washington in whom the President had implicit confidence and who from the nature of his position and function could hold the relation of confidential adviser and executive. . . . He became the President's

11. *War Investigating Commission*, I, 119; VI, 2848; VII, 3293-94. *Correspondence*, I, 119. For an example of Corbin's coordination of the bureaus, see Memorandum Assigning Volunteers to Camps, May 15, 1898, File No. 80916, AGO Records. Gen. Henry W. Lawton to Adj. Gen. Corbin, November 8, 1898, Box 1A; John D. Long to Secretary of War Elihu Root, July 21, 1903, Thomas H. Carter to Root, August 1, 1903, John W. Griggs to Root, August 10, 1903, Francis E. Warren to Root, September 13, 1903, *The New York Times*, October 24, 1909, clipping, Box 8; *Nebraska State Journal*, May 1, 1898, and *The Mail and Express Illustrated Saturday Magazine*, June 25, 1898, both clippings in 1898 Scrapbook, Box 10, Corbin Papers. Brig. Gen. James H. Wilson to Commissary General John F. Weston, July 18, 1899, Box 44, Wilson Papers. Dunn, *Harrison to Harding*, I, 251-52.

counsellor and adjutant. In all the work of organizing, planning and operating the President relied on his judgment and execution. They were in constant consultation. I have not infrequently called at the White House on some errand late at night, and found them conferring together. This was blended with his regular work as Adjutant General, but was beyond it. Much of his most important and valuable service was in giving the President the benefit of his knowledge and judgment, and in carrying out the President's wishes and commands through the proper channels, and his part had no record.

In July, Secretary Alger asked Congress to advance Corbin as well as all his successors in office to the rank of major general and thereby give formal recognition to The Adjutant General's role as chief of the staff. Congress failed to comply with the request, but Corbin continued to expand his power as acting commander of the Army.[12]

Alger and Corbin early began trying to liberate the War Department from the toils of its peacetime procedures. At the beginning of the war, Alger restored to corps and department commanders much of the administrative discretion taken from them by previous changes in the regulations. Throughout the conflict, he supported commanders who took initiative in promoting the welfare of their men or the success of their missions. Corbin, who transmitted to Alger and the bureaus the demands and complaints of line commanders, helped to speed and simplify the movement of supplies. Probably as a result of his influence, the bureau chiefs avoided their peacetime practice of countermanding or reducing field commanders' requisitions. Line officers later testified almost unanimously to the staff's cooperative attitude. In June, at the War Department's request, Congress allowed the Quartermaster and Ordnance bureaus to discard their cumbersome contract system when emergencies required rapid purchasing, and the bureaus took full advantage of their new freedom. Gradually, too, the Quartermaster and Medical departments enlarged the discretionary authority of their officers outside Washington by allowing them to purchase and issue supplies without clearing every transaction with the bureau chiefs.[13]

12. The quotation is from Charles Emory Smith to Secretary of War Elihu Root, August 12, 1903, Box 8, Corbin Papers. Grenville M. Dodge to "Dear Horton," September 8, 1909, C. H. Grosvenor to Mrs. Edyth P. Corbin, September 11, 1909, Edgar S. Dudley to Lt. Gen. H. C. Corbin, September 19, 1906, F. V. Greene to Col. H. H. Sargent, October 27, 1909, Box 1A; J. A. T. Hull to Root, August 14, 1903, John W. Griggs to Root, August 10, 1903, James Wilson to Root, August 14, 1903, Francis E. Warren to Root, September 13, 1903, Box 8, Corbin Papers. In order to fill out the historical record, Root collected testimonials to Corbin's role from many officials of McKinley's government. By mid-June, Corbin had established himself in the President's confidence. See John J. McCook to Maj. Gen. James H. Wilson, June 20, 1898, Box 15, Wilson Papers. *Army and Navy Journal,* August 27, 1898, and February 25, 1899. For material on the effort to make Corbin and his successors major generals, see *Memorandum of the Military Service of Brig. Gen. Henry C. Corbin* (Pamphlet, 1900), 18-21, Box 7, Corbin Papers.

13. *War Investigating Commission,* I, 685; III, 141-42, 240, 255-56, 310, 337-38; IV, 845-46, 851-52, 984-86, 1259; VI, 3110; VII, 3299, 3325. *RSW, 1898,* I, 13; IV, 245-46. GO 66, HQA, June 9, 1898,

From Secretary Alger down, War Department officials worked hard and unselfishly to master the situation in which they found themselves. If they were at times misguided or unimaginative, they nevertheless served honorably; none used his post to enrich himself. Thanks to their efforts, the Army's central administration muddled through the crisis. Gradually, as the department emerged from the initial confusion, its actions took on system and purpose. Through trial and error and often, as Corbin exemplified, through able men's simply looking around them and doing what was necessary, the early maldistribution of responsibilities was overcome. Perceptive officers undertook tasks as they came to their attention, and, as the Army's missions took on clearer definition, the War Department used its personnel more efficiently. Further, experience with large-scale operations improved the performance of officers at every point along the chain of command.

II

The formation of that chain of command by the appointment of generals and staff officers constituted one of the War Department's most urgent and complicated undertakings during the first weeks of mobilization. Under the law of April 22, the states commissioned the regimental and company commanders of their Volunteers while the President selected a specified number of major generals, brigadier generals, and staff officers for each division actually formed. The President also appointed all officers of the United States Volunteer Cavalry, Infantry, Engineers, and Signal Corps. In July a series of acts of Congress authorized additional officers for the bureaus, some of them Volunteers and others Regulars, all to be selected by the President. In all, the White House and the War Department controlled about 1,000 Regular and Volunteer commissions, many of which carried with them substantial prestige and power. The task of distributing this bounty proved difficult and time-consuming for the harried chiefs of the War Department.[14]

During May and June, the months in which the Army took shape, more than 25,000 applicants for commissions, many of whose applications were reinforced by endorsements from influential friends in politics and the

GO/AGO, 1898. Risch, *Quartermaster Corps*, 517-19, 525. Chief Q. M. Guy Howard to the Quartermaster General, September 20, 1898, and Lt. Col. J. B. Bellinger, Report of the Quartermaster Depot at Tampa, May 18-August 31, 1898 (hereafter cited as Bellinger, Tampa Report), both in File No. 115533, OQMG Records. Maj. Gen. J. R. Brooke to Adj. Gen. Corbin, April 23, 1898, and Corbin to Brooke, April 25, 1898, File No. 75583; Corbin to Brooke, June 7, 1898, File No. 87702; Brig. Gen. L. A. Carpenter to Corbin, September 10, 1898, File No. 147555, AGO Records. *Army and Navy Journal*, April 23, 1898. *The New York Times*, May 22, June 4 and 5, 1898.

14. Alger, *Spanish-American War*, 32-33. Risch, *Quartermaster Corps*, 517. *War Investigating Commission*, I, 122, 194-95; II, 784. GO 52, HQA, May 24, 1898; GO 96, HQA, July 13, 1898; GO/AGO, 1898.

business community, descended on the War Department. Cabinet officers, senators, representatives, governors, and state politicians all interceded on behalf of constituents or relatives. Even President McKinley took a personal interest in scores of cases and often directed particular appointments or promotions or secured a special favor for some old Ohio friend. Applicants and highly placed callers on behalf of applicants occupied so much of Secretary Alger's business day that he absented himself from his office in the mornings and remained at home where he could read his correspondence without distractions. He and Adjutant General Corbin saved much of their administrative work for evenings and Sundays, when their offices were closed to the public. Not until mid-July did they finish parceling out the commissions, and only then did the importunate mob cease to jam the corridors of the War Department.[15]

President McKinley closely supervised Army appointments. A master builder of political coalitions, he used Army commissions to recognize and reward sections and interest groups, thereby consolidating their support for his Administration. He saw to it that each state received a share of the commissions roughly proportional to its population and importance. Political opponents accused McKinley and Alger of favoring their home states of Ohio and Michigan in making appointments, but those states received no more than their share. McKinley was careful to give Democrats, and especially Southern Democrats, a large portion of the ranking military appointments. He did so for two reasons: First, he wanted to increase Southern support for his Administration and its policies; second, as the first war President since Appomattox, he wanted to demonstrate that sectional animosity was a thing of the past, that Blue and Gray now stood united against the national enemy. To implement this policy, McKinley awarded major generals' commission to Joseph Wheeler of Alabama and Fitzhugh Lee of Virginia, both distinguished Confederate cavalry leaders and influential Southern Democrats. Lesser Confederate veterans received brigadier generals' stars. Yet, while McKinley took politics into account in distributing commissions, he also insisted on military ability in the men he chose. He scrutinized applicants' records carefully and favored those with Regular Army or National Guard experience. Often, as in his choice of Wheeler and Lee, military fitness went hand in hand with political expediency.[16]

15. Alger, *Spanish-American War*, 29-33, 39-40. Bigelow, *Santiago Campaign*, 5-6. *Army and Navy Journal*, April 30, 1898. *The New York Times*, May 27 and June 17, 1898. For examples of political intervention in appointments, see the following: J. Pierpont Morgan to Secretary Alger, May 19, 1898; Alger to Judge Philip T. Van Zile, July 17, 1898, Alger Papers. Secretary of the Treasury Lyman J. Gage to Alger, June 4, 1898, Box 1, Gage Papers; this is only one of many such letters in Gage's papers. John Addison Porter to Alger, May 2, 3, 5, 10, 12, 13, and 14, 1898; Porter to Adj. Gen. Corbin, June 17, July 7, 8, and 13, August 2 and 12, 1898; George B. Cortelyou to Corbin, July 19, 1899, McKinley Papers. This is only a small sampling of the letters on military patronage in the President's papers.

16. *Army and Navy Journal*, February 25 and April 8, 1899. *The New York Times*, May 6 and 29, 1898. Morgan, *Road to Empire*, 68-69. Maj. Gen. Joseph Wheeler, *The Santiago Campaign, 1898*, 3-4. John Addison Porter to Secretary Alger, May 18 and 23 and June 28, 1898; Memorandum, June 10, 1898, on officer appointments, unsigned; Charles T. O'Ferrall to President McKinley, June 22, 1898; John Addison Porter to Adj. Gen. Corbin, August 2 and 3, 1898, McKinley Papers.

Statistics on the awarding of commissions reveal the Administration's bias in favor of the professional soldier. Of 26 major generals of Volunteers commissioned during the war, 19 were promoted Regular Army officers; the remaining 7 came from civil life. Out of 102 brigadier generals, 66 came from the Regular Army and 36 from civilian occupations. Of the civilians appointed, most had served in the Civil War or brought experience in the Regular Army or National Guard as a qualification. Several were West Point graduates who had left the Army to enter business and politics and now were recalled in the emergency. McKinley officered the United States Volunteer Cavalry, Engineer, and Immune regiments largely from the Regular Army. The Hull bill created vacancies in the Regular service for 195 second lieutenants, and to fill them McKinley for the first time drew upon the graduates of military courses in the land-grant colleges. The editor of the *Army and Navy Journal,* a spokesman for the Uptonian reformers, praised McKinley's Army appointments and rejoiced that "the organization and discipline of our volunteer forces has been entrusted to soldiers and not to politicians."[17]

Of all McKinley's military appointments, his nominations for Volunteer staff positions aroused the most controversy. The law of April 22 and the later legislation that enlarged the bureaus created over 400 temporary staff posts for the President to fill. About half of the appointees he took from the Regular Army, either by promotions of officers already in the staff bureaus or by transfers of line officers to the supply departments. Under the President's supervision, Alger and Corbin selected the rest from civilian applicants, apportioned among the states according to population. They secured from each applicant a statement of his age, education, and military experience and required each to present an endorsement from his senator or congressman. Corbin then prepared a list of the most promising applicants, from which the President made the final selections.[18]

Sharp-eyed critics detected many prominent Republican names on the lists of staff officers so chosen. They found there the names of sons of such party leaders as former President Benjamin Harrison, Secretary Alger, and James G. Blaine as well as the name of a grandson of Ulysses S. Grant. In all, twenty or thirty relatives of Republican governors, senators, congressmen

17. The quotation is from *Army and Navy Journal,* May 7, 1898; see also issues of May 28, June 4, 11, and 25, and August 2, 1898, and February 18 and August 5, 1899. *The New York Times,* May 21, 23, and 25, June 20 and 24, 1898. *War Investigating Commission,* I, 114. Alger, *Spanish-American War,* 34-36. Wilson, *Under the Old Flag,* II, 416-17. Maj. Gen. Miles to Secretary Alger, April 30, 1898, File No. 192302, AGO Records. Adjutant General Corbin nominated many Regular officers for their Volunteer commissions; see Corbin to Miles, April 21, 1898, Box 1A, Corbin Papers.

18. *RSW, 1898,* I, 257. *War Investigating Commission,* I, 120; VII, 3297-98. Alger, *Spanish-American War,* 34-36. *Army and Navy Journal,* May 21, 1898. *The New York Times,* May 13 and 18, 1898. Anna B. Kilbourne to President McKinley, May 11, 1898, McKinley Papers. Hugh L. Scott to Mrs. Scott, May 30, 1898, Box 1, Scott Papers.

Courtesy National Archives

Major General Joseph Wheeler
(Painting by Aimé Dupont)

144

Courtesy USAMHI

Major General Fitzhugh Lee

and local officials held staff commissions. Opposition politicians and editors cried favoritism and claimed that untrained civilians were being promoted over the heads of experienced and deserving career soldiers. *The New York Times* wailed that these appointments would "debauch the army by notifying its officers that preferment in the staff departments . . . goes by favor and not by merit. It is inexcusable and outrageous."[19]

While McKinley's solicitude for the sons and nephews of prominent Republicans deserved censure, the critics of his civilian staff appointments exaggerated the extent of the abuse of his power to appoint officers and ignored the personnel problem the President faced. McKinley did not in fact by-pass qualified Regulars to lavish these posts upon influential amateurs. He appointed over 200 Regulars to Volunteer staff positions, many of them to the highest ranks. He could have appointed more only by disbanding most of the Regular regiments and distributing their officers throughout the Volunteer Army. As it was, he left some regiments with only one commissioned officer to a company. Because there were not enough Regulars to staff all the troop organizations, and because the country lacked a reserve officer training program, McKinley necessarily used civilians. Most of the civilian appointees went into the lower ranks of the staff bureaus. Regulars dominated the higher grades and held the more responsible positions. In the Quartermaster and Subsistence departments, to which many civil appointees were assigned, Regulars commanded all of the major purchasing and supply depots and acted as chief quartermasters and commissaries of all army corps. Professionalism, not political expediency, governed the Administration's policies regarding selection of officers, and President McKinley used most of the country's available military talent effectively.[20]

Throughout its ranks, the army formed in 1898 contained excellent human material. The mixed lot of immigrants, drifters, adventurers, and refugees from poverty who filled the Regular regiments impressed observers as alert, tough, and superbly disciplined. The Volunteer rank and file, while they lacked the military experience and physical conditioning of the Regulars, also displayed soldierly promise. Mostly single men in their early twenties, they came from a broad variety of civil occupations, although farmers, clerks,

19. The quotation is from *The New York Times*, May 24, 1898; see also issues of May 20 and 21 and June 1 and 2, 1898. *Army and Navy Journal*, May 21 and June 4, 1898. R. Heber Newton to President McKinley, May 24, 1898; John Brown Simpson, "A Methodist and Veteran Republican," to McKinley, May 25, 1898, McKinley Papers.

20. *War Investigating Commission*, I, 114. RSW, 1898, I, 278, 531, 533-34, 555-61, 688. Alger, *Spanish-American War*, 32. *Army and Navy Journal*, May 28, 1898. *The New York Times*, May 24, 1898. John Addison Porter to John Brown Simpson, June 10, 1898, and to R. Heber Newton, June 10, 1898, McKinley Papers. Early in the war, the War Department asked Congress for authority to recall retired officers to fill staff jobs, but Congress, evidently eager to make room for Volunteers, refused the authorization. See Alger, *Spanish-American War*, 33, and *Army and Navy Journal*, June 25 and August 27, 1898.

and laborers predominated. Few of the Volunteers underwent the test of battle, but those who did, acquitted themselves well. A captain of Regular cavalry, not predisposed in favor of Volunteers, wrote of the Second Massachusetts Regiment on the march in Cuba: "They were about as brown, and looked almost as hardy, as the Regulars. They went through mud and water, well closed up, at a good swinging gait." After watching them in camp and battle, this officer concluded that the Volunteers of 1898 "were much better soldiers than Volunteers of our Civil War with the same length of service." Another Regular in Cuba praised the courage and discipline of the Rough Riders and the First Illinois Infantry. British officers who watched Volunteers from the western states in action at Manila spoke favorably of their discipline and steadiness under fire, their resourcefulness, and their willingness to take initiative, but they deplored the men's disregard for camp sanitation.[21]

One English observer saw broader implications in the performance of the American Volunteers. "Here . . .," he wrote, "is a fact for military nations to ponder—that the Volunteer in America is as good a fighter as the Regular. The military strength of the country must then be measured not by the size of its army, but by its capacity to produce volunteers and maintain them." Given the large population and the economic resources of the United States, he went on, that capacity was all but unlimited, and it made the United States one of the world's great military powers.[22]

Volunteer officers, especially those appointed by the states, made a less favorable impression upon knowledgeable observers than did their men, and some of them failed under the weight of responsibility. Many Volunteer officers, politicians who feared to offend voters back home, did not maintain strict discipline. A captain of Engineers in Puerto Rico saw one such officer meekly accept a tongue-lashing from an enlisted man in a public street. Others proved to be indifferent administrators. They neglected to inspect their camps, failed to requisition needed supplies, and ignored the often deplorable state of their men's food and health. A few displayed irresponsibility and cowardice. A drunken colonel from South Carolina, ordered to move his regiment from one camp to another, had his men take down their tents a day early, a bit of forehandedness that left the men shelterless throughout a night of drenching rain. During the invasion of Puerto Rico,

21. The quotation is from Bigelow, *Santiago Campaign*, 98. John H. Parker, *History of the Gatling Gun Detachment, Fifth Army Corps, at Santiago*, 178-85. *RSW, 1899*, I, Pt. 3, pp. 432, 443-44, 495. Oregon Adjutant General, *Seventh Biennial Report of the Adjutant General of the State of Oregon to the Governor and Commander-in-Chief, 1899-1900*, 26. For a British comment, see Charles Sidney Clark, "The Volunteer in War," *JMSI*, XXIV, 469-74 (reprinted from *United Service Magazine*, London). Anna Northend Benjamin, "Christian Work in Our Camps," *The Outlook*, LIX, 566-69. *The New York Times*, May 22, 1898.

22. Clark, *JMSI*, XXIV, 474.

the colonel, the lieutenant colonel, a major, and a captain of the Sixth Massachusetts Infantry were dismissed from command by General Miles for hiding in their tents or malingering on the transports while their men fought. To the credit of the Volunteers, the incompetents and the cowards were only a tiny minority of the whole, and by one means or another their superiors got rid of them. Most of the Volunteer officers lacked only training and experience. The best of them soon acquired the first qualification, and had the war lasted longer and required more fighting, those who survived would have gained the second.[23]

III

The responsibility for clothing, arming, and equipping the assembling troops fell most heavily upon the Quartermaster and Ordnance departments. The unexpected call for 125,000 Volunteers, followed in May by further enlargements of the Army, caught both bureaus with their clothing and weapon stock piles reduced by peacetime economy drives to a level barely sufficient for the 25,000-man Regular establishment. Since the bureau chiefs did not anticipate at the outset the assembly of such a large force and since preparation of the coast defenses seemed the immediately more urgent task, they had spent little of their shares of the Fifty Million appropriation to remedy these deficiencies. Quartermaster General Ludington in mid-March ordered his depots to accelerate production of clothing and tentage, purchased small quantities of extra material, and scouted market conditions in the industries upon which his bureau would draw in war, but not until April 20 and 25 did he issue large contracts for uniform cloth and tent canvas. Before Congress called for armed intervention in Cuba, Chief of Ordnance Brig. Gen. Daniel W. Flagler ordered a speed-up in rifle production, but he canceled it almost immediately, under the delusion that his department's existing reserve, supplemented by the usual daily output of the arsenals, would be ample for the small force contemplated. Not until late April did he order the production of 129,000 sets of infantry equipment. The Quartermaster's Department on April 30 could clothe and equip perhaps 25,000 additional troops. The Ordnance Department had available at the same time some 53,000 Krag-Jörgensen rifles and 15,000 carbines, but it had cartridge belts, knapsacks, and personal accoutrements for only 20,000 men. The equipment of the state reserves, the bureaus learned as the Volunteers streamed into camp, was woefully inadequate.[24]

23. *RSW, 1898*, II, 638. *War Investigating Commission*, III, 724. *Correspondence*, I, 373-76. *Army and Navy Journal*, September 24, 1898. Hugh L. Scott to Mrs. Scott, July 29, 1898, Box 1, Scott Papers. Maj. John R. Brooke to Adj. Gen. Corbin, September 8, 1898, File No. 128803; Eugene Ellicott to Asst. Adj. Gen. Heistand, May 12, 1899. File No. 236869, AGO Records. Alger, *Spanish-American War*, 34, 36. Funston, *Memories*, 153, describes a rough-and-ready method for weeding out incompetents.

24. *RSW, 1880*, I, xi-xii; *1881*, I, 10; *1883*, I, 11; *1898*, I, 449; IV, 14, 69-70. *War Investigating Commission*, I, 126-30, 196, 198, 437; II, 801; IV, 1111; VI, 2625-27, 2857-58; VII, 3139, 3149. Cruse, *Apache Days and After*, 255-56. Risch, *Quartermaster Corps*, 522, 535. *Army and Navy Journal*, March 12 and 19, 1898.

Assured ample funds by a Congress that appropriated over $130 million for the Quartermaster's Department alone, the bureaus lost no time in attacking the shortages of supplies. In peacetime, both departments manufactured most of their supplies in their own plants, using raw or semifinished materials bought from private contractors. Both now increased production at their arsenals and depots by hiring additional workers and installing new machinery. At the Quartermaster Department's clothing plant in Philadelphia, for example, the commanding officer for the first time supplemented the hand sewing of uniforms with the work of electric cutting and stitching machines. The Ordnance Department's Springfield Armory, which manufactured the Krag rifle, increased its work force during the war from less than 600 men to over 1,800 and established two 10-hour shifts per day. Daily rifle production rose from 120 in mid-March to 363 in mid-August. By adding more workers and machines, Frankford Arsenal at Philadelphia increased its daily production of .30-caliber rifle cartridges from 48,000 to 180,000. The equipment plant at Rock Island and the other arsenals reported similar expansion.[25]

The enlargement of government plants, however, proved insufficient to meet the needs of the war-swollen Army, and both Quartermaster and Ordnance departments made large contracts with private manufacturers for items they had previously turned out only in their own shops. The Quartermaster's depots at Philadelphia, New York, Saint Louis, Chicago, Boston, and Jeffersonville in Indiana, all acted as purchasing agencies, letting contracts for over 100 different pieces of clothing and equipment. Additional offices that had been opened to deal with the emergency tapped the markets of other major cities. The San Francisco depot purchased on the Pacific Coast much of the clothing and also many of the tents, wagons, and ambulances used by the Manila expedition. Except in extreme emergencies, purchasing officers called for bids on major supply orders. They gave manufacturers from twenty-four hours to ten days to reply, depending on the circumstances. The depot quartermaster who was to order the purchase opened the bids, inspected the samples of goods offered, and sent all the documents to Washington with his recommendation for the award. After reviewing these materials, the Quartermaster General almost invariably ratified his subordinate's recommendation and ordered him to complete the contract. This time-consuming procedure produced little but delay, and late in the war General Ludington began delegating full contracting powers to his subordinates. With this authority in hand, depot quartermasters awarded

25. *War Investigating Commission*, I, 127; II, 791-95; V, 2186-87. *RSW, 1893*, I, 19-20; *1898*, I, 15; IV, 13-16, 28-30, 32-39, 70-72, 76, 86-90. Maj. G. S. Bingham to the Quartermaster General, August 14, 1899, File No. 133396, OQMG Records. Alger, *Spanish-American War*, 23. Risch, *Quartermaster Corps*, 456-57, 521, 526-27. *The New York Times*, May 15 and 30, 1898. The Engineers and the Signal Corps also bought small amounts of their own specialized equipment but encountered no serious difficulties in obtaining all they needed. See *War Investigating Commission*, I, 194, 201; II, 781, and *RSW, 1898*, I, 902-3.

contracts to the lowest bidder who offered articles of standard quality for rapid delivery, but they sometimes paid a higher price for earlier delivery of better goods. At least on the government's side, no frauds marred the purchasing effort. For the most part, the goods furnished under these contracts proved to be of good quality, and careful bargaining by quartermasters kept the prices paid for clothing and animals at about the prewar level. In all, the Quartermaster's Department secured about two-thirds of its clothing and tentage and all of its vehicles and animals from private sources. Quartermaster General Ludington and his staff expressed satisfaction with the results of the contract system and urged more extensive and systematic resort to it in future emergencies.[26]

The Ordnance Department drew upon private contractors for millions of rounds of small-arms ammunition, thousands of artillery shells and fuses, and tens of thousands of cartridge belts, haversacks, mess kits, and horse accoutrements. Over 130 different firms supplied infantry and cavalry equipment. Shell and powder manufacturers enlarged their plant capacity, not only meeting the Army's immediate needs but enhancing the ability of their industry to respond effectively to subsequent emergencies. Following contracting procedures similar to those of the Quartermaster's Department, Ordnance officers bargained to keep prices down and, as far as their limited numbers permitted, made rigid inspections to maintain quality. Yet, General Flagler expressed less satisfaction with the contract system than did his colleague Ludington. One source of this discontent was the cost of Ordnance stores from private plants, which was higher than that for the same material made in government arsenals. Another was that few firms could produce all the components of such complex items as shrapnel shells and fuses. Parts turned out in widely scattered locations had to be brought to the arsenals for assembly into finished projectiles, a clumsy, time-consuming procedure. General Flagler concluded at the end of hostilities that the government should enlarge its own ordnance manufacturing capacity rather than rely primarily on private sources in wartime.[27]

Production delays and an inability to secure quickly the specialized military goods that had no civilian market plagued both bureaus and dictated early policies regarding supplies. General Ludington discovered, for example, that only a few firms at the outset could manufacture Army uniform fabrics and tent canvas, which were heavier and stronger than the common civilian products. He at once ordered all the standard materials he could obtain and tried to induce additional companies to start their manufacture.

26. War Investigating Commission, I, 138-41; V, 2184-85; VI, 2643, 2692-95, 2702; VII, 3140, 3763. RSW, 1898, I, 382-83, 385, 450-60. Risch, Quartermaster Corps, 526-27. Depot QM O. F. Long to the Quartermaster General, August 22, 1899. File No. 133396, OQMG Records. Army and Navy Journal, June 18, 1898. Russell A. Alger to Col. Curtis Guild, November 12, 1901; and Elihu Root to Alger, July 16, 1903, Alger Papers.

27. RSW, 1898, IV, 14, 20, 28-29, 38-39, 48-49, 70-71.

To meet immediate needs, however, he instructed his purchasing officers to buy up all the blue cloth that approached in quality the Army's rigid specifications and all the available tent canvas. The depot converted these materials into shirts, trousers, blouses, and tents, and camp quartermasters issued the resulting substandard items to the regiments as they streamed in. The uniforms, while they often wore out quickly or faded to strange and motley hues, at least covered the soldiers' nakedness. As to the tents, one quartermaster remarked, "It was thought better to have a poor tent than no tent at all." As rapidly as he could, General Ludington replaced these first issues with uniforms and tents of standard quality, but he could not do so quickly enough to escape the press's accusations of corruption and furnishing shoddy goods.[28]

An economy drive, back in Cleveland's second administration, had necessitated the sale of many of the Army's big six-mule supply wagons to save the cost of maintaining them. Now, under emergency conditions, Ludington made compromises in quality in order to remedy the desperate shortage of transportation in the camps. Without animals and vehicles in adequate numbers, the Army could neither maneuver in the field nor supply itself in camp. Fortunately, animals were readily available. Boards of artillery and cavalry officers and quartermasters' agents quickly secured at reasonable prices the 10,000 cavalry horses, 2,500 artillery horses, 17,000 draft mules, and 2,600 pack mules that were put into service during hostilities. The purchase of vehicles was less simple. The Army needed about 5,000 wagons to supply its divisions but had on hand at the start of mobilization less than 1,200, all in use by Regular regiments. Since no civilian demand existed for the sturdy six-mule vehicles normally used by the Army and so blithely sold during the economy drive, very few were obtainable, and only seven firms in the country manufactured them. These firms, having received few orders since the economy drive, had no stock piles of seasoned wood in the proper shapes and sizes for assembly. Hence, when the war began they could not resume production quickly. Ludington ordered all the big wagons the manufacturers could turn out and, to meet the immediate emergency, bought over 3,600 of the lighter four-mule wagons that were in manufacture to be sold commercially to farmers. To simplify the furnishing of spare parts, he bought only from large firms in lots of several hundred. Besides the farm wagons, he eventually secured 600 of the standard vehicles. The smaller farm wagons broke down often, wore out quickly,

28. *War Investigating Commission*, I, 128-29; IV, 885, 1238-39, 1262; V, 2187-89; VI, 2647-48, 2651-53, 2697-99; VII, 3139-40. *RSW, 1898*, I, 381-85, 450, 456-57. Alger, *Spanish-American War*, 23-24. Funston, *Memories*, 162-63, describes an early issue of uniforms and how they faded. Risch, *Quartermaster Corps*, 522-23, 525-27. Q. M. Gen. Marshall I. Ludington to Adj. Gen. Corbin, May 13, 1898, and Asst. Adj. Gen. William H. Carter to the Quartermaster General, May 17, 1898, File No. 81388, AGO Records. *The New York Times*, May 10, 1898.

and could not bear as much weight as the regulation type. Divisions that were equipped with them needed more than the usual allowance of vehicles to move their baggage. In many instances, the troops did not receive the extra wagons, and at the time of the armistice in mid-August the transportation shortage still had not been fully remedied in most camps.[29]

The Ordnance Department, as the result of its long-standing policy of spending most of its scanty annual artillery appropriation on hard-to-construct barrels and breech mechanisms, entered the war with ample stocks of cannon of all calibers, for which arsenals and private contractors rapidly furnished carriages, limbers, and ammunition wagons. By using its existing reserve of completed 3.2-inch fieldpieces, the bureau at once equipped each of the 14 Regular field batteries with its regulation number—six—and each of the 16 Volunteer batteries with four guns. It also put together a formidable siege train from the twenty-five 5-inch guns, twenty 7-inch howitzers, and twenty-five 3.6-inch mortars that stood ready in government arsenals, fully supplied with carriages and accessories, at the outbreak of war. During March and April Secretary Alger had sent most of these guns to strengthen the coast defenses, but early in May he ordered them concentrated at Tampa to equip batteries for the expected siege of Havana. By June 7 artillerymen at Tampa had organized two batteries of these heavy weapons that consisted between them of four cannon, four howitzers, and eight mortars. These units went to Santiago with the Fifth Corps while the formation of additional batteries went forward at Tampa. Besides field and siege cannon, the Ordnance Department issued to the troops twelve Hotchkiss guns, about sixty Gatling guns, and assorted other small-caliber rapid-fire weapons, which more than proved their worth in Cuba and the Philippines.[30]

The Ordnance Department encountered its most frustrating and damaging shortages and production delays in the securing of smokeless ammunition and up-to-date infantry small arms, and the two problems were closely related. Years of limited appropriations had prevented the Ordnance Department from stock-piling the smokeless powders that its officers by 1898 had developed for every weapon in the arsenals. Also, the war had caught most of the private manufacturers upon whom the government relied for its powder supply in the midst of converting their plants for production of the new explosive, a process totally different from the making of charcoal powder. When mobilization began, only three firms, two in the East and

29. *War Investigating Commission*, I, 130-31; IV, 1129-30, 1134; VI, 2608, 2624-26, 2628-29; VII, 3141-42. *RSW, 1898*, I, 385-86. Chief Q. M. Guy Howard to the Quartermaster General, September 20, 1898, File No. 115533, OQMG Records. Maj. Gen. J. R. Brooke to Adj. Gen. H. C. Corbin, June 9, 1898, File No. 159902, AGO Records. Cruse, *Apache Days and After*, 264-67. Risch, *Quartermaster Corps*, 535-39.

30. *War Investigating Commission*, II, 800; VI, 2857, 2868. *RSW, 1898*, IV, 9, 20-23, 31, 246. *The New York Times*, May 19, 1898. Circular No. 11, Headquarters of the Army, July 8, 1898, in *GO/AGO, 1898*.

one on the Pacific Coast, were fully tooled for smokeless powder; the works of a fourth producer had blown up on March 22. In response to wartime demand, many producers speeded conversion of constructed new plants, but most of the additional facilities were not ready in time to meet the immediate emergency. With production capacity thus limited, the Army and Navy worked out a priority system for allotting the available smokeless powder. In the first months of preparation, they used all the supply to make cartridges for the battleships' heavy guns and ammunition for the Krag-Jörgensen rifle, which could fire only smokeless powder. For the coast-defense guns, the field artillery, and the old-model rifles of the Volunteers, the Chief of Ordnance purchased an emergency reserve of charcoal powder, ample stocks of which were readily obtainable. During May he began buying smokeless powder for the field artillery, and still later he ordered smokeless cartridges for the Volunteers' Springfield rifles. None of this smokeless ammunition was available for issue until after the first expeditions had sailed for Santiago and Manila. In fact, ammunition for small arms remained in short supply throughout the duration of hostilities. For example, General Miles wanted to establish a reserve of 500 rounds of rifle ammunition per soldier, but the total amount delivered would have provided each of the over 275,000 men under arms with less than half that allowance. However, since most of the Army never entered combat, the shortage had no serious consequences.[31]

The limited supply and slow delivery of smokeless cartridges complicated the difficulties created by the Ordnance Department's shortage of Krag-Jörgensen rifles, a shortage that resulted in part from years of congressional parsimony and in part from General Flagler's initial expectation that only a small force would be mobilized. When the war began, the Ordnance Department had barely enough Krags on hand for the expanding Regular regiments. The National Guard possessed none of the new rifles because Congress, in spite of the War Department's pleas, had never voted funds for the Guard's rearmament. Springfield Arsenal, the only government plant that could manufacture the Krag, rapidly expanded its facilities, work force, and output, but it could not enlarge production sufficiently to rearm the Volunteers as they were mustered in. The Krag's manufacture could not be farmed out to private companies because they lacked the machinery and the license to use certain crucial patents. The Volunteers therefore would have to be issued some other firearm. The Ordnance Department could have purchased for them other magazine rifles of American or foreign manufacture, as General Miles proposed, but the foreign weapons might be intercepted

31. Alger, *Spanish-American War*, 13. *War Investigating Commission*, I, 197-98; II, 800; VI, 2850-51. *RSW, 1898*, IV, 13-14, 19-20, 22, 52-53. *Army and Navy Journal*, March 26, 1898. *The New York Times*, June 9 and 13, 1898. Asst. Adj. Gen. J. C. Gilmore to Adj. Gen. Corbin, May 20, 1898, File No. 81953, AGO Records.

at sea by Spanish warships or impounded by neutral governments, and the American rifles fell short of Army standards of accuracy and durability. At any event, the reserve of smokeless cartridges was increasing no more quickly than was the supply of Krags; if another weapon that required the same propellant had been issued to the Volunteers, they would have had no ammunition for it. Late in May, the ammunition shortage even prevented the issue of 20,000 of the available Krags to the First Corps. During the first two and one-half months of war, therefore, the Ordnance Department limited the distribution of Krags to the Regulars and to the Rough Riders, who benefited from Theodore Roosevelt's political influence.[32]

To arm the Volunteers, the Ordnance Department resorted to the .45-caliber Springfield rifle, which the Regulars had discarded for the Krag-Jörgensen. A single-shot breechloader, the Springfield used charcoal powder to propel its heavy slug and, in the hands of trained men, was an accurate, powerful weapon. Most National Guard regiments carried the Springfield in 1898, and the Ordnance Department had over 260,000 of them in storage at its arsenals. Because the Springfield fired charcoal powder, ammunition for it could be obtained at once. Further, the Ordnance Department had developed a smokeless cartridge for it, which contractors could begin manufacturing as soon as more urgent needs had been met. The Springfield thus seemed to the authorities a sensible stopgap in the emergency. Moreover, many officers of both line and staff considered the Springfield a match in combat for repeaters like the Krag. The extreme effective ranges of the two rifles were about the same, approximately two miles for each weapon. At the shorter distances at which most firing was done, the Springfield's 500-grain bullet would hit harder than the 220-grain slug of the Krag. Army fire tactics in the nineties placed greater value on accuracy than they did on rapid shooting. The Krag, while it had a five-shot magazine, was supposed to be used as a single-loader in all combat situations except the climactic moment of delivering or repelling a charge. The Springfield's lack of a magazine thus seemed only a marginal deficiency, and its firing rate of fifteen rounds per minute was expected to be rapid enough for most battle conditions. Besides, the Springfield's simpler breech mechanism, in the opinion of many Regular and National Guard officers, made it less likely than the Krag to get out of order under the rough handling of inexperienced Volunteers.[33]

32. *War Investigating Commission*, II, 800; VI, 2862. *RSW, 1894*, I, 63, and *1895*, I, 26, contain pleas that the militia be rearmed with the Krag. *RSW, 1898*, IV, 8, 85. Maj. Gen. J. R. Brooke to Adj. Gen. Corbin, May 26 and 27, 1898, Corbin to Brooke, May 27 and 28 and June 1, 1898, File No. 84218; Maj. Gen. Nelson A. Miles to Secretary Alger, July 1, 1898, File No. 192302; Maj. Gen. Coppinger to Corbin, July 19, 1898, and Corbin to Coppinger, July 20, 1898, File No. 260048, AGO Records. Brig. Gen. Daniel W. Flagler to Alger, April 11, 1898, Alger Papers. Flagler to Maj. Gen. James H. Wilson, June 20, 1898, Box 8, Wilson Papers. During the weeks after the passage of the Fifty Million Bill, the War Department considered arming the Volunteers with Winchester repeaters but dropped the plan; see *Army and Navy Journal*, March 12 and 19, 1898. Roosevelt, *Rough Riders*, 8-9.

33. *War Investigating Commission*, I, 197; II, 800; III, 232-33; VI, 2852-53; VII, 3267. *RSW, 1882*, I, xvii; *1892*, III, 28; *1897*, III, 27-28; *1898*, IV, 10-12, 51, 53, 237. Chief of Ordnance A. R.

Courtesy USAMHI

Stacked Springfields at Camp Thomas

During the first three months of the war the Ordnance Department outfitted the Volunteers with the Springfield and built up a supply of both charcoal and smokeless ammunition for it. At the same time, the bureau pressed its efforts to increase production of the Krag and prepared to replace the Volunteers' Springfields with the magazine rifle as regiments were designated for service at the front. This process began in July, when the Ordnance Department issued Krags to many of the Volunteer regiments assigned to the invasion of Puerto Rico. Even then, the supply of smokeless cartridges was barely adequate to furnish a minimum battle allowance for each man thus rearmed. Employed extensively in combat in Cuba and the Philippines, the Springfield, according to commanders' reports, proved inferior to the Krag in only two respects. Its charcoal powder created clouds of smoke, which exposed the troops' positions when they fired, and the flatter trajectory of the Krag bullet made the new weapon easier to aim at long ranges than the Springfield.[34]

Besides furnishing the soldier with weapons and ammunition, the Ordnance Department supplied him with his cartridge belt, canteen, haversack, knapsack, and eating utensils, and it furnished saddles and harness for the cavalry and artillery. Because the cloth and leather parts deteriorated if stored for long periods, the bureau never stockpiled these materials in peacetime. Instead, the Chief of Ordnance sought to build up at government arsenals sufficient machinery to turn out large quantities of equipment in the weeks immediately preceding any callup of troops. Congressional tightfistedness during the nineties had prevented completion of the equipment plant at Rock Island Arsenal, and this lack of plant capacity, along with the absence of advance information on the size of the projected war force, left the Ordnance Department in 1898 without resources to meet the immediate demand. The bureau struggled to make up for lost time. At Rock Island, the commander increased his work force to almost 3,000, installed additional machinery, and by mid-August had pushed output to 6,000 sets of infantry, cavalry, and artillery equipment per day. The Chief of Ordnance also ordered thousands of sets of infantry, cavalry, and artillery equipment from contractors, but few firms brought to their production any experience in this line. Consequently, their deliveries fell behind schedule and many of their

Buffington to Adj. Gen. Corbin, April 7, 1899, File No. 228078; Corbin to Rep. Robert J. Gamble, May 22, 1899, File No. 238300, AGO Records. Blunt, *Harper's Weekly*, XXXVII, 619. For prewar National Guard comment on the advantages of the Springfield, see Maine Adj. Gen., *Report for 1898*, 75-76. Capt. C. J. Crane, "The New Infantry Rifle," *JMSI*, XIX, 488-95, expresses prewar Regular Army doubts about the Krag.

34. Brig. Gen. Daniel W. Flagler to Maj. Gen. James H. Wilson, June 20, 1898, Box 8, Wilson Papers. Memorandum, Office of the Chief of Ordnance, July 17, 1898, File No. 105774; Maj. Gen. J. C. Breckinridge to Adj. Gen. Corbin, October 20, 1898, File No. 174154, AGO Records. *War Investigating Commission*, VI, 2864. *RSW, 1898*, IV, 12-13. *Correspondence*, I, 353. GO 144, HQA, September 16, 1898, in *GO/AGO, 1898*.

goods were of poor quality. Cartridge belts presented a special problem. Just before the war the Ordnance Department had begun issuing a new woven cartridge belt of design superior to any previously in use. However, it had bought all of these belts from a single firm, the only one in the country able to weave them, and that firm could not expand its limited production facilities rapidly enough to meet wartime demand. The Ordnance Department perforce had to accept substandard belts from other companies, some of which were delivered with loops too large to hold the cartridges. Nevertheless, by the end of August the bureau had secured enough equipment to outfit the whole Army, but slow deliveries, especially of mess kits, caused bitter complaint in the camps.[35]

Responsibility for feeding the troops rested upon the Subsistence Department, which purchased and issued the components of a ration set by act of Congress to protect the enlisted man from food-faddist commanders and the War Department from entrepreneurial pressures. The Army in fact used three different rations, each of which constituted a monotonous but, by the standards of that day, well-balanced diet. The garrison ration, issued to troops in barracks or permanent camps, consisted of fresh meat (mostly beef), bread or flour, fresh vegetables according to the locality and season, green coffee, salt, pepper, sugar, vinegar, candles, and soap. The field ration, for troops on the march, contained bacon, hardtack, canned or otherwise preserved vegetables, roasted coffee, and the same seasonings and accessories as the garrison ration. Troops traveling on trains and ships or stationed where they could not cook received the travel ration: canned beef, hardtack, canned baked beans, roasted coffee, and sugar, with canned tomatoes added on long journeys. The Army at that time had no equivalent of the prepared C-rations and K-rations of later wars. The Subsistence Department was experimenting with an emergency ration of bacon, pea meal, hardtack, ground coffee, seasonings, and plug tobacco in a compact wrapping, but few soldiers received it in the Spanish War. Beyond adding canned salmon to the meat ration, Commissary General Charles P. Eagan made no major changes in the Army's diet. Years of service in the line before joining his bureau had established his faith in the basic staples, and he rejected the prepared foods and concentrated diets pressed upon him by inventors and promoters.[36]

Only in the method of furnishing fresh beef did Eagan attempt major innovation. In past wars and campaigns, troops in the field had driven herds of cattle along with them and slaughtered animals as needed to make up

35. Alger, *Spanish-American War*, 22-23. *War Investigating Commission*, I, 198; II, 801, 807; VI, 2857-59, 2866. *RSW, 1898*, IV, 7, 14-16.

36. *War Investigating Commission*, I, 151, 551; VI, 2956-57. *RSW, 1898*, I, 550-53, 643. *Army Regulations, 1895*, Paragraphs 1251 and 1252. Undated manuscript headed "Subsistence," Box 1A, Corbin Papers. Circular No. 1, Office of the Commissary General of Subsistence, May 16, 1898, and GO 15, HQA, June 7, 1898, both in *GO/AGO, 1898*. Risch, *Quartermaster Corps*, 506-7.

the daily ration. This system was wasteful and in overseas operations, especially in devastated Cuba, impractical. The meatpacking industry's new technologies of refrigeration and canning offered alternatives that seemed healthful and economical. To feed the men in the home camps and wherever possible overseas, Eagan relied on refrigerated beef, frozen dressed carcasses shipped from the packing houses in specially equipped railroad cars and transport vessels. Where he could not use refrigerated beef, Eagan resorted to a canned substance called "fresh roast beef," which had been part of the Army ration since the late 1870s but little used until 1898. Actually a boiled beef, steam-cooked and canned by most of the major packers, canned roast beef was designed as an ingredient for stews and formed a regular part of the diet of Western hunters, cowboys, and prospectors. The United States Navy purchased about 500,000 pounds of it annually, and European Powers imported huge amounts of it to feed their soldiers. The product appeared to Eagan and his subordinates to be an economical, easily transported substitute for fresh beef and a palatable one as well. Col. John F. Weston of the Subsistence Department wrote to Eagan late in March that he had combined canned beef with the vegetable components of the field ration to produce a stew "fit for the immortal gods and not beneath the notice of a general." This report was to prove overoptimistic; it seemed that the preferences of the rank and file were not those of gods or generals.[37]

An aggressive, hard-driving administrator, Eagan adjusted quickly to the need to purchase foodstuffs rapidly and in huge quantities. Early in April, before Eagan took over the Subsistence Department, his predecessor had obtained from departmental and depot commissaries throughout the country accurate lists of the major food suppliers, with a detailed record of which ration components each firm could furnish on short notice. As soon as the troops began concentrating, Subsistence officers in Chicago and other food-processing centers, with the aid of this information, issued contracts for millions of pounds of meat, vegetables, flour, and all the myriad substances required to feed an army. Whenever possible, they advertised for bids on large orders, but they bought freely in the open market when immediate action was necessary. For items of regular consumption, such as meat and vegetables, purchasing commissaries contracted on a monthly basis. The supplier agreed to ship during that period, at an agreed-upon rate, to camps designated by the commissary, all that the Army required of that particular ration component. For refrigerated beef, General Eagan usually dealt directly with the larger packers. Corps and division commissaries often purchased fresh bread and vegetables from firms in the vicinity of their camps.[38]

37. The quotation is from Col. J. F. Weston to Commissary General Charles P. Eagan, March 24, 1898, in Alger, *Spanish-American War*, 388-89; see also 390-91. Risch, *Quartermaster Corps*, 449, 529. *War Investigating Commission*, I, 557; IV, 1558-59; VI, 2939, 2948. *Army and Navy Journal*, March 4, 1899.

38. *War Investigating Commission*, I, 546-47; IV, 1556-58; VI, 2949. *RSW, 1898*, I, 553. Alger, *Spanish-American War*, 380. Risch, *Quartermaster Corps*, 529. *Army and Navy Journal*, May 28, 1898.

The American food industry easily met the Army's demands, and the officers and men usually found their rations ample in quantity and adequate in quality, although Volunteers, fresh from civilian life, often complained of the monotony of the Army diet. In the home camps, the only serious food shortages resulted from spoilage of supplies en route, distribution difficulties within the camps, and poor cooking and management of the ration by regimental and company officers and cooks. Minor complaints arose about some specific ration components. The practice of issuing green, unground coffee, for example, created difficulty for troops in the field, who often lacked facilities for roasting and grinding it. Insp. Gen. J. C. Breckinridge thought that the ration should include a soft drink with which the men could quench their thirst in hot climates where the water was scarce or unpotable. The loudest, most widespread, and most bitter complaints descended upon the canned roast beef from which Commissary General Eagan had expected so much. Often issued in hot weather to troops who lacked equipment for cooking it, the stuff proved at best tasteless and at worst, to quote Theodore Roosevelt, "nauseating." Even hungry men could not choke it down in its uncooked state. Around this beef grew, later in the war, the scandal that wrecked Eagan's career.[39]

In spite of the miscalculations caused by the early uncertainty about the size of the wartime Army and in spite of the delays while producers retooled to make specialized military items, the bureaus manufactured and purchased the necessary supplies rapidly and with a minimum of confusion and wasted motion. As early as the middle of June, tens of thousands of uniforms, thousands of tents, hundreds of wagons, and arms and accoutrements in proportion were on their way to the camps. By mid-August, the Quartermaster and Ordnance departments had procured and issued enough material to supply each soldier with a rifle, full outfit of cartridge belt, canteen, haversack, and mess kit, and his complete allowance of clothing and tentage. The Ordnance Department had accumulated enough ammunition to equip the overseas expeditions and to provide a small training allowance for troops in the United States, although it still lacked a full battle reserve for every man in the Army. However, difficult as it had been to obtain supplies and start them in the direction of the camps, this phase of equipping the troops was easier than the next—getting the supplies and equipment to the men who needed them.[40]

39. War Investigating Commission, III, 84-85, 111, 230, 329-30, 721-22, 751; IV, 844-45, 854-55, 1110, 1243-44, 1260; VI, 3107, 3110. RSW, 1898, II, 221. Maj. Gen. J. R. Brooke to Secretary Alger, May 31, 1898, File No. 87864; Commissary General Charles P. Eagan to Alger, September 23, 1898, File No. 136786; Lt. Col. Frank D. Baldwin to the Adjutant General of Camp George H. Thomas, August 20, 1898, Maj. Gen. J. C. Breckinridge to Adj. Gen. Corbin, October 20, 1898, File No. 174154, AGO Records. Alger, Spanish-American War, 421-22. For a Volunteer regiment's experience with food at Chickamauga, see Creagher Fourteenth Ohio, 100-101. Roosevelt, Rough Riders, 61, expresses the consensus in Shafter's army on Eagan's canned beef.

40. War Investigating Commission, I, 129, 131, 197; II, 800-801; VI, 2649-50, 2654, 2850. RSW, 1898, I, 383-84; IV, 13, 16, 25-26. Alger, Spanish-American War, 24. Q. M. Gen. Marshall I. Ludington

IV

Under orders of the generals in command of departments, corps, and camps, staff officers in the field were supposed to distribute food and equipment to the troops and report supply needs or shortages to their superiors and to their bureaus in Washington. This system of administration in the field suffered a near breakdown in the first weeks of the Spanish War, and from its failure stemmed most of the supply deficiencies that made army life miserable for so many soldiers. Difficulties in correlating supply distribution with strategy, lack of transportation facilities of all sorts, and undermanned, inexperienced camp staffs formed an almost insurmountable barrier between the weapons, food, and clothing so laboriously obtained by the bureaus and the men who needed them. It was in the field, rather than in Washington, that the worst effects of thirty years of centralized administration and congressional penny-pinching became acutely evident.

The Quartermaster and Ordnance departments changed their supply distribution systems as the Administration's war strategy and mobilization plans changed. In compliance with the original plans, they sent stores for the Regulars directly to the regiments in camp or to Fort McPherson and San Francisco, the principal collecting points for recruits. They founded their initial plans for supplying the Volunteers on two assumptions: that the regiments, as Miles proposed, would remain in their states until fully outfitted; and that the bureaus would merely be completing the outfits of troops already partially clothed and equipped by the states that raised them. At the suggestion of Generals Ludington and Flagler, the War Department's general orders of April 30 and May 5 required the quartermaster and ordnance officer of each Volunteer regiment, as soon as it entered federal service, to determine how many state supplies the unit had and how much additional material it needed to complete its equipment. The officers would then requisition the additional stores from the War Department by sending their estimates to Washington. The bureaus then would dispatch the required arms, clothing, and accoutrements to the state camps. The federal government would give the state authorities receipts for all National Guard property their regiments took into the Volunteer service and would later reimburse the states in money or in kind. To guide Volunteer officers in

---

to Col. J. G. C. Lee, May 14, 1898, and to Depot Q. M. at Jeffersonville, Ind., May 14, 1898, File No. 99478, OQMG Records. Asst. Adj. Gen. Heistand to Commanding General at Chickamauga Park, July 15, 1898, File No. 102388, AGO Records. *Army and Navy Journal*, June 17, 1898. *The New York Times*, June 2 and 3, 1898.

determining their needs, a War Department order of May 10 listed, item by item, the proper equipment for an infantryman, a cavalryman, and an artilleryman.[41]

This procedure soon proved unworkable. The procedures of exchanging receipts and filing reports and requisitions were grossly inefficient for so large an army, and they threatened to swamp the Washington offices in a flood of paper. Because some states withheld militia equipment from their Volunteers and because so much state material was discovered, on inspection, to be obsolete or worn out, the initial supply estimates became all but useless as guides to bureau action. After McKinley decided on an early offensive, regiments began leaving their state camps before receiving all the equipment they had requisitioned. The bureaus, having acted on the President's first plans, had sent small lots of supplies to widely separated places, only to have them arrive after the units for which they were designated had departed. The bureau chiefs soon realized also that they did not have enough qualified officers to supervise simultaneous operations in forty-five different states. When the War Department in mid-May ordered most of the regiments to a few large camps, the bureaus welcomed the decision and adjusted their procedures to it. They established depots at the major concentrations and shipped articles to them in bulk, often direct from the factories. From these depots the supply officers then filled the requisitions of individual regiments.[42]

The movement of troops and supplies to the large camps by rail presented few difficulties. Lines crisscrossed all parts of the nation, and the railroad companies by the late nineties had perfected systems for through service and for the transfer of cars from one road to another. The government simply made the contracts for transportation and let the companies assemble and move the trains. Early in May, Secretary Alger considered bringing a railroad executive into the Quartermaster's Department to coordinate rail transportation, but Col. Charles W. Bird, the veteran quartermaster who oversaw those matters within the bureau, conducted the first movements of Regulars and Volunteers so efficiently that Alger dropped

41. Chief of Ordnance D. W. Flagler to Secretary Alger, April 30, 1898, File No. 76880; Q. M. Gen. M. I. Ludington to Adj. Gen. Corbin, May 4, 1898, File No. 80457, AGO Records. GO 31, HQA, April 30, 1898; GO 41, HQA, May 10, 1898, GO/AGO, 1898.

42. War Investigating Commission, I, 129; III, 128, 133; VI, 2647, 2865; VII, 3142. RSW, 1898, I, 405; IV, 23-24, 245-46. While it used depots in the camps for distribution, the Ordnance Department throughout the war tried to earmark specific lots of weapons and equipment for specific regiments; see RSW, 1898, IV, 5-6, 23. Chief of Ordnance D. W. Flagler to Secretary Alger, May 11, 1898, and Adj. Gen. Corbin to Flagler, May 16, 1898, File No. 79040, AGO Records. The New York Times, June 3, 1898. Ohio Adj. Gen., Report, 1898, 641-42, describes his state's bookkeeping problems.

the idea of a civilian "czar" and left Bird in charge. Most Quartermaster contracts for the rail carriage of passengers and freight were negotiated by the department, camp, and depot quartermasters at the points of origin of the shipments, with the Quartermaster General or Colonel Bird intervening from Washington occasionally to secure a lower rate or faster service. For example, if a regiment was to go by rail from Camp Thomas to an Atlantic embarkation port, Adjutant General Corbin would inform General Ludington of the fact and indicate when the regiment should move. Ludington then passed the information to the depot quartermaster at Chickamauga, who arranged for the trains and told the regimental commander when to have his gear packed and his men at the station. Unlike Civil War soldiers, who often rode in boxcars, troops in the Spanish-American War, by government order, traveled in day coaches or, on long trips, in sleeping cars. If assigned such accommodations, a single infantry regiment required six trains to carry its men, equipment, and animals.[43]

When the first contingents were being transported, the officers discovered that it was easier to place men and stores on trains and start them to the camps than to get them unloaded when they arrived. None of the assembly camps had adequate warehouses or sidings in the first and busiest weeks, and the hurried shipment to them of thousands of troops and carloads of equipment in late May and early June resulted in monumental traffic jams. Adding to the confusion, the forwarding of freight shipments to the camps was poorly coordinated. Depot quartermasters dispatched carloads of material to the concentration points without informing anyone on the ground of what was on the way or when it would arrive. Boxcars with no indication on their sides of what they contained reached the camps days and sometimes weeks ahead of the bills of lading that itemized their cargoes. The southern railroads that served most of the principal camps and embarkation ports were less wealthy and technically efficient than their northern counterparts. Occasionally they ran short of locomotives and rolling stock, so they delayed troop movements while they borrowed equipment from more affluent lines. Disputes arose between troops and railroad workers about the loading of regimental animals and baggage; cavalrymen especially complained about the railroadmen's mistreatment of their beloved horses.[44]

43. *War Investigating Commission*, I, 132, 440-41, 505; III, 134-39; VI, 2607-8, 2767-68, 2777-78. *RSW, 1898*, I, 386-87, 437. *The New York Times*, May 4, 9, and 17, and June 1, 1898. Alger, *Spanish-American War*, 21-22. Risch, *Quartermaster Corps*, 540-41, 543-44.

44. *War Investigating Commission*, I, 522, 525, 533-34, 536, 538-39; IV, 1237-38; VI, 2610, 3103. *Correspondence*, I, 294, 296, 317. Risch, *Quartermaster Corps*, 540-41. For a cavalryman's complaint, see Bigelow, *Santiago Campaign*, 29-30. Lt. Col. J. B. Bellinger, Report of the QM Depot at Tampa, May 18-August 31, 1898, File No. 115533, OQMG Records.

Army officers and railroad executives soon eliminated most of the obstacles to the smooth, rapid movement of troops and stores. At the principal camps, the railroads, usually at their own expense, installed additional platforms and sidings. Their shipping agents cooperated with the depot quartermasters to prevent pile-ups of supplies. Early in June, Quartermaster General Ludington ordered all shipping officers to send a list of the contents of each freight car ahead of it to its destination, and a month later he directed them to tack signs on the outsides of boxcars that carried Army stores, indicating the nature of the goods within. In telegraphic contact with railroad traffic managers, depot quartermasters followed rush shipments through to their destinations, thus reducing the change of their being lost or delayed. Troop commanders and supply officers almost unanimously praised the efficiency and spirit of cooperation displayed by the railroad companies and their employees. The chief quartermaster at Camp Thomas said of the railroadmen with whom he dealt that "their services went far beyond mere business effort, and partook of the character of friendly, zealous and interested aid in forwarding the government business." During the war months, the railroads moved, in all, over 17,000 officers and 435,000 men in reasonable comfort, without serious accident, and at rates for both freight and passengers far lower than those charged civilian shippers.[45]

The railroad corporations with which the War Department dealt were organized and staffed for grand-scale endeavors and followed administrative procedures adapted to the smooth movement of large numbers of people and large quantities of freight. The same could not always be said of the War Department's own supply bureaus. Those agencies worked diligently to move supplies into the camps with the least possible delay, but circumstances, their own mistakes, and clumsy procedures often partially nullified their efforts. The shortage of many items at the outset, combined with the need to launch overseas expeditions within a month of the first call for troops, forced delays in the shipment of scarce articles to Chickamauga, Jacksonville, and Camp Alger. The first uniforms, tents, wagons, and medical kits went to Tampa and San Francisco in order to outfit the invasion units, while regiments in the reserve camps struggled along with the bare minimum of equipment and sometimes less than the minimum. At Camps Thomas and Alger, the bureaus at first failed to cooperate effectively with the troop commanders, more through misunderstanding and confusion over authority than through obstructive malice. Commissaries,

45. The quotation is from Col. J. G. C. Lee to the Quartermaster General, September 11, 1898, File No. 115533, OQMG Records; in same collection, see Capt. D. A. McCarthy to the Quartermaster General, August 5, 1899, and Lt. Col. C. A. McCanley to the Depot Q. M. at Philadelphia, August 24, 1898, File No. 133396. *War Investigating Commission,* I, 132, 524; III, 126, 139, 434; IV, 958; VI, 2609, 2611-12; VII, 3152; VIII, 519-20. *RSW, 1898,* 387. Risch, *Quartermaster Corps,* 541-42.

medical officers, and ordnance specialists everywhere complained that whenever transportation was short the Quartermaster's Department, which shipped the stores of all other bureaus as well as its own, discriminated in favor of its own material. The Ordnance Department's issue procedures proved too rigid for wartime efficiency. At Tampa, for instance, the depot commander would not permit regiments to draw rifles for recruits in advance of the men's arrival; he would not even requisition the weapons until the recruits actually reached camp. Most crippling of all their procedural deficiencies was the bureaus' heavy reliance on requisitions from unit commanders and camp depots in determining the distribution of supplies. In contrast to the procedures in World War I, when the bureaus maintained a constant flow of stores to the front based on estimates of need, in 1898 they waited for requests from the field before sending out equipment. This overreliance on requisitions led to much unnecessary correspondence and created endless, frustrating delays in the delivery of needed stores.[46]

In distributing stores, the Subsistence Department outperformed the other bureaus, partly because it could obtain ample stocks at the outset of the war and partly because Commissary General Eagan broke free of the requisition system. As soon as the troops began to concentrate, Eagan established a Subsistence depot under the command of an experienced Regular officer near each camp. This officer drew stores from purchasing commissaries in the large cities and contracted locally for fresh vegetables and bread. He kept his depot stocked with rations sufficient to meet the day-to-day needs of the troops and to build up a reserve of sixty days' food for the entire command. On the basis of weekly reports from each depot, General Eagan sent in additional stores to maintain the sixty days' reserve. The depot at Camp Thomas also kept on hand 350,000 to 400,000 travel rations for issue to regiments ordered overseas. As a result of Eagan's system, camp commanders complained, not of an insufficiency of food, but rather of an oversupply. For example, Maj. Gen. J. R. Brooke at Camp Thomas declared that General Eagan had swamped him with rations and that he lacked storage space for the supplies pouring in upon him.[47]

46. *War Investigating Commission*, I, 199, 540; III, 81; IV, 984-85, 1110-11, 1237-38, 1433. Adj. Gen. Corbin to Maj. Gen. J. R. Brooke, May 24 and 27, 1898, and Brooke to Corbin, May 25 and 31 and June 4, 1898, File No. 84218; Corbin to Brooke, June 13, 1898, File No. 89371; Maj. Gen. Miles to Gen. J. C. Gilmore, June 7, 1898, File No. 90846; Brooke to Corbin, June 17, 1898, File No. 96332; Brig. Gen. L. A. Carpenter to the Adj. Gen., IV Corps, September 10, 1898, and Brig. Gen. Robert H. Hall to the Adj. Gen., IV Corps, September 10, 1898, File No. 147555; Maj. Gen. Fitzhugh Lee to Corbin, June 5, 1898, File No. 160137, AGO Records. Risch, *Quartermaster Corps*, 666, describes the supply system in World War I.

47. *War Investigating Commission*, I, 152-53, 204, 547, 552, 554, 556; III, 132, 329; IV, 844-45, 1243, 1559; VI, 2940, 2950, 3072. *RSW, 1898*, I, 554, 560-61, 582. General Brooke's complaint of an overabundance of food and the Commissary General's reply to it are in Maj. Gen. J. R. Brooke to Adj. Gen. Corbin, May 17, 1898, and Commissary General Charles P. Eagan to Corbin, May 17, 1898, File No. 81048, AGO Records. *The New York Times*, May 22, 1898.

Even had all the bureau chiefs been as efficient and aggressive as General Eagan, administrative breakdowns within the assembly camps would have deprived soldiers of needed supplies. Sprawling over square miles of ground and filled with untrained men under inexperienced officers, the great troop concentrations presented an administrative problem that was almost insurmountable, considering the staff and resources available to the War Department at the outset. The shortage of wagons, for example, hampered the distribution of supplies over such large areas. Because of the rapid changes in war strategy and mobilization plans, the camps took form before commanders, staffs, and supplies could reach them. Maj. Gen. William M. Graham, commanding the Second Corps, did not arrive at Camp Alger until May 19. He found there five or six regiments camped helter-skelter over the ground, no staff officers, and no supplies. Major General Brooke at Camp Thomas complained repeatedly that he lacked officers to control the thousands of Volunteers who were being sent to him. Camp administration under these conditions was often at least haphazard. "The United States troops who arrive in Tampa," a journalist wrote, "are dumped out at a railway siding like so many emigrants. No staff officer prepares anything in advance for them. Regiments go off in any direction that suits them, looking for the nearest place where they may cook their pork and beans."[48]

In every camp a critical shortage of trained staff officers prevented efficient management. The bureaus had entered the war with barely enough officers to man their Washington headquarters, staff the geographical departments, and run the purchasing and manufacturing depots. Most of these officers, their responsibilities and the need for their skills increased by the emergency, could not be spared for field service. The Volunteer law of April 22 and later legislation created on paper a full staff for the wartime Army, but the selection and commissioning of its members required time. Most of these Volunteer staff officers did not reach the assembly camps until late June or early July, long after the formation of the divisions and brigades they were supposed to administer. When they did arrive, they needed additional weeks to learn their jobs. In the first weeks of mobilization, during which the need for a large, competent staff was most urgent, the work of distributing supplies in each camp fell on a few Regular quartermasters, commissaries, and ordnance officers. The 20,000-man Philippine expedition, preparing for combat in hostile country 4,000 miles from home, could be allotted only three experienced quartermasters. The chief quartermaster at Camp Thomas, with almost 60,000 troops under his care, had only four officers to assist him.[49]

48. The quotation is from *The New York Times*, June 12, 1898. *War Investigating Commission*, III, 213-14; IV, 853, 883. Chief Q. M. Guy Howard to the Quartermaster General, September 20, 1898, File No. 115533, OQMG Records. Maj. Gen. J. R. Brooke to Adj. Gen. Corbin, May 30, 1898, File No. 87702, AGO Records. Bigelow, *Santiago Campaign*, 33-35.

49. *War Investigating Commission*, I, 112, 116, 122-23, 126-27, 148-49, 194-95, 200-201, 791; II, 784; III, 54, 84-85, 125, 127-28, 140, 246, 259; IV, 883-84, 886-87, 954, 962; VI, 2702, 2861,

This handful, themselves inexperienced in managing divisional and corps formations, were brutally overburdened. The depot quartermaster at Camp Thomas considered the emergency ended when he could reduce his work day from nineteen hours to fifteen. The depot commissary at the same camp wrote: "I have arranged matters so that I sleep until about 5 o'clock in the morning, and go to bed usually not later than midnight." Tired, overworked men inevitably made mistakes and lost their tempers, and the inexperience of the Volunteers on the new divisional and brigade staffs "made it impossible to get proper requisitions for supplies, and caused great confusion, adding to the difficulty in finding out just what was wanted, and making impossible an intelligent disposition of the supplies on hand." Lt. Col. Curtis Guild, Inspector General of the Seventh Corps, summed up the effect upon the soldiers of this staff shortage and correctly placed the blame for it:

> Men imperfectly trained or utterly ignorant have been placed in highly important positions, with the health and lives of soldiers dependent upon them, for the excellent reason that enough trained army surgeons, quartermasters, commissaries, ordnance officers, inspectors, etc., with a large trained corps of enlisted men in each department, did not exist, and halftrained volunteers had to be allowed to try. The private soldier has had to pay for the unwillingness of Congress to provide and keep on hand a sufficient corps of trained men to feed, clothe, arm, and nurse him.[50]

The Regular supply officers, eagerly if often clumsily aided by their Volunteer assistants, strove manfully to counteract the effects upon the welfare of the troops of delayed, fragmentary shipments of stores and undermanned, inexperienced staffs. The slow delivery of many items by the contractors meant that small lots of clothing, arms, and equipment were constantly trickling into the camps. As rapidly as the material came in, commissaries, quartermasters, and ordnance officers issued it, ingeniously stretching the inadequate amounts. The depot quartermaster at Tampa, for instance, developed his own rationing system to assure that each man received immediately at least one complete outfit of clothing. Quartermaster and Commissary officers at Tampa, Camp Thomas, and Camp Alger dispensed

2960, 3100; VII, 3153-54, 3207-8, 3270, 3297-98. *RSW, 1898,* 878-79; II, 221, 223, 480, 664; IV, 10, 24. Risch, *Quartermaster Corps,* 516-17, 519. GO 52, HQA, May 24, 1898; GO 96, HQA, July 13, 1898, *GO/AGO, 1898.* Lt. Col. J. B. Bellinger, Report of the Q. M. Depot at Tampa, May 18-August 31, 1898, Col. J. G. C. Lee to the Quartermaster General, September 11, 1898, and Lt. Col. J. W. Pope to the Quartermaster General, November 16, 1898, File No. 115533, OQMG Records. Hugh L. Scott to Mrs. Scott, August 7, 1898, Box 1, Scott Papers. J. F. Weston to Brig. Gen. James H. Wilson, August 3, 1899, Box 26, Wilson Papers.

50. The first quotation is from *War Investigating Commission,* IV, 854-55; see also IV, 847, 1132. The second quotation is from Lt. Col. J. W. Pope to the Quartermaster General, November 16, 1898, File No. 115533, OQMG Records. The third quotation is from *RSW, 1898,* II, 638. Capt. D. A. McCarthy to the Quartermaster General, August 5, 1899, File No. 133396; Col. J. G. C. Lee to the Quartermaster General, September 11, 1898, File No. 115533, OQMG Records. Hugh L. Scott to Mrs. Scott, June 2 and August 18, 1898, Box 1, Scott Papers.

with much of the regulation paper work in order to speed the distribution of supplies. To get around the initial lack of division and brigade staffs, they issued food, clothing, and equipment directly to the regiments. This practice produced traffic jams of wagons and work details around the depots, but it saved time and allowed regiments to draw needed supplies as soon as they reached camp. In midsummer, as the crisis eased and staff organizations neared full manpower, the bureaus restored the more systematic procedures prescribed in regulations. Considering the handicaps under which they labored, the camp depots issued an astonishing amount of equipment in a short time. The Quartermaster's Department at Camp Thomas, for example, between May and September of 1898 received and issued over 180 ambulances and 2,000 wagons, with their animals and harness. It also issued over 1,300,000 articles of clothing, 54,700 pieces of equipment, and over 143,600 tents of all types. In every five to ten days during the period of greatest activity, its wagons hauled some 2 million pounds of stores.[51]

Line officers, Regular and Volunteer alike, often revealed themselves as ineffectual administrators. Corps and division commanders drawn from the Regular Army, who had never before had charge of any contingent larger than a regiment and who were used to referring every problem to Washington, failed to take strong control over their staffs and were slow to use the independent powers granted them by Secretary Alger. Few of them, except for those who had commanded corps or divisions in the Civil War, even knew how to organize their personal staffs. All too often, inexperienced commanders, confused by the War Department's maldistribution of responsibilities, stood by helplessly while their subordinates wrangled and their camps fell into confusion. General Brooke, for example, commanded the Department of the Gulf and the entire camp at Chickamauga as well as his own First Corps. With two independent staffs under him and many diverse responsibilities, he all but lost control of Camp Thomas. His quartermaster squabbled with his medical officers over the number of hospital tents the surgeons should be allowed and supply officers at First Corps Headquarters undercut division commanders by issuing orders directly to their staffs. Outside of his own corps, Brooke neglected the sanitary condition of the camp, which steadily worsened as the summer wore on. Maj. Gen. Fitzhugh Lee's management of the Seventh Corps at Jacksonville, by contrast, showed what an officer experienced in controlling large formations could accomplish. From the begin-

51. *War Investigating Commission*, I, 203; III, 127-28, 141-42, 256, 337-38, 721-22; IV, 845-46, 851-52, 883-84, 1238, 1259; VI, 3066-67, 3070. *RSW, 1898*, I, 898-99; IV, 245-46. Maj. J. W. Pullman to the Quartermaster General, August 4, 1898, Lt. Col. J. B. Bellinger, Report of the Q. M. Depot at Tampa, May 18-August 31, 1898, Col. J. G. C. Lee to the Quartermaster General, September 11, 1898, Chief Q. M. Guy Howard to the Quartermaster General, September 20, 1898, File No. 115533 OQMG Records. For a running day-by-day account of supply issues at Camp Thomas, see File No. 159902, AGO Records; also in same collection, Brig. Gen. L. A. Carpenter to the Adj. Gen. at Huntsville, Ala., September 10, 1898, File No. 147555. Hugh L. Scott to Mrs. Scott, July 11, 1898, Box 1, Scott Papers. *The New York Times*, May 22 and June 5, 1898.

ning, he enforced harmony among his staff officers, rigorously inspected his camps, and quickly corrected sanitary or administrative flaws. His camp, as a result, seemed to visitors orderly and well run, even though the Seventh Corps, like all the others, suffered from shortages of equipment and clothing.[52]

In every camp, crowded, dirty company streets, ill-spaced tents, and piles of unissued supplies testified to the administrative inadequacies of state-appointed Volunteer regimental and company officers. All too many of these gentlemen failed to master supply procedures; they neglected to requisition needed equipment; and they rarely inspected their men's tents and kitchens. Even the most conscientious of them lacked understanding of how the Army operated. In the Volunteer regiments of the Eighth Corps, "scarcely an officer knew how to make out a paper upon which to secure for his men a single article of supply. They could not even be relied upon to render a return of the number and condition of the men over whom they exercised supervision." Completely defeated by the issuing procedures, a Kansas officer lined up his men in front of several newly arrived boxes of clothing and told them, "Here, you fellows, you need these things; just break open the boxes and help yourselves." When the Volunteers did obtain supplies, they often wasted food and mistreated equipment. Their abuse of teams and riding animals drove veteran quartermasters to despair. Since the states had full control over the commissioning of regimental and company officers, the Army could do little about their deficiencies except educate them in their duties, which camp commanders and Regular staff officers diligently tried to do. The whole experience seemed to Regulars to confirm the correctness of Emory Upton's contention that the federal government must appoint all Army officers and train them in peacetime up to a uniform standard of competence.[53]

Administrative incompetence and neglect in the regiments came near to nullifying the efforts of Commissary General Eagan to furnish the soldiers

52. *War Investigating Commission*, III, 92, 105-6, 112, 142, 313, 336-39, 344, 706-7; IV, 853, 884; 1112-13, 1122-23, 1404-5; V, 1731; VI, 2720-21, 2724-25, 3070-71, 3078, 3090; VIII, 368-70. Maj. Gen. J. R. Brooke to Adj. Gen. Corbin, June 8, 1898, File No. 215311; Corbin to the Surgeon General, November 10, 1898, File No. 150307, AGO Records. Palmer, *America in Arms*, 119, stresses the inexperience of Regulars of the 1890s in controlling large formations. Risch, *Quartermaster Corps*, 515. Wilson, *Under the Old Flag*, II, 422, describes how an experienced officer organized his personal staff. *The New York Times*, June 13, 1898, comments on the efficiency of Lee's command at Jacksonville.

53. The first quotation is from *War Investigating Commission*, VIII, 178; see also I, 111-12; III, 11-12, 83-84, 92-93, 142, 230-31, 250, 252, 327-28, 332; IV, 846-47, 937, 984-85, 1123-24, 1352, 1354; VIII, 98-99, 368-70. The second quotation is from *"The Fighting Twentieth": History and Official Souvenir of the Twentieth Kansas Regiment*, 20, 27. Maj. Gen. John R. Brooke to Adj. Gen. Corbin, September 8, 1898, File No. 128803, AGO Records. Bellinger, Tampa Report, and Lt. Col. J. G. C. Lee to the Quartermaster General, September 11, 1898, File No. 115533, OQMG Records. Hugh L. Scott to Mrs. Scott, May 29, 1898, Box 1, Scott Papers. GO 84, HQA, June 29, 1898, *GO/AGO, 1898*. Brig. Gen. Thomas M. Anderson, "Supply and Distribution," *JMSI*, XXIX, 204. Bigelow, *Santiago Campaign*, 41-42. *Army Regulations, 1895*. Paragraphs 233-39, 252, 257, 266, and 269, detail the pivotal role in Army administration played by regimental and company commanders.

Courtesy USAMHI

Company Kitchen, Camp Alger

with ample and palatable food. The Subsistence Department had no control over the preparation of the soldiers' meals. Its depots issued the raw material to the regiments in bulk, usually at ten-day intervals, and left the preparation of meals to the soldiers. According to Army regulations, each company in camp was to mess as a unit, with men from the ranks detailed to prepare the food under the close supervision of the company commander. Only partially satisfactory in the Regular service, this system broke down completely in many Volunteer regiments. Company commanders failed to requisition the rations to which their men were entitled. Usually unsupervised by their officers, inexperienced, unenthusiastic cooks reduced good meat and vegetables to unpalatable messes that were ruinous to the digestions and dispositions of their comrades. Often, the cooks failed to budget supplies properly, gorging the men during the first days of a ration period and starving them during the last. In a single brigade, one properly administered regiment would live well on the Army ration; the regiment next to it in camp, issued the same supplies, would seethe with resentment of hunger and inedible meals. Corps commanders did their best to remedy the situation by distributing copies of the manual for Army cooks and even preparing simple meals for untrained chefs to follow, but their efforts fell considerably short of success.[54]

Recognizing the threat to health and morale posed by bad cooking, Commissaries General, seconded by progressive-minded line officers, had agitated for twenty years for the enlistment and training of professional Army cooks. In May of 1898 Commissary General Eagan renewed the campaign, and Congress at last responded. On July 7 Congress authorized the enlistment of a "competent" cook for each company, troop, and battery in the Regular and Volunteer forces. The cook was to receive the rank and pay of a corporal and under his captain's supervision would prepare the unit's food. On July 12 the War Department ordered each regimental commander to enlist cooks for his companies, either from civilian life or from the men already in service. Candidates for the job must give a "practical exhibition" of their cooking skills, using components of the Army's ration. While it represented a minor victory for military reformers, the law did little to alleviate the immediate plight of the troops. Recruitment of cooks went slowly. Many Volunteers who continued to suffer under the ministrations of bungling chefs filled letters to their families, their congressmen, and their home-town newspapers with complaints of starvation and bad food.[55]

54. *War Investigating Commission*, I, 554-55; III, 219, 230, 252-53, 331, 333, 351, 655, 667; IV, 846, 936, 1245-47, 1260-61. *RSW, 1898*, II, 209, 212, 481, 637-38. *Army and Navy Journal*, October 8, 1898, and July 15, 1899. GO 110, HQA, August 1, 1898, *GO/AGO, 1898*. *Army Regulations, 1895*, Paragraphs 280 and 1258. Brig. Gen. James R. Lincoln to Adj. Gen. Corbin, September 12, 1898, and Brig. Gen. Jacob Kline to Corbin, September 24, 1898, File No. 147555, AGO Records.

55. *War Investigating Commission*, I, 550-51. *RSW, 1880*, I, xv; *1881*, I, 4: *1883*, I, 12; *1884*, I, 14-15; *1885*, I, 22; *1886*, I, 27; *1888*, I, 21; *1892*, I, 15; *1898*, II, 221. GO 94, HQA, July 12, 1898; Circular No. 47, HQA, November 10, 1898, *GO/AGO, 1898*. *Army and Navy Journal*, June 25, 1898. Powell, *United Service*, II, 230-31, 233.

V

Although the months of May and June were for many soldiers a nightmare of mislaid requisitions, lost supplies, scarcities, delays, and discomfort, the confusion in Washington and in the camps gradually subsided. As production of military supplies increased, an ever larger stream of goods flowed into the assembly camps. The new staff officers, inexperienced as they were, proved eager to learn. Gradually they mastered their duties and thereby removed part of the administrative burden from the hard-pressed Regulars. Regimental administration slowly improved under the pressure of necessity, and with the aid of camp and field experience that was often painful. By mid-August, most of the regiments called out early in May were approaching battle readiness. Units that had assembled under the second call for Volunteers reported little trouble in obtaining clothing and equipment.[56]

Under the conditions prevailing in 1898, the organization, officering, and equipment within three months of even a stationary force of 275,000 men constituted a remarkable achievement for the War Department—and it was only one part of the dual task President McKinley had imposed on his straining military machine. At the same time the War Department was struggling with problems of supply and administration in the home camps, it launched and pressed to victory overseas campaigns on opposite sides of the world.

56. *War Investigating Commission*, I, 133; III, 233, 663-64; IV, 936-37, 956, 962, 1110, 1240; VI, 2960, 3100; VII, 3142, 3283, 3297-98. *RSW, 1898*, II, 221. Brig. Gen. Robert Hall to Adjutant General, 2nd Division, IV Corps, September 10, 1898, Lt. Col. M. W. Day to Adjutant General, IV Corps, September 12, 1898, Brig. Gen. James R. Lincoln to Adj. Gen. Corbin, September 12, 1898, Lt. Col. S. M. Whiteside to Adjutant General, IV Corps, September 23, 1898, Brig. Gen. J. K. Hudson to Adjutant General, 2nd Division, IV Corps, September 15, 1898, File No. 147555; Maj. Gen. J. F. Wade to Corbin, July 19, 1898, File No. 159902, AGO Records. Col. W. T. Patten to the Quartermaster General, August 16, 1898, File No. 115533, OQMG Records. Col. Colson to Brig. Gen. Sanger, September 9, 1898, Box 7, Scott Papers. Bigelow, *Santiago Campaign*, 10-11. *The New York Times*, June 12 and 19, 1898.

6

Organizing the Invasion Forces

By the last week of May, the War Department had settled on a system for assembling and equipping the Volunteers, and it had begun the organization of expeditions against Manila and Havana. The Administration's commitment to the attack on the Philippines remained constant, but scarcely had the Army's preparations for the descent on Havana got under way when still another shift in strategy threw the service off balance again. For the third and final time in the war, Cervera's elusive Spanish squadron altered American plans of campaign.

The Navy had located Cervera's vessels off Martinique on May 13. Three days later, the United States consul at Curacao reported the Spaniards' arrival there. Then the Navy's scout vessels, few in number and poorly deployed, lost Cervera once more. Evading the American fleet, Cervera's cruisers and torpedo-boat-destroyers early on May 19 slipped into the harbor of Santiago de Cuba, a city on the island's southern coast and capital of its rugged, thinly populated easternmost province. On the same day, the Army's Signal Corps received news of the squadron's whereabouts from a confidential agent in the Havana telegraph office. The fleet moved quickly to bottle up Cervera. Steaming at full speed into the Caribbean, the armored squadron that had remained on the Atlantic seaboard to ward off Spanish raids blockaded Santiago on May 28 and confirmed Cervera's presence there. Admiral Sampson arrived with his force on June 1. While the entire armored fleet thus massed off Santiago, lighter ships maintained the watch on Havana and other Cuban ports.

Sampson's fleet had trapped Cervera, but it could not reach him to destroy him. Cervera's ships lay at anchor in Santiago harbor, a bottle-shaped bay enclosed both inland and to seaward by hills and entered from the sea through a narrow twisting channel between high cliffs. Spanish forts armed with heavy cannon commanded the narrow harbor mouth, and mines blocked the tortuous channel. The city of Santiago, fortified against the insurgents, lay near the head of the harbor on its eastern side, invisible from Sampson's ships. If the American battleships tried to steam into the bay and engage Cervera, they would risk disastrous losses from Spanish mines and gunfire. Sampson therefore confined his efforts to sealing up the harbor mouth and bombarding its guardian forts. To keep the Spanish vessels imprisoned, Navy volunteers tried to sink the old collier *Merrimac* in the middle of the entrance channel, but the forts' batteries sank the ship at an ineffectual position. Early in June, Sampson's lighter ships entered and secured the lower end of Guantánamo Bay, east of Santiago, for use as a refuge from storms and as a coaling station. To secure this base, a Marine battalion of 600 men landed on the east shore of the bay on June 10, established a camp, and fought several victorious skirmishes with Spanish infantry. The Marines thus could claim the honor of having secured the first permanent American foothold in Cuba.[1]

So long as it remained intact in Santiago, Cervera's squadron kept Spanish resistance alive in the Caribbean and restricted American freedom of action. Still supposed to be capable of operating at full speed and power, the Spanish ships tied down most of the American fleet in blockading them. Given favorable weather conditions, the Spaniards might slip out of Santiago, elude the armored vessels, and attack the weaker ships blockading Havana or Cienfuegos. With the Army's assistance, the Navy could eliminate this threat. Troops landed east or west of the harbor entrance could storm and silence the Spanish batteries and thus allow the fleet to clear the mines from the channel, steam into the harbor, and crush Cervera. The Navy Department therefore asked that the troops at Tampa, intended for the assault on Havana, move instead to Santiago to help destroy the Spanish fleet.[2]

A movement against Santiago could bring diplomatic as well as military benefits. With the Army still not ready to attack Havana, here was a chance to establish a foothold in Cuba early. For this purpose, Santiago offered a worthwhile and vulnerable target. Cuba's third city in size and importance, it contained 45,000 inhabitants and was served by one of the island's best harbors. It had no road or rail connection with Havana, 500 miles to the west, and the Cuban rebels who infested its mountainous, undeveloped hinterland could prevent the other Spanish garrisons in eastern Cuba from marching to its rescue. Thus, the 10,000 Spaniards who garrisoned the town would have to defend it without hope of major reinforcement. They should be easy prey for the almost 20,000 American troops who were nearing battle readiness at Tampa.[3]

1. Alger, *Spanish-American War*, 48, 221-26. Chadwick, *Spanish-American War*, I, 236, 243-91, 293-307, 314-18, 321-34, 337-43, 345-46, 348-67, 373-75, 379-88. Long, *New American Navy*, III, 5-6. Mahan, *Lessons*, 96-99, 138-40, 155-72. *War Investigating Commission*, VI, 2935. *The New York Times*, May 29 and 30, 1898.

2. Alger, *Spanish-American War*, 62. Chadwick, *Spanish-American War*, I, 220-21. Mahan, *Lessons*, 61-62, 76, 84-85, 95. Nunez, *Guerra*, III, 134. Miles, *The North American Review*, CLXVIII, 525. *War Investigating Commission*, I, 245. *Correspondence*, I, 16. American naval strategy seems at first glance to have been absurdly overcautious, but our strength, while greater than that of Spain, was not sufficiently so to permit the taking of unnecessary risks. A single severe setback could have crippled the battle fleet and produced dangerous diplomatic and psychological effects. Also, McKinley and his advisers, Civil War veterans almost to a man, remembered Bull Run and did not want to be responsible for a similar disaster.

3. *Army and Navy Journal*, June 11, 1898. *The New York Times*, May 27 and June 1 and 3, 1898. *Correspondence*, I, 14-15.

Once their attention had been focused on eastern Cuba, American civilian and military leaders also looked with new interest at Puerto Rico, Spain's other major colony in the Western Hemisphere. Located some 500 miles east of Cuba and evidencing little of the larger island's political turbulence, Puerto Rico was of great strategic value. In the immediate crisis it provided a base for the Spanish fleet within easy striking distance of Cuba; if it fell to the Americans, naval relief of Spanish forces in Cuba would be impossible. In the future, from Puerto Rican harbors the American fleet could command the approaches to the projected isthmian canal. Possession of the island thus would contribute to the attainment of a major objective of United States foreign policy. From the beginning of the war advisers to the President had urged him to seize Puerto Rico. Among them, Philip C. Hanna, United States consul in San Juan at the outbreak of war, waxed most eloquent and circumstantial. While repeatedly suggesting an invasion of the island, Hanna pointed out that Spain had stationed only about 5,000 troops in Puerto Rico, that the climate was more healthful than Cuba's, and that the people favored the United States. He claimed that 10,000 American soldiers could overrun the island, which would provide the United States with a useful naval base and a docile Caribbean colony. Initially, Puerto Rico received little attention in American plans for war with Spain, centered as they were on Cuba and Havana. However, the shift of the military center of gravity from Havana to Santiago revived talk of invading the smaller Spanish possession.[4]

To adjust American strategy to the altered naval situation, President McKinley on May 26 held another of his White House councils of war, which was attended by Secretaries Alger and Long, General Miles, and three naval officers. The Navy's delegation included Captain Mahan, now a member of the Naval War Board. The conference decided to abandon temporarily the attack on Havana. Instead, the United States would launch a campaign against Santiago and Puerto Rico. At the close of the meeting, Secretary Alger directed General Miles to prepare detailed plans for the Army's operations against those objectives. The decision represented a victory for Miles, whose favorite war strategy the Administration had now adopted.[5]

In two memoranda written on May 26 and 27, supplemented a month later by a third, Miles, in response to Alger's directive, laid out his proposed plan of campaign. He suggested that the available force of Regulars attack

4. *Army and Navy Journal*, May 7, 1898. Long, *New American Navy*, I, 205. Mahan, *Lessons*, 27-28. Lt. Gen. John M. Schofield, "General Schofield's Experiences in McKinley's Administration," undated memoir in Box 93, Schofield Papers. Andrew van Bibber to Secretary Alger, April 19, 1898, File No. 75270; Theodore Kellogg to President McKinley, May 10, 1898, File No. 80180; Consul Philip C. Hanna to Assistant Secretary of State William R. Day, May 4, 9, 12, and 14, June 6, 1898, and to Assistant Secretary of State J. B. Moore, May 28, 1898, File No. 82865; Hanna to Day, April 20, 1898, File No. 505104, AGO Records.

5. Alger, *Spanish-American War*, 48. Mayo, *America of Yesterday*, 196-97. *The New York Times*, May 27, 1898.

Santiago and aid the Navy in destroying Cervera's fleet. Next, the Santiago expedition, reinforced from the United States if necessary, would attack Puerto Rico with Navy support. Miles expected Puerto Rico to fall with little fighting. After taking that objective, he said—going considerably beyond the decisions of the May 26 conference—the land and sea forces should return to Cuba and capture, one by one, the deep-water ports on the island's northeast coast. Through these ports the United States could send large quantities of arms and supplies to the rebels, whose main armies operated in this region. With the supply shipments, Miles continued, should come 10,000 to 15,000 Regular cavalry and field artillery. This corps, mounted and hence highly mobile, should join the freshly equipped Cubans in a drive westward through the fever-free plateau country of central Cuba. This allied army would overrun the Spanish garrisons in its path and sweep away Spanish sovereignty in most of Cuba. At the end of its victorious march it would bring Havana under siege. Such an offensive, Miles reasoned, should require most of the summer. By the time the cavalry reached Havana's environs, the rainy season would have ended. If the capital did not then surrender, the Volunteers, fully equipped and with three months' training behind them, could land near the city and complete Spain's defeat.[6]

Miles's elaborate plan brought him once again into conflict with McKinley and Alger. The President and the Secretary of War adopted only those parts of Miles's proposal that carried out the decisions of May 26. They decided to attack Santiago at once with the Regulars of the Fifth Corps and to strike at Puerto Rico as soon as Santiago fell, using for this second operation as much of the Fifth Corps as remained battleworthy, supplemented by reinforcements from the United States. They postponed the attack on Havana until autumn and indicated that Major General Lee's Seventh Corps, then concentrating at Jacksonville, would lead it.[7]

However, at Alger's vehement urging, the President rejected Miles's proposed drive westward through central Cuba. Alger, an experienced cavalryman (Miles had spent most of his career in the infantry), stressed the enormous logistical problems that would attend any such venture. The government, he said, lacked ships to carry the expedition's 10,000 or 15,000 horses. At the end of an ever-lengthening supply line and unable to live off the devastated countryside, the force would require 90 tons of food and forage per day, all of which would have to come through one or two small ports and be carried to the front over the region's inadequate roads. Alger

6. Maj. Gen. Miles to Secretary Alger, May 26 and 27 and June 24, 1898, in Alger, *Spanish-American War*, 49-55.

7. Alger, *Spanish-American War*, 59. Miles, *The North American Review*, CLXIX, 125-26. *War Investigating Commission*, III, 90, 320; VII, 3249. *Correspondence*, I, 263. *RSW, 1898*, II, 583. *The New York Times*, June 8, 1898. Brig. Gen. William Ludlow, Chief Engineer of the V Corps and one of the authors of the Mariel attack plan, opposed the move upon Santiago as wasting force upon a secondary objective; see Ludlow to Adj. Gen. Corbin, June 5, 1898, Box 1, Corbin Papers.

pointed out that many of the Spanish-held towns the cavalry were supposed to capture were strongly fortified. If committed in central Cuba, the horse soldiers might bog down in sieges or suffer crippling losses in frontal attacks. Finally, Alger asked, why march part of the army 350 miles overland to Havana—a trek that would require two or three months—when they could reach the city in a day by ship from the United States and land under cover of naval cannon? The President accepted Alger's reasoning and vetoed Miles's cavalry foray.[8]

In three telegrams, sent between May 26 and 30, the War Department ordered Major General Shafter at Tampa to embark his Fifth Corps and prepare to sail for Santiago. A fourth War Department message on May 31 specified Shafter's mission. He was to sail to Santiago under naval convoy, land his troops near the city, and so operate as to capture or destroy the Spanish garrison and aid the fleet in eliminating Cervera's squadron.[9]

The War Department reinforced Shafter's Fifth Corps with all the other troops then ready for field service. Most of the remaining Regulars east of the Mississippi entrained for Tampa. On May 30 General Miles directed the Regular regiments at Mobile to embark and join the army of invasion. At the same time, he ordered the Rough Riders to Tampa, along with eight of the most nearly equipped Volunteer regiments at Camp Thomas. The Volunteer infantry were to receive at Tampa whatever additional arms and accoutrements they needed before they boarded ship with the Fifth Corps. With these reinforcements, Shafter would have about 25,000 troops under his command.[10]

II

Preparations for deploying armies on foreign shores had begun long before the Administration made its final selection of objectives for attack. Acting largely on their own initiative, the bureau chiefs even before the declaration of war started assembling transports, weapons, clothing, and equipment for possible invasion forces. General Miles, the Military Information Division, and the troop commanders collected intelligence about the Army's probable objectives and sought the military assistance of dissident

8. Alger, *Spanish-American War*, 52-57. Secretary Alger to President McKinley, May 26, 1898, McKinley Papers.

9. Alger, *Spanish-American War*, 63-65, prints the text of the four orders to Shafter.

10. *Correspondence*, I, 17-18, 30-31, 539. *War Investigating Commission*, VI, 3066. Hugh L. Scott to Mrs. Scott, June 2, 1898, Box 1, Scott Papers. Asst. Adj. Gen. J. C. Gilmore to Adj. Gen. Corbin, May 29, 1898, File No. 85802; Maj. Gen. J. R. Brooke to Corbin, May 30, 1898, File No. 87702; Maj. Gen. Miles to Maj. Gen. J. J. Coppinger, May 30, 1898, File No. 192302, AGO Records. *The New York Times*, May 31 and June 2 and 3, 1898. Bellinger, Tampa Report, File No. 115533, OQMG Records.

elements in Spain's colonies. As a result of these preparations, American troops by late June were closing in on Santiago and Manila while the expedition against Puerto Rico made ready in training camps and embarkation ports.

To assure rapid equipment of the troops designated for the first attacks, the Quartermaster and Ordnance departments gave them first claim on all scarce supplies. As wagons began to arrive from the manufacturers, the Quartermaster General dispatched most of them to Tampa for the Cuban expedition and released to the reserve camps only the number needed to haul stores from the railroad sidings to the regiments. The Chief of Ordnance established special issuing depots at Tampa and San Francisco, upon which all units ordered to those ports for embarkation could draw to complete their equipment. To keep these depots fully stocked, he delayed shipments to other camps. In late May and early June, when the War Department ordered regiments to the front from Camps Thomas and Alger, the camp commanders applied a similar priority system. At Camp Thomas, for example, General Brooke diverted all his clothing and ordnance stores to the First Corps, which had been designated for overseas duty, and he took weapons and equipment from some of his regiments to complete the outfit of others.[11]

Shortages of indispensable articles hampered the Army's preparations at every turn, but few produced more suffering among the soldiers or were harder to overcome than the shortage of tropical uniforms for the invasion troops. Before 1898 the Quartermaster's Department had issued no special hot-weather uniform. In the warmer parts of the South and Southwest, soldiers had worn the standard blue wool suit with minor modifications. The nearest clothing to a light-weight summer uniform that the Army issued was a brown canvas fatigue suit, which the Quartermaster's Department had begun issuing in 1883.[12]

Early in April, on General Miles's recommendation, Quartermaster General Ludington adopted a variation of the canvas suit for wear by troops sent to hot climates and contracted for the manufacture of an experimental lot of 10,000 of them. A month later, as the Volunteers poured into the assembly camps, Ludington clothed them in the traditional blue wool. At the same time, he tried to place orders for more of the canvas uniforms, only to encounter frustrating delays. He had wanted them manufactured from khaki, the closely woven, lightweight brown cotton used by the British in warm climates with great success, but no American firm could weave or dye that fabric. Ludington perforce fell back on light canvas, but even that

11. *War Investigating Commission*, II, 803, 807; IV, 1262, 1433; VI, 2626, 2865, 3070-72. *RSW, 1898*, IV, 15, 23-24, 245-46. Adj. Gen. Corbin to Maj. Gen. J. R. Brooke, June 13, 1898, File No. 89371; Corbin to Brooke, July 6, 1898, File No. 159948, AGO Records.

12. Risch, *Quartermaster Corps*, 503-5.

proved hard to obtain. Depot quartermasters rejected several bids on large lots of the brown uniform because the samples of fabric were of such poor quality. Not until June 8 did the depot quartermaster at New York, satisfied at last with the cloth offered, issue contracts for 50,000 of the suits. To tide the Army over until the new uniform was delivered in quantity, the Quartermaster General reduced the weight of the cloth in the standard trousers, shirts, and blouses, hoping thereby to adapt the blue uniform to hot climates. He also bought and issued huge quantities of light cotton underwear.[13]

The size of the armies that were to attack Santiago, Puerto Rico, and Manila and the amount of equipment they would take with them depended absolutely on the capacity and number of ships that could be found to transport them. Quartermaster General Ludington and his subordinates, responsible under the *Army Regulations* for providing all forms of transportation including ocean-going steam vessels, did most of the work of chartering, purchasing, and fitting out troopships. In emergencies, field commanders supplemented the bureaus' efforts by chartering steamers on their own authority. Early in June, McKinley and Alger gave Maj. Gen. Merritt at San Francisco "the widest latitude" in securing transports for his expedition. Deeply concerned about the shipping problem, Secretary Alger tried to use his connections in the business community to obtain additional vessels at the lowest possible cost.[14]

Long before McKinley, Alger, and Miles decided on a plan of campaign, Quartermaster General Ludington had begun his search for troopships. On March 24 he ordered his depot commander at New York to make a survey of shipping lines operating between East Coast ports and the Caribbean. The depot officer was to ascertain and report on the number of vessels these companies owned, their capacity, and the number that would be available for charter at short notice. On March 29 the depot commander submitted his lists of ships. Late in April, with the government committed to a descent upon Cuba, depot quartermasters in the Atlantic and Gulf ports, often with the aid of Navy officers, began inspecting steamers for charter. On the basis of their reports and recommendations, the Quartermaster General's Office in Washington made the final arrangements with the owners. The bureau hired ships at a fixed rate per day, proportional to their tonnage. The companies manned the steamers and provided food for Army officers aboard, while the government furnished coal and water. As soon as the vessels were turned over to the Army, depot

13. *War Investigating Commission*, I, 422; VI, 2648. *RSW, 1898*, I, 385, 457. Risch, *Quartermaster Corps*, 524. *Army and Navy Journal*, April 9 and 23 and June 11 and 18, 1898. *The New York Times*, June 1, 9, and 10, 1898.

14. Risch, *Quartermaster Corps*, 452. Lee, *JMSI*, XV, 257. *Correspondence*, I, 10; II, 692, 722. *War Investigating Commission*, I, 469. Adj. Gen. Corbin to Mr. Boyd, May 8, 1898, File No. 79898, AGO Records. Secretary Alger to G. M. Dodge, June 24, 1898, Alger Papers. Abstract of evidence given by Mr. Baker, President of National Steamship Company, in Frank J. Hecker Papers.

quartermasters at the ports of delivery or at the points where they were to load troops began fitting them up to carry men, animals, and supplies.[15]

Inexperience, the inadequacies of the United States merchant marine, and technical obstacles hindered the assembly of a transport fleet. Without prior practice in such work and lacking even a set of sea transport regulations to guide them, quartermasters made mistake after mistake in fitting out ships and estimating their capacity. Foreign flag vessels, under international law, could not be chartered for military use, a fact that forced Ludington and his officers to rely on the meager American merchant marine. Well represented in Congress, East Coast shipowners blocked the transfer of foreign vessels to American registry for use in the Caribbean because they feared that, once under the United States flag, such ships would enter the profitable coastal trade. However, the shipping lobby allowed such transfers in the Pacific. Further reducing the Quartermaster General's range of choice, the roomy, powerful vessels used on the trans-Atlantic routes drew too much water to enter Cuban or Puerto Rican harbors; even the southern Atlantic ports of the United States, from which the Army wanted to embark, could not accommodate them. The Quartermaster's Department thus had to depend upon the small, slow vessels that plied the Gulf and the Caribbean in peacetime, most of which were little suited to carrying men and animals in large numbers.[16]

In preparing the Caribbean fleet, General Ludington ran afoul of the Administration's changing Cuban strategy and of his own reluctance to accumulate shipping that might not be needed. Trying to conform to War and Navy Department plans, Ludington during the first weeks of mobilization chartered only enough steamers for General Shafter's 6,000-man reconnaissance in force. The sudden decision early in May to attack Havana with 70,000 troops required a hurried expansion of the transport fleet. The Quartermaster's Department now began chartering every available merchantman in its attempts to supply transportation for at least 25,000 men, the planned first wave of the invasion. Chartering at New York and other Atlantic and Gulf ports, the bureau by the end of May had taken under contract

15. *War Investigating Commission*, I, 133-34, 441, 447, 467, 470, 475; V, 2191-92; VI, 2411-13, 2415, 2612-13, 2788, 2793-94. *Correspondence*, II, 653-54, 695. Risch, *Quartermaster Corps*, 545, 547. The Navy before 1890 had made an extensive survey of American merchant shipping and its potential military uses, but the Army ignored the Navy's information and made its own surveys; see *Army and Navy Journal*, December 17, 1898. By June 30, 1898, the Quartermaster's Department had spent over $1,300,000 on ship charter fees; see *RSW, 1898*, I, 389.

16. Capt. Carroll A. Devol, "Supply and Distribution," *JMSI*, XXIX, 208. Capt. W. E. Birkheimer, "Transportation of Troops by Sea," *JMSI*, XXIII, 438-39. *War Investigating Commission*, I, 445, 467; V, 2193; VI, 2612, 2620. *RSW, 1899*, I, Pt. 2, pp. 223, 234. *Correspondence*, I, 41, 43-44. Risch, *Quartermaster Corps*, 545-47. *The New York Times*, May 9, 24, and 25, June 10, 11, 18, and 23, 1898.

Loaded Transports moving out into Tampa Bay, sailing for Santiago.

most of the usable vessels. The crews who installed bunks and crude ventilation, cooking, and lavatory facilities aboard these first troopships put haste before thoroughness, as the expedition was supposed to sail as soon as possible and the voyage to Havana would be short. The quartermaster in charge of fitting out transports at New York recalled: "These ships had to go at once. I would have anywhere from three to five days to take a ship and fit her up to go to sea. . . . It was a rush order." Many vessels steamed out of New York Harbor for Tampa with workmen still hammering away below decks.[17]

Besides securing transports, the Quartermaster's Department had to find landing craft with which to deposit men, horses, guns, vehicles, and stores on enemy beaches. Neither the Navy nor the Army in 1898 owned specialized boats for this purpose. For landing troops, Army commanders planned to use the transports' lifeboats and borrowed Navy steam launches. For disembarking freight and heavy equipment, Quartermaster General Ludington decided to employ steam lighters, diverted from their peacetime tasks in

17. The quotation is from *War Investigating Commission*, V, 2415; see also I, 444-46, 468-70, 474-75; V, 2194, 2213; VI, 2410-13, 2417, 2612, 2620; VII, 3155-56. Chadwick, *Spanish-American War*, II, 11. Miley, *In Cuba*, 9-11. Col. A. S. Kimball to Adj. Gen. Corbin, May 11, 1898, File No. 253334, AGO Records. *The New York Times*, May 8, 10, 11, 14, and 25, 1898. *Washington Post*, April 29, 1898.

American harbors. On April 30, without prior orders and with commendable initiative, Ludington set in motion a search for these craft. The results were disappointing. After canvassing the length of the Atlantic Coast, his subordinates found only three usable lighters. Most of the others drew too much water to approach the shores of Cuba. To make up for the shortage of lighters, quartermasters in the Gulf ports hired flat-bottomed, decked barges. Chartered sea-going tugs were to tow these clumsy hulks to Cuba and then back and forth between ships and shore. On the assumption that the troops would land in the sheltered bay of Mariel, the Cuban expedition's chief engineer, Brig. Gen. William Ludlow, loaded a train of pontoons and two engineer companies on the chartered steamer *Alamo*. Designed for use in bridging rivers, the pontoons could be employed also in building temporary docks at Mariel, thereby supplementing the Quartermaster Department's equipment. The diversion of the invasion force to Santiago, where the troops had to land in rough water on an open coast, rendered Ludlow's preparations useless.[18]

On the Pacific Coast, the Quartermaster's Department, working in cooperation with Secretary Alger and General Merritt, rounded up steamers for the Manila expedition. The small number of American-flag vessels that plied the Pacific made this task difficult; to add to the difficulties, most of the available ships were away from their home ports, on long voyages to Asia or South America. Their owners could deliver them to the Army only a few at a time as they straggled home from the distant ports. On the positive side, the steamers finally secured—most of them passenger ships built for voyages to hot regions—were larger and better suited for troop-carrying than were the Caribbean transports. By threatening reluctant owners with seizure of their vessels, the authorities by June 30 had secured for the Eighth Corps fourteen steamers with a total troop capacity of about 14,000 men. As soon as these ships returned to West Coast ports, the Quartermaster's Department took them over, converted them for transport work, and sent them off a few at a time with detachments for Manila.[19]

The authorities at San Francisco carefully prepared the transports for their month-long 7,000-mile run to the Philippines. Upon the charter of each vessel, officers from the Quartermaster and Medical departments and from the line inspected her, determined her passenger capacity, and specified in detail the alterations needed to fit her for carrying troops. Crews under command of the depot quartermaster then installed bunks, ventilators,

18. *War Investigating Commission*, I, 447, 500-504; VI, 2615, 2619-20; VII, 3789-90.

19. *Correspondence*, II, 654, 659-61, 667-68, 670-72, 683, 721-22. *War Investigating Commission*, I, 446; VI, 2786. *RSW, 1898*, I, 388; *1899*, I, Pt. 2, p. 476. Col. Charles Bird to the Quartermaster General, August 12, 1898, File No. 115533, OQMG Records. Risch, *Quartermaster Corps*, 546-47. *Army and Navy Journal*, March 25, 1899. *The New York Times*, May 10 and 28 and June 9, 1898.

electric lights, bathing and toilet facilities, and galleys large enough for preparing and serving at least two hot meals per day. Each transport carried fresh meat for the voyage, either frozen in refrigerators or live in pens on deck. Each had a fully equipped clinic staffed with surgeons and hospital corpsmen. Because of the length of the voyage, the Eighth Corps took along no landing craft other than the small boats of its transports. In disembarking, the corps would supplement them with whatever boats could be borrowed from the Navy or commandeered locally.[20]

Besides its responsibility to obtain transports, the War Department had to select bases at which to embark men and supplies. The Manila expedition had at its disposal the railroad terminals, storehouses, and wharves of San Francisco, the metropolis of the Pacific Coast, but no such commodious base was available to the Cuban and Puerto Rican expeditions. For the operations in the Caribbean, Secretary Alger and his colleagues wanted a port that could be easily protected from Spanish naval raids and was as close as possible to Cuba, the principal theater of operations. The state of Florida, which juts out to within 90 miles of Havana, as yet contained few large cities and railroads, while the well-developed ports of the Gulf and Atlantic coasts lay far from Cuba, across sea lanes exposed to harassment by the enemy. Almost by administrative gravitation, the Army selected Tampa, on Florida's west coast, as its Caribbean port of embarkation. Early in April the joint strategy board had urged Tampa's use, and part of the Regular Army assembled there under the orders of April 15. Later in April, the War Department selected these regiments for Shafter's reconnaissance in force and sent ships and stores to Tampa for them. When, early in May, the Administration decided on the 70,000-man blow at Mariel and Havana, it seemed sensible to Alger and his associates to assemble the additional steamers and troops at Tampa and to mass there most of the expedition's supplies. Thus, they committed the Army to embark through Tampa.[21]

A city of 26,000 people in 1898, Tampa had many of the features the Army required in a Caribbean base. It was closer to Havana by sea than any other usable port. Lying at the head of a deep bay, it was safe from Spanish raids. Tampa's harbor, with 21 feet of water in its channel, could accommodate large steamers, and thirteen vessels at a time could load at the city's main wharf. However, ten miles of sandy, roadless country crossed by only a single line of railroad track separated Tampa's campground, railroad terminals, and warehouses from the wharves on the bay at Port Tampa. This bottleneck created infinite difficulties in the embarkation of a large force.[22]

20. *War Investigating Commission*, I, 446, 653; III, 96, 108; VIII, 179-80. *RSW, 1898*, I, 389, 403, 580-81, 713; *1899*, I, Pt. 2, p. 476, Pt. 4, pp. 226-27. John F. Bass, "San Francisco," *Harper's Weekly*, XLII, 642.

21. *War Investigating Commission*, I, 245; VII, 3263, 3278. Alger, *Spanish-American War*, 65, 69-70, 82, 328. Risch, *Quartermaster Corps*, 550-51.

22. *War Investigating Commission*, III, 443; VI, 2668. *RSW, 1898*, II, 591-92. Alger, *Spanish-American War*, 65. Chadwick, *Spanish-American War*, II, 3.

III

Officials in Washington were acutely aware that the expeditions would be marching and fighting over unfamiliar, ill-mapped terrain among alien peoples. Accordingly, they spent much time collecting information about the Spanish colonies they planned to attack, and their efforts were supplemented by those of the various field commanders. In the cases of Santiago and Manila, this work was bound up with the task of establishing cooperation with native rebels.

The Military Information Division had been amassing information on Spain's colonies since long before the war, and the opening of actual hostilities removed the restraints on outright espionage. Early in April, two officers of the division, Lts. Andrew S. Rowan and Henry H. Whitney, left Washington on Caribbean scouting missions. Rowan stationed himself initially at Kingston in neutral Jamaica and Whitney joined Sampson's fleet. Between April 23 and May 13, Rowan, with the aid of Cuban agents at Kingston, stole into Santiago Province, where he conferred with General Calixto García. Rowan then slipped out of Cuba again, accompanied by two of García's staff officers. Rowan brought back with him valuable information about Cuba's terrain and the condition of one of the principal insurgent armies. Whitney, disguised as a British merchant seaman, entered Puerto Rico on May 15. At the risk of his life (if the Spaniards had caught him out of uniform—as he was—they would have had every right under the laws of war to shoot him), he spent two weeks reconnoitering southern Puerto Rico. He reached Washington again on June 9 with accurate information on Spanish troop dispositions, the topography of the country, the condition of the harbors, and the political attitude of the inhabitants. Later in the war, he returned to the island in uniform with General Miles's invading army.[23]

The Signal Corps scored some of the war's most important intelligence coups. In charge of monitoring overseas cable messages, its officers in the United States collected valuable data on Spanish ship movements. Its station at Key West received reports almost daily from an agent in the Havana telegraph office. This courageous, unknown spy gave the Americans their first word that Cervera had taken refuge in Santiago.[24]

Expedition commanders supplemented material from the Washington bureaus with the results of their own independent investigations. At Tampa, General Shafter pored over histories of earlier campaigns in the West Indies. He studied with special attention the unsuccessful British attack on

23. Chadwick, *Spanish-American War*, II, 358-59. Miles, *The North American Review*, CLXIX, 125. *RSW, 1898*, II, 10.

24. *RSW, 1898*, I, 893. *War Investigating Commission*, VI, 2935.

Santiago in 1741. He also conferred at length with Cuban refugees and officers from the Santiago area, who told him much about the terrain and advised him on the best landing places. Members of his staff closely interrogated Col. Frederick Funston of the Twentieth Kansas Infantry, who had fought in eastern Cuba with the insurgents. General Miles based his strategy in Puerto Rico in part on the reports of Lieutenant Rowan and in part on the dispatches of the former United States consul at San Juan, who furnished much detail on the military and political situation in the island. At San Francisco, General Merritt set up an intelligence bureau at his headquarters and scoured the nation for maps of the Philippines and books about them. He consulted the few American civilian experts on the Islands and sought information from businessmen who had traded in Manila. Merritt drew every fact he could from State Department consular reports, and he telegraphed a series of questions to Admiral Dewey concerning Manila's garrison and terrain. Using material copied from the *Encyclopedia Britannica* to supplement data from their own files, officers of the Military Information Division answered these questions as accurately and thoroughly as Dewey in his observations from the scene.[25]

Once the expeditions landed in enemy country, they scouted and patrolled extensively. At Santiago, General Shafter's Chief Engineer, Col. George M. Derby, took charge of reconnaissance. With six staff and line officers, most of them graduates of the command school at Fort Leavenworth, Derby daily scouted the area between the army's beachhead and the city. Assisted by infantry patrols, parties of Cubans, and hired civilian spies, Derby's officers ascertained the positions of the Spanish defenders and built up the first detailed topographical map to be made of the Santiago region. In Puerto Rico, General Miles's engineers, aided by friendly Puerto Ricans, did equally extensive work. One of the rewards was the discovery, in the course of their explorations, of a strategic mountain trail that was unknown to the Spaniards. Eighth Corps officers at Manila, their reports supplemented by information from a spy in the city who had been hired by Admiral Dewey, mapped the terrain around the Philippine capital and located the Spanish defenses. In all three theaters, each American general, although operating in the area for the first time, had at his disposal more military and topographical information than did the Spaniards who had campaigned in the Islands for years.[26]

25. Funston, *Memories*, 156-57. Herbert H. Sargent, *The Campaign of Santiago de Cuba*, II, 7. Miles, *The North American Review*, CLXVIII, 528. *RSW, 1898*, II, 149. *Correspondence*, II, 645-46, 649-52, 654-56, 665-66, 675-76, 682, 689-91, 710-19. *The New York Times*, June 4, 1898. Consul Philip C. Hanna to Assistant Secretary of State John Bassett Moore, May 28, June 7, and July 22, 1898, File No. 82865, AGO Records. John A. Porter to Maj. Gen. Wesley Merritt, May 12, 1898, McKinley Papers. For the encyclopedia incident, see Edward M. Coffman, *The Hilt of the Sword: The Career of Peyton C. March*, 14.

26. *War Investigating Commission*, VII, 3200, 3235. *RSW, 1898*, II, 54, 161. *Army and Navy Journal*, October 29, 1898. *Correspondence*, II, 779-80. Alger, *Spanish-American War*, 121-22, 132-34. Wheeler, *Santiago Campaign*, 264. Wilson, *Under the Old Flag*, II, 442.

Before General Shafter sailed for Santiago, General Miles secured for him the cooperation of the Cuban Gen. Calixto García, whose army, the largest and best trained of the insurgent forces, dominated the hills behind the city. Since early April Miles had maintained constant contact with García and other rebel leaders, communicating with them through Lieutenant Rowan and through other messengers smuggled in and out of Cuba. On June 2, while Shafter's troops were embarking, Miles asked García by letter to bottle up the outlying Spanish garrisons near Santiago and to bring a force down to the coast to assist the American landing. García complied with both requests. His troops besieged every major Spanish post in eastern Cuba and thus blocked any attempt to reinforce Santiago. García then brought 5,000 more of his men down to the coast west of Santiago to meet Shafter. Though of little value in frontal attacks, during the campaign these ragged Cuban soldiers harassed the Spanish garrison, dug trenches for the Americans, and furnished invaluable aid in scouting the enemy positions. In accord with McKinley's policy, both sides treated their cooperation as a strictly military arrangement between local commanders. In the American view at least, acceptance of their aid implied no recognition of the rebels' political authority.[27]

At Manila, also, a native army awaited the arrival of the Americans. These were troops of a newly proclaimed Republic of the Philippines, led by the Republic's dictator-president Emilio Aguinaldo. Nationalist rebellion, provoked by Spanish misrule and organized by young, European-educated Filipinos, had flared into open warfare in 1896 in Luzon, the archipelago's principal island on which Manila stood. From the ensuing guerrilla campaign, Aguinaldo emerged as generalissimo and popular symbol of the revolt. Late in 1897 an agreement between the Spanish governor Primo de Rivera and Aguinaldo temporarily ended the fighting. In return for Spain's promises of reform in the government of the Islands and for the payment of 800,000 Mexican dollars into the rebels' treasury, Aguinaldo and thirty leading insurgents left Luzon for exile in Hong Kong. The truce quickly broke down. The Spaniards paid half of the agreed indemnity but kept none of their other promises, so the rebels in the Islands and at Hong Kong renewed their agitation. During February and March of 1898 fighting resumed in Luzon.

The leaders in exile saw in the impending war between the United States and Spain potential benefits for their cause, while to Commodore Dewey, preparing at Hong Kong for a possible assault on Manila, the insurgents appeared to be likely allies. Before Dewey's squadron sailed for Manila,

---

27. *RSW, 1898*, II, 15-17, 597. *War Investigating Commission*, VII, 3212. Miles, *The North American Review*, CLXVIII, 526-28, 758-59. *The New York Times*, May 27, 1898. Chadwick, *Spanish-American War*, I, 336, 387. Funston, *Memories*, 63-65, describes García and his troops. García was at odds with the Cuban revolutionary government at the time of the Santiago campaign; see Healy, *United States in Cuba*, 30-31.

the rebels held a series of meetings with the Commodore and with the American consuls at Singapore and Hong Kong. As a result of these talks, Dewey in mid-May allowed Aguinaldo and his colleagues to return to the Philippines on an American warship. After landing near Manila, Aguinaldo soon raised all of southern Luzon against Spain. With weapons from captured Spanish arsenals he equipped an army, and about 15,000 local militia, recruited by the Spaniards to resist the Americans, joined him with their rifles and equipment. Aguinaldo's army, a more formidable fighting force than the Cuban guerrilla bands, rapidly overwhelmed the scattered Spanish detachments in the countryside. Early in June, with about 12,000 troops, the Filippino general laid siege to Manila. Although his men lacked the training and equipment to storm the city, they prevented the entry of food and supplies and exchanged sporadic fusillades with the Spanish defenders.[28]

In Cuba, the United States and the rebels shared a common goal: expulsion of Spain from the island. In the Philippines, on the other hand, the absence of a firm American policy prevented cooperation between the Army and Aguinaldo. Dewey and the consuls at Singapore and Hong Kong had conferred with the Filipino nationalist without prior permission or policy guidance from Washington. While seeking his military cooperation, they had led Aguinaldo to believe that the United States was committed to Philippine independence. The McKinley Administration, however, was as yet committed to nothing in the Philippines. The President eventually might claim all or part of the archipelago for the United States; he might recognize Aguinaldo's government; or he might return the Islands to Spain. During the weeks of active warfare, McKinley's main concern seems to have been to retain the power of decision. On May 26 Secretary of the Navy Long, at the President's direction, cabled Admiral Dewey: "It is desirable, as far as possible, and consistent for your success and safety, not to have political alliances with the insurgents or any faction in the Islands that would incur our liability to maintain their cause in the future." In its instructions to the American consul at Singapore in June, the State Department declared that the United States would take temporary control of the Philippines as part of its war against Spain and would expect all inhabitants of the Islands to submit to that control. If any of them wished to help the Americans in the fight, their aid would be accepted, provided they placed themselves under American command and asked no political commitments.[29]

28. *RSW, 1898*, II, 40, 55; *1899*, I, Pt. 4, pp. 337, 365-66. U.S., Congress, Senate, *A Treaty of Peace between the United States and Spain*, Senate Doc. No. 62, 55th Cong., 3d sess., 1899, pp. 319-22, 333-34, 336-38, 341-42. *War Investigating Commission*, III, 98-99. Teodoro A. Agoncillo, *Malolos: The Crisis of the Republic*, 1-84, 118-45, 215-74. Alger, *Spanish-American War*, 332, 343-48. Chadwick, *Spanish-American War*, II, 365-66. Nunez, *Guerra*, V, 169-70, 177, 206, 229-31. Wolff, *Little Brown Brother*, 23-27, 45-47, 76-77.

29. The order to Dewey is quoted in Long, *New American Navy*, II, 109-10, and in Chadwick, *Spanish-American War*, II, 366; see also II, 367-68. State Department correspondence and instructions are in *Treaty of Peace*, 338-39, 342-43, 353-57. Agoncillo, *Malolos*, 146-55. Wolff, *Little Brown Brother*, 67-68.

In accord with these instructions, Admiral Dewey, after Aguinaldo landed in Luzon, withheld recognition of his government. He turned over to the nationalist leader some Spanish arms his squadron had captured and he allowed Filipino troops to move across the bay by boat, but he avoided combined operations with the insurgents. General Merritt sailed for Manila with positive orders not to ally with Aguinaldo. He conducted his campaign without regard to the Filipino army and even avoided a conference with its general. The siege of Manila developed into a curious triangular contest in which the American fleet and the Eighth Corps fought the Spaniards while simultaneously maneuvering to deny the Filipinos a share in the spoils of victory. The Filipinos meanwhile used the strategic situation created by Dewey's success to forward their own cause.[30]

IV

In the manner of their departure from the United States, the Santiago and Manila expeditions presented a study in contrast. The Fifth Corps embarked in haste and confusion, leaving behind men and equipment; the Eighth Corps boarded ship methodically and in order, taking along all the supplies intended for it. The circumstances in which the two expeditions set forth—the Fifth Corps hurriedly, to attack an objective decided upon only hours before sailing orders arrived, the Eighth Corps deliberately, to approach an objective clearly defined for weeks—account for most of the difference in performance. Nevertheless, many of the differences resulted from the personalities, the military experience, and the administrative capacities of the expedition commanders, for upon them fell the ultimate responsibility for transforming aggregations of men, material, and ships into invasion forces.

Maj. Gen. William Rufus Shafter of the Fifth Corps typified the senior Regular officer of the 1890s. Born in rural Michigan in 1835, he entered the Army in 1861 as a volunteer. He fought well against the Confederates and earned the Medal of Honor for gallantry during his Civil War service. Joining the Regulars in 1866, he campaigned against the Indians and proved himself to be a competent company and regimental commander. Slowly he advanced through the ranks of the peacetime Army and received his brigadier general's star in 1897. When mobilization began in 1898, he commanded the Department of California, with his headquarters at San Francisco. His rank and seniority in the Army brought him his commission as major general of Volunteers and command of the elite Fifth Corps. Critics of the McKinley Administration attributed Shafter's rise to the fact that he came from Michigan, the home state of Secretary Alger, with whom Shafter

30. *Correspondence*, II, 779-80. *Treaty of Peace*, 369. Agoncillo, *Malolos*, 174. Alger, *Spanish-American War*, 333, 350. Chadwick, *Spanish-American War*, II, 367-68.

had been associated previously in G.A.R. activities. However, if Shafter had a sponsor in the War Department, it was Adjutant General Corbin, an old frontier comrade and close friend. In fact, Alger, Corbin, and Miles all regarded Shafter as a level-headed and aggressive officer. He was their unanimous choice to lead the first attack on Cuba.[31]

In appearance and manner, the general who would plant the Stars and Stripes on Cuban soil was less than heroic. A heavily built, short-legged man with a massively proportioned head and thick, grayish-white mustache, Shafter had gone grossly to fat during his sedentary years of garrison command. On the eve of his embarkation for Santiago, according to his chief commissary, he "couldn't walk two miles in an hour, just beastly obese." His laconic speech and crude manners alienated many who came in contact with him, and he had a reputation for bullying his subordinates. Yet, others who worked with him credited him with determination and quickness of decision. Shafter's worst failing as a commander, one he shared with most Regulars of his generation, was a lack of experience in organizing and maneuvering large formations. Never, before taking command at Tampa, had he directed so many men—25,000 infantry, cavalry, and artillery—in an independent campaign. His inexperience became evident during the weeks of preparation at Tampa. He did little to bring order to his base; he failed to draw clear lines of responsibility for staff officers and troop commanders; at times he overlooked important details. Fortunately for him, his staff contained experienced, hard-working Regulars whose willingness to take initiative and to improvise in emergencies partially compensated for their superior's mistakes and oversights. Shafter had the good sense to give them wide freedom of action.[32]

The Fifth Corps, composed as it was of most of the Regular infantry, cavalry, and field artillery, the Rough Riders, and eight of the best-trained and -equipped Volunteer infantry regiments, contained the Army's elite troops, but it had serious weaknesses as a fighting force. Its individual units,

31. Charles Dudley Rhodes, "William Rufus Shafter," *DAB*, XVII, 15-16. Chadwick, *Spanish-American War*, II, 6. Miley, *In Cuba*, 1-2. *Army and Navy Journal*, December 24, 1898, and February 4, 1899. *Washington Post*, April 29, 1898. *New York Times Magazine*, June 26, 1898. William R. Shafter to R. A. Alger, August 31, 1889; Alger to Shafter, November 16, 1896; Maj. Gen. Miles to Alger, March 19, 1897; Adj. Gen. Corbin to Alger, November 16, 1900; Alger to Corbin, November 19, 1900, Alger Papers. Shafter to Congressman C. H. Grosvenor, May 4, 1900, Box 1, Corbin Papers. Box 1A of the Corbin Papers contains duplicates of Corbin to Alger, November 16, 1900, and of Alger's reply of November 19.

32. The quotation is from J. F. Weston to Maj. Gen. James H. Wilson, June 7, 1898, Box 26, Wilson Papers; see also Weston to Wilson, July 14, 1899, Box 26, Wilson Papers. Chadwick, *Spanish-American War*, II, 6. Cruse, *Apache Days and After*, 277. George Kennan, *Campaigning in Cuba*, 246-47. Miley, *In Cuba*, 9. Parker, *Gatling Gun Detachment*, 20-32, 37, 56-60, 211-12. Wheeler, *Santiago Campaign*, 6, 196-97. Wilson, *Under the Old Flag*, II, 419, 428. *Army and Navy Journal*, June 11 and December 24, 1898. Theodore Roosevelt to Henry Cabot Lodge, March 9, 1899, in *Roosevelt-Lodge Correspondence*, I, 394. *War Investigating Commission*, III, 8-9; VI, 2623, 2926-27, 2931-32; VII, 3638-39, 3791. *RSW, 1898*, II, 600. *The New York Times*, June 14 and 15, 1898.

especially the Regulars and the Rough Riders, had achieved a high standard of training. Their battalion and company officers seemed to observers to be alert and competent. Yet, none of these troops had held brigade or divisional maneuvers before their embarkation. An officer with the expedition doubted whether even regiments of the same brigade "have ever practiced attacking together, and whether half of them have ever practiced attacking at all as regiments." The Fifth Corps, like the rest of the Army, suffered from a shortage of experienced staff, especially in the Medical Department, and frequent transfers of key men during the weeks of preparation did nothing to increase its cohesion. The corps sailed for Santiago as a collection of efficient small units, not as a fully integrated fighting machine.[33]

Tampa, Shafter's base, presented throughout May and June an appalling spectacle of congestion and confusion in which the Army's haste and mismanagement made almost insurmountable the port's already formidable obstacles to rapid, orderly embarkation. Neither the War Department nor General Shafter put one man in charge of the port or gave anyone power to coordinate the work of staff and line. Troop commanders and staff officers all went their separate ways, frequently frustrating each other's endeavors. After the decision to attack Havana, the War Department poured men and supplies into Tampa without regard for the city's limited terminal and warehouse capacity. Trainloads of food, clothing, and weapons backed up on sidings as far north as Columbia, South Carolina, while the quartermasters at Tampa lacked wagons with which to haul material from the cars and buildings in which to put it. The delayed arrival of bills of lading forced supply officers to open scores of boxcars in their search for urgently needed stores. By May 18, more than 1,000 freight cars jammed the yards at Tampa and Port Tampa, and they were being emptied at a rate of only two or three a day. In irritating contrast to the general cooperativeness of their industry with the Army, the two rival railroad companies that served Tampa feuded bitterly with each other as each tried to monopolize the profitable government traffic. Their battle reached its climax when the Plant System, which controlled the single track to Port Tampa, refused to let its competitor's cars pass over it. The Plant System's employees quit their obstructions of traffic only after the military authorities threatened to seize the company's facilities.[34]

33. The quotation is from Bigelow, *Santiago Campaign*, 72; see also 13-14, 38-39, 46-47. Alger, *Spanish-American War*, 286-87. Kennan, *Campaigning in Cuba*, 3-4. Roosevelt, *Rough Riders*, 53-56. Wheeler, *Santiago Campaign*, 82-83. *RSW, 1898*, I, 788; II, 148. *War Investigating Commission*, I, 664; VI, 3040-43; VII, 3241. *Correspondence*, I, 24. John A. Porter to Secretary Alger, May 30, 1898, McKinley Papers. Bellinger, Tampa Report, File No. 115533, OQMG Records. *The New York Times*, June 4, 1898.

34. *War Investigating Commission*, I, 133, 522-23; III, 434-37, 444; V, 1842, 1851-53; VI, 2611, 2947; VII, 3193, 3639-40, 3667. *Correspondence*, I, 25. Alger, *Spanish-American War*, 66, 68. Kennan, *Campaigning in Cuba*, 49. Miley, *In Cuba*, 22-25, 27. Risch, *Quartermaster Corps*, 549. Theodore Roosevelt to Henry Cabot Lodge, June 10 and 12, 1898, *Roosevelt-Lodge Correspondence*, I, 306, 308-9. Bellinger, Tampa Report, File No. 115533, OQMG Records. Maj. Gen. William R. Shafter to Adj. Gen. Corbin, June 7, 1898, Box 1, Corbin Papers.

Courtesy USAMHI

Major General William R. Shafter (right) with Brigadier General William Ludlow at Tampa.

The congestion and confusion were at their worst on May 26, when the Fifth Corps began loading its guns, wagons, animals, and supplies onto steamers for the voyage to Santiago. Because everything had to be funneled down that single railroad track to Port Tampa, the stowing of the baggage was not completed until the small hours of June 7. Only then could the troops start marching aboard. The movement of the regiments to their transports, too, had been poorly planned. Col. C. F. Humphrey, Shafter's chief quartermaster, who had charge of the operation, had not thought through the details of bringing almost 20,000 men down the railroad line to the wharf, and he failed to notify the regimental commanders of the sketchy arrangements he had made. Interference from Washington compounded the confusion. Under pressure from Secretary of the Navy Long, who chafed at the Army's slowness and feared that Cervera would escape from Santiago before the Fifth Corps could arrive, President McKinley and Secretary Alger on the night of June 7, after regiments had been embarking all day, telegraphed Shafter to sail at once with whatever troops then were on board. In his endeavors to comply with these instructions and at the same time

191

to take as many men as possible, Shafter tried to rush too many troops through Port Tampa too rapidly. The embarkation turned into a huge, slow-moving stampede. Regiments appropriated each other's trains in their haste to reach the docks and arrived at the port in the wrong order for boarding the steamers. Thousands of sweating, shouting, cursing men milled about on the wharf. The Rough Riders, who had captured a coal train for the ride to the port, seized a transport on their own initiative, barely winning a race to the gangplank against a slightly less aggressive unit. Largely without guidance from the corps commander, the regiments sorted themselves out and swarmed onto ships, piling their baggage into the holds in confused heaps.[35]

The Quartermaster's Department had assembled for the Fifth Corps 31 transports, most of them small, shallow-draught coastal freighters, plus 2 water boats and 1 collier. Assisted by the Engineers, the department had furnished for landing craft 3 small steam lighters, 1 sea-going tug, and 2 decked barges. Shafter had discovered before the embarkation that this heterogeneous armada could not carry all of his 25,000 men. Therefore, the troops who swarmed into Port Tampa on June 7 included only the Regulars, the Rough Riders, and two Volunteer infantry regiments—in all, about 17,000 men. The rest of the Volunteers remained at Tampa, along with most of the expedition's ambulances, many of its wagons, the cavalry's horses, and tons of regimental baggage and hospital stores—all left behind so that as many troops as possible could sail. Even with the force and its impedimenta thus reduced, the steamers were dangerously overcrowded.[36]

By midday on June 8, most of the soldiers had found places in the cramped holds. They spent the next week sweltering on shipboard in Tampa Bay while the Navy investigated and found incorrect a report that Cervera had escaped to sea. On June 14 the expedition at last sailed. The Quartermaster's Department had fitted the ships for the short, thirty-hour voyage from Tampa to Mariel by installing only wooden bunks, rudimentary toilet and washing facilities, boilers for heating coffee, and little else for the comfort of the men. In vessels so ill fitted and then overcrowded, the week-long, 1,000-mile journey to Santiago became for the soldiers an ordeal of

35. Alger, *Spanish-American War*, 71. Bigelow, *Santiago Campaign*, 52. Miley, *In Cuba*, 4, 19-22, 25, 27-34. Risch, *Quartermaster Corps*, 551-52. Roosevelt, *Rough Riders*, 57-60. *War Investigating Commission*, V, 2060; VI, 2657-60, 2776, 2777; VII, 3193, 3232, 3603-6, 3640-41, 3651-52, 3667-68. *Correspondence*, I, 9, 22-23, 29-31. *RSW, 1898*, IV, 245. Theodore Roosevelt to Henry Cabot Lodge, June 12, 1898, *Roosevelt-Lodge Correspondence*, I, 307. Bellinger, Tampa Report, File No. 115533, OQMG Records. *The New York Times*, June 14, 1898.

36. *War Investigating Commission*, I, 134, 468-69; V, 1848, 2052-53; VI, 2414-15, 2657, 3037; VII, 520-21. *RSW, 1898*, I, 388, 391, 704; II, 12, 148-49. Chadwick, *Spanish-American War*, II, 19-20. Risch, *Quartermaster Corps*, 546-47. Lt. Col. Smith S. Leach to the Chief of the Third Division, General Staff, December 22, 1905, File No. 342, Records of the Joint Army-Navy Board (hereafter cited as Army-Navy Board Records).

jammed decks and passageways, scanty, uncooked food, smelly, ill-ventilated bunkrooms, and putrid water. Only unbroken calm weather, which permitted most of the men to remain on the upper decks in the fresh air, prevented mass suffering and even death as the fleet steamed slowly toward Cuba.[37]

During the two weeks of embarkation and waiting at Tampa, General Miles had hovered at Shafter's side. Miles had become increasingly restless and uncomfortable as his authority in the Administration dwindled, so he had left Washington for Tampa on May 30 to help untangle the confusion at the Florida base. His presence seems to have had little effect on conditions at Tampa, and events during his stay further alienated Miles from Alger and the bureau chiefs. Soon after reaching Tampa, Miles telegraphed to the bureau chiefs an inquiry about the supplies at Tampa and a complaint about the railroad congestion. This routine communication leaked to the newspapers, which blew it up into a stinging rebuke of the bureaus by the Commanding General. Apologies and explanations followed, but the incident left hard feelings between Miles and the staff chiefs, who blamed him for the release of the telegram. At the same time, Miles continued to question the Administration's strategy by suggesting that the Fifth Corps attack Puerto Rico instead of Santiago. President McKinley rejected Miles's proposal. Early in the war, McKinley and Alger had given Miles supreme command of the Caribbean striking force and had authorized him to accompany it or any part of it in the field. While at Tampa, Miles decided to sail with the Fifth Corps and to take direct control of the attack on Santiago. On June 5 he cabled Washington for permission to do so but phrased his request so it seemed like a demand for authority to strike at Puerto Rico. For this reason and because they believed they already had given Miles all the command authority he needed, neither McKinley nor Alger answered Miles's telegram. When Shafter sailed on June 14, Miles remained behind at Tampa. Soon thereafter he returned to Washington, convinced he had been kept away from the front by malice in the Administration.[38]

37. Alger, *Spanish-American War*, 72-75. *Correspondence*, I, 31-32, 35. *War Investigating Commission*, I, 134-35, 446, 497-500; III, 108; VI, 2412, 2414, 2614, 2657; VII, 3191, 3242; VIII, 520-21. *RSW, 1898*, II, 149, 592. Lt. Col. Smith S. Leach to the Chief of the Third Division, General Staff, December 22, 1905, File No. 342, Army-Navy Board Records. Two eloquent personal accounts of life aboard these ships are: Bigelow, *Santiago Campaign*, 50-51 and 76-77, and Theodore Roosevelt to Henry Cabot Lodge, June 12, 1898, *Roosevelt-Lodge Correspondence*, I, 308.

38. *Army and Navy Journal*, April 23 and June 25, 1898. *The New York Times*, May 28 and 31, June 2 and 10, 1898. *War Investigating Commission*, VII, 3206, 3248, 3564-65. *Correspondence*, I, 21, 26, 48, 264. Alger, *Spanish-American War*, 59-61, 66-69. Leech, *Days of McKinley*, 241. Miles, *Serving the Republic*, 275-76, and *The North American Review*, CLXVIII, 528. V. L. Mason to Col. B. F. Montgomery, July 28, 1900; R. A. Alger to Adj. Gen. Corbin, August 6, 1900, Alger Papers. *Chicago Record*, June 18, 1898, clipping in 1898 Scrapbook, Box 19, Corbin Papers. John J. McCook to Maj. Gen. James H. Wilson, June 30, 1898, Box 15, Wilson Papers. Commissary General Charles P. Eagan to Adj. Gen. Corbin, June 10, 1898, File No. 88399, AGO Records. Miles really was another victim of the War Department's failure clearly to define command responsibilities. Had Alger and McKinley at the start given Miles charge of the Cuban invasion and relieved him of all other duties, the General's relations with his political superiors probably would have been harmonious.

Miles returned to the capital to make known his views on organizing the army that was to reinforce the Fifth Corps and attack Puerto Rico. The ever-cautious McKinley had ruled on June 4 that the second expedition must be strong enough to take Puerto Rico without the aid of the Fifth Corps, and organization of the new force proceeded on that principle. On June 18 McKinley, Alger, and Miles agreed that the second expedition, which would consist of about 30,000 men, should be drawn from three of the partially equipped corps in the home camps. About 12,000 of the troops were in Tampa—regiments that had been left behind by Shafter and were now under control of the Fourth Corps. Some 16,000 Volunteers from the First Corps at Camp Thomas and 6,000 more from the Second at Camp Alger—all of whom were approaching battle readiness by mid-June—would constitute the balance of the force. Of this second expeditionary force, all but a few regiments would be Volunteers. The regiments from Camp Alger and as many men from Tampa as were needed were to follow the Fifth Corps to Santiago; the rest of the troops would invade Puerto Rico.[39]

On June 26 Secretary Alger formally named General Miles to command the new expedition and set Puerto Rico as its target. At the same time, he instructed camp commanders to prepare the selected units for immediate field service. The commanders did so by stripping stay-at-home regiments of supplies and by stopping issues to all units except those headed overseas. By the last week of June the first contingents of the new expedition were beginning to move. On June 23 and 26, three regiments from the Second Corps sailed from Newport News to join Shafter. On June 30 a shipload of Regular recruits and an Illinois Volunteer regiment left Tampa for Santiago and six batteries of Regular field artillery and a District of Columbia infantry regiment boarded ships at the Florida base.[40]

V

The confusion at Tampa contrasted sharply with the order and efficiency of the Eighth Corps' preparations at San Francisco, and the contrast demonstrated the importance of the strong hand of an experienced commander. Major General Shafter's ineptness at Tampa was in direct contrast to the skills of Maj. Gen. Wesley Merritt at San Francisco. Merritt, in charge

39. *Correspondence*, I, 46, 48, 55-57, 263-64, 268. *RSW, 1898*, II, 207-8. Alger, *Spanish-American War*, 298-99. Secretary Alger to President McKinley, June 18, 1898, McKinley Papers; another copy of this document is in the Alger Papers. Maj. Gen. J. R. Brooke to Adj. Gen. Corbin, June 25, 1898, File No. 159902; Brig. Gen. Henry V. Boynton to C. A. Boynton, June 14, 1898, File No. 160115, AGO Records. *The New York Times*, June 8 and 16, 1898. Mayo, *America of Yesterday*, 200.

40. *Correspondence*, I, 44-47, 53, 58-60, 62-65, 67, 69-72, 268-70, 540. Adj. Gen. Corbin to Maj. Gen. W. M. Graham, June 21, 1898, File No. 91142; Corbin to Graham, June 22 and 24, 1898, File No. 94795, AGO Records. *War Investigating Commission*, III, 128, 232; IV, 887; VI, 3067. Alger, *Spanish-American War*, 299-300. Wilson, *Under the Old Flag*, II, 432-33.

General Merritt (seated, center) with his staff en route to Manila.

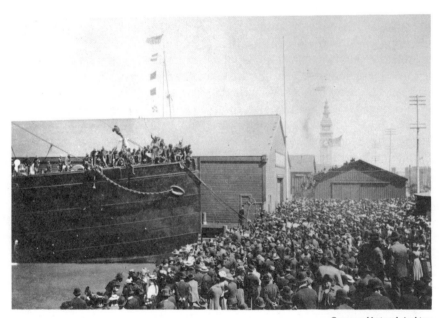

Camp Merritt, Cal. Transport Indiana *receiving troops and freight at Pacific Mail Docks on eve of departure. Crowd bidding farewell. June 27, 1898.*

of the Manila expedition, was the second-ranking officer of the Regular establishment. Unlike most of the generals of 1898, he had graduated from West Point. Divisional command in the Civil War had given him the practice in administering and maneuvering large formations that Shafter so conspicuously lacked. Rumor had it that Merritt resented his assignment to Manila as less than his rank deserved, but whatever discontent he may have felt did not diminish the energy with which he prepared his force for its adventure. Before leaving Washington for San Francisco, he conferred at length with McKinley, Alger, and Miles. He pressed the War Department for funds for emergency supply purchases, for field and mountain artillery, and for a force of engineers. Through insistent demands on the War Department, he secured able generals to assist him and built up a competent staff heavily weighted with Regulars. He was fortunate also in his Volunteer regimental officers, many of whom had served in the National Guard or in the Regular Army.[41]

Under instructions from the War Department, Maj. Gen. Henry C. Merriam of the Department of California, who had his headquarters at San Francisco, transformed his staff into a supporting command of the Manila expedition, thus assuring Merritt at least a minimum of coordination and unification of responsibility at his base. Merritt made good use of Merriam and of the officers of the Eighth Corps. He assigned to Merriam, assisted by the commander of each contingent destined for overseas duty, the task of housing, equipping, and training the troops. He placed his own second in command, Maj. Gen. Elwell S. Otis, in charge of chartering and fitting out transports. Merritt organized his corps on a functional basis rather than adhering rigidly to the prescribed divisional and brigade structure. Knowing that the slow arrival of ships would force his corps to sail in several sections of varying size, Merritt postponed the formation of permanent divisions until his army reached Manila. He sent out each detachment as a self-contained command with its own complement of staff and medical personnel. The troops awaiting transportation at San Francisco constituted the "Independent Division," an administrative and training formation from which separate regiments were taken to organize the expeditions to Manila. While encamped around San Francisco, the soldiers of this division completed their equipment and underwent intensive drills, which included regimental battle exercises. Late in July, after both Merritt and Otis had sailed for the Philippines, the War Department placed the Independent Division under control of the Department of California, and it continued to feed regiments to the Eighth Corps.[42]

41. Alger, *Spanish-American War*, 327. Wolff, *Little Brown Brother*, 92. *Army and Navy Journal*, May 28, 1898. *The New York Times*, May 21, 1898. *War Investigating Commission*, I, 675; III, 102, 112-13; VII, 3270-71. *Correspondence*, II, 639, 643-47, 657-60, 665-67, 674, 678-79, 681-83, 696-98.

42. *Correspondence*, II, 647, 725, 734-35. *War Investigating Commission*, III, 109; VII, 3265. Chadwick, *Spanish-American War*, II, 373. Funston, *Memories*, 158, 169-70. *The New York Times*, May 20, 22, 28, 29, and 31, 1898.

On May 25 the vanguard of the expedition, 2,500 men in three steamers, sailed for Manila. A second contingent of 3,500 left on June 15, and 4,600 more troops, accompanied by General Merritt, passed outward through the Golden Gate on June 27 and 29. Additional regiments left San Francisco during July and August, but only the first three groups reached Manila in time to fight Spanish forces.[43]

The embarkation of all these contingents proceeded in good order, according to a well worked out system. Each Manila-bound regiment received its transport assignment well in advance of departure, and its quartermaster and commissary supervised the loading of stores and baggage. The officers tried to fill the holds so that material likely to be needed first at Manila was loaded last, for easy access at their destination. Often, the late delivery to the docks of bulky items and the need to trim the vessels carefully for the long and possibly rough voyage disrupted these plans, but, compared to the indiscriminate piling in of baggage that occurred at Tampa, the loading of the Eighth Corps transports was a model of precision. When the time for departure came, the regiments marched in good order from their camps through the city's streets to the wharves. The crowds that gathered along the line of march to watch them go aroused the only confusion and excitement that attended these movements. Because of the thorough manner in which the ships had been prepared for the journey, the men of the Eighth Corps crossed the Pacific in relative comfort, although there were complaints from some transports of overcrowding and of limited bathing facilities. Stringent sanitary precautions during the voyage prevented major outbreaks of disease, and the troops reached Manila in fighting condition.[44]

VI

The Santiago and Manila expeditions and the later expedition against Puerto Rico all left the country as well equipped as the available material, the restricted shipping, and the state of American military and industrial technology permitted. Regulars in all theaters went into battle with the up-to-date Krag-Jörgensen rifle and smokeless ammunition. In Cuba and the Philippines, the Volunteers carried the old Springfield, but the state regiments that went to Puerto Rico in July and August received Krags before they entered combat. All expeditions took with them more heavy weapons than

43. Alger, *Spanish-American War*, 328-29. *RSW, 1898*, I, 269. *Correspondence*, II, 742, 748-49, 751.

44. *Correspondence*, II, 704, 717-18, 767-77. *War Investigating Commission*, III, 95-97, 107-8; VII, 3272. *RSW, 1899*, I, Pt. 2, pp. 476-78. Anderson, *JMSI*, XXIX, 202-3. Devol, *JMSI*, XXIX, 211-12. *Army and Navy Journal*, September 10, 1898. *The New York Times*, May 24 and 25 and June 4 and 15, 1898. Lt. Col. J. W. Pope to the Quartermaster General, November 16, 1898, File No. 115533, OQMG Records.

they could bring to bear on the enemy. The Fifth Corps sailed for Santiago with 16 light field guns, 8 large-caliber siege pieces, 8 field mortars, 4 Gatling guns, 1 Hotchkiss revolving cannon, and 1 experimental dynamite gun. Still more artillery followed with the reinforcements sent to Cuba after the battles of San Juan and El Caney. The Puerto Rico expedition eventually accumulated 106 guns and mortars of various calibers and 10 Gatlings, many of them weapons intended for Santiago and diverted from there when the Spanish garrison surrendered. The Eighth Corps crossed the Pacific with 16 light field guns, 6 small mountain guns, and an assortment of Gatlings and rapid-fire weapons. All the expeditions had more ammunition than they had occasion to use although the artillery and the Volunteers had to fire black powder because of the late procurement and issue of the smokeless variety.[45]

Because of the delays in production, only 5,000 of the new brown tropical uniforms reached the Fifth Corps before it sailed for Santiago. Most of Shafter's troops had to sweat out the campaign in the standard heavy wool shirts and trousers, although Quartermaster General Ludington on July 6 sent down a shipload of the new uniforms for them. Later expeditions fared better with respect to clothing. The regiments that embarked for Puerto Rico wore the canvas suits, which by the start of that campaign in July were being delivered in large numbers. The troops of the Eighth Corps took with them to Manila light canvas or duck suits and an ample supply of tropical underclothing, much of it purchased on the West Coast. By the end of August, Secretary Alger could report that over 80,000 canvas uniforms had been issued to the soldiers. These first tropical uniforms left much to be desired. They fitted poorly and wore out quickly. The men complained that they were almost as hot as the regulation blue. Throughout the war, Secretary Alger and General Ludington urged manufacturers to begin producing a true cotton khaki, but their efforts did not bear fruit until after Spain gave up the fight.[46]

The expeditions received large stocks of food, medical stores, vehicles, pack and draught animals, and engineering and communications equipment. Each unit that went to Santiago or Puerto Rico took with it a three- or four-months' supply of the essential ration components. Troops bound for Manila carried food for six months. Under contract with the Subsistence Department,

45. *War Investigating Commission*, IV, 956. *RSW, 1898*, IV, 247. *Correspondence*, I, 399; II, 638-39, 666, 742. *Treaty of Peace*, 425. Chadwick, *Spanish-American War*, II, 19-20, 300. Wilson, *Under the Old Flag*, II, 442.

46. *War Investigating Commission*, I, 442-43; III, 104-5; VI, 2649, 3102. *Correspondence*, I, 82; II, 777-79. Alger, *Spanish-American War*, 284. Risch, *Quartermaster Corps*, 524. Anderson, *JMSI*, XXIX, 203-4. *Army and Navy Journal*, August 27 and October 8 and 15, 1898. *The New York Times*, May 18 and June 4 and 10, 1898. Capt. E. B. Harrison to Maj. J. N. Carson, August 24, 1898, File No. 115533, OQMG Records. Charles A. Moore to Secretary Alger, August 4, 1898, Alger Papers.

refrigerator ships delivered fresh American beef to the forces in the Caribbean and Australian beef and mutton to the army at Manila. The Medical Department lavishly outfitted the expeditions with hospital furniture, surgical instruments, and medicines. The division hospitals of the Fifth Corps received most of the available ambulances, hospital tents, and wagons, only to leave the bulk of them behind at Tampa for lack of space on the transports. Medical stores included an individual first-aid packet for each soldier. According to surgeons at Santiago, widespread use of these dressings on the firing line saved the lives of scores, possibly hundreds, of wounded men. Engineer detachments accompanied each expedition and carried with them as much construction and siege gear as they could load on their ships. At Santiago, in Puerto Rico, and at Manila, men of the Signal Corps made heroic and successful efforts to keep army detachments and headquarters linked with telegraph and telephone lines. In Cuba, they dredged up the severed end of an undersea cable off Guantánamo, thereby establishing direct telegraph communication between General Shafter's headquarters and the War Department.[47]

On June 20 Shafter's transports dropped anchor off Santiago. Ten days later, the first 2,500 men of the Eighth Corps reached Manila.[48] These expeditions had departed from their bases in the United States as well prepared for their missions as the limited time and resources allowed. The War Department, aided by the Navy and the State departments, had done its best to inform commanders about the conditions they would encounter. Within the restrictions imposed by the President's policy, the military authorities had established favorable political conditions for the invasions. It now rested with the troops and their commanders to meet and surmount the ultimate test of battle.

47. *War Investigating Commission*, I, 548, 571, 594, 597, 653, 682-83, 686; II, 781; IV, 960-62; V, 1969; VI, 2927-28, 2930-32, 3029-31; VII, 3238-39; VIII, 404-5. *RSW, 1898*, I, 562-63, 565-66, 575-76, 579-81, 692, 694, 704, 712-13, 797, 851-52, 877-78, 880-91, 895-97. Chadwick, *Spanish-American War*, II, 19-20. Miley, *In Cuba*, 93-94. Risch, *Quartermaster Corps*, 530. Maj. Gen. J. R. Brooke to Adj. Gen. Corbin, September 8, 1898, File No. 128803, AGO Records. Bellinger, Tampa Report, File No. 115533, OQMG Records.

48. Alger, *Spanish-American War*, 83-84. Chadwick, *Spanish-American War*, II, 369.

7

The Army in Combat

I

In Cuba, Puerto Rico, and the Philippines, the Army assisted the operations of the Navy and exploited its victories. At Santiago, in the war's longest, hardest campaign, Shafter's Fifth Corps had to overcome obstacles of climate and terrain as well as surmount the fierce resistance of the Spaniards, who were fighting to protect their fleet, which determined their strategic ability to continue the war. At Puerto Rico and Manila the Army's role was to exploit on land the Navy's command of the sea by rounding up at the cost of minimal casualties the isolated Spanish garrisons. Yet, each of these apparently simple operations had military and, in the Philippines, political complications of its own.

After establishing the broad objectives of each of the campaigns, the War Department, at President McKinley's behest, gave its field generals wide discretion in the conduct of operations and enjoined them to cooperate closely with their Navy counterparts. The final instructions, issued on May 23 to Brig. Gen. Thomas M. Anderson, commanding the vanguard of the Manila expedition, typified the department's delegation of tactical decision-making:

> The Secretary of War directs that General Anderson . . . on arrival [at Manila] will confer fully with Admiral Dewey as to whole situation and dispose of the troops so as to have them under the protection of the guns of the Admiral's fleet until the arrival of the main force of the army under General Merritt and General Otis. Importance of the speedy return of transports going with these troops should be kept in view. This instruction is not intended to deprive General Anderson of the fullest discretion after consultation with Admiral Dewey. Hearty co-operation with the senior officer of the Navy is enjoined. He must, however, be governed by events and circumstances of which we can have no knowledge. The President and Secretary of War rely upon the sound judgment of the officer in command.[1]

The War Department defined General Shafter's missions at Santiago so broadly as to invite a major Army-Navy dispute over the purposes and tactics of the campaign. Shafter, according to the War Department's order to him of May 31, was to

> proceed under convoy of the navy to the vicinity of Santiago de Cuba, land your force . . . east or west of that point as your judgment may dictate . . ., and move it onto the high ground overlooking the harbor or into the interior, as shall best enable you to capture or destroy the garrison there, and cover the navy as it sends its men in small boats to remove torpedos, or with the aid of the navy, capture or destroy the Spanish fleet now reported to be in Santiago harbor.

1. Text of the instructions to Anderson is in *Correspondence*, II, 668-69.

The order gave Shafter wide latitude in the conduct of the campaign but urged him to move as rapidly as possible, once ashore, and thus reduce the length of time his men would be exposed to tropical diseases. It permitted Shafter to cooperate with the Cuban rebel troops near Santiago whose aid General Miles was then securing. Once his initial objectives had been attained, Shafter, if his losses had not been too great, could remain at Santiago; or he could re-embark his corps and move to Puerto de Banes, a rebel-held harbor on Cuba's north coast, "reporting by the most favorable means for further orders and future important service."[2]

While Navy officers envisioned the Santiago operation as limited to open-ing the harbor to the fleet and assuring Cervera's destruction, the War Depart-ment's order to Shafter, stressing as it did the capture of the city and its garrison as well as the elimination of the Spanish squadron, appeared to authorize an extensive land campaign in eastern Cuba. Shafter so construed it. He assumed he was to overrun and occupy the whole Santiago region. As soon as he reached Cuba, he asked the War Department to send him more horses for his cavalry so that mounted columns could "gather in some small bodies of troops in the interior." All but ignoring the Navy, once he got his men ashore, Shafter directed his operations as much to winning a decisive land battle as to aiding in the capture of the enemy cruisers. In the light of McKinley's insistence after May 2 on a large land campaign in Cuba and of the President's decisions and orders during the actual battles and siege, there is every reason to believe Shafter correctly deduced and carried out his Commander-in-Chief's intentions.[3]

II

Shafter's troops were the first major Army contingent to set foot on Spanish colonial soil and to engage the enemy. After his transports dropped anchor off Santiago on June 20, Shafter spent the next two days concerting plans with Admiral Sampson and with the Cuban General García and prepar-ing his soldiers for disembarkation. On June 22 the advance units of his corps, supported by Navy gunfire and by a simultaneous land attack by García's Cubans, went ashore at the small port of Daiquirí, 17 miles east of San-tiago. To divert the Spaniards' attention, the fleet also shelled several other coastal points while transports maneuvered menacingly off shore. The Spaniards offered no resistance at Daiquirí. Unsure where Shafter would land, their commander had scattered his men in small detachments along 50 kilometers of coastline east and west of the harbor mouth. The 300 Spaniards at Daiquirí, without artillery to answer the Navy's cannon and menaced from the rear by the Cubans, withdrew before dawn on June 22. Only the heavy surf and a shortage of small boats hindered Shafter's disembarkation.

2. For text of Shafter's orders, see Alger, *Spanish-American War*, 63-65.

3. Alger, *Spanish-American War*, 86-88. Chadwick, *Spanish-American War*, I, 359. Goode, *With Sampson*, 177-78. Miley, *In Cuba*, 15-16. Shafter's request for cavalry mounts is in *Correspondence*, I, 60.

Courtesy National Archives

Ninth U.S. Infantry landing at Siboney, Cuba, June 25, 1898.

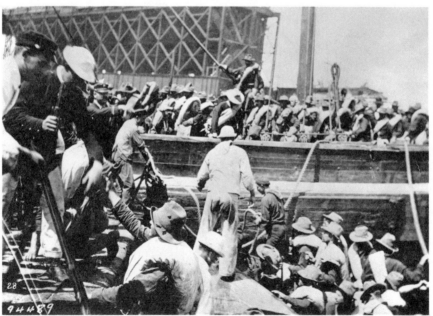

Courtesy National Archives

Landing at Daiquirí with ore loading pier in the background.

Using the Navy's steam launches, the transports' lifeboats, and other light craft, about 6,000 troops struggled ashore through the breakers on the first day of the invasion, with a loss of two men drowned when their boat capsized. The artillery horses and pack mules suffered more severely. Since small boats could not carry them, the soldiers pushed them overboard from the transports and left them to swim to the beach. Thirty of them drowned or were dashed against the rocks. Late in the day, the first troops ashore drove the Spanish garrison out of Siboney, a small port west of Daiquirí, and gave the army a second landing point eight miles closer to Santiago. During the next three days, the rest of the American troops and 4,000 of García's Cubans, brought around on transports from their camp west of the harbor, landed through Daiquirí and Siboney, followed by draught and pack animals, field guns, wagons, and supplies. By June 26 General Shafter had his two infantry divisions, his dismounted cavalry division, and his independent infantry brigade, plus assorted cavalry, artillery, engineer and signal units, and the bulk of García's army, on shore and ready for action.[4]

From its landing places, the Fifth Corps could move in two directions. It could march along the coast road toward the fort of El Morro, which guarded the entrance to Santiago Bay, storm El Morro with the Navy's assistance, and thus open the harbor to the fleet. Or, the corps could move inland, along a second road running north and west from Siboney toward the city of Santiago at the head of the bay, and make the city the point of attack. In a letter dispatched to Secretary Alger on May 26, General Miles had advocated the second course of action. The Fifth Corps, he wrote, should land at Daiquirí and march on Santiago. By seizing the high ground that surrounded the city to the east and north, the Fifth Corps could trap the garrison against the bay and assure its destruction or capture. Artillery planted on the same hills would render the bay untenable for Cervera's vessels and would force them to run out to sea under Sampson's guns.[5]

Admiral Sampson and his staff, who saw destruction of Cervera's squadron as the principal object of the campaign and who considered the city and its garrison of little military importance, favored the advance along the beach toward El Morro and expected Shafter to undertake it. Shafter, however, before his troops went ashore, decided to follow Miles's plan. He had several reasons for doing so. Miles's strategy would assure a more complete victory by encircling the city garrison, and it would win for the Army a larger share of credit for the final triumph on both land and sea. Reports from American intelligence and from García's Cubans indicated that the

4. *War Investigating Commission*, III, 302-5; VI, 2658; VII, 3196, 3198, 3200, 3653-54, 3669-70. *RSW, 1898*, I, 406; II, 149-50. Alger, *Spanish-American War*, 78-86, 90-101. Goode, *With Sampson*, 180. Miley, *In Cuba*, 26, 76-77. Nunez, *Guerra*, IV, 46-49, 54-56, 74, 76, 79-80, 102-3, 111-12.

5. Maj. Gen. Nelson A. Miles to Secretary Alger, May 26, 1898, in Alger, *Spanish-American War*, 49-50.

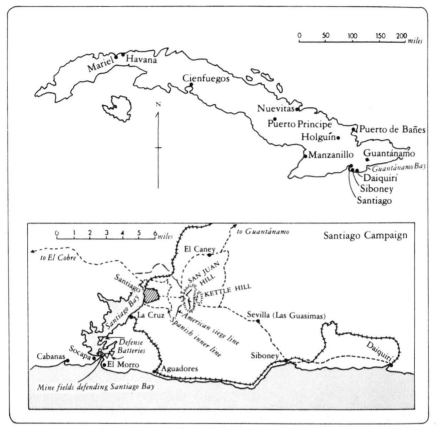

Map 2.   Cuba and the Santiago Campaign

Spaniards had massed most of their troops near El Morro; therefore, a drive inland would strike the weaker part of the Spanish line. Finally, Shafter's orders stressed capture of the town and its defenders; the President clearly wanted a strong American showing on land in Cuba. Impelled by all these considerations, Shafter went inland. Navy officers later criticized him for doing so and complained that he failed to inform them of his plans until his troops began their attack on July 1, but Shafter's notes to Admiral Sampson in late June clearly indicated his intentions.[6]

The garrison at Santiago presented only a weak obstacle to the carrying out of Shafter's plans. About 12,000 Spanish troops held the city and posts in its vicinity, and they were isolated by impassable roads, Cuban

6. Alger, *Spanish-American War*, 83-84, 88-91, 123, 225. Chadwick, *Spanish-American War*, II, 13-14, 22-25. Goode, *With Sampson*, 177-79, 187-88. *Correspondence*, I, 19-20, 25. *War Investigating Commission*, III, 7. George J. Tanham, "Service Relations Sixty Years Ago," *Military Affairs*, XXIII, 145. Shafter sent Admiral Sampson two letters, one on June 25 and the second on June 26, clearly indicating that he planned to attack Santiago from the northeast; see Chadwick, II, 58-59, and Alger, 124-25.

guerrillas, and mountainous jungle terrain from their 24,000 countrymen scattered elsewhere in eastern Cuba. Worse, Santiago's defenders were short of food and ammunition. While most of them carried modern repeating rifles, they had no machine guns and few artillery pieces. About a third of the garrison were Cuban loyalist militia and volunteers, poorly disciplined, demoralized, and unreliable. Throughout the campaign, General Arsenio Linares, the Spanish commander, had persisted in trying to hold too many places with too few men. Besides defending the ridges north and east of the city, he garrisoned the forts at the harbor entrance and distributed much of his force among numerous outposts on both sides of the bay. When General García's army withdrew from the west side of the harbor to join Shafter at Siboney, it left behind small detachments to harass the Spaniards. Their activities convinced Linares that García's main force was still on that side of the bay, and he immobilized many troops to ward off a non-exsistent menace. His lines east of the bay, where Shafter had landed, remained dangerously thin.[7]

Supply difficulties promised more trouble for the Americans than did the enemy. The Fifth Corps had been organized and equipped for a campaign in the open country around Havana, where it could march over relatively well kept roads and use the sheltered harbor of Mariel for landing men and stores. Neither harbors nor roads were available at Santiago. Siboney and Daiquirí, the expedition's landing points and supply bases, were mere huddles of buildings where breaks in the steep shoreline cliffs offered access to the interior, and they lacked usable wharves and sheltered anchorages. All stores and equipment had to come in over open beaches pounded by high waves, which also set the anchored transports to plunging and drifting, causing many collisions. Inland, the natural obstacles proved even more formidable. The countryside around Santiago consisted of irregular hills overgrown with trees and brush and cut by innumerable creeks and ravines. Movement through it was all but impossible for large bodies of troops unless they followed the roads and trails. If Shafter marched from Siboney to Santiago, about 15 miles to the northwest, all of his men, guns, and wagons would have to follow a single road—really a trail—worn out of the encroaching jungle by generations of Cubans on foot and horseback. Barely wide enough for a single wagon, unpaved, and studded with boulders, this road climbed up and down ridges, forded countless streams, and in low-lying areas often lay at the bottom of ravines and along creek beds. At best, it was almost impassable for heavy vehicles. The daily downpours of the Cuban rainy season, which began about a week after the Fifth Corps landed, blocked the road with flooding streams and transformed whole sections

7. Alger, *Spanish-American War*, 122-23. Chadwick, *Spanish-American War*, II, 42-44, 71-72. Nunez, *Guerra*, IV, 50-52, 84-91, 98-100, 117-118, 137-40. Sargent, *Campaign of Santiago*, II, 102, 130, 134-35.

of it into mud in which wagons sank to their axles. Poor and thinly populated in normal times, the Santiago region had been devastated by war and offered neither food nor fodder to the invading army. Over the whole sad countryside lay the shadows of malaria and yellow fever.[8]

Neither on the water nor on shore did Shafter have transportation or equipment to overcome these obstacles. Of his improvised fleet of landing craft, one lighter broke down at Tampa; the sea-going tug deserted the convoy on the first night of the voyage; and one of the barges parted its towline and vanished into the Caribbean. In response to Shafter's repeated pleas, the Quartermaster's Department on June 25 began chartering additional tugs and sending them to Cuba with barges in tow. The long ocean voyage was too much for these harbor craft; few of them completed the run to Santiago. Of the barges that did arrive, most were wrecked in the surf at Daiquirí or Siboney within a few days. During most of the campaign, the expedition's landing craft were reduced to only one small steam lighter with which to disembark rations, ammunition, wagons, and other bulky freight. On land, the 200 wagons the Fifth Corps had brought along proved to be almost useless in the rough terrain. Scores of them remained untouched in the transports' holds throughout the advance and siege because the narrow road could not accommodate them and because there were no lighters to disembark them. After the rainy season began, much of the task of maintaining the reserves of food and ammunition at the front fell upon the sturdy mules of the expedition's seven pack trains, the only transport able to negotiate the quagmire trails. The work of these strong, stubborn animals enabled the Fifth Corps to survive, but there were not enough of them to resolve the transportation problem.[9]

The shortage of lighters made the land transportation problem all but insurmountable. Shafter's two engineer companies had aboard their transport *Alamo* most of the construction gear needed to put the road in working condition, but if Shafter used his only lighter to bring this material to land, his commissaries could not keep rations moving ashore rapidly enough to prevent hunger among the troops on the beach. The equipment, accordingly, stayed in the *Alamo*'s hold. Using whatever material they could find

8. *RSW, 1898,* I, 406; II, 160, 592-93, 599. *War Investigating Commission,* I, 360-61; V, 2059-60; VI, 2415, 2662-64, 2678; VII, 3200-3201, 3604, 3668-71. *Correspondence,* I, 120-21. Alger, *Spanish-American War,* 119-22, 170. Chadwick, *Spanish-American War,* II, 42, 50, 76. Miley, *In Cuba,* 79-81. Sargent, *Campaign of Santiago,* II, 9-11. Wheeler, *Santiago Campaign,* 47, 183-84. *Army and Navy Journal,* May 27, 1899. Gen. Guy V. Henry to Adj. Gen. Corbin, July 12, 1898, Box 1, Corbin Papers. Maj. C. H. Heyl to Corbin, August 3, 1898, File No. 108220, AGO Records.

9. *RSW, 1898,* I, 389, 391, 405-6; II, 616. *War Investigating Commission,* I, 146, 447; V, 1844-47, 2055-56; VI, 2615, 2657, 2662; VII, 3195, 3642-44; VIII, 527. *Correspondence,* I, 54, 56, 58, 104, 113, 115, 120, 129, 146. Alger, *Spanish-American War,* 118-19, 293. Kennan, *Campaigning in Cuba,* 229, 242-43. Miley, *In Cuba,* 85-88. Parker, *Gatling Gun Detachment,* 189-91. *Army and Navy Journal,* August 27, 1898. Col. Charles Bird to the Quartermaster General, August 12, 1898, File No. 115533, OQMG Records.

on shore and assisted from time to time by infantry units, the engineers struggled heroically to improve the road and the pier facilities. They improvised a small wharf at Siboney and restored to operation a narrow-gauge railroad that ran a short distance inland from Siboney. They spent days widening the road and resurfacing its worst stretches, but the line of communication remained at best tenuous. To keep his force in action under these conditions, General Shafter rigidly limited the amounts and types of supplies unloaded from the ships and sent to the front. He allowed to go forward only ammunition, some medical stores, and hardtack, canned meat, and coffee, the essential ration components. He ordered all other heavy material, including camp equipment and cooking utensils, left on the beach or on the steamers. In the fear that they would bog down in the road and cut his only artery of supply, he made no attempt to move his siege cannon to the front, which denied his troops the support of their big guns.[10]

The Fifth Corps thus fought in self-imposed privation. The troops had to survive the battle and siege on scanty, monotonous rations, with pup tents and tree branches for shelter and their personal mess kits for cooking. If they fell sick or wounded, they received barely adequate medical attention from ill-equipped, understaffed field hospitals. In battle, they assaulted fortifications with only rapid-fire guns and light fieldpieces for support. All the equipment needed to remedy these conditions lay a few hundred yards off shore in the steamers' holds, kept from the soldiers by lack of transportation facilities. Most of the expedition's camp furniture, tents, cooking gear, and medical stores did not reach land until the Spanish surrender opened Santiago Bay to the transports, and some of this equipment remained on the ships until they returned to the United States. For one example, a shipload of tropical uniforms, enough for every man in the corps, arrived at Siboney on July 10 and lay untouched for two weeks while the men in the trenches sweltered in wool trousers and flannel shirts.[11]

This situation was not the fault of General Shafter or of the staff on the scene, all of whom struggled to surmount problems not of their own making. The attack on Santiago had been decided upon suddenly, in response to the Navy's plea for help. The War Department had neither the time nor the planning agency to work out in detail the strategy of the campaign,

10. *War Investigating Commission*, V, 1847-50, 2052, 2055-56; VI, 3108-10; VII, 3197-98. *RSW, 1898*, I, 406-7, 538; II, 161. *Correspondence*, I, 66-67. Alger, *Spanish-American War*, 118-19. Miley, *In Cuba*, 80, 84-89. Parker, *Gatling Gun Detachment*, 191. Sargent, *Campaign of Santiago*, II, 87-88. Wheeler, *Santiago Campaign*, 245-46, 262-63. *Army and Navy Journal*, August 13 and 27 and October 29, 1898.

11. *War Investigating Commission*, I, 363, 489-90, 708-11; III, 6, 16; VI, 2416-17, 3038-39, 3107. *RSW, 1898*, I, 705, 786. Alger, *Spanish-American War*, 284-86. Bigelow, *Santiago Campaign*, 64, 85, 99-100, 136-38, 142-43. Kennan, *Campaigning in Cuba*, 131-33, 245-46. Capt. Charles J. Goff to the Quartermaster General, September 29, 1898, File No. 115533, OQMG Records. Maj. Gen. William R. Shafter to Adj. Gen. Corbin, August 16, 1898, Box 1, Corbin Papers. Capt. W. C. Brown to Col. Theodore Roosevelt, September 7, 1898, Vol. 3, Theodore Roosevelt Paper.

to study the terrain of the area, and to determine the transportation requirements of an army that was to fight under those conditions for the objective set. Shafter's force until May 26 was being organized and equipped to operate under very different conditions. Once aware of the new situation, War Department officials made every effort to send Shafter what he needed, but the campaign, fought as it was by improvisation, ended before these efforts produced results.

As soon as they disembarked, Shafter's brigades began pushing inland on the road from Siboney. Advance elements of the cavalry division fought the campaign's first skirmish on June 24 at Las Guásimas, 3½ miles from the coast, mauling a Spanish detachment in retreat toward Santiago. The skirmish, in which the Rough Riders distinguished themselves for their steadiness under fire, cost 16 Americans killed and 52 wounded; Spanish losses totaled about 250. After this engagement, no Spanish troops remained between Shafter's beachhead and Santiago's outer defenses.[12]

Shafter spent the next week in assembling his army near the Las Guásimas battlefield. The Spaniards meanwhile fell back to the eastern outskirts of Santiago, to a line running from the fortified village of El Caney on the left through San Juan Ridge in the center to Aguadores, a small settlement on the seashore about five miles east of El Morro. From these positions, they protected Santiago's line of communications with the interior and screened their main fortifications encircling the city. Shafter planned to delay his attack on this position until he could secure his supply line and until the vanguard of the second Caribbean expedition arrived to reinforce him. The first of these troops, half a brigade of Michigan Volunteer infantry from Camp Alger, disembarked at Siboney on June 27. Aware from the reports of refugees from Santiago of the misery within the Spanish lines, Shafter was confident that time and hunger would weaken further the Spanish defense.

Two days after the reinforcements landed, Shafter abruptly changed his plans and decided on an immediate further advance. His decision was precipitated by Cuban reports that 8,000 Spanish troops from Manzanillo, a large garrison west of Santiago, had broken through an insurgent covering force and were marching to reinforce Linares, bringing along a cattle herd and other supplies. They should reach Santiago on July 2 or 3. To prevent this strengthening of the garrison, Shafter decided to attack Santiago's outer defenses at once. Shafter, in his reports and directives, specified no firm objective for this operation, but he appears to have intended not much more than to secure a favorable position for subsequent assault or siege and for intercepting the Manzanillo reinforcements. In his only prebattle statement of his intentions, he cabled the War Department on 29 June:

12. *War Investigating Commission*, III, 4; VII, 3251. Alger, *Spanish-American War*, 102-10, 112, 115-17. Nunez, *Guerra*, IV, 107-10. Wheeler, *Santiago Campaign*, 242.

"Expect to put division on Caney road, between that place and Santiago, day after tomorrow, and will also advance on Sevilla [Siboney] road to San Juan River [a stream just east of the heights] and possibly beyond."[13]

Shafter's plan of attack, based on extensive reconnaissance of Santiago's approaches by his own troops and García's Cubans, employed the only two practicable routes of advance through the jungle-covered country which separated his corps from the city. The plan called for Major General Wheeler's dismounted cavalry division and the 1st Infantry Division under Brigadier General Jacob F. Kent to advance directly on San Juan heights along the road the army had followed from Siboney. This movement was to begin only after Brigadier General Henry W. Lawton's 2d Infantry Division, some three miles farther north, attacked and captured El Caney, thereby opening another line of march to Santiago along the road from Guantanamo. Lawton, who had scouted El Caney extensively, believed that he could secure the place in about two hours. His division then would move on Santiago, with Wheeler and Kent joining in on his left. The three divisions together would clear the Spaniards off the San Juan heights and bring the city under close siege. Meanwhile, as a diversion, the newly landed Michigan Volunteers would feign an attack along the shore from Siboney toward Aguadores. Brigadier General John C. Bates's independent brigade of two Regular regiments was to constitute the corps reserve. García's Cubans were to follow Lawton's march and help him seal off Santiago from the north. To support the main attacks, Shafter attached a battery of field artillery and the Gatling guns to Wheeler's and Kent's divisions and another field battery to Lawton. He held the corps' remaining two batteries in reserve at his headquarters. At the time when Shafter made his plan, and until the advance began on July 1, the information reaching the Fifth Corps commander indicated that San Juan Hill was weakly held if at all and that the El Caney garrison was unlikely to put up determined resistance. Hence, Shafter and his division commanders prepared for a lightly opposed forward movement rather than for a setpiece assault on fortified positions.[14]

The Fifth Corps spent the day and much of the night of June 30 moving into its jumpoff positions, Lawton's division near El Caney and Wheeler's and Kent's at El Poso, an abandoned sugar plantation about three miles east of Santiago where high, open ground provided a position for their supporting artillery and a view of San Juan Hill. At 6:15 the next morning, July 1, 1898, Lawton's guns opened fire on El Caney, signalling the start of the Spanish-American War's only major land engagement.[15]

13. *RSW*, *1898*, II, 152-53. *Correspondence*, I, 59-60, 64; quotation is from p. 68, Alger, *Spanish-American War*, 117-18, 123-27. Chadwick, *Spanish-American War*, II, 67-68. Wheeler, *Santiago Campaign*, 262-63.

14. Graham A. Cosmas, "San Juan Hill and El Caney, 1-2 July 1898," in Charles E. Heller and William A. Stofft, eds., *America's First Battles, 1776-1965*, 123 (hereafter Cosmas, "San Juan Hill and El Caney").

15. Unless otherwise noted, the following account and analysis is based on Cosmas, "San Juan Hill and El Caney," 125-46.

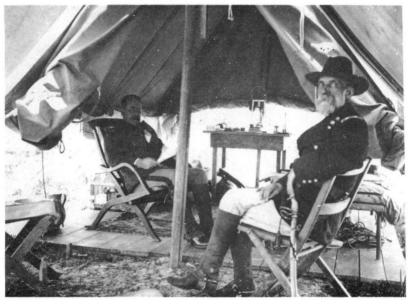

Wheeler and one of his brigade commanders in Cuba.

U.S.A. Transports at Siboney, Cuba.

Courtesy National Archives

Capron's Battery in action on July 10, 1898, during siege of Santiago, Cuba.

Courtesy National Archives

Pack mules of the Fifth Corps supply train.

Courtesy National Archives

United States troops going to the front.
Scene near Major General Shafter's Headquarters during advance on Santiago, Cuba.

Courtesy National Archives

U.S. Pack Train marching to the front during advance on Santiago, Cuba.

Command and control problems and deployment difficulties hampered the Fifth Corps as it went into the attack. General Shafter had planned to direct the action in person from horseback; but after several days of activity in the Cuban heat, illness and exhaustion prostrated the elderly, overweight commander. During the fighting, he remained at the main corps headquarters, relying on messengers and a telephone line to El Poso to keep abreast of the action. At El Poso, the Fifth Corps adjutant general, Lieutenant Colonel Edward J. McClernand, who was familiar with Shafter's plans and intentions, set up an advance command post to coordinate the San Juan attack. Shafter's involuntary absence from the front created confusion because he had issued only verbal instructions to his division commanders. He considered a written operation order unnecessary, he later declared, because his generals "were experienced officers, who only needed to know the general plan, which was simple." In fact, without Shafter's personal guidance, commanders hesitated at crucial points in the action. Further complicating the situation, General Wheeler, the senior division commander, also fell ill and was unable to join his division until late in the day. His replacement, Brigadier General Samuel S. Sumner, seems to have been unfamiliar with the overall corps plan.

Even with all its commanders healthy, the corps would have had difficulty in fighting, due to the transitional state of the Army's tactics and command and control procedures. The units that went into action on July 1, at least the Regulars, were well trained in the open order infantry tactics which the Army had adopted during the previous two decades in response to the increased lethality of modern firepower; however, they had practiced them only at company and battalion level. Shafter and his division commanders, without experience in conducting an open-order corps-size attack, fell back on the methods of the Civil War. Especially at San Juan, they put more men into the attack than the frontage could accommodate and kept their men in close order columns too far into the lethal zone of the Spaniards' Mauser rifles. They also failed to brief their small unit commanders, on whose initiative the effective execution of the new tactics depended, on the overall plan and their units' missions. Most troops went into action with only such general instructions as: "Keep well closed up and . . . be in immediate readiness for action." In a style appropriate to a Napoleonic or Civil War battle, division and brigade commanders simply rode forward at the heads of their columns until they could see the enemy, made plans on the spot, and then issued orders either in person or through aides as regiments marched up. The result, especially when the action took unexpected turns, was much confusion and slow response to the situation, as well as heavy casualties among commanders and aides as they tried to distribute orders under fire.

Shafter's attack columns had sufficient artillery support for their missions, but the gunners labored under a doctrine that lagged behind technological change. In 1898 the U.S. Army possessed no system for indirect fire that would permit batteries located out of sight of the enemy to deliver accurate bombardment under the direction of forward observers. American artillerymen still relied on direct fire visually controlled by the battery commander and were supposed to push their guns right up to the infantry skirmish line—a nearly suicidal maneuver in the face of modern small arms. The same reliance on direct fire, combined with an absence of rapid communications, prevented the Fifth Corps from employing the guns of Sampson's warships to assist its attack.[16]

These American operational limitations, combined with the difficult terrain, the heat, and the determined resistance of small numbers of entrenched Spanish infantry armed with bolt-action smokeless powder rifles, made the overrunning of Santiago's outer defenses a bloody day-long process. General Linares attempted only a delaying action along his outer line. Since the Cubans prevented the Spaniards from patrolling beyond their defenses and the jungle concealed as well as hampered American movements, Linares on July 1 seemed uncertain of the main axis of the American attack and, until mid-day, even of whether a major attack in fact was in progress. He made no attempt to augment the 500 troops holding El Caney and reinforced the single company holding San Juan Hill only after the American advance on the position was underway. Even with these reinforcements, which included the Spaniards' only two modern fieldpieces, no more than 600 men opposed Wheeler's and Kent's divisions. However, hundreds more Spanish troops in the main trench line before Santiago joined in the fighting after the Americans reached the crest of San Juan Hill.

Lawton took all day, not two hours, to reduce El Caney. Expecting only feeble resistance, he deployed his division as much to prevent a Spanish withdrawal as to storm the position. Lawton initially employed his artillery ineffectively, scattering its fire among a number of targets. The garrison, protected by slit trenches, blockhouses, and fortified buildings, with barbed wire entanglements blocking the approaches to their position, showed no disposition to retreat. Lawton's first assault, conducted by only one of his three brigades, was halted by intense Spanish rifle fire. The American troops spent the morning in sporadic firefights with the defenders, suffering a steady toll of dead and wounded as they tried to work their way forward through thickets and open fields. Finally, around 12:30 P.M., Lawton, whom Shafter had reinforced with Bates's brigade, launched a concentrated infantry and artillery attack on a large stone blockhouse that was the key to the defenders' position and captured it. As this blockhouse was falling, Shafter, trying to restore his original plan, sent Lawton a message, more a suggestion than

16. American infantry and artillery doctrine of the 1890s are discussed in Cosmas, "San Juan Hill and El Caney," 114-15.

an order, urging him to leave a force to screen the rest of the Spanish position and push his division and Bates's brigade on toward Santiago to assist Kent and Wheeler, who had just taken San Juan Hill. Lawton rejected this proposal, claiming his troops were too heavily engaged to withdraw. He spent another two hours reducing El Caney by rifle and artillery fire rather than direct assault. In the end the survivors of the garrison attempted to escape from the town but were shot down or forced to surrender by Lawton's encircling troops. Only then, around 4:30 P.M., did American soldiers actually enter El Caney.

The divisions attacking San Juan Hill also had their difficulties. To reach the ridge from their starting position at El Poso, the troops had to traverse a narrow road bordered by woods and thick brush, ford two streams, and then cross an open field. Once they left the high ground at El Poso, they could not see their objective until they reached the edge of the field and, because of the undergrowth, could not deploy from their march columns. On the other hand, the defenders of the ridge could not see the Americans either and hence until around noon were uncertain whether a serious attack was taking place.

In position since dawn, the divisions—Wheeler's under temporary command of General Sumner—waited for a couple of hours listening to Lawton's gunfire at El Caney. As it became apparent that Lawton was going to be delayed there, Colonel McClernand, after securing Shafter's permission, around 8:00 A.M. started the infantry and dismounted cavalry forward along the road, the cavalry division in the lead. As the divisions began marching along the trail, their supporting battery at El Poso opened fire on San Juan Hill, precipitating an artillery duel with the Spanish guns on the ridge and in the fortifications. For a couple of hours, this was the only firing as the cavalry and infantry, moving slowly, pressed forward along the trail and began their deployment in front of the ridge, the cavalry to the right of the road and the infantry, who pushed their column up alongside that of the cavalry, to the left.

At around 11:00 A.M., as the cavalry were completing their deployment in front of the ridge and the infantry were beginning theirs, the Spanish riflemen, in the trenches and a blockhouse on San Juan Hill, and on Kettle Hill, an elevation in front of the main ridge facing the cavalry, opened fire. What precipitated their action was the arrival at the head of the American column of a Signal Corps reconnaissance balloon, sent forward by Shafter's chief engineer, Colonel George F. Derby, over the objections of the balloon detachment commander, in an effort to obtain more information about the Spanish position. The tethered balloon, walked forward along the trail by its crew, became entangled in the trees and could neither be raised nor lowered. It soon came down, riddled with bullets and shell fragments, but not before it had revealed the Americans' position to the Spaniards. Its short flight, however, did generate one useful piece of intelligence; the location of a trail branching off the main road that facilitated the deployment of Kent's division.

Kent and Sumner, realizing for the first time that San Juan Hill was strongly defended, now completed their attack deployment under a steady fire from the Spanish trenches and from snipers hidden in trees along the road and on the edges of the open ground in front of the ridge. Sumner, whose cavalry already were partially deployed, made no attempt to cover the infantry's maneuver with suppressive fire, evidently out of uncertainty whether Shafter really intended him to attack. As the troops struggled forward along the trails, across the steeply banked streams, and through the thickets, bullets and shrapnel took a steady toll of dead and wounded. The one Volunteer infantry regiment in the assault, the 71st New York, trying to move along the trail found by the balloon, lost its cohesion under this fire. General Kent and his staff, unable to restore order, herded the New Yorkers off the trail into the brush to allow Regular regiments to go past.

By about one o'clock, a long American firing line was facing the hill and threatening to turn the Spaniards' right flank. A growing volume of Krag-Jörgensen fire swept the crests of San Juan and Kettle Hills. Shafter meanwhile sent the corps' two reserve field artillery batteries forward to El Poso to support the attack, but by the time the guns unlimbered the final assault was underway. More immediately effective was Captain John H. Parker's battery of four Gatling guns, which Shafter had attached to the attack force. Parker's guns opened fire at about 1:15 P.M., directing streams of bullets at the Spanish trenches and blockhouse. Under cover of Parker's fusillade, the blue-clad cavalrymen and infantrymen began moving up the hill in long, loose skirmish lines. The infantry division started on its own and the cavalry advanced after Sumner requested and received permission from McClernand.

The assault went in against a Spanish force that already was pulling back. Around noon, the defenders' two artillery pieces had run out of shrapnel, their most effective projectile. Their infantry suffered heavy casualties from the Americans' artillery, rifle, and Gatling fire, and Kent's division threatened to envelope their flank and enfilade their route of withdrawal to their main line. The evidence is unclear whether the Spaniards acted under orders or spontaneously. After directing an initially heavy fire at the advancing Americans, they quickly abandoned their positions. Only their dead and wounded remained in the trenches as the cavalry swept successively over Kettle Hill and part of San Juan Hill and the infantry overran the main portion of San Juan Hill and the Spanish blockhouse.

Although San Juan Hill was secured by about 1:30 P.M., fighting continued for the rest of the afternoon. Spanish infantry and artillery in the main defenses kept up a steady fire on the captured crest and attempted a couple of counterattacks, quickly broken up by American rifles and Gatling guns. The Americans returned the fire while gathering their dead and wounded and beginning to entrench their own positions. General Wheeler, who resumed command of his division late in the afternoon, took charge of consolidating the new front line. He called forward wagon loads of ammunition, rations, and entrenching tools.

By sundown, Shafter's troops had eliminated the Spaniards' covering line east of Santiago and seized the high ground overlooking the city. This success, however, had cost the Fifth Corps over 1,300 casualties. During the night, Shafter brought Lawton's division and Bates's brigade up from El Caney, by a roundabout march via El Poso, to join the line on the San Juan heights. He and his officers agreed that the Spaniards' main defenses were too strong for their tired, depleted force to take by storm, and they prepared for a siege. The Spaniards, on their part, showed no disposition to counterattack. Fighting on July 2 consisted only of exchanges of rifle and artillery fire from the trenches.[17]

The ferocity of the Spaniards' resistance on July 1 and the number of their own casualties depressed many American officers. Theodore Roosevelt, whose Rough Riders had helped storm San Juan Ridge, wrote to his friend Henry Cabot Lodge soon after the battle: "We have won so far at a heavy cost; but the Spaniards fight very hard and charging these entrenchments against modern rifles is terrible. We are within measurable distance of a terrible military disaster." Maj. Gen. Joseph Wheeler of the cavalry division, Shafter's second in command, while confident that the Americans could hold San Juan Hill, believed that an assault on the Spanish second line would cost at least 3,000 casualties. None of the American commanders realized how few enemies they had fought on July 1. Shafter, for example, thought that at least 12,000 Spaniards had opposed his troops at San Juan and El Caney.[18]

On the day after the battle, Shafter, afflicted with gout and debilitated by an attack of malaria, seriously considered abandoning his line of advance. He proposed to Wheeler that the corps shift to its left from San Juan Hill and attack the forts at the harbor entrance. Wheeler strongly opposed such a move, arguing that the ridge furnished an excellent artillery position

17. Cosmas, "San Juan Hill and El Caney," 143-44. *War Investigating Commission*, III, 6; VII, 3234. *RSW, 1898*, II, 155, 173. Alger, *Spanish-American War*, 166-71. Miley, *In Cuba*, 121. Parker, *Gatling Gun Detachment*, 138-50. Wheeler, *Santiago Campaign*, 274, 282, 284-85. *Army and Navy Journal*, October 29, 1898.

18. The quotation is from Theodore Roosevelt to Henry Cabot Lodge, July 3, 1898, in *Roosevelt-Lodge Correspondence*, I, 317, and Morison, *Roosevelt Letters*, II, 846. Wheeler, *Santiago Campaign*, 46, 87. *RSW, 1898*, II, 157.

and that an assault on the forts would result in "enormous" American losses. With both ends of his line exposed to possible counterattack and with the threat of the advancing Manzanillo column hanging over him, Shafter called a meeting of his division commanders during the night of July 2 and suggested withdrawal from the ridge to a more easily defended line closer to Siboney. The division commanders unanimously voted against retreat. They expressed confidence that they could hold their positions. After two hours of discussion, Shafter decided to keep his troops where they were for another twenty-four hours. At the end of that time, he would review the situation again and make a final decision to stand or fall back. Early in the morning of July 3, Shafter expressed his hesitation in a long telegram to Washington. He informed the War Department that he had Santiago invested from the north and east but that his line was thin and his troops had suffered heavy losses. He could not storm the town with his present force, he continued, and he was "seriously considering" withdrawal to a position 5 miles nearer Siboney, where he could supply his troops more easily.[19]

Shafter's dispatch, which reached Washington at 11:45 A.M. on July 3, caused consternation at the War Department, where President McKinley and Secretary Alger had waited throughout the preceding three days for news by telegraph from Santiago. Shafter's civilian superiors responded with speed and resolution to the apparent setback. Twenty-five minutes after the arrival of Shafter's report, Secretary Alger sent a reply. He urged Shafter to hold San Juan Hill if he possibly could, as "the effect upon the country would be much better than falling back," but he authorized Shafter to retreat if he deemed it necessary to preserve his army. Alger promised to send his field commander reinforcements "at once."[20]

Troops from Tampa and Camp Alger, earlier selected for the second Caribbean expedition, had been embarking to join Shafter since June 23. Part of the Camp Alger contingent had landed at Siboney in time to fight on July 1. The Administration now ordered a second brigade to Santiago from Camp Alger, and on July 3 it directed General Brooke to prepare one of his divisions at Chickamauga for immediate embarkation. Alarmed by Shafter's apparent despondency and by reports of his poor health, President McKinley on July 3 ordered General Miles to accompany these reinforcements to Santiago, there to "give such orders as might be required for the welfare and success of the army." The authorities also tried to remedy

19. Shafter's July 3 report is in *Correspondence*, I, 74-75; see also I, 123. *War Investigating Commission*, VII, 3204. Alger, *Spanish-American War*,176-77. Chadwick, *Spanish-American War*, II, 110. Hagedorn, *Wood*, I, 179. Miles, *Serving the Republic*, 281-82. Wheeler, *Santiago Campaign*, 286-87, 310. Joseph Wheeler to Theodore Roosevelt, March 9, 1899, Vol. 5, Roosevelt Papers. Maj. Gen. Leonard Wood to R. A. Alger, March 21, 1900, Box 28, Wood Papers.

20. Alger, *Spanish-American War*, 172-75, 177. Miles, *The North American Review*, CLXVIII, 750-51. *Correspondence*, I, 70-74.

Shafter's shortage of landing craft and transportation by sending to Cuba additional tugs, lighters, and steamers loaded with Army Engineers, laborers, tools, pack mules, and wagons. Under a contract with the Quartermaster's Department that was signed on July 10, a New York firm organized a construction corps for Santiago. The force, to consist of 100 mechanics and 250 unskilled laborers with a full outfit of derricks, pile drivers, and building materials, was to travel to Cuba on a government steamer accompanied by two sea-going tugs and a fleet of lighters.[21]

III

An acute shipping shortage prevented the departure of most of these reinforcements. The shortage had become apparent even before the crisis at Santiago, and Secretary Alger and Quartermaster General Ludington had taken drastic steps to alleviate it, but their efforts came too late to avert near paralysis in the Caribbean during the first weeks of July.

The need for more ships in the Caribbean had become evident as soon as the Fifth Corps embarked. Limited space on his vessels had forced Shafter to leave behind 10,000 of his men and much needed equipment; ships would have to be found to take these troops and stores to Santiago. If it were to operate independently of the Fifth Corps, the 30,000-man army destined to attack Puerto Rico also required a fleet of its own. In its attempts to secure additional transports by charter, the Quartermaster's Department met frustration. The assembly of the first fleet had exhausted the supply of American-flag steamers on the Atlantic and Gulf coasts. The shipping companies were, in their turn, chartering foreign vessels to conduct their commercial business. Between June 6 and July 3, quartermasters could pry loose from their owners only nine more ships. In Congress, the opponents of transfers of registry remained adamant. Late in June the Navy Department loaned to the Army its scout cruisers *Harvard*, *Yale*, and *Columbia*, ocean liners armed and equipped for duty with the fleet. No longer needed by the Navy, now that Cervera was bottled up, these vessels could carry 1,000 troops each, and they could make the round trip between East Coast ports and Cuba in seven or eight days. The Army also purchased from the Navy the steamer *Rita*, which had been captured while trying to run the blockade of Cuba. These vessels provided invaluable additional capacity, but still more shipping was needed.[22]

21. *Correspondence*, I, 35-36, 51, 55, 65-66, 76-77, 81-82, 92, 94-95, 100, 107, 111-12, 118, 126-27, 131-33, 137. *RSW, 1898*, I, 391. *War Investigating Commission*, I, 448. Alger, *Spanish-American War*, 185. Miles, *Serving the Republic*, 282-83. Col. Frank J. Hecker to Secretary Alger, January 9, 1899, Alger Papers. Bellinger, Tampa Report, and Col. Charles Bird to the Quartermaster General, August 12, 1898, File No. 115533, OQMG Records. Adj. Gen. Corbin to Maj. Gen. William M. Graham, June 24 and 30, 1898, File No. 91142, AGO Records.

22. *War Investigating Commission*, I, 475-76; VI, 2613-14. *RSW, 1898*, I, 389. *Correspondence*, I, 49, 75, 95, 101, 103, 284. Alger, *Spanish-American War*, 249-50. The *Rita* was secured through

Shafter's fleet, it turned out, could not be used as had been planned, for a second trip. On June 23 General Miles ordered Shafter to unload his transports as rapidly as he could and to start them northward to Tampa under Navy escort for his reinforcements and supplies. Shafter and his quartermasters found it impossible to carry out this order. Lacking wharves and lighters, they could not stock-pile food, medical stores, and ammunition on the beach. The daily discharge from the ships barely kept up the army's current needs. The transports had to remain at anchor off Daiquirí and Siboney, functioning as storehouses for the troops at the front. Not until late June did a few of Shafter's ships start north. Most did not leave Santiago until the siege had ended.[23]

Even before he knew Shafter's ships could not be used, Secretary Alger acted boldly to meet the emergency. About June 15 he decided to supplement the charter system by purchasing a permanent government transport fleet. By purchase, the Army could acquire foreign-flag vessels, which would assume American registry automatically when bought by the government. Congress would not object to Alger's device because government-owned vessels would not enter the coasting trade, which Congress was protecting. To direct the purchase of ships, Alger brought into the War Department a Detroit business associate, Frank J. Hecker, a shrewd, experienced banker and railroad executive. On June 20 Alger gave Hecker full authority to buy or charter steamers, hire crews for them, and fit them for the transport service. On July 18, to provide Hecker with military rank, Alger and Quartermaster General Ludington established the new Transportation Division within the Quartermaster's Department. The division had two branches. One, under the direction of Hecker, who received a colonel's commission in the Volunteer Army, controlled all water transportation; the other, headed by a veteran Regular, Col. Charles Bird, oversaw the movement of troops by rail. To avoid conflict of authority within the division, both Hecker and Bird reported directly to the Quartermaster General.[24]

---

the efforts of Major General Wilson; see Wilson, *Under the Old Flag*, II, 436-37. *The New York Times*, June 3, 5, 7, 8, 9, 11, 18, and 25, 1898. Secretary of the Navy John D. Long to Secretary Alger, June 20, 1898, Alger Papers. Long to the Commanding Officer of the *Yale*, June 20, 1898, Maj. Guy Howard to Adj. Gen. Corbin, June 20 and 21, 1898, File No. 94795; Maj. Gen. Miles to Alger, June 19, 1898, File No. 192302; Miles to Quartermaster General Ludington, June 14, 1898, File No. 221674, AGO Records. Col. Charles Bird to the Quartermaster General, August 12, 1898, File No. 115533, OQMG Records.

23. *Correspondence*, I, 50, 55, 70, 73, 75, 80, 98, 110, 120-23, 167, 169, 173.

24. *War Investigating Commission*, I, 472, 478-79; VI, 2417, 2607, 2767-68. *RSW, 1898*, I, 437-38. War Department Order of July 18, 1898, published in GO 122, WD, August 18, 1818, *GO/AGO, 1898*. Leech, *Days of McKinley*, 294-95. Risch, *Quartermaster Corps*, 546. Col. Charles Bird to the Quartermaster General, August 12, 1898, File No. 115533, OQMG Records. Secretary Alger to Frank J. Hecker, June 20, 1898, Alger Papers. Maj. Gen. James H. Wilson to A. G. Robinson, April 6, 1899, Box 43, Wilson Papers. *The New York Times*, June 25, 1898. New York *Evening Post*, August 3, 1898, clipping in Frank J. Hecker Papers.

Between June 20 and July 25 Hecker bought fourteen large steamers on the Atlantic Coast. All but three of these vessels had sailed under foreign registry before their purchase by the Army. Seven new British-built steamers, secured in one lot from the Atlantic Transport Company, formed the nucleus of the permanent Caribbean fleet. Used in peacetime to haul live cattle across the ocean and designed, as British law required, for easy conversion to troop-ships, these vessels boasted electric lighting and modern high-speed engines. Five of them could carry 1,000 men and 1,000 animals each per voyage; each of the other two had room for 800 soldiers and as many animals. Assorted large passenger steamers and freighters and a refrigerator ship rounded out the purchased fleet, which could carry, in all, 14,000 troops and 7,000 horses and mules. Hecker also bought two big steamers on the Pacific Coast for the Manila run. One of them, the *Scandia* of the Holland-American Line, had just completed a voyage to ferry Russian troops to Port Arthur when the Army acquired her. A variety of tugs, barges, and lighters completed the list of Hecker's purchases. In all, he spent over $16,500,000 on ships. They were worth the price. They helped to relieve the immediate shipping shortage, and they were to prove invaluable in meeting the overseas commitments that grew out of the Spanish war.[25]

At the urging of General Miles, who had been appalled by the conditions on Shafter's transports, the Quartermaster's Department fitted out its second Caribbean fleet more carefully and thoroughly than it had the first. In both purchased and chartered steamers, Quartermaster crews installed hammocks instead of wooden bunks. The hammocks could be taken down during the day, thus affording the soldiers freedom of movement on the berth decks and permitting easier cleaning and better ventilation. Most of the new ships also were fitted with electric lights and fans and extra cooking equipment. As the vessels of Shafter's fleet returned from Santiago during July and August, the Quartermaster General ordered them refitted according to the new pattern. The ships so equipped proved more comfortable than the first lot of transports, but complaints continued to come from the troop commanders. General Brooke, for example, thought that the 18-inch-wide space allotted for each hammock was too small. "A man in his coffin is allotted 22 inches," he wrote, "but in these boats he is allowed 18 inches."[26]

25. *War Investigating Commission*, I, 139, 479, 481-83, 485-86, 488, 491; VI, 2416, 2614, 2768-74, 2785-87. *RSW, 1898*, I, 389-90, 392, 438-39. Risch, *Quartermaster Corps*, 546. *The New York Times*, June 25, 1898. Charles H. Cramp to Secretary Alger, November 18, 1898, and Alger to Cramp, November 22, 1898, Alger Papers. Quartermaster Summerhayes to Frank J. Hecker, July 9, 1898; R. N. Baker to Alger, July 11, 1898; Hecker to George D. Meiklejohn, July 25, 1898, Hecker Papers. Col. Charles Bird to the Quartermaster General, August 12, 1898, File No. 115533, OQMG Records.

26. The quotation is from *War Investigating Commission*, I, 511-12; see also I, 446, 471-73, 480, 482, 484-85, 487, 490, 492-94, 496-97, 510-11; IV, 959-60; VI, 2413-14; VIII, 577-58. *Correspondence*, I, 35-36, 38-39, 41, 45, 266-67, 317. *RSW, 1898*, I, 388-90; II, 139. Risch, *Quartermaster Corps*, 548. Col. Charles Bird to the Quartermaster General, August 12, 1898, and Bellinger, Tampa Report, File No. 115533, OQMG Records.

Besides securing more ships, Army authorities in the field and in Washington tried to bring order out of the chaos at their southern base and to speed up the embarkation of men and stores. At Tampa, the depot quartermaster, Capt. J. B. Bellinger, fully supported by his superiors in Washington and by troop commanders on the scene, waged a determined, successful fight against congestion and disorganization. Bellinger, who took up his duties late in May, was a tough, experienced Regular, and he staffed his depot with veteran officers and clerks. He rented or had built additional warehouses and set up animal corrals and wagon repair shops. He simplified his bureau's issuing procedures so as to move needed stores quickly to the regiments. Bellinger launched a vigorous attack on the mass of loaded freight cars that were clogging Tampa's terminals and yards. He hired horsemen to ride along the miles of sidings, open up the cars, and identify their contents. As soon as his riders located several carloads of wagons, Bellinger had his men take them out and assemble them. Then he used the wagons to haul stores from the rest of the cars to his new warehouses. Under the Army's urging, the railroads suspended their feuding and installed additional sidetracks and terminal facilities at Tampa and its port, which permitted the efficient handling of a larger volume of traffic. The Quartermaster General in Washington made sure that advance notice of all supply shipments reached Tampa before the shipments themselves. By June 15 Quartermaster crews were emptying 70 boxcars per day, and by the end of the month the freight blockade had disappeared. Bellinger also tried to improve embarkation methods at Port Tampa for both men and stores, but in this he was only partially successful.[27]

As Shafter's embarkation dramatically demonstrated, the railroad bottleneck between Tampa and its port made impossible the rapid shipment from there of a large army. This fact General Shafter, Captain Bellinger, and other officers stationed at Tampa reported to the War Department. In response, Secretary Alger early in June decided to abandon Tampa as an embarkation port for troops and to use instead northern cities, which offered more extensive railroad and wharf facilities. This plan would mean a longer voyage for Caribbean-bound transports, but any disadvantages that ensued could be accepted, now that Cervera's squadron was trapped and larger steamers were coming into service.

Alger's plan received support from Major General Brooke, who commanded the troops at Camp Thomas. Brooke argued that inland cantonments like Chickamauga were more comfortable and healthful for the soldiers than camps in the hot coastal lowlands, and he urged that his men be kept at Camp Thomas until they were needed at the front, at which time they could go by train to northern ports to meet their ships. General Miles objected

27. Bellinger tells his own story in Tampa Report, File No. 115533, OQMG Records. *War Investigating Commission,* I, 523-25; III, 437; VI, 2611-12, 2698, 2701, 2703-4; VII, 3152; VIII, 519-20. *Correspondence,* I, 53. Risch, *Quartermaster Corps,* 542. *The New York Times,* June 6, 1898.

to the change of base. He wanted the troops from Camp Thomas who were assigned to the Puerto Rico expedition brought south and encamped in Florida to await embarkation at Tampa and Miami. As was becoming common practice in the War Department, Alger overruled Miles and followed Brooke's advice. Regiments already in southern stations embarked at Tampa, but those in northern camps met their ships at New York, Newport News, and Charleston. They left their camps one brigade at a time, moving only when transports were ready at their embarkation ports. The system worked smoothly; it prevented pile-ups of men and supplies on the docks and kept the soldiers out of the damp heat of the coastal summer.[28]

These changes in policy and administration assured the eventual assembly of an adequate transport fleet and prevented a repetition of the Fifth Corps's scramble to the ships at Tampa, but they did not solve the immediate problem of augmenting the troops at Santiago quickly. With Shafter's vessels immobilized off Santiago, reinforcements could depart only as rapidly as the new ships came into service. They did so only a few at a time, straggling into the embarkation ports in twos and threes between June 20 and the end of July. In mid-July, Shafter's vessels began arriving at Tampa, but during the crisis of the campaign, more men and equipment were ready in mainland camps and ports than the War Department could muster ships to carry to the front.[29]

As many troops as could, quickly embarked and left for Cuba, many of them on the borrowed Navy cruisers. Three regiments from Camp Alger and a regiment from Tampa had departed before July 1. Six batteries of field artillery and a District of Columbia infantry regiment, with additional equipment and supplies for the Fifth Corps, sailed from Tampa on July 3. A regiment from Camp Alger left New York on July 6, and two more, accompanied by General Miles, departed from Charleston three days later. Transportation of these troops required all the ships immediately available. The rest of the force at Tampa and a brigade from Chickamauga, which had moved to Charleston, waited in camp for transports until the close of the campaign. The construction crew from New York did not get away until July 17, and it arrived at Santiago too late to assist Shafter's hard-pressed quartermasters and engineers.[30]

28. *Correspondence*, I, 32-33, 35, 37-39, 45, 47, 73, 76-77, 82-83, 85-86, 91, 93-94, 98, 144, 274, 278, 294, 301, 306, 312, 320, 328. Alger, *Spanish-American War*, 177-78. Quartermaster Humphrey to the Quartermaster General, May 24, 1898, File No. 85540; Maj. Gen. J. R. Brooke to Adj. Gen. Corbin, June 8, 1898, File No. 215311; Secretary of the Navy Long to the Commanding Officer of the *Yale*, June 21, 1898, Asst. Adj. Gen. George H. Hopkins to Secretary Alger, June 23, 1898, Maj. Gen. W. M. Graham to Corbin, June 24, 1898, and Quartermaster Guy Howard to Corbin, June 25, 1898, File No. 94795; Brooke to Corbin, July 4, 1898, File No. 98440; Corbin to Mr. M. E. Ingalls, July 20, 1898, File No. 133959, AGO Records. Bellinger, Tampa Report, Capt. E. B. Harrison to Maj. J. N. Carson, August 24, 1898, File No. 115533, OQMG Records. G. M. Dodge to Alger, July 7, 1898, Alger Papers.

29. *War Investigating Commission*, I, 134, 481, 487-88, 495; VI, 2420. *Correspondence*, I, 56, 88, 96, 98, 111, 174, 184, 190, 194, 198, 275, 304-6, 330, 332-33. Adj. Gen. Corbin to Maj. Gen. W. M. Graham, June 24, 1898, File No. 91142; Maj. Guy Howard to Corbin, June 20, 21, and 24, 1898, and A. S. Crowinshield to Corbin, June 24, 1898, File No. 94795, AGO Records. Bellinger, Tampa Report, File No. 115533, OQMG Records.

30. *Correspondence*, I, 80-81, 95, 97, 100-103, 105-6, 108, 109, 112, 115, 117, 119-20, 127, 132-33, 138. Wilson, *Under the Old Flag*, II, 434-35. *Army and Navy Journal*, July 9, 1898. Col. Frank J.

IV

Neither General Shafter nor his superiors in Washington realized how badly the Spaniards had been hurt in the battles of San Juan and El Caney. If the Americans had suffered heavy casualties, so had their opponents. Of the 500 defenders of El Caney, hardly a surviving soldier escaped wounds or capture. The units defending San Juan Hill lost between 30 and 50 per cent of their men. General Linares, who had, in person, led the fight for the ridge, was out of action with a severe arm wound and many lower-ranking officers had died in the battle. At sundown on July 1, barely 300 men, 100 of them convalescents from the military hospital, held the Spanish trenches on Santiago's outskirts. Had the Americans mounted another attack, they would have swept into the city almost unopposed. During the second day's fighting, the Spaniards, by abandoning all their positions west of the harbor except the Socapa battery at the entrance, concentrated enough troops in Santiago to secure the inner defenses, but the hopelessness of their situation became increasingly apparent. The garrison had run short of ammunition; only 190 rounds per man remained after the battle. Food stocks were low; the soldiers lived on a daily ration of rice, oil, sugar, coffee, and brandy while the civilians starved. The fall of El Caney had left the city reservoir in American hands and severed communication with the farming villages in the hills to the north. Most important, the American capture of the ridges north and east of town made a successful defense of Santiago impossible. American rifles and rapid-fire guns on the heights could overwhelm the Spanish works, situated on lower ground, thus assuring victory to the Fifth Corps if it attacked again in force. The American positions also blocked the garrison's retreat inland. If driven from their second line, the Spaniards must surrender, die where they stood, or be pushed into the bay. If the Americans could bring up their heavy guns, they could drop shells on the warships in the harbor. With good reason, General José Toral, who succeeded the wounded Linares in command, telegraphed his superiors in Havana on July 2 that Santiago's situation was "becoming more and more untenable."[31]

On the night of July 2, Shafter had decided to remain in his present situation for twenty-four hours, but if, at the end of that period, conditions had not improved, he would order a retreat. Well within that time, the extent of his success on July 1 and the weakness of the Spanish position became dramatically evident. In response to Toral's report on Santiago's precarious condition, the Spanish authorities at Havana ordered Admiral Cervera's squadron to leave the doomed city and run for safety in the open sea. Early on July 3, while Alger and McKinley were reading Shafter's

---

Hecker to Secretary Alger, January 9, 1899, Alger Papers. Bellinger, Tampa Report, File No. 115533, OQMG Records.

31. General Toral is quoted in Chadwick, *Spanish-American War*, II, 123-24; see also II, 40-42, 121. Nunez, *Guerra*, IV, 52-54, 58-59, 132-33, 145-53, 211-14, 218-19, 224-25. Wheeler, *Santiago Campaign*, 89, 195. Gen. Guy V. Henry to Adj. Gen. Corbin, July 12, 1898, Box 1, Corbin Papers.

pessimistic thoughts of retreat, Cervera's four cruisers and two torpedo-boat-destroyers steamed down the bay in single file and out through the narrow channel, in a gallant dash for freedom. The waiting American squadron closed in, and within three hours and forty minutes, Admiral Sampson's gunners had destroyed or set on fire every Spanish vessel. Naval command of the Caribbean now belonged to the United States, and the principal objective of the Santiago campaign had been achieved.[32]

On land, also, Shafter's situation visibly improved on July 3. The long-dreaded Spanish relief column from Manzanillo entered Santiago that evening by slipping into town from the west through a gap between Shafter's right flank and the bay shore and brushing aside García's Cubans, who tried to block the way. However, instead of 8,000 troops, the relief force, commanded by Col. Frederico Escario, numbered only 3,500. They had marched 150 miles over jungle trails under constant harassment by the Cubans, but, on arrival, their numbers and condition were not enough to break the siege; they merely increased the number of Spaniards in the American trap. At 1:16 A.M. on July 4, Shafter felt secure enough to telegraph the War Department that he would "hold my present position." Later in the day he told Washington that, while he could maintain the siege, he could not storm the city with the force on hand and he repeated his request for reinforcements.[33]

With the destruction of Cervera's ships, the Santiago campaign entered a stage that demanded new strategic decisions by both sides. For the Americans, the question arose whether to continue the campaign at all. The naval objective of the operation had been achieved on July 3. Should the Army now persist in the siege of a town to which American commanders previously had accorded little military value? On July 5, before he sailed for Cuba, General Miles proposed abandonment of the attack. With the Spanish squadron eliminated, he wrote to Secretary Alger, the Fifth Corps with all available reinforcements should invade Puerto Rico, which Miles called "the gateway to the Spanish possessions on the Western Hemisphere." A White House council of war on July 6 discussed and rejected Miles's proposal. In a series of telegrams, Secretary Alger ordered General Shafter to proceed with the reduction of Santiago. He gave Shafter complete discretion in determining the method and time of attack and offered him all the men, guns, and equipment at the Administration's disposal. The McKinley Administration thus affirmed its commitment to a land campaign in Cuba. If naval considerations forced the substitution of Santiago for Havana

32. Alger, *Spanish-American War*, 178-79, 244-45. Chadwick, *Spanish-American War*, II, 122-23. Nunez, *Guerra*, IV, 183. Miles, *The North American Review*, CLXVIII, 751-52.

33. *Correspondence*, I, 78. Alger, *Spanish-American War*, 180, 186. Nunez, *Guerra*, IV, 57-58, 216. Wheeler, *Santiago Campaign*, 291-92, 363-64. Miles, *The North American Review*, CLXVIII, 751.

as the initial objective, then that city, instead of the capital, would be seized and held as part of the American drive for an independent role in determining Cuba's future.[34]

The Spaniards also had decisions to make. Governor-General Ramón Blanco y Arenas at Havana, Spanish supreme commander in Cuba, had ordered Santiago defended only to protect Cervera's fleet. He attached little importance to holding the city for its own sake, and he wanted to save its garrison for service elsewhere. Accordingly on July 2, the same day that he ordered Cervera to run for safety, Blanco directed General Toral to defend Santiago as long as possible and then to try to negotiate or fight a way out for his troops and march to Manzanillo or Holguín. To assist Toral in breaking out, Blanco began organizing a new relief column at Holguín.[35]

Shaped by these decisions in Washington and Havana, the siege of Santiago continued. Both armies kept to the shelter of their earthworks. For the Spaniards, an assault was out of the question, and General Shafter preferred to wait for reinforcements before launching his men once more against repeating rifles and barbed wire. Shafter's troops strengthened their line on San Juan Hill and its neighboring ridges by deepening their trenches and positioning cannon and Gatling guns to sweep the Spanish works below. The condition of the road from Siboney prevented Shafter's artillerymen from bringing forward their heavy siege guns, but they were able to haul 8 light mortars up from the coast to supplement the 16 field guns already in position. While fortifying his line, Shafter gradually extended it to the right to complete the entrapment of the Spaniards. By July 9 the right flank of the Fifth Corps rested on the bay shore west of Santiago, thus closing the garrison's last escape route. During the afternoon of July 10 and the morning of July 11, the two armies fought the campaign's last battle, which consisted entirely of rifle and artillery exchanges from the trenches. Since they were fighting from the higher ground, the Americans had all the best of it and drove many Spaniards from their positions with well-directed rifle and machine-gun fire. The Fifth Corps in this engagement lost 2 dead and 2 wounded; the Spaniards lost 7 killed and over 50 wounded.[36]

34. *Correspondence*, I, 82, 84, 87, 89-90, 271. Alger, *Spanish-American War*, 186, 300-301. Miles, *The North American Review*, CLXVIII, 752-55.

35. Chadwick, *Spanish-American War*, II, 114-15, 123-24. Nunez, *Guerra*, IV, 220. Gen. José Toral to Gen. Blanco, July 13, 1898, Blanco to Gens. Linares and Toral, July 13, 1898, translations in File No. 1497505, AGO Records.

36. *Correspondence*, I, 81-82, 89-90, 92, 122-23, 125, 130. *War Investigating Commission*, VII, 3201-2, 3237-38. *RSW, 1898*, II, 157. Alger, *Spanish-American War*, 181-83, 192, 196-97. Chadwick, *Spanish-American War*, II, 209-10. Miley, *In Cuba*, 126. Nunez, *Guerra*, IV, 212, 215-16, 221-24. Parker, *Gatling Gun Detachment*, 163-67. Theodore Roosevelt to Henry Cabot Lodge, July 10, 1898, *Roosevelt-Lodge Correspondence*, I, 322.

During most of the siege, a truce, which had been called to permit negotiations between the opposing commanders, kept the guns quiet. On July 3, after the Spanish fleet steamed out to its doom, General Shafter sent General Toral a demand that he surrender both the town and his troops. If Toral refused, Shafter threatened, he would shell the city. Toral rejected the surrender demand but indicated an interest in further parleys. On various pretexts, the generals spun out their bargaining, for each felt that delay served his purposes. Toral was playing for time to delay as long as possible the day when he must surrender, make a suicidal attempt to break out of the trap, or face an American attack he knew he could not repel. On his part, General Shafter was waiting for reinforcements; he did not yet believe his force strong enough to storm the city.[37]

On July 8 Toral made a counteroffer to Shafter's repeated demands for surrender. He would evacuate Santiago, Toral declared, if the Americans would allow him and his troops to march unmolested to Holguín with all their weapons and euipment. This offer, which would save the garrison while losing the city, conformed to Toral's orders from General Blanco. Shafter on July 9 transmitted Toral's proposal to Washington and urged its acceptance to save lives and bring a quick end to the siege. President McKinley and Secretary Alger rejected Shafter's advice. They ordered him to secure unconditional surrender of the garrison either by siege or by assault, as Shafter thought best. However, at Alger's suggestion, the new demand for surrender bore an offer to transport Toral's troops back to Spain at the expense of the United States Government as soon as they laid down their arms. While unorthodox, this proposal made sense under the circumstances. The prospect of being sent home instead of languishing in an American prison camp might soften the Spaniards' resolution; if transported back to Spain, the Santiago troops would be removed from the war and would be unable to return to the Caribbean battle area while the American fleet controlled the seas. Shafter transmitted the new proposal to Toral, who rejected it. Amid the deadlock thus produced, the fire fight of July 10-11 occurred.[38]

Besides bargaining with his Spanish opponent, Shafter was negotiating during the siege with Admiral Sampson. Neither officer had authority over the other, Army-Navy cooperation at Santiago depended entirely upon mutual agreement. While Santiago was under siege, the commanders of the two forces could not agree on tactics for finishing off the trapped garrison. Beginning on July 2, General Shafter repeatedly urged Sampson to attack

37. *Correspondence*, I, 78-79, 92, 99, 101, 105. Alger, *Spanish-American War*, 176-77, 182-85, 187-88. Wheeler, *Santiago Campaign*, 128-29. James H. Wilson to Col. Edward J. McClernand, March 26, 1910, Box 14, Wilson Papers.

38. *Correspondence*, I, 116-19, 125, 130. Alger, *Spanish-American War*, 192-98, 276-77. Charles Emory Smith to R. A. Alger, January 13, 1902, Alger Papers. Unsigned note, dated November 23, 1898, in McKinley Papers.

the forts at the harbor entrance with his battleships. By fighting their way into the harbor, Shafter said, the battleships could take the garrison in the rear and force an immediate surrender. Admiral Sampson refused, fearing the loss of irreplaceable ships to mines planted in the narrow channel. If the Army had stormed the forts at the start of the campaign, Sampson argued, the squadron could clear away the mines and go in, but until the Army did its part he would not risk the fleet's few armored vessels. Pleading a lack of troops, Shafter in turn declined to attack the forts. The stalemate continued throughout the siege, and neither commander changed his position. Sampson would agree only to bombard the city from the sea at long range when the Army renewed its assault; Navy guns joined in the shelling on July 10 and 11, their fire guided by Army observers on San Juan Hill. The firing had no appreciable effect on the enemy.[39]

The interservice dispute spread from the front at Santiago to the Cabinet in Washington, where Secretary Alger upheld Shafter and Secretary of the Navy Long defended Sampson. President McKinley, consistent with his policy of leaving tactical decisions to the officers on the scene, simply ordered Shafter and Sampson to work out the problem between themselves. On July 13 the dispute exploded in the Cabinet in a bitter personal exchange between Secretary Alger and Captain Mahan of the Navy strategy board. Mahan, angered by Alger's criticism of the fleet's caution, scolded the Secretary for his ignorance of naval problems. According to Secretary Long, who witnessed the incident, President McKinley seemed pleased at the discomfiture of his Secretary of War.[40]

On July 12 General Toral renewed his offer to evacuate Santiago in return for free passage to Holguín for his troops. Once again, General Shafter, supported now by General Miles who had just landed at Siboney, urged his superiors in Washington to accept the Spanish offer. Both Shafter and Miles stressed the desirability of avoiding an assault, with its accompanying heavy casualties, and advocated Toral's formula as a quick, cheap way of ending the campaign. On July 13 Secretary Alger, at the President's direction, rejected the Spanish proposal. He ordered Shafter and Miles to secure the unconditional surrender of the garrison and repeated the Administration's offer to ship the Spaniards home, once they submitted to the United States. If he could not secure a capitulation on those terms, Alger told Miles, he should "assault, unless in your judgment an assault would fail. . . . Matter should be settled promptly."[41]

39. *Correspondence*, I, 87-89. The Army's side of the dispute is argued fully in Alger, *Spanish-American War*, 87, 189-92, 226-35, 239. Chadwick, *Spanish-American War*, I, 354; II, 202-8, 229-30. Tanham, *Military Affairs*, XXIII, 145-47.

40. Long describes the Cabinet clash in Mayo, *America of Yesterday*, 203-4; see also 201 and 205-6. *Correspondence*, I, 89, 91, 94, 134-36, 141. Alger, *Spanish-American War*, 189, 233-34, 236-38. Chadwick, *Spanish-American War*, II, 202-3.

41. The quotation is from *Correspondence*, I, 136; see also 133-34. Alger, *Spanish-American War*, 198-201. Mayo, *America of Yesterday*, 203-4. Miles, *Serving the Republic*, 288, and *The North American Review*, CLXVIII, 756. Olcott, *McKinley*, II, 49-51.

For both armies, the crisis of the siege had arrived. American and Spanish troops alike were approaching the limits of physical endurance. A shortage of manpower required both Shafter and Toral to keep all of their soldiers on constant duty in the trenches. C ɪɪɪadequate rations of food and water, Americans and Spaniards suffered alternate periods of baking sun and drenching rain. In the lines of the Fifth Corps, men went temporaly insane from the relentless heat. On July 13 General Toral reported to Havana that he could not evacuate Santiago because his troops, their feet swollen by hours on watch in flooded trenches, could not march. Dysentery, malaria, and the dread yellow fever thinned the ranks of both armies.[42]

By July 12, when he urged acceptance of Toral's evacuation offer, General Shafter realized that his position was becoming more and more precarious. Cuban scouts reported a 6,000-man Spanish relief column forming at Holguín, and the Fifth Corps's supply system was collapsing. Almost 40,000 people now depended for survival on Shafter's commissaries. They included roughly 20,000 American troops, García's 4,000 insurgents, and about 16,000 civilian refugees who had fled Santiago to escape shelling and starvation and now huddled in misery around El Caney. Increasingly heavy rains had washed out large sections of the road from Siboney, and almost 50 per cent of the Army's teamsters and packers had fallen ill. Without their services, neither wagons nor mule trains could work at full efficiency. Shafter had to stop food deliveries to the refugees at El Caney because his quartermasters could not push enough rations to the troops at the front. At sea, the hurricane season threatened. If a storm should drive the transports from the coast, the Fifth Corps, with no reserves of food on shore, very soon would approach starvation. Time had run out for General Shafter. Unable to sustain a siege much longer, he must attack or see his men starve, sicken, and collapse. He urged acceptance of Toral's offer to escape from his dilemma, but the Administration vetoed that solution.[43]

At this critical point, the reinforcements ordered to Shafter in response to the news of San Juan Hill at last began to arrive. On July 9 and 10, the infantry and artillery from Tampa and another infantry regiment from New York reached Siboney and Daiquirí. The infantry at once marched to strengthen the line of San Juan Hill, but the shortage of lighters and the condition of the road prevented the artillery from moving up. On July 11, General Miles, with 1,500 more infantry from Camp Alger, arrived off Siboney.

42. *War Investigating Commission*, I, 365-66, 368-69. *RSW, 1898*, II, 597. Alger, *Spanish-American War*, 202-3. Nunez, *Guerra*, IV, 233-34. Maj. Gen. W. R. Shafter to Secretary Alger, July 13, 1898, Alger Papers. Gen. Toral to Gen. Blanco, July 13, 1898, translation in File No. 1495705, AGO Records.

43. *Correspondence*, I, 125-132. *War Investigating Commission*, VII, 3199. Alger, *Spanish-American War*, 199-200, 233, 236-37. Chadwick, *Spanish-American War*, II, 217. Hagedorn, *Wood*, I, 180. Miley, *In Cuba*, 154. Nunez, *Guerra*, IV, 217-18. Gen. Guy V. Henry to Adj. Gen. Corbin, July 12, 1898, Box 1, Corbin Papers. Col. Leonard Wood to Mrs. Wood, July 15, 1898, Box 190, Wood Papers.

The next day, the Commanding General rode inland to Shafter's headquarters. His presence, Col. Leonard Wood wrote, "was like a tonic; it braced all hands up."[44]

After joining Shafter in his request to Washington that the Spaniards be permitted to march out, Miles, in accord with Secretary Alger's peremptory orders, took steps to bring a quick end to the siege. He and Shafter arranged a face-to-face meeting with General Toral for noon on July 13. At this conference, held between the lines under a huge ceiba tree, the Americans gave Toral until noon of the following day to surrender the city and his troops. If Toral had not acted by that time, Miles and Shafter said, they would attack. To support this threat, Shafter's divisions prepared for a new battle, and Miles arranged with Admiral Sampson to land all the reinforcements still on transports, west of the harbor entrance. From that point, these troops could storm the harbor forts and allow the fleet to enter. Together, the land and sea forces could bring the city garrison under fire from the flank and rear while Shafter's men struck from San Juan Hill. Such a concerted assault would render the Spanish position untenable. Early on July 14 the Army transports, escorted by warships, assembled off the coastal village of Cabanas, the point selected for Miles's fresh invasion.[45]

The attack, well planned and certain to be decisive, never took place. Realizing that he had run out of time and room to maneuver, General Toral requested permission to surrender from Governor-General Blanco at Havana; Blanco gave it. Hours before the scheduled opening of the new battle, Toral informed the Americans of his orders, and they canceled plans for the assault. During the next two days commissioners from the two armies worked out the final surrender agreement, which was called a "capitulation" as a concession to Spanish pride. In return for the Americans' promise to ship all the prisoners back to Spain, Toral surrendered not only the garrison of Santiago but also the troops at Guantánamo and at six smaller posts in eastern Cuba, all of whom Toral commanded. These outlying detachments, isolated in roadless terrain, besieged by Cubans, and dependent on Santiago for supplies and reinforcements, were doomed as soon as Santiago fell. At noon on July 17 the Santiago garrison laid down their arms while picked units of the Fifth Corps raised the Stars and Stripes over the municipal palace. Their comrades, formed for parade along the old siege lines, gave vent to yells of triumph.[46]

44. The quotation is from Col. Leonard Wood to Mrs. Wood, July 15, 1898, Box 190, Wood Papers. *Correspondence*, I, 122-23. *RSW, 1898*, II, 19, 258, 597. Alger, *Spanish-American War*, 197, 200-201. Chadwick, *Spanish-American War*, II, 216-17. Miles, *Serving the Republic*, 285-86.

45. *Correspondence*, I, 136-38. *RSW, 1898*, I, 804; II, 18-22. Alger, *Spanish-American War*, 204-20. Chadwick, *Spanish-American War*, II, 223-24. Miles, *Serving the Republic*, 286-90, and *The North American Review*, CLXVIII, 755-56. Wheeler, *Santiago Campaign*, 177.

46. Alger, *Spanish-American War*, 210-11, 217-20, 277. Miles, *Serving the Republic*, 290-92. Nunez, *Guerra*, IV, 229-32, 234-35. Parker, *Gatling Gun Detachment*, 171-73. Wheeler, *Santiago Campaign*, 180-82. Gen. Blanco to Gen. Toral, July 15, 1898, and Gen. Blanco to the Minister of War, July 17, 1898, translations in File No. 1497505, AGO Records.

The soldiers had reason to cheer. At the cost of 243 officers and men killed in action and 1,445 wounded, they had established American sovereignty over the entire eastern end of Cuba. They had taken, in all, nearly 24,000 prisoners, about half of them Spanish regulars and the rest local militiamen and volunteers. Their operations had forced Spain's only battle fleet out to sea to destruction and had rendered Spain helpless to resist further American attacks on her colonies and even on her own coasts. General Shafter spoke the truth when he declared the war "virtually closed" with the capture of Santiago.[47]

V

General Miles on July 15 left Shafter to complete the occupation of Santiago and returned to Siboney to organize the attack on Puerto Rico. The War Department had planned to use part of the Fifth Corps in this operation, but Shafter's troops, worn out and infected with malaria and dysentery, were not fit for another campaign. The only troops available at Santiago for immediate action were those Miles had planned to disembark west of the harbor entrance. Still aboard their ships, they included two Volunteer infantry regiments, five Regular field batteries, and small detachments of Regular recruits, engineers, and men from the Signal Corps and Hospital Corps. They numbered, in all, about 3,400.[48]

On July 17 Miles asked the War Department for permission to start at once for Puerto Rico with this force and a strong Navy escort. Miles believed that, with support from the guns of the warships, his vanguard could seize a beachhead on the island and cover the landing of additional troops dispatched direct from the United States. Such a movement, Miles pointed out to Secretary Alger, would secure an American foothold in Puerto Rico before Spain sued for peace, as she was likely to do, now that she had lost both her fleet and Santiago. After initial hesitation, McKinley and Alger approved Miles's plan, although they warned him that reinforcements from the United States could not join him in Puerto Rico within less than a week. The General then spent two days quarreling with Admiral Sampson about the size and composition of his naval convoy. President McKinley, out of patience at last with the interservice wrangling, on July 20 told the Navy to give Miles the ships he wanted. The next day, Miles's transports, accompanied by a battleship and several lighter warcraft, steamed away from Santiago and set course for Puerto Rico.[49]

47. Maj. Gen. W. R. Shafter to Secretary Alger, August 4, 1898, Alger Papers. Alger, *Spanish-American War*, 296-97. *Correspondence*, I, 152-53. William T. Stead to Secretary of the Treasury Lyman J. Gage, July 16, 1898, Box 1, Gage Papers.

48. *Correspondence*, I, 144, 146, 273, 283, 293, 304. *War Investigating Commission*, VII, 3225.

49. *Correspondence*, I, 154-55, 280-88, 299, 303. *RSW, 1898*, II, 29. Alger, *Spanish-American War*, 250-54, 301-7. Chadwick, *Spanish-American War*, II, 266, 269-70, 275-80. Miles, *The North American Review*, CLXIX, 126-27. Tanham, *Military Affairs*, XXIII, 147-48.

Using the borrowed Navy cruisers, the newly purchased steamers, and returning vessels of the Santiago fleet, regiments from Chickamauga and Tampa embarked to join Miles. These troops had been assigned to the Puerto Rico expedition as early as mid-June, and one brigade from Camp Thomas, diverted to reinforce Shafter, had been camped at Charleston awaiting transports since early July. The regiments from Chickamauga all embarked at northern ports under Secretary Alger's new transportation policy, which now proved its worth. On July 20 the brigade at Charleston sailed, followed from Newport News on July 28 by General Brooke and a second brigade of his First Corps. A third brigade from Chickamauga reached Newport News two days after Brooke's vessels left. By July 28 six transports had departed from Tampa, carrying two Regular infantry regiments and detachments of artillery and cavalry, all from the Fourth Corps. Additional troops awaited at Tampa for the return of more of General Shafter's transports, when they, too, could leave for the front. During the first week of August, the First Volunteer Engineers from New York and contingents of infantry and artillery from Newport News and Tampa put to sea. A report from General Miles on August 10 that he needed no more troops and also the diversion of shipping to Santiago to bring home the fever-ridden Fifth Corps prevented the rest of the First and Fourth corps from sailing for Puerto Rico.[50]

Before Miles left Cuba, the War and Navy departments had agreed that his expedition should land at Cape Fajardo on Puerto Rico's north coast, within easy reach of San Juan, the island's capital and strongest fortress. At sea on July 22, Miles changed his objective. Instead of attacking Cape Fajardo, where he had reason to believe the Spaniards were expecting him and were concentrating to meet him, he proposed to strike at Ponce on the southern coast, the island's largest city, and thereby avoid facing the enemy's strongest position. Miles knew from intelligence reports, including those of Lieutenant Whitney, that Spain had few troops in the Ponce area, that southern Puerto Rico contained rich stores of food and fodder, and that the local citizenry favored the United States. From Ponce, a well-paved road covered the 70 miles to San Juan.[51]

Miles persuaded the commander of his Navy escort to agree to the change of plan. The invasion fleet sighted Puerto Rico late on July 24 and while daylight lasted steamed in the general direction of San Juan to deceive

50. *Correspondence*, I, 140, 144-46, 153, 205, 237, 275-79, 286-88, 290-95, 304, 306-10, 312-13, 315-17, 319-21, 323-29, 332-37, 340-41, 343, 349-51, 354-55, 360, 362-66, 368, 370, 377, 510. *War Investigating Commission*, I, 496, 510; VII, 3294-95. Alger, *Spanish-American War*, 305. Chadwick, *Spanish-American War*, II, 284. Wilson, *Under the Old Flag*, II, 439-40. Asst. Adj. Gen. J. A. Johnston to the Chief of Ordnance, July 23, 1898, File No. 103944, AGO Records. Bellinger, Tampa Report, File No. 115533. OQMG Records.

51. *Correspondence*, I, 318-19, 321-22. *RSW, 1898*, II, 29-30. Alger, *Spanish-American War*, 306-7. Chadwick, *Spanish-American War*, II, 284-88, 298-300. Miles, *The North American Review*, CLXIX, 128-29.

Spanish coast-watchers. After dark, except for a cruiser left off the north coast to divert reinforcements to Ponce, the fleet, with lights out to prevent observation, turned about and steamed southward around the southwest end of the island. Early in the morning of July 25, Navy launches and the small boats of the transports put the troops ashore at the minor port of Guánica, 15 miles west of Ponce. After a brief, bloodless skirmish, the few Spanish defenders fled the town and surrendered to the Americans a deep, sheltered harbor in which the ships could unload. A second skirmish the following day, again without American casualties, gave Miles's troops possession of the main road to Ponce. On July 27 the first of Miles's reinforcements from the United States, the brigade from Charleston under Maj. Gen. James H. Wilson, arrived off Guánica. Miles left this brigade on their transports and sent them, on July 28, steaming into Ponce harbor with the battleship *Massachusetts* in support. Simultaneously, the troops from Guánica attacked the city by land. Outmaneuvered and hopelessly outnumbered, the Spanish garrison retreated toward San Juan after only a token resistance. Puerto Rico's largest city had fallen to the Americans.[52]

After he entered Ponce, Miles issued a proclamation addressed to the people of Puerto Rico. In it, he declared that the United States Army had come, not to make war upon the Puerto Ricans, but to liberate them from Spanish oppression. He promised that personal and property rights would be respected insofar as the exigencies of war allowed. Either because they were glad to be freed from oppression or because they recognized the winning side when they saw it, most of the inhabitants of southern Puerto Rico cheerfully collaborated with the American forces. They furnished guides for attack columns and brought in animals, carts, food, and forage for the invading army. The Puerto Rican volunteers, who constituted almost half of the Spanish garrison in the island, deserted en masse, either dispersing to their homes or going over to the Americans.[53]

In the midst of a friendly population Miles consolidated his position, assisted by a steady stream of reinforcements from the United States. Wilson's 3,500 men had landed on July 28. Three days later, Brig. Gen. Theodore Schwan, at the head of 2,800 Regular infantry, cavalry, and artillery from Tampa, came ashore at Ponce. General Brooke brought in over 5,000 more men, mostly Volunteer infantry, between August 3 and 5 and disembarked them at Miles's order at Arroyo, 40 miles east of Ponce. From there, they could move against the flank of any Spanish force that tried to block the main highway to San Juan. Additional small contingents, which arrived during the next three weeks, built Miles's command up to 17,000 officers and men,

52. *Correspondence*, I, 322. *RSW, 1898*, II, 30-31. Alger, *Spanish-American War*, 305-6. Miles, *The North American Review*, CLXIX, 129-32. Nunez, *Guerra*, V, 94-96.

53. *Correspondence*, I, 341, 351, 359. *RSW, 1898*, II, 31-32. Miles, *The North American Review*, CLXIX, 132-33. Nunez, *Guerra*, V, 83, 91-92, 101.

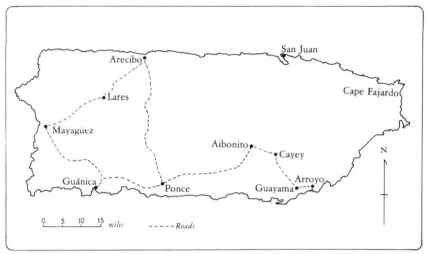

Map 3.   The Puerto Rico Campaign

amply supported by rapid-fire guns and artillery. Miles's army contained
elements of the First, Second, and Fourth corps. The deployment of these
units into Puerto Rico from widely separated camps within three weeks
demonstrated the Army's growing skill at amphibious campaigning and
showed that Secretary Alger's efforts to end the transport shortage were
producing the desired results.[54]

The lack of transportation and supplies that had turned the siege of
Santiago into a nightmare for the Fifth Corps did not plague the Puerto
Rico expedition. All contingents of Miles's army left the United States fully
supplied with food, canvas suits, tentage, wagons, ambulances, and medical
stores. By capturing two sheltered harbors in the first days of the invasion,
Miles's force did not have to disembark across open beaches. The seizure
of 80 small lighters at Guánica and Ponce and the arrival late in July of
the engineering expedition from New York, which had been originally intended for Shafter, assured quick solutions of the army's landing and construction problems. The Medical Department complained of a shortage of
surgeons and nurses, but supplies of all kinds were ample and the available
staff more than sufficed to treat the campaign's few casualties.

Deficiencies in organization and procedure did, of course, become evident. Troop commanders complained that transport crews smashed or lost
Amy stores while embarking them or stowed material in the holds in ways
that prevented efficient unloading. From some transports came reports of
overcrowding and bad food. One of General Brooke's brigades became

54. *Correspondence*, I, 333, 378, 392, 402. *RSW, 1898*, I, 270; II, 228. *War Investigating Commission*, VII, 3255. Alger, *Spanish-American War*, 308, 310-11. Miles, *The North American Review*,
CLXIX, 133-34.

separated from its wagons during the voyage and had to struggle through the campaign with a train improvised from native ox-carts. None of these misfortunes seriously disrupted operations. Since Puerto Rico, unlike Cuba, had not been devastated by war before the Americans landed, temporary shortages of food and transportation could be filled by local purchase or rental.[55]

While his forces disembarked, Miles carefully mapped his advance against San Juan. The chain of low mountains that lies in an east-west direction through the middle of the island separates Ponce from the capital; these mountains constituted the chief barrier to Miles's march. The Spaniards, who had concentrated near Cape Fajardo at the start of the campaign, were now regrouping in the mountains. A force of about 1,300 took position at Aibonito and blocked the pass through which the highway to San Juan crossed the range. Miles's final attack plan demonstrated his skill at analyzing and making use of terrain as well as his penchant for isolating and enveloping rather than storming enemy strong points. He organized four assault columns. The first, under Brigadier General Schwan, was to circle the mountain barrier at its western end by marching northward from Guánica, along the coast. On Schwan's right, a second column was to cross the mountains over a trail that was unknown to the Spaniards, which Miles's engineers had discovered. These two columns were to meet at Arecibo, a port on the north coast that was connected to San Juan by rail. There, they would be reinforced by troops brought by sea from Ponce, thus giving the army a base close to the enemy's fortress. Meanwhile, Major General Wilson, with a third column, was to march directly up the highway toward Aibonito while General Brooke advanced from Arroyo with a fourth detachment to cut the road behind the Spaniards. Together, the four columns would outflank and envelop the strongest Spanish positions, drive the enemy into San Juan, and destroy Spanish sovereignty throughout Puerto Rico. Isolated and beleaguered by land and sea, San Juan itself soon must fall.[56]

After some preliminary maneuvers, Miles's four columns opened their offensive on August 9 against weak resistance. With the defection of the local volunteers, no more than 8,000 Spanish regulars remained to face the

55. *War Investigating Commission*, I, 174-75, 577-78, 592, 596-97, 621, 623-25, 628-29, 652; II, 781, 785; IV, 958-59; V, 1970; VII, 3225, 3255-56; VIII, 556-62. *RSW, 1898*, I, 734-35, 759; II, 31, 39, 227. *Correspondence*, I, 291-92, 350. Alger, *Spanish-American War*, 306-8. Creagher, *Fourteenth Ohio*, 124-26. Chadwick, *Spanish-American War*, II, 295. Miles, *The North American Review*, CLXIX, 130. Risch, *Quartermaster Corps*, 554-55. Maj. Gen. J. R. Brooke to Adj. Gen. Corbin, September 8, 1898, File No. 128803, AGO Records. Capt. E. B. Harrison to Maj. J. N. Carson, August 24, 1898, Capt. Frank L. Polk to the Chief Quartermaster, I Corps, August 30, 1898, Bellinger, Tampa Report, File No. 115533, OQMG Records. Brig. Gen. Guy V. Henry to Secretary Alger, October 15, 1898; Col. Frank J. Hecker to Alger, January 9, 1899, Alger Papers. W. B. Averill to Mr. Van Etten, August 12, 1898, Hecker Papers.

56. *War Investigating Commission*, VII, 3254. Alger, *Spanish-American War*, 310-11. Miles, *The North American Review*, CLXIX, 134. Nunez, *Guerra*, V, 96-98. *Army and Navy Journal*, May 7, 1898.

Americans. The Spanish commanders, making the same mistake their colleagues had in Cuba, tried to hold too many places with too few troops. As a result, none of their detachments was strong enough to stop the American column sent against it or to prevent envelopment by the more numerous attackers. The western column under General Schwan made the most spectacular advance. In eight days, Schwan's men marched 92 miles, fought two sharp skirmishes, captured nine towns, and took 192 Spanish prisoners. The column sent through the mountains along the newly discovered trail also achieved its objective without difficulty. Steadily and methodically, Wilson and Brooke closed in on Aibonito. The only serious threat to the completeness of Miles's triumph came from Admiral Sampson, whom Miles accused of planning to bombard San Juan into surrender before his troops could reach it. On August 9 Miles asked the President to keep the fleet away from San Juan until the Army arrived, and the President complied.[57]

Although marred by Miles's "dog-in-the-manger" treatment of the Navy and transformed for the troops into little more than a field maneuver by the Spaniards' weakness, the Puerto Rican campaign was well planned and aggressively conducted. When an armistice ended the fighting on August 12, Miles's troops, at a cost of 4 dead and about 40 wounded, had overrun most of Puerto Rico and had rendered untenable any Spanish position outside the fortress of San Juan. Those Spaniards who had not been surrounded and captured were streaming back into the capital in total defeat. San Juan remained in Spanish hands when the campaign ended, but Miles's victory more than sufficed to support a demand by the United States that Spain surrender Puerto Rico as part of the peace settlement.[58]

VI

While Miles's troops swept toward San Juan, Merritt's soldiers, half a world away, closed in on Manila. The vanguard of the Eighth Corps, 2,500 men in three transports commanded by Brigadier General Anderson, sailed from San Francisco on May 25 under escort by the cruiser *Charleston* and reached Manila on June 30. The flotilla stopped off on the way to capture the small Spanish island of Guam. Guam's 60 defenders, unaware until the Americans arrived that war had begun, surrendered without firing a shot.[59]

57. *RSW, 1898*, II, 34-36. *Correspondence*, I, 380. Chadwick, *Spanish-American War*, I, 229; II, 316. Miles, *The North American Review*, CLXIX, 134-37. Nunez, *Guerra*, V, 6-7, 48-49, 82-83, 90, 92-94, 98-102, 104-5, 107-8. Tanham, *Military Affairs*, XXIII, 148.

58. *Correspondence*, I, 393, 399. *RSW, 1898*, II, 36. Alger, *Spanish-American War*, 316-17.

59. *RSW, 1898*, II, 54. Chadwick, *Spanish-American War*, II, 373-74. Wolff, *Little Brown Brother*, 97-98.

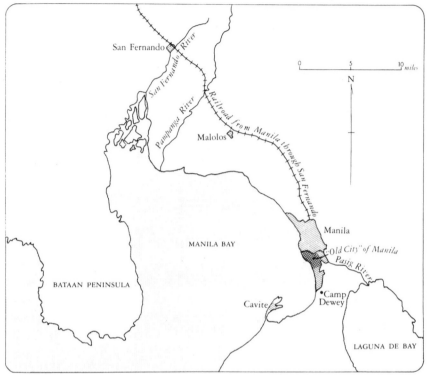

Map 4.   The Philippines: Central Luzon and the Manila Area

At Manila, Anderson confronted a complex political and military situation. The city contained over 300,000 people in 1898 and was the commercial and cultural as well as the political capital of the Philippines. Lying on
the east shore of the wide bay where Dewey had fought his naval battle,
it was divided in two by the Pasig River, which flowed into the bay from
the east. On the Pasig's south bank, surrounded on three sides by the river
and the bay, stood the "Old City," a massive stone fortress built in the
eighteenth century. North and south of the Pasig, newer suburbs sprawled
out from the ancient walls. Flat, swampy land, crossed by few paved roads,
surrounded Manila. Located as it was at the water's edge, Manila could not
be defended against a fleet that commanded the bay, and the Spaniards had
made new defensive preparations. Of more than 100 guns in the city's shore
defenses, only 4 were modern breechloaders. Again following the strategy
that had lost Cuba and Puerto Rico, the Spaniards, who had over 20,000
troops available in the Philippines, assembled fewer than 13,000 of them
to protect Manila. The rest were scattered throughout the Islands in
ineffective, vulnerable detachments.[60]

60. *Correspondence*, II, 690-91. Agoncillo, *Malolos*, 198. Alger, *Spanish-American War*, 325.
Nunez, *Guerra*, V, 118-26, 170, 175-76, 193-96. Wolff, *Little Brown Brother*, 20-21.

With the arrival of Anderson's command, two separate and independent military forces held Manila under siege. Since the battle of May 1, Admiral Dewey's warships had controlled Manila Bay, and naval landing parties had occupied the town and arsenal of Cavite, located at the end of a narrow peninsula that thrust out into the bay south of Manila. By threatening bombardment of the defenseless city, Dewey could have forced its surrender at any time, but until Anderson's men arrived he lacked troops to garrison it. On land, Aguinaldo's Filipino nationalists ringed the city. About 12,000 strong, they exchanged occasional volleys with the Spaniards, who had erected a line of trenches and blockhouses to resist them. On July 1 they forced the Spaniards to abandon the city waterworks.[61]

In accord with the Administration's policy, the Army commanders at Manila avoided cooperation with Aguinaldo. General Anderson conferred once with the Filipino leader on July 1 and found that he was displeased at the landing of United States troops who, he thought (rightly), intended to deprive him of the fruits of his previous victories. When he arrived, late in July, General Merritt avoided even this limited contact and never met or spoke with Aguinaldo. Aguinaldo, in his turn, tried to prevent the Americans from securing local animals and vehicles for a supply train, but under American pressure he eventually abandoned this effort. Both Anderson and Merritt came to regard Aguinaldo as a potential enemy, and they reported their suspicions of him to the War Department.[62]

During the first days of July, Anderson's 2,500 men disembarked at Cavite. They took over the stone buildings of the Spanish arsenal for barracks and storehouses, conducted drills and practice marches, reconnoitered the countryside, and built scaling ladders out of bamboo for use in the final assault on the walls of the fortress. The attack on Manila would necessarily be made from the south, along the beach. To secure a base nearer the Spanish lines than Cavite, which was 27 miles from Manila by road, General Anderson on July 15 transferred part of his force by water to a point on the bay shore north of the arsenal. There, on low-lying ground behind the Filipino siege line and only 3 miles from Manila's southernmost suburb, the troops established Camp Dewey, the main American base for the campaign. When the second contingent of the Eighth Corps arrived under Brig. Gen. Francis V. Greene, its 3,500 men disembarked at Camp Dewey. General Merritt reached Manila on July 25 and was followed six days later by 4,800 more troops under Brig. Gen. Arthur MacArthur, who also went ashore at Camp Dewey.[63]

61. *Correspondence*, II, 779-80. *RSW, 1898*, II, 40. Agoncillo, *Malolos*, 156-68. Chadwick, *Spanish-American War*, II, 363. Nunez, *Guerra*, V, 173-76, 207-15. Wolff, *Little Brown Brother*, 107-9.

62. *Correspondence*, II, 743, 777-79, 809. *RSW, 1898*, II, 40, 54; *1899*, I, Pt. 4, pp. 336-40. Alger, *Spanish-American War*, 348-50, 358-61. Anderson, *JMSI*, XXIX, 205-6.

63. *Correspondence*, II, 690-91, 742, 777-80. *War Investigating Commission*, III, 97-99, 101. *RSW, 1898*, I, 39, 41, 54-55, 60-61. Agoncillo, *Malolos*, 174. Alger, *Spanish-American War*, 331-32. Sexton, *Soldiers in the Sun*, 30-31.

The Eighth Corps arrived in the Philippines during the monsoon season, a period of torrential daily rains that turned the countryside into a vast swamp while high winds raised waves in the bay and surf on the beaches. In spite of these conditions, Merritt's troops managed to land their supplies and set up camps that were at least a degree more comfortable than the squalid trenches of Santiago. At Cavite, supplies could be brought ashore over the arsenal's wharf, and at Camp Dewey a conveniently located creek mouth offered a sheltered landing place. Merritt's quartermasters, using Navy launches and the transports' boats and supplementing them with captured Spanish steamers and primitive Filipino lighters called *cascos*, improvised a fleet of landing craft. They disembarked troops, guns, and stores with no loss of life and small loss of property. Because General Merritt thought animals could not survive the long voyage to Manila, the Eighth Corps had brought with it few horses, mules, or wagons. Merritt's quartermasters had planned to improvise supply trains with local animals and vehicles. In spite of Aguinaldo's obstructionism, they collected enough pony carts, buffalo-drawn sledges, and Chinese coolies to meet the army's need for ground transportation. Like their comrades in Cuba, the men of the Eighth Corps had only their pup-tents for shelter, but they were able to floor them with bamboo to keep out the dampness of the ground. They enjoyed adequate rations, and the monotony of salted and canned meat was occasionally broken by issues of fresh beef from the refrigerator ship in the bay. The expedition's hospitals proved more than equal to the demands of the campaign, and their equipment and efficiency impressed critical British officers present at Manila to observe how the Yankees carried on colonial war. The health of the troops reflected the sound management of the expedition. On August 13, when the final attack on Manila began, only 124 men out of more than 8,000 then on shore were in hospitals, over half of them with wounds.[64]

By late July, with the first three expeditions well organized, Merritt considered himself ready to attack Manila. First, he had to clear away the insurgents entrenched between Camp Dewey and the city. This task he entrusted on July 28 to Brigadier General Greene, who negotiated directly with the rebel commander of that sector so as to avoid any recognition of Aguinaldo's government. Greene evaded a maneuver by Aguinaldo to force American recognition and persuaded the Filipinos to shift to their right. Early on July 29, troops from Camp Dewey occupied 400 yards of the rebels' trenches facing the Spanish lines. That night, the Americans, dissatisfied with the Filipinos'

---

64. *Correspondence*, II, 680-82, 684-85, 687-89, 698, 777-79, 781-82, 807, 810-11. *RSW, 1898*, I, 851, 878; II, 39, 41, 55, 61; *1899*, I, Pt. 4, p. 340. *War Investigating Commission*, I, 152; III, 101-4, 112; VII, 3268. Alger, *Spanish-American War*, 340-41. Anderson, *JMSI*, XXIX, 206-7. Chadwick, *Spanish-American War*, II, 393. Latshaw, "Medical Service," 88-89, 91-92. Sexton, *Soldiers in the Sun*, 32-34. Lt. Col. J. W. Pope to the Quartermaster General, November 16, 1898, File No. 115533, OQMG Records. For a British view of the VIII Corps at Manila, see Capt. S. S. Long, "A Few Short Notes on the Administration of the United States Army in the Philippines," *JMSI*, XXV, 125-35, reprinted from *Journal of the United Service Institution in India*.

fortifications and position, advanced 100 yards closer to the Spaniards and dug new trenches. Later, they extended their front another 800 yards inland and masked a section of the insurgents' line.[65]

The Filipinos had surrounded Manila since early June, but neither they nor the Spaniards had engaged in much fighting, apart from occasional sporadic exchanges of shots. However, between July 30 and August 7 the Spaniards subjected the Americans nightly to rifle and artillery fusillades, and Merritt's troops replied in kind. They lost 12 killed and over 50 wounded in these exchanges. The nightly firing ceased on August 7, when Admiral Dewey, at Merritt's urging, threatened to bombard the city with his heavy guns if the Spaniards continued. While the skirmishing went on in the trenches, General Merritt brought MacArthur's force ashore at Camp Dewey and organized the whole army into a division. Commanded by General Anderson, the division comprised two brigades, one under General Greene and the other under General MacArthur. One infantry regiment and some heavy artillery garrisoned Cavite.[66]

Early in August, General Merritt and Admiral Dewey, using the Belgian consul as a go-between, opened secret negotiations with General Fermin Jaudenes, the Spanish commander in Manila. Cut off from reinforcement by Dewey's squadron and surrounded on land by Americans and Filipinos, Jaudenes knew his position was hopeless. If the city was to fall, he preferred that it be to the Americans rather than to the Filipinos, whose retaliation for the Spaniards' past atrocities he and his army dreaded. Jaudenes therefore was quite willing to surrender, but he feared disciplinary action from his own government if he yielded without a battle. (His predecessor had been removed late in July for discussing capitulation with Dewey.) The Spanish general refused to submit until attacked, but he agreed with the Americans on rules to reduce the destructiveness of the coming battle, the end of which was all but prearranged. Jaudenes promised that if the American fleet did not shell the city and if Merritt kept the Filipinos out of the land attack, the Spaniards would fight only for their outer line of trenches and blockhouses. They would not defend the thick walls of the inner citadel or use its heavy guns. The two sides also arranged that, once the land battle started, Dewey's flagship would steam toward the inner city and demand surrender by flag signals. Jaudenes then would raise a white flag on the walls and allow the Americans to enter the citadel. Following this formula, Dewey and Merritt on August 9 sent a note to Jaudenes to demand surrender of the city. As planned, the Spaniard rejected the ultimatum, and the Americans began preparing for the assault.[67]

65. Treaty of Peace, 363, 367. RSW, 1898, II; 41, 63-65. Agoncillo, Malolos, 177-79. Alger, Spanish-American War, 333-34.

66. RSW, 1898, II, 41, 55, 63-66, 678. Correspondence, I, 556. Alger, Spanish-American War, 334-35, 340-41. Chadwick, Spanish-American War, II, 400-401.

67. RSW, 1898, II, 41-42. Correspondence, II, 781-82. Agoncillo, Malolos, 186-93. Alger, Spanish-American War, 334-36. Chadwick, Spanish-American War, II, 402, 408-11. Sexton, Soldiers in the Sun, 38. The New York Times, June 9, 1898.

Working closely with Admiral Dewey, Merritt and his subordinates carefully planned their attack so as to assure success, regardless of how stubbornly the Spanish resisted. The operation promised to be a complex one, whether or not the attack met opposition, as the Americans had to maneuver both to capture the city and to keep Aguinaldo's forces out of it. For this reason, Merritt, in contrast to Shafter before San Juan and El Caney, issued detailed written instructions to his division and brigade commanders, specifying unit objectives, routes of advance, and the tactics to be followed.

Under the plan, the infantry of the Eighth Corps, Greene's brigade on the left along the bay and MacArthur's on the right inland, were to strike the south end of the Spanish outer line. Dewey's ships, steaming offshore just ahead of Greene's advance, were to support the troops with cannon and machine-gun fire. (This was possible at Manila, as it had not been at San Juan Hill, because the vessels, steaming close to the flat shoreline, could employ direct fire at the Spanish positions.) Merritt intended the Navy's guns, supplemented by Army field batteries, to break the enemy defense. He ordered the infantry to go forward only after the shelling had silenced the Spanish guns. The assault plan took account of a probable early surrender by the Spaniards. Six companies of Oregon Volunteers and Merritt's headquarters would remain aboard a Navy warship during the attack, ready to disembark directly into the walled city if the Spaniards raised the white flag. On the night of August 12 Merritt requested Aguinaldo by letter to keep his troops out of the battle, and he instructed Greene's and MacArthur's brigades to occupy Manila's suburbs north and south of the Pasig River as soon as possible after they broke the Spanish line. They were to keep out of the suburbs any Filipino troops who tried to enter. The attack was set for August 13. Orders to the regiments went out on the 12th, and that night engineers crept forward to cut the barbed wire in front of the Spanish trenches and to clear paths for the assault through the thick underbrush. Anderson, Greene, and MacArthur had not been informed of Merritt's and Dewey's arrangements with General Jaudenes, so they expected and prepared for a hard battle. Later, when they learned of the arrangements for surrender, they still believed that their strategy would have prevailed, although at greater cost in American lives, had the Spaniards fought it out.[68]

At about 9:30 A.M. on August 13, a day of heat, clouds, and periodic drenching rain, Dewey's ships opened fire on the Spanish outer line. From then on, the Battle of Manila went according to plan. After an hour's shelling by the fleet, Greene's and MacArthur's men attacked the Spanish trenches and blockhouses, routing their defenders in a sharp skirmish that

68. *RSW, 1898*, II, 42, 56, 71, 82-83. *Correspondence*, II, 782. Agoncillo, *Malolos*, 182, 188-89, 195. Alger, *Spanish-American War*, 331, 334, 336-38.

cost the Americans 5 dead and 44 wounded. Around 11:30 A.M. General Jaudenes hoisted his surrender flag on the citadel's walls, but the troops opposing Greene and MacArthur did not see it and continued fighting for a brief period. In response to the surrender signal, Merritt's officers went ashore from their steamer into the walled city to arrange the terms of capitulation, followed by the Oregon troops, who guarded the public buildings and began disarming crowds of Spanish soldiers. Aguinaldo's insurgents, defying Merritt's request to their leader, joined the attack and raced Greene's and MacArthur's brigades for possession of the suburbs. With help from the Spaniards, who held their lines until the Americans arrived, Greene secured the districts north of the Pasig, but south of the river and east of the walled city, the rebels overran part of the suburbs before MacArthur could move into position to bar them entirely. By the end of the day, Merritt's troops controlled the citadel and most of the suburbs. They faced outward in a semicircle, their backs to the bay and surrounded by angry but confused Filipinos. The following day, August 14, Jaudenes signed the formal articles of capitulation, under which he surrendered Manila with 13,000 troops, 22,000 stand of arms, and an assortment of artillery pieces. As a reflection of the McKinley Administration's desire to retain political freedom of choice in the Philippines and of the Spaniards' fear of the insurgents, one clause of the surrender agreement required that the weapons given up by the Spanish prisoners be returned to them if the American army evacuated Manila.[69]

VII

While Merritt's troops were fighting their way into Manila, diplomats in Washington were concluding an armistice between the United States and Spain. Her Caribbean fleet lost, Spain sued for peace on July 18. Discussions ended August 12 in a protocol dictated by President McKinley. The agreement enjoined an immediate cease-fire on all fronts. The Spanish army would at once evacuate Cuba and Puerto Rico and allow American forces to occupy those islands. Spain ceded to the United States Puerto Rico and Guam, and she relinquished sovereignty over Cuba, leaving that island's ultimate political fate to be settled by the Americans and the Cuban insurgents. Spain also agreed that United States forces would occupy the city and bay of Manila until the future of the Philippines was decided by the formal peace conference, which would meet in Paris on October 1. Late in the afternoon of August 12, President McKinley cabled his proclamation of the armistice to American commanders in Cuba, Puerto Rico, and the Philippines and ordered an immediate halt in military operations. Because

69. *RSW, 1898*, II, 40-44, 68-71, 677-78. *War Investigating Commission*, III, 100; VII, 3267-68. *Correspondence*, II, 765. Agoncillo, *Malolos*, 199, 203-10. Alger, *Spanish-American War*, 337-40. Chadwick, *Spanish-American War*, II, 421-22. Nunez, *Guerra*, V, 222-24. Sexton, *Soldiers in the Sun*, 43-44, 46. Wolff, *Little Brown Brother*, 125.

of the international date line, August 12 in Washington was August 13 at Manila, the day of Merritt's attack, and slow cable communications prevented the cease-fire order from reaching the Philippine capital until August 16. The armistice thus failed to prevent the Battle of Manila, which the terms of the protocol rendered unnecessary.[70]

The terms of the protocol signaled complete victory by the United States over Spain. In winning this victory, the Army, as its commanders had expected before the war, had played only a secondary role. By the Spaniards' own admission, the loss of their Caribbean and Pacific fleets brought over their surrender. Without her fleets, Spain could not relieve or supply her colonial armies. They must starve, be wiped out in battle, or surrender. Spain's own coasts now lay open to raids by American warships, and Spanish statesmen feared that such raids would set off revolution against the monarchy.[71]

At the cost in all theaters of 281 officers and men killed and 1,577 wounded, the Army had performed adequately the limited but vital tasks assigned to it. Its troops drove Cervera's squadron from its refuge at Santiago to destruction under Sampson's guns, and their presence and successes in Puerto Rico and at Manila enforced the McKinley Administration's claim to United States sovereignty over those strategic points. The Regulars and the Rough Riders acquitted themselves well in the Santiago battles, and the state Volunteer regiments showed gratifying steadiness under fire in Puerto Rico and the Philippines. Although deficiencies in supply and transportation crippled the Fifth Corps at Santiago, they resulted more from the circumstances under which that campaign was launched and the terrain in which it was carried on than from exceptional military incompetence. The other expeditions, operating under more favorable conditions, suffered few major supply or equipment shortages. Army-Navy cooperation, however, clearly needed improvement. No system had been devised for commanding sea and land forces in joint operations, and the services had feuded at Santiago and competed for glory in Puerto Rico. They worked well together at Manila primarily because no major disagreements arose over military and political tactics.[72]

70. Alger, *Spanish-American War*, 341-42. Chadwick, *Spanish-American War*, II, 423-25, 427-41. Mayo, *America of Yesterday*, 210. Morgan, *McKinley*, 396-97. Memorandum signed by President McKinley, July 26, 1898, McKinley Papers. *Correspondence*, I, 220, 222, 322-23, 327, 383, 385, 389; II, 750.

71. Chadwick, *Spanish-American War*, I, 89n. Nunez, *Guerra*, III, 142-45. Olcott, *McKinley*, II, 57-58. Gen. Blanco to the Minister of War, July 9, 13, and 14, 1898, and to the President of the Council of Ministers, July 14, 1898, Minister of War to Blanco, July 12, 1898, and President of the Council of Ministers to Blanco, July 12, 1898, translations in File No. 1495705, AGO Records.

72. For Army-Navy cooperation at Manila, see Tanham, *Military Affairs*, XXIII, 141-42. For casualty statistics, see *RSW, 1898*, I, 273, or *War Investigating Commission*, I, 114.

Tested in combat for the first time, the new weapons and equipment adopted by the Army during the previous decade proved durable and efficient. The Ordnance Department early in September asked officers who had served at Santiago, where the hardest and longest sustained fighting had occurred, for their evaluation of their men's arms and accoutrements. In the officers' replies, the Krag-Jörgensen rifle received almost universal praise. The Santiago veterans also expressed satisfaction with the light field gun, although they called for minor improvements in the carriage and the sights. They roundly condemned the use of black powder in battle, and most urged replacement of the Springfield with the Krag in all regiments as soon as possible. The cartridge belts, haversacks, and other pieces of personal equipment furnished by the Ordnance Department received favorable comment, but some officers urged that a light portable entrenching tool be attached to the infantryman's outfit. British correspondents with the Army praised the simplicity of American field equipment; they pointed out that the American soldier on campaign, unlike his British or European counterpart, was not burdened with elaborate parade gear or with tools for polishing buttons and shining boots.[73]

In directing and supporting operations, the War Department in the main performed competently. Except for insisting, under presidential orders, on total victory at Santiago, it allowed the field commanders to shape their tactics to fit the situation. As the strenuous efforts to reinforce and resupply Shafter exemplified, Alger and the bureau chiefs were more than generous in meeting commanders' requests for men and material. Far from ignoring General Miles's advice, as they later were accused of doing, McKinley, Alger, and the bureau chiefs helped the Commanding General to wage the Puerto Rican campaign entirely according to his own plans. Success overseas, however, had its price. Preoccupied with the conduct and support of military operations, the War Department had paid too little attention to a developing crisis in the Medical Department and the training camps. That crisis, which exploded into public attention about the time the armistice was signed, did much to give the Army's administration during the Spanish-American War its subsequent unsavory reputation.

73. *RSW, 1898*, IV, 13, 26-27, 235-40. *The New York Times*, May 22 and June 12, 1898. V Corps officers reported that at Santiago the Krag had been fired mostly as a single-loader, with the magazine seldom employed for rapid fire; see *RSW, 1898*, IV, 237.

8

Sickness and Scandal

I

Late in July of 1898, John Hay, who had observed the conflict from his diplomatic post in London, wrote to his friend Theodore Roosevelt: "It has been a splendid little war; begun with the highest motives, carried on with magnificent intelligence and spirit favored by that fortune which loves the brave. It is now to be concluded, I hope, with that . . . good nature which is . . . the distinguishing trait of the American character."[1]

By the time Hay penned his complacent comments, the Army's part in the war had begun to appear less than splendid to Hay's countrymen across the Atlantic, and very little of that characteristic American good will was being shown toward Secretary Alger and the other chiefs of the War Department. For the Army, the war ended in sickness, confusion, and complaint. Disastrous epidemics drove the Fifth Corps from Santiago in panic flight and ravaged the assembly camps of the Volunteers. Public complaints about neglect of the soldiers mounted during the weeks after the armistice, while personal feuds rent the high command. The men who had guided the Army to victory became in the popular mind incompetents and criminals and the name of the Secretary of War synonymous with all that was rotten in the public service. The medical and administrative deficiencies in the Army that came to light during July and August and gave rise to the storm of abuse were for the most part the inevitable consequences of tropical campaigning and hasty mobilization. This fact could not, however, save official reputations.

II

To bring troops into battle as rapidly as they did, Secretary Alger and the bureau chiefs, with the full concurrence of President McKinley, had used scarce resources to equip some units and branches of the Army thoroughly while neglecting others. In July and August the neglected elements began breaking down. The collapse centered in the Medical Department and in the mass of troops called out in the beginning for no good military reason and held throughout the summer in camps of reserve.

Although it was headed by one of the nation's most distinguished scientists and contained probably the best-educated body of surgeons in the country, the Medical Department labored under crippling political and

1. John Hay to Theodore Roosevelt, July 27, 1898, Vol. 3, Roosevelt Papers.

administrative handicaps. It possessed little authority or prestige within the Army. Line and staff alike scorned medical officers as "nobody but doctors," and surgeons during the 1880s had had to wage a fierce bureaucratic battle for the right even to use military titles. Because of the department's low status, Secretaries of War and Commanding Generals regularly gave low priority to its requests for legislation, men, and money. The Quartermaster's Department, which shipped all medical supplies, frequently lost or mishandled important materials. Line commanders paid little attention to their hospitals unless neglect bred disaster. General Shafter boasted that in all his Army career he had never seen or signed a medical supply requisition. "The doctors," he said, "know what is wanted and they get it." Surgeons in camp and field had no power to enforce their recommendations for sanitation, and commanders often brushed aside their warnings and suggestions and even belittled the medics as stuffy old women who tried to coddle the soldiers. General Brooke recalled, after the war, how his chief surgeon at Camp Thomas had annoyed him by repeatedly "thrashing over old straw" on matters of health. The camp's appalling sick rate demonstrated the results of Brooke's traditional Army attitude.[2]

Even had Surgeon General Sternberg and his subordinates enjoyed the full cooperation of all other branches and bureaus, the medical science upon which they relied so confidently was as yet undeveloped. Physicians still had much to learn about the detection of yellow fever, malaria, and typhoid—the scourges that afflicted the Army in 1898—and their knowledge of how these diseases were spread included many gaps and misconceptions. For example, Army surgeons, like their civilian colleagues, often confused malaria with the early stages of yellow fever or diagnosed typhoid as malaria. Since they failed to recognize the first cases among their patients, they acted too late to check many epidemics. When they did act, mistaken theories on the manner in which the diseases spread led them to take the wrong measures to prevent infection and contagion. The mosquito went unrecognized as the carrier of yellow fever and malaria, so surgeons attributed outbreaks of these tropical maladies to a variety of conditions including impure water, occupation of infected buildings, and the digging of trenches, which supposedly set free a miasma locked up in the soil. Surgeons who were battling typhoid understood that polluted water and filthy camps facilitated the spread of the disease, but they had not yet learned that typhoid is contagious and that the germ can remain virulent for a long time in places once occupied

2. Shafter is quoted in *War Investigating Commission*, VII, 3192; Brooke's remarks are in VI, 3096-97; see also, I, 174: IV, 1469; VI, 2820-21, 2984, 3083-87, 3098-99; VII, 3152. Gibson, *Soldier in White*, 189. Hagedorn, *Wood*, I, 223. Latshaw, "Medical Service," 18-19, 21, 122. Maj. Walter Reed, Maj. Victor C. Vaughan, and Maj. Edward O. Shakespeare, *Abstract of Report on the Origin and Spread of Typhoid Fever in U.S. Military Camps during the Spanish War of 1898* (hereafter cited as *Reed Report*), 180; Surg. Gen. George M. Sternberg to Adj. Gen. Corbin, December 16, 1901, File No. 411152, AGO Records.

Surgeon General George M. Sternberg, U.S. Army.
Appointed Surgeon General, U.S.A., May 30, 1893, retired June 8, 1902.

by typhoid victims. Guided as they were by incomplete, incorrect information, medical officers in 1898 could not have checked epidemics even under the best of conditions. In the campaigns of the Spanish-American War they worked under many material and administrative handicaps, some of their own making and some the result of too-rapid mobilization and peacetime penny pinching.[3]

During the first months of the war, the Medical Department encountered many difficulties—some of its own making—in distributing medicines, hospital equipment, and surgical supplies to the camps. Like the other bureaus, it entered the conflict with supplies and equipment barely sufficient for the peacetime Army. Like the other bureaus, it placed large orders for all kinds of material as soon as mobilization began. Plagued by delays in manufacturing important items and by slow deliveries, Surgeon General Sternberg, during the first weeks of the war, borrowed medical stores from the states and enforced a priority system to assure full outfits for the invasion troops. Neither he nor his subordinates, however, worked out an efficient distribution system for such easily obtained articles as bedding, surgical thermometers, hospital foods, and medicines, which surgeons in the camps used in large quantities. The officers in charge of medical supply depots, pleading a lack of storage space, waited for requisitions to arrive from the camps and then purchased only enough of the required items to fill their immediate needs. Since the surgeons in the field, inexperienced as they were in administering large hospitals, usually underestimated their supply needs, chronic shortages of everything from thermometers to bedsheets afflicted the sick among the troops. At Chickamauga, Camp Alger, and Jacksonville, regimental and division surgeons turned for necessities to the Red Cross and other private relief agencies because, as one Army doctor put it, "they honored requisitions at once and the United States government did not."[4]

Along with its inefficient supply service, a shortage of surgeons and hospital corpsmen crippled the Medical Department. The bureau entered the war with barely enough officers to staff the standing Army. Similar to the other bureaus, it received a large wartime reinforcement, commissioned in part by the President and the bureau chief and in part by the state governors. Congress on May 12 also permitted the Surgeon General to supplement his uniformed personnel with an unlimited number of civilian contract

3. *RSW, 1898*, I, 784; *1899*, I, Pt. 2, pp. 614-15, 625. *War Investigating Commission*, III, 27, 618; IV, 908, 919-20; V, 2350; VI, 3045. *Correspondence*, I, 303. Latshaw, "Medical Service," 12, 114-15, 117-18. *Reed Report*, 188-90, 194-203, 208. Brig. Gen. James H. Wilson to Col. Stephen H. Olin, August 28, 1899, Box 44, Wilson Papers.

4. The quotation is from *War Investigating Commission*, IV, 1540-41; see also I, 114-15, 173-74, 637, 643, 680-82, 684-85, 701; III, 261-62, 309-10, 312-13, 491, 494-95; IV, 1118-19, 1250, 1402-3, 1532; V, 1722, 1732-33, 1738-39, 1964, 2317-20, 2322-23; VI, 2627, 2797, 2805-6, 2812-13, 2819, 2827-28, 2835-36, 2971-74, 2977, 3002-3; VII, 3317, 3319-20, 3772. *RSW, 1898*, I, 691-94, 755-76, 768, 772, 798. Risch, *Quartermaster Corps*, 538.

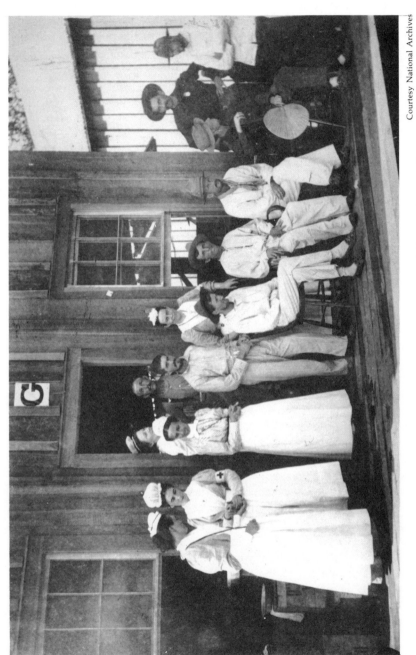

Camp Thomas, Chickamauga Park, Sternberg Hospital, Third Army Corps. Nurses and convalescent patients.

Courtesy National Archives

surgeons. For lack of both time and officers for examining boards, Sternberg appointed Volunteer surgeons and contract doctors from civil life after only the sketchiest assessment of their professional qualifications. Further, many of the Volunteer regimental surgeons, commissioned by the states from the National Guard, owed their positions more to political influence than to medical accomplishments. The civilians so selected, many of them graduates of medical schools as yet little influenced by modern scientific doctrines, were in large part ignorant of bacteriology and of the principles of sanitation. Those who were conversant with up-to-date techniques knew little of Army supply procedure or hospital administration. To offset such handicaps, most of the new appointees made diligent efforts to master their duties. Surgeon General Sternberg placed his few Regulars in the highest ranking and most responsible posts in camps and hospitals, and they in turn devoted as much time as they could afford to training their subordinates. Nevertheless, as was the case in all the bureaus, a qualified staff large enough for the war-swollen Army did not emerge until after the effects of its absence at the beginning were all too tragically evident.[5]

To provide nurses, stretcher-bearers, and ambulance drivers, the Medical Department tried to enlarge its small but highly trained Hospital Corps. Strenuous efforts to attract civilian recruits and to persuade medically qualified Volunteers to transfer from line regiments resulted in frustration. By August 31, although the Hospital Corps had grown from its peacetime strength of 791 to almost 6,000 men, the corps still had barely half the number required for the Army of 275,000, and most of the recruits lacked training and experience. In their search for attendants in the camp hospitals, commanders temporarily detailed squads of infantrymen for ward duty. These detail men, usually the dregs of their units, were worse than useless in caring for patients, and their neglect of elementary sanitary precautions helped spread typhoid through the camps. Driven by despair to innovation, Surgeon General Sternberg for the first time in the Army's history employed large numbers of female nurses in military hospitals. By September 15 over 1,100 of these professionally qualified women were working in wards in the United States and overseas. Their devoted, capable efforts won over the conservative Army surgeons who previously had viewed with grave doubts this female intrusion into the male world of the military. The Surgeon General brought a woman physician, Dr. Anita Newcomb McGee, into his bureau as chief of nurses. Although this appointment signaled the arrival of the female nurse as a permanent addition to the military establishment, the full benefits of the innovation were not felt until many Army hospitals had neared collapse for lack of trained attendants.[6]

5. *War Investigating Commission*, I, 169-70, 571-72, 635, 643; III, 89, 238, 315-16; IV, 1139, 1419-20, 1533; V, 1742, 1977; VI, 2813-14, 2848, 2988, 3002; VII, 3288. *RSW, 1898*, I, 688-89, 703, 745, 747; *1899*, I, Pt. 2, p. 560. Gibson, *Soldier in White*, 187-88, 193-94. Latshaw, "Medical Service," 10-14, 21-22, 28-29, 141-43. GO 152, HQA, May 24, 1898, in *GO/AGO, 1898*.

6. *War Investigating Commission*, I, 169-72, 636-37, 649, 654, 671-75, 723; III, 492-93; IV, 1404, 1532; V, 1695, 1744-45, 1979, 1981-83; VI, 2824-27, 2995, 2999; VII, 3168, 3170-74. *RSW, 1898*, I,

Hospital organization in the field became a disruptive problem for Sternberg and his subordinates. Each regiment, Regular and Volunteer, reached the assembly camps with its own self-contained hospital. Early in May, as corps and divisions took shape, the Medical Department, following a plan perfected in the Civil War, began consolidating the regimental surgeons, corpsmen, and supplies of each division into a single 200-bed field hospital. These division hospitals, moving with the troops on campaign and able to break down into brigade sections when necessary, were to collect the regiments' sick and wounded for treatment and send the worst cases to large base or general hospitals for intensive care. In the Civil War, this system had left the regiments unencumbered with sick and wounded; it had assured efficient medical administration; and it had provided sustained attention for men who needed it. Army surgeons in 1898 expected the system to operate efficiently again.[7]

Surgeon General Sternberg had little trouble in establishing and staffing his base hospitals, six of which were in operation by August 31. Under his supervision, the Quartermaster's Department purchased and fitted out a superbly equipped hospital ship, the *Relief*, for Caribbean service. But in the camps, the division hospitals from the beginning floundered in dissension and disorder. Shortages of equipment and trained personnel delayed their organization, and the removal of surgeons from their regiments left too few doctors with the troops for proper supervision of hygiene. The breakup of the regimental establishments met determined opposition from Volunteer colonels and surgeons, who obstructed the program at every stage and by every means they could devise. Once formed—despite this opposition—the division hospitals existed in a state of continuing administrative chaos. The lack of Regular medical officers forced the Surgeon General to place newly recruited Volunteers in charge of many of these hospitals, and the complexities of requisitioning supplies, keeping the records of hundreds of patients, and training raw medical corpsmen were clearly beyond their capabilities. In the great Volunteer concentrations, these division hospitals were the only installations for treating the sick. The epidemics of the late summer caught them with their many deficiencies still uncorrected.[8]

689-90, 709, 714, 745, 754-55; *1899*, I, Pt. 2, p. 376. Latshaw, "Medical Service," 29-31, 120-21, 147-48. GO 58, HQA, May 31, 1898; GO 126, HQA, August 25, 1898, *GO/AGO, 1898*.

7. Latshaw, "Medical Service," 6-7. *War Investigating Commission*, I, 180, 571-72, 643-44, 649-50, 653-54; III, 264, 312; V, 1979-80; VI, 2817, 2819. *RSW, 1898*, I, 703, 736.

8. *War Investigating Commission*, I, 180-81, 644, 648-49, 655-56; III, 90, 309, 315-16; IV, 955, 1113-14, 1407-8, 1420; V, 1731-32, 1757-58; VI, 2817, 2831-34, 2981-82, 2992-94; VII, 3372-74. *RSW, 1898*, I, 398, 694-96, 703, 708, 711-12, 714, 737-38, 745, 753-54, 768; *1899*, I, Pt. 2, pp. 552-53. Latshaw, "Medical Service," 141. National Relief Commission, *Report of the Executive Committee of the National Relief Commission* (hereafter cited as *National Relief Commission*), 162. Maj. Gen. J. R. Brooke to Adj. Gen. Corbin, September 8, 1898, File No. 128803, AGO Records.

An aggressive Surgeon General, wise in the ways of politics and administration, might have overcome at least some of his bureau's deficiencies, but Dr. George M. Sternberg was a research scientist, not an organizer. A kind man who felt obliged to console every distraught relative of a sick soldier who called on him for reassurance, Sternberg devoted his time and energy to small details and delegated many important tasks to his subordinates. He issued voluminous, technically excellent instructions for camp sanitation but left their enforcement entirely to the surgeons in the field. His office called for no regular supply reports, and Sternberg later stated that he knew nothing of the shortages in the camps until they were mentioned in the newspapers. In late June and again in late July, he sent officers of his bureau to inspect the assembly camps, but he never saw any reports of deteriorating sanitation. He admitted that the documents might have been lost in the confusion of his office.[9]

Along with the near collapse of the medical service went a breakdown in the Inspector General's Office, the Army's agency for detecting trouble in any area or command and reporting it to the high command. For years, the Inspector General had struggled with The Adjutant General for control of the reports from inspecting officers in the field. By early 1898 The Adjutant General had won out. With all inspection reports channeled to The Adjutant General's office, the Army was left without a central, independent receiving point for information. The Inspector General at the same time lost almost all control over his subordinates outside Washington. The confusion that developed during the war completed the disruption of this bureau. Following the example of Insp. Gen. Joseph C. Breckinridge, who received a major general's stars and went to Cuba with the Fifth Corps, many officers of the bureau left it for line commissions in the Volunteers. Under these circumstances, coordinated inspection of the growing Army was impossible, and aside from sporadic visits to camps and hospitals by boards appointed by Secretary Alger, the officials in Washington had few direct sources of information on conditions in the field. In the camps, some commanders used the inspectors on their staff to good effect; many others did not. This disintegration of the inspection service allowed abuses in the camps to accumulate unnoticed and, among other damage, undermined the Army's defenses against disease.[10]

9. *War Investigating Commission*, I, 609, 687; VI, 2798-2801, 2803, 2821, 2823, 2844; VIII, 221. Alger, *Spanish-American War*, 412-14. Gibson, *Soldier in White*, 205-6. Surg. Gen. George M. Sternberg to Adj. Gen. Corbin, June 28 and July 29, 1898, Files No. 88877 and 107839, AGO Records.

10. *War Investigating Commission*, I, 124, 188, 269; III, 344; IV, 1265; V, 1772-73, 1779-80; VI, 2800-2801, 2821-22, 3068; VII, 3372-74, 3767. *RSW, 1898*, I, 361-63; II, 565-71. GO 11, HQA, March 23, 1898; GO 81, HQA, June 27, 1898, *GO/AGO, 1898*. Maj. Gen. William R. Shafter to Secretary Alger, August 10, 1899; Alger Papers. Shafter to Adj. Gen. Corbin, August 16, 1898, Box 1, Corbin Papers. For the maneuvering over the inspection reports, see Files No. 84952, 88156, 88877, 89168, 107840, 187505, 239634, AGO Records. *The New York Times*, June 3, 1898.

III

Disease wrecked the Fifth Corps at Santiago almost before General Shafter could consolidate his victory over the Spaniards. After the formal occupation of the city on July 17, most of the American troops, now about 20,000 in number, encamped in the surrounding hills. The ordeal of battle and siege had left its mark on the conquerors. The soldiers were filthy and exhausted; their uniforms hung on them in malodorous rags, while their swollen feet protruded from split and battered shoes. During the two or three weeks immediately following the capitulation, the army's living conditions gradually improved. The Navy opened Santiago Bay to shipping on July 19, so the expedition's transports, along with supply steamers from the United States, could enter and unload at the city's wharves. Fresh meat and vegetables now varied the soldiers' campaign diet. Summer uniforms at last arrived. Tents and cooking utensils not seen since the landing on June 22 began to reach the regiments. By the end of July, the shortages and discomforts of the siege were being remedied, but yellow fever, malaria, and dysentery had begun their deadly advance through the camps.[11]

The specter of an epidemic had haunted General Shafter ever since the landing at Daiquirí. During the siege, the threat became actuality when, on July 6, surgeons discovered cases of yellow fever at Siboney. Their reports were among the factors that led Shafter and Miles to press for acceptance of Toral's evacuation offer. After Santiago fell, men sickened by the hundreds, a few with yellow fever, most with malaria, typhoid, and dysentery. On July 27 General Shafter reported over 4,000 of his troops in hospitals. Four days later, the death rate had reached 15 per day. Shafter suspended the customary rifle volleys and bugle calls at burials lest their frequency undermine morale. He and his surgeons feared that the few cases of yellow fever would multiply into a large-scale epidemic.[12]

While apprehension focused on yellow fever, it was the milder and less feared malaria that crippled the Fifth Corps. The disease rarely killed soldiers who contracted it, but it left them weak, emaciated, hollow-eyed, and unable to digest their food. Often, it struck in combination with dysentery. Contrary to the expectations of their officers, who had thought that malaria victims would recover quickly, Shafter's troops degenerated into a mob of shambling scarecrows. The daily sick reports, which took account only

11. *Correspondence*, I, 171, 174, 192, 198, 242, 275, 279. *War Investigating Commission*, I, 375-77; VI, 3110; VII, 3210, 3672. *RSW, 1898*, I, 407, 785, 825; II, 647-48, 667. Kennan, *Campaigning in Cuba*, 215, 267. Miley, *In Cuba*, 187-88. Parker, *Gatling Gun Detachment*, 197. Charles Johnson Post, *The Little War of Private Post*, 259, 266-67, 273-75, 288-89. Wheeler, *Santiago Campaign*, 204, 359-61. Maj. Gen. William R. Shafter to Secretary Alger, August 4, 1898, Alger Papers.

12. *Correspondence*, I, 137, 140, 171, 174-75, 178, 183, 185, 187, 193, 195, 197, 206, 211-12, 214, 218-19, 223-24. *RSW, 1898*, I, 705, 804-5; *1899*, I, Pt. 2, pp. 602-3. *War Investigating Commission*, VI, 3049. Kennan, *Campaigning in Cuba*, 213-14. Miley, *In Cuba*, 215. Post, *Little War*, 249, 260-61.

of men actually in hospitals, understated the extent of the disaster. Most of the sick never reached the hospitals. Afflicted with recurrent fever and acute diarrhea, men stumbled glassy-eyed through their duties until they collapsed and stretcher-bearers, themselves sick, carried them away. As the musicians fell ill, the bugle calls that regulated camp life became fainter and more confused by wrong notes. The wavering calls sounded to one imaginative New York soldier like "the ghastly echo of a thinning and dying army corps."[13]

The Fifth Corps's surgeons worked heroically to heal the sick and safeguard the well, but the shortages of manpower and equipment that had prevailed throughout the campaign reduced the effectiveness of their efforts. The expedition had reached Santiago with ample medical stores, but the surgeons could not secure enough boats to bring all their supplies ashore or vehicles to haul them to the front. With the army's transportation shortage forcing the imposition of rigid priorities, the surgeons' needs were, as usual, relegated to the bottom of the list. Begging and borrowing boats when they could and dragging equipment to the front by hand when necessary, they had one of the corps's three division hospitals in operation close to the firing line when the attack started on July 1. With material from the others, they improvised a base hospital at Siboney and converted one of the transports, the *Olivet*, into a hospital ship. The surgeons drew invaluable stocks of bedding and special foods from a Red Cross steamer that reached Siboney on June 26, complete with its own landing craft. The surgeons, assisted by Red Cross doctors and nurses and by hospital corpsmen, worked unceasingly to care for the more than 1,400 wounded that poured in from San Juan Hill and El Caney. Only 13 men died of wounds after being brought back from the line, a tribute to the medics' success in preventing the infections that had turned Civil War hospitals into chambers of horror. While the wounded still crowded the improvised wards at Siboney, the sick began coming in. Within a week of the battles, Maj. Benjamin F. Pope, the corps's Chief Surgeon, faced total paralysis of his hospital's services because his few surgeons and corpsmen were exhausted and medical supplies were wholly depleted.[14]

13. The quotation is from Post, *Little War*, 261; see also 253, 264-65, 283, 340. *War Investigating Commission*, I, 374-75; III, 49, 52; IV, 909; V, 1678, 2131; VI, 3045; VII, 3210. Alger, *Spanish-American War*, 426. Dr. Carroll Dunham, "Medical and Sanitary Aspects of the War," *The Review of Reviews*, XVIII, 415-27. Parker, *Gatling Gun Detachment*, 198-99. Roosevelt, *Rough Riders*, 202-3. Wheeler, *Santiago Campaign*, 205. Theodore Roosevelt to Henry Cabot Lodge, July 19 and 31, 1898, *Roosevelt-Lodge Correspondence*, I, 326, 331-32.

14. *War Investigating Commission*, V, 1967, 2383-94; VI, 2806, 3031-34, 3042, 3050-51; VII, 3209-10, 3252; VIII, 526. *RSW, 1898*, I, 5, 704-5, 779-80, 793-95, 800-803. Bigelow, *Santiago Campaign*, 143-45. Kennan, *Campaigning in Cuba*, 115, 147-48. Latshaw, "Medical Service," 45, 47-48, 50-51.

In anticipation of another battle and also because he wanted to clear his overcrowded wards, Major Pope, with the approval of General Shafter and of the authorities in Washington, late in the siege began sending convalescent sick and wounded back to the United States on returning transports. During July he dispatched eight such ships, carrying hundreds of patients. The results of this policy were unfortunate. The steamers were not equipped to transport sick men, and the hospital at Siboney could spare few surgeons and corpsmen and little material to care for the men on board. While Major Pope intended to send only convalescents, many sick soldiers, seeing a chance to get home, slipped onto the ships and then relapsed; some died during the voyage. Transports from Cuba steamed into Tampa and New York loaded with suffering troops. War correspondents who had hitched rides on the returning ships filled their reports to their papers with tales of horror. President McKinley, outraged by the stories of negligence and filth, on August 1 ordered an investigation by Army authorities and the punishment of any officers who could be proved at fault. The condition of these fever ships from Santiago gave dramatic notice to the American people that something had gone wrong with the Army's administration.[15]

Efforts to prevent a yellow fever epidemic began with the arrival of General Miles at Siboney. Following the advice of experts on his staff who believed the disease was contracted by the troops occupying contaminated buildings and camping on polluted ground, Miles on July 11 ordered the whole village of Siboney burned; work details at once applied the torch to all structures in the village. To relieve the shortage of attendants in the Siboney hospitals, Miles brought the entire Twenty-fourth Infantry down from the siege line after the Spaniards' surrender. These Negro Regulars uncomplainingly nursed yellow fever patients at the risk of contracting the disease themselves. Once the capitulation freed the troops from the trenches, General Shafter, under instructions from Miles, began separating suspected yellow fever victims from their units and shifting regiments to new camps on supposedly clean soil. The regiments were to move every time new yellow fever suspects appeared in their ranks. This practice, approved by the best medical thought of the time, theoretically would permit the army to march away from the fever and eventually to escape it altogether.[16]

15. *Correspondence*, I, 83, 93, 190-91, 197-99. *War Investigating Commission*, I, 186-87; VI, 3045-48. *RSW, 1898*, I, 705-6, 785-86. Bigelow, *Santiago Campaign*, 149-151. Wheeler, *Santiago Campaign*, 309-10. A. H. Doty to Surgeon General Sternberg, July 21, 1898, President McKinley to Secretary Alger, August 1, 1898, Adj. Gen. Corbin to Maj. C. H. Heyl, August 1, 1898, and Heyl to Corbin, August 3, 1898, File No. 108220, AGO Records. The investigating officer found no single man to blame for conditions on the transports. He attributed them to the congestion and shortages at Siboney.

16. *RSW, 1898*, I, 733, 739; II, 23, 25-27. *War Investigating Commission*, I, 615; V, 1966, 1974; VI, 3049; VII, 3252-53. Miley, *In Cuba*, 216. Miles, *Serving the Republic*, 293. Wheeler, *Santiago Campaign*, 342-43. Maj. Gen. William R. Shafter to Secretary Alger, November 30, 1898, Alger Papers.

In response to urgent pleas from Shafter, the War Department rushed additional doctors, nurses, and medical stores to Santiago. The new hospital ship *Relief*, her outfitting having been completed late in June, sailed from New York on July 2 with 20 surgeons and over 700 tons of supplies on board. She reached Siboney on July 7, to be greeted as a savior by the desperate surgeons. During the weeks after the surrender, other vessels from the United States brought in still more equipment, along with 65 additional doctors— some Regulars and the rest civilians under contract—and 129 nurses, many of them women. Gradually the hospitals around Santiago assumed a semblance of order and efficiency.[17]

Besides sending medical staff and supplies to Santiago, President McKinley and Secretary Alger had to resolve a more perplexing choice: Should the Fifth Corps stay in Cuba while it fought the epidemic, or should it return at once to the United States for recuperation? Until the armistice, military considerations dictated keeping the Fifth Corps in Cuba. At Santiago, Shafter's troops could guard the 24,000 Spanish prisoners, and they might undertake additional campaigns to strengthen the American hold on eastern Cuba. Medical and political circumstances also pointed to the advisability of leaving the Fifth Corps in position. Confused as they were about the means and manner by which yellow fever spread, officials and ordinary citizens alike feared that the Fifth Corps, if brought home while still infected, would bring the fever with it and start an epidemic in the United States. They preferred that the troops remain in Cuba until certified as free of the disease. Suggestions that the Fifth Corps be encamped for a rest on the New England coast brought indignant protests from the region's congressmen, and the South reacted with terror to the prospect of even a few yellow fever convalescents arriving from Cuba. Reflecting the popular fears, the Medical Department in mid-July went so far as to order the disinfection of all mail passing from Santiago to the United States. Not only might Shafter's troops infect the country, Secretary Alger feared, they might contaminate the transports that carried them northward and render the whole Caribbean fleet unusable. On the basis of all these considerations, Alger on July 13 and 14 told General Shafter to begin quarantining yellow fever suspects and shifting camps. When the regiments stopped producing new yellow fever cases, Alger said, they could be sent back to the United States. Alger expected no early return of the Fifth Corps. He thought it must remain at Santiago "until the fever has had its run."[18]

17. *Correspondence*, I, 72, 74, 107, 155, 164, 169, 177, 182, 186-87, 192, 195, 200, 208, 341. *RSW*, *1898*, I, 705, 733, 803, 805; *1899*, I, Pt. 2, p. 522. *War Investigating Commission*, I, 664; IV, 3040, 3044, 3050-51; VII, 3170. Alger, *Spanish-American War*, 291. Surgeon General Sternberg to Maj. George H. Tourney, June 22, 1898, File No. 108220, AGO Records.

18. Alger, *Spanish-American War*, 255-59. *Correspondence*, I, 135-36, 141, 144, 153, 179, 189, 191, 199, 357. *War Investigating Commission*, III, 26; VI, 2842. James M. Harding to Secretary Alger, April 4, 1898, File No. 74028, AGO Records. Maj. Gen. William R. Shafter to Alger, August 4, 1898, Alger Papers, discusses a possible attack on Holguín. The United States by 1898 had an elaborate quarantine system to keep out diseases from abroad; see Walter Wyman to Secretary of the Treasury Lyman J. Gage, November 28, 1898, McKinley Papers.

Initially, reports from the front indicated that Alger's policy would work and that the condition of the Fifth Corps was far from critical. General Shafter on July 13 and General Miles on July 18 and 21 expressed confidence that the corps, by moving its camps to high, clean ground, could shake off the fever. Miles warned, however, that if the change of camps failed the Fifth Corps might have to go north, regardless of the danger of an epidemic. In reports to Washington and private letters to friends, Shafter's officers until the end of July gave little indication that their men were approaching physical collapse. Many of them, including Col. Theodore Roosevelt of the Rough Riders, described their troops as ready for further action and tried to have their units sent to Puerto Rico to join General Miles's campaign. No one pointed out to the authorities in Washington that malaria, not yellow fever, was sweeping the camps and that it was leaving the soldiers too weak to perform even routine fatigue duties. Unversed in the effects of malaria, War Department officials, in the absence of realistic reports from the field, did not foresee the collapse of the corps.[19]

Under the illusion that all was going well at Santiago, Secretary Alger began leisurely preparations for the eventual return of the Fifth Corps to the United States. He told Shafter on July 23 that the troops would start northward to rest and prepare for another campaign as soon as it seemed medically safe to move them. Shafter in reply expressed hearty approval of an early departure from Santiago, but he transmitted no sense of crisis and reported that his men were shifting camp to escape the fever. To replace Shafter's troops at Santiago, the War Department readied United States Volunteer infantry regiments for embarkation. Composed of men supposedly immune to yellow fever, these units had been intended from the beginning for tropical garrison duty. On July 28 Secretary Alger, on Surgeon General Sternberg's recommendation, selected 5,000 acres of rolling ground at Montauk Point, the eastern tip of Long Island, for the expedition's rest and recuperation camp. Army officers from New York City had chosen this site early in June. Well watered and breezy, it was remote enough from population centers for effective quarantine, and troops coming from Santiago could disembark there without passing through any of the port cities. The War Department initially planned a camp of modest size at Montauk, through which a few of Shafter's regiments at a time would be repatriated. On August 1, at Shafter's recommendation, the War Department ordered part of the dismounted cavalry division to sail for Montauk. If these troops remained free of yellow fever upon arrival, others could follow them.[20]

19. *Correspondence*, I, 142-43, 283, 303. *War Investigating Commission*, IV, 989, 993; VI, 3048; VII, 3771. Theodore Roosevelt to Secretary Alger, July 23, 1898; Alger to Roosevelt, August, 1898; Roosevelt to Charles W. Eliot, August 23, 1898, in Morison, *Roosevelt Letters*, II, 859-60, 869. Wheeler, *Santiago Campaign*, 205, 351, 354, 357-58, 364-65. Maj. Gen. William R. Shafter to Alger, July 13, 1898; Roosevelt to Alger, July 31, 1898; J. S. Farrar to Alger, August 1, 1898, Alger Papers. Brig. Gen. William Ludlow to Adj. Gen. Corbin, June 5, 1898, Box 1, Corbin Papers, expresses the early underestimation of the threat of malaria. Charles Dick to President McKinley, July 20, 1898, McKinley Papers.

20. *Correspondence*, I, 158, 167, 172-75, 184-85, 188-89, 196. *War Investigating Commission*, I, 215-16; III, 23; VI, 2465, 2842; VII, 3770, 3784-85. *RSW, 1898*, I, 785. Alger, *Spanish-American*

On August 2 the content of Shafter's dispatches abruptly changed; and so did War Department policy. On that day, Shafter reported that an epidemic of yellow fever was "liable to occur" and that to avoid it the corps should come north "as rapidly as possible while the sickness is of a mild type." On August 3, in a long telegram, he finally detailed the disintegration of his corps. The changes of camp, Shafter said, had not stamped out the fever; instead, they had exhausted men already weakened by malaria and left them susceptible to more dangerous ailments. Shafter at last admitted that about 75 per cent of his troops had had malaria and that the Fifth Corps had become "really an army of convalescents." Further changes of camp would be impossible because the men were too physically broken to march. A full-scale yellow fever epidemic had not yet started, Shafter said, but if one struck now, with the men weakened as they were, the death rate would be appalling. "In my opinion," he concluded, "there is but one course to take, and that is to immediately transport the Fifth Corps . . . to the United States. . . I am sustained in this view by every medical officer present."[21]

Secretary Alger responded without hesitation to his field commander's urgent plea. Immediately upon the arrival of Shafter's August 3 report, he authorized Shafter to send to Montauk all the troops he could spare from duty at Santiago. Additional orders on August 4 and 5 gave Shafter full control of all transports then in Santiago harbor and directed other vessels to him from Puerto Rico and from American ports.[22]

On August 3, before sending his long telegram to Washington, Shafter had called a council of his general officers and chief surgeons, at which he told them what he intended to do and asked for their support. His subordinates emphatically concurred in Shafter's judgment that the weakened troops must leave Cuba at once or die by the hundreds of yellow fever. All three division commanders and several of the brigadiers then drafted and signed a letter to Shafter in which they reiterated in blunt language the main points of the corps commander's telegram, and Shafter forwarded the document to Washington in support of his own dispatch. The corps and division chief surgeons prepared a similar message of their own to accompany Shafter's wire. Somehow, a copy of the generals' letter fell into the hands of an Associated Press correspondent at Shafter's headquarters, who at once wired its text to his bureau in the United States.[23]

War, 259-61. Wheeler, *Santiago Campaign*, 347-48. *Army and Navy Journal*, June 25, 1898. G. M. Dodge to Secretary Alger, undated, probably June or July, 1898, Alger Papers. Adj. Gen. Corbin to the Commanding General, Department of the East, May 15, 1898, File No. 80916; Brig. Gen. Royal T. Frank to Corbin, June 2, 1898, File No. 194225, AGO Records.

21. Shafter's August 3 telegram is in Alger, *Spanish-American War*, 263-64; see also 262. *Correspondence*, I, 194. Miley, *In Cuba*, 215-22. Leonard Wood to Secretary Alger, July 30, 1898, Alger Papers. Charles Dick to President McKinley, July 25, 1898. McKinley Papers.

22. Alger, *Spanish-American War*, 264-65. *Correspondence*, I, 201, 203-7.

23. Alger, *Spanish-American War*, 265-68, 271. Miley, *In Cuba*, 220-23. *RSW, 1898*, I, 823. Hagedorn, *Wood*, I, 201, quotes Wood's recollection that Shafter himself gave the reporter a copy of the letter.

On the morning of August 4, the text of the generals' letter—soon labeled the "Round Robin"—appeared on front pages across the nation. The Administration had kept secret the first reports of the condition of the Fifth Corps, so the "Round Robin" gave an astonished public its earliest detailed account of the pitiable state of the heroes of Santiago. Publication of the "Round Robin" embarrassed American diplomats, then in the midst of armistice talks with the Spaniards. It also discredited the War Department. The appearance of the "Round Robin" coincided with the Administration's announcement on August 4 that Shafter's troops would return home at once. Although McKinley and Alger had made that decision on the basis of Shafter's report, which reached Washington several hours before the "Round Robin," the conjunction of the two items in the newspapers convinced numbers of Americans that a callous government had left brave soldiers to sicken and die and had acted to save them only after the officers on the scene by-passed regular channels and carried their case through the press to the people.[24]

Shafter's alarming messages, combined with the "Round Robin" furor, stampeded McKinley and Alger into a serious mistake. On August 3 construction of the rest camp at Montauk Point barely had begun. The Administration should have postponed the embarkation of any large number of men at Santiago until the tents, hospitals, and other facilities for their reception were well on their way to completion. Shafter's troops, with additional medical aid from the United States, could have held out at Santiago for a week or two longer. However, in the hope that the camp at Montauk would be finished by the time the first transport dropped anchor off Long Island, the President and the Secretary allowed Shafter to start his men north at once.[25]

The first shipload of troops left Santiago on August 7; others followed as rapidly as the men could embark. To move his troops, Shafter used the eight vessels of his original fleet, which remained at Santiago, augmented by other transports sent from the United States and Puerto Rico. So great was the official sense of urgency about the evacuation that the War Department diverted to Santiago ships intended to carry regiments to Ponce and thus deprived Miles of part of his planned force. Day after day, weary, sick, but happy soldiers swarmed onto the home-bound steamers. Only the severely ill and the yellow fever suspects remained behind, complaining bitterly that they were being callously left to die in a strange land. (On the contrary, specially equipped transports brought most of them home before the end of August.) Fleeing the scene of its triumphs as though a military enemy pursued it, the Fifth Corps left behind its tents, wagons, ammunition, and

24. Alger, *Spanish-American War*, 265, 269-73. Mayo, *America of Yesterday*, 212. Olcott, *McKinley*, II, 81-82. *Army and Navy Journal*, August 13, 1898.

25. Chadwick, *Spanish-American War*, II, 259-61, argues that the panicky rush of the V Corps northward was not medically necessary.

heavy equipment. As Shafter's regiments departed, the immune United States Volunteers of the permanent garrison arrived, and the ships that brought them joined the evacuation fleet. The Spanish prisoners left Santiago at the same time as their late American antagonists. They sailed for Spain aboard vessels hired from a Spanish company by the War Department to take the soldiers home under the terms of the surrender agreement. By August 25 the entire corps had left Santiago for Montauk, and on that day General Shafter and his staff, among the last to go, boarded their transport.[26]

Meanwhile, work proceeded on the rest camp at Montauk. Officers from the headquarters of the Department of the East at New York City had negotiated the land-use contract early in June with the tract's owner, the Long Island Railroad Company. Representatives of the railroad and the Quartermaster's Department signed the final agreement on August 2, after a conference between Secretary Alger and the Long Island's president, Frank Baldwin. Under the agreement, the government leased about 5,000 acres of the railroad's land at Montauk until May 31, 1899, at a total rent of $15,000. The Army received free use of the company's docks, buildings, and other facilities on the site. The railroad agreed to install sidings, warehouses and terminals at the camp at its own expense, and in return, the Army agreed to use no other private carrier than the Long Island Railroad between New York City and the camp. The Quartermaster, Medical, and Subsistence departments at once sent officers to Montauk, contracted for lumber and construction materials, and began digging wells. On August 4 Secretary Alger placed Brig. Gen. Samuel B. M. Young, a Fifth Corps officer invalided home early in the campaign, in command of the camp. Young reached Montauk the next day. The railroad company sent trainloads of workmen and equipment to the site and started construction of four and one-half miles of new sidings, along with warehouses and station buildings. When completed, the installation, named Camp Wikoff after an officer killed at San Juan Hill, was to consist of a detention camp at which newly arrived regiments would be quarantined until proven free of yellow fever and a larger general camp where the troops would rest and recover their strength. Each camp was to contain a large hospital.[27]

26. *Correspondence*, I, 211-14, 216, 219-21, 224-26, 232-35, 237, 239-45, 248-49, 253, 255, 359-61, 382, 384, 395, 402. *War Investigating Commission*, VI, 2788-92. *RSW, 1898*, I, 393-95; *1899*, I, Pt. 2, pp. 521-22. Alger, *Spanish-American War*, 278-79. Miley, *In Cuba*, 228. Post, *Little War*, 291-96. Parker, *Gatling Gun Detachment*, 202-4. Wheeler, *Santiago Campaign*, 205, 267-69. Col. Charles Bird to the Quartermaster General, August 12, 1898, File No. 115533, OQMG Records. Lt. Col. Valary Harvard to the Surgeon General, August 24, 1898, in J. A. Porter to William C. McCloy, September 20, 1898, McKinley Papers.

27. *War Investigating Commission*, I, 217; III, 409, 415, 420; V, 1856-57, 1887-88, 1955-57; VI, 2465-67, 2474, 2478, 2761-62, 2783; VII, 3785-87; VIII, 592-96. *RSW, 1898*, I, 570-71, 829, 974. Alger, *Spanish-American War*, 425-26. GO 120, WD, August 15, 1898, *GO/AGO, 1898*.

Congestion at the railroad terminal, the late arrival of men and supplies, and strikes among the Army's hired laborers slowed the construction
of hospitals, warehouses, and floored tents for the soldiers. The Quartermaster's Department required several weeks to collect sufficient wagons for
the camp, and the resulting transportation shortage further retarded progress. On August 8, compounding the confusion, 3,500 cavalrymen and
over 5,000 horses and mules, detachments and mounts of the cavalry division at Santiago left behind in Florida in June for lack of shipping, descended
on the camp. The War Department had ordered them up from Tampa to
escape a typhoid outbreak and in the mistaken belief that they could help
in preparing Camp Wikoff. Actually, their trains blocked the sidings and
delayed the arrival of building materials, construction crews, and camp staff.
To compound the confusion, most of the troops reached Montauk ahead
of their tents and baggage.[28]

When the regiments from Santiago began disembarking on August 14
after a voyage that was comfortable on some transports and miserable on
others, they found no facilities ready for them. The emaciated, exhausted
soldiers stumbled ashore into a welter of confusion. They slept on the ground
in tents that lacked floors and bedding. Sometimes they endured for days
on short rations. In the half-completed, understaffed hospitals, sick men
went untended for twenty-four hours at a time. They lay on blankets on
the grass while workmen hammered, sawed, and pounded around them.[29]

Nevertheless, the War Department was striving vigorously to put Camp
Wikoff in order. When Maj. Gen. Joseph Wheeler, second in command of
the Fifth Corps, landed at Montauk on August 15, President McKinley placed
him in charge of the camp and authorized him to do everything he thought
necessary to make the soldiers comfortable. Wheeler remained in command
until General Shafter arrived early in September. He made free use of his
authority, purchasing tons of special foods for sick men and convalescents
and hiring additional doctors and nurses for the hospitals. He also had a
steam laundry and a bakery installed in the camp. Secretary Alger visited
Camp Wikoff on August 24 and again at the end of the month. He untangled
conflicts of authority and ordered extra issues of clothing and supplies to

28. *War Investigating Commission*, I, 133; III, 19-20, 409, 415; V, 1794-96, 1892-93, 1957-58;
VI, 2467-68, 2635-36, 2763-64, 2783-85; VII, 3278-79, 3770-71. *RSW, 1898*, I, 571, 829-31, 837;
II, 208. Alger, *Spanish-American War*, 261-62, 424-25. Bellinger, Tampa Report, File No. 115533,
OQMG Records. Maj. Gen. S. B. M. Young to Col. Frank J. Hecker, and Hecker to Young, un-
dated notes in Hecker Papers.

29. *Correspondence*, I, 225, 227-29, 241-42. *War Investigating Commission*, III, 400-401, 413,
415-16, 420-21, 606, 624-25; IV, 769-70, 805-6, 1208, 1225, 1273, 1282, 1473-74, 1479, 1487, 1514,
1521-22; V, 2010, 2013-14, 2403. *RSW, 1898*, I, 572, 840, 842, 848. Parker, *Gatling Gun Detachment*, 215. Post, *Little War*, 309-24. "Barbarism at Montauk," *Harper's Weekly*, XLII, 890.
W. A. Rogers, "Camp Wikoff," *Harper's Weekly*, XLII, 890. Theodore Roosevelt to Henry Cabot
Lodge, September 4, 1898, *Roosevelt-Lodge Correspondence*, I, 341.

the troops. Further to dramatize the Administration's concern, President McKinley and Surgeon General Sternberg toured the camp. The Quartermaster's Department chartered steamers to move men and stores to and from New York City, piped running water to every regiment, and sent in vast quantities of tentage, clothing, and other material. Surgeon General Sternberg authorized his subordinates at Wikoff to hire extra doctors and nurses when they needed them and to draw supplies directly from the medical depot at New York without first sending their requisitions to Washington for his approval. Private relief societies and local citizens, aroused by reports of the soldiers' suffering, established diet kitchens and recreation tents, overran the camp with volunteer workers, and donated tens of thousands of dollars and tons of food, liquor, and other articles for the comfort and convenience of the soldiers.[30]

Under these determined if disordered ministrations, conditions at Camp Wikoff slowly improved. The Medical Department enlarged its hospital facilities and brought in scores of contract surgeons and about 300 female nurses. Regiments that arrived from Santiago after the middle of August found tents ready for them and water piped to their company streets. So many soldiers gorged on rich foods furnished by the private relief agencies that many did not even bother to draw their regular Army rations.[31]

Abuses continued to plague Camp Wikoff throughout its existence. Traffic on the Long Island Railroad, which was operating twice its normal number of trains per day, remained slow and congested. There never seemed to be enough wagons at the camp's sidings, so supplies piled up at the railroad depot for lack of vehicles to move them. The hospitals, which treated over 10,000 patients in thirty days could not entirely overcome their initial confusion. Complaints—usually justified—of overcrowding, lax administration, incompetent attendants, and unsanitary conditions came from them throughout their harassed existence. Quarantine regulations collapsed completely. In camps and hospitals, officers, enlisted men, patients, and visitors mingled freely in cheerful disregard of the possibility of contagion. A War Department order of August 9 that allowed surgeons to furlough convalescents to their homes produced trouble and heartbreak. In trying to relieve their overcrowded wards, surgeons at Montauk sent hundreds of men off prematurely, and sick, sometimes dying, stragglers from Camp

30. *War Investigating Commission*, I, 218-19, 443, 553; III, 18, 49-50, 55, 409, 616; V, 1698, 1892, 1930, 2036, 2146, 2283, 2345-48; VI, 2776, 2784. *RSW, 1898*, I, 177, 389, 392, 573-74, 693, 831, 833, 839, 842-43, 848-49. *Correspondence*, I, 256. Alger, *Spanish-American War*, 425-29. Post, *Little War*, 324-25, 327-29. Wheeler, *Santiago Campaign*, 206, 208-12, 219-21. *Army and Navy Journal*, September 10, 1898. Maj. Gen. Joseph Wheeler to Secretary Alger, August 28, 1898, Alger Papers.

31. *War Investigating Commission*, III, 608, 621-24, 645, 746-47, 766-67; IV, 1226, 1480, 1495; V, 1896, 1901-2, 1930, 2224. *RSW, 1898*, I, 706-7, 832-33, 838, 840-41, 846-47, 849. *Army and Navy Journal*, September 10, 1898. Roosevelt, *Rough Riders*, 220.

Wikoff collapsed in passenger cars and railroad stations all across Long Island. An atmosphere of noise, confusion, and indiscipline permeated the whole camp. Relatives who visited it in search of sick or convalescent soldiers could not even find signs to direct them to the various brigades and divisions.[32]

In late August and early September, the Volunteer regiments of the Fifth Corps left for their home states on furloughs, at the end of which they were to be mustered out of the Army. The Regular units also began to return to the posts they had left when mobilized in April. To end the scandal of sick soldiers dropping in streets and on station platforms, Asst. Surg. Gen. Charles R. Greenleaf early in September established a medical examining board at each Montauk hospital. The boards examined each convalescent who applied for furlough and granted leave only to men deemed well enough to travel. At the same time, surgeons transferred over 1,000 of the camp's sick to hospitals in New York, Boston, Philadelphia, Providence, and other northeastern cities. The shelter and care afforded patients who remained at Montauk improved radically. By September 23 only seven Regular regiments remained at Camp Wikoff, and the hospitals were emptying rapidly. On October 3 General Shafter announced the formal disbanding of the Fifth Corps. Twenty-five days later, the last unit, a Volunteer signal company, left the now empty dunes of Montauk. From first to last, about 21,000 soldiers had passed through Camp Wikoff. They left behind 257 dead, most of them victims of disease. The survivors recovered at least partially from the ravages of their Santiago ordeal.[33]

Through a mixture of scientific ignorance, misunderstanding between the field commander and his superiors in Washington, and poor distribution of responsibility, the War Department had bungled the return of Shafter's troops to the United States. Well publicized, the failure left scandal and bitterness in its wake. The "Round Robin" affair had set off a wave of public apprehension about Army management, and reports from Camp Wikoff transformed apprehension into indignation. Montauk lay close enough to New York City for scores of newspapermen and hundreds of relief workers

32. *War Investigating Commission*, I, 131, 183, 219; III, 24-25; IV, 1510-12; V, 1691-94, 1794-95, 1889-91, 1895-96, 2009, 2037, 2044-48, 2050-51, 2071-73, 2075-78, 2133-42, 2189-90, 2222-23, 2225-26, 2247, 2250, 2255, 2289-90, 2342-43, 2351-52; VI, 2447, 2449, 2451-52, 2470-73, 2491, 2499-2500, 2502, 2570, 2650-51. *RSW, 1898*, I, 707-8, 832. GO 114, HQA, August 9, 1898, *GO/AGO, 1898*. Col. F. J. Hecker to Secretary Alger, undated, Hecker Papers. Mrs. Louise E. Hogan to George B. Cortelyou, October 29, 1898, McKinley Papers.

33. *War Investigating Commission*, I, 219; IV, 1274; V, 1894-95. *RSW, 1898*, I, 832-34, 839, 846-47, 849-50. *Correspondence*, I, 257. *Army and Navy Journal*, September 24, October 8, and November 5, 1898. Roosevelt, *Rough Riders*, 228-29. Wheeler, *Santiago Campaign*, 212-13, 222-27. Chief Signal Officer Greely to Lt. Col. Montgomery, August 19, 1898, Box 1A, Corbin Papers. Dr. John W. Brauman to J. Addison Porter, September 10, 1898, McKinley Papers. GO 137, WD, September 5, 1898; GO 143, HQA, September 14, 1898; GO 146, HQA, September 17, 1898, *GO/AGO, 1898*.

and ordinary citizens to visit it. These observers brought back shocking tales of suffering, neglect, and incompetence. One seasoned worker among the disadvantaged burst into tears when he tried to describe camp conditions to a meeting of his organization. Under instructions from partisan editors, some journalists exaggerated Camp Wikoff's deficiencies and played down the government's efforts to remedy them, but the truth was damaging enough to the War Department. In spite of reassuring statements from General Wheeler and others in authority that everything possible was being done for the soldiers, thousands of citizens who visited or read about Camp Wikoff formed the unshakable conviction that men who had risked all for their country had been betrayed by those in power. Events in the great Volunteer camps provided further evidence to support this belief.[34]

IV

Of the more than 200,000 Volunteers called out in April and May, no more than 35,000 left the country or were even assigned to expeditions before the armistice in August. Political favoritism influenced the selection of regiments for the few front line assignments. The two Volunteer brigades sent to the Caribbean from Camp Alger, for example, included Ohio and Michigan regiments in which President McKinley and Secretary Alger had personal interest. After the fall of Santiago and the opening of armistice talks had indicated the hardest fighting had ended, Volunteer officers, assisted by politicians from their home states, campaigned vigorously for active duty for their units. Senators, congressmen, and governors deluged the War Department with pleas on behalf of innumerable regiments, batteries, and battalions, urging that they be sent to Puerto Rico or Manila. Secretary Alger tried to give each state some political recognition. He reinforced Miles and Merritt with regiments from states that were not yet represented at the front. On August 2 he ordered the formation of a special, oversized division for service in Puerto Rico. The dispatch of this division, composed of eighteen regiments from all the assembly camps, would have mollified the states that were still unsatisfied, but reports from General Miles that he required no more troops and the need for ships to evacuate the Fifth Corps from Santiago forced cancellation of this project.[35]

34. Alger, *Spanish-American War*, 430-31, 447-48. Wheeler, *Santiago Campaign*, 213-19. *War Investigating Commission*, III, 401; V, 1653, 1900-1902, 2349. J. H. Ladew to President McKinley, August 30, 1898, McKinley Papers. *Army and Navy Journal*, September 10, 1898. For examples of popular reporting on Camp Wikoff, see: "Barbarism at Montauk," *Harper's Weekly*, XLII, 890; and Rogers, *Harper's Weekly*, XLII, 890.

35. Alger, *Spanish-American War*, 19. *Correspondence*, I, 308, 311, 323-24, 329-32, 336, 339-40, 343, 345-49, 351, 353-57, 362-63, 370, 377; II, 728, 734-35, 740-41, 743-44, 747, 749, 752-55. Frederick D. Grant to Secretary Alger, August 6, 1898; Mrs. Ida H. Grant to Alger, August 14, 1898, Alger Papers. John J. McCook to Maj. Gen. James H. Wilson, July 19, 1898, Box 15, Wilson Papers. Two-thirds of the Volunteer units raised never left the country, even for occupation duty; see *Correspondence*, I, 538-628.

The rest of the Volunteers sat out the war in camp, most of them at Chickamauga, Camp Alger, Jacksonville, and Tampa. They spent many hours at target practice, company, battalion, regimental, and brigade drills, and at Camp Thomas, in large-scale combat maneuvers. Policing and maintenance of the camps also occupied some of their time, but not enough, as it developed. In their free hours, the troops visited nearby cities on passes (Chattanooga for Camp Thomas, Washington, D.C., for Camp Alger), attended shows and revival meetings in camp, and set up regimental canteens that dispensed beer and other refreshments. Camps Thomas and Alger soon acquired a dirty fringe of fly-by-night saloons, greasy restaurants, gambling dens, and bordellos. A burlesque theater held forth on the edge of Camp Alger until the corps commander, disgusted by its "immoral exhibitions," ordered it closed.[36]

The Volunteers endured in these camps many of the shortages and hardships of a field campaign. The War Department deliberately withheld from them such amenities as board floors for their tents, on the theory that the soldiers needed toughening for field service. The slow manufacture and delivery of many items and the priority given issues to the Fifth and Eight corps left the great Volunteer concentrations short of clothing, arms, tents, camp equipment, and cooking gear until well into July. At Chickamauga and Camp Alger, the quartermasters lacked wagons to haul their stores from the railroad terminals. In the same camps, a tent shortage forced six or eight soldiers to sleep in shelters designed for four. For weeks, at Jacksonville, men ate with their fingers and used shingles and pieces of board for plates because of delays in the arrival of tin plates, knives, and forks. Supplies gradually dribbled into the depots, and camp staff worked long hours distributing them. By the time all the men had received their first issues of clothing and equipment, the original equipment had begun to break and wear out, and the incoming shipments barely sufficed for replacements. Except for the Subsistence Department, which maintained lavish stock piles, all the supply bureaus in the camps issued material as rapidly as it arrived. Under this policy, they found it impossible to accumulate reserves.[37]

36. *War Investigating Commission*, I, 208; V, 1759; VI, 3101. *Correspondence*, I, 530. GO 84, HQA, June 29, 1898, *GO/AGO, 1898*. Acting Insp. Gen. J. P. Sanger to Secretary Alger, June 3, 1898, File No. 88310; Lt. Col. Frank D. Baldwin to the Adjutant General, Camp Thomas, August 20, 1898, File No. 174154; Asst. Adj. Gen. J. C. Gilmore to Adj. Gen. Corbin, May 3, 1898, File No. 192302, AGO Records. Creagher, *Fourteenth Ohio*, 101-9. *National Relief Commission*, 100-101. *The New York Times*, May 26, 1898.

37. *War Investigating Commission*, I, 119-20; II, 805-6, 808; III, 127, 129, 231, 336-39, 721-22; IV, 883-84, 940-41, 1238; V, 1769-70; VI, 2654, 2717, 2864, 3067; VII, 3150-52; VIII, 302. *RSW, 1898*, I, 700; II, 653. Maj. Gen. J. R. Brooke to Adj. Gen. Corbin, June 17, 1898, File No. 96332; Brooke to Corbin, July 13, 1898, File No. 102388; Brooke to Corbin, June 24 and July 1, 1898, File No. 159902; Brooke to Corbin, July 7, 1898, File No. 159948; Maj. Gen. W. M. Graham to Corbin, June 7, 1898, File No. 160143, AGO Records. Col. J. G. C. Lee to the Quartermaster General, September 11, 1898, File No. 115533, OQMG Records. Holbrook, *Minnesota in the War*, 75. *National Relief Commission*, 99-100. Hugh L. Scott to Mrs. Scott, July 11, 1898, Box 1, Scott Papers.

Observers commented with distaste on the pervasive filthiness of Camps Thomas and Alger. The noisome conditions had several causes. As a result of the supply shortage, the soldiers lacked shovels with which to dig latrines and refuse pits; they had no disinfectants to control germ-bearing insects; and they had no kettles in which to boil drinking water. In both camps, the Regular commanders, disregarding the well-established rule that troops in the field must be widely dispersed for proper sanitation, packed too many men into too few acres of ground. Regiments often dug latrines and garbage pits within yards of their kitchens, hospitals, and living quarters. At Camp Thomas, a stratum of limestone less than two feet below the surface of the ground prevented the digging of sinks deep enough for the absorption of their contents. In rainy weather, the shallow pits flooded and overflowed, sluicing sewage through the camps. In spite of the drilling of scores of wells, both camps suffered from water shortages. The soldiers, with barely enough water for cooking and drinking, were unable to wash frequently. At Camp Alger, troops had to march seven miles to the Potomac River and back for their weekly baths. Above all, through their carelessness and indiscipline, the Volunteers polluted the camps. Regimental and company officers failed to enforce regulations controlling the use and maintenance of latrines and neglected the disposal of refuse, and higher commanders made little effort to end such slackness. In many regiments, the men threw garbage on the ground near their tents and defecated in the surrounding woods. Near the camp of the Third United States Volunteer Cavalry at Chickamauga, a board of inspecting officers reported, "It was quite impossible to walk through the woods . . . without soiling one's feet with fecal matter."[38]

Conditions were better in the smaller camps at Tampa, San Francisco, and Jacksonville. At Tampa, the experienced Regulars kept their tents strictly policed. They camped on sandy ground that absorbed liquid waste and dried quickly after rains, and they had ample water, piped from the city. Only the intense summer heat and constant, heavy rains rendered Tampa undesirable as a permanent camp. At San Francisco, the Eighth Corps encamped on dry ground and had sufficient water, but their principal camp,

38. The quotation is from *Reed Report*, 184; see also 179-81, 187, 221. *War Investigating Commission*, I, 207-10; II, 773-74; III, 214-16, 218-21, 226, 260-61, 701-2; IV, 854, 962-63, 1109, 1117, 1142, 1248, 1284, 1401; V, 1737, 1743, 1759-60; VIII, 254-56. *RSW, 1898*, I, 698-700, 742, 748-50, 757, 761-62; II, 645. Dunham, *Review of Reviews*, XVIII, 415-27. Latshaw, "Medical Service," 118-19. Parker, *Gatling Gun Detachment*, 175-78, details the sanitation violations committed by a Volunteer regiment at Santiago. Unsigned copy of report of Board of Officers to Adj. Gen. Corbin, June 2, 1898, File No. 88156; W. M. Beckner to A. S. Berry, June 9, 1898, File No. 92556; H. V. Boynton to Hon. John H. Tweedale, August 6, 1898, File No. 110114; Maj. Gen. J. R. Brooke to Corbin, September 8, 1898, File No. 128803; Maj. Gen. W. M. Graham to Corbin, June 7, 1898, File No. 160143; Maj. James Parker to the Adj. Gen., Camp Thomas, August 19, 1898, Lt. Col. Frank D. Baldwin to the Adj. Gen., Camp Thomas, August 20, 1898, File No. 174154, AGO Records. Col. J. G. C. Lee to the Quartermaster General, September 11, 1898, File No. 115533, OQMG Records. Hugh L. Scott to Mrs. Scott, August 11, 1898, Box 1, Scott Papers. H. V. Boynton to Brooke, September 17, 1898, and to Maj. Gen. James H. Wilson, October 1 and 13, 1898, Box 4, Wilson Papers.

located on the seaward outskirts of the city, was too crowded, and cold ocean breezes frequently brought in dense fog and clouds of blowing sand. Near Jacksonville, Maj. Gen. Fitzhugh Lee and his 30,000 men of the Seventh Corps erected what was by 1898 standards a model assembly camp. By choosing the ground himself, Lee established his troops on sandy, absorbent soil, close to Jacksonville's rail terminals, lumber yards, and commercial facilities. A Civil War veteran who was experienced in commanding large formations, he kept his staff busy and harmonious and enforced strict sanitation. He had running water from the city's system piped to each of his regiments and purchased in Jacksonville lumber and fittings for bath houses, hospitals, and tent floors. While other camps deteriorated to squalor and confusion, Lee's troops stayed at Jacksonville in relative comfort and trained for the attack on Havana that was never launched.[39]

With the opening of peace talks in July and the signing of the armistice in August, discipline and morale among the Volunteers began to break down. Men who had been keyed up all summer by the prospect of action, agitated by repeated rumors of movement, and sometimes marched to the railroad stations and back again under conflicting orders felt betrayed by the sudden, anticlimactic end of the war. The government that had called them out and imposed hardships upon them had, after all, no need for them. A Regular on the staff at Camp Thomas wrote: "Everybody is disgusted after working in the most enthusiastic way for over two months to have it all go for nothing. . . . The enthusiasm has gone out of this army and they all want to go home." Bored, homesick soldiers refused to obey orders, insulted their officers, and even struck them. An Illinois regiment mutinied at Camp Thomas. Hundreds of Volunteers brawled en masse at San Francisco. In Washington and Jacksonville, drunken soldiers on leave rioted in the streets. Volunteers circulated petitions and wrote letters to congressmen and home-town newspapers demanding the discharge of their regiments.[40]

From the first days of mobilization, troop commanders and medical officers had watched apprehensively for the appearance of typhoid in these great concentrations. They recalled its ravages in Civil War armies, and the well-informed among them knew that typhoid had felled almost 10 per cent of the Prussian army during the war of 1870-1871. From Civil War

39. *War Investigating Commission*, I, 211-12, 214-15; III, 8, 81, 90-92, 94, 109-10, 313, 340, 447; VI, 3026. *RSW, 1898*, II, 223. Funston, *Memories*, 160-61. *Army and Navy Journal*, May 28 and September 24, 1898. *The New York Times*, June 1 and 23, 1898. Brig. Gen. William Ludlow to Adj. Gen. Corbin, May 11, 1898, Box 1, Corbin Papers. Secretary Alger to Maj. Gen. Miles, June 13, 1898, File No. 89369, AGO Records.

40. The quotation is from Hugh L. Scott to Mrs. Scott, August 4, 1898; see also Scott to Mrs. Scott, July 29 and August 7, 1898, Box 1, Scott Papers. *War Investigating Commission*, IV, 850, 1109, 1121. *RSW, 1898*, II, 462. Creagher, *Fourteenth Ohio*, 92, 109-10. *National Relief Commission*, 106-7. *Army and Navy Journal*, July 30 and September 10, 1898. Maj. Gen. J. C. Breckinridge to Adj. Gen. Corbin, October 20, 1898, File No. 174154, AGO Records. Members of the 1st Ohio Volunteer Cavalry to President McKinley, August 31, 1898, McKinley Papers.

Courtesy National Archives

*Major General
Grenville M. Dodge,
U.S. Volunteers.
(Photo probably
earlier than 1898)*

Courtesy National Archives

Secretary of War Alger tours Camp Wikoff.

Courtesy USAMHI
*Dentistry in
Camp Thomas.*

Courtesy USAMHI

Washday in Camp Thomas.

experience, they expected the Volunteers to neglect sanitation and thus make themselves dangerously vulnerable to the scourge. Yet for the first two and one-half months of war, the new Army seemed surprisingly, gratifyingly healthy, in spite of camp hardships. Sick rates remained low—less than 6 per cent of the total strength at Camp Thomas — and few typhoid cases appeared. Many officials expressed confidence that the Army would avoid a major epidemic, but a few experienced surgeons warned that poor sanitation would bring an increase in sickness.[41]

Much of the optimism of June and early July in fact rested on a false basis. Typhoid outbreaks follow a seasonal cycle, rare in spring but more frequent and deadly during the middle and late summer. The troops had yet to pass through the season of greatest danger. Then, too, more typhoid existed in the camps than the surgeons realized. They had made the mistake, all too common in medical practice at the time, of diagnosing many of the first typhoid cases as malaria or other mild fevers. Investigators later concluded that almost every regiment brought to camp a few men who were infected with typhoid. Many had the disease in its incubatory stage, when none of its symptoms were evident. Before falling sick themselves, they scattered typhoid bacteria through kitchens, tents, and latrines. Flies, poor sanitation, and the lack of disinfectants did the rest; the germs, once deposited, lived and remained dangerous for a long time. When the doctors at last realized the disease was upon them, no real chance remained of checking its spread.[42]

Beginning in late July, typhoid cases increased the sick rate in every camp. An officer wrote from Camp Thomas on August 4: "The typhoid fever is getting very bad. There are 300 cases in this Division and a thousand men on the sick report. The other troops are worse off yet." In fact, the number of sick at Camp Thomas grew from about 2,200 on July 25 to 3,600 on August 8 and 4,400 on August 15. Every large camp suffered severely, although Jacksonville, with better sanitation, felt the full fury of the epidemic later than did the other concentrations. Regiments quartered in their home states underwent small epidemics of their own.[43]

41. *War Investigating Commission*, I, 612-14; VI, 3069; VII, 3360-61. *RSW, 1898*, I, 739-40, 750-51. Gibson, *Soldier in White*, 195-96. *National Relief Commission*, 75. *Reed Report*, 211-12. Report of board of officers to The Adjutant General, June 2, 1898, File No. 88156. Surgeon General Sternberg to Adj. Gen. Corbin, July 15, 1898, File No. 98439, AGO Records. C. D. Shelton to Chase S. Osborn, June 20, 1898, Osborn Papers. *The New York Times*, May 30, June 12 and 16, 1898.

42. *Reed Report*, 8-9, 167-75, 177-79, 181-86, 202-3, 210-11, 220, 228-30, 232-33. *RSW, 1898*, I, 698, 701; *1899*, I, Pt. 2, p. 558. *War Investigating Commission*, IV, 1117; VI, 2822. Alger, *Spanish-American War*, 448. Latshaw, "Medical Service," 120, 124.

43. The quotation is from Hugh L. Scott to Mrs. Scott, August 4, 1898; see also Scott to Mrs. Scott, August 11, 1898, Box 1, Scott Papers. *War Investigating Commission*, I, 208; III, 83, 225, 309, 319; IV, 1136-37; VII, 3275; VIII, 164-65. *RSW, 1898*, I, 713-14, 737, 757-58, 761, 771; II, 176-77, 208-9, 220. Alger, *Spanish-American War*, 448-50. Gibson, *Soldier in White*, 190. Maj. Gen. John J. Coppinger to Adj. Gen. Corbin, July 29, 1898, File No. 104623; Coppinger to Corbin, July 18, 1898, File No. 106275; President B. R. Cowan, Army and Navy League, to President McKinley, July 29, 1898, File No. 107022; Maj. James Parker to the Adj. Gen. of Camp Thomas, August 19, 1898, File No. 174154; Maj. Gen. J. C. Breckinridge to Corbin, August 23, 1898, File No. 196334; Breckinridge to Corbin, September 1, 1898, File No. 239473; Breckinridge to Corbin, August 19, 1898, File No. 242989, AGO Records.

At Camps Thomas and Alger, the division hospitals, plagued from the start by organizational disputes and equipment shortages, collapsed under the influx of patients. Their failure, as a medical officer put it, was that "of a frog to become an ox suddenly." Designed as traveling field hospitals that would send their worst cases to base hospitals, these installations, even fully manned and equipped, lacked the staff and the supplies to care for the severely ill. As the epidemic developed, surgeons in the division hospitals evacuated many of their typhoid patients to Army base hospitals or to civilian institutions. On July 28, however, with the general hospitals already overcrowded, Surgeon General Sternberg ordered that the sick be treated in the camps. In many ill-equipped division hospitals, this order resulted in jammed wards, inadequate care for patients, and shortages of cots, bedding, bedpans, medicines, and innumerable other necessities. At Camp Thomas, typhoid patients sometimes lay in their own filth for as long as twenty-four hours because the hospitals lacked clean linen with which to change their beds. At San Francisco, civilian hospitals took many of the sick from the Eighth Corps, and at Jacksonville, where the crisis came later, the resourceful General Lee used the delay to equip his hospitals lavishly. Yet, overcrowding characterized even the best Army hospitals.[44]

Once aware that a crisis existed, the Medical Department acted energetically to control it. Surgeon General Sternberg sent additional supplies and equipment, scores of contract doctors, and hundreds of female nurses to the division hospitals and transformed them into semi-permanent institutions for the treatment of the seriously ill. He gave his chief surgeons in the camps wide authority to purchase needed supplies in their localities. Both to relieve the camp installations and to receive casualties from the Caribbean, Sternberg late in July ordered the construction of a new 1,000-bed general hospital at Fort Monroe, Virginia, and on August 1 he ordered one of 750 beds erected at Camp Thomas. He also expanded six post hospitals into general hospitals. On August 10, at the suggestion of Commissary General Eagan, the War Department adopted a more efficient system for supplying special food to patients who could not digest the standard rations. The Red Cross and other private relief organizations, as they had in Cuba and at Montauk, sent surgeons, nurses, and supplies of their own to the camps, thereby furnishing welcome aid to the hard-pressed Army medics.[45]

44. The quotation is from Col. Dallas Bache, "The Place of the Female Nurse in the Army," *JMSI*, XXV, 34-15. *War Investigating Commission*, I, 181, 651, 713; II, 773-76; III, 84, 86, 264-65, 310, 320, 448-66, 489-90, 507-12, 703-4; IV, 1248, 1250, 1406-7, 1417-18, 1420-21, 1531, 1538; V, 1763; VI, 2986-87, 3000-3001; VII, 3372; VIII, 221, 254-56. *RSW, 1898*, I, 709-11, 745, 768-69; II, 177; *1899*, I, Pt. 2, p. 376. *National Relief Commission*, 68, 92-93, 159. Lt. Col. Frank D. Baldwin to the Adj. Gen., Camp Thomas, August 20, 1898, File No. 174154; Maj. Gen. J. C. Breckinridge to Adj. Gen. Corbin, August 19, 1898, File No. 242989, AGO Records. *Army and Navy Journal*, September 24, 1898.

45. *War Investigating Commission*, I, 181-82, 184, 553, 650, 653-56, 658, 687, 701, 730-31; III, 150-53, 264, 310-11, 316-17; VI, 2654, 2819, 2828, 2839, 2951; VII, 3169-70, 3180-81; VIII, 167-69. *RSW, 1898*, I, 710-11, 714-18, 724-25, 732. Latshaw, "Medical Service," 143-44. *Reed Report*, 3. George Kennan to J. Addison Porter, June 12, 1898, McKinley Papers. GO 116, WD, August 10, 1898; GO 136, WD, September 3, 1898, *GO/AGO, 1898*.

Besides dealing with the exigencies of the present, Sternberg tried to provide against future epidemics. On August 18 he commissioned a board of three medical officers, headed by Maj. Walter Reed, to visit and inspect the disease-ridden camps. Reed and his colleagues were to investigate sanitation methods and recommend improvements as well as to determine the exact causes of the outbreak and spread of typhoid. Sternberg hoped that the Reed board would close many of the existing gaps in medicine's knowledge of typhoid etiology, making easier and more certain the prevention of subsequent epidemics. Reed and his companions set out at once on their journey of inspection and research.[46]

Line commanders, urged on by peremptory orders from the War Department to secure "the commencement, continuance, . . . and practical accomplishment" of a camp cleanup, issued and enforced stringent new sanitary regulations. On August 2 Secretary Alger sent Major General Breckinridge, recently returned from Santiago, to restore order, hygiene, and morale at Camp Thomas, where the departure of General Brooke for Puerto Rico in July had left a condition close to anarchy. Breckinridge put crews to work deepening and disinfecting latrines, burning garbage, and cleaning up hospitals and camps. To revive morale and occupy the soldiers' time and energies, he organized parades, sports, and practice marches. Following the theory applied in Cuba, he ordered regiments to move their camps to fresh ground and to space their tents more widely. Maj. Gen. William M. Graham, commanding Camp Alger, took similar steps, as did General Lee at Jacksonville. Early in August, on orders from Secretary Alger, General Graham marched one of his divisions across country to a new campsite at Thoroughfare Gap, Virginia. The march turned into a fiasco. Heavy rains deluged the toiling column, alternating with hours of suffocating heat. A wagon train with provisions failed to arrive, so the men went supperless the first day out of their old camps. Stragglers from the poorly disciplined regiments committed thefts and acts of vandalism along the line of march, and enraged Virginia farmers descended on the War Department with claims for damages. The movement of the division reduced crowding at Camp Alger, but that was all that could be said for it.[47]

46. *RSW, 1899*, I, Pt. 2, p. 626. Alger, *Spanish-American War*, 415. Latshaw, "Medical Service," 115-17, 125.

47. The quotation is from GO 117, WD, August 10, 1898, *GO/AGO, 1898. War Investigating Commission*, III, 218, 221; IV, 1109, 1240-41, 1258, 1431; V, 1761, 1791. *RSW, 1898*, I, 731, 743, 771-72; II, 582-83, 653-54. *Army and Navy Journal*, August 27, 1898. Adj. Gen. Corbin to Commanding General at Camp Thomas, August 5, 1898, File No. 108493; Maj. James Parker to the Adj. Gen. at Camp Thomas, August 19, 1898, Maj. Gen. J. C. Breckinridge to Corbin, October 20, 1898, File No. 174154; Corbin to Breckinridge, August 7, 1898, File No. 192880; Breckinridge to Corbin, August 23, 1898, File No. 196334, AGO Records. Quartermaster Guy Howard to the Quartermaster General, September 20, 1898, File No. 115533, OQMG Records.

The march from Camp Alger formed part of a massive redeployment of the troops in the United States, designed to place them in healthful, comfortable new camps. Secretary of War Alger ordered the movements on the recommendations of surgeons and troop commanders and in response to political pressure from citizens who wanted their boys taken out of sites the press had labeled death traps. During July and August, the divisions of the Fourth Corps, minus a few regiments that had sailed for Puerto Rico, moved from Tampa to Fernandina in northeast Florida to escape rain, typhoid, and malaria. As part of the same movement, the cavalry detachments of the Fifth Corps made their disruptive descent upon Camp Wikoff. On August 2 the Secretary directed General Graham to transfer the Second Corps from Camp Alger and Thoroughfare Gap to a new site near Middletown in central Pennsylvania. A division of the First Corps had gone to Puerto Rico in July. On August 8 Alger instructed General Breckinridge to send one of that corps's remaining divisions from Camp Thomas to Lexington, Kentucky, and the other to Knoxville, Tennessee. Meanwhile, under direction from their local commanders, the troops at San Francisco moved to cleaner, more comfortable camp grounds. Extreme heat and clouds of mosquitoes rendered Fernandina unsatisfactory as a campsite; therefore, on August 11 Secretary Alger reassigned the Fourth Corps to Huntsville in northern Alabama. On August 28 he transferred the Third Corps from Camp Thomas to Anniston, Alabama. Of the large troop formations, only the Seventh Corps at Jacksonville remained in its original camp.[48]

In executing these troop movements, both the War Department and the field commanders made strenuous efforts to avoid a repetition of the chaos at Montauk. Boards of Army officers selected each new campground and contracted with the neighboring municipalities for piped water, terminal

48. *War Investigating Commission*, I, 213-14; II, 773-74; III, 240-41; IV, 1252; V, 1760-61, 1792; VII, 3274, 3355-75; VIII, 164-65, 246. *RSW, 1898*, I, 711-12; II, 176-77. *Correspondence*, I, 146, 519, 530, 534, 547. Alger, *Spanish-American War*, 417. *National Relief Commission*, 101. *Reed Report*, 100. *army and Navy Journal*, August 27, 1898. Brigade Surgeon Edward Martin to the Chief Surgeon, IV Corps, July 21, 1898, Maj. Gen. J. J. Coppinger to Adj. Gen. Corbin, July 21 and 29, 1898, File No. 104623; Coppinger to Corbin, July 15, 1898, Corbin to Coppinger, July 17, 1898, File No. 106275; L. B. Budinger to Corbin, August 1, 1898, File No. 109530; Clayton Wolcott to President McKinley, August 1, 1898, File No. 110180; Gov. W. O. Bradley to Corbin, August 10, 1898; J. S. Crawford and G. M. Curtis to Corbin, August 13, 1898, File No. 111290; Mrs. G. W. Lane to McKinley, August 20, 1898, File No. 115065; Margaret D. Adsit to McKinley, August 26, 1898, File No. 121361; Maj. James Parker to the Adj. Gen. at Camp Thomas, August 19, 1898, File No. 174154; Brig. Gen. L. A. Carpenter to the Adj. Gen. at Huntsville, Ala., September 10, 1898, File no. 147555; Corbin to Maj. Gen. Breckinridge, August 10, 1898, and memorandum, same date, signed by Corbin, File No. 192307; Brig. Gen. L. H. Carpenter to the Adj. Gen. at Fernandina, August 11, 1898, Coppinger to Corbin, August 17, 1898, Corbin to Coppinger, August 24, 1898, File No. 235978; Corbin to Breckinridge, August 22, 1898, File No. 242989, AGO Records. Bellinger, Tampa Report, File No. 115533, OQMG Records. Clem Studebaker to McKinley, July 19, 1898; John A. Porter to Secretary Alger, July 23, 1898, McKinley Papers.

facilities, and, in some places, structures for warehouses and hospitals. At the Middletown site, named Camp George Gordon Meade after the victor of Gettysburg, crews from the Pennsylvania Railroad worked closely with Army Engineers, drilling wells, installing pipelines and pumps, laying sidetrack, and erecting warehouses. Under instructions from Secretary Alger, commanders and their staffs preceded their men to the new camps. They supervised the preparations and delayed the movement of the main body of their troops until facilities were ready. The generals tried to have hospitals and supply depots stocked and in operation when the regiments arrived. All the units traveled by rail to their new camps. General Graham sent only one of his regiments per day from Camp Alger to Camp Meade, thus avoiding congestion and traffic jams at both ends of the journey. By mid-September, with no serious delays or blunders, all of the corps had occupied their new stations and left the old camps vacant except for cleanup details and a few hospitals still filled with typhoid patients.[49]

The camps that were occupied in late summer were markedly improved over those into which troops had moved earlier. With the exception of the Fourth Corps's temporary stopping point at Fernandina, all of them lay in high, rolling country, cool, dry, and healthful. They had ample pure water, usually piped from wells or city mains to the company streets. The Quartermaster's Department at the sites began flooring the soldiers' tents and furnished enough additional canvas to end overcrowding. Camp commanders, believing that congestion had contributed to disease and squalor, spaced their men's tents far apart and kept latrines and garbage dumps well away from kitchens and dining areas. They enforced strict cleanliness everywhere.[50]

49. *War Investigating Commission*, I, 212-13, 266; III, 240, 721; IV, 1131-32, 1329-30; V, 1792. *RSW, 1898*, I, 522-23, 743; II, 208, 225. *Correspondence*, I, 288-89, 510. *Army and Navy Journal*, August 6 and September 10, 1898. Hugh L. Scott to Mrs. Scott, August 23 and 28, 1898. Box 1; Mayor J. B. Simrall to Brig. Gen. Sanger, August 15, 1898, Special Orders No. 79, Headquarters of Camp George H. Thomas, August 18, 1898, Box 7, Scott Papers. Chief Quartermaster Guy Howard to the Quartermaster General, September 20, 1898, Bellinger, Tampa Report, File No.115533, OQMG Records. Adj. Gen. Corbin to Maj. Gen. J. C. Breckinridge, August 8, 1898, File No. 88326; Breckinridge to Corbin, August 17, 1898, File No. 117694; Col. Charles R. Greenleaf, Maj. George H. Hopkins, Maj. F. G. Hodgson, and 1st Lt. Edgar Jadwin to Corbin, June 14, 1898, File No. 121918; Brig. Gen. R. T. Frank to the Adjutant General of Camp Thomas, August 26, 1898, File No. 130705; Corbin to Chiefs of the Staff Bureaus, August 10, 1898, Corbin to Breckinridge, August 11 and 19, Breckinridge to Corbin, August 11, 16, and 19, 1898, File No. 192307; Chief Surgeon Girard to Surgeon General Sternberg. August 19, 1898, File No. 192892; Breckinridge to Corbin, August 21, 1898, File No. 242989; Maj. Gen. J. J. Coppinger to Corbin, August 13, 1898, File No. 235978; Maj. Gen. J. H. Wilson to Corbin, July 16, 1898, File No. 236362; Adj. Gen. Stewart of Pennsylvania to Secretary Alger, August 5, 1898, File No. 247950, AGO Records. For details of the troop movements, see the following, in AGO Records: I Corps, Files No. 88326, 117060, 174154, 192307, and 242989; II Corps, Files No. 192881, 192890, and 192892; IV Corps, File No. 235978.

50. *War Investigating Commission*, I, 129, 212-13, 220-21; III, 216, 222-23, 226, 242, 249-51, 724; V, 1723-24, 1792. *RSW, 1898*, I, 700; II, 482, 645, 662. *National Relief Commission*, 114-18, 156. Wilson, *Under the Old Flag*, II, 460-61. Brig. Gen. Robert H. Hall to the Adj. Gen., 2nd Division, IV Corps, September 10, 1898, File No. 147555, AGO Records.

Having been educated by bitter experience, everyone responsible for the well-being of the troops displayed a newly aroused concern with sanitation and medical facilities. Surgeon General Sternberg received regular reports on sanitation from corps chief surgeons, and corps and division commanders made frequent inspections of their camps and hospitals to seek out and correct even minor deficiencies. In the Volunteer regiments, the officers kept a closer watch on kitchens, garbage dumps, and latrines. At the suggestion of surgeons and line officers, Secretary Alger in September ordered regimental hospitals re-established. With their own staffs, ambulances, and tents, these installations could care for all the less severe cases and thus reduce the burden on the division hospitals. To expedite movement of necessary equipment, the Surgeon General allowed his chief surgeons to send supply requisitions directly to the depots instead of routing them first to Washington for his approval. This reform, along with the accumulation of larger stock piles of supplies, permitted the rapid and lavish equipment of the hospitals in the new camps. When the Third Division of the First Corps moved to Lexington from Camp Thomas, its entire division hospital, which was filled with typhoid patients, remained behind. At Lexington, the divisional surgeons enjoyed the gratifying experience of requisitioning and receiving promptly the outfit for a complete new hospital. Temporary staff and equipment shortages developed at some camps, but the filth, confusion, and lack of necessities that had plagued the troops in July and August did not recur.[51]

The health of the Army gradually improved. The disease mortality rate, which reached 5.89 men per 1,000 in September, dropped to 1.51 per 1,000 in November and had fallen to .71 per 1,000 by April of the following year. Army general hospitals early in December reported that, for the first time in many weeks, hundreds of their beds were empty. During all this time, Major Reed and his typhoid board traveled about, inspecting camps, interviewing troop commanders and surgeons, and studying the medical history of every typhoid-stricken unit. Their full report did not appear until 1904. When it did, it significantly extended the medical profession's knowledge of causes and spread of typhoid.[52]

The lessons learned and the administrative improvements made as a result of the epidemics could not palliate the fact that the Army in 1898 had suffered a shattering medical disaster. According to the Reed board, none of

51. *War Investigating Commission,* I, 181, 183, 654, 685; IV, 1115-16, 1119, 1139-40; VI, 2837. *RSW, 1898,* I, 189, 714, 732, 738-39. *National Relief Commission,* 115. *Army and Navy Journal,* August 27, 1898. GO 151, HQA, September 22, 1898; GO 178, HQA, November 8, 1898, *GO/AGO, 1898.* Asst. Adj. Gen., 3rd Division, I Corps, to Maj. J. D. Griffith, Chief Surgeon, 3rd Division, September 26, 1898; Griffith to Asst. Adj. Gen., 3rd Division, October 13, 1898, Box 7, Scott Papers. Lt. Col. A. C. Girard to Adj. Gen. Corbin, September 23, 1898, File No. 130677; Maj. John L. Phillips to the Adj. Gen., II Corps, October 13, 1898, File No. 138737, AGO Records.

52. *RSW, 1899,* I, Pt. 2, p. 626. *Alger, Spanish-American War,* 450-51. Latshaw, "Medical Service," 123-25. *Reed Report,* 6-9. *Army and Navy Journal,* December 3, 1898.

the measures taken against typhoid had been effective in halting its rampage. The disease simply burned itself out after attacking all the men susceptible to infection. Almost 21,000 soldiers contracted the disease, which struck over 90 per cent of the Volunteer regiments, and about 1,500 men died. Counting the victims of other ailments, around 2,500 officers and men perished of sickness during the short war, ten times the number killed in action. The United States Army was not alone in suffering mass losses from disease; other armies of the period also fell victim to typhoid and similar epidemic illnesses. The British in South Africa, for example, lost 5,800 soldiers to typhoid out of 31,000 who contracted the disease. Nevertheless, the spectacle of American boys suffering by the thousands and dying by the hundreds in camps on their own country's soil while under the care of their own government shocked and angered the public. The people demanded explanations the War Department could not give and impatiently rejected the excuses it offered.[53]

V

During the prewar months of preparation and during the first few weeks of mobilization, the War Department received much public praise for its vigorous, seemingly competent response to the international crisis. The editor of the *Army and Navy Journal* as late as June 4 extolled "the rapidity with which the emergencies have been met by the staff departments and other authorities."[54]

Beginning in June, however, the tone of public comment swiftly changed. Ordinary soldiers and their relatives, politicians, war correspondents, and editors soon mounted a campaign of criticism against the War Department. Initially they focused their attacks on discomfort and the shortages of equipment in the assembly camps. Then the correspondents at Santiago, led by the popular Richard Harding Davis, began cabling home blistering denunciations of General Shafter's tactics, supply management, and personal conduct. The "Round Robin," the Montauk debacle, and the typhoid epidemic lengthened the list of grievances against the War Department and increased the number and shrillness of its detractors.[55]

53. *RSW, 1898*, I, 273-74, 720-22; *1899*, I, Pt. 2, p. 16. *War Investigating Commission*, I, 266; III, 217. Alger, *Spanish-American War*, 417-18. Chadwick, *Spanish-American War*, II, 483. Gibson, *Soldier in White*, 190, 214-15. Latshaw, "Medical Service," 105, 115, 149. *Reed Report*, 185-86, 190-92.

54. *Army and Navy Journal*, June 4, 1898.

55. *Army and Navy Journal*, June 11 and July 23, 1898. *The New York Times*, May 28 and 30, June 2, 3, and 13, 1898. *Correspondence*, I, 106, 172. Alger, *Spanish-American War*, 281-83, 295. Dunham, *Review of Reviews*, XVIII, 415-27. Bennett L. Jackson, "The Army and the Press: from the American revolution through World War I" (Master's thesis, University of Wisconsin, 1963), 180-182. Kennan, *Campaigning in Cuba*, 225-36, joins the attack on Shafter. Leech, *Days of McKinley*, 297. Davis's blast at Shafter is printed in an unidentified newspaper clipping in folder

Disaffected Army officers fed a steady stream of facts and accusations to the civilian critics and sometimes used them to strike at enemies within the service. Long before the conflict with Spain, officers had made a habit of leaking to newspapers or to friendly politicians information that was derogatory to rivals and superiors. Tensions arising out of the war increased this divisive activity. Many of Shafter's subordinates at Santiago honestly doubted his fitness for command and believed him guilty of serious military blunders, and they let reporters know their feelings. Because the war was too limited in scope and duration to allow every officer a chance for action, rank, and distinction in the field, fierce competition developed for the few choice assignments. Officers who fared poorly were quick to denounce and undercut their more fortunate colleagues. West Point graduates, for instance, accused Secretary Alger of discriminating against them in assigning officers to important commands and of favoring men who had entered the service as Volunteers in the Civil War. (Most of this apparent discrimination resulted, in fact, from the way in which the officer corps had been reorganized after Appomattox and from Alger's and McKinley's adherence to seniority in distributing commands.) Concerned about rank and promotion, many officers looked forward in mutual suspicion to the inevitable postwar political battle over Army reorganization. Hugh L. Scott, a young staff officer at Camp Thomas, expressed the prevalent gloomy forebodings: "The Vols out here are getting their fences ready to get into the Regular Army when it is enlarged & we old fellows will go to the wall again. I wouldn't wonder if this war does not injure our promotion more than we can recover in our own life time by infiltration of Vols who have a pull." All of this military quarreling and backbiting contributed to the atmosphere of scandal and conflict that enveloped the War Department and the Army.[56]

marked "Shafter" in Box 1, Corbin Papers. See also Buffalo, N.Y., *Enquirer*, July 12, 1898, and *Chicago Interocean*, July 10, 1898, both clippings in 1898 Scrapbook, Box 10, Corbin Papers. Spencer Borden to President McKinley, August 22, 1898, McKinley Papers, expresses the widespread feeling that Shafter had blundered. Hugh L. Scott to Mrs. Scott, May 30, 1898, Box 1, Scott Papers. Files No. 88039, 88338, 88877, 89760, 96677, 96678, 98508, 106644, 110707, 114168, and 114405, AGO Records, contain samples of the complaints reaching the War Department.

A widespread but mistaken belief that disease in the camps resulted directly from poor food and clothing and from wrong choice of sites increased public bitterness against the War Department. For comment on this point, see: *RSW, 1898,* I, 647; *War Investigating Commission,* VII, 3599-3600; Parker, *Gatling Gun Detachment,* 193; Latshaw, "Medical Service," 119-20, 123; and *Reed Report,* 173-76, 220-21.

56. The quotation is from Hugh L. Scott to Mrs. Scott, August 18, 1898; see also Scott to Mrs. Scott, August 7, 1898, Box 1, Scott Papers. Maj. Gen. William R. Shafter to Adj. Gen. Corbin, August 16 and September 26, 1898, and August 22, 1900, Corbin to Brig. Gen. Theodore Schwan, October 19, 1899, Box 1; San Francisco *Evening Post,* June 24, 1898, clipping in 1898 Scrapbook, Box 10, Corbin Papers. New York *Evening Post,* August 3, 1898, clipping in Hecker Papers. Joseph Wheeler to President McKinley, October 16, 1899, McKinley Papers. Maj. Gen. John M. Schofield to Secretary of War Daniel S. Lamont, April 8, 1893, Box 57, Schofield Papers, complains of

Although politicians and editors of the Democratic opposition predictably led the assault on the War Department, by the end of August articulate citizens of all parties and most professions had joined the chorus of indignation. Even the clergy entered the field of military controversy. The pastor of the church attended by Vice-President Garrett A. Hobart denounced Secretary Alger in a sermon that caused the indignant Hobart to resign his membership in the congregation. The War Department, cried its enemies, had starved the soldiers; it had elevated incompetents to command who wasted their men's lives in botched battles; it had left the survivors to die miserably of disease in fly-infested, comfortless hospitals. Critics pointed to the bitter contrast between the clean efficiency of the Navy's war and the bloody squalor of the Army's. Americans who were traveling abroad, it was said, read with embarrassment the foreign press's accounts of their Army's miserable failure.[57]

Examination of the records shows that much of the indictment of Army mismanagement was distorted and overdrawn. Civilians indoctrinated in a romantic view of war blamed its grim realities on mistakes by those in charge. Soldiers, when they found that the perennial camp complaints drew an interested audience, responded with tall tales of horror and hardship. The newspapers sent few reporters to cover the relatively well managed Puerto Rico and Manila operations. They concentrated on the difficulties at Santiago and by doing so presented to the public only a partial and prejudiced description of the Army's efforts. Correspondents in the field often spread camp rumor as fact and vilified officers whom they disliked. The tactless Shafter quarreled with many reporters and suffered, as a result, from savagely hostile coverage in important journals. The War Department made no systematic effort to inform the people about its problems of mobilization and supply, and the newspapers devoted little space to those matters.[58]

---

prewar leaks to the press. Robert H. Hall to Maj. Gen. James H. Wilson, December 22, 1898, Box 11; Gen. J. P. Sanger to Wilson, March 7, 1900, Box 22; Wilson to Col. John J. McCook, December 10, 1898, to F. M. Kelley, December 19, 1898, to Maj. Campbell E. McMichael, December 21, 1898, and to Col. Bluford Wilson, December 22, 1898, Box 43; Wilson to Col. Bluford Wilson, July 18, 1899, Box 44, Wilson Papers. *Army and Navy Journal*, June 11, 18, and 25, 1898. Wilson, *Under the Old Flag*, II, 415-16, 418-19. For expressions of lack of confidence in Shafter, see: Rutherford Corbin to Adj. Gen. Corbin, July 7, 1898, Box 1A, Corbin Papers; J. F. Weston to Maj. Gen. James H. Wilson, June 7 and October 22, 1898, Box 26, Wilson Papers; and Col. Leonard Wood to Mrs. Wood, July 15, 1898, Box 190, Wood Papers.

57. Alger, *Spanish-American War*, 433-36, describes the Hobart incident, along with other attacks on the War Department. Gibson, *Soldier in White*, 197-99. Leech, *Days of McKinley*, 305. *Army and Navy Journal*, October 1, 1898. Examples of press attacks on the War Department abound in the 1898 Scrapbook, Box 10, Corbin Papers. Rowland Snelling to C. S. Osborn, May 11, 1899, Osborn Papers, expresses a foreign view of the Army scandals. John J. McCook to Maj. Gen. James H. Wilson, August 11, 1898, Box 15, Wilson Papers.

58. Jackson, "Army and Press," 166-78, 182-85, 187, 191, 197-98, analyzes the quality of war reporting and the Army's information policies, or the lack thereof. Alger, *Spanish-American War*, 423. Gibson, *Soldier in White*, 217. Johnson, *Unregimented General*, 245, recounts Army troubles with the press during the Indian wars. Sexton, *Soldiers in the Sun*, 79-81. *War Investigating Commission*, III, 317, 345-46; VII, 3299. *Correspondence*, I, 176-77; II, 834. *Army and Navy Journal*, August 13, September 17, and October 1, 1898, July 22, 1899.

Although much of the criticism of the Army can be written off as distortion, falsification, and exaggeration, much was certainly wrong in the Army's administration. The question was not whether mistakes and abuses had occurred but, rather, whether all or most of them could be, in fairness, blamed on dishonesty or incompetence in the War Department. The record points away from this simple method of accounting for the tragedies at Santiago, Montauk, and the Volunteer camps. Certainly no official, from McKinley and Alger down, had made every decision correctly or anticipated every possible contingency, but neither had anyone cynically neglected his duties or deliberately betrayed the public trust. The complex, fluctuating political and military circumstances of the conflict, the deficiencies of an as yet primitive medical science, and a generation of public and congressional neglect of the Army were the principal causes of the war's waste and disorder. A national debate on military policy and organization was much needed.

The nation was treated instead to a search for scapegoats. The people, impatient with the details of staff organization and Army administration, wanted villains identified and punished, and the politicians and editors set to work to meet the demand. New York State, where Theodore Roosevelt was running for governor on his Santiago battle record, typified the popular mood. "Taking it as a whole," the candidate wrote of the voters, "New York cares very little for the war now that it is over, except that it would like to punish somebody because the Republican administration did not handle the War Department well."[59]

The scapegoat-hunters quickly selected Secretary Alger as villain-in-chief. As early as May 18, *The New York Times* had called for his removal and had urged President McKinley to replace him with a "serious" Secretary of War. The *Times* repeated its demand at regular intervals, and gradually newspapers and politicians of both parties took it up. By September Alger had become so unpopular throughout the country that Republican candidates, fearing defeat in the fall elections, pleaded with McKinley to remove the Michigan albatross from the party's collective neck. In the popular vocabulary of the day, the word "Algerism" emerged as a synonym for

59. The quotation is from Theodore Roosevelt to Henry Cabot Lodge, October 16, 1898, in *Roosevelt-Lodge Correspondence*, I, 356-57; see also 310. For examples of the search for scapegoats, see the following: Alger, *Spanish-American War*, 432-33. Gibson, *Soldier in White*, 192-93, 200-204. Dunham, *Review of Reviews*, XVIII, 415-27. "How to Do It and How Not to Do It," *The Nation*, LXVII, 196. Morgan, *McKinley*, 424-25. *Army and Navy Journal*, July 16 and October 1, 1898. Clippings in 1898 Scrapbook, Box 10, Corbin Papers. Edward Eggleston to President McKinley, August 2, 1898; Senator George F. Hoar to McKinley, September 8, 1898, McKinley Papers. The staff bureaus, and especially the civilians given Volunteer commissions in them, were favorite targets of abuse, in which line officers often joined. See, for example, Hugh L. Scott to Mrs. Scott, August 18, 1898, Box 1, Scott Papers. A staff officer defends himself and his colleagues in Col. J. G. C. Lee to the Quartermaster General, September 11, 1898, File No. 115533, OQMG Records.

corruption and incompetence anywhere in government. The specific charges against Alger were vague. His detractors simply blamed him for every supply shortage, every mistake, every tactical blunder, regardless of whether it could be traced directly to his decision or action. Repeatedly, Alger's enemies hinted that personal financial interests had influenced his official conduct, but they never brought forward specific evidence of venality. His critics sometimes attributed to Alger policies the reverse of those he actually had supported. The *Times*, for example, accused him of trying to withhold Regulars from the Manila expedition, an attempt actually made by General Miles. While Alger had proposed keeping the troops at northern camps until they embarked for Santiago and Puerto Rico and Miles had wanted to send more men south, newspaper stories reversed their positions. In reality, Alger had made few major decisions. Usually, he rubber-stamped the advice of field commanders and bureau chiefs, and he executed faithfully the orders of President McKinley, who dictated all the major military policies.[60] Nevertheless, removal of Alger became in the public mind the one act that would redeem the Army. As an editor put it:

> The smaller fry can be investigated afterward. . . . Sweep Alger out of the way first. Remove the polluting influence of Michigan politics and the rest will follow as a matter of course. Algerism is at the bottom of the war scandals. Remove Alger and you administer to Algerism its death blow.[61]

A vain and choleric man, Alger responded self-righteously and ineffectually to the chorus of criticism. He took pride in the work of his department. He wrote to a supporter: "When we think of calling for an army from civil life, gathering it together, arming and equipping it, when there was no equipment for it, fighting battles all the way from Manila to Porto Rico, and closing the whole matter in three months, we realize it is something that has never before been equalled, and I doubt if it ever will be." Alger belittled sickness and hardship as inevitable accompaniments of war and insisted that no important decision had been wrong. He made no distinction between politically motivated slanders and reasoned criticisms of the

60. *The New York Times*, May 9, 18, 22, 23, 28, 30, and 31, June 2, 5, 8, 10, 14, and 15, 1898. Leech, *Days of McKinley*, 311-12. Theodore Roosevelt to Maria Longworth Storer, February 18, 1899, in Morison, *Roosevelt Letters*, II, 950. Henry Cabot Lodge to Roosevelt, July 6 and September 1 and 23, 1898; Roosevelt to Lodge, September 4, 1898, *Roosevelt-Lodge Correspondence*, I, 319-20, 338, 341, 347. H. V. Boynton to Adj. Gen. Corbin, July 21, 1899, Box 1A; *Chicago Record*, June 18, 1898, and other clippings in 1898 Scrapbook, Box 10, Corbin Papers. Peter Balmat to President McKinley, August 20, 1898; Spencer Borden to McKinley, August 22, 1898; Josiah Hartzell to McKinley, August, 1898; Walter A. Halbert to McKinley, August 30, 1898; New York *Evening Post*, September 9, 1898, clipping; *The Times* (London), July 14, 1899, clipping, McKinley Papers. Lt. Gen. J. M. Schofield, "General Schofield's Experiences in McKinley's Administration," Box 93, Schofield Papers. John J. McCook to Maj. Gen. J. H. Wilson, August 11, 1898, Box 15; Wilson to McCook, November 13, 1898, and to Anthony Higgins, December 22, 1898, Box 43, Wilson Papers. For an example of the President's role in crucial decisions, see Alger, *Spanish-American War*, 262.

61. Clipping in 1898 Scrapbook, Box 10, Corbin Papers.

conduct of operations, but rejected both as reflections on his personal integrity. Urged on by sympathetic friends, he insisted that he would never resign under fire, that he would continue in office until the facts vindicated him. He issued long statements to the newspapers that detailed with statistics the work done by the staff bureaus, and he blamed all the Army's shortcomings on the lack of supplies at the outset, the inexperience of the Volunteers, and the natural hardships of tropical campaigning. Alger found defenders among Civil War veterans, Republican politicians, and newspaper editors. A few critics of the Army's administration indirectly supported him by blaming previous military policy, not current personnel, for the service's deficiencies. Most citizens, however, found the Secretary's defensive fulminations unconvincing. In spite of Alger's denials, the conduct of the war had included failures and mistakes; and the people wanted to know why.[62]

Faced with this attack on his subordinate, President McKinley took an evasive course. He had early lost confidence in Alger's advice, yet he had used the loyal Secretary as his agent for controlling the Army. Through Alger, McKinley had overruled General Miles and other professional soldiers on such crucial questions as the size of the Volunteer Army, the invasion of Cuba in the rainy season and the prolongation of the siege of Santiago. In the war's aftermath of suffering and confusion, McKinley seems to have lost faith in his own military judgment. After all, he had led the country into war when he knew the Army was not ready; thus, he could not openly admit that the policies followed by Alger were his own and then explain and defend them. Instead, McKinley pursued three lines of evasive action at the same time. First, he refused publicly to repudiate Alger or to demand his resignation but insisted that he would not abandon the Secretary in his time of troubles. Second, he took highly publicized steps to correct, or appear to correct, Army abuses. On September 3 he visited Camp Wikoff to see at first hand the condition of the troops; later in the month, he dispatched Alger, Sternberg, and other officials on a tour of the southern camps. He sent a personal agent, Mrs. Louise L. Hogan, to visit the camps and recommend measures for the comfort of the soldiers. Third, McKinley carefully

62. The quotation is from Secretary Alger to Chauncey M. Depew, August 19, 1898, Alger Papers. Alger to Gen. G. M. Dodge, May 21 and July 23, 1898; Alger to W. Livingstone, June 4, 1898; Chauncey M. Depew to Alger, August 8, 1898; J. McGavney to Alger, August 8, 1898; Redfield Proctor to Alger, August 11, 1898; Alger to Gov. H. S. Pingree, August 13, 1898; J. C. Spooner to Alger, August 16, 1898; Alger to Depew, August 18, 1898; Depew to Alger, August 20 and September 8, 1898; W. Youngblood to V. L. Mason, September 29, 1898; Arthur A. Leslie to Alger, October 10, 1898; Alger to St. Clair McKelway, May 17, 1899; Alger to W. H. Alger, June 29, 1899; Stenographic Report of Interview between Alger and Nelson Hersh of the New York *World*, October 12, 1898, indicates Alger's attitude toward his critics, Alger Papers. In self-defense, Alger began inquiring personally into even minor complaints about Army conditions; see *Correspondence*, II, 834. A pro-Alger speech by a Civil War veteran is printed in Alger, *Spanish-American War*, 419-24. Leech, *Days of McKinley*, 293, 305, 314. *Army and Navy Journal*, August 27, September 3, and November 12, 1898. *The New York Times*, May 27, 1898. For a variety of comments on Alger, see clippings in 1898 Scrapbook, Box 10, Corbin Papers.

dissociated himself from Alger and the War Department. He assumed the public role of concerned, objective citizen who was waiting for the facts to come in before passing judgment on his own agents. He did nothing to check criticism of Alger in the Republican press, and in private conversation with General Schofield, who thought the Santiago campaign had been botched, McKinley gave the impression that an incompetent Alger had made wrong decisions without his knowledge. This skilled, subtle performance prevented the mud that was being thrown at the War Department from splashing on the rest of the Administration, but it left Alger understandably confused and angry.[63]

On September 8, probably under the President's direction, Alger asked for the appointment of a commission composed of "from five to seven . . . of the most distinguished soldiers and civilians that can be selected" to investigate every aspect of the Army's administration and to discover and report the truth about the conduct of the war. President McKinley at once approved the request and set about forming the commission. He strove to persuade General Schofield to serve, but Schofield declined, since he suspected that the creation of the commission was a political maneuver rather than a first step toward the Army reform he considered essential. To head the commission McKinley finally selected Gen. Grenville M. Dodge of Iowa, an experienced Civil War commander who was prominent in business and in Republican party affairs. A close friend of Alger, Dodge had corresponded with him throughout the war, praising his efforts and commending him for correct decisions. In letters to the newspapers, Dodge dismissed most criticism of the War Department as unfair and blamed corps, camp, and regimental commanders for existing Army abuses. Because he had taken a public position in the controversy, Dodge expressed reluctance to serve on the commission, but McKinley, evidently trusting his honesty, tact, and party loyalty, forced the job upon him. Of the other eight members eventually chosen, six were active or retired soldiers, among them Brigadier General Wilson,

63. Gibson, *Soldier in White*, 206-7. Leech, *Days of McKinley*, 292-93, 311, 313, 321. Morgan, *McKinley*, 395-96. Olcott, *McKinley*, II, 89. All of these authors, with the partial exception of Leech, take McKinley's supposed loyalty to Alger at face value; I do not. For glimpses of McKinley in his various roles, see the following: Charles F. Gauvreau, *Reminiscences of the Spanish-American War in Cuba and the Philippines*, 53. Wheeler, *Santiago Campaign*, 219, 221. *War Investigating Commission*, VII, 3771. *Army and Navy Journal*, September 10 and 24, October 1, 1898. Capt. W. I. Davenny to Secretary Alger, September 23, 1898; J. H. Gallinger to Alger, October 4, 1898; statement signed by Alger, November 26, 1900; Beriah Wilkins to Alger, December 4, 1901; G. W. Ruthen to Alger, August 24, 1903, Alger Papers. Adj. Gen. Corbin to Rep. Charles H. Grosvenor, February 4, 1907, Box 1, Corbin Papers. John A. Porter to Edward Eggleston, August 5, 1898; *Brooklyn Times*, August 31, 1898, clipping; Mrs. Louise E. Hogan to President McKinley, September 20, 1898, and to George B. Cortelyou, October 29, 1898; Cortelyou to Mrs. Hogan, October 8, 1898, and to Secretary Alger, April 25, 1899; undated draft of letter from McKinley to Alger, probably July, 1899, McKinley Papers. Schofield recounts his talk with McKinley in his "Experiences in McKinley's Administration," Box 93, Schofield Papers. Hugh L. Scott to Mrs. Scott, September 21, 1898, Box 1, Scott Papers.

Chief of Engineers, whose bureau had escaped public attack. Two civilians, ex-Governor Urban A. Woodbury of Vermont, and Dr. Phineas T. Connor of Ohio, completed the commission's roster.[64]

From its formation, the purpose of the Dodge Commission, as the investigating body came to be called, remained obscure. In his instructions to the commission's members, issued on September 27, the President did not ask them to propose Army reforms. He treated them instead as a grand jury called to seek out the guilty. Enjoining them to probe every bureau and agency of the War Department, McKinley declared that "The people of the country are entitled to know whether or not the citizens who so promptly responded to the call of duty have been neglected or maltreated by the Government to which they so willingly gave their services. If there have been wrongs committed, the wrongdoers must not escape conviction and punishment." If this were the commission's purpose, General Schofield pointed out in refusing to join it, the investigation amounted to little more than an extralegal witch hunt, in which men would be tried and condemned without the legal safeguards provided in a regular civil or military court. In fact, the appointment of the Dodge Commission was for McKinley an evasive political maneuver. Uninterested in leading a campaign for military reform, he hoped the investigation would silence public agitation, at least until after the congressional elections in November.[65]

Although the political opposition denounced its work as a white-wash and although many Army officers, in the fear that controversy would damage their careers, avoided its sessions, the Dodge Commission achieved the results McKinley desired. During October, November, and the first week of December, the commission's members delved into every detail of the Army's administration except for the politically and diplomatically sensitive subjects of military policy and strategy. They closely questioned Secretary Alger and the bureau chiefs and collected reams of records and correspondence. They visited Chicago, Cincinnati, Detroit, Harrisburg, New York, Boston, Philadelphia, Tampa, and other cities to take testimony from officers of every grade and from enlisted men, nurses, charity workers, and

64. Alger's request for an investigation is printed in *War Investigating Commission*, I, 237. Grenville M. Dodge to Secretary Alger, May 25, June 10 and 24, July 7, and August 11, 1898, Alger Papers. Edward Atkinson to President McKinley, August 25, 1898; Dodge to McKinley, August 17 and September 10, 1898, McKinley Papers. McKinley to Lt. Gen. J. M. Schofield, September 9, 13, and 14, 1898, Schofield to McKinley, September 10, 13, and 14, 1898; Dodge to Schofield, September 14, 1898, Box 41; "General Schofield's Experiences in McKinley's Administration," Box 93, Schofield Papers. Alger, *Spanish-American War*, 376. Leech, *Days of McKinley*, 313-14. Morgan, *McKinley*, 424-26. The other members of the commission were Col. James A. Sexton, Col. Charles Denby, Capt. Evan P. Howell, Gen. James A. Beaver, and Maj. Gen. Alexander McD. McCook.

65. McKinley's instructions are quoted in *War Investigating Commission*, I, 5, 237. Lt. Gen. J. M. Schofield to President McKinley, September 18, 1898, Box 41; and "General Schofield's Experiences in McKinley's Administration," Box 93, Schofield Papers, express Schofield's concern for legality.

concerned citizens. They inspected the Army camps then in use and toured the sites of those which had been abandoned before the commission's formation. The long parade of witnesses failed to disclose any spectacular instances of stupidity or corruption in high places, and such newspaper heroes of the Santiago campaign as Leonard Wood and Henry W. Lawton testified that the War Department had done its best in difficult circumstances. Partly as a result of the commission's work, Republican politicians in the weeks before the election reported an encouraging shift in public opinion in favor of Alger and the Administration. The party easily retained its congressional majority in the November voting.[66]

VI

On December 21, after several delays and postponements, Major General Miles at last appeared before the Dodge Commission, then in session in Washington. Rumors in the press had predicted that his testimony would be sensational; it was. Miles, hero of the Civil War and the Indian campaigns, Commanding General of the Army, conqueror of Puerto Rico, brought to light for the first time in the investigation what looked like a specific instance of wrongdoing by the War Department. His testimony came at the end of months of frustration for the Commanding General and brought to an ugly climax his long-simmering feud with Alger, the bureaus, and the McKinley Administration.[67]

Miles's sailing for Santiago on July 9 with the reinforcements for General Shafter had not ended his troubles with the War Department. Disagreements continued to dog his movements. Before leaving Washington, Miles told McKinley and Alger that he would not supersede Shafter in direct command of the Fifth Corps unless Shafter, whose reported ill health had caused the Administration much concern, was too sick to remain on duty. Miles repeated this statement to reporters at Charleston shortly before his embarkation. On July 8 Alger cabled Shafter that Miles was on his way to Santiago "but with instructions not to in any manner supersede you as commander of the

66. *War Investigating Commission*, I, 108-11; III, 86-88; VII, 3284-85. *Army and Navy Journal*, October 1 and 15, November 12, 1898. H. H. Kohlsast to Secretary Alger, October 13, 1898, Alger Papers. S. B. Elkins to President McKinley, September 23, 1898; S. K. Donavin to McKinley, October 21, 1898; J. M. Babcock to McKinley, November 10, 1898, McKinley Papers. Hugh L. Scott to Mrs. Scott, November 13, 1898, Box 1, Scott Papers. William E. Barrows to Maj. Gen. James H. Wilson, November 18, 1898, Box 3; Wilson to Col. John J. McCook, December 10, 1898, Box 43, Wilson Papers. Henry Cabot Lodge to Theodore Roosevelt, September 8, 1898, in *Roosevelt-Lodge Correspondence*, I, 343. Roosevelt to Paul Dana, January 14, 1899, in Morison, *Roosevelt Letters*, II, 912-13. Alger, *Spanish-American War*, 376-77. Dawes, *Journal*, 170. Hagedorn, *Wood*, I, 228-30. Leech, *Days of McKinley*, 315. Morgan, *McKinley*, 426.

67. Alger, *Spanish-American War*, 377-78. *War Investigating Commission*, I, 80. Unidentified clipping, 1898 Scrapbook, Box 10, Corbin Papers.

forces in the field . . . so long as you are able for duty." Alger sent this message to reassure Shafter that the Administration did not plan to remove him, and it did no more than echo Miles's own public remarks. At Santiago, Miles as Commanding General of the Army issued all his orders to the Fifth Corps through Shafter and concurred in most of Shafter's plans, including the proposal to let the Spanish garrison march out. Yet, when Shafter informed him of Alger's July 8 telegram, Miles quickly convinced himself it had been a secret dispatch sent to undermine his authority. He added it to his growing list of grievances against the Secretary. A further insult came at the conclusion of Miles's swift, victorious campaign in Puerto Rico. On August 17 he requested permission to arrange the surrender and evacuation of San Juan by the beaten Spaniards, only to be informed by Washington that a special military commission, set up under the terms of the armistice, would deal with such matters. Added to all of Miles's specific grievances was his awareness of the increase of Corbin's authority within the Administration and the diminution of his own. Newspaper rumors of an Alger-Corbin conspiracy to undercut Miles and eventually remove him from his post reinforced his suspicions for the able Adjutant General.[68]

On August 11, with his Puerto Rico campaign rolling smoothly toward victory, Miles had launched his first public attack on his enemies. Through a friendly newspaper reporter, W. J. Whelply of *The Kansas City Star*, who interviewed him at his field headquarters, Miles accused Alger of undermining his authority at Santiago. He also claimed that the War Department had ignored his plans for suppressing the yellow fever epidemic, had garbled his dispatches in releasing them to the press, and had withheld ships and landing craft from his Puerto Rican operations. When he landed at New York on September 7 upon his return from Puerto Rico, Miles issued a second statement. In it, he asserted that the war had been fought according to his strategic plans, and he claimed credit for the victory at Santiago as well as for the conquest of Puerto Rico. Critics of the War Department seized on Miles's remarks as proof of what they had asserted all along: that Alger and Corbin had conspired against Miles and tried to prevent this honest, brilliant fighting man from winning the war quickly and cheaply. In a gross oversimplification, they attributed all of the Army's deficiencies to Alger's and Corbin's disregard for or suppression of Miles's advice. Since Miles on

68. Miles's remarks to the reporters are in *Kansas City Star*, July 9, 1898; see also issue of July 13, 1898. The July 8 telegram is in *Correspondence*, I, 110; see also I, 218-19, 290, 396, 398. Alger, *Spanish-American War*, 204-55. Miles, *Serving the Republic*, 292-95. For comment on the "conspiracy" against Miles, see: Dunn, *Harrison to Harding*, I, 247. Adj. Gen. Corbin to R. A. Alger, November 16, 1900, Alger Papers; another copy of this letter is in Box 1A, Corbin Papers. Alger to Corbin, November 19, 1900, Box 1A; *Chicago Times-Herald*, June 20, 1898; *Mail and Express*, June 22, 1898; Elmira (N.Y.) *Advertiser*, June 24, 1898; Los Angeles *Herald*, July 9, 1898; and other unidentified clippings in 1898 Scrapbook, Box 10, Corbin Papers.

September 7 claimed that the war had been fought according to his plan, this view contained inconsistencies, but that fact did not disturb those who wanted to believe in Miles's virtue and Alger's villainy.[69]

The press blew up even the most innocuous incidents into War Department attacks on Miles. In early September, for example, the Mayor of New York asked that the troops from Camp Wikoff and those returning from Puerto Rico be paraded through the city before leaving for their posts and their home states. President McKinley agreed to the request, provided the commanders at Camp Wikoff considered their men physically fit for the march. He consulted the officers at Montauk and also General Miles, when Miles reached New York. After an exchange of telegrams, all the officers concerned, including Miles, decided the parade would not be practicable, and the President canceled it. The newspapers told this commonplace story differently. Miles, they said, had recommended the parade and McKinley initially had approved it, only to change his mind under the sinister influence of Corbin, who wanted to deny Miles the honor of leading the heroes of Santiago up Broadway.[70]

Alger greeted reports of Miles's interview on August 11 with outward blandness. He told newspapermen that he doubted the authenticity of the story, but his display of equanimity concealed bitter anger. When Miles issued his second statement, Alger abruptly dropped plans to take the General along on his tour of the southern camps, and when Miles returned to Washington, the Secretary avoided speaking to him. Rumors spread that Miles would be court-martialed for insubordination or removed from command of the Army, but until he appeared before the Dodge Commission, an uneasy truce prevailed in the War Department. After Miles arrived in Washington on September 8, he issued no more statements. He ignored Alger and maintained outwardly cordial relations with the President. Nevertheless, tension and hostility continued to increase, watched anxiously by junior officers who feared the quarrel would divide the service and damage their careers. At reviews and ceremonies during the autumn, the President openly snubbed Miles. Miles, on his part, seethed with anger and looked for

69. *Kansas City Star*, August 23 and 24, 1898. *New York Tribune*, September 6 and 8, 1898. *Army and Navy Journal*, July 2, September 10, and November 19, 1898. Maj. Gen. Miles to Secretary Alger, September 7, 1898, File No. 192302, AGO Records. Miles, *Serving the Republic*, 304-5. Ranson, *Military Affairs*, XXIX, 187. For newspaper comments, see clippings in 1898 Scrapbook, Box 10, Corbin Papers.

70. President McKinley to Secretary Alger, September 6, 1898; Alger to McKinley, September 8, 1898, Alger Papers. Mayor Robert A. Van Wyck to McKinley, September 6, 1898, McKinley to Mayor Van Wyck, September 6, 1898, Adj. Gen. Corbin to Maj. Gen. W. R. Shafter, September 6, 1898, Shafter to Corbin, September 7, 1898, Corbin to Maj. Gen. Miles, September 10, 1898, Miles to Corbin, September 10, 1898, Maj. Gen. Bates to Miles, September 11, 1898, Assistant Secretary of War George D. Meiklejohn to Miles, September 12, 1898, Miles to Secretary Alger, September 12, 1898, File No. 202272, AGO Records. For newspaper comment on the incident, see 1898 Scrapbook, Box 10, Corbin Papers.

a chance to strike at the Administration. After a conversation with Miles in October, Shafter warned his friend Corbin that the General "was wild with suppressed rage. . . . He was breathing vengeance on the Department and will do all he can to raise trouble. He talked and acted like an insane man."[71]

Miles found his issue in the quality of the Army's refrigerated and canned beef. Refrigerated beef, as soon as commissaries learned how to store and transport it, had become during the war the most popular component of the ration in all theaters and camps. Canned roast beef, on the other hand, used by the Fifth Corps at Santiago and by units in the United States, Puerto Rico, and the Philippines, was the least popular. Often forced by field conditions to eat it as it came from the can, the soldiers quickly learned to hate its bland taste, and the damp heat at Santiago caused the meat to spoil almost as soon as the cans were opened. The packers foisted on the Army at least a few bad lots of the meat, cans containing scraps of gristle, pieces of rope, and even dead maggots. With complete justification, the troops loathed the product, and officers and enlisted men alike complained bitterly about its frequent issue.[72]

Miles had heard his first complaints about Army beef during his trip to Tampa in June. He continued receiving them throughout the war, mostly referring to the hated canned roast beef. On September 20, after his return to the United States, Miles directed every Regular regimental commander whose unit had served in Cuba or Puerto Rico to forward to Army headquarters his evaluation of canned beef as a ration. The resulting reports unanimously and in strong language condemned the meat. Miles also received an alarming report on the refrigerated beef. It came from a Volunteer surgeon on his staff, Dr. William H. Daly, a Pittsburgh physician in civil life and long a friend of the General. Mrs. Miles considered Daly, whom contemporaries accused of trying to extort bribes from would-be Army contractors, a bad influence on her husband, but the General trusted him.

71. The quotation is from Shafter to Corbin, October 23, 1898, Box 1, Corbin Papers; see also newspaper clippings in 1898 Scrapbook, Box 10, Corbin Papers. *Kansas City Star*, August 24, 25, and 28, 1898. *New York Tribune*, August 27 and 31, September 9 and 10, 1898. R. A. Alger to Senator George F. Hoar, February 8, 1902, Alger Papers. The worries of career officers are expressed in Hugh L. Scott to Mrs. Scott, September 7, 1898, Box 1, Scott Papers.

72. *War Investigating Commission*, I, 154-55; II, 862-63; III, 330; IV, 1244, 1557-59; VI, 2938-39, 2948, 2959-60, 3089, 3110; VII, 3210, 3283-84, 3601, 3610-13, 3664-65; 3749-52. *RSW, 1898*, I, 562-63. *Food Furnished by the Subsistence Department to Troops in the Field*, Senate Doc. No. 270, 56th Cong., 1st sess., 1900 (hereafter cited as *Beef Court*), II, 1899. Alger, *Spanish-American War*, 384-85, and "The Food of the Army during the Spanish-American War," *The North American Review*, CLXXII, 39-58. Hagedorn, *Wood*, I, 229n. Roosevelt, *Rough Riders*, 61. *Army and Navy Journal*, January 21, February 18, March 4, 18, and 25, April 29; 1899. Theodore Roosevelt to Maj. Gen. Miles, January 9, 1899, and to Gen. George B. Davis, February 28, 1899, in Morison, *Roosevelt Letters*, II, 903, 952-54. Armour and Company to R. A. Alger, January 18, 1901, Alger Papers. Capt. W. C. Brown to Roosevelt, September 7, 1898, Vol. 3, Roosevelt Papers. Ship provisioners long had considered canned roast beef unsuitable for tropical use; see *War Investigating Commission*, VIII, 447. Eagan's failure to find this out reflected the Army's inexperience with tropical warfare and the weakness of its planning.

Daly had traveled to Tampa with Miles and accompanied him in the invasion of Puerto Rico. In September, with several other officers, he made an inspection trip to Camp Thomas. In all these places, Daly saw and ate beef that tasted to him of boric and salicylic acid, poisonous chemicals sometimes injected into meat to preserve it. Daly had eaten such preserved meat previously on a western hunting trip and remembered the taste. In Puerto Rico, he claimed later, he made a chemical analysis of the suspect beef and found acid traces in it. Daly reported his suspicions orally to Miles during August, and on either September 21 or October 21 (the exact date became confused), he detailed his suspicions and his evidence to the General in a letter that claimed the Army's meat contained harmful chemicals. While many officers complained about the canned beef, Daly seems to have been the only one to suspect the refrigerated variety. The great "Embalmed Beef" furor was to rest on his allegations.[73]

By the end of October at the latest, Miles held apparently strong evidence against both varieties of ration beef. At this time the Army still issued both types to the troops in large quantities. His obligations to the men under his command seemingly required Miles to report his facts immediately to McKinley, if not to Alger, and to demand swift investigation and remedial action. Miles made no such report. Until he met the Dodge Commission, he kept his information to himself and quietly built his case for two months while the soldiers were eating presumably poisoned meat. Driven by a mixture of motives, Miles had decided to use beef as his issue for public attacks on his enemies. He opposed in principle any departure from traditional meat supply methods, and he seems genuinely to have suspected Alger and Eagan of corruption. Too, he was smarting with injured pride, and he wanted revenge for the real and fancied slights he had endured. Politically ambitious but naive, he hoped to ride his revelations into the White House.[74]

On December 21, before the Dodge Commission, Miles opened his assault. His testimony touched on many matters, including criticism of the site of Camp Alger and of Shafter's tactics at Santiago, but the beef material constituted its sensational core. Miles introduced the meat issue in response to a general question about the quality of his supplies in Puerto Rico. He said that poor food had been "one of the serious causes of so much sickness

73. *Beef Court*, I, 14, 15-16. *War Investigating Commission*, I, 168; VII, 3258-59, 3582-83, 3707-11, 3713; VIII, 412-18. The text of Daly's "Embalmed Beef" letter is in Alger, *Spanish-American War*, 396-98; see also 398-402. Johnson, *Unregimented General*, 346, comments on Mrs. Miles's distrust of Daly. Statement by H. V. Boynton, October, 1902, Alger Papers. The charge of corruption against Daly is repeated in H. V. Boynton to Maj. Gen. James H. Wilson, May 24, 1899, Box 4, Wilson Papers.

74. *Beef Court*, I, 14, 21; II, 1887. *War Investigating Commission*, I, 153-54; VII, 3768. Alger, *Spanish-American War*, 377, 383, 405-10. Johnson, *Unregimented General*, 345-46. Leech, *Days of McKinley*, 316. Morgan, *McKinley*, 380. Ranson, *Military Affairs*, XXIX, 188. For Miles's views on beef supply, see *New York Tribune*, July 20, 1898, and Miles to Secretary Alger, February 6, 1899. File No. 197829, AGO Records. John J. McCook to Maj. Gen. James H. Wilson, April 7, 1899, Box 15, Wilson Papers.

and distress on the part of the troops." He criticized Commissary General Eagan for abandoning the Army's traditional beef on the hoof in favor of the new processed meats and declared that there was "some serious defect in that refrigerator beef, and also the canned beef that was furnished." From that point, in answer to leading questions from the commission, he supported his charges with the introduction of the adverse reports on canned beef and Daly's letter alleging chemical treatment of the frozen carcasses. While he did not openly attribute corrupt motives to Alger and Eagan, he implied them, and he argued (incorrectly) that the canned beef was not legally part of the Army ration.[75]

Immediately after testifying, Miles left Washington for Cincinnati to spend the Christmas holidays at the home of his wife's cousin. At Cincinnati, he met an enthusiastic reception from the press and populace. Emboldened by his apparent popularity, he continued his offensive. On December 22 he elaborated on his charges concerning the Army's supply of beef to a reporter for the sensationalist *New York Journal*. The *Journal*'s headline the next day read: "Miles Makes Grave Charges against the Administration—Poisons Used In Beef Made the Soldiers Ill—Tons of Bad Meat Sent to Troops in Porto Rico—These Charges, He Declares, Contain Only A Few Of The Facts Which Has Gathered." Miles's allegations revived the languishing public campaign against the War Department. Here, supported by unimpeachable authority, was at last a specific instance of malfeasance, and the Administration's enemies made the most of it.[76]

According to Secretary Alger, Miles's charges about beef struck Commissary General Eagan "with the suddenness and sharpness of a blow from an assassin's knife out of the dark." In his efforts to keep the soldiers fed, Eagan had driven himself to exhaustion throughout the summer. Miles's hints of corruption and the vituperative press attacks on Eagan they inspired aroused the hot-tempered Commissary General to rage. Miles further provoked Eagan by coldly snubbing the bureau chief's request on December 27 for clarification of his *Journal* interview. Frantic with fury, Eagan sought a way to strike back at his accuser. He considered challenging Miles to a duel but in the end settled for a public rebuttal before the Dodge Commission. Eagan had testified before the commission prior to Miles's appearance. He now requested and obtained a rehearing. Consulting no one, Eagan carefully prepared a long statement, which he read to the commission on

75. Miles's testimony is in *War Investigating Commission*, VII, 3256-61, 3263. *Army and Navy Journal*, December 24, 1898. Alger, *Spanish-American War*, 384-86. Johnson, *Unregimented General*, 347.

76. *New York Journal*, December 23, 1898, printed in *Beef Court*, III, 1922-24. Alger, *Spanish-American War*, 378-79. Johnson, *Unregimented General*, 347-48. Ranson, *Military Affairs*, XXIX, 187-88. For an example of anti-Administration press comment, see J. B. Bishop, "Get the Beef Contracts," *The Nation*, LXVII, 217-18.

January 12, 1899. The bulk of the statement consisted of a lengthy defense of canned and refrigerated beef, both of which Eagan declared to be sound, nutritious foods. He insisted that none of the beef contained poisonous chemicals. Growing more and more upset as he read, at times almost in tears, Eagan charged that Miles had maligned him and his department by implying corruption and neglect of duty. He called Miles's remarks on this point

> a scandalous libel, reflecting upon the honor of every officer in the Department who has contracted for or purchased this meat, and especially and particularly on the Commissary-General—myself. In denouncing General Miles as a liar when he makes this statement . . ., I wish to make it as emphatic and as coarse as the statement itself. I wish to force the lie back into his throat, covered with the contents of a camp latrine. I wish to brand it as a falsehood of whole cloth, without a particle of truth to sustain it, and unless he can prove his statement he should be denounced by every honest man, barred from the clubs, barred from the society of decent people, and so ostracized that the street bootblacks would not condescend to speak to him, for he fouled his own nest, he has aspersed the honor of a brother officer without a particle of evidence or fact to sustain in any degree his scandalous, libelous, malicious falsehood.

Lest anyone remain in doubt about his attitude toward Miles, Eagan further on called the Commanding General a liar "with as black a heart as the man who blew up the Maine possessed." The commission forced Eagan to delete the most abusive passages from his statement before accepting it into the record, but reporters who covered the hearing took down and published the unexpurgated outburst.[77]

Eagan's verbal assault on General Miles destroyed the Commissary General's career. For military men, Eagan's abusive language toward this superior in rank reduced the entire issue to one of insubordination, and on this question the Army had no choice but to unite against the Commissary General. Reluctantly, Secretary Alger arranged Eagan's court-martial for conduct unbecoming an officer and prejudicial to good order and discipline. A board of officers headed by Major General Merritt, recently returned from Manila, tried the case late in January and inevitably found Eagan guilty. Eagan's counsel could do little but plead for leniency on grounds of extenuating circumstances. The court sentenced Eagan to dismissal from the service but privately recommended clemency to the President. On February 7, 1899, McKinley announced his confirmation of the court's verdict. At the same time, in recognition of Eagan's long, loyal service to the nation and of the extreme pressures that had provoked his outburst, the President commuted Eagan's sentence to suspension from rank and duty with full pay for six

---

77. The official record of Eagan's statement is in *War Investigating Commission*, I, 89-91, and VII, 3564-99. The quoted remarks, which are deleted from the official version, are in *Army and Navy Journal*, January 14, 1899, and GO 24, HQA, February 7, 1899, in *GO/AGO, 1899*. For the circumstances surrounding Eagan's outburst, see the following: *Army and Navy Journal*, January 28, 1899. Alger, *Spanish-American War*, 379-82. Leech, *Days of McKinley*, 642. Commissary General C. P. Eagan to Adj. Gen. Corbin, December 24, 1898, Alger Papers.

years, which meant until Eagan's retirement. This was as close as the government could come to apologizing to Eagan for what Miles had done to him. Eagan left Washington in mid-March to join his son in business in Honolulu. Col. John F. Weston, an experienced, progressive-minded Regular who had distinguished himself at Santiago, replaced him as head of the Subsistence Department. Ironically, Weston was the officer who first suggested feeding the troops canned roast beef.[78]

Though not publicly abusive, Secretary Alger raged at Miles in private and urged McKinley to remove him from command of the Army. McKinley, who did not want a direct conflict with Miles and his backers, the influential Sherman family, and whose legal power to oust Miles without a court-martial was questionable, refused to do so, but for practical purposes he set the General aside and turned still more frequently to Corbin for military advice. Meanwhile, the Dodge Commission launched a painstaking inquiry into the condition and quality of the Army's beef. Its members took lengthy testimony from officers who had served in Cuba and other theaters. Their testimony confirmed the Army's hatred for canned beef but contained unanimous expressions of approval for the refrigerated variety. Only Dr. Daly, who proved to be less than convincing on the stand, alleged evidence of embalming. Solemnly, in formal session, the commission members opened cans of beef from Army storehouses and tasted their contents. They collected samples of refrigerated beef from all camps and posts that were using it and had them analyzed by government chemists, who found not a trace of harmful preservatives. In their report to the President, issued on February 9, the commission members declared that Miles's charges of chemical treatment of the refrigerated beef were without foundation. They concluded that canned beef was legally part of the Army ration and a nutritious food, but they questioned the wisdom of issuing it in hot climates and in the field where the men could not cook it. In letters to friends, General Dodge bitterly condemned Miles for not reporting his suspicions at once and for overstating his charges when finally he did present them.[79]

78. For a running account of the court-martial and for editorial comments on the Eagan case, see *Army and Navy Journal*, January 14, 21, and 28, February 4 and 11, March 11, April 8 and 29, June 3, 1899. GO 24, HQA, February 7, 1899, in GO/AGO, 1899. Alger, *Spanish-American War*, 381-83. Leech, *Days of McKinley*, 318. Redfield Proctor to Secretary Alger, February 4, 1899, Alger Papers. For Col. Weston's views on canned beef, see Weston to the Commissary General, March 24, 1898, in Alger, *Spanish-American War*, 388-89. Until Eagan's retirement, Weston had to work as "Acting" Commissary General, doing a brigadier general's job with the rank and pay of a colonel; see Weston to Maj. Gen. James H. Wilson, February 9, 1899, Box 26, Wilson Papers.

79. Russell A. Alger to Senator George F. Hoar, February 8, 1902, Alger Papers. Morgan, *McKinley*, 427. *War Investigating Commission*, I, 163-67; II, 853-66: VII, 3601-2, 3703, 3711, 3713, 3723-24. Grenville M. Dodge to Gen. H. V. Boynton, March 23, 1899, Box 1A, Corbin Papers. Dodge to Boynton, March 28, 1899, and to President McKinley, Arpil 20, 1899, McKinley Papers. McKinley's inability to remove Miles without first proving him guilty of gross malfeasance illustrated the basic weakness of the Army command system, about which Schofield had warned a decade earlier.

Ignoring the Dodge Commission, Miles reopened the battle on a new front. He told reporters early in February that he had "overwhelming" new evidence the refrigerated beef was embalmed, including affidavits from men who saw the dastardly work being done. His presidential aspirations now dominated Miles's reasoning, as both Democrats and anti-McKinley Republicans talked with apparent seriousness of making him their standard-bearer. Miles went so far as to offer Theodore Roosevelt second place on his ticket, in the event that some faction nominated him. On February 8 he largely nullified the popular impact of the Dodge report by asking the President to appoint a military court of inquiry to investigate the whole beef issue. The next day, McKinley formed a board of officers "to investigate certain allegations of the Major-General Commanding the Army in respect to the unfitness for issue of certain articles of food furnished by the Subsistence Department to the troops in the field." Acting as a regularly constituted court of inquiry, the board would determine the facts in the case and recommend any further action its members deemed desirable. Meantime, the President again rejected Alger's demand that he dismiss Miles.[80]

The beef court, composed of officers from the line and the Corps of Engineers, held its first session on February 20, with General Miles as opening witness. Miles produced none of the new evidence at which he had hinted, and he began backing away from his earlier allegations. He repudiated his newspaper interviews of December 23 and February 1, and he denied any implication of fraud in his remarks about Alger and Eagan. In fact, he altered or repudiated so many of his statements that the court found it difficult to establish just what his charges were. The members of the court went over all the ground previously covered by the Dodge Commission. They interrogated witnesses; they visited packing plants; they tasted beef and had it analyzed by government chemists. On April 29, 1899, the court issued its report. As had the Dodge Commission, it dismissed as groundless Miles's charge that the refrigerated beef contained preservative chemicals. The court declared canned roast beef a wholesome food but condemned its large-scale issue in the tropics without adequate prior experiments, calling it "a colossal error" by Gerald Eagan "for which there is no palliation." The court added, however, that Eagan's mistake had resulted from no other motive "than the earnest desire

80. Miles hinted at new evidence in an interview printed in the New York Herald, February 1, 1899, reproduced in Beef Court, III, 1924-26; see also I, 5. Miles almost at once repudiated this interview; see Army and Navy Journal, February 4 and 25, 1899. Alger, Spanish-American War, 383-84. Leech, Days of McKinley, 319. Henry Adams to Elizabeth Cameron, December 18, 1898, and January 15 and February 5, 1899, in Letters of Henry Adams, 1892-1918, Worthington C. Ford, ed. (hereafter cited as Adams Letters), II, 197, 202-3, 213-14. Theodore Roosevelt to Henry Cabot Lodge, August 10, 1899, Roosevelt-Lodge Correspondence, I, 416, recounts Miles's invitation to Roosevelt to join his ticket. Russell A. Alger to Senator George F. Hoar, February 8, 1902, Alger Papers. J. P. Sanger to President McKinley, September 23, 1898, McKinley Papers. John J. McCook to Maj. Gen. James H. Wilson, April 7, 1899, Box 15, Wilson Papers. Miles to Alger, February 8, 1899, File No. 199028, AGO Records.

to procure the best possible food for the troops." The court reserved its harshest words for General Miles. It found that

> the Major-General Commanding the Army had no sufficient justification for alleging that the refrigerated beef was embalmed or was unfit for issue to troops. It also finds that he committed an error in that having belief or knowledge, as claimed, that the food was unfit, that it caused sickness and distress, that some of it was supplied under the pretence of experiment, that other beef was embalmed, he did not immediately report such knowledge or belief to the Secretary of War to the end that a proper remedy might be promptly applied.[81]

For practical purposes, the court's verdict ended the beef controversy. Although Miles talked bravely for a while of demanding still another inquiry and although as late as 1911 he referred in his memoirs to the "scandal" of the Army's "corrupt food supply," most of his contemporaries, regardless of their attitudes toward the War Department, concluded that he had lost his battle. Secretary Alger, General Dodge, and ex-Governor Woodbury all urged McKinley to remove Miles from command, but the President refused, declaring that he did not want to make a martyr out of the General. Instead of firing Miles, the President isolated and ignored him. Army officers who made the mistake of supporting Miles during the controversy now found themselves in disfavor, their careers in jeopardy. They included Inspector General Breckinridge, a long-time ally of the Commanding General, who, as a contemporary put it, "tied himself and his office to Miles, and sank with him."[82]

The Army itself was the chief victim of the beef controversy. The quarrel completed the fragmentation of the high command and left Miles in open opposition to the President he supposedly served. It embittered Secretary Alger against both Miles and McKinley, who Alger believed had treated his enemy too leniently. The scandal wrecked the career and reputation of

81. The quotations and Miles's testimony are in *Beef Court*, I, 6-8, 18-19: II, 1858, 1877-78, 1884-86, 1889-90, 1892-93. *Army and Navy Journal*, February 11 and April 22, 1899. Alger, *Spanish-American War*, 390-92, 394, 402-3, 409. GO 91, WD, May 6, 1899, *GO/AGO, 1899*. Eagan resented the court's condemnation of his use of canned beef; see Charles P. Eagan to Russell A. Alger, November 3, 1899, Alger Papers.

82. Miles's comment is in *Serving the Republic*, 304. Henry Adams to Elizabeth Cameron, February 5 and 12, 1899, in *Adams Letters*, II, 215-17. *Army and Navy Journal*, April 22 and May 13, 1899, and J. B. Bishop, "The Beef Verdict," *The Nation*, LXVIII, 347-48, express the prevalent journalistic view that the case was closed. Russell A. Alger to Senator George F. Hoar, February 8, 1902, Alger Papers. Urban A. Woodbury to President McKinley, January 14, 1899; Grenville M. Dodge to McKinley, April 20, 1899, McKinley Papers. J. F. Weston to Maj. Gen. James H. Wilson, April 28, 1899, Box 26; Wilson to Maj. Gen. David Stanley, April 4, 1899, Box 43, Wilson Papers. For the troubles of Inspector General Breckinridge, see H. V. Boynton to Wilson, December 18, 1898, and May 24, 1899, Box 4, Wilson Papers. Also Inspector General Breckinridge to Theodore Roosevelt, July 24, 1899, Vol. 6, Roosevelt Papers. For Breckinridge's attacks on the bureaus, see *Army and Navy Journal*, January 14, 1899.

loyal, efficient Commissary General Eagan, who had deserved better from his country. Above all, it left an ineradicable stain upon the prestige of the service. The sensational charges, not the sober refutations, stuck in the minds of thousands of ordinary citizens. For them, the odor of rotten beef would always hang over the history of the war with Spain.[83]

83. For comments on the results of the scandal, see: Alger, *Spanish-American War*, 405-6. *Army and Navy Journal*, February 4 and April 15, 1899. Henry Adams to Elizabeth Cameron, February 19, 1899, *Adams Letters*, II, 219. Russell A. Alger to Senator George F. Hoar, February 8, 1902, Alger Papers. Brig. Gen. James H. Wilson to Commissary General John M. Weston, May 8, 1899, Box 44, Wilson Papers.

9

An Army for Empire

I

On February 9, 1899, in the midst of the beef controversy, the Dodge Commission issued its report on the Army's administration. The commission, its judgments backed by volumes of testimony and documents, reviewed in detail the work of each staff bureau, the conduct of each overseas campaign, and the formation and administration of each principal camp. Dodge and his colleagues found the War Department guiltless of deliberate negligence or major corruption. They blamed most of the war's administrative mistakes and supply shortages on the country's failure to maintain a well-equipped force in peacetime, but they sharply criticized the railroad tieup at Tampa and the inadequacy of Shafter's transport fleet. They insisted that intelligent planning and proper management could have prevented these and other misfortunes. The commissioners suggested many improvements in the Army's organization and methods, most of them familiar to military reformers. They called for the maintenance of adequate supply stockpiles, for federal examinations for all Volunteer officers, for better field training of the National Guard, and for the enlargement and reorganization of the supply and medical bureaus. Following the advice of General Schofield, they urged that the President be allowed to select a compatible Commanding General.[1]

The commission's members sharply differed in their evaluations of the performance of Secretary Alger. General Dodge and the majority wanted to praise his conduct in office, but a vocal minority insisted on condemning him. Faced with the threat of a minority report, the pro-Alger faction agreed to a paragraph that acknowledged Alger's honesty and industry but declared that "there was lacking in the general administration of the War Department . . . that complete grasp of the situation which was essential to the highest efficiency and discipline of the Army."[2]

1. For the commission's principal conclusions, see *War Investigating Commission*, I, 111-14, 124, 147-48, 153, 189, 199-200, 209, 221-22. Dodge thought the War Department had done well, but that many military reforms were needed. See: Grenville M. Dodge to Secretary Alger, February 21, 1899, and October 6, 1902; also Dodge to Col. H. J. Gallagher, June 22, 1899; all in Alger Papers. Dodge to President McKinley, April 20, 1899, McKinley Papers. Major General Wilson, who had complaints of his own about the conduct of the war, thought the commission's document a "fair report"; see Wilson to Col. John J. McCook, April 30, 1899, Box 44, Wilson Papers.

2. The quotation is from *War Investigating Commission*, I, 116. For the divisions on the commission, see Urban A. Woodbury to R. A. Alger, February 21, 1903, Alger Papers, and Brig. Gen. J. H. Wilson to Col. John J. McCook, April 30, 1899, Box 44, Wilson Papers.

The Dodge report pictured conscientious officials struggling manfully—and in the main successfully—to overcome difficulties that were largely not of their own making. During the last months of 1898 and the first half of 1899, the performance of the War Department and the Army it administered went far to confirm the correctness of the commission's verdict.

The mid-August armistice did not end the war for the Army. Technically, the United States remained at war with Spain until early February 1899, when the Treaty of Paris was ratified. While American and Spanish diplomats negotiated in Paris, the War Department partially demobilized, reorganized, and redeployed the Volunteer Army. It planned and executed the replacement of the Spanish army in Cuba with an American occupation force. It reinforced the Eighth Corps in the Philippines and then mobilized additional troops for a new war in those islands. In the course of these efforts, the War Department and the Army displayed little of the confusion, waste, and disorder that had marred the buildup during the spring of 1898. Instead, they responded with methodical efficiency to the new challenges of overseas empire.

For President McKinley and his military advisors, the first order of business after the August 12 armistice was reduction of the Volunteer Army. Predictably, the great majority of the Volunteers, especially those whose regiments had sat out the war in camp, demanded immediate discharge, their pleas quickly taken up by their political representatives. McKinley, however, needed to retain at least a portion of the Volunteer Army to secure Cuba, Puerto Rico, and Manila and to dissuade the Spaniards from stiffening their negotiating posture; and under the law he could do so as long as the United States remained technically at war with Spain. Accordingly, McKinley on August 18 ordered the discharge of 100,000 Volunteers, about half the total number raised. To ensure public acceptance and state support of his policy, the President mustered out the Volunteers by entire regiments, with the number of discharges distributed among the states in proportion to population as the original Volunteer calls had been. He released at once all the Volunteers who had campaigned in Cuba and Puerto Rico and allowed the governors, "so far as consistent with the public interests," to select the other regiments from their states for discharge, with the proviso that they give preference to units that had been longest in service. To mollify "bring-the-boys-home-now" sentiment further, McKinley permitted individual transfers between regiments remaining in service and those being discharged. Under his guidance, the War Department released hundreds of men from the Army upon individual application, many for reasons of hardship and others for reasons of political expediency.[3]

3. Alger, *Spanish-American War*, 19, 39. Holbrook, *Minnesota in War*, 41-42, 84-85. *Correspondence*, I, 400-401, 404-405; II, 783, 785. *RSW, 1898*, I, 7, 261; II, 640. *RSW, 1899*, I, Pt. 4, pp. 43-44. J. A. Porter to Corbin, September 7, 1898; Col. B. F. Montgomery to President McKinley, October 11, 1898; Corbin to Cortelyou, December 1, 1898; McKinley Papers. In the same collection, see John A. Porter to Secretary Alger, August 26, November 28, December 1, 10, and 12, 1898, and January 3 and 4, 1899, for a small sampling of McKinley's intervention to secure individual discharges, often on political grounds. *Army and Navy Journal*, August 20 and September 3, October 1 and 8, 1898.

During September, the War Department selected for muster out over 70 infantry regiments. It also discharged almost all the Volunteer artillery and cavalry, including the Rough Riders and the other two U.S. Volunteer cavalry regiments, because these troops were the most expensive to maintain and the regular establishment contained enough cavalry for the Army remaining in service. Reversing the process by which they had entered the Army, the state units designated for discharge travelled by rail from their federal camps to state rendezvous, where they turned in their arms and equipment, completed their reports and returns, and received their final pay and discharge papers. Under a War Department policy, most of the men of each regiment went home on furlough as soon as their unit reached its state camp, for 60 days if they had served overseas and 30 if they had remained in the United States. The War Department intended these furloughs as a combined bonus and paid vacation for the troops, at the end of which they came back to camp for formal muster out. Aside from the inevitable difficulties caused by incomplete records, missing soldiers, and lost equipment, not to mention the recordkeeping complications of the furlough system, the demobilization went forward relatively smoothly. In the major federal camps, there was a constant coming and going of regiments, as units destined for muster out left for home and more recently enlisted regiments came in from state rendezvous to replace them. Most returning regiments, even ones that had never fired a shot in anger, received a heroes' welcome from their home towns, with parades, bands, and patriotic oratory. Many returned Volunteers re-entered their states' National Guards, adding a leavening of camp and field experience to the state militia.[4]

With reduction of the Army under way, McKinley, Alger, and Corbin early in September turned their attention to the reorganization and redeployment of the troops remaining in service. The Regulars who had fought at Santiago were dispersing from Montauk to their permanent posts, and the Seventh Corps had no pressing reason to move from Jacksonville. However, tens of thousands of Volunteers and a few Regulars at Lexington, Knoxville, Huntsville, and Camp Meade had to take new stations farther south to escape the rigors of the oncoming winter and prepare for the occupation of Cuba. A board of officers headed by Brigadier General Theodore Schwan of the Adjutant General's Department and including representatives of the Medical and Quartermaster Departments and the Engineers, after a tour of

4. *RSW, 1898*, I, 261-62; IV, 5; *RSW, 1899*, I, Pt. 2, p. 12. GO 124, WD, August 20, 1898; GO 130, HQA, August 29, 1898; *GO/AGO, 1898. Army and Navy Journal*, September 3, 10, 17, and October 26, 1898. Chief Quartermaster Guy Howard to the Quartermaster General, September 20, 1898, File No. 115533, OQMG Records, describes turbulence in the II Corps. Holbrook, *Minnesota in War*, 43-44, describes a typical state homecoming. Maj. Gen. James H. Wilson to Senator Stephen B. Elkins, January 2, 1899, Box 43, Wilson Papers, complains about the state of training and discipline of the retained regiments, which had been mustered in late in the war with Spain.

potential southern campsites, developed detailed plans for reorganization and relocation of these troops. On October 7, the War Department, following the Schwan board's recommendations, discontinued the Third, Fifth, and Sixth corps; reassigned their remaining troops to the First, Second, and Fourth corps; and directed the three reconstituted corps to stations in the hill country of Alabama, Georgia, and South Carolina. Profiting from the mistakes of the summer, the War Department spread the troops among many small camps, with no more than a division assigned to any one locality. This arrangement reduced Army demands upon the host communities' transportation and public utilities systems and facilitated the maintenance of proper sanitation. Separate orders on October 8 and 21 reorganized the Seventh Corps, which had been reduced in size by the muster out of the regiments, into two divisions and directed it to shift camp from Jacksonville to Savannah, selected by the War Department as the embarkation port for the Cuban army of occupation.[5]

The execution of this redeployment presented a dramatic contrast to the chaotic days of May and June. To guide the corps commanders in their planning and operations, Secretary Alger furnished to each of them copies of the Schwan board's surveys of his organization's campsites. He also ordered commanders and their staffs to precede their troops to the new stations by at least ten days and insisted that hospitals, water systems, and supply depots be in place before a single regiment left the old camps. During late October and early November, engineers, wagon trains, and medical and signal detachments descended upon the new winter campsites. Construction crews laid water pipe and erected wooden hospitals, warehouses, kitchens, bath houses, and mess halls. Quartermaster and subsistence officers set up their depots. When the troops themselves changed station, each regiment travelled by rail with all its transportation and equipment, with departures and arrivals scheduled to prevent congestion at any point. In nine days, the 21,000 officers and men of the Second Corps, with over 2,000 horses and mules and hundreds of tons of baggage, transferred themselves by train from Camp Meade to Georgia and South Carolina without major untoward incident. The movement of the Seventh Corps from Jacksonville to Savannah, according to a newspaper correspondent,

5. For troop locations in September, 1898, see tables in File No. 121918, AGO Records. The report of the Schwan board, with accompanying records and correspondence, is in the same file. GO 163, HQA, October 7, 1898; GO 166, HQA, October 13, 1898; GO 171, HQA, October 21, 1898, *GO/AGO, 1898*; GO 163 also can be found in *Correspondence*, I, 257-58, see also I, 510, 519, 530, 534-35, 548. *Army and Navy Journal*, September 3 and 10, October 1 and 8, 1898. Selection of Savannah: Col. Frank J. Hecker to Quartermaster General Ludington, September 29, 1898, Hecker Papers. *RSW, 1898*, II, 639. For preference for smaller camps, see: Acting Inspector Gen. J. P. Sanger to Alger, June 3, 1898, File No. 88310, AGO Records; *War Investigating Commission*, VI, 3103; and *RSW, 1898*, II, 8, 209, 565, and 664.

is made with a steadiness, evenness, and thoroughness that would do credit to old campaigners. System and discipline are shown in every action. When a regiment arrives the unloading and setting up is done neatly and expeditiously. This is the result of the training the men have had in camp and shows an immense improvement over anything done by the Volunteers before.[6]

The Army's new efficiency stemmed in good part from more thorough planning, exemplified by the work of the Schwan board, and to the fact that the War Department increasingly delegated the details of operations to its field commanders while providing them with the necessary authority to do their jobs. Brig. Gen. Joseph P. Sanger, a division commander in the First Corps, told the Dodge commission: "Commanders are taking things into their own hands more, and just the moment they did that, and got rid of much red tape, things came along all right." The corps commanders of the reorganized Volunteer Army—Major General Wilson (First Corps), Major General Graham (Second Corps), Major General Wheeler (Fourth Corps), and Major General Lee (Seventh Corps)—all were veterans of the early days of the mobilization. They made the most of their hard-won experience and new freedom of action.[7]

The corps commanders had the support of supply bureaus which at last possessed adequate stocks of materiel and which had done much to improve their own operating procedures. The Quartermaster Department, for example, by early December had on hand a full supply of clothing, tentage, and equipment for 250,000 troops. Its private contractors were prepared to fill quickly any large new military orders. Enough horses, mules, and wagons were available to give each corps its full allowance of field transportation. Continuing to manufacture and purchase all types of supplies, Quartermaster General Ludington planned to stockpile permanent reserves for an Army of 100,000 men. Early in October, anticipating the movement to winter camps, he began distributing warm clothing to the troops and called for bids on the construction of 60 prefabricated wooden hospitals.[8]

6. Quotation is from *Army and Navy Journal*, November 5, 1898; see also issues of October 22 and November 19, 1898. GO 163, HQA, October 7, 1898, *GO/AGO, 1898*. Draft letter from Adj. Gen. Corbin to Corps Commanders, October, 1898; File No. 121918; Asst. Adj. Gen. Reichman, II Corps, to Corbin, November 6, 1898, File No. 156090; Maj. Gen. S. B. M. Young to Corbin, December 10, 1898, File No. 175230; Corbin to Asst. Adj. Gen. Carter, October 14, 1898, and to Commanding Generals, I and II Corps, October 28, 1898, File No. 299587; all in AGO Records. Capt. W. C. R. Colquhoun, Report of Augusta Depot, June 30, 1899, File No. 133396; and File No. 119092; both in OQMG Records. *War Investigating Commission*, I, 211. *RSW, 1898*, I, 521, 528-29; II, 211-13; *RSW, 1899*, I, Pt. 2, pp. 402-403. Maj. Gen. J. F. Wilson to Henry Cabot Lodge, October 25, 1898, Box 43, Wilson Papers. Wilson, *Under the Old Flag*, II, 461-62.

7. Sanger quotation is from *War Investigating Commission*, IV, 1113.

8. *War Investigating Commission*, VI, 2629, 2642-43, 2647, 2699; VII, 3143-45, 3148. *RSW, 1899*, I, Pt. 2, pp. 238-39. *Army and Navy Journal*, October 1, 1898.

The Ordnance Department also came out of the war with expanded reserves of all types of weapons and equipment, with enhanced productive capacity at its arsenals, and with a fully tooled up private manufacturing sector upon which to draw. Improvement was especially evident in the small arms situation. By the end of 1898, over 150,000 Krag rifles were in the hands of troops or ready for issue. Springfield Arsenal had doubled its manufacturing capacity for the rifle to 300 a day. During the following year the Ordnance Department opened a new cartridge plant at Frankford Arsenal in Philadelphia and started construction of a second rifle works at Rock Island, Illinois. With plans afoot to build up a reserve of 500,000 Krags, the Chief of Ordnance during the fall of 1898 rearmed with the magazine rifle all the Volunteer regiments bound for Cuba. He would have done the same for the Volunteers at Manila, but the Eighth Corps commander delayed taking this step on the assumption his state troops soon would return to the United States.[9]

The Medical Department took full advantage, not only of ample stockpiles and streamlined administrative procedures, but also of the fact that the summer's epidemics and scandals had instilled in War Department officials and line commanders a new appreciation of the importance of the medics' functions to the Army as a whole. Surgeon General Sternberg improved his supply system by enlarging his existing depots at New York, Saint Louis, and San Francisco and opening additional ones at Atlanta and Savannah to serve troops in the new southern camps and those bound for Cuba. His bureau worked out with the Subsistence Department an improved system for providing special diets for patients in Army hospitals, a task hitherto mired in confusion and conflicts of authority. The Medical Department expanded its support of troops in camp and field by re-establishing regimental dispensaries to treat minor injuries and ailments while at the same time reinforcing the division hospitals. Many of the latter, in the new camps, were housed in centrally heated prefabricated wooden buildings. The hospitals' enlarged staffs now regularly included female nurses. To relieve the camp hospitals if necessary and to care for patients from Cuba and Puerto Rico, General Sternberg opened 1,000-bed base hospitals at Fort Monroe and Savannah in December. He ordered construction of another, of 500 beds, at San Francisco to care for sick and wounded from the Philippines. The hospital ship *Relief* continued in service in the Caribbean.[10]

9. *RSW, 1898,* I, 203, 211; II, 641. *RSW, 1899,* III, 5-7, 17-20, 25, 27-28, 32, 521. *War Investigating Commission,* I, 197; VI, 2850-52, 2860. *Correspondence,* II, 758, 837-38, 992-93. *Army and Navy Journal,* November 19 and December 24, 1898. GO 144, HQA, September 16, 1898, *GO/AGO, 1898.* Ch of Ordnance D. W. Flagler to Alger, September 12, 1898, File No. 158861; Maj. Gen. F. Lee to Corbin, October 20, 1898, File No. 142834; Corbin to Gen. Douglass, January 3, 1899, File No. 243319; all in AGO Records. Maj. Gen. J. H. Wilson to Flagler, October 21, 1898, Box 43, Wilson Papers. For a British survey of the increase in American ordnance production capacity, see C. S. Clark, "Naval and Military Progress of the United States," *JMSI,* XXV, 421.

10. *RSW, 1898,* I, 696-97, 739. *RSW, 1899,* I, Pt. 2, pp. 363-64, 377-82, 396-401, 407-408, 412-14, 558. *War Investigating Commission,* III, 493; VI, 2759. For the development of the system for rationing the sick, see GO 125, HQA, July 8, 1899, and GO 137, HQA, July 26, 1899, both in *GO/AGO, 1899.*

Courtesy USAMHI

Main Street, 1st Brigade Hospital, Camp Conrad, Columbus, Georgia, December 25, 1898.

Courtesy USAMHI

Winterized Tents, probably Camp Shipp, Alabama, Fall 1898.

Sternberg took advantage of increased high-level attention to medical matters to strengthen his department's authority over camp sanitation. To ensure himself of adequate information on camp conditions, the Surgeon General on December 2, 1898, appointed one of his assistants, Colonel Charles R. Greenleaf, Medical Inspector of the Army. Greenleaf regularly toured Army installations and reported in detail to Sternberg on general troop health, hospital conditions, and the efficiency of Medical Department personnel. Indicating the War Department's increased concern with preventing disease, Secretary Alger on December 31 ordered the chief surgeon of every command to make a weekly sanitary inspection of the soldiers under his care and forward his findings and recommendations both to his immediate commanding officer and to the Surgeon General. Alger at the same time ordered monthly inspections of all Army hospitals.[11]

On November 29, 1898, with its reorganization and redeployment substantially completed, the Army contained some 178,000 officers and men, 63,000 of them Regulars. It was becoming a well equipped, efficiently managed force. The new southern camps proved generally satisfactory, with ample space for the troops, good drainage, and plenty of pure water, all elements missing from the first assembly camps. A correspondent wrote in February of the brigade at Albany, Georgia: "The camp is very healthy, and the troops present a vastly different appearance from those at our great camps last summer." Older camps, such as that at San Francisco for Manila-bound troops, also displayed steady improvement in housing, sanitation, discipline, and water supply. On his inspection tours, Colonel Greenleaf found the soldiers everywhere well housed, clothed, and fed, the hospitals fully organized and supplied, and the camps cleaner than they ever had been before. However, Greenleaf's reports, and those of command surgeons, continued to contain complaints of sanitary negligence on the part of line officers, both Regular and Volunteer. Nevertheless, there was to be no repetition of the great typhoid epidemic of 1898.[12]

II

Besides reducing and redeploying the Army created for the war with Spain, the McKinley administration during the autumn launched a campaign for a permanent Regular Army of 100,000 men, the size force the President and his advisors considered necessary to occupy and defend America's

11. *War Investigating Commission*, VI, 2821-22. *RSW, 1899*, I, Pt. 2, pp. 556-57, 560-62. GO 194, HQA, December 31, 1898, *GO/AGO, 1898*.

12. *RSW, 1898*, II, 176-77, 640. *RSW, 1899*, I, Pt. 1, p. 3, Pt. 2, pp. 396, 402-403, 406, 556-58, Pt. 3, p. 193. *War Investigating Commission*, I, 114, 153; III, 224, 721, 751; IV, 1131. *Army and Navy Journal*, December 17, 1898, January 28, February 11 and 25, 1899. Maj. Gen. J. H. Wilson to Capt. Erskine Hewitt, December 11, 1898, Box 43, Wilson Papers.

new island dependencies. Such expansion of the Regular Army enjoyed substantial support in Congress and the press and among the relatively small public interested in military affairs. The Navy's Admiral Mahan, whose earlier writings had mentioned the Army only in passing, now acknowledged the need for "an adequate and extremely mobile army" to cooperate with the Navy in maintaining the nation's position as a world power. Even the National Guard, which had blocked Army expansion the previous spring, no longer actively opposed it. With their wartime role in the Volunteer Army secured by the Act of April 22, 1898, the Guardsmen, preoccupied with reestablishing and improving their state organizations, took little part in the new military debate. The few who did participate generally favored enlargement of the Regular force.[13]

During late November, Secretary Alger, Adjutant-General Corbin, and their congressional ally, Representative John A. T. Hull, drafted a bill which provided for a 100,000-man Army, the additional strength to come from a modest increase in the number of infantry and cavalry regiments, from adding a fully manned third battalion to each regiment, and from doubling the artillery to meet both field and coast defense requirements. The bill made no change in the command system or staff organization. However, it abolished artillery regiments in favor of a corps headed by a general officer and containing a prescribed number of coast and field batteries, a reform urged by artillery officers since the early 1880s.

This bill ran afoul of a complex of political forces. Military reformers criticized its lack of major command and staff reorganization, but they disagreed among themselves, in the press and before congressional committees, about what changes were desirable. The widespread press and public distrust of Secretary Alger prejudiced many members of Congress against any measure originating in his department. Most important, congressional Democrats quickly rallied against the bill, both because they opposed in principle any permanent increase of the standing Army and because they were trying to block the administration's annexation of the Philippines which the enlarged Army was intended to support. Committee hearings and floor debates dragged on into the new year, even as the Senate battle over ratification of the Treaty of Paris with its Philippine annexation provisions reached its climax. The Republicans pushed the Hull bill through the House of Representatives, but that was as far as it got. With only three weeks left in the session, with the peace treaty ratified and the wartime Volunteers and Regulars now due for discharge, and with a Democratic Senate filibuster in prospect, the administration, on Febuary 22, 1899, withdrew its bill in favor of an alternative proposal drafted by the Democrats on the Senate Military Affairs Committee.

13. This section, unless otherwise noted, is based on Graham A. Cosmas, "Military Reform after the Spanish-American War: The Army Reorganization Fight of 1898-1899," *Military Affairs*, XXXV, no. 1 (February, 1971), 12-18.

The compromise measure, which became law on March 2, left Army organization as it was except for giving three full battalions to each existing infantry regiment and adding two batteries to each of the seven artillery regiments. It permitted the President to keep the Regular Army at 65,000 men until July 1, 1901 and to organize and officer 35,000 Volunteers, recruited either from the United States or from the new dependencies, to serve until the same date. The bill also provided for retention of Volunteer generals and staff officers throughout the period of temporary expansion. However, at the insistence of anti-militarist Democratic senators, the final version of the bill required that, on July 1, 1901, the Army be reduced to a permanent strength of less than 30,000 men, too few to man the additional battalions and batteries the bill authorized.

The act of March 2, 1899, thus contributed nothing to long-term military reform. Nevertheless, it did meet the immediate emergency, and in an essentially Uptonian manner. It allowed the continuation in service for up to two years of an Army of 100,000 men, including new Volunteer regiments raised entirely under federal auspices. It authorized the temporary retention in the officer corps of the ablest Volunteer generals and staff officers. To ease the transition between the old Army and the new in the Philippines, the law permitted the President to retain Spanish War Volunteer regiments there for up to six months after the proclamation of peace, if the men agreed to remain. Military reformers, both uniformed and civilian, with an adequate force assured for the next two years, had a breathing space in which to resolve their own differences and develop solutions to the tangled questions of command and staff restructuring. Senator Henry Cabot Lodge, a strong expansionist and proponent of military preparedness, summed up: "The Army bill is, of course, a makeshift, but we get the main thing, which is the troops. The reorganization will take place next winter, and I think will then be . . . done much better than we could have done now."[14]

III

Even as it reorganized the existing Regular and Volunteer force and sought legislation creating a new one, the War Department proceeded with the occupation of Cuba, Puerto Rico, and the Philippines. Securing Puerto Rico was a simple matter of returning to the United States the Volunteer regiments of General Miles's invasion force and replacing them with a much smaller contingent of Regulars. The tasks in Cuba and the Philippines were more complicated. In Cuba, the War Department had to conduct a large-scale occupation closely synchronized with a Spanish military withdrawal. In the Philippines, ratification of the Treaty of Paris resulted in armed conflict

14. Henry Cabot Lodge to Theodore Roosevelt, March 15, 1899, in *Roosevelt-Lodge Correspondence*, I, 395. Text of the act of March 2, 1899 is in *RSW, 1899*, I, Pt. 2, pp. 57-60.

between the American occupying force and the nationalist troops of Emilio Aguinaldo, necessitating for the U.S. Army what amounted to a new mobilization for a new war.

To carry troops overseas and support them once there, the War Department during the autumn of 1898 established a permanent organization for the transport service it had improvised during the war. Secretary Alger and his associates took this action in part to improve operating efficiency and in part to ward off a Navy Department bid to take over the entire sea transport mission. On November 16, Alger set up an Army Transport Service as a division of the Quartermaster's Department. The new service, under regulations prepared by a board of officers headed by Brigadier General William Ludlow on the basis of those used by the British Navy, operated and maintained the Army's troop and supply ships and managed the embarkation and disembarkation of troops and stores. At two home ports, New York for the Atlantic and Caribbean and San Francisco for the Pacific, General Superintendents fueled, manned, and maintained Army transports and loaded and dispatched them as military requirements dictated. Each transport, whether government owned or chartered, sailed under charge of a quartermaster, assisted by a surgeon and commissary. Except in technical matters of navigation and seamanship, the province of the vessel's master, the quartermaster directed the movements and daily routine of his transport. If steaming under Navy escort, he was to conform to the sailing orders of the squadron commander.[15]

While the Transport Service set up its port facilities and recruited a staff of former merchant marine personnel, Quartermaster General Ludington began taking the vessels purchased during the war out of service a few at a time for stem-to-stern conversion into troop-carriers of the most up-to-date design. The first three of these ships, the *Grant*, *Sherman*, and *Sheridan*, each with a capacity of more than a regiment, entered service early in 1899, in time to carry 5,000 Regular infantry to the Philippines. Conversion of additional steamers soon followed, so that within a couple of years the Army possessed a transport fleet that was a match in quality, if not size, for that of any European power. For large troop movements, the Quartermaster's Department continued to need chartered vessels; the Transport Service managed the securing and outfitting of these ships without major difficulty.[16]

15. For the Navy challenge, see: *Army and Navy Journal*, December 17 and 24, 1898; *War Investigating Commission*, III, 306-307; IV, 952; VI, 2418-19; VII, 3289-90. Development of Transport Service: *RSW, 1899*, Pt. 2, pp. 234-35, 546-47. Brig. Gen. William Ludlow to Corbin, August 27, 1898, File No. 115913; Quartermaster General Ludington to Corbin, September 6, 1898, File No. 122525; and Ludlow and 1st Lt. W. C. Rivers to Corbin, October 26, 1898, File No. 145788; all in AGO Records. *Regulations for the Army Transport Service* (Pamphlet in File No. 287644, AGO Records), *passim*.

16. *RSW, 1898*, I, 390-92, 697. *RSW, 1899*, I, Pt. 2, pp. 158-61, 163-64, 223, 235, 547. *Correspondence*, II, 752-53, 875. *War Investigating Commission*, VI, 2416, 2621, 2772-73; VIII, 521-22. *Army and Navy Journal*, October 22 and December 17, 1898, January 21, February 11, March 18, May 13 and 20, and August 26, 1899. Lt. Col. J. W. Pope to the Quartermaster General, November 16, 1898, File No. 115533; Col. J. W. Scully to the Quartermaster General, September 20, 1899,

Building on the experience of 1898, the Army developed increasing sophistication in embarking expeditionary forces for both Cuba and the Philippines. For the large Cuba occupation army, the War Department employed Savannah as its main embarkation port for troops while sending much construction material and heavy freight through Charleston and Tampa. At Savannah, Major J. B. Bellinger, the port quartermaster, used his summer's experience at Tampa in organizing a smooth-running base. Within 60 days, he embarked over 25,000 officers and men, along with more than 7,000 animals and thousands of tons of cargo, without serious delay or major accident. San Francisco, already well-established as the base for the Eighth Corps, handled most troops and cargo for the Philippines, although a few reinforcements sailed for the islands from New York via the Suez Canal. In embarking troops, the War Department routinely followed the practice it had instituted to prevent a repetition of the Fifth Corps's difficulties at Tampa. It kept regiments at their camps and stations until their transports were in port and only then started them by rail to the coast to meet their ships. This procedure, coordinated by telegraph between the Adjutant General's office and the geographical department commanders, kept up a generally smooth flow of troops with minimal congestion at the ports.[17]

The planning and execution of the American occupation of the major part of Cuba—all the island, in fact, outside the portion of Santiago Province captured in Shafter's campaign—constituted the War Department's most complex and difficult task during the fall of 1898. During September and October, an Evacuation Commission of Army and Navy officers, appointed by President McKinley under the armistice terms, arranged with the Spanish authorities for the gradual removal of their 120,000 troops from the island, beginning at the eastern and western ends and working toward Havana. At the same time, the commission, assisted by a board of officers from the War Department staff bureaus, oversaw preparations for the introduction of the American army of occupation. That army was to be large. At the commission's recommendation, the War Department earmarked some 50,000 troops, from the newly reorganized and redeployed First, Second, and Seventh corps, for deployment to Cuba. McKinley, Alger, and the evacuation commission's chairman, Major General James F. Wade, hoped that dispatch of such a large force at the outset would prevent outbreaks of disorder as the Spanish

File No. 133396; OQMG Records. Risch, *Quartermaster Corps*, 566-67. GO 3, HQA, January 9, 1899, *GO/AGO, 1899*. A British writer thought the American transport fleet superior to those of all other powers except Great Britain; Clark, *JMSI*, XXV, 424.

17. *Army and Navy Journal*, November 19 and 26, 1898, April 1 and 22, May 13, June 17, and July 15, 1899. Capt. R. L. Brown to Maj. J. B. Bellinger, June 30, 1899; Maj. Bellinger to the Quartermaster General, June 30, 1899; and Deputy Quartermaster General Humphrey to the Quartermaster General, August 21, 1899; all in File No. 133396, OQMG Records. Asst. Adj. Gen. W. H. Carter to Brig. Gen. Carpenter, November 5 and 6, 1898, File No. 153143; Adj. Gen. Corbin to Maj. Gen. Lee, December 1, 1898, File No. 243302; Corbin to Commanding General, I Corps, December 10, 1898, File No. 243307; all in AGO Records. Movements to the Philippines can be followed in *Correspondence*, II, 829-1041.

withdrew and overawe any Cubans disposed to challenge United States authority. They expected to reduce the force rapidly as conditions stabilized.[18]

The occupation planners, determined to prevent epidemics like those which had wrecked the Fifth Corps, decided to introduce the American occupation troops only a few at a time, as required to replace departing Spanish garrisons. Since the Spanish withdrawal began slowly, this procedure kept the bulk of the American force out of the island until the relatively disease-free late fall and winter. In the meantime, commanders, staff officers, and engineer troops spread out across Cuba. They located and prepared camp-sites, hospitals, and supply depots and began the Herculean task of cleaning up and repairing Havana and other war-ravaged, disease-ridden cities. The flow of American regiments into the island began slowly during November and accelerated in December, as the Spanish withdrawal gained momentum. For the most part, the influx went smoothly, except for inevitable delays caused by weather and some difficulty setting up the large Seventh Corps camp at Marianao on the outskirts of Havana. On January 1, 1899, the day the Spanish Governor-General formally transferred sovereignty over Cuba to the new American military governor, Major General John R. Brooke, 23,000 American troops were in the island. Within a month, the force built up to its peak strength of about 45,000. Thereafter, its numbers rapidly declined, as Cuba remained peaceful and President McKinley recalled the Spanish War Volunteers to the United States for muster out. By the end of 1899, the occupation force consisted of about 11,000 troops, all Regulars.

The United States soldiers occupying Cuba, and those in Puerto Rico and the Philippines, were better housed and equipped for tropical service than those who served in the improvised wartime campaigns; and they had the benefit of more extensive medical support. Regiments of the Cuban occupation force brought with them large hospital tents, one for every six men, with precut lumber for frames and floors. They lived in these shelters for the first three months of the occupation. After the Volunteers left, the smaller permanent garrison moved into renovated Spanish barracks or newly constructed posts, such as Camp Columbia at Havana. Troops in Cuba, Puerto Rico, and the Philippines now possessed a variety of hotweather clothing, including uniforms of white duck, khaki, and a lightweight version of the traditional blue. The Quartermaster's Department, however, continued to have difficulty obtaining satisfactory khaki cloth for the preferred field uniform. Although regiments in the Philippines were outfitted with excellent suits from established British suppliers in Hong Kong, Singapore, and Bombay, those in the Western Hemisphere had to make do with the product of inexperienced American manufacturers, which faded to a variety of

18. This discussion of the occupation of Cuba is drawn from Graham A. Cosmas, "Securing the Fruits of Victory: The U.S. Army Occupies Cuba, 1898-1899," *Military Affairs*, XXXVIII, No. 3, pp. 85-91.

shades when washed and often was too light for durability. Tropical equipment also was influenced by contemporary medical misconceptions. Hence, every soldier received a heavy flannel "belly band" to be worn around his waist to prevent chills to the bowels, which supposedly caused dysentery and malaria.[19]

Surgeon General Sternberg equipped the overseas garrisons lavishly; and command surgeons enforced rigorous sanitary precautions. Each occupation regiment went to Cuba with its own fifteen- or twenty-bed hospital. Each division hospital had a capacity of 1,000 patients. In Cuba, and also in Puerto Rico and at Manila, the Medical Department renovated Spanish military hospitals to serve as general hospitals and convalescent facilities. To ensure adequate supply, the Surgeon General during 1899 set up and stocked depots at Havana, San Juan, and Manila. At overseas stations, surgeons and troop commanders cleaned and disinfected every structure used by the Army, installed new camp and municipal water and sewage systems, and enforced upon both soldiers and civilians rigid standards of garbage removal and waste disposal. These precautions checked the ravages of typhoid, dysentery, and many other diseases in the tropical garrisons. However, yellow fever remained unconquered until Major Walter Reed identified its mosquito carrier in 1901.[20]

The Philippine War, which began along the Eighth Corps's lines around Manila on the night of February 4, 1899, tested a portion of the Army in hard tropical combat and found it more than able to carry out its mission. In the initial campaigns, which involved conventional operations against the massed troops of Emilio Aguinaldo, both Regulars and Spanish War Volunteers attacked skillfully and aggressively. Repeatedly, they drove the Filipinos from their fortified positions. The troops of the Eighth Corps responded resourcefully to tactical surprises and learned to march and fight in heat that prostrated regiments newly arrived from the United States.[21]

19. *RSW, 1899*, I, Pt. 2, pp. 154-55, 239, 243-44, 450, 454, 505-506, 515-17, 523-26, 581-82, Pt. 3, pp. 124-25, 127, 222-23, 313-14, 494, and Pt. 4, pp. 39-40. *War Investigating Commission*, III, 83, 104, 339-40; VI, 2648-49; VII, 3154, 3156-57, 3192, 3211-12, 3271. *Correspondence*, II, 794, 797, 902, 1024, 1028. 1042-43. GO 26, HQA, February 9, 1899; GO 87, HQA, May 3, 1899; *GO/AGO, 1899*. For housing of colonial garrisons, see Files No. 115533, 133396, and 137361, OQMG Records; and Files No. 138133, 157472, 164171, 194178, 194708, 221646, 228955, and 243531, AGO Records. For documents, reports, and correspondence on the tropical uniform, see Files No. 115533, 121944, 132523, and 133396, OQMG Records. For "belly bands" and their uses, see Capt. Matthew F. Steele, "Some Notes on the Clothing and Equipment of the Soldier for Service in the Tropics," *JMSI*, XXIX, 22-23.

20. *RSW, 1898*, I, 735, 740, 852; II, 36. *RSW, 1899*, I, Pt. 2, pp. 314-15, 364, 451-52, 498, 503-507, 514-17, 522-23, 526-27, 597-98, 603-12, Pt. 3, pp. 437-38, 495, Pt. 4, p. 40. *Correspondence*, I, 215, 217, 373, 378, 381; II, 795, 802, 833, 839, 842, 885, 893. Latshaw, "Medical Service," 92-98. Board on Garrisons in Cuba to Corbin, October 21, 1898, File No. 132015; Maj. Gen. J. R. Brooke to Corbin, February 8, 1899, Corbin to Brooke, February 10, 1899, File No. 201560; AGO Records. Lt. Col. J. W. Pope to the Quartermaster General, August 11, 1899, File No. 133396, OQMG Records. Hagedorn, *Wood*, I, 242-45, describes efforts to control yellow fever at Santiago.

21. *RSW, 1899*, I, Pt. 2, p. 21, Pt. 3, pp. 439, 443-46, Pt. 4, p. 175. *Correspondence*, II, 874. Lt. Col. James Parker, "Some Random Notes on the Fighting in the Philippines," *JMSI*, XXVII, 325-26. *Army and Navy Journal*, July 22, 1899. While effective in combat, the troops, especially the Spanish War Volunteers, often looted and committed acts of vandalism behind the lines. Their indiscipline seriously hampered the American effort to win the confidence of the Filipinos.

Courtesy National Archives

*Major General
John R. Brooke*

Courtesy National Archives

American Troops entering Havana, Cuba, January 1, 1899.

American logisticians were equally efficient. The corps chief quarter-master, Lt. Col. J. W. Pope, although he was, at the outset, short of men, draught animals, and standard Army vehicles, improvised supply trains by supplementing his few wagons with native buffalo and pony carts and employing hundreds of Chinese coolies. During the offensive north of Manila, pony carts loaded with rations and ammunition kept up with each regiment's firing line, and a divisional train of wagons and buffalo carts followed the combat forces along the railroad, which formed the axis of the advance. Engineers marched with the wagons and repaired roads and bridges on their route. The Quartermaster's Department also repaired and operated the railroad, improvised fleets of supply barges on the rivers, and built the Eighth Corps a navy of shallow-draught gunboats. Working closely with the quarter-masters, Subsistence and Ordnance officers kept their bureaus' supplies moving to the front. Signal Corpsmen, often stringing line under fire, kept the mobile columns in constant telegraphic contact with headquarters in Manila. Surgeons and hospital corpsmen with first-aid supplies accompanied every unit into battle and treated the wounded at field dressing stations. Using ambulances, horse litters, and Chinese stretcher-bearers, medical officers evacuated seriously wounded men to the railhead for transportation to the base hospitals in Manila. Late in the northern campaign, they constructed and staffed a forward base hospital in the town of San Fernando, at the farthest limit of the army's advance. In Luzon, the bureaus demonstrated what they could accomplish if given seasoned personnel, an adequate base of operations, and timely inclusion in campaign planning.[22]

By mid-summer of 1899, the Eighth Corps had driven Aguinaldo's main army away from Manila into central Luzon and had secured a few footholds in the outlying islands. The Filipino army had been much reduced by casualties and desertion, and the nationalist political leadership had suffered a number of defections of prominent men to the Americans. Nevertheless, these early successes had cost the Eighth Corps 361 officers and men killed in action, 438 more dead of disease, and 1,412 wounded—casualties that already equalled the combat losses of the entire war with Spain. Aguinaldo's force remained in the field in Luzon and the other islands. The

22. Capt. C. G. Sawtelle, Jr., to the Chief Quartermaster, Dept. of the Pacific and VIII Corps, February 6, March 19, and May 31, 1899; Lt. Col. J. W. Pope to the Quartermaster General, August 11, 1899; File No. 133396, OQMG Records. Maj. R. H. Fitzhugh to Adj. Gen., 2d Division, VIII Corps, March 20, 1899; Dep. Surg. Gen. H. Lippincott to Adj. Gen., Dept. of the Pacific and VIII Corps, April 2, 1899; Lt. Col. J. R. McGinness to Adj. Gen., Dept. of the Pacific and VIII Corps, April 4, 1899; McKinley Papers. *RSW, 1898*, I, 852. *RSW, 1899*, I, pt. 2, pp. 451-52, 462-65, 467, 745-46, 798-99, Pt. 3, pp. 440-41, 444-45, Pt. 4, pp. 101, 227. Latshaw, "Medical Service," 92-93, 100-103. Risch, *Quartermaster Corps*, 568. Parker, *JMSI*, XXVII, 327-28. *Army and Navy Journal*, May 27, 1899, quotes Maj. Gen. Arthur MacArthur in praise of the supply departments. See also in this connection Theodore Roosevelt to Maj. J. H. Parker, February 13, 1900, Morison, ed., *Roosevelt Letters*, II, 1181-82.

Filipino leader and his hard-core followers showed no signs of giving up and still enjoyed the support of most of their countrymen. It was clear that a long, costly struggle lay ahead.[23]

The McKinley administration by mid-summer was well on the way to mobilizing forces for that struggle. This involved replacing the Spanish War Volunteers, who constituted about three-fourths of the 20,000-man Eighth Corps and now were due for return to the United States and muster out, as well as enlargement of the corps for its war mission. Even before the outbreak of hostilities, the War Department had started six Regular infantry regiments for Manila. Other Regular infantry, artillery, and cavalry units followed during the early months of 1899, along with thousands of men recruited under the new Army reorganization act to replace temporary wartime enlistees among the Regulars already in the islands. Early in July, after Maj. Gen. Elwell S. Otis, the Eighth Corps commander, asked for a full 40,000 troops to subdue the Philippines, the War Department, with no more Regulars available for deployment, began organizing the first ten U.S. Volunteer infantry regiments authorized under the March reorganization act.[24]

What amounted to an exchange of armies went forward smoothly during the summer, as weather forced a pause in active campaigning in Luzon. A steady stream of transports shuttled between Manila and San Francisco, carrying Regulars outward bound and returning state Volunteers on the homeward voyage. The Volunteers awaited muster out in previously prepared camps at San Francisco and after discharge travelled individually to their homes, at government expense. Meanwhile, the War Department organized its new Volunteer regiments at various Army posts. The Army recruiting service enlisted men for these units. President McKinley appointed their officers, selecting them from among Regulars and Volunteers on the basis of their records in the war with Spain. To equip the regiments promptly the Quartermaster's Department dispatched complete outfits of clothing, tentage, and equipment to their rendezvous well in advance of the recruits' arrival. The Ordnance Department issued them Krag-Jörgensen rifles. These regiments departed for the Philippines during the early autumn.

23. *RSW, 1899*, I, Pt. 1, pp. 12, 23, 34-35, Pt. 4, pp. 133-35, 139-48, 152-57, 161-64. *Correspondence*, II, 969, 980, 986, 991, 997, 999, 1004-1005, 1011, 1013, 1019, 1027, 1029, 1033-35, 1037, 1039-40, 1051, 1058, 1060, 1076, 1105. J. G. Schurman to Secretary of State John Hay, July 4, 1899; Maj. Gen. Otis to Alger, July 8, 1899; Commissioner Denby to Hay, July 17, 1899; McKinley Papers. Agoncillo, *Malolos*, 489-93, 540-41, 585-88.

24. *RSW, 1899*, I, Pt. 1, p. 5, GO 35, HQA, March 3, 1899; GO 56, HQA, March 27, 1899; GO 82, HQA, April 26, 1899; GO 83, HQA, April 28, 1899; GO 107, HQA, June 13, 1899; GO 108, HQA, June 13, 1899; GO 109, HQA, June 15, 1899; GO 113, HQA, June 20, 1899; *GO/AGO, 1899. Correspondence*, II, 929, 932-33, 936-37, 968-69, 999, 1004, 1013. *Army and Navy Journal*, February 25, March 4, and April 1, and 22, June 3, 17, and 24, 1899. "Memorandum for the Adjutant General to Submit to the Acting Secretary of War," with endorsement by Asst. Secretary of War G. D. Meiklejohn, June 6, 1899, Corbin to Maj. Gen. Otis, June 15, 1899, File No. 242889; Corbin to Maj. Gen. Brooke, June 6, 1899, File No. 248666; AGO Records.

Well-trained and led for the most part by officers of high quality, these units proved effective in combat, and also in the even more difficult work of pacification and counterguerrilla operations.[25]

San Francisco became the support base for the army at Manila. At the Presidio, where Maj. Gen. Shafter now commanded the Department of California and directed the logistical effort, well-appointed new camps sprang up to house outward-bound Regulars and U.S. Volunteers and returning state regiments. Scheduled by Shafter in cooperation with the Army Transport Service and the other department commanders, the two-way flow of troops proceeded with little of the disorder and delay Shafter's Fifth Corps had endured at Tampa. Besides the soldiers, thousands of tons of Manila-bound cargo passed through San Francisco and other West Coast ports. By late August, the quartermaster depot at San Francisco had dispatched to the Islands a full year's supply of clothing and equipage for the Eighth Corps. From large reserves, the depot could respond swiftly to unexpected demands. To enhance Otis's mobility, the Quartermaster's Department sent out hundreds of horses and mules, scores of wagons, carts, and ambulances, and thousands of cavalry mounts. The Ordnance Department built up a West Coast stockpile of 10,000 sets of infantry arms and accoutrements, 10 million rounds of smallarms ammunition, and a variety of other stores, to be forwarded to Manila as General Otis called for them. The Subsistence Department loaded rations on every departing transport to establish a six-months' reserve of nonperishables at Manila. (The Army in the Philippines drew fresh meat, vegetables, and other perishables from local markets and, in the case of meat, from Australia and New Zealand.) The Medical Department early in March dispatched its hospital ship *Relief* to Manila from New York via the Suez Canal. Transports sailing from San Francisco carried additional surgeons, corpsmen, and supplies. As a result of this effort, when good campaigning weather returned in November, General Otis had well over 40,000 well supplied, fully equipped troops ready for action in Luzon.[26]

25. Corbin to Acting Secretary of War, June 20, 1899; Acting Secretary of War Meiklejohn to McKinley, June 24, 1899; McKinley Papers. GO 122, HQA, July 5, 1899; GO 124, HQA, July 8, 1899; *GO/AGO, 1899. Army and Navy Journal*, July 1, 8, 15, 22, and 29, 1899. *RSW, 1899*, I, Pt. 2, pp. 16, 21, 31, 38. *Correspondence*, II, 1029, 1030-31, 1041, 1044, 1046-47. Maj. Gen. W. R. Shafter to Alger, July 10, 1899, Alger Papers. Shafter to Corbin, August 10, 1899, Box 1, Corbin Papers. Col. Pettit to Corbin, July 22, 1899, File No. 137883, OQMG Records; this file also covers development of the supply system for the new regiments. Parker, *JMSI*, XXVII, 325-26, assesses the fighting quality of the U.S. Volunteers.

26. *Correspondence*, II, 874, 884, 929, 949, 951, 963, 969, 1012-14, 1017-18, 1021-22, 1024, 1026, 1042. *RSW, 1899*, I, Pt. 2, pp. 21-22, 156, 162, 467-68, 553; III, 5. *Army and Navy Journal*, November 19, 1898; April 4, May 27, June 3 and 10, 1899. Corbin to Shafter, June 10, 1899; Shafter to Corbin, June 10, 1899, File No. 242889, AGO Records. Ch Quartermaster, Dept. of California, to the Quartermaster General, August 8, 1899; Depot Quartermaster O. F. Long to the Quartermaster General, August 22, 1899; File No. 133396, OQMG Records. Shafter to Corbin, August 10, 1899, Box 1, Corbin Papers.

Courtesy USAMHI

20th Kansas Camp at the Presidio, San Francisco.

IV

The Army's display of tactical and administrative efficiency during the first half of 1899 did nothing to improve the reputation and political position of Secretary Alger. Most Americans, their image of the Army's administration irrevocably tarnished by the disease-ridden aftermath of the Spanish War and by the beef scandal, disregarded the findings of the Dodge Commission and the court of inquiry into the beef supply. They continued to regard the War Department as a welter of confusion and a sinkhole of corruption and to blame Alger for the supposed mess. Republican politicians continued to warn President McKinley of his war minister's unpopularity with the voters and to urge the President to get rid of him.[27]

Neither Alger nor his enemy Miles in fact deserved much credit for the Army's success in meeting the new challenges of overseas empire. Absorbed ever since the previous autumn in their bitter feud, the two men refused even to speak to one another. When they communicated at all, they used intermediaries. To avoid involvement in this personal battle, McKinley bypassed both men. Acting as his own Secretary of War and his own Commanding General, he managed the Army himself under an informal but effective command system that he evolved under the pressures of the war and of the Alger-Miles conflict. McKinley oversaw every detail of the Army's operations, from the selection of Cuban campsites and the appointment of occupation commanders to the conduct of battles in the Philippines. He pressed continually for advance planning and careful attention to sanitation. On questions of Army administration, supply, and personnel, he relied on the counsels of Corbin, now Commanding General in all but name and rank. Overseas, the President gave Army and garrison commanders, carefully chosen for loyalty to his Administration and his policies, wide freedom of action on all matters, and he made certain that the bureaus met the commanders' every demand for men and equipment. Through friends on their staffs, Corbin cross-checked the performance of these commanders. In consultation with Corbin and the field generals, the President made most of his decisions without consulting Alger and Miles, and he ignored or overruled their advice when they offered it.[28]

27. James S. Kirk to Secretary of the Treasury Lyman J. Gage, February 25, 1899; William M. Osborne to President McKinley, March 3, 1899; John K. Gowdy to McKinley, March 22, 1899; Charles Ledyard Norton to J. A. Porter, March 31, 1899; Grenville M. Dodge to Gen. H. V. Boynton, March 28, 1899, and to McKinley, April 20, 1899; Gen. H. V. Boynton to McKinley, April 25, 1899, McKinley Papers, Henry Cabot Lodge to Theodore Roosevelt, July 12, 1899, Richard C. Parsons to Roosevelt, July 15, 1899, Vol. 6, Roosevelt Papers. John J. McCook to Maj. Gen. J. H. Wilson, January 18 and April 7, 1899, Box 15, Wilson Papers. For other contemporary expressions of dismay at War Department inefficiency and of desire for Alger's removal, see *Adams Letters*, II, 206, 210, 213, 218, and 220, and *Roosevelt-Lodge Correspondence*, I, 399-400, 411-12. See also Morgan, *McKinley*, 428-29.

28. McKinley's command system has to be pieced together by tracing many administrative actions and decisions. The following materials are revealing: President McKinley to Secretary Alger,

Throughout the spring of 1899 McKinley waged a covert but bitter contest of wills against his increasingly useless war minister. The President wanted and needed a new Secretary of War, one better informed than Alger about the legal complexities of colonial government and one who could regain for the War Department the public confidence Alger had lost. However, McKinley could not simply fire Alger, because his political opponents would plausibly construe such action as a confession of military mismanagement. Then, too, McKinley, a kindly man who took matter of conscience seriously, was in moral debt to Alger. Throughout the Spanish War he had imposed his own will upon the Army through the loyal Secretary. Later, he had failed to take responsibility when disaster and scandal clouded the prosecution of the war and the people blamed the mismanagement on Alger. If anything, McKinley had acquiesced in and even encouraged such placing of the blame, thereby allowing the burden to fall on his Secretary. Alger now ruthlessly exploited McKinley's conscience-stricken hesitation. Convinced of his own rectitude and contemptuous of the President's behavior in the dispute with Miles, which he considered cowardly, Alger refused to resolve McKinley's dilemma by resigning. He continued to go through the motions of managing his department. He signed orders, toured the Caribbean garrisons, and in May instituted a "Secretary's Cabinet," a weekly meeting of the bureau chiefs to coordinate their work. Time and again he repeated that he would not quit under fire, that he would stay on until the record vindicated him or at least until 1901, when he could withdraw gracefully at the change of administrations. Without influence in the War Department and treated with bare civility by the President and the other members of the Cabinet, Alger persisted through the spring and into the early summer.[29]

September 8, 1898, File No. 121918; Endorsement of President, dated October 29, 1898, on Maj. Gen. J. F. Wade to Adj. Gen. Corbin, October 19, 1898, File No. 143728; Corbin to Maj. Gen. J. R. Brooke, December 30, 1898, File No. 243520, AGO Records. Alger to Maj. Gen. William Ludlow, February 20, 1899, Alger Papers. Gen. Theodore Schwan to Corbin, August 21, 1899, Box 1; *New York Herald*, clipping dated 1899, Box 1A, Corbin Papers. Hugh L. Scott to Mrs. Scott, May 3, 1899, Box 1, Scott Papers, testifies to the power junior officers believed Corbin had over promotions. Anthony Higgins to Maj. Gen. J. H. Wilson, June 26 and July 9, 1899, Box 11; Wilson to Col. W. E. Wilder, November 10, 1898, Box 43; Wilson to W. L. Bull, April 28, 1899, and to H. W. Gause, July 25, 1899, Box 44; Wilson to Col. LeGrande Cannon, October 14, 1899, Box 45, Wilson Papers. *Army and Navy Journal*, October 29, 1898. Dunn, *Harrison to Harding*, I, 246-74. Wilson, *Under the Old Flag*, II, 472-73. For specific Presidential overridings of Alger, see Files No. 242889 and 243502, AGO Records, and *Correspondence*, II, 988-89.

29. Leech, *Days of McKinley*, 366-67, 369-70, 373-74. Morgan, *McKinley*, 429. Olcott, *McKinley*, II, 89-90. Secretary Alger to W. H. Alger, June 29, 1899; Beriah Wilkins to Alger, December 14, 1901; Alger to Senator George F. Hoar, February 8, 1902, Alger Papers. Corbin claimed McKinley decided on Alger's removal as early as December, 1898; see Maj. Gen. Corbin to Representative Charles H. Grosvenor, February 4, 1907, Box 1, Corbin Papers. Note signed by President McKinley, July 19, 1899, and draft of letter from McKinley to Alger, July, 1899, McKinley Papers. Otto Carmichael to C. S. Osborn, July 18, 1899, Box 4; John J. McCook to Wilson, April 7, 1899, Box 15; Wilson to Senator William P. Frye, April 3, 1899, Box 43; Wilson to Gen. S. Cadwallader, July 26, 1899, Box 44, Wilson Papers. *Army and Navy Journal*, March 25 and May 13, 1899, describes Alger's administrative activities.

An ill-conceived political venture by Alger in his home state permitted McKinley to end the agony. In Michigan, a factional feud between a conservative machine headed by Senator James McMillan and an insurgent coalition led by militant reform governor Hazen S. Pingree divided the Republican party. Alger had designs on the boss's Senate seat. Although the Secretary had been on bad terms with the Senator, he believed that he held McMillan's promise to withdraw in his favor in 1900. Accordingly, on a trip to Michigan in late April, Alger launched his senatorial campaign. When McMillan promptly announced his own candidacy for re-election, Alger openly allied with Pingree against him. Seen in relation to the complexities of Michigan politics, the association made sense. Both Alger and Pingree hated McMillan and desired his defeat. Alger had always maintained a more friendly relationship with Pingree than had other orthodox Michigan Republicans. During the war, Pingree, who had supervised closely the organization of Michigan's Volunteers, stoutly defended Alger's management of the Army. However, Pingree had, since the armistice, publicly criticized McKinley's foreign and domestic policies, and he tried to associate Alger with these attacks. Although Alger went out of his way to separate himself from Pingree on these issues, it appeared to the press and public by early July that McKinley's Secretary of War had joined the President's political enemies.[30]

McKinley now could demand Alger's resignation for reasons unrelated to Army administration and acceptable to his own tender conscience, but Alger still refused to admit the hopelessness of his position. On July 12 he repeated to newspapermen his intention to remain in the Cabinet. Still unwilling himself to do what had to be done, McKinley deputized his tactful and urbane but ailing Vice-President, Garrett A. Hobart, to tell Alger his time in office had run out. A close friend of Alger, Hobart invited the Secretary in mid-July to spend the weekend at his summer home in Long Branch, New Jersey. There, he told Alger that the President resented his attempt to unseat a senator who was loyal to the Administration and wished him to leave the Cabinet. On his return to Washington on July 19, Alger had a final acrimonious interview with McKinley and submitted his

30. Stephen B. Sarosohn, "The Regulation of Parties and Nominations in Michigan: The Politics of Election Reform" (Ph.D. dissertation, Columbia University, 1953), 66-73, 77, 81-83, describes the factions among Michigan Republicans and Alger's position among them. Alger gives his version of the Senate fight in a posthumously published interview in *Milwaukee Journal*, January 24, 1907. *Army and Navy Journal*, April 29, 1899, recounts the trip to Michigan during which Alger's Senate bid evidently took shape. Kalamazoo (Michigan) *Telegram* January 26, 1907, clipping in Obituary Scrapbook; Hazen S. Pingree to Secretary Alger, August 16, 1898, and July 3, 1899; Alger to Pingree, July 5, 1899, Alger Papers. Alger to Chase S. Osborn, May 8 and 15, 1899; Osborn to Alger, May 11 and 18, 1899; Pingree to Alger, May 23, 1899; A. H. N. Jenkins to Osborn, June 28, 1899; H. H. Frausshauser to Osborn, June 28, 1899; Ralph Stone to Osborn, August 26, 1899, Osborn Papers. These and other letters in the Osborn collection reveal the extent of Pingreeite backing for Alger, based more on a desire to defeat McMillan than on devotion to the beleaguered Secretary of War. On Alger's political foray, see also Leech, *Days of McKinley*, 368-70, and Morgan, *McKinley*, 429.

resignation, to take effect whenever the President wished. That same day McKinley, in a short note that made only perfunctory mention of Alger's loyal service, set August 1 as the date for the Secretary's relinquishing of the post to which he had clung so long and to so little purpose. McKinley, his Cabinet, and Republican leaders throughout the country greeted Alger's resignation with relief. On the other hand, the editor of the *Army and Navy Journal*, who had grown increasingly sympathetic to the beleaguered Secretary as the Army's efficiency improved, commented:

> The ancient Israelites had a practice of transferring their transgressions to the head of a goat when they became too heavy, and sending the animal into the wilderness bearing the sins of the people with him. Now that a similar vicarious transfer of our evils of military administration has been made in the case of Secretary Alger it is to be hoped that we shall have rest for a time from indefinite and vociferous charges against our military administrators.[31]

Until August 1 Alger remained the nominal but inactive head of the War Department. On the day appointed for his leaving office, he ceremoniously turned over his post to his successor, Elihu Root, an able, intelligent, tactful New York corporation lawyer whom McKinley had selected to develop a system of government for the new American colonies rather than to reform the Army. That same evening, aboard his private railroad car, the former Secretary left Washington for Detroit. His fellow Michiganders, many of whom attributed his dismissal to a sinister Eastern conspiracy, welcomed him to his home city with a parade of thousands of well-wishers and a reception in the City Hall's corridors, which were packed with his sympathizers. In September Alger withdrew from the Senate race rather than fight a party-wrecking and, in the opinion of most experts, losing battle to unseat McMillan. He spent the first two years of his retirement writing his memoir, *The Spanish-American War*, a defense of his actions as Secretary of War and of the War Department's operations. In 1902, when McMillan died, the governor of Michigan sent Alger to the Senate to serve out the boss's term, and in the following year the Michigan legislature elected Alger to the seat in his own right. He remained in the Senate until his death in January, 1907, a popular if not especially influential figure.[32]

31. The quotation is from *Army and Navy Journal*, July 29, 1899; see also issues of May 6 and July 15 and 22, 1899. For an officer's retrospective praise of Alger, see Cruse, *Apache Days and After*, 272. Leech, *Days of McKinley*, 376-78, and Morgan, *McKinley*, 274, 429-31, recount the final events of Alger's tenure. For Alger's version, see statement signed by him and dated November 26, 1900, Alger Papers, and interview in *Milwaukee Journal*, January 24, 1907. Secretary Alger to President McKinley, July 19, 1899; McKinley to Alger, July 19, 1899, copies in both Alger and McKinley Papers, are the resignation documents. For expressions of relief at Alger's departure, see Dawes, *Journal*, 196, and Olcott, *McKinley*, II, 90.

32. For Root's selection, see Dunn, *Harrison to Harding*, I, 154-58; Philip C. Jessup, *Elihu Root*, I, 215; and Morgan, *McKinley*, 431-32. For the transfer ceremony, see *Army and Navy Journal*, August 5, 1899. The Detroit welcome is recounted in exhaustive detail in Scrapbook of Clippings, Alger Papers. For Alger's subsequent political activities, see *Milwaukee Journal*, January 24, 1907; R. A. Alger to William Jackson, September 8, 1899, Alger Papers. Alger to C. S. Osborn, May 15, 1899; Otto Carmichael to Osborn, May 17, 1899, Osborn Papers. Sarasohn, "Regulation of Parties," 82-83, 99.

Alger in 1899 had left to Root an Army far different in size and circumstances from the force he had inherited a little more than two years previously. Instead of 25,000 soldiers scattered in small detachments over the continental United States, the Army Root took over consisted of almost 100,000 men, two-thirds of them deployed at overseas stations and more than 30,000 engaged in or on their way to combat in rice fields and jungles half a world away. Its generals governed Cuba, Puerto Rico, and the conquered portions of the Philippines, shouldering as they did so a weight of responsibility and a range of duties unequaled since Reconstruction. With its stock piles of equipment and weapons much enlarged, the Army now had its own navy of troop transports, hospital ships, lighters, launches, and river gunboats. The mobilization for the war with Spain had left behind it an expanded production capacity, both governmental and private, for military goods of all types and trained reserve of tens of thousands of ex-soldiers, many of whom had returned to the ranks of the National Guard. Most important, the war and the events stemming from it had seasoned the officer corps by giving generals, staff officers, and regimental and company commanders experience in administering and maneuvering large formations, in some cases under fire. These officers, Regulars and Volunteers alike, could now meet future emergencies with a sure hand. General Shafter, who himself had had much to learn, summed up the Army's improved state when he wrote in 1900: "We are getting used to war now and have the necessary appliances and means to do with."[33]

As Secretary of War, Root quickly imparted new strength and purpose to his office. From the issuance of his first annual report in 1899, he established a cohesive agenda for Army reform. However, beyond reviving the officers's schools, suspended during the Spanish War, and creating an Army War College, Root made no immediate radical changes in the day-to-day administration of the Army. Personal and power relationships within the War Department also changed little. Root, like Alger, found it impossible to work with General Miles and relied on Adjutant General Corbin as a *de facto* chief of staff. The staff bureaus continued to function along the lines established at the end of the Spanish-American War. They made continuous incremental improvements in weapons, equipment, and administrative methods. Root himself was preoccupied during his first three

33. The quotation is from Maj. Gen. William R. Shafter to Adj. Gen. Corbin, August 22, 1900, Box 1, Corbin Papers. Secretary Root in November of 1899 expressed satisfaction at the state of the Army; see *RSW, 1899*, I, Pt. 1, pp. 22 and 55. *War Investigating Commission*, I, 114. The improvement of armament stock piles and production capacity is detailed in *RSW, 1898*, IV, 13-14, 21; *1899*, I, Pt. 1, pp. 36-37; III, 17-20, 25, 27-28, 32. Clark, *JMSI*, XXV, 420-22, 424, describes the Army's increased efficiency from a British viewpoint, finding the improvements impressive. After the Spanish War, British military planners revised upward their estimates of American power; see Kenneth Bourne, *Britain and the Balance of Power in North America, 1815-1908*, 352-53.

Courtesy U.S. Army Center of Military History

Secretary of War Elihu Root
(by Raimundo de Madrazo)

years in office with resolving the political status of Cuba, establishing an American colonial policy, and ending the war in the Philippines, which degenerated into a prolonged, frustrating guerrilla conflict. Only with these problems behind him could Root, beginning in 1901, concentrate on the campaign for Army reform that earned him his deserved reputation as one of the greatest Secretaries of War.[34]

V

During five hectic months in the spring and summer of 1898, the United States liquidated Spain's colonial empire in the Caribbean and the Far East and began her march to world power. In that period, the War Department, suddenly confronted with the task of waging trans-oceanic campaigns and securing and ruling an empire, performed well. Handicapped by lack of stock piles of supplies and a reserve of trained officers and men, required to conduct operations in tropical regions never previously invaded by large numbers of American troops, and haunted by diseases as yet unconquered by medical science, the department committed many errors while solving its immediate problems. Yet, much that went wrong could not fairly be blamed on organizational or managerial inadequacies. The constant fluctuations in the size of the planned expeditionary force—fluctuations that were imposed by the President and Congress—disrupted most of the War Department's advance preparations for the emergency. McKinley's substitution after the Battle of Manila Bay of an aggressive land strategy for the more cautious one advocated by General Miles, which he had previously endorsed and made the basis of initial Army preparations, contributed much to the haste, confusion, and improvisation that attended the dispatch of the Santiago expedition. The President's decision to use the limited number of trained men and the scanty supplies available at the outset for early overseas attacks made unavoidable the shortages and administrative inadequacies of the training camps at home. Had policy decisions been made differently and had more resources been provided, even so, the long-standing contempt of line commanders for the Medical Department and the deficiencies and disagreements of turn-of-the-century medical science would have assured confusion and suffering where typhoid and yellow fever struck.

34. Root's activities can be followed through the annual reports of the War Department for the years 1899 through 1904. These have been published in consolidated form in Elihu Root, *Five Years of the War Department* (Washington: Government Printing Office, 1904). Root's relations with Miles are traced in Ranson, *Military Affairs*, XXIX, 190-93, 197-99. Miles retired for age in August, 1903. For Root's reliance on Corbin, see Root to Chairman of the House Committee on Military Affairs, February 19, 1900, in *Memorandum of the Military Services of Brigadier-General Henry C. Corbin* (1900), 18-19, in Box 7, Corbin Papers, as well as numerous other letters in the same collection. Corbin left the Adjutant General's office in 1903, after the General Staff absorbed most of its functions. Returning to the line, he commanded successively the Division of the Atlantic and the Division of the Philippines. He retired in 1906 and died three years later.

As Secretary Alger never tired of reminding his critics, the War Department achieved much in spite of its handicaps. It organized and dispatched, within two months of the start of mobilization, expeditions sufficiently large and well-equipped to secure the government's objectives in Cuba, Puerto Rico, and the Philippines. By mid-August it had assembled and outfitted almost 300,000 Regular and Volunteer troops, soldiers whom qualified observers considered to be much more efficient than any previous American force at a comparable length of time after enlistment. When the initial shortages of staff and supply were remedied late in 1898, when experience had taught officers to manage large forces and respect the advice of their surgeons concerning sanitation, and when political conditions permitted more accurate anticipation of the demands to be imposed on the Army, the War Department settled rapidly into purposeful routine and reacted with little fumbling or lost motion to the new challenge of the Philippine Insurrection.

Secretary Alger and General Miles contributed relatively little to this favorable result. Alger, a conscientious if only sporadically efficient administrator, pressed the bureaus for decisive action and tried to promote cooperation between them, but his unreliability as a policy adviser to the President, his choleric impulsiveness, and his conflict with General Miles quickly reduced his influence over most of his department's work. The collapse of public confidence in him further undermined his control over events and policies. Miles's feud with Alger, combined with his arrogant assertion of his right to command and his disagreement with McKinley over strategy, canceled the Commanding General's effectiveness. However, the virtual abdication of both its nominal chiefs had little effect on War Department operations because other men took over their functions. President McKinley acted throughout the war as his own Secretary of War, and Adjutant General Corbin, probably the department's most capable administrator, served him loyally and well as chief of staff. Supported by competent bureau chiefs and field commanders and assisted by hard work and desperate improvisation in the lower ranks of staff and line, McKinley and Corbin brought the War Department and the Army through the crisis the President's vacillating policies had helped to create.

The influence of Corbin and the determination of McKinley and Alger to uphold the authority of their field commanders largely prevented line-staff antagonism from adversely affecting the management of the war effort, and all concerned gradually broke the stultifying grip of administrative overcentralization. If camp and army commanders failed to obtain from the bureaus the supplies they needed, it was usually because of shortages or transportation bottlenecks, not stinginess or second-guessing of commanders' decisions by the bureaus' chiefs. McKinley and Alger encouraged and supported independent action by commanders; the chief obstacle to such action was the slowness of the officers themselves to break the peacetime habits of caution and passivity. The effectiveness of the Commanding General's office collapsed during the war because Miles ignored Schofield's warning that the military professional must adapt his plans and advice to the political goals of his civilian superiors. It is worth noting, however, that when Miles took the field in Puerto Rico, he enjoyed the same breadth of tactical discretion and the same unhesitating logistical support that Shafter and Merritt received in their operations.

McKinley, Alger, Miles, and Corbin strove to organize the Army on the principles elaborated by Emory Upton and his followers. Only resistance by the National Guard prevented them from using an expansible Regular Army as the expeditionary force. Congress, in its Army legislation, at least partially accepted that vital component of the Regulars' program. When compelled to create a Volunteer Army, the War Department retained for the Regulars control over every aspect of its formation but the selection of its regimental and company officers, and Adjutant General Corbin checked the states' tendency to spawn politically inspired units of less than battle strength. The United States Volunteer Cavalry, Signal Corps, and Immune Infantry represented an advance toward Upton's goal of an all-federal citizen army. The War Department and Congress also took a first step toward defining the permanent military role of the National Guard, although their decision on this issue did not please the Regulars. In commissioning Volunteer generals and staff officers, McKinley, Alger, and Corbin reserved as many posts as they could for Regulars, thus adhering to Upton's doctrine that the standing Army should command the wartime Army. In the course of putting the enlarged Army in the field, the advocates of many minor reforms, for example the introduction of trained company cooks, won their battles. The appointment by Secretary Alger of boards of officers to select campsites and to plan troop deployments indicated an increasing concern within the War Department with advance analysis of problems and with administrative coordination.

When implemented under the conditions of 1898, however, many of these Uptonian policies actually contributed to the War Department's difficulties. The doctrine elaborated by Schofield and rigidly adhered to by Miles that the Army should play only a limited role in overseas offensive wars helped to restrict the scale of early preparations and to assure the assignment of priority to coast defense. The Regulars' preference for waging wars with compact forces containing a high percentage of career men, a preference they shared at that time with the officers of every major Western Power, contributed to administrative chaos when it collided at the last moment with the desire of both President McKinley and the National Guard for greater numbers and a share of commands for non-Regulars. The monopolization of higher commands by Regulars who were inexperienced in exercising such authority did not guarantee military efficiency, and it prevented the fullest use of qualified Civil War veterans like James H. Wilson. These facts did not necessarily invalidate Uptonian doctrines, but they did indicate that Upton's ideas could be applied effectively in war only if they were fully adhered to in peace as well, a conclusion quite acceptable to the Regulars.[35]

During the debates on Army reorganization in the winter of 1898-1899, soldiers and civilians disagreed on whether the emergencies of the war demonstrated the need for the command and staff reforms advocated by Upton and his followers. Spokesmen for the line—always the center of agitation for staff reform—predictably blamed all the war's calamities on permanent staff appointments and the bureaus' independence of the Commanding General. They urged that the Commanding General, assisted by a general staff, be given authority over every branch of the Army and that all staff posts be filled by short detail from the line. Just as predictably, staff officers argued that the established system had won the war and, therefore, there was no reason to change it.[36]

Because so many other circumstances than the structure of the War Department worked against military efficiency in 1898, a definitive case cannot be proved on either side of this argument. Certainly a general staff dominated by followers of Upton and holding the prevalent view of the Army's limited role in an offensive war would have produced mobilization plans similar to those made by the existing system and would have stumbled into the same disruptive political collision with the National Guard. The existence of such a staff by itself would not have remedied the prewar lack of funds, equipment, and trained men, nor would it have persuaded McKinley to hold military operations to the slow pace dictated by the Army's unreadiness. Once assured sufficient funds and manpower, the bureaus cured many of their own deficiencies and by mid-1899 were cooperating effectively to support complex operations in a distant overseas theater. In the field, the effectiveness of both line and staff depended more on the competence and aggressiveness of corps and division commanders than it did on institutional arrangements in Washington.

35. Alfred Vagts, *A History of Militarism: Civilian and Military*, 377-78, comments on the pre-1914 Regulars' fear of a genuine mass army, even in countries like Germany, which had conscription. The condescension of American Regulars toward Civil War veterans recalled from civilian pursuits is expressed in Adj. Gen. H. C. Corbin to Maj. Gen. William R. Shafter, September 1, 1900, Box 1, Corbin Papers.

36. For the clashing line and staff viewpoints, see the following: *Army and Navy Journal*, June 4, August 27, September 17, October 1, 15, and 29, November 5, 12, and 26, December 10, 17, and 24, 1898, and February 25 and March 4, 1899. Andrews, *Independent*, LI, 456-59. Alexander S. Bacon, "Is Our Army Degenerate?" *The Forum*, XXVII, 11-23. Alfred E. Bates, "The Army—Its Staff and Supply Departments," *The Conservative Review*, III, 162-89. Lt. John H. Parker, "Some Lessons of the War from an Officer's Standpoint," *The Review of Reviews*, XVIII, 427-31, and "Our Army Supply Departments and the Need of a General Staff," *The Review of Reviews*, XVIII, 686-95. *RSW, 1898*, I, 262-63. *War Investigating Commission*, IV, 1241; V, 1981-83; VI, 2848-49, 2867, 2933, 2940-42, 2955-56; VII, 3146-48, 3291.

One still, of course, could make an excellent case on general principles for a more rational distribution of authority within the War Department and for the creation of a full-fledged planning agency. The point is that, for most Army officers and civilian military theorists, the experiences of the war with Spain served only to support policy positions that had been previously taken. For disciples of Upton, especially, the conflict confirmed doctrines; it did not change them. As Secretary Root acknowledged, the Army reforms instituted during his tenure merely codified these established principles. The officer who drafted Root's Army Reorganization Act of 1901 admitted to copying much of it from old bills in the War Department's files. The General Staff Act of 1903 owed much to the command proposals of Schofield. The Dick Militia Act of the same year wrote into law the federal recognition of and aid to the National Guard long favored by both Regulars and guardsmen. On the crucial question of the National Guard's relation to the Volunteer Army, the Dick Act, in spite of a campaign by Root for an all-federal Volunteer force, merely repeated the provisions of the law of April 22, 1898.[37]

As it had done in the Civil War and would do again in World Wars I and II, the War Department in 1898 responded to crisis with improvisation, trial, and error, followed by a growing mastery of the circumstances that confronted it. To military reformers, to political opponents of the McKinley Administration, to much of the press, and to many honestly indignant and bewildered citizens, the resulting disorder of the war effort in itself sufficed to convict of incompetence or worse the men who managed it. But war is not conducted and military policy is not made in a vacuum. Military decisions always reflect the social and political context in which they are reached. In 1898 that context was one of transition accompanied by confusion. The United States was groping her way into the complicated game of international power and diplomacy, aware of her strength and desirous of using it, but unsure for what purposes. McKinley's vacillating strategy and war aims, together with the fluctuating demands they imposed on the armed services, mirrored the larger national uncertainty. At the same time, the Army itself was undergoing change as the new generation of professional officers tried to adapt its organization to the needs of a modern industrial nation and the state militia sought a new role and reason for being. The simultaneous transitions in foreign relations and in military thought interacted in complex ways during the Spanish-American War. At the focus of these clashing forces, the officials of the War Department strove, in the main successfully, to forge an army for empire.

37. Root himself acknowledges the derivative nature of his reforms, in *RSW, 1899*, I, Pt. 1, pp. 45-46. For the drafting of the Act of 1901, see William H. Carter to Gen. James H. Wilson, May 19, 1915, Box 6, Wilson Papers. Text of the act is in *RSW, 1901*, I, Pt. 2, pp. 79-87. The evolution of the General Staff Act can be traced in Carter, *General Staff*, 1-63; for additional comment, see Huntington, *Soldier and State*, 252-53. On the Dick Act, see Elbridge Colby, "Elihu Root and the National Guard," *Military Affairs*, XXIII, 20, 29-33; and *RSW, 1899*, I, Pt. 1, pp. 52-54; *1901*, I, Pt. 1, pp. 25-27; *1902*, I, 34, 36-40; *1903*, I, 73-80.

Bibliography

Primary Sources

I. Manuscript Collections

A. National Archives, Washington, D.C.
   Records of The Adjutant General's Office, Record Group 94
   Records of the Joint Army-Navy Board, Record Group 225
   Records of the Office of the Quartermaster General, Record Group 92
B. Library of Congress, Washington, D.C.
   Tasker H. Bliss Papers
   William Conant Church Papers
   Henry Clark Corbin Papers
   Lyman J. Gage Papers
   William McKinley Papers
   Theodore Roosevelt Papers
   John M. Schofield Papers
   Hugh L. Scott Papers
   James Harrison Wilson Papers
   Leonard Wood Papers
C. William L. Clements Library, Ann Arbor, Michigan
   Russell Alexander Alger Papers
   Frank J. Hecker Papers
D. Michigan Historical Collections, Ann Arbor, Michigan
   Chase S. Osborn Papers
   William H. Withington Papers
E. U.S. Army Military History Institute, Carlisle Barracks, Pa.
   Samuel B. M. Young Papers

II. United States Government Documents and Publications

Congressional Record. Vol. XXXI. 55th Cong., 2d sess., 1898.

Department of War. *Abstract of Report on the Origin and Spread of Typhoid Fever in U.S. Military Camps during the Spanish War of 1898*, Walter Reed, Victor C. Vaughan, and Edward O. Shakespeare. Washington, D.C., 1900.

————. *Regulations for the Army of the United States, 1895.* Washington, D.C., 1895.

————. The Adjutant General's Office. *General Orders and Circulars, Adjutant General's Office, 1898.* Washington, D.C., 1899.

————. *General Orders and Circulars, Adjutant General's Office, 1899.* Washington, D.C., 1900.

————. *Correspondence Relating to the War with Spain and Conditions Growing out of the Same, . . . between The Adjutant General of the Army and Military Commanders in the United States, Cuba, Porto Rico, China, and the Philippine Islands, from April 15, 1898, to July 30, 1902.* Washington, D.C., 1902. 2 vols.

Department of War, Root, Elihu. *Five Years of the War Department.* Washington, D.C., 1904.

Department of War, Military Information Division. "Poder Militar y Naval de Los Estados Unidos en 1896." *Selected Professional Papers Translated from European Military Publications.* Publication No. 18, Washington, D.C., 1898.

_____. *The Organized Militia of the United States, 1897.* Publication No. 19, Washington, D.C. 1898.

House of Representatives. *Annual Report of the Secretary of War, 1877, 1880-1903.* House Executive Documents, 45th through 58th Congresses. Washington, D.C., 1877, 1880-1903.

_____. *Report of the Board on Fortifications and other Defenses Appointed by the President of the United States under . . . the Act of Congress Approved March 3, 1885.* House Document No. 49. 49th Cong., 1st sess., 1886.

_____. *House Report No. 795.* House Reports, Miscellaneous. 55th Cong., 2d sess., 1898, Vol. 3.

_____. *House Report No. 1138.* House Reports, Miscellaneous. 55th Cong., 2d sess., 1898. Vol. 4.

_____. *Views of the Minority to Accompany H.R. 11022,* Representatives James Hay, N. N. Cox, T. M. Jett, and Mark A. Smith. House Report No. 1709, Pt. 2. 55th Cong., 3d sess., 1899.

Senate. *Reorganization of the Army.* Senate Report No. 555. 45th Cong., 3d sess., 1879.

_____. *A Treaty of Peace between the United States and Spain.* Senate Document No. 62. 55th Cong., 3d sess., 1899.

_____. *Food Furnished by Subsistence Department to Troops in the Field.* Senate Document No. 270. 56th Cong., 1st sess., 1900.

_____. *Report of the Commission Appointed by the President to Investigate the Conduct of the War Department in the War with Spain.* Senate Document No. 221. 56th Cong., 1st sess., 1900. 8 vols.

_____. *The Military Policy of the United States,* Bvt. Maj. Gen. Emery Upton. Senate Document No. 494. 62d Cong., 2d sess., 1912.

_____. *Creation of the American General Staff,* Maj. Gen. William Harding Carter. Senate Document No. 119. 68th Cong., 1st sess., 1924.

_____. Foreign Relations Committee. *Affairs in Cuba: Message of the President of the United States on the Relations of the United States to Spain, and Report of the Committee on Foreign Relations, United States Senate, Relative to Affairs in Cuba.* 55th Cong., 2d sess., 1898.

III. State Government Documents and Publications

Maine, Adjutant General of. *Annual Report of the Adjutant General of the State of Maine for the Year Ending December 31, 1894.* Augusta, 1895.

_____. *Annual Report of the Adjutant General of the State of Maine for the Year Ending December 31, 1898.* Augusta, 1902.

Massachusetts Adjutant General's Office. *Annual Report of the Adjutant General of the Commonwealth of Massachusetts for the Year Ending December 30, 1895.* Boston, 1896.

Michigan Adjutant General. *Record of Service of Michigan Volunteers in the Civil War, 1861-1865.* Kalamazoo, 1905.

New Hampshire, Adjutant General of. *Biennial Report of the Adjutant General of the State of New Hampshire, October 1, 1898, to October 1, 1900.* Manchester, 1900.

New York Adjutant General's Office. *New York in the Spanish-American War, 1898.* 3 vols. Albany, 1900.

Ohio, Adjutant General of. *Annual Report of the Adjutant General to the Governor of the State of Ohio for the Fiscal Year Ending November 15, 1897.* Norwalk, 1898.

———. *Annual Report of the Adjutant General to the Governor of the State of Ohio for the Fiscal Year Ending November 15, 1898.* Columbus, 1899.

Oregon, Adjutant General of. *Seventh Biennial Report of the Adjutant General of the State of Oregon to the Governor and Commander-in-Chief, 1899-1900.* Salem, 1900.

IV. Newspapers

Army and Navy Journal, 1898-1899.
Detroit Free Press, 1892.
Kansas City (Mo.) *Star,* 1898.
Milwaukee Journal, 1907.
The New York Times, 1897-1898.
The New York Tribune, 1898.
The Washington Post, 1898.

V. Books

Adams, Henry, *Letters of Henry Adams, 1892-1918.* Edited by C. Worthington Ford. 2 vols. Boston and New York, 1938.

Alger, Russell Alexander. *The Spanish-American War.* New York and London, 1901.

Bigelow, John, Jr. *Reminiscences of the Santiago Campaign.* New York and London, 1899.

Carter, William Harding. *The American Army.* Indianapolis, 1915.

Creagher, Charles E. *The Fourteenth Ohio National Guard—the Fourth Ohio Volunteer Infantry.* Columbus, 1899.

Cruse, Thomas. *Apache Days and After.* Caldwell, Ida., 1941.

Dawes, Charles G. *A Journal of the McKinley Years.* Edited by Bascom N. Timmons. Chicago, 1950.

Dunn, Arthur Wallace. *From Harrison to Harding.* 2 vols. New York and London, 1922.

"The Fighting Twentieth:" History and Official Souvenir of the Twentieth Kansas Regiment. Topeka, 1899.

Funston, Frederick. *Memories of Two Wars: Cuban and Philippine Experiences.* New York, 1914.

Gauvreau, Charles F. *Reminiscences of the Spanish-American War in Cuba and the Philippines.* Rouses Point, N.Y., 1915.

Goode, W. A. M. *With Sampson through the War.* New York, 1899.

Kennan, George. *Campaigning in Cuba.* New York, 1899.

Kennon, L. W. V. *The Army: Its Employment during Time of Peace and the Necessity for Its Increase.* Monograph No. 2, U.S. Infantry Society. Washington, D.C., n.p., 1896.

Kidd, James H. *Personal Recollections of a Cavalryman.* Ionia, Mich., 1908.

Lodge, Henry Cabot, ed. *Selections from the Correspondence of Theodore Roosevelt and Henry Cabot Lodge, 1884-1918.* 2 vols. New York and London, 1925.

Long, John D. *The New American Navy.* 2 vols. New York, 1903.

Mahan, Alfred Thayer. *The Interest of America in Sea Power, Present and Future.* Boston, 1897.

_____. *Lessons of the War with Spain and Other Articles.* Boston, 1899.

Mayo, Lawrence S., ed. *America of Yesterday as Reflected in the Journal of John Davis Long.* Boston, 1923.

Miles, Nelson A. *Serving the Republic.* New York and London, 1911.

Miley, John D. *In Cuba with Shafter.* New York, 1899.

National Relief Commission. *Report of the Executive Committee of the National Relief Commission.* Philadelphia, 1900.

Parker, John H. *History of the Gatling Gun Detachment, Fifth Army Corps, at Santiago.* Kansas City, Mo., 1898.

Post, Charles Johnson. *The Little War of Private Post.* Boston, 1960.

Roosevelt, Theodore. *The Rough Riders.* New York, 1899.

_____. *The Letters of Theodore Roosevelt.* Edited by Elting E. Morison and others. 8 vols. Cambridge, Mass., 1951.

Schofield, John M. *Forty-Six Years in the Army.* New York, 1897.

Sheridan, Philip Henry. *Personal Memoirs of P. H. Sheridan,* 2 vols. New York, 1888.

Sherman, William T. *Memoirs of W. T. Sherman, Written by Himself.* 2 vols. New York, 1875.

Upton, Emory. *The Armies of Asia and Europe.* New York, 1878.

Wheeler, Joseph. *The Santiago Campaign, 1898.* Philadelphia, 1899.

Wilson, James Harrison. *Under the Old Flag: Recollections of Military Operations in the War for the Union, the Boxer Rebellion, etc.* 2 vols. New York and London, 1912.

VI. Articles

Alger, Russell Alexander. "The Food of the Army during the Spanish War." *The North American Review,* CLXXII (January, 1901), 39-58.

Allen, 1st Lt. Henry T. "The Central Military Administrations of Five Great Powers." *JMSI,* XIX (July, 1896), 63-82.

_____. "The Organization of a Staff Best Adapted to the United States Army." *JMSI,* XXVIII (March, 1901), 169-83.

Anderson, Col. Thomas M. "Military Service Reform." *JMSI,* XII (September, 1891), 980-87.

_____. "Supply and Distribution." *JMSI,* XXIX (September, 1901), 198-207.

Andrews, Avery D. "Army Controversies," *The Independent,* LI (February 16, 1899), 456-59.

Ayres, James Cooper. "The National Guard and Our Sea-Coast Defense." *The Forum,* XXIV (December, 1897), 416-21.

Bache, Col. Dallas. "The Place of the Female Nurse in the Army." *JMSI,* XXV (November, 1899), 307-28.

Bachelor, Lt. Joseph B., Jr. "A United States Army." *JMSI,* XIII (January, 1892), 54-74.

Bacon, Alexander S. "Is Our Army Degenerate?" *The Forum,* XXVII (March, 1899), 11-23.

"Barbarism at Montauk." *Harper's Weekly,* XLII (September 10, 1898), 890.

Barry, Capt. Herbert. "In What Way Can the National Guard be Modified so as to Make it an Effective Reserve to the Regular Army in Both War and Peace?" *JMSI,* XXVI (March, 1900), 189-231.

Bass, John F. "San Francisco." *Harper's Weekly,* XLII (July 2, 1898), 642.

Bates, Alfred E. "The Army—Its Staff and Supply Departments." *The Conservative Review*, III (March, 1900), 162-89.

Bend, Gen. W. B. "In What Way Can the National Guard be Modified so as to Make It an Effective Reserve to the Regular Army in both War and Peace?" *JMSI*, XXVII (November, 1900), 371-79.

Benjamin, Anna Northend. "Christian Work in Our Camps." *The Outlook*, LIX (July 2, 1898, 566-69.

Benjamin, Charles F. "The Artillery and the Ordnance." *JMSI*, VIII (December, 1887), 361-80.

Best, 1st Lt. Clermont L., Jr. "Wanted: A Fitting Artillery Organization," *JMSI*, XVII (November, 1895), 502-22.

Bingham, Capt. T. A. "The Prussian Great General Staff and What It Contains that is Practical from an American Standpoint." *JMSI*, XIII (July, 1892), 666-76.

Birnie, Capt. Rogers. "Gun Making in the United States." *JMSI*, XII (1891), 385-526.

Bishop, J. B. "Get the Beef Contracts." *The Nation*, LXVII (March 23, 1899), 217-18.

————. "The Beef Verdict." *The Nation*, LXVIII (May 11, 1899), 347-48.

Blunt, Stanhope E. "The United States Magazine Rifle." *Harper's Weekly*, XXXVII (July 1, 1893), 619.

Boies, Col. H. M. "The Defense of a Free People in the Light of the Spanish War." *JMSI*, XXIV (January, 1899), 15-27.

Carbaugh, Lt. H. C. "Federal Duty and Policy as to Organizing and Maintaining an Adequate Artillery Force for the United States." *JMSI*, XXI (September, 1897), 257-63.

Chester, Capt. James. "Impending Changes in the Character of War." *JMSI*, XIX (July, 1896), 83-89.

Clark, C. S. "Naval and Military Progress in the United States." *United Service Magazine* (London). Reprinted in *JMSI*, XXV (November, 1899), 420-25.

————. "The Volunteer in War." *United Service Magazine* (London). Reprinted in *JMSI*, XXIV (May, 1899), 468-74.

"Comment and Criticism: Organization of Militia Defense." *JMSI*, XIII (November, 1892), 1174-82.

"Comment and Criticism." *JMSI*, XXII (February, 1898), 429-40.

"Henry Clark Corbin, Lieutenant-General, United States Army." *Army and Navy Life and the United Service*, IX (September, 1906), reprint in Box 8, Corbin Papers.

Crane, Capt. C. J. "The New Infantry Rifle." *JMSI*, XIX (November, 1896), 488-95.

Devol, Capt. Carroll A. "Supply and Distribution." *JMSI*, XXIX (September, 1901), 208-15.

Duncan, Lt. George B. "Reasons for Increasing the Regular Army." *The North American Review*, CLXVI (April, 1898), 448-59.

Dunham, Dr. Carroll. "Medical and Sanitary Aspects of the War." *The Review of Reviews*, XVIII (October, 1898), 415-27.

Foote, Lt. S. M. "Based on Present Conditions and Past Experiences, How Should Our Volunteer Armies be Raised, Organized, Trained, and Mobilized for Future War." *JMSI*, XXII (January, 1898), 1-49.

————. "Our Volunteer Armies—A Reply." *JMSI*, XXII (May, 1898), 639-42.

Fox, John, Jr. "Volunteers in the Blue-Grass." *Harper's Weekly*, XLII (June 18, 1898), 591.

Frazier, Lt. Col. Walter S., Jr. "The National Guard National in Name Only." *JMSI*, XX (May, 1897), 518-23.

Gibbon, Gen. John. "Needed Reforms in the Army." *The North American Review*, CLVI (February, 1893), 212-219.

Giddings, Maj. Howard A. "How to Improve the Condition and Efficiency of the National Guard." *JMSI*, XXI (July, 1897), 61-75.

Gilchrist, Col. James G. "The Reorganization of Our State Troops." *JMSI*, XXIII (November, 1898), 418-26.

Glassford, Capt. W. A. "Based on Present Conditions and Past Experiences, How Should Our Volunteer Armies be Raised, Organized, Trained, and Mobilized for Future Wars." *JMSI*, XXII (May, 1898), 471-81.

_____. "Porto Rico and a Necessary Military Position in the West Indies." *JMSI*, XXVIII (January, 1901), 15-19.

Green, Capt. Lewis D. "The Nicaragua Canal in Its Military Aspects." *JMSI*, XXVI (January, 1900), 1-14.

Greene, Francis V. "The New National Guard." *The Century Magazine*, XXII, New Series, No. 4 (February, 1892), 483-98.

_____. "The Important Improvements in the Art of War during the Past Twenty Years and Their Probable Effect on Future Military Operations." *JMSI*, IV (1883), 1-41.

Griffin, Lt. Eugene. "Our Sea-Coast Defense." *JMSI*, VII (December, 1886), 405-65.

Hains, Lt. Col. Peter C. "Should the Fixed Coast Defenses of the United States be Transferred to the Navy?" *JMSI*, XV (March, 1894), 233-56.

Harbord, Lt. J. G. "The Necessity of a Well Organized and Trained Infantry at the Outbreak of War, and the Best Means to be Adopted by the United States for Obtaining such a Force." *JMSI*, XXI (July, 1897), 1-27.

Hawthorne, Lt. H. L. "A Central American Inter-Oceanic Canal and Its Strategic Importance to the United States." *JMSI*, X (November, 1889), 576-91.

Holabird, Bvt. Brig. Gen. Samuel B. "Some Thoughts about the Future of our Army." *The United Service*, VIII (January, 1883), 17-36.

"How to Do It and How Not to Do It." *The Nation*, LXVII (September 15, 1898), 196.

Howard, Gen. Oliver O. "A Plea for the Army." *The Forum*, XXIII (August, 1897), 641-52.

Hull, John A. T. "The Hull Army Bill." *The Forum*, XXV (June, 1898), 386-402.

_____. "The Organization of the Army." *The North American Review*, CLXVIII (April, 1899), 385-98.

"Increase in Our Artillery Urgently Needed." *Scientific American*, LXXVII (November 13, 1897), 306.

King, Col. C. W. "United States Guard, Why Not?" *JMSI*, XXII (May, 1898), 642-51.

King, Maj. William R. "The Military Necessities of the United States and the Best Provisions for Meeting Them." *JMSI*, V (December, 1884), 355-95.

Ladd, Lt. E. F. "A Special Service Corps for the Quartermaster's Department." *JMSI*, XIV (September, 1893), 1008-18.

Lee, Bvt. Lt. Col. J. G. C. "Reform in Army Administration." *JMSI*, XI (July, 1890), 529-43.

_____. "Centralization and Decentralization in Army Affairs." *JMSI*, XII (July, 1891), 744-54.

_____. "Suggestions for Consideration, Relative to the Quartermaster's Department, U.S. Army." *JMSI*, XV (March, 1894), 257-80.

Long, Capt. S. S. "A Few Short Notes on the Administration of the United States Army in the Philippines." *JMSI*, XXV (July, 1899), 125-35.

Low, A. Maurice. "Amateurs in War." *The Forum*, XXVI (October, 1898), 157-66.

MacPherson, Ernest. "The Reorganization of the National Guard." *JMSI*, XXV (November, 1899), 329-35.

Mason, Victor L. "New Weapons of the United States Army." *The Century Magazine*, XLIX, New Series, No. 4 (February, 1895), 570-83.

Mawson, Harry P. "The National Guard." *Harper's Weekly*, XXXVI (September 3, 1892), 858.

Merritt, Bvt. Brig. Gen. Wesley. "Important Improvements in the Art of War in the Last Twenty Years and their Probable Effect on Future Military Operations." *JMSI*, IV (1883), 172-87.

Michie, Peter S. "The Personnel of Sea-Coast Defense." *JMSI*, VIII (March, 1887), 1-17.

Miles, Maj. Gen. Nelson A. "Our Coast Defenses." *The Forum*, XXIV (January, 1898), 513-19.

_____. "The War with Spain." *The North American Review*, CLXVIII (May, 1899), 513-29, and (June, 1899), 749-60; CLXIX (July, 1899), 125-37.

Parker, Lt. Col. James. "Some Random Notes on the Fighting in the Philippines." *JMSI*, XXVII, No. 108 (November, 1900), 317-340.

Parker, Lt. John H. "Some Lessons of the War from an Officer's Standpoint." *The Review of Reviews*, XVIII (October, 1898), 417-31.

_____. "Our Army Supply Departments and the Need of a General Staff." *The Review of Reviews*, XVIII (December, 1898), 686-95.

_____. "National Guard Problem." *The Forum*, XXVIII (October, 1899), 190-96.

Parkhurst, Lt. C. D. "The Practical Education of the Soldier." *JMSI*, XI (November, 1890), 946-52.

Powell, Capt. William H. "The National Guard, and the Necessity for Its Adoption by the General Government." *The United Service*, XII (January, 1885), 19-31.

_____. "Army Reform." *The United Service*, II, New Series, No. 3 (September, 1889), 225-33.

Price, Capt. George F. "The Necessity for Closer Relations between the Army and the People, and the Best Method to Accomplish the Result." *JMSI*, VI (December, 1885), 303-30.

Rice, Col. James M. "The National Guard—What It Is and Its Use." *JMSI*, XV (September, 1894), 909-36.

Rodenbough, Bvt. Brig. Gen. Theodore F. "Militia Reform without Legislation." *JMSI*, II, No. 8 (1881), 388-420.

Rogers, W. A. "Camp Wikoff." *Harper's Weekly*, XLII (September 10, 1898), 890-93.

Sanger, Maj. William Cary. "Organization and Training of a National Reserve for Military Service." *JMSI*, X (March, 1889), 32-83.

_____. "The Army Organization Best Adapted to a Republican Form of Government, which Will Ensure an Effective Force." *JMSI*, XIV (November, 1893), 1145-81.

Scherer, Lt. Louis C. "Limitations of the National Guard." *JMSI*, XVIII (March, 1896), 267-84.

Schofield, Maj. Gen. John M. "Notes on the Legitimate in War." *JMSI*, II, No. 5 (1881), 1-9.

Sharpe, Lt. A. C. "Organization and Training of a National Reserve for Military Service." *JMSI*, X (March, 1889), 1-31.

Sherman, Gen. William T. "The Militia." *JMSI*, X (March, 1885), 1-26.

Steele, Capt. Matthew F. "Some Notes on the Clothing and Equipment of the Soldier for Service in the Tropics." *JMSI*, XXIX, No. 112 (July, 1901), 14-23.

Stone, J. Hamilton. "Our Troops in the Tropics—From a Surgeon's Standpoint." *JMSI*, XXVI (May, 1900), 358-69.

Stuart, Lt. Sidney C. "Some Principles of Organization Adapted to the Conditions Affecting the Maintenance, Instruction and Efficiency of Our Coast Artillery." *JMSI*, XII (November, 1891), 1224-36.

_____. "The Army Organization Best Adapted to a Republican Form of Government, which Will Ensure an Effective Force." *JMSI*, XIX (March, 1893), 231-78.

Wagner, Lt. Arthur L. "The Military Necessities of the United States and the Best Provisions for Meeting Them." *JMSI*, V (September, 1884), 237-71.

_____. "The Military and Naval Policy of the United States." *JMSI*, VII (December, 1886), 371-403.

_____. "An American War College." *JMSI*, X (August, 1889), 287-304.

"War with the United States." *JMSI*, XVIII (May, 1896), 669-73.

Weaver, Lt. E. M. "Some Thoughts with Reference to the Organization of Our Artillery." *JMSI*, X (September, 1889), 466-77.

_____. "The Military Schools of the United States." *The United Service*, III, New Series, No. 5 (May, 1890), 457-69.

Wetmore, W. Boerum. "The National Guard Bill in Congress." *The United Service*, VI (March, 1882), 337-42.

Whistler, Lt. G. N. "The Artillery Organization of the Future." *JMSI*, V (September, 1884), 324-30.

White, William Allen. "When Johnny Went Marching Out." *McClure's Magazine*, XI (June, 1898), 198-205.

Williams, Capt. Arthur. "Readiness for War." *JMSI*, XXI (September, 1897), 225-56.

Williams, Leonard. "The Army of Spain: Its Present Qualities and Modern Virtues." *United Service Magazine* (London). Reprinted in *JMSI*, XXI (September, 1897), 349-53.

Wilson, Maj. George S. "The Army: Its Employment during Time of Peace and the Necessity for Its Increase." *JMSI*, XVIII (May, 1896), 477-506.

Wingate, Gen. George W. "The Reorganization of Our State Troops: Comment and Criticism." *JMSI*, XXIII (November, 1898), 552-55.

_____. "The Defense of a Free People in the Light of the Spanish War." *JMSI*, XXIV (March, 1899), 321-24.

Wisser, Lt. J. P. "A Decennium of Military Progress." *JMSI*, XVIII (March, 1896), 235-54.

Zalinski, Capt. E. L. "The Army Organization Best Adapted to a Republican Form of Government, which Will Ensure an Effective Force." *JMSI*, XIV (September, 1893), 926-77.

Zogbaum, Rufus Fairchild. "Official and Social Life of the Army and Navy in Washington." *Harper's Weekly*, XXXVII (August 12, 1893), 767, 770.

Secondary Sources

I. Books

Agoncillo, Teodore A. *Malolos: The Crisis of the Republic.* Quezon City, P. I., 1960.

Ambrose, Stephen E. *Upton and the Army.* Baton Rouge, 1964.

Bald, F. Clever. *Michigan in Four Centuries.* New York, 1954.

Baxter, Albert. *History of the City of Grand Rapids, Michigan.* New York and Grand Rapids, 1891.

Bernardo, C. Joseph, and Eugene H. Bacon. *American Military Policy: Its Development since 1775.* Harrisburg, Pa., 1955.

Bingham, S. C. *Early History of Michigan with Biographies of State Officers, Members of Congress, Judges and Legislators.* Lansing, 1888.

Bourne, Kenneth. *Britain and the Balance of Power in North America, 1815-1908.* Berkeley and Los Angeles, 1967.

Chadwick, Rear Adm. French Ensor. *The Relations of the United States to Spain: The Spanish-American War.* 2 vols. New York, 1911.

Coffman, Edward M. *The Hilt of the Sword: The Career of Peyton C. March,* Madison and Milwaukee, Wis., and London, 1966.

Dennis, Alfred L. P. *Adventures in American Diplomacy, 1896-1906.* New York, 1928.

Derthick, Martha. *The National Guard in Politics.* Cambridge, Mass., 1965.

Farmer, Silas. *History of Detroit and Wayne County and Early Michigan.* Detroit and New York, 1890.

Fletcher, Marvin. *The Black Soldier and Officer in the United States Army, 1891-1917.* Columbia, Mo., 1974.

Ganoe, William Addleman. *The History of the United States Army.* Rev. ed. New York and London, 1942.

Gibson, John Mendinghall. *Soldier in White: The Life of General George Miller Sternberg.* Durham, N.C., 1958.

Grenville, John A. S., and George Berkeley Young. *Politics, Strategy, and American Diplomacy: Studies in Foreign Policy, 1873-1917.* New Haven and London, 1966.

Hagedorn, Hermann. *Leonard Wood: A Biography.* 2 vols. New York and London, 1931.

Healy, David F. *The United States in Cuba, 1898-1902: Generals, Politicians, and the Search for Policy.* Madison, 1963.

Heitman, Francis B. *Historical Register and Dictionary of the United States Army.* 2 vols. Washington, D.C., 1903.

Holbrook, Franklin F. *Minnesota in the Spanish-American War and the Philippine Insurrection.* Saint Paul, 1923.

Hotchkiss, George W. *History of the Lumber and Forest Industry of the Northwest.* Chicago, 1898.

Howard, Michael. *The Franco-Prussian War: The German Invasion of France, 1870-1871.* New York, 1961.

Huntington, Samuel P. *The Soldier and the State: The Theory and Politics of Civil-Military Relations.* Caravelle Editions. New York, 1964.

Jessup, Philip C. *Elihu Root.* 2 vols. New York, 1938.

Johnson, Virginia W. *The Unregimented General: A Biography of Nelson A. Miles.* Boston, 1962.

LaFeber, Walter. *The New Empire: An Interpretation of American Expansion, 1860-1898.* Ithaca, 1963.

Leech, Margaret. *In the Days of McKinley.* New York, 1959.

MacGregor, Morris J., and Bernard C. Nalty, eds. *Blacks in the United States Armed Forces: Basic Documents.* 13 vols. Wilmington, Del., 1977.

May, Ernest R. *Imperial Democracy: The Emergence of America as a Great Power.* New York, 1961.

————. *The Ultimate Decision: The President as Commander-in-Chief.* New York, 1960.

Millis, Walter. *Arms and Men: A Study of American Military History.* Mentor Books, New American Library, Inc. New York, 1958.

————. *The Martial Spirit.* Boston and New York, 1931.

Monaghan, Jay. *Custer: The Life of General George Armstrong Custer.* Boston, 1959.

Morgan, H. Wayne. *America's Road to Empire: The War with Spain and Overseas Expansion.* New York, London, and Sydney, 1965.

————. *William McKinley and His America.* Syracuse, 1963.

Nalty, Bernard C. *Strength for the Fight: A History of Black Americans in the Military.* New York, 1986.

Nunez, Severo Gómez. *La Guerra Hispanoamericana.* 5 vols. Madrid, 1899-1902.

Olcott, Charles S. *The Life of William McKinley.* 2 vols. Boston and New York, 1916.

Palmer, Gen. John McAuley. *America in Arms: The Experience of the United States with Military Organization.* New Haven, 1941.

Riker, William H. *Soldiers of the States: The Role of the National Guard in American Democracy.* Washington, D.C., 1957.

Risch, Erna. *Quartermaster Support of the Army: A History of the Corps, 1775-1939.* Washington, D.C., 1962.

Sargent, Herbert H. *The Campaign of Santiago de Cuba.* 3 vols. Chicago, 1914.

Sexton, Capt. William Thaddeus. *Soldiers in the Sun: An Adventure in Imperialism.* Harrisburg, Pa., 1939.

Sprout, Harold, and Margaret Sprout. *The Rise of American Naval Power, 1776-1918.* Rev. ed. Princeton, 1942.

Tuchman, Barbara W. *The Guns of August.* New York, 1962.

Vaghts, Alfred. *A History of Militarism: Civilian and Military.* The Free Press, The Macmillan Co. New York, 1967.

Weigley, Russell F. *Towards an American Army: Military Thought from Washington to Marshall.* New York and London, 1962.

Wolff, Leon. *Little Brown Brother: How the United States Purchased and Pacified the Philippine Islands at the Century's Turn.* Garden City, N.Y., 1961.

II. Articles

Bethel, Elizabeth. "The Military Information Division: Origin of the Intelligence Division." *Military Affairs*, XI (Spring, 1947), 17-24.

Boylan, Bernard L. "The Forty-Fifth Congress and Army Reform." *Mid-America*, XLI (July, 1959), 173-86.

Brown, Richard C. "General Emory Upton—the Army's Mahan." *Military Affairs*, XVII (Fall, 1953), 125-31.

Chamberlain, Robert S. "The Northern State Militia." *Civil War History*, IV (June, 1958), 105-18.

Colby, Elbridge. "Elihu Root and the National Guard." *Military Affairs*, XXIII (Spring, 1959), 28-34.

Cosmas, Graham A. "San Juan Hill and El Caney, 1-2 July, 1898," in Charles E. Heller and William A. Stofft, eds., *America's First Battles, 1776-1965.* Lawrence, Kan., 1986, 109-48.

————. "Military Reform after the Spanish-American War: The Army Reorganization Fight of 1898-1899." *Military Affairs*, XXXV, No. 1 (February, 1971), 12-18.

————. "Securing the Fruits of Victory: The U.S. Army Occupies Cuba, 1898-1899." *Military Affairs*, XXXVIII, No. 3 (October, 1974), 85-91.

Fletcher, Marvin. "The Black Volunteers in the Spanish-American War." *Military Affairs*, XXXVIII, No. 2 (April, 1974), 48-53.

Halle, Louis J. "1898: The United States in the Pacific." *Military Affairs*, XX (Summer, 1956), 76-80.

Ranson, Edward. "Nelson A. Miles as Commanding General, 1895-1903." *Military Affairs*, XXIX (Winter, 1965-1966), 179-200.

Robertshaw, James Malcolm. "History of Company C Second Mississippi Regiment, Spanish-American War." In Dunbar Rowland, ed., *Publications of the Mississippi Historical Society: Centenary Series*, Vol. I, 429-41. Jackson, Miss., 1916.

Seager, Robert II. "Ten Years before Mahan: The Unofficial Case for the New Navy, 1880-1890." *Mississippi Valley Historical Review*, XL (December, 1953), 491-512.
Tanham, George J. "Service Relations Sixty Years Ago." *Military Affairs*, XXIII (Fall, 1959), 139-48.
Todd, Frederick P. "Our National Guard: An Introduction to Its History." *Military Affairs*, V, 73-86, 152-70.

III. Unpublished Materials.

Jackson, Bennett L. "The Army and the Press: From the American Revolution through World War I." Master's thesis, The University of Wisconsin, 1963.
Latshaw, George William. "Military Medical Service during and Immediately after the Spanish-American War, 1898-1901." Master's thesis, The University of Wisconsin, 1958.
Sarasohn, Stephen B. "The Regulation of Parties and Nominations in Michigan: The Politics of Election Reform." Ph.D. dissertation, Columbia University, 1953.

Index

C

Calhoun, Secretary of War John C., 14-15
California, Department of, 196, 314
California, volunteer policy of, 111
Camps, U.S. Army
general, 162-67, 267, 276-78; reforms, 300-301
Camp Alger, Va., 108, 120, 124, 129, 129n.48, 137, 163, 166, 178, 219, 224, 267; conditions at, 250, 266-68, 274-75
Camp Columbia, Cuba, 307
Camp Cuba Libre, Fla., 129 see also Jacksonville, Fla.
Camp George Dewey, P.I., 239-41
Camp George Gordon Meade, Pa., 276, 299
Camp George H. Thomas, Ga., 129, 129n.48, 165-66, 178, 194, 223-24; conditions at, 267-69, 272-73 see also Chickamauga, Ga.
Camp Wikoff, Long Island, N.Y.; conditions at, 262-66, 275, 283, 288
Cape Fajardo, Puerto Rico, 233, 236
Cape Tunas, Cuba, 103
Cape Verde Islands, 96, 111
Cardenas, Cuba, 103
Caribbean, as strategic area, 29-30, 111
Caribbean fleet, U.S., 220-22, 258
Cartridge belts, supply of, 157
Casualties of U.S. Army: at Santiago, 232
in Puerto Rico, 237
at Manila, 242-43
total in Spanish War, 244
from disease, 277-78
Cavalry: school for officers, 4
U.S. Volunteer, 127
Cavite, P.I., 239-40
Central American canal: as factor in U.S. diplomacy, 29-31, 64; as factor in war plans, 175
Cervera, Adm. Pascual de
commander of Spanish fleet, 96, 104, 111, 121-22, 173-74, 192, 204, 220
destruction of his fleet, 225-26
Chadwick, Capt. French Ensor, xv
Charleston, S.C., 137, 224, 233
Chickamauga Park, Ga.: general, 91-92, 98, 108
as training camp, 116, 118, 120, 124, 126, 135
conditions at, 137, 164, 224, 233, 250, 267-68
see also Camp George H. Thomas

Chief of Ordnance, 134, 137, 148; and Cuban expedition, 178, 302
Chief of Staff, in European armies, 16-17
Cienfuegos, Cuba, 103, 174
Cleveland, Grover, 13, 63
Coast defense of U.S., 31-35; strengthening of, 75-80, 85
Columbia, S.C., 137
Command systems: European vs. U.S., 14-21
Commanding General of the Army (U.S.): position and duties of, 14-16, 25, 27
conflict with Secretary of War, 16-18, 22, 24-25
Commissary Department: under Eagan, 60
Committee on Military Affairs, 82-85, 89, 92-93
Connor, Dr. Phineas T., 285
Cooks, Army, 170
Coppinger, Maj. Gen. John J., 126n.41
Corbin, Henry C., Adjutant General, xvi-xvii
biography of, 57-59
judgment of Alger, 52
organization of Army, 82-84, 88, 91-92, 105, 108, 118, 122, 128
and Hull bill, 84, 88, 92, 305
and Army administration, 133-34, 139-40, 140n.12, 141-43, 162, 189
expansion of War Department's authority, 134, 139, 287-88, 316, 323
reorganization, 295, 320
Corps, Army: general, 126-27, 135
I Corps, 126, 128, 135, 167, 194
in Puerto Rican campaign, 233, 275, 277
in Cuba, 308
II Corps, 126, 129, 194, 275, 300, 308
III Corps, 126, 129, 275, 300
IV Corps, 126, 129, 233, 275-76, 300
V Corps, 126, 176, 188-90, 198-99, 201
during Cuban campaign, 204, 206-10, 214, 218, 224-25, 227, 230-32, 244
sickness in, 247, 255-64, 275
disbanding of, 265, 300
VI Corps, 126, 300
VII Corps, 126, 129, 167, 176, 269, 275, 299-300
in Cuba, 308-9
VIII Corps, 112-13, 126, 129, 168, 185, 188, 194, 196-98
during Philippine Islands campaign, 239-40, 242
in camp, 268-69, 275
during Philippine Insurrection, 310, 312-13

at Santiago, 123, 174, 204, 228-29
conference with Shafter, 202
conflict with Miles, 232, 237
San Antonio, Texas, 108
San Francisco, Calif., 108
port of embarkation for the Philippines, 111,
113, 137, 182-83, 194, 196, 307-8, 314
headquarters of VIII Corps, 126, 196
camp at, 268-69, 304, 313-14
hospital at, 302
San Juan, Puerto Rico: defenses of, 73
Sampson at, 111
objective of campaign, 233-34, 236-37
reinforcements for, 234
during U.S. occupation, 310
San Juan Hill, Cuba, 131
defenses of, 209-10
battle at, 214-18
casualties at, 218, 225
during siege, 229, 231
Sanger, Brig. Gen. Joseph P., 301
Sanitation in Army camps, xv, xvii, 167; as
factor in disease control, 252, 268, 272,
275-77, 304; overseas camps, 310
Santiago campaign, xv, xvii, 135, 137,
173-77, 182-99; combat phase of, 201-2,
204-10, 214-19
Santiago de Cuba
strategy at, 127, 173-77, 185, 206-7
black troops at, 131
as military objective, 174-78, 184-86, 192,
198, 204-5, 209, 224
investment of, 209-10, 219
Spanish losses at, 225-26
siege of, 226-30
surrender of, 231-32
disease at, 255, 257, 259
U.S. departure from, 260-62
Savannah, Ga., 137, 300; port of embarkation for Cuba, 308;
hospital at, 302
Schofield, Lt. Gen. John M., xvii
system of command, 22, 24
reform of Army, 27-28, 32
retirement, 27, 55
and Corbin, 58
intervention in Cuban plans, 64, 75, 94
as advisor to McKinley, 94-95, 97, 133-34,
297
departure from Washington, 134, 134n.2
and Alger, 284-85

Schwan, Brig. Gen. Theodore, 234, 236-37,
299
Schwan board, 300-301
Scott, Hugh L., 279
Secretary of War, xvi-xvii; responsibilities of,
13-14, 16, 19, 25;
conflicts with Commanding General, 16,
18, 22; response to reformers, 45
Seventy-first New York, 118, 217
Sexton, Col. James A., 285n.64
Shafter, Maj. Gen. William R.
commander of Cuban expedition, 103,
117-18
V Corps commander, 126n.41, 188
biography of, 188-89
during Santiago campaign, 177, 185-86,
190-93, 199, 201-2, 204-10, 219-21,
225-31, 286-87
in combat, 214-19
and epidemics in V Corps, 248, 255-65
criticism of, 278-79
postwar activities of, 289, 314, 320
Sheridan, Gen. Philip: and Miles, 55
Sherman, Senator John, 52, 54
Sherman, Mary Hoyt (Mrs. Nelson A. Miles),
54
Sherman, Gen. William T.: and reform, 2,
21, 38; and Miles, 54
Siboney, Cuba, 204, 206-10, 219, 227, 229-30;
hospitals at, 256-57
Sicard, Rear Adm. Montgomery, 115
Signal Bureau, U.S. Army, 12
Signal Corps, U.S. Army: functions of, 12-13
preparations for war, 77, 173
and cables from Cuba, 173, 184, 199
during combat, 199, 216-17
in Puerto Rico, 232
in Philippines, 312
Signal Corps, U.S. Volunteer, 127
Smallpox: as factor in war plans, 96
Smokeless powder. See Ammunition
Socapa, Cuba, 225
Spain
military weakness of, xv
in Cuba, 63-66, 90
Spanish forces in Cuba, 70-71, 95
strategy, 72-74
colonies of, 72-73
negotiations for surrender at Santiago,
226-32
peace treaty with, 243-44, 298, 305